Overlay, Overlay

Overlay, Overlay

How to Bet Horses Like a Pro
Angel Cordero, Jr., Woody Stephens, P.G. Johnson and Richard Migliore Share Their Handicapping Secrets

Bill Heller

Bonus Books, Inc., Chicago

© 1990 by Bonus Books, Inc.
All rights reserved

94 93 92   5 4 3

Library of Congress Catalog Card Number: 89-81941

International Standard Book Number: 0-933893-86-8

Bonus Books, Inc.
160 East Illinois Street
Chicago, Illinois 60611

Printed in the United States of America

With love, to my wife, Anna, and our son, Benjamin.
Anything is possible.

Contents

Foreword

Clearly, it is no coincidence that so many of the illustrative races on the following pages took place at Saratoga. The author, you see, is as much a part of the Saratoga race scene as the handmelons, the baths and the discos.

Of course, I've never encountered the author of this book at the baths or the discos, nor have I observed him wasting his time on such luxuries as food. He is much too busy devoting every waking hour to separating winners from losers at the "day track" on Nelson Avenue. Bill Heller puts more emotion, more energy, more drive into those twenty-four days at Saratoga than Reigh Count, Can Do Cazzie or John Piesen do in twenty-four years. The man literally lives and breathes jockey ratings, inside speed and signs of life theories.

Bill is not exactly what I would describe as a gracious loser; every defeat is taken as a personal affront to his manhood, every losing photo an absolute disaster.

For example, Bill never has forgiven me for 1982 when I beat him out by one winner at Saratoga on a closing-day, ninth race disqualification.

Read and enjoy Bill's book. I know I did. But don't ever watch a race with him. He curses. He screams. He stamps his feet. He pounds his fist. And that's while the horses are still in the gate!

If you get the idea that Bill takes his work seriously, he does. And he should. There's nothing funny about a losing day at the race-track. Yet, on the other hand, I've never known anyone who enjoys winning as much as Bill.

I think Bill enjoyed writing *Overlay, Overlay*. I know you'll enjoy reading it.

John Piesen
New York Post
February 1990

Preface

There was a kingdom, a wonderful kingdom. The kingdom had produced generations of happy people for centuries. There were meaningful jobs, security, comfort and a general well-being.

One day, the king decided his utopia must be preserved for posterity. He gathered the kingdom's scholars.

"You must find," he instructed them, "just what it is that makes our society perfect. You must put it down in print, so future generations can learn from us."

The scholars dispersed and set about the king's task. They conducted thousands of interviews, did months of research, and, finally, after three years, returned to the king with a set of eight books.

The king took the eight books home and pored over them. He was delighted with what he read and told the scholars so when he reconvened them a week later. "You have a marvelous understanding of our society," the king told them. "Your work is exemplary, and I am very proud. Yet eight books are too many. Can you take what you have found and condense it into one single book?"

Again, the scholars dispersed. They worked for months, condensing the essence of the eight separate volumes into a single book.

They returned to the king, and he read the book at home that night. The next morning, he again talked to the scholars, who eagerly awaited the monarch's response. "I am immeasurably proud of your work," he told them. "You are all highly commended. But one book is still too much. Can you condense it into one chapter?"

The scholars went back to work and returned two weeks later with one chapter. The king kept the scholars waiting in the garden while he read it. He walked into the garden and said, "This is wonderful. But it must be condensed into a single page."

A week later, the scholars brought the king a single page. He read it in front of them. "I'm thrilled," he said. "But I wonder, can you condense this into a single sentence, one sentence which would describe to all who read it why our society is perfect?"

The scholars returned the following day and presented the king with a sheet of paper, blank except for a single sentence. The king read it and smiled. "You have done it," he said.

The single sentence was: "There ain't no such thing as a free lunch."

What does this have to do with horse racing? Plenty.

So many books about handicapping advertise self-proclaimed revolutionary methods or systems which guarantee you'll make a profit at the track. The books brag of how their authors have been able to retire with their profits; buy several yachts, and spend half of each year in Tahiti.

It's just not so. There are systems from here to doomsday ranging from simplistic if not idiotic approaches to elaborate and exhausting works of well-known national handicappers. They all have one thing in common: they don't work. Not consistently. There are no secrets, no hidden tricks, and most certainly of all, no sure thing.

There is no free lunch.

One day at the Albany (N.Y.) *Times Union*, the newspaper I worked and handicapped for from 1973 to 1984, I received a copy of a gimmick book. It was a beautiful piece of work; there were eighty pages used to camouflage a single point, that the best way to handicap races was to figure out a horse's average earnings per start. Eighty pages, and the only piece of useful information was a single sentence, one less useful than the scholars' description of their utopia. Average earnings per start is just a single item in a whole school of handicapping, one which relies on a horse's class. A lot of other factors are involved in determining class, and plenty of other schools of handicapping do exist. They are headed by professionals who have been handicapping their whole lives. There are schools of form and speed and trips and visual handicapping. And there are methods of handicapping by workouts, equipment changes, jockeys, trainer patterns, odds on the tote board and even potential exacta and quinella payoffs posted on TV monitors at the track. Everything. You name it, and there's a handicapper who believes his or her sole method can turn a profit.

But there are no physical laws of certainty governing your chances of handicapping winners. If there were, racetracks wouldn't be in business. It's that simple.

Racetracks are in business because bettors lose money and win money and are willing to donate 14 to 25 percent of their action every day while doing it. That percentage, called the takeout, supports the track and feeds the government revenue. It is constant, every race, every day. Often, beginners at the track or at off-track betting parlors don't understand this principle. They see a long shot come in and think the track or Off-Track Betting (OTB) made a million-dollar killing on that particular race. It doesn't work that way. The track gets its takeout of the total money wagered, called the handle, every race at a fixed percentage regardless of what the winner pays. The winning payoff—as are all payoffs—is determined by the odds the bettors establish with their own money, be it in win, place and show pools or exacta or trifecta betting.

Because of that, wagering on horse racing is a highly advantageous form of gambling. Bettors establish the odds by the money they bet, and regardless of those odds, bettors collect every race.

Thus, it's not a case of the bettors en masse vs. the track or OTB. It's bettors vs. bettors; one person matching his system based on speed figures against another guy's passion for class handicapping, against someone else betting license plate numbers. One of them wins every race. Never do the same people win all the time. That's why after one race, some stranger next to you at the track will offer an explanation of how he—genius that he is—came up with that particular winner. The next race, he's the one with his tickets crumpled, his face screwed up in a malevolent pout looking very capable of murdering you if you were to pose the innocent question, "What happened?"

What happens is very simple if we strip ourselves of illusions and deal with reality. There is no guarantee, no tip sheet, no system, no friend in the world who will provide you with one winner after the next consistently.

What can I provide you with? I can provide you with an understanding of what the game is all about. I've enlisted the thoughts of some of the most well known horsemen in America—jockeys Angel Cordero, Jr., and Richard Migliore, trainers Woody Stephens and Phil Johnson, and racing officials Tommy Trotter and Lenny Hale—to supplement the insights I've gathered in a seventeen-year career as racing writer, columnist, public handicapper and fan. There is much to learn.

Knowledge is a potent weapon at the race track. So, too, is a healthy perspective and a philosophy of gambling which makes you comfortable.

Can I consistently provide you with winners? No way. I'm no smarter than other professional handicappers and, I'm sure, a lot of amateurs. But, boy, I love going to the races, and I love handicapping them. Somewhere along the line, reality belted me across the face and said, "Bill, you are NOT going to win 10 million dollars playing horses."

Somewhere farther down the line, I said, "That's okay." I love racing and the challenge of handicapping. There is no thrill quite as sweet as correctly figuring out which horse is ready to win, and how the race is going to go, and then seeing it happen after you've made your opinions in print with your name on them.

When you handicap in a newspaper, sometimes you must pick chalk, the favorites. But I've spent a career looking for the 2 to 1 favorite who should be 4 to 5, or the 6 to 1 shot who should be the 5 to 2 favorite. What I want is a winner who is an overlay, a horse paying more than he should for any of a myriad of reasons. You'll get more winners by strictly playing favorites, even though favorites on a national average never win more than 30 to 40 percent of the time in both thoroughbred and harness racing.

There are times to bet favorites. We will look for those times, but more often we'll search for the second, third, fourth or maybe eighth choice we believe can win after an intelligent bout of handicapping.

If you get one 5 to 1 winner on a racing program and bet it well, you're set. If you can get two 4 to 1 shots who should have been 2 to 1, you're way ahead.

I'll arm you with enough knowledge to peg those types of horses. Sometimes they'll win, and sometimes they'll lose. No guarantees. No free lunch. But handicap one of them a day and you're smiling. Shoot for two of them. Overlay. Overlay.

Acknowledgments

If you're lucky, you get to meet and come to know a person as nice as John Piesen of the *New York Post*. When he was asked questions by an anxious newcomer to the Saratoga Pressbox, he not only answered them but continued to help the neophyte, myself, year after year. Do the foreword for this book? Of course he would. He's still helping me. Thanks John.

Another member of the *New York Post*, long-time friend Gerard Bray, waded through the book's rough draft and provided useful suggestions. So did Bob Gersowitz.

Howie Blank, Barry Ikler and Gene Espeland provided proofreading.

Steve Schwartz's entire staff in the New York Racing Association Press Office helped locate charts and photos. A special thanks to a tireless member of Steve's staff, Shirley Day Smith. Her devotion to her work is as good an endorsement of thoroughbred racing as there is.

Special thanks, too, to John Deneen and Larry Razbadouski of Bonus Books.

Trainers Woody Stephens and Phil Johnson, jockeys Angel Cordero, Jr., and Richard Migliore, Arlington Park and Gulfstream Racing Secretary Tommy Trotter and Lenny Hale, NYRA's Senior Vice President, Racing, all found time to cooperate despite their hectic schedules.

Mark Cusano, annually one of the best handicappers at Saratoga, and the staff at the *Daily Racing Form,* helped locate charts.

Last and never least, my wife, Anna, worked diligently through all the rewrites and revisions. Thanks Honey.

What Is an Overlay?

CHAPTER 1 An overlay is any horse going off at higher odds than he deserves. We'll confine our consideration of overlays to those horses who have a legitimate chance in the race we're handicapping. For example, a horse we don't think has a chance might figure to go off at odds of 15 to 1. But the tote board says 50 to 1 with only a minute left before post time. Certainly, this horse is an overlay. That should not, however, alter our evaluation of him as a non-contender.

What we're searching for is the contending horse we like who is an overlay. If we have handicapped a race of twelve horses down to three contenders, we'll consider betting one of those three horses. Through handicapping, we'll have approximations of odds we feel each of our three contenders should be. For example, we decide the horse we like the most should be 2 to 1; the second of our choices should be 3 to 1, and the final contender should go off 5 to 1. A couple of minutes before post time, with the betting almost completed, those three horses are the following prices in order: 4 to 5, 3 to 1 and 8 to 1. The horse at 4 to 5 is an underlay, the exact situation we try to avoid at all times, with an underlay being defined as a horse at a price we perceive as too low for his relative chance to win.

Now we're getting into the topic of value. In trying to find legitimate overlays, we want horses that have more value than the rest of the bettors believe: a 4 to 1 chance we think should be 2 to 1, or a 10 to 1 shot we feel should be 4 to 1. If we're correct in our handicapping, we're getting greater value than we should. If we're wrong, we lose.

In our example, the horse who is the 4 to 5 favorite might have the highest probability of winning but the least value of our three contenders. If we like our second choice as much, or almost as much, as the first, we'll bet him. If we think our third choice is almost as good or as good as the first two, we'll likely bet him. If we feel the favorite is appreciably stronger than the other two contenders, we'll skip the race. We expected 2 to 1 and will not bet this horse at 4 to 5. There is simply no value for our perceptions about the race. Even if the 4 to 5 favorite wins, it does not mean he had value as a wager. Remember, we want more for our money, not less.

Overlays abound every day at every racetrack in the country. The difficulty is honing our handicapping skills to pinpoint them, a process which entails a strong knowledge of all aspects of handicapping.

This book will take you step by step through all the prominent factors of handicapping. As a bettor, you must take every edge you can to outsmart the other bettors you're competing against. The majority of money wagered in every race—which produces a favorite—is only correct roughly a third of the time. That's the percentage of winning favorites. In two-thirds of all the races you handicap, a nonfavorite is ready to win.

We aren't against betting favorites, as long as they have value. Probably the exact opposite of our philosophy is the plunger who bets tens of thousands of dollars to show on an extremely heavy favorite. Such a bettor is shooting for an immediate five percent on his return ($2.10 is the minimum return on a show, and/or win and place bet). That bettor could be getting 6 to 7 percent interest at the bank without risking so much money. Instead, he or she wants an immediate return at 5 percent. When we see this type of situation develop, an inordinate amount of money in the show pool on one horse, we'll bet another contender in the race to show and hope the heavy favorite runs out. When that happens, the show prices are boxcar figures. You've occasionally seen a horse paying $10.40, $5.20 and $20.40 across the board after a heavy favorite runs out of the money. When you take advantage of it, you're turning a conservative show bet into a generous return. If the favorite does run in the money and our horse does, too, we'll get the same small profit ratio as the chalk player. Only we might have invested a fraction as much. That is the inherent value of any overlay and the disadvantage of any underlay. If there is an underlay, by definition it must create overlays. Let's find them.

My First Overlay

2

Everybody remembers their first overlay, right? My philosophy of handicapping and betting took painful years to evolve. They were painful because I paid for each lesson with losing tickets. But right at the start of my gambling career, I learned to appreciate the overlay.

Despite growing up less than fifteen miles away from Monticello Raceway, I didn't make my initial trip to a track until I was in high school in Liberty, New York.

Making my first visit to Monticello, a harness track, seemed natural, almost a reflex reaction when my first opportunity came. The offer to go to the track came from an unlikely source, my conservative friend, Gary Holmes. Gary wasn't the gambling type. He never drank, never smoked, and only cursed after he became better acquainted with myself and another high school buddy, Lenny. Gary would go to the races simply because he enjoyed watching the horses race. Gambling never crossed his mind. It certainly crossed mine when I first heard the call to post. I don't know why I fell in love so quickly with horse racing. Subsequent talks, discussions and arguments with my mother led her to conclude it was in my blood.

My father had a short and unsuccessful fling as a horseplayer, but uncharacteristically, thanks to great pressure from my mom, lost interest. My Uncle Hymie, who had been mayor of Liberty, owned harness horses many years ago. My first exposure to racing came when one of my uncle's horses was in a race televised from Yonkers. My brother and I were allowed to stay up late to watch the great event, only to see the driver of my uncle's horse fall out of the sulky somewhere on the backstretch.

My uncle, unwittingly, could have had a lot to do with my inculcation simply by giving me a summer job in the Triangle Diner, a popular restaurant he owned opposite world-famous Grossinger's Hotel. I started working at the diner in the summer of my fifteenth year. Originally, I was a soda jerk, but I was soon promoted to general bimbo and part-time cashier. As a cashier, one of my duties was to sell Monticello Raceway programs at the register to those hard-core addicts who needed it with their eggs, toast and coffee to start the morning.

Inevitably, I became acquainted with my uncle's regular customers, some of whom frequented Monticello. One of them, a middle-aged, harmless looking cab driver named Blinky, was the steadiest racegoer I've ever seen. Blinky was a long-time friend of my dad and probably had a lot to do with his involvement in racing since my dad worked most of his adult life at the Triangle. Blinky's story was told to me many times in lecture form by my mom and my uncle. From their accounts, Blinky had lost a loving family and a great job because he had a weird set of priorities, namely, the track came first. I used to think the story was an exaggeration until one night Blinky called my father collect from Miami, Florida, begging for money to replace lost wagers at Hialeah.

After a couple more summers working at my uncle's diner, I learned how Blinky would operate. To get money in the morning, he would drive customers non-stop to places as far away as New York City (100 miles). Then he'd come back that night to take a stab at Monticello. When I worked the night shift, I'd always see Blinky at the diner. On rare occasions, he'd be bubbling over, telling of how he had the Daily Double a dozen times and made a killing. More often, though, he'd walk into the diner with a kind of shocked expression on his face. I later learned the expression: you just can't believe you didn't have that No. 5 horse in the last race. It would've gotten you even for the night. Thoughts of a very sad Blinky filled my mind in terror when my mom demanded, "Do you want to grow up to be another

Blinky?" I hoped not. He seemed the loneliest person in the world. Yet, I just loved the track.

I probably wouldn't have developed deep feelings for racing if not for that first night with Gary. Having just five dollars in my pocket, I persuaded Gary to break his policy of nonintervention and split a couple of bets. He picked the horses because I had no idea how to read the program. Gary and I won twelve dollars each, a healthy profit for a sixteen-year-old. My eyes lit up like bumpers on a pinball machine.

That was minor league compared to the following summer when I discovered the true meaning of overlay. Gary's interest in racing faded; mine grew. I'd go to the track with either my cousin, Potsy, or another friend, Mark. Potsy introduced me to a new thrill in life: making the Double. Potsy was a track veteran who had the misfortune of finishing his work shift—he was a waiter at the Triangle—at 7:30. By the time he finished with his customers and changed, it was 7:45, fifteen minutes before post time. Going with him to the track was not only making a wager, but daring death to smite you down as Potsy did eighty-five on the Quickway, Route 17, to make the first race.

Looking for a safer way to enjoy the races, I became track partners with Mark. Mark's grandfather was convinced I was a bad influence on Mark. My mom was convinced Mark was a bad influence on me. Our partnership thrived.

The last time I went to the track with Gary had been profitable because of a New Zealand horse named Dromana. Gary talked me into betting her, and she won at 12 to 1.

I returned to the track a week later with Mark and was amazed to see the price on Dromana: 9 to 1. Despite her victory in her last start, the betting public must have determined a slight rise in class would compromise her chances. It didn't in the slightest.

Dromana won again, and Mark and I hit a perfecta worth $167.40. Dromana should have been about 4 to 1; the perfecta (the same bet as an exacta when the bettor must pick the first two finishers in exact order) should have paid about $50.00. I still have the win picture. My first overlay.

Attacking the Beast

3 For the uninitiated, the *Daily Racing Form* is an intimidating, confusing mixture of numbers, dates and times. But learning how to read the *Form* is a must. And it's not hard at all.

The *Form* has detailed explanations of how to read the vast amount of information provided. What's being offered to the handicapper are the essential facts on breeding, a horse's record, and a past performance line of up to ten of its most recent races. Beginners are advised to read the explanations in the *Form* and to keep in mind that each past performance line is a vital one chronicling what the horse did or failed to do in his race, his odds, any difficulties he may have encountered, and the final time of the race. We'll refer to the past performance lines as PPs.

Depending on where in the country you purchase your *Form*, you may notice some differences in the PPs shown in this book and the ones in your *Form*. For example, the Midwest edition has a slightly different layout for its PPs. Also, comments are not supplied for each PP shown (although problem races are often noted in an explanatory line under the PP line), nor are the weights or the distances separating the top three finishing horses given. So, make sure you have a complete understanding of your edition's PPs. With that accomplished, you will have no problem understanding and using the information and strategies contained in this book.

Even the most skilled and time-tested handicappers can be guilty of a crucial mistake when studying the *Form*. ALWAYS, repeat, always, start at the line at the bottom of a horse's PPs. Then work your way up through his races, evaluating the most recent race last. This alone will give you an immediate edge over many bettors who simply judge a horse by its most recent race or two, thereby missing potentially important information from other races. Reading PPs in the way I describe also gives you a feel for how a horse is coming into today's race. It may tip off a trainer's pattern of getting a horse ready for a certain race. It may show how a horse performed in the same class previously. Evaluating past performances and odds also provides insight. Suppose a horse went off at odds of 2 to 1 in a race for $25,000 claimers five starts ago. Say he won that race by two lengths, then moved up in higher claiming company or allowance company and was dull in four races. Now, the horse is back in a class where he's previously won. And he was bet well when he won. Is he being bet heavily this time in the same $25,000 claimer? Or are bettors ignoring his previous win in the same class? If the horse is completely dead on the board (e.g., 5 to 1 morning line and going off at 20 to 1), it might be an indication the horse has some physical problems, which would explain the return to the $25,000 claiming price. But if the horse is between 4 to 1 and 6 to 1, he's probably simply being overlooked. By looking at all the horse's PPs, we know he can win in this class and did so easily at 2 to 1. If he's 4 to 1 or higher, he may just be the overlay we're looking to catch. But we wouldn't have known of his previous win in the same class if we only skimmed the horse's last one or two races from the top of his PPs.

Start on the bottom. It'll help you get to the top.

Here's a step-by-step method of handicapping from the *Form*.

1. Get early scratches and cross out these horses from all races.

2. Go to the graded entries immediately before the PPs. Check each race for equipment changes, either blinkers on or blinkers off, and indicate the change for each horse in the entries with a notation above his PPs, B's on or B's off.

3. Check the graded entries for jockeys. If there is a jockey change, write the new jockey's name over the PPs.

4. Cross out late scratches and write in late jockey changes.

5. Start at the bottom PP for each horse and glance quickly through his lines to note any layoffs longer than a month. Do this by drawing a line in the PPs between the race before the layoff and subsequent new races.

6. You're now ready to rock. As you evaluate each horse, be sure to note any races in common with other horses in this race.

Here's a glossary of useful terms.

Types of Bets

Daily or Instant Double—pick winners of two successive races, usually the first two of the day known as the Daily Double.

Exacta (also called perfecta)—pick two horses in exact order.

Exacta Box—pick two horses to finish 1-2 in either order. An exacta box of two horses will cost twice as much as a straight exacta bet; an exacta box of three horses costs six times as much. For example, a $2 bet of a 2-1 exacta costs $2. A $2 exacta box of 2-1 costs $4. A $2 exacta box of 1-2-3 costs $12.

Exacta Wheel—pick one horse to win and cover every other horse in the race for second.

Pick 3, Pick 4, Pick 5, Pick 6—pick winners of that many consecutive races.

Quinella—pick two horses to finish 1-2 in either order.

Triple (also called trifecta)—pick three horses in exact order.

Triple Box—pick three horses to finish 1-2-3 in any order. A $2 triple box of three horses costs $12, six times as much as a straight triple bet; a triple box of four horses costs $48.

Triple Key—pick one horse to finish first, second or third and cover a specific number of horses in the rest of the field to complete the triple; e.g., in a 10 horse field, key the No. 6 horse to win and use four other horses to finish second or third; for $2 triples, the cost is $24; add a fifth horse to box underneath the No. 6 horse and the cost is $40.

Betting Information
Entry—two horses with the same owner (and/or trainer) coupled as one for wagering

Even Money—odds of 1 to 1. Bet $2 and win $2

Field—two or more horses coupled for wagering

Daily Racing Form Comments for Winning Horses
Driving—all out

Easily/Handily—self-explanatory

Ridden out—jockey continues to ride the horse hard but doesn't use his whip

Daily Racing Form Comments for Losing Horses
Bolted—horse made sudden, sharp move to the extreme outside of the course

Bore out/in—instead of racing in a straight line, horse veered outside or inside

Broke through—horse broke through the starting gate before the start (horse is then either reloaded into the gate or scratched pending a quick evaluation by a veterinarian)

Brushed—made physical contact with another horse

Came again—horse was passed, but regained ground on the horse who passed him (which few horses do)

Checked—more serious extension of steadied

Dull—horse's effort wasn't sharp

Eased—horse was beaten so badly the jockey eased him to a stop

Evenly/Even try—horse neither gained nor lost significant ground

Gamely—horse displayed courage in a close finish

Greenly—horse showed inexperience by racing erratically

Hung—horse appeared to be making a winning move then failed to sustain it

Impeded/bothered—horse was physically impeded/bothered by another horse, who may have been disqualified (DQ)

Lacked room—close presence of other horses in front and/or alongside him prevented him from beginning or continuing to advance

Lost whip—jockey lost the whip

No threat—didn't seriously threaten winning horse

Prominent—horse was a factor for much of the race

Rallied—closed well

Saved ground—horse raced on the inside around a turn, thus covering less distance

Shuffled back—horse lost ground because of traffic problems in front of him

Steadied—jockey had to physically stop his riding motion because of traffic problems

Taken up—extreme extension of steadied

Unruly—horse made like Flicka, acting up, either while being saddled or being loaded into the starting gate

Used up—expended its energy early in the race prompting or setting the pace

Wide—horse lost ground on a turn because he was far from the rail

Willingly—horse continued to gain ground

Daily Racing Form Information about Workouts
B—breezing (not at full speed)
BG—breezing from the starting gate
H—handily (full speed)
HG—handily from the gate
(d)—around dogs, pylons placed on the course to prevent horses from digging up the inside part of a course; any workout around dogs means the horse raced a greater distance around a turn.

Daily Racing Form Track Conditions

fst—fast
gd—good
sly—sloppy
my—muddy

yl—yielding turf course
sf—soft turf course
fm—firm turf course
hd—hard turf course

Points of Call

PPs in the *Form* give the final time of the winner and fractions for the horse in front at different points. These points of call show a horses position and length behind the leader. One length equals one-fifth of a second, thus a horse two lengths behind has a time two-fifths of a second slower than the leader. The stretch call in all races is made one-eighth of a mile from the finish. Here are the points of call and fractional times for commonly run distances.

Points of Call

Distance of Race	1st call	2nd call	3rd call	4th call	5th call	Fractional Times Given At:		
5 furlongs	start	3/16	3/8	stretch	finish	1/4	1/2	finish
5¹/₂ furlongs	start	1/4	3/8	stretch	finish	1/4	1/2	finish
6 furlongs	start	1/4	1/2	stretch	finish	1/4	1/2	finish
6¹/₂ furlongs	start	1/4	1/2	stretch	finish	1/4	1/2	finish
7 furlongs	start	1/4	1/2	stretch	finish	1/4	1/2	finish
1 mile	1/4	1/2	3/4	stretch	finish	1/2	3/4	finish
1 mile 70 yards	1/4	1/2	3/4	stretch	finish	1/2	3/4	finish
1¹/₁₆ miles	1/4	1/2	3/4	stretch	finish	1/2	3/4	finish
1¹/₈ miles	1/4	1/2	3/4	stretch	finish	1/2	3/4	finish
1³/₁₆ miles	1/4	1/2	3/4	stretch	finish	1/2	3/4	finish
1¹/₄ miles	1/4	1/2	1 mile	stretch	finish	1/2	1 mile	finish
1⁵/₁₆ miles	1/4	1/2	1 mile	stretch	finish	1/2	1 mile	finish
1³/₈ miles	1/4	1/2	1 mile	stretch	finish	1/2	1 mile	finish
1¹/₂ miles	1/4	1/2	1¹/₄	stretch	finish	1/2	1¹/₄	finish
1⁵/₈ miles	1/4	1/2	1³/₈	stretch	finish	1/2	1¹/₄	finish
2 miles	1/2	1 mile	1³/₄	stretch	finish	1/2	1³/₄	finish

Framework and Tips

CHAPTER 4 Handicapping can't be done without a framework. You must have a series of beliefs in the process of handicapping, which is nothing more than trying to logically deduce a winner from available information.

An extremely negative framework pervading many racetracks is the opinion every race, regardless of the outcome, is fixed. Frankly, I've never had much sympathy for bettors who cannot accept responsibility for their own losing bets. Losing will occur many times, but we understand we will also have our share of winners whose value hopefully will outweigh the losers. Again, this touches upon the theme of value for your wager, which is the foundation of this book.

As for people who say every race is fixed, I pose this question: if you believe that to be true, why do you bet on the horses? Would you play poker if you knew beforehand the deck was stacked against you? Of course not. But it's much easier subscribing to the paranoia of an inherently unfair system than accepting the realities of gambling on horses: namely, an acceptance of defeat when it happens.

I'm not trying to peddle the naive notion every horse in every race is a "go." I am suggesting the country's better tracks, those with higher purses, offer racing where most, if not all the horses entered, have some chance of winning. If you believe otherwise, put this book down.

Our framework is defined: handicapping alone can and will determine winners, and on the way to cashing tickets, we accept the reality we will lose some of our bets.

That still leaves the thorny question: what about tips?

Tips, a potentially fatal disease, are called by other names: hot horse, can't miss, sure thing, and the ever popular inside information.

A tip is a piece of information about one horse in a race, usually suggesting how well he is going to do. Frequently, valid information such as a good workout—which may be public knowledge—is the essence of a tip. Other times, tips stem from information not publicly known, perhaps a workout not included or reported erroneously in the *Daily Racing Form*, or the fact a horse's poor last race was because of sickness or because the horse was purposely given an easy race by the trainer.

The tip passes the word that the horse is a "go" this time. But by the time you've heard it, thousands of dollars have probably been poured in on the animal, lowering his odds. Consider this: if you possess such valuable inside information, how many other people know the exact same thing?

When a horse shows up short on the tote board, that is a lower price than he deserves, there is a self-perpetuating factor unleashed. Many bettors at the track who haven't yet made a wager see the so-called hot horse and jump aboard to bet it, lowering the odds even farther. As we've already established, we're looking for the horses at a price of greater value, not one depreciated by word of mouth.

Countless times, I've seen horses off layoffs hammered down in the wagering to much lower prices than they deserve. Generally, as will be noted later in the book, a horse racing from a layoff—four weeks of inactivity are a lot, six are suspicious and eight or more are too many—is not a sound investment, let alone if he's going off as a heavy favorite. We'll pass and possibly bet a different horse whose odds are higher than they deserve because of the dump on the layoff horse. Remember, underlays create overlays.

As reliable as tips may sound, as pure as the intentions of the donor who gave the horse to you may be, tips invariably will interfere with your handicapping and invite economic disaster. If the tip is such a good thing, we will duly note it as we go about the handicapping process. But if you subjectively listen to tips, you're creating a no-win situation. Bet on some of them and become angry when other ones come in. You'll never be right all the time, but you will be playing horses who are underlays, lower in price than they should be and the exact opposite of what this book is about.

Be strong. Be resolute. Wear earmuffs if you're weak. Just follow the simple rule: no tips, and you'll never have to judge whether it's good or bad information.

As a two-time owner of a harness horse and a close friend of several owners, let me offer personal insight on how rotten inside information can be.

A trainer I know well at Saratoga Harness had four horses entered one fall evening in 1983. Of the four, the one with the apparent best chance of winning was a 3-year-old filly in the seventh, a filly I had owned in a partnership with two good friends. One of them went back to the paddock before the races to discuss the filly's chances. As was custom, the trainer sent out some money to bet on his horses. He sent out $100 to win on the horse he trained in the fourth. The horse ran out of the money at 9 to 2. He sent out $25 to win on a mare he owned himself. She finished second in the fifth race at 7 to 1. The trainer sent out $50 to win on a 4 to 5 shot in the tenth who finished second. The trainer didn't send out a penny on the 3-year-old filly, who was listed at 3 to 1 on the morning line, opened at 19 to 1 from OTB money, went off 9 to 1 and won by a head to return $21.80.

So much for tips vs. looking for overlays. Friends of the trainer were destroyed betting his tips conveyed through the owner. Any bettor searching for an overlay that evening would have zeroed in on the 3-year-old filly. Her own trainer didn't.

The Three Schools of Handicapping

5 Each major school of handicapping, class, speed and form, has its merits and weaknesses. We'll examine each school—as well as other aspects of handicapping including trips, workouts, changes and weight. We want to extract the best from each school and use it in our handicapping.

One thing this book will not do is offer a magic formula assigning points for this and points for that, having you dabbling in calculus to compute winners. Assigning points, which is the basis of any system, is much too subjective. Why is one factor worth one to five points and another worth one to three? What is the justification for assigning the range of points in each category?

Systems which produce a final number or figure for a horse through a subjective point system are inherently flawed. We will not deal with absolutes, nor will we delude ourselves into believing anyone is capable of such powers. Deal with reality. There are no guaranteed formulae or systems which work consistently. Instead, there are subjective judgments of varied importance. Hopefully, with a sound understanding of the important factors of handicapping, we will tie together our judgments to form intelligent opinions about each horse in each race we handicap.

We will look at each school as a question we must answer in our handicapping. Class asks the question, "How good is this horse, and how well is he capable of racing?" Speed asks, "How fast is the horse capable of racing?" Form asks, "How well is this horse capable of racing *today*?" Other factors ask different questions, some of them rather obvious. Changes ask, "Will a change, be it equipment, jockey or trainer, or racing surface, help this horse?"

Enough with questions. Let's look for some answers.

Class

6 Defining a horse's class means determining the quality of his past performances. To do so, we must have a firm understanding of classifications; an idea of the difference in the quality of racing at different tracks, and, ultimately, a subjective value system we can use.

Our value system may not be an exact copy of the next person's; however, there shouldn't be a vast difference of opinion when two handicappers evaluate a horse's class. In other words, we should all agree a Secretariat has more class than a lifetime $10,000 claimer. Ditto for a stakes horse compared to a maiden. The arguments start when handicappers project class, offering their opinions of how much class a horse will exhibit because of his breeding. We will use breeding as one of our handicapping tools, especially with turf racing, but in general, when we handicap for class we will stick solely to what the horse has accomplished on the track. Past performances only. Keep in mind if class was solely determined on projections because of breeding, every six-figure yearling purchased would be a champion. It doesn't happen that way, as a quick review of sales prices and results will indicate. A John Henry can evolve into a champion despite his obscure breeding. If a horse has demonstrated a certain high level of class on the track, his lineage becomes irrelevant.

The first step of measuring class is understanding the conditional system racetracks use. In general, there are two types of racing at every track: 1) claimers, where a horse can be purchased right out of the race by another horseman for the specified claiming price entered, and 2) everything else, which includes maiden races, allowances, handicaps and stakes.

The first classification every thoroughbred encounters is a maiden race. This means non-winners of a pari-mutuel race. Maiden races can be held for claimers. These races are simply called maiden claimers. Horsemen who desire to race their maidens without a claiming price put their entries into races called maiden special weights. After a horse wins a maiden race, he or she will either move into allowance or stakes company, or be placed in a claimer.

Unlike the easier-to-read conditions of harness racing, thoroughbred racing's conditions make it difficult for the beginner. The lowest level of allowance races is for horses who have never won a race "other than maiden, claimer or starter." The condition simply means non-winners of two races lifetime excluding claiming races and starter handicaps. If a thoroughbred wins his way out of this condition, he will have to move up the allowance level to tougher competition: non-winners of three. If a horse keeps winning at ascending allowance levels, he will ultimately race his way out of allowance company, because conditions for allowance races aren't usually written for non-winners of seven or eight races lifetime. This will force the trainer of such a horse to seek more challenging allowance conditions, find a handicap where the weights are assigned by a track's racing secretary, try stakes company, or go into claimers.

A special category of handicap races is the starter handicap. These races are specifically for horses that have started at a certain claiming level sometime during the current season. Starter handicaps are raced infrequently at most tracks.

For a quick review, the normal progression for a horse who doesn't start in a claimer is: maiden, non-winners of one other than maiden, non-winners of two other than maiden, non-winners of three, etc., with a step in stakes company anywhere along the line. Figuring out allowance conditions is sometimes difficult because the *Daily Racing Form* simply puts "Alw" for an allowance race without specifying the conditions. Three years ago, the *Form* made it even harder by not including the purse of such allowance races. Now the

Form does include the purses, so we can safely infer in past performance lines (PPs) that "Alw 40000," an allowance race with a purse of $40,000, is a higher class than "Alw 20000," an allowance with a purse of $20,000.

Unfortunately, purses in allowance races for state-breds (horses bred in the home state of the track) are often inflated, making across-the-board comparisons difficult. A horse running in a state-bred allowance with a purse of $30,000 may have faced easier competition than a horse in an open allowance race of $20,000. To determine that, we must have a strong estimate of the quality of various state-bred programs.

An excellent example is B.C. Sal, a 6-year-old that was entered in the Williamson, a $20,000 stakes race for New York-breds at Finger Lakes, July 15, 1989. B.C. Sal had a career record of 42-14-6-7 and earnings of $514,546. His lifetime average earnings per start is $12,251. Much of his earnings came from races such as the Williamson, which was restricted to New York-breds (indicated in the Form by the capital letter S, for state-bred, framed by a box immediately before the condition of the race). In the last decade, New York State has made significant progress in its thoroughbred breeding program, but still is not remotely competitive—nor is any other state of the Union—with Kentucky. *The Blood-Horse*, thoroughbred racing's weekly breeding magazine, showed in its Dec. 16, 1989 issue that forty-one of the fifty top sires in North America by 1989 earnings were from Kentucky. For leading active sires by lifetime earnings, forty-one of fifty were from Kentucky. Florida had four; California and Canada had two each, and New York had one.

In previous years, B.C. Sal had made several starts at the New York Racing Association tracks, Aqueduct, Belmont and Saratoga. Some of them were in open (non-restricted) races. What was B.C. Sal's class in open company? It's shown quite dramatically by his only PP not at Finger Lakes. It's a line we might have missed if we glanced from the top of his PPs instead of the bottom. At Aqueduct, Nov. 19, 1988, B.C. Sal raced in a $35,000 claimer. He was fifth by six and three-quarters lengths at odds of 6 to 1.

B.C. Sal's enormous lifetime average earnings per start is useful in state-bred races such as the Williamson. In open races, it's not. A better indication of his class in open company is his performance in a $35,000 claimer.

A more frequent obstacle in the *Form* is its listing of claiming races by claiming price, not the purse of the race, in PPs. "Clm 10000" means a claiming race with a claiming price of $10,000, not a purse of $10,000. To compare purses of claiming and allowances races, we must examine past charts, the track program or the *Form*.

The same problem occurs with stakes races, which are listed by their names in PPs instead of by purses. The beginner may know the Kentucky Derby is a harder race than a $50,000 allowance race, but what about less known and out-of-town stakes? The best stakes races are classified into three grades with Grade I the highest. That helps in many cases, but the only complete solution is familiarity, which breeds knowledge in handicapping, not contempt. The more familiar one becomes with racing in its entirety, the easier time he'll have pegging the relative value and quality of ungraded stakes.

With an understanding of the classification system used in thoroughbred racing, we can now address the two principal questions class asks:

1. How good is this horse?
2. How well is he capable of racing?

The record the horse has compiled and the quality of his performances supply answers. Does he win or finish in the money a high percentage of the time? If he does, what is the quality of the competition? These are the substantive components of class.

Since the *Form* provides lifetime records and earnings as well as those of the current season and the previous year, we have significant data on not only the horse's present abilities but also the ability he has shown in the past.

Let's compare two horses.

Land Between and Las Manitas were 4-year-old fillies, each with twenty-one career starts, when they were entered in separate races the same day at Belmont Park, May 29, 1989.

Land Between was entered in a $17,500 claiming race with a purse of $17,000. Las Manitas was entered in a $41,000 handicap.

Obviously, Las Manitas will show superior class just from the placement of the two horses by their trainers. Can we actually determine that? Yes.

Land Between — Ch. f. 4, by Full Pocket—Syrian Circle, by Damascus
$16,500 Br.—Hurstland Farm (Ky)
Tr.—Klesaris Robert P
Own.—Gold N Oats Stable
115 — Lifetime 21 1 4 2 $35,820 — 1989 8 0 2 0 $10,820 — 1988 13 1 2 2 $25,000

10May89- 1Bel sly 1 1/16 :45⅗ 1:10⅗ 1:44⅖ ⒻClm 22500 6 1 12 1½ 22½ 49 Cordero A Jr b 115 *1.70 71-19 StdyStt1177½MggiTonght112noDvousDutchss1151½ Set pace, tired 7
29Apr89- 1Aqu fst 1 :46⅕ 1:11⅗ 1:39 ⒻClm 22500 2 3 41¼ 32½ 31½ 2hd Cordero A Jr b 115 2.60 71-27 CrmllSwts112hdLndBtwn1153½ShnncckLss1171¼ Checked, drifted 7
10Apr89- 1Aqu fst 7f :22⅖ :45 1:23⅘ ⒻClm c-16500 7 2 42 31 1hd 2¾ Samyn J L b 115 5.50 81-27 Carmella Sweets 113¾ Land Between1154FlorDeLuna1171 Gamely 7
1Apr89- 9Aqu fst 6f :22⅗ :46⅖ 1:11⅘ ⒻClm 16500 5 7 75½ 76 57 45¾ Lovato F Jr b 115 4.10 75-20 Saucy Voyage 1123¼FastaDancer1152Mogumby115½ Lacked room 8
22Mar89- 9Aqu fst 7f :22⅘ :46 1:24⅘ ⒻClm 16500 2 11 72¾ 95 63½ 54 Antley C W b 115 9.00 73-22 ShDnHmWrng1172¼HrWy112nkCyclpsWmn117nk Steadied,in tight 11
19Feb89- 4Aqu fst 6f ⊡:23 :47⅕ 1:13 ⒻClm 17500 1 6 63 65 67 65¼ Lovato F Jr 117 11.80 74-25 There's a Way 113hd Lady Seul 1171¼ MaxBanker117nk No factor 7
6Feb89- 4Aqu fst 1 1/16 ⊡:48 1:13⅕ 1:46⅘ ⒻClm 22500 6 3 41½ 43 58 49¾ Santos J A 115 6.20 65-17 Dusty Donna 1152 Tarnish Miss 110½ Gucci Gal 1157¼ Evenly 7
28Jan89- 1Aqu fst 1⅛ ⊡:49 1:14⅕ 1:54⅖ ⒻClm 22500 6 4 54¾ 43½ 54 53¼ Thibeau R J Jr 115 17.90 67-22 Grudge Match 115¾ Social Secret 1171¼ Dusty Donna 1171¼ Tired 8
28Dec88- 9Aqu fst 6f ⊡:22⅘ :46 1:12 ⒻClm 22500 6 11 95 97 66 65½ Hernandez R Z 114 20.80 78-21 You'llbesurprised 1112½ Her Way 107nk Scarlet Leaf 116¾ Outrun 11
8Dec88- 1Aqu fst 6f ⊡:23⅗ :47⅗ 1:13⅕ ⒻClm 20000 2 10 43 43½ 410 48½ Samyn J L 116 26.80 69-21 DrlingDutch1113½You'llbesurprised1112½ⒹHrWy1112½ Even effort 12
8Dec88-Placed third through disqualification

Las Manitas — Dk. b. or br. f. 4, by Faraway Son—Maimiti, by Never Bend
Br.—Brant P M (Ky)
Tr.—Lukas D Wayne
Own.—Brant P M
116 — Lifetime 21 8 5 3 $181,757 — 1989 6 2 1 0 $58,168 — 1988 12 4 3 3 $103,189

6May89- 9GS fst 6f :21⅖ :44 1:08⅗ 3↑ⒻBdrs Cup H 7 7 69 59 614 614¼ Allen K K 113 13.80 85-16 Safely Kept 1082¾ Social Pro 1167 Kerygma 117hd Outrun 9
6May89-Grade III
21Apr89- 8Aqu fst 1 :45⅖ 1:10⅖ 1:37 3↑ⒻAlw 47000 1 3 32 21½ 33½ 45 Krone J A 119 2.20 76-23 BoldWench114½WhosDoubt1192¾AWinkAndANod1191¾ Weakened 6
26Feb89- 8Aqu fst 6f ⊡:22⅗ :46 1:10⅘ 3↑ⒻCorrection H 6 1 51½ 54½ 32 45¼ Krone J A 114 3.90 85-24 CageyExubernce122¾Hedgebout1154½RoylRexson111hd Weakened 6
5Feb89- 8Aqu fst 6f ⊡:22⅗ :46 1:10⅘ 3↑ⒻBerlo H 5 1 11 12 11½ 2¾ Krone J A 114 *1.00 89-18 Hedgeabout 114¾ Las Manitas 1141 Bodacious Tatas 110¾ Gamely 5
23Jan89- 8Aqu fst 6f ⊡:22⅕ :45⅗ 1:10⅕ ⒻHandicap 1 4 42 2hd 13 11½ Krone J A 112 4.70 93-21 Las Manitas 1121½ Avie's Gal 1223½ Bodacious Tatas1132½ Driving 7
7Jan89- 5Aqu fst 6f ⊡:23 :46⅗ 1:11⅖ ⒻClm 100000 4 1 1½ 1hd 11 1¾ Krone J A 122 2.10 87-19 Las Manitas 122¾ Tis Michelle 1222 Fine Timing 118nk Driving 6
10Dec88- 5Aqu fst 6f ⊡:22 :45⅕ 1:11⅗ 3↑ⒻClm 75000 5 3 31½ 32½ 31 11¾ Santos J A 115 *1.00 86-22 LasManitas1151¾Vanessa'sPride115¾ElizabethStevens115¾ Driving 7
2Dec88- 1Aqu fst 6f :22⅖ :46 1:11⅗ 3↑ⒻClm 100000 1 3 2hd 52½ 43 33¾ Santos J A 120 3.00 78-26 MarinneTheres1092¾FineTiming1131LsMnits120no Lacked fin. bid 6
18Nov88- 8Aqu gd 7f :23 :46⅕ 1:24 3↑ⒻHandicap 5 4 21½ 21 67 710½ Cordero A Jr 113 5.40 70-30 Hedgeabout 114¾ Starita 1133½ Pasampsi 110hd Tired 9
30Oct88- 7Aqu fst 1 :46⅖ 1:11⅖ 1:37⅖ 3↑ⒻAlw 47000 3 1 11½ 11½ 2hd 43¼ Romero J A 112 2.70 76-23 TopsInTps1152¾DewnsAdvocte115nkBristlin'Belle115nk Weakened 8
LATEST WORKOUTS May 26 Bel 4f fst :49 B — May 19 Bel 5f fst 1:01⅖ H — Apr 9 Bel tr.t 4f gd :49⅕ B — Mar 30 Bel tr.t 5f fst 1:02⅗ H

Land Between shows a lifetime record of 21-1-4-2. This means she's had twenty-one starts, one win, four seconds and two thirds. Her lifetime earnings are $35,820.

Las Manitas has a lifetime record of 21-8-5-3 with earnings of $181,757. Las Manitas has earned more than five times as much as Land Between in the exact same number of career starts.

Let's compare average earnings per lifetime start and use that as an indication—but not an ironclad rule—of class. Land Between's average earnings per lifetime start are $1,705; Las Manitas' are $8,655. This shouldn't be interpreted as Las Manitas having five times as much class as Land Between, yet it certainly indicates she has demonstrated significantly more class in her career.

Average earnings per lifetime start lose validity as a tool of comparison when we compare horses of extremely varied backgrounds—a proven 5-year-old with dozens of starts compared to a 3-year-old in his first season of racing.

Occasionally, a single victory proves to be an economic fluke when a horse wins a gigantic purse. A good example was 31 to 1 longshot Wild Again winning the inaugural $3 million Breeders' Cup

Classic in 1984. Thoroughbred purses are divided by percentage among the top finishers in two formats: 1) sixty, twenty, twelve and eight to the top four, or 2) fifty, twenty-five, twelve, eight and five among the top five. Wild Again's Breeders' Cup victory inflated his average earnings per lifetime start to an incredibly high number, one which dwarfed not only his peers but champions of previous seasons, too.

As we'll do with overinflated purses for races restricted to horses bred in one state, we'll note such aberrations when we discover them in our handicapping.

Is there another way to further verify Las Manitas' superior class to Land Between's? Again, the answer is yes, an answer produced by examining each horse's ten past performance lines as they appeared in that afternoon's *Form*.

Land Between's lifetime record is one win in twenty-one starts, an obviously poor percentage. In 1989, she had eight starts with only two finishes in the money, two seconds.

Horses demonstrate class by winning races and by the level of competition they compete against.

Remembering that we start at the bottom with the least recent race, let's examine how Land Between is approaching the race, which is at a distance of $1^1/_{16}$ miles.

Land Between has been a busy filly, one who has received little rest while racing in each of the last six months in New York at Aqueduct and Belmont Park. Back on December 8, she competed in practically the same level of claiming price, $20,000, and finished fourth by eight and one-half lengths at odds of 26 to 1. The *Form's* comment was "Even effort," while indicating she was placed third through a disqualification of one of the fillies who beat her.

It's important to note the race was a sprint at six furlongs.

Land Between was subsequently entered in a moderately higher claimer (from $20,000 to $22,500) at six furlongs, $1^1/_8$ miles and $1^1/_{16}$ miles; and then back to six furlongs in a $17,500 claimer. It didn't seem to matter much. She was sixth, fifth, fourth and sixth. Nor did the jockey matter. Her trainer used a different jockey in each race.

Perhaps out of frustration, her trainer made an equipment change, adding blinkers, March 22, indicated by the letter "b" before the weight. The blinkers didn't help either. Land Between finished fifth that day and fourth the next although the *Form* noted traffic problems in each race: "Steadied, in tight" then "Lacked room."

Finally, on April 10 at seven furlongs in a $16,500 claimer, Land Between lit the board, finishing second by three-quarters of a length. From that race, she was claimed for $16,500 by trainer Bob Klesaris for Gold N Oats Stable. The claim is indicated by the letter "c" appearing before the claiming price.

Klesaris tried Land Between in two longer races and switched jockeys from Jean-Luc Samyn to Angel Cordero, Jr. Despite moving up in claiming price from $16,500 to $22,500, Land Between finished second by a head at a mile at odds of 5 to 2, lower odds than her preceding eight races.

In her last start, she was bet down even more, going off as the favorite at 8 to 5 on a sloppy track at $1^1/_{16}$ miles. For the only time in her ten PPs, she made the lead, opening a clear advantage while setting torrid fractions. They were too torrid. After a half in :45 3/5 and six furlongs in 1:10 3/5, she tired to finish fourth by nine lengths. The *Form*'s comment: "Set pace, tired."

Today her trainer drops her from a $22,500 tag to $16,500 while keeping her at $1^1/_{16}$ miles. Regardless, an evaluation of Land Between's class is an easy one: that of a $16,500 to $22,500 claimer.

Let's move on to Las Manitas, handled by America's annual leading trainer the last several years, D. Wayne Lukas.

Las Manitas has also been in three claiming races, once for $75,000 and twice for $100,000. She also raced in two allowance races, two unnamed handicap races and three stakes races. Only her latest effort, a distant sixth in the Grade III Garden State Park Breeders' Cup Handicap, was in a graded race.

Eight of her ten PPs are sprints, seven at six furlongs and one at seven when she finished seventh. In her two other races at a mile, she was fourth twice.

By starting at the bottom of her PPs, we can't help but notice Las Manitas' performance in sprints. At today's distance of six furlongs, she shows three wins, one second and one third in seven races.

We also see she was given a breather from February 26 to April 21 after she finished a tiring fourth. In her first race back, Las Manitas ran another tiring fourth. This was not totally unexpected since horses frequently need one race back after a layoff. Her next start was her poor performance at Garden State, but this was against higher caliber fillies than she had been racing against.

In the last two years, she's won a healthy six of eighteen, finishing in the money thirteen times. She has shown the class of a $100,000 priced claimer, competitive at the top allowance level and marginally competitive in minor stakes. Her class is much greater than Land Between's.

Having demonstrated that a stakes horse is classier than a modest claimer isn't going to produce an Eclipse Award for brilliance. We don't need to compare horses in different races, rather horses in the same race.

Let's look at the May 29, 1989, running of the $589,000 Metropolitan Handicap (Grade I) at Belmont Park. The one mile Metropolitan is the first leg of the Handicap Triple Crown (the other legs are the Suburban and Brooklyn). In handicaps, the racing secretary determines the weight each horse will carry, assigning the highest weight to the best horse and the lowest to the worst. On The Line and Seeking the Gold were co-high weights at 126 pounds, conceding 11 to 14 pounds to the other six horses in the Metropolitan.

Seeking the Gold and Dancing Spree were coupled as an entry because they had the same owner. An entry simply means you get both horses with one bet. Entry-mates are assigned numbers 1 and 1A for betting, but that does NOT mean either had the No. 1 post.

We'll examine the field, concentrating on class, in post position order.

8 BELMONT

1 MILE. (1.33) 96th Running THE METROPOLITAN HANDICAP (Grade I). Purse $500,000 added. 3-year-olds and upward. By subscription of $1,000 each, which should accompany the nomination; $4,000 to pass the entry box, $4,000 to start, with $500,000 added. The added money and all fees to be divided 60% to the winner, 22% to second, 12% to third and 6% to fourth. Weights, Wednesday, May 24. Starters to be named at the closing time of entries. Trophies will be presented to the winning owner, trainer and jockey. Nominations close Wednesday, May 10 with 25 nominations.

Coupled—Seeking the Gold and Dancing Spree.

Finder's Choice ✱ — **Dk. b. or br. c. 4, by Buckfinder—Trial Landing, by Solo Landing**
Own.—Locust Hill Farm — **Br.—Janney Mr–Mrs S S Jr (Ky)** — **Tr.—Hadry Charles H** — **115**

Lifetime 18 7 1 3 $254,736 — **1989** 4 2 0 2 **$105,100** — **1988** 13 4 1 1 **$142,136** — **Turf** 2 0 1 0 **$14,270**

6May89- 9Pim	fst	1 1/16	:46⅕	1:10	1:40⅘	3↑Riggs H	1	3	$3^{3½}$	$3^{1½}$	1^{4}	1^{8}	Desormeaux K J	115	*.80	100-10	Finder'sChoice115^{8}MasterSpeaker115^{2¾}Arugula114^{hd}	Going away	6
6May89-Grade III																			
15Apr89-11Pim	sly	1⅛	:46⅘	1:11	1:49⅖	3↑Campbell H	5	3	$3^{1½}$	2^{hd}	$2^{2½}$	$3^{9¼}$	Desormeaux K J	118	1.70	86-15	LittleBoldJohn126^{nk}TemplrHill111^{9}Finder'sChoice118^{9}	Weakened	7
15Apr89-Grade III																			
18Mar89-11Lrl	gd	1 1/16	:46⅕	1:11⅕	1:42⅘	Alw 36000	2	4	$2^{2½}$	2^{2}	1^{hd}	1^{3}	Desormeaux K J	119	*1.70e	95-21	Finder'sChoice119^{3}Baldski'sChoice122^{nk}TemplrHill114^{6}	Drew off	7
20Feb89-10Lrl	fst	7f	:22⅕	:45⅖	1:22⅘	3↑Gen George	2	9	5^{3}	5^{2}	2^{3}	$3^{1½}$	Desormeaux K J	117	26.00	95-15	Little Bold John 122½ Oraibi 119^{1} Finder's Choice 117no	Fin. well	13
17Dec88- 9Pha	fst	1	:46⅗	1:11	1:37⅖	Flintlock	5	3	3^{1}	2^{2}	$3^{2½}$	$6^{4¾}$	Rocco J	122	*.80	82-18	Regal Hero 115^{hd} Front Page 115^{2½} Wolverine 115^{1½}	Weakened	9
24Nov88- 9Lrl	fst	1 1/16	:48⅖	1:12⅗	1:43	Annapolis	4	3	$3^{½}$	$1^{½}$	1^{hd}	$1^{1½}$	Desormeaux K J	119	*1.30	94-18	Finder's Choice 119^{1½} Bid for a Star 119^{3} Sir Riddle 122^{4}	Driving	7
13Nov88- 9Lrl	yl	1 1/16 Ⓣ	:49⅕	1:14⅖	1:46⅘	Japan H	4	7	6^{6}	$6^{6½}$	$2^{2½}$	2no	Desormeaux K J	114	6.80	63-37	Arlene'sVlentine116^{no}Finder'sChoic114^{2¾}BoldndLuck112^{1¼}	Nosed	14
23Oct88-10Lrl	fm	6f Ⓣ	:22⅕	:45⅖	1:10⅖	3↑Laurel Dash	11	8	5^{9}	5^{10}	$4^{4½}$	$6^{3½}$	Antley C W	117	26.20	86-15	Steinlen 124no Mac's Fighter 117½ Fourstardave 117½	Weakened	11
24Sep88-10Lrl	fst	6½f	:22⅗	:45⅘	1:17	Mrylnd Cty H	7	8	6^{5}	$6^{5¾}$	$6^{5¼}$	4^{3}	Ferrer J C	114	9.00	92-17	Teddy Drone 116^{1¼} King's Nest 121^{1¼} Trap Line 114½	Mild rally	8
27Aug88- 3Mth	fst	6f	:21⅘	:44⅖	1:08⅘	Alydar	4	5	5^{5}	$6^{4¾}$	$5^{4¾}$	4^{5}	McCarron C J b	122	2.30	91-12	TeddyDrone118^{1}MedievlVictory122^{3}SolidBryn118^{1}	No solid resp.	6

LATEST WORKOUTS **May 19 Pim 5f fst 1:03⅕ B** **May 13 Pim 4f fst :50⅖ B** **May 4 Pim 4f fst :47⅘ B** **Apr 29 Pim 5f fst 1:02⅖ B**

Triteamtri *

B. c. 4, by Tri Jet—Special Team, by Specialmante
Br.—Warner Marvin L (Fla)
Tr.—Frankel Robert

Own.—Warner M L Jr

115 Lifetime 18 6 3 1 $446,330 | 1989 4 1 1 0 $233,900 | 1988 9 2 1 1 $141,148 | Turf 14 5 2 1 $212,430

2Apr89- 8SA fst 1⅛ :45⅘ 1:09⅕ 1:47⅕ S Brndino H 6 3 $3^{2\frac{1}{2}}$ $3^{4\frac{1}{2}}$ 6^{11} 6^{13} Stevens G L 118 4.90 80-15 Ruhlmann $119^{1\frac{1}{4}}$ Lively One $120^{3\frac{1}{2}}$ Saratoga Passage116^{2} Faltered 6
2Apr89-Grade II

5Mar89- 8SA fst 1¼ :46⅕ 1:34 1:58⅘ S Anita H 10 1 $1^{1\frac{1}{2}}$ 1^{1} 2^{hd} $2^{1\frac{3}{4}}$ Stevens G L 116 40.80 93-07 Martial Law$113^{1\frac{3}{4}}$Triteamtri116^{hd}StylishWinner113^{no} Game effort 11
5Mar89-Grade I

11Feb89- 7SA my 1 :47⅕ 1:12⅕ 1:38⅕ Pmpi Ct H 4 1 1^{1} 1^{4} 1^{6} 1^{10} Stevens G L 118 3.70 77-31 Triteamtri 118^{10} Gorky $117^{4\frac{1}{2}}$ He's A Saros $118^{\frac{1}{2}}$ 5

15Jan89- 8SA fst 1⅛ :46⅘ 1:10⅕ 1:47⅖ S Fernando 4 10 $7^{3\frac{1}{2}}$ $4^{2\frac{3}{4}}$ $7^{7\frac{1}{4}}$ 8^{8} Meza R Q 120 24.60 84-11 MiPreferido123^{hd}Spedrtic$120^{4\frac{1}{2}}$PrcivArrognc120^{no} Stumbled start 12
15Jan89-Grade I

13Nov88- 8Hol fm 1⅛ Ⓣ:47 1:11 1:48⅖ Hol Dby 4 3 3^{2} 1^{hd} 2^{hd} 9^{3} Cordero A Jr 122 *3.80 83-14 Silver Circus 122^{hd} Raykour 122^{hd} Dr. Death $122^{\frac{1}{2}}$ Led, tired 14
13Nov88-Grade I

8Oct88- 8Kee fm 1⅛ Ⓣ:47⅕ 1:12⅘ 1:53 3↑Kee Brd Cup 6 3 $3^{2\frac{1}{2}}$ 2^{1} $2^{\frac{1}{2}}$ $6^{9\frac{1}{2}}$ Romero R P b 122 *1.80 67-19 Niccolo Polo $126^{\frac{1}{2}}$ Pollenate 126^{3} Eve's Error 126^{1} Well up, tired 10
8Oct88-Grade III

3Sep88- 9Mth fm 1⅛ Ⓣ:48 1:11⅘ 1:49⅘ 3↑Longfelow H 1 2 1^{hd} 1^{hd} $1^{1\frac{1}{2}}$ 1^{2} Romero R P b 112 2.90 98-07 Triteamtri 112^{2} Wanderkin $117^{1\frac{3}{4}}$ Arrived On Time 111^{hd} Driving 9
3Sep88-Grade II

24Aug88♦4Deauville(Fra) gd*1 1:38 Ⓣ Prix Quincey(Gr3) $5^{5\frac{1}{4}}$ Legrix E 124 6.50 — — Always Fair $120^{2\frac{1}{2}}$ Foreign Survivor 120^{2} Zelphi $124^{\frac{3}{4}}$ Evenly 13

26Jun88♦3Longchamp(Fra) gd*1¼ 2:05⅘ Ⓣ GrandPrix deParis(Gr1) 6^{4} Carson W 128 19.00 — — FijarTango $128^{\frac{3}{4}}$ Pasakos 128^{1} Welkin $128^{\frac{3}{4}}$ Mild late bid 10

29May88♦5Longchamp(Fra) yl*1⅛ 1:54 Ⓣ PrixJeanPrat(Gr1) 3^{2} Eddery P 128 13.00 — — Lapierre $128^{1\frac{1}{2}}$ FijarTango $128^{\frac{1}{2}}$ Triteamtri 128^{nk} Prom thruout 8

LATEST WORKOUTS ●May 24 Hol 6f fst 1:11⅗ H ●May 19 Hol 7f fst 1:21⅗ H ●May 14 Hol 1 fst 1:39⅖ H May 9 Hol 6f fst 1:11⅘ B

Its Acedemic

Ch. h. 5, by Sauce Boat—After School, by Arts and Letters
Br.—Vogel Hortense & M (Ky)
Tr.—Barrera Luis

Own.—Vogel M

112 Lifetime 32 8 7 8 $402,818 | 1989 8 3 3 1 $226,518 | 1988 13 4 1 3 $131,480 | Turf 1 0 0 0

19May89- 8Bel fst 1 :47 1:10 1:35 3↑Handicap 6 2 3^{3} 2^{3} 2^{2} $3^{2\frac{3}{4}}$ McCauley W H 121 3.10 87-16 True and Blue $119^{\frac{3}{4}}$ForeverSilver122^{2}ItsAcedemic121^{hd} Bid, wknd 6

29Apr89- 8Aqu fst 1¼ :49⅕ 1:38⅕ 2:02⅗ 3↑Excelsior H 2 2 2^{1} 1^{hd} 1^{1} $2^{1\frac{3}{4}}$ Nelson D 113 3.20 81-27 Forever Silver$111^{1\frac{3}{4}}$ItsAcedemic113^{1}JackOfClubs$113^{2\frac{3}{4}}$ Weakened 5
29Apr89-Grade II

1Apr89-10Hia fst 1¼ :46⅘ 1:34⅕ 1:59⅖ 3↑Widener H 5 5 5^{12} 8^{16} 7^{12} $7^{20\frac{3}{4}}$ Nelson D 114 9.90 75-14 Cryptoclearnce$122^{3\frac{1}{2}}$SlewCitySlew118^{nk}MiSelecto114^{hd} No factor 8
1Apr89-Grade I

18Mar89- 8Aqu gd 1⅛ :48⅗ 1:12⅘ 1:50 3↑Grey Lag H 3 4 $5^{2\frac{1}{2}}$ $4^{2\frac{1}{2}}$ 1^{1} $2^{\frac{3}{4}}$ Nelson D 116 *.90 84-30 Lay Down $112^{\frac{3}{4}}$ Its Acedemic $116^{4\frac{1}{4}}$ Congeleur 113^{5} Game try 6
18Mar89-Grade III

20Feb89- 8Aqu fst 1⅛ ⊡:48⅗ 1:13⅕ 1:51⅕ 3↑Stymie H 7 4 4^{4} 2^{hd} 1^{hd} $1^{2\frac{1}{4}}$ Nelson D 113 *1.10 86-27 Its Acedemic $113^{2\frac{1}{4}}$ Congeleur 113^{7} Lord OfTheNight115^{5} Driving 7
20Feb89-Grade III

28Jan89- 8Aqu fst 1⅛ ⊡:48 1:13⅗ 1:50 3↑Assault H 3 7 $6^{3\frac{1}{2}}$ 5^{3} 1^{1} $1^{2\frac{1}{2}}$ Nelson D 111 2.70 92-22 Its Acedemic $111^{2\frac{1}{2}}$ Congeleur $113^{1\frac{1}{2}}$LordOfTheNight116^{4} Driving 7
28Jan89-Grade III

18Jan89- 8Aqu fst 1⁷⁰ ⊡:48 1:12⅖ 1:41 Alw 41000 1 2 $2^{1\frac{1}{2}}$ $6^{3\frac{1}{4}}$ $1^{\frac{1}{2}}$ $1^{1\frac{1}{2}}$ Nelson D 115 1.80 95-16 Its Acedemic$115^{1\frac{1}{2}}$TurningForHome$115^{1\frac{3}{4}}$Worryation$115^{7\frac{3}{4}}$ Driving 7

7Jan89- 8Aqu fst $1\frac{1}{16}$ ⊡:46⅘ 1:11⅕ 1:42⅘ 3↑Aqueduct H 1 5 $5^{5\frac{1}{2}}$ 4^{6} 3^{1} 2^{1} Nelson D 110 18.60 94-19 LordOfTheNight114^{1}ItsAcedemic$110^{4\frac{3}{4}}$TruendBlue$113^{2\frac{3}{4}}$ Game try 6
7Jan89-Grade III

10Dec88- 7Aqu fst 6f ⊡:22⅗ :46⅕ 1:10⅗ 3↑Alw 36000 2 2 $5^{1\frac{3}{4}}$ $4^{1\frac{1}{2}}$ $2^{\frac{1}{2}}$ $1^{1\frac{1}{4}}$ Hernandez R Z 115 3.50 91-22 ItsAcedemic$115^{1\frac{1}{4}}$CutterSam$108^{6\frac{3}{4}}$Embrace'sSybling$115^{3\frac{1}{2}}$ Driving 7

26Nov88- 7Aqu fst 6f :22 :45 1:09⅖ 3↑Alw 41000 3 4 $5^{3\frac{3}{4}}$ $4^{3\frac{1}{2}}$ $4^{5\frac{1}{2}}$ 5^{8} Hernandez R Z 115 25.00 85-22 Lord Of TheNight$115^{6\frac{3}{4}}$CutterSam$108^{\frac{3}{4}}$WrongDoctor115^{nk} Outrun 7

LATEST WORKOUTS ●May 26 Bel tr.t 7f gd 1:30 B May 14 Bel tr.t 5f fst 1:04⅖ B May 8 Bel tr.t 5f fst 1:03⅘ B Apr 24 Bel tr.t 1 fst 1:45⅖ B

On The Line

Ch. h. 5, by Mehmet—Male Strike, by Speak John
Br.—International Thbrd Breeders Inc (Fla)
Tr.—Lukas D Wayne

Own.—Klein E V

126 Lifetime 29 12 6 1 $916,610 | 1989 4 ɜ 1 ʋ $320,680 | 1988 5 4 0 1 $327,000 | Turf 4 0 0 0 $10,625

6May89- 8Aqu fst 7f :21⅘ :43⅘ 1:21⅖ 3↑Carter H 6 3 $3^{1\frac{1}{2}}$ 4^{2} 3^{1} 1^{nk} Stevens G L b 125 *.60 94-19 On The Line 125^{nk} True and Blue $114^{\frac{1}{2}}$Dr.Carrington$110^{1\frac{1}{4}}$ Driving 8
6May89-Grade I

5Apr89- 8SA fst 6½f :21⅘ :44⅕ 1:14 Ptro Grnd H 4 8 2^{1} $2^{\frac{1}{2}}$ 1^{hd} $1^{\frac{3}{4}}$ Stevens G L b 125 *1.00 100-14 On The Line $125^{\frac{3}{4}}$ Ron Bon 116^{2} Jamoke $114^{\frac{1}{2}}$ Bobbled start 10
5Apr89-Grade III

29Jan89- 8SA fst $1\frac{1}{16}$:46⅖ 1:10⅕ 1:41 S Pasqual H 3 1 $1^{1\frac{1}{2}}$ 1^{1} $1^{1\frac{1}{2}}$ 1^{nk} Stevens G L b 123 *.60 96-16 On The Line 123^{nk}MarkChip$114^{2\frac{1}{2}}$StylishWinner113^{5} Held gamely 6
29Jan89-Grade II

14Jan89- 8SA fst 7f :22⅖ :44⅗ 1:20⅗ S Carlos H 2 2 1^{3} $1^{2\frac{1}{2}}$ 1^{hd} $2^{1\frac{1}{4}}$ Stevens G L b 126 *.30 96-11 CherokeeColony$119^{1\frac{1}{4}}$OnTheLin126^{3}HppyInSpc116^{hd} Second best 6
14Jan89-Grade II

30Dec88- 8SA fst 6f :21⅖ :43⅗ 1:07⅗ Pal Vrdes H 1 4 2^{hd} 2^{hd} $1^{\frac{1}{2}}$ $1^{2\frac{1}{2}}$ Stevens G L b 124 *.70 100-12 On The Line $124^{2\frac{1}{2}}$ Claim $118^{1\frac{1}{4}}$ Basic Rate $115^{2\frac{1}{2}}$ Drew off 6
30Dec88-Grade III

17Dec88- 8Hol gd 6f :22⅕ :45⅕ 1:09⅕ 3↑Tf Express H 2 3 3^{3} 3^{1} 1^{hd} $1^{5\frac{1}{2}}$ Stevens G L b 121 *.80 96-17 On The Line $121^{5\frac{1}{2}}$ Little Red Cloud $115^{1\frac{1}{2}}$ Faro $118^{\frac{1}{2}}$ Easily 6

2Dec88- 8Hol fst 6f :21⅘ :44⅗ 1:09⅕ 3↑Alw 35000 9 1 $6^{3\frac{3}{4}}$ 5^{2} 3^{2} $1^{\frac{1}{2}}$ Stevens G L b 114 *1.70 96-15 On The Line $114^{\frac{1}{2}}$ Claim $112^{\frac{1}{2}}$ Caballo De Oro $114^{1\frac{3}{4}}$ Driving 9

7Feb88- 8SA fst 1¼ :45⅗ 1:35⅕ 2:00⅖ C H Strb 4 2 $2^{\frac{1}{2}}$ $3^{\frac{1}{2}}$ $3^{3\frac{1}{2}}$ 3^{11} Santos J A b 119 7.00 76-16 Alysheba 126^{3} Candi's Gold 117^{8} On The Line $119^{8\frac{1}{2}}$ Weakened 6
7Feb88-Grade I

17Jan88- 8SA sly 1⅛ :46⅗ 1:10⅗ 1:49 Sn Frndo 4 1 $1^{2\frac{1}{2}}$ $1^{1\frac{1}{2}}$ 1^{1} $1^{\frac{1}{2}}$ Santos J A b 120 1.40 84-17 On The Line $120^{\frac{1}{2}}$ Candi's Gold $123^{8\frac{1}{2}}$ Grand Vizier 114^{1} Driving 5
17Jan88-Grade I

ᶜDec87- 8SA fst 7f :22⅕ :44⅖ 1:21 Malibu 4 2 1^{1} $1^{1\frac{1}{2}}$ 1^{5} $1^{7\frac{1}{2}}$ Cordero A Jr b 117 8.00 95-16 On The Line $117^{7\frac{1}{2}}$ Temperate Sil $126^{\frac{3}{4}}$ Candi's Gold $123^{\frac{1}{2}}$ Easily 9
26Dec87-Grade II

LATEST WORKOUTS May 23 Bel 5f fst 1:01 H Apr 26 Hol 5f fst 1:00⅗ H Mar 30 SA 5f fst :59⅗ H

Proper Reality Dk. b. or br. c. 4, by In Reality—Proper Princess, by Nodouble
Own.—Winn Mrs James A Br.—Winn Mrs James A (Fla) Tr.—Holthus Robert E
117 Lifetime 13 8 1 1 $987,800 1989 5 2 1 1 $236,980 1988 7 5 0 0 $745,000

13May89- 9Pim fst 1 3/16 :46⅖ 1:10 1:53⅕ Pim Specl H 1 5 55¼ 33 1hd 22 Bailey J D 118 13.90 99-10 Blushing John 1172 Proper Reality1181½Granacus113½ Drifted out 12
15Apr89- 6OP fst 1⅛ :47 1:11⅕ 1:49 Oaklawn H 5 7 74¾ 63¼ 43½ 52¼ Bailey J D 121 3.60 86-21 SlewCitySlew118½Stlwrs113noHomebuildr1151½ Bumped taken up 8
15Apr89-Grade I
25Mar89- 9OP fst 1 1/16 :49⅖ 1:13⅘ 1:43 Razorback H 3 2 2hd 1hd 31 34½ Bailey J D 123 *.20 81-24 Blushing John 1171½ Lyphard'sRidge1113ProperReality1234 Tired. 5
25Mar89-Grade II
4Mar89- 9OP sly 1 1/16 :47⅖ 1:12⅕ 1:44 Essex H 6 3 33½ 31½ 11 15 Bailey J D 120 *.20 81-28 Proper Reality1205ContactGame1111¼Lyphard'sRidge1123¼ Easily 6
11Feb89- 9OP fst 6f :21⅘ :45⅕ 1:09⅕ H Springs 2 6 52¼ 31 1hd 13 Bailey J D 112 *.40 94-20 ProperRelity1123Homebuilder121noBeAgnt1182 Wide str. handily 9
4Jun88- 6Spt fst 1⅛ :45⅕ 1:10 1:50⅕ Ill Derby 4 4 310 210 12 14 Bailey J D 124 *.30 94-17 Proper Reality 1244 Jim's Orbit 1226ClassicAccount1122½ Handily 6
4Jun88-Grade II
21May88- 8Spt fst 1 1/16 :47⅖ 1:12⅖ 1:44⅖ Nash Mem H 4 6 53½ 3½ 11 17½ Bailey J D 125 *.70 92-22 Proper Reality1257½Drouilly'sBoy1181½DeeLance12115 Ridden out 6
7May88- 8CD fst 1¼ :46⅘ 1:36 2:02⅕ Ky Derby 12 10 55½ 23 23½ 43¾ Bailey J D 126 27.20 82-11 Winning Colors 121nk Forty Niner 1263 Risen Star 126½ Bid hung 17
7May88-Grade I
23Apr88- 9OP fst 1⅛ :46⅖ 1:11 1:48⅖ Ark Derby 1 6 62¾ 61¼ 41½ 11¼ Bailey J D 118 3.20 91-14 Proper Reality 1181¼ Primal 1151¼ Sea Trek123½ Boxed in 2nd trn 8
23Apr88-Grade I
2Apr88- 9OP fst 1 1/16 :45⅗ 1:10⅖ 1:42⅗ Rebel 2 5 42 73¾ 54½ 43 Bailey J D 119 2.30 85-16 Sea Trek 1121 Din's Dancer 114¾ Notebook 1221¼ Boxed 2nd trn 10
LATEST WORKOUTS May 26 Bel 3f fst :36⅕ B ●May 6 Pim 6f sly 1:14⅕ H Apr 12 OP 4f fst :50⅖ B ●Apr 5 OP 6f fst 1:12⅖ H

Forever Silver * Gr. c. 4, by Silver Buck—Disabled Maid, by Correlation
Own.—Chevalier Stable Br.—DMD Properties & Samara Farm (Fla) Tr.—Shapoff Stanley R
113 Lifetime 35 6 7 7 $300,860 1989 10 3 2 1 $169,260 1988 16 2 4 4 $105,280 Turf 8 1 0 3 $23,650

19May89- 8Bel fst 1 :47 1:10 1:35 3↑Handicap 3 4 56 65½ 64½ 2¾ Vasquez J 122 2.90 89-16 TruendBlue119¾ForevrSilvr1222ItsAcdmic121hd Angled in stretch 6
29Apr89- 8Aqu fst 1¼ :49⅕ 1:38⅕ 2:02⅗ 3↑Excelsior H 1 4 45 41½ 21 11¾ Krone J A 111 3.80 83-27 Forever Silver 1111¾ Its Acedemic 1131JackOfClubs1132¾ Driving 5
29Apr89-Grade II
12Apr89- 8Aqu fst 1 :45⅘ 1:10⅕ 1:35⅘ 3↑Alw 47000 6 5 43 52¾ 2hd 11½ Krone J A 121 2.70 87-19 ForvrSilvr1211½DncingPrtns1212½ThMdDoctor1211 Altered course 7
18Mar89-10Hia fst 1⅛ :47⅕ 1:10⅘ 1:47⅖ 3↑Seminole H 4 4 42½ 63 54½ 54¾ Vasquez J 113 31.10 89-18 SirLeon1122½FastForward115hdIntensiveCommnd111no No threat 9
18Mar89-Grade II
11Mar89- 6Hia fst 1⅛ :47 1:11⅖ 1:49⅗ Alw 23500 1 6 85¼ 72¼ 2hd 22 Vasquez J 119 *2.80 81-21 Sir Leon 1132 ForeverSilver1191ArcticHoneymoon1134¾ Bid,wknd 8
25Feb89- 4GP fst 1 1/16 :47 1:12⅗ 1:46 Alw 30500 1 4 48 31½ 11½ 1¾ Vasquez J 117 3.40 71-28 Forever Silver 117¾ Birdies Dee Cee 1192½ Festive 1176¼ Driving 6
11Feb89- 5GP fst 1 1/16 :47⅘ 1:12⅘ 1:45⅕ Alw 29000 5 3 54½ 54 32½ 42¾ Vasquez J 115 17.10 72-25 [DH]BoldMidway1172½[DH]FastForwrd1192½RonStevens117nk Rallied 7
21Jan89- 9GP fm 1 1/16 Ⓣ:46⅘ 1:10⅖ 1:42 Alw 28000 11 9 1014 912 88¾ 85½ Penna D 115 37.20 84-09 Jimmy's Bronco 122¾ Kings River II 115¾ Lay Down119hd Outrun 11
13Jan89- 8GP fm *1 1/16 Ⓣ 1:45⅕ Alw 20000 4 8 916 1012 87½ 35½ Vasquez J 117 5.20 74-23 MetroMoon1174½FullyAttuned1171ForeverSilver1171 Wide, rallied 10
3Jan89- 9Crc fm *1 Ⓣ:49⅖ 1:14⅖ 1:38⅕ Alw 22900 1 7 74½ 76 67½ 66 Samyn J L 115 9.60 76-20 Set a Record 115hdMiamiSlick118¾Baldski'sStar112hd No menace 8
LATEST WORKOUTS May 13 Bel 5f fst 1:00⅘ H ●Apr 26 Bel 4f fst :46⅘ H Apr 21 Bel 6f fst 1:13⅗ H Apr 10 Bel tr.t 5f fst 1:00 H

Seeking the Gold * B. c. 4, by Mr Prospector—Con Game, by Buckpasser
Own.—Phipps O Br.—Phipps O (Ky) Tr.—McGaughey Claude III
126 Lifetime 14 8 5 0 $2,177,420 1989 1 1 0 0 $24,600 1988 12 6 5 0 $2,145,620

20May89- 7Bel fst 7f :22⅕ :45 1:21⅗ 3↑Alw 41000 3 3 21½ 21 1½ 1nk Perret C 121 *.30 94-17 Seeking the Gold 121nk Sewickley 1248 Cliff Flower1141¼ Driving 5
5Nov88-10CD my 1¼ :47⅘ 1:38⅗ 2:04⅘ 3↑Br Cp Class 9 6 612 52 2hd 2½ Day P 122 5.80e 72-20 Alysheba 126½ Seeking the Gold 1225 Waquoit 126nk Gamely 9
5Nov88-Grade I
25Sep88-10LaD fst 1¼ :49⅕ 1:39 2:03⅘ Super Derby 4 2 2½ 2hd 2hd 1nk Day P 126 *.70 82-19 SeekingtheGold126nkHappysIrkToms1261½LivelyOne126nk Driving 9
25Sep88-Grade I
20Aug88- 8Sar fst 1¼ :48⅗ 1:37⅘ 2:01⅖ Travers 1 1 3½ 32 22 2no Day P 126 2.50 93-09 FortyNiner126noSeekingtheGold126¾Brian'sTime1265½ Fin. strong 6
20Aug88-Grade I
30Jly88- 9Mth fst 1⅛ :47⅗ 1:11⅖ 1:47⅗ Haskell H 3 3 32 2hd 2hd 2no Day P 125 2.60 96-10 Forty Niner 126no Seeking the Gold 1254 Primal 117½ Bumped 5
30Jly88-Grade I
2Jly88- 8Bel fst 1⅛ :47 1:11⅕ 1:48 Dwyer 4 3 33 32½ 11 11¾ Day P 123 *.30 87-20 Seeking the Gold 1231¾ Evening Kris1192GayRights1231¼ Driving 7
2Jly88-Grade I
29May88- 8Bel fst 1⅛ :45⅖ 1:09⅕ 1:47⅗ Peter Pan 7 2 21 2hd 1hd 12 Day P 120 *.70 89-17 Seeking the Gold 1202 Tejano 1261¼ Gay Rights 117nk Driving 7
29May88-Grade II
7May88- 8CD fst 1¼ :46⅘ 1:36 2:02⅕ Ky Derby 8 6 23½ 35 45½ 75 Romero R P 126 15.90 81-11 Winning Colors 121nk Forty Niner 1263 RisenStar126½ Weakened 17
7May88-Grade I
23Apr88- 8Aqu fst 1⅛ :46⅘ 1:10⅖ 1:47⅕ Wood Mem 1 3 34½ 2½ 1hd 21½ Romero R P 126 *2.30 97-12 PrivteTrms1261½SkingthGold126noChrokColony126½ Held gamely 10
23Apr88-Grade I
9Apr88- 7Aqu fst 1 :45 1:10 1:34⅘ Gotham 3 5 45 42 32½ 2¾ Romero R P 114 *.60 91-19 PrivteTerms126¾SeekingtheGold1145PrfctSpy1213 Altered course 8
9Apr88-Grade II
LATEST WORKOUTS May 27 Bel 4f fst :48⅕ B May 19 Bel 3f fst :36⅕ B May 14 Bel 5f fst 1:01⅖ B May 8 Bel 5f fst 1:01⅘ H

Dancing Spree * Ch. c. 4, by Nijinsky II—Blitey, by Riva Ridge
Own.—Phipps O Br.—Phipps O (Ky) Tr.—McGaughey Claude III
113 Lifetime 18 5 2 6 $173,300 1989 6 1 2 2 $93,151 1988 12 4 0 4 $80,149 Turf 6 0 0 2 $13,303

6May89- 6CD my 7f :22⅖ :45⅕ 1:24 C D H 4 11 1211 84¾ 2hd 14 Day P b 116 *1.70 86-17 DancingSpree1164Carborundum117½BroadwayChief1151 Drew out 13
14Apr89- 8Kee fst 7f :23 :45⅘ 1:22⅘ 3↑Com Brd Cup 6 8 77¼ 72 32½ 32¾ Cordero A Jr b 115 2.50 91-15 Sewickley 115¾ Irish Open 1182 DancingSpree1153½ Jostled, start. 9
1Apr89- 8Aqu fst 1 :46⅕ 1:10⅗ 1:35⅗ 3↑Westchstr H 2 4 32½ 1hd 1½ 2hd Antley C W b 112 2.10 88-20 Lord OfTheNight115hdDancingSpree1124¾Congeleur1121¾ Drifted 8
1Apr89-Grade III
3Mar89- 9GP fst 6f :22 :44⅕ 1:09⅕ 3↑Hallandale H 1 6 67¼ 56¼ 32½ 22¼ Perret C b 114 4.60 91-20 Miami Slick 1122¼ Dancing Spree 1143 TheRedRolls112½ 2nd best 6
5Feb89-10GP fst 1⅛ :47⅘ 1:11⅗ 1:50⅕ 3↑Donn H 3 4 55 64¼ 66¼ 811 Perret C b 114 21.80 70-25 Cryptoclernce1211½SlwCitySlw1183½Priml1174½ Failed to respond 12
5Feb89-Grade I
21Jan89-10GP fst 7f :22 :44⅖ 1:23⅕ 3↑Super Bowl H 3 10 89¼ 77½ 41¾ 31 Perret C b 114 16.30 87-21 [D]MiamiSlick112¾Prospector'sHalo115nkDncingSpree114½ Rallied 11
1Dec88- 8Aqu fst 1⅛ :47⅖ 1:12⅖ 1:51⅕ 3↑Alw 29000 5 3 1hd 11 12½ 14 Vazquez J J5 b 112 *.60 79-26 Dancing Spree 1124FluorescentLou1153Binn'sFargo11712 Driving 5
5Nov88- 7Aqu fst 1 :46⅗ 1:11 1:36⅖ 3↑Alw 31000 5 2 1hd 11 12½ 16¾ Vazquez J J5 b 110 2.60 84-26 DncingSpree1106¾[DH]RunToDylight117[DH]MedivlRivl115hd Driving 7
14Oct88- 7Bel fst 1 1/16 :46⅕ 1:11⅕ 1:43⅘ 3↑Alw 31000 1 5 32 21 34½ 37¼ Cordero A Jr 114 5.70 76-23 MakeLuck1162½PortWashington1145DancingSpree114¾ Off slowly 7
28Sep88- 8Bel fm 1⅜ Ⓣ:49⅕ 1:39⅘ 2:16⅗ 3↑Alw 31000 7 6 69 75 85¼ 67 Santos J A 113 5.40 72-20 Hodges Bay 113no Reincarnate 1172¼ Anchor Bay 1104 Outrun 9
LATEST WORKOUTS May 16 Bel 4f sly :48⅖ B May 5 CD 3f my :36⅕ B Apr 30 CD 4f fst :48 H Apr 24 Kee 4f fst :51 B

Finder's Choice—115—The 4-year-old from Maryland-based trainer Charles Hadry had a career record of 18-7-1-3 with earnings of $254,736, an average of $14,152. In 1989, he had two wins and two thirds in four starts, earning $105,100, an average of $26,275. We'll note that in the six PPs showing from 1988, Finder's Choice hadn't raced in a graded stakes. He had in 1989, finishing third in the Grade III Campbell Handicap and first by eight lengths in his last race, the Grade III Riggs Handicap, when he equaled the course record at $1^1/16$ miles indicated by a speed rating of 100. (Speed ratings are discussed in Chapter 8.)

Triteamtri—115—Another 4-year-old with the same number of career starts as Finder's Choice, eighteen, with a record of 6-3-1 and earnings of $446,330, an average of $24,796. In 1989, he had a win and a second from four starts and earnings of $233,900, an average of $58,475. Triteamtri shipped to the U.S. in 1988 after competing in Europe, where all racing is on turf. His accomplishments on grass are considerable, but not relevant to today's race on dirt. Triteamtri made his final three 1988 starts at Monmouth, Keeneland and Hollywood Park on turf.

In 1989, he raced exclusively on dirt for California trainer Bobby Frankel. The results were mixed: eighth by eight lengths in the Grade I San Fernando, first by ten lengths in an ungraded stakes at 1 mile, an excellent front-running second in the Grade I Santa Anita Handicap at $1^1/4$ miles, and a dull sixth by thirteen in the $1^1/8$ mile San Bernadino Handicap (Grade II), April 2.

His showing in the Santa Anita Handicap at odds of 40 to 1 was an indication of considerable class. Triteamtri, though, had two strikes against him: he hadn't raced in nearly two months and he had never raced in New York. Not racing in New York can be an extremely significant factor in handicapping because of New York State's drug policy which prohibits the use of bute, a painkiller, and Lasix (furosemide), a diuretic which helps bleeders. Most other tracks in the country permit one or both.

Its Acedemic—112—The lightweight of the field had a lifetime record of 32-8-7-8 and career earnings of $402,818, an average of $12,588. Yet this 5-year-old has improved drastically. Prior to 1988, Its Acedemic had made $44,820 in his career. In his 4-year-old season, he won $131,480. With eight starts in 1989, he had a record of 3-3-1 and had made $226,518, for an average of $28,314.

While also displaying versatility by winning races from six furlongs to 1$1/8$ miles, Its Academic had won two of three high-level allowance races and had been first twice and second twice in four Grade III stakes races. Trainer Luis Barrera then stepped Its Acedemic up to a Grade I race, the 1$1/4$-mile Widener Handicap at Hialeah, April 1, 1989. Its Acedemic got a fair amount of respect from bettors, who sent him off at 9 to 1, but finished seventh by twenty and three-quarters lengths to Cryptoclearance, one of the top older horses in the country. The *Form's* comment was "No factor." If Its Acedemic had a bad start or traffic problems during the race, we rely on the *Form* to tell us in its comment. We prefer seeing each horse's races ourselves to document any problems. You can do it if you go to the races daily, or if you have a track which televises replays you can tape daily on a VCR.

Was the distance too long for Its Acedemic? After all, the Metropolitan is a mile. Its Acedemic answered that question in his next race, running a strong second at 1$1/4$ miles in the Grade II Excelsior Handicap back at Aqueduct. We'll conclude distance wasn't what beat Its Acedemic at Hialeah, rather the Grade I competition.

His final race before the Met was a so-so third in a one mile handicap at Belmont. Tempering Its Acedemic's blatant improvement is the fact that he hasn't won in his last four races. His last win was February 20.

On the Line—126—One of a barn full of trainer D. Wayne Lukas and owner Eugene Klein's stable of stars, this 5-year-old made $916,610, an average of $31,607, while finishing 12-6-1 in 29 career starts. Subtract four starts on turf, where he never finished in the money while making $10,625, and On The Line's dirt record (25-12-6-1) and average earnings ($36,239) are even more impressive.

In the last two years, he had won seven of nine, with the only losses a distant third to 1988 Horse of the Year Alysheba in the 1$1/4$ mile Charles H. Strub Stakes and a second by one and one-quarter lengths in his 1989 debut to Cherokee Colony as the 3 to 10 favorite in the seven furlong San Carlos Handicap. He followed that with wins in Grade II, Grade III and Grade I stakes, the last a neck victory in the seven furlong Carter Handicap at Aqueduct as the 3 to 5 favorite. His average earnings in 1989 were $80,170.

On The Line had won at 1$1/8$ and 1$1/16$ miles in California, yet clearly was at his best sprinting. In the seven sprints in his ten PPs, he had six wins and a second.

The mile distance of the Met is as fair a test as any in horse racing, too far for pure sprinters and too short for true distance horses. On The Line seemed well-suited for it.

Proper Reality—117—The 4-year-old had just thirteen lifetime starts, yet won nearly $1,000,000 ($987,800) while compiling a record of 8-1-1 and average earnings of $75,984. His 2-1-1 record in five starts in 1989 earned $236,980, an average of $47,396.

Proper Reality won his only start as a 2-year-old (derived by subtracting twelve starts as a 3 and 4-year-old from his career total of thirteen starts) and was pointed to the Kentucky Derby via the Arkansas route of prep races at Oaklawn Park. Proper Reality was a dull fourth by three lengths in the Rebel Stakes, but bounced back to win the Grade I 1^{1}/$_{8}$ mile Arkansas Derby by one and one-quarter lengths. Dismissed at odds of 27 to 1 in the Kentucky Derby, Proper Reality stalked winner Winning Colors from second, tiring a little at the end to finish fourth by three and three-quarters, a half length behind third place finisher Risen Star, who subsequently won the Preakness and Belmont Stakes.

Proper Reality went to softer spots at Sportsman's Park in Chicago, taking a minor stakes by seven and one-half lengths then the Grade II 1^{1}/$_{8}$ mile Illinois Derby by four lengths as the 3 to 10 favorite.

Proper Reality suffered a fracture in his left front leg in the race and didn't race again as a 3-year-old.

Be wary of horses attempting to come back from serious injuries. Even those who do return to the races many times don't make it all the way back to their previous level of ability.

Proper Reality had five 1989 races to judge. He won two minor stakes at Oaklawn easily as an odds-on favorite, then finished third by four and a half lengths as the 1 to 5 favorite to Blushing John in the Grade II Razorback Handicap while spotting the winner six pounds. In the Grade I Oaklawn Handicap, Proper Reality was fifth by two and a quarter to Slew City Slew (who beat Its Acedemic by seventeen and a quarter lengths when second in the Widener Handicap). He again carried more weight than the winner (three pounds) and had the comment "Bumped, taken up" in the *Form*. Taken up means the jockey stopped riding for an instant and took tight hold of the reins. In his last race, the Pimlico Special Handicap, Proper Reality, carrying one pound more than the winner, was second by two to Blushing John, who set a track record with the victory in 1:53 1/5 for the 1³/₁₆ miles (a significant record because the Preakness is run at the same distance). The *Form* said Proper Reality "Drifted out," a sign of a horse tiring by not running in a straight line.

Yet his effort in the Pimlico Special was fast enough to come within one-fifth of a second of the old track record (two lengths meant his time was two-fifths of a second slower than Blushing John). And he was a clear second, one and one-quarter lengths ahead of third-place Granacus, in a field of twelve.

In the Met, instead of giving weight, Proper Reality carried nine pounds less than On The Line and Seeking the Gold.

Forever Silver—113—In thirty-five lifetime starts, Forever Silver was 6-7-7 with earnings of $300,860, an average of $8,596. Reflecting his improvement, he was 3-2-1 in ten starts, accumulating $169,260 for an average of $16,926, in 1989.

Forever Silver moved up through the allowance ranks to run fifth by four and three-quarters lengths in the Grade II Seminole Handicap at Hialeah then first by one and three-quarters against Its Acedemic in the Grade II Excelsior. Spotting Its Acedemic a pound, he beat him again by two lengths when second in a handicap at Belmont in his last start.

Seeking the Gold—126—The obvious heavy-hitter had tons of class evident in his outstanding career, 14-8-5-0 lifetime with earnings of $2,177,420, an average of $155,530. His best race was his final one in 1988, when he finished second by half a length to Horse of the Year Alysheba in the $3 million Breeders' Cup Classic.

But in 1989, Seeking the Gold had just one start, a hard earned neck decision in a $41,000 allowance race at Belmont. Trainer Shug McGaughey used the race for a prep for the Met.

Dancing Spree—113—Seeking the Gold's stablemate was another improving 4-year-old just beginning to reach his potential. His lifetime numbers were 18-5-2-6 for earnings of $173,300, an average of $9,627. In 1989, he was 6-1-2-2, making $93,151, an average of $15,525. He won his last race, a minor stakes at Churchill Downs, by four lengths.

Questions not dealing with class were important. Was Seeking the Gold ready to beat Grade I horses off a lone allowance race? Was On The Line at his best at a mile? Could both of them concede nine pounds to Proper Reality?

Yet the crucial element in handicapping this race was a consideration of class.

Both Seeking the Gold and Proper Reality were in sharp form when they met in the 1988 Kentucky Derby at equal weights. Proper Reality was fourth, one and a quarter lengths ahead of Seeking the Gold in seventh.

Seeking the Gold subsequently developed into a superior 3-year-old; Proper Reality was injured. Their meeting in the Kentucky Derby was more than a year earlier. Yet their performances in the Derby indicated Proper Reality had the class to beat Seeking the Gold and win this race. This belief was further strengthened by careful examination of Proper Reality's races in 1989.

The entry of Seeking the Gold and Dancing Spree was bet down to 4 to 5. On The Line was 5 to 2. Proper Reality 4 to 1.

Proper Reality was an overlay.

In a marvelously dramatic duel through the stretch, Proper Reality veered out of traffic late, cut to the inside under jockey Jerry Bailey and beat Seeking the Gold to the wire by a nose. Dancing Spree was just another nose back in third.

Determining class doesn't have to be a difficult endeavor. Sometimes, it's actually easy.

The first race at Belmont Park, July 14, 1989, was a six furlong race for $50,000 claimers. Two scratches left a field of six.

Starting at the bottom of his PPs, we find that The Real Virginian has been extremely competitive in $50,000 claimers, showing a record of 1-2-3 in seven starts, all sprints. His lone miss was a fourth at seven furlongs. Today's race is at six. Thus, he's had six previous starts not only at the same claiming price, but also at the same distance.

Two starts back, The Real Virginian won a $50,000 claimer and was claimed by trainer John "Butch" Lenzini. In his lone race for Lenzini, The Real Virginian was moved up to $75,000, where he finished sixth by four and a half. Lenzini dropped him right back to the level where he's proved he can win.

And he did, at odds of 5 to 2, paying $7.20. Was he an overlay? No. Four of his five rivals had shown competitive races in higher company than $50,000. But he had clearly demonstrated the class to compete at the $50,000 claiming level.

As a point of information, the word 'claimer' sometimes has a negative connotation or is misinterpreted as an indication of inferior horses, horses with less class. Horses who compete in extremely high-priced claimers, $50,000 to $100,000, intermittently hold their own against allowance horses and occasionally make successful forays into stakes. Kemolina is a good example:

8 BELMONT

WIDENER TURF COURSE
1 1-16 MILES
BELMONT PARK
START
FINISH

1 1/16 MILES. (Turf). (1.39 1/5) ALLOWANCE. Purse $33,000. Fillies and mares, 3-year-olds and upward which have never won three races other than Maiden, Claiming or Starter. Weights, 3-year-olds, 116 lbs. Older, 122 lbs. Non-winners of two races other than Maiden or Claiming at a mile or over since June 15 allowed 3 lbs. Of such a race since then, 5 lbs.

Coupled—Miss Evans and Eau Forte.

***Kemolina** — **B. m. 5, by Kenmare—Timolina, by Timmy My Boy**
Br.—Wetherill Succ Mrs E C (Fra)
Own.—Happy Hill Farm — **Tr.—Preger Mitchell C**

119 — Lifetime 23 5 1 3 $83,610 — 1989 3 2 1 0 $44,180 — 1988 7 1 0 1 $18,720 — Turf 21 5 1 3 $83,610

1Jly89- 3Bel	fm	1	Ⓣ:46 2/5 1:10 1/5 1:35 1/5	3↑ⒻAlw 31000	1	6	4²	2²	2²	1nk	McCauley W H	117	5.80	89-15	Kemolin117nkRiverofTime117 1 1/4 SisterMrgry117 1 1/4	Up final strides 9
1Jun89- 5Bel	fm	1 1/16	[T]:48 2/5 1:11 4/5 1:42	ⒻClm 75000	2	3	5 1 3/4	3 1 1/2	3 1/2	1nk	McCauley W H	113	11.90	91-13	Kemolina 113nk Dance in a Veil 116 2 1/2 EnergySquare114 1 3/4	Driving 10
21May89- 5Bel	gd	1 1/16	[T]:47 4/5 1:12 3/5 1:44 4/5	ⒻClm 70000	4	6	6¹¹	7 7 1/2	4 5 1/2	3⁵	McCauley W H	113	14.10	72-20	Native Candy 113 2 1/4 [D]Pia's Baby 113 2 3/4 Kemolina 113 1 1/4	Rallied 10
21May89-Placed second through disqualification																
2Dec88- 5Aqu	fst	7f	:23 2/5 :46 4/5 1:25	3↑ⒻClm 50000	1	8	6 2 3/4	8 5 3/4	8⁹	8 10 1/4	McCauley W H	117	19.70	66-26	Golden T.Dancer117 3/4 AdorableAngel114noGentleWorld113 1/2	Outrun 8
15Oct88- 6Bel	fm	1 1/16	Ⓣ:47 3/5 1:12 1/5 1:43 4/5	3↑ⒻAlw 31000	3	7	6 4 1/2	5 3 1/2	4 3/4	4³	McCauley W H	117	48.30	74-27	Podeica 117¹ Highland Penny 114 3/4 [D]Fineza 114 1 1/4	Outrun 11
15Oct88-Placed third through disqualification																
29Sep88- 8Bel	fm	1	Ⓣ:45 4/5 1:10 2/5 1:35 1/5	3↑ⒻAlw 31000	7	9	8 5 3/4	4²	4 3/4	5⁶	McCauley W H	117	21.80	83-14	Majeboo 117 1 1/4 Belle Et Deluree 114 1/2 Trojan Desert 117⁴	Outrun 10
31Aug88- 2Bel	fm	1	Ⓣ:48 1:12 2/5 1:37 3/5	3↑ⒻClm 80000	5	5	5 2 3/4	7⁷	7¹³	7¹⁶	Davis R G	114	4.80	61-2C	Far East 114no Rare Lead 122⁶ Le Beau Monde 114 1 1/4	Off slowly 8
11Aug88- 9Sar	fm	1 1/8	Ⓣ:47 3/5 1:11 2/5 1:48 1/5	3↑ⒻClm 45000	4	7	5 4 1/4	6 3 1/4	2hd	1 1 1/2	Davis R G	117	5.50	86-23	Kemolina 117 1 1/2 LuckyTouch115²FatefulProspect113 1 1/4	Drew clear 11
14Jly88- 7Bel	fm	1 1/16	Ⓣ:46 1:09 4/5 1:42 2/5	3↑ⒻAlw 31000	7	3	3¹	2hd	8 6 1/2	9 8 1/2	Davis R G	117	18.70	75-14	Popol Vuh 117nk Tunita 111 3/4 Fineza 116 1 1/4	Tired 10
27Jun88- 6Bel	fst	6f	:22 2/5 :45 3/5 1:09 1/5	3↑ⒻAlw 28000	4	6	6 5 1/2	6 5 1/2	5⁹	5¹⁷	Davis R G	117	24.30	76-18	Classic Crown 109 1 3/4 Lake Valley114 7 3/4 SeattleSmooth109²	Outrun 6

LATEST WORKOUTS Jly 22 Bel 4f fst :50 3/5 B — Jly 16 Bel 4f fst :50 4/5 B — Jly 12 Bel 3f fst :36 H — ●Jun 29 Bel 3f fst :34 4/5 H

On Sept. 29, 1988, she moved from an $80,000 claimer to a $31,000 allowance, both on grass at the same distance, and improved her performance from seventh by sixteen lengths to fifth by six. On July 1, 1989, she followed a neck victory in a $75,000 claimer on the grass with a neck victory in a $31,000 allowance grass race.

At the other end of the spectrum, maiden claimers frequently are overinflated in value and don't compete well at the same claiming level once they've won a race.

Distinctions of class among top horses may be subtle.

The seventh race at Saratoga, Aug. 5, 1988, matched six turf specialists in a $47,000 1³/₁₆ miles grass handicap. Since it was a handicap, weights were assigned by the racing secretary. There were only seven pounds separating lightweight Hodges Bay from topweight Silver Voice, at 108 and 115. In between were Major Beard (113), Barood (111), El Senor (111) and Blew By Em (110). The small difference in weight assignments reflect a closely-matched field.

Could we separate one of the six on class?

In post position order were Major Beard, a 4-year-old who was fourth by four lengths in his last start, a similar $47,000 handicap at Belmont Park, against good grass horses, Broadway Tommy, Heritance and Fuller's Folly. Though sent off as the 8 to 5 favorite, Major Beard beat just one horse, Dawn o' The Dance.

Blew By Em was a 3-year-old winless in five starts in 1988, including a dull sixth in the Hawthorne Derby.

Barood had been idle since running tenth by nine lengths in the Grade I Bowling Green Handicap. He was beaten by two and a quarter lengths by El Senor.

Hodges Bay was a talented 3-year-old off a strong second in the Lexington Stakes against other 3-year-olds.

El Senor won his third start back, then finished fifth by six and three-quarters to Coeur de Lion in the Bowling Green and fourth by six and a half to Glaros, two lengths behind third-place Coeur de Lion, in the Grade II Tidal Handicap, also at 1³/₈ miles, with blinkers added.

Silver Voice was third by eight in his last start July 4 in the one mile Poker Stakes on the turf at Belmont.

Hodges Bay and Blew By Em were 3-year-olds facing older, tougher horses. Barood was beaten by El Senor in his last. Major Beard and Silver Voice hadn't run well in softer spots. El Senor had paid his dues in decent yet unspectacular fashion against the top competition Grade I and Grade II stakes attract. His fifth in the Bowling Green was in a field of thirteen. His fourth in the Tidal Handicap was in a six horse field, but he was four and three-quarters lengths closer to Coeur de Lion while getting three less pounds (seven from ten).

El Senor had been facing superior horses and should have been the favorite. When allowed to go off at 7 to 2, he was definitely an overlay. He rallied strongly along the hedge to beat Major Beard by a neck and return $9.60.

Inside with Lenny Hale and Tommy Trotter

CHAPTER 7 Lenny Hale, Senior Vice President of Racing for the New York Racing Association, is one of three men in America entrusted with the responsibility of determining *The Blood-Horse* Free Handicap, which gauges the ability of horses by age and sex and projects what they've accomplished on a theoretical scale of weights with the top horse weighted the heaviest.

Hale is in good company. His co-workers are Thomas Robbins, Racing Secretary at Santa Anita, and Jimmy Kilroe, Senior Vice President at Santa Anita.

In previous years while he was Racing Secretary for NYRA, Hale teamed with Tommy Trotter, Racing Secretary at Arlington Park and Gulfstream Park, and Kilroe to do the Jockey Club Experimental Handicap, which, since 1934, annually weights the nations's top 2-year-old colts and fillies. "As far as I'm concerned, they are the two best (racing secretary) handicappers in the country," Hale said.

Hale, forty-two, began working with thoroughbreds in Joseph Magner's stable in Delaware. An active horseman who owns and rides show jumpers, Hale trained thoroughbreds in West Virginia and Maryland. He served as Assistant Starter and Starter in Florida and New Jersey, then worked as a Paddock Judge, Patrol Judge and Placing

Judge before joining the NYRA as Assistant Racing Secretary, working under Trotter. Hale became Racing Secretary in 1979; was named an NYRA Vice President in 1983, and was promoted to Senior Vice President two years later. In 1983, Hale was honored with the Red Smith Good Guy Award, presented by the New York Turf Writers.

Fundamental to the duties of a racing secretary is a healthy understanding of class as it relates to weighting horses for any race classified as a handicap, be it a Grade I stakes or a starter handicap.

"One little rule of thumb," Hale said. "Horses beat each other all the time, but class horses generally overcome their problems, like not being 100 percent sound. Sometimes his heart will take over.

"It's tough to describe class, but you can see it when it's there. It's what separates horses whenever they have equal ability. A horse with a class edge will usually win. Horses of equal ability and class will beat each other.

"A horse doesn't have to be a stakes winner to have class. There are top-level claimers who have class and get into a habit of winning, horses such as King's Swan and Creme De La Fete. They give everything they've got. Another example is Clarinet King, who's now a riding horse. He just gave it the best he had every race."

Hale cited class as a key factor in performances by two contemporary champions: "Class is what got Easy Goer second in the Breeders' Cup Juvenile [in 1988 at Churchill Downs] and the Kentucky Derby, because both races were over a track he didn't even want to stand on. When Churchill Downs gets wet, it becomes greasy. I walked on the track. It's not like Belmont because Belmont has a great deal of sand. It's abrasive and keeps horses from sliding. Personal Ensign wasn't happy with the track that day either."

Regardless, Personal Ensign got the job done. She completed her undefeated career with a courageous last second surge to beat Winning Colors in the 1988 Breeders' Cup Distaff.

"Everybody says what's the difference, because all horses in a race have to run on it," Hale said. "But some horses handle an off track better."

In doing just one component of *The Blood-Horse* Experimental Weights, such as 2-year-olds, Hale spends three to four weeks. "We go through about six hundred 2-year-olds," he said. "It's tedious because you don't want to miss anything. Older horses have at least raced against each other."

When horses who haven't raced against each other converge in a handicap race, the racing secretary encounters his most difficult obstacle. "The problem sometimes comes when a horse carried, say 126 pounds, in a non-graded stakes and comes here and shows up in, say the Woodward," Hale said. "You know he's not going to win carrying the same weight against these stakes horses. Then, how much weight do you drop a horse? It's a dilemma. Once horses race against each other, they kind of weight themselves."

In handicap stakes races, the racing secretary tries to assign weights to ideally create a blanket finish of horses of different ability. It's a difficult task. "We try to bring horses together by weights," Hale said. "It's the only tool we've got."

The guidelines many racing secretaries use is equating one pound to one length in a distance race longer than a mile and two pounds to one length in sprints.

For example, if horses A and B carry the same weight in a $1^1/8$ mile race and A beats B by one length, then, A would be assigned one pound more than B if they raced against each other again in a handicap longer than one mile.

If A and B carry the same weight in a sprint and A beats B by one length, A would be assigned two pounds more if they met again in a handicap sprint.

Trotter uses guidelines of one pound equal to one length for races longer than $1^1/8$ miles; two pounds equal to one length for races from a mile to $1^1/8$ miles, and three pounds equal to one length for sprints under one mile.

A moment of joy for a racing secretary comes when the weights he assigned in a high-profile stakes race produces an exciting finish. Not surprisingly, Hale thus cites the 1976 Marlboro Handicap as his favorite race. At the time, Hale was Assistant Racing Secretary to Trotter. The Marlboro brought together three-time Horse of the Year Forego (then 6 years old) and the high speed 3-year-old Honest Pleasure, fresh off a stakes and track record victory in the Travers. "Tommy and I did the weights separately, which we did for every race, and we agreed completely," Hale said. "We had the same weight for the top four finishers."

Racing on the lead over a sloppy track, Honest Pleasure, carrying 119 pounds, seemed to have the race won with a clear lead at the sixteenth pole. Forego, however, was just beginning to roll under the impost of 137 pounds. Storming down the center of the track like a runaway locomotive, Forego passed Honest Pleasure on the last step before the wire. "Class, that's what carried Forego to win," Hale said. Hale's right. Forego showed a substantial dislike for a sloppy track almost his entire career, but won over the off track that day.

Trotter also has fond memories of that race: "I'll always remember it. Any time there's a photo finish, you feel like you've done your job and you're pleased with it. You can watch that race time and time again, and you can't believe that Forego got up there in time. And, it was on a track he didn't like."

Another of Trotter's favorite races was the 1961 Jerome Handicap, won by Carry Back. "I think there were six horses within a length," Trotter said. "The key to greatness in a horse is when he carries high weight and is able to win with it."

Trotter, sixty-three, served as Racing Secretary at NYRA for fourteen years and is considered one of the nation's most influential racing officials. He's been doing the Experimental Handicap for twenty-one years and is also on the Thoroughbred Owners & Breeders Association Committee which grades all stakes races in North America. Of more than 2,700 stakes races conducted at 42 different racetracks in North America in 1989, 439 were designated as graded. In an October 1989, interview, he explained his thoughts on class and how it relates to his handicapping in assigning weights: "It's not easy to define class. First of all, we run through past performances. Then we select who's going to be the top weight. You can always distinguish the class. Your top weight is a horse who's been winning and carrying the weight. That's your starting point. From your top weight, you try to reach out and make assumptions on the other horses, see if any of them raced against your top weight. Then you make a judgment how many pounds separate them. If two horses haven't raced against each other, you make comparisons of how they raced against the same opponents."

Trotter explained the history of the Jockey Club Experimental Handicap: "At one time, it was done for the purpose of running two stakes races, one at six furlongs and one at a mile and a sixteenth, at Jamaica Race Track in the 1940s. It was a prediction for 3-year-olds. Weights were done for 2-year-olds at the end of one year, then announced the following January 12th. In order for a horse to be eligible to run in either of those two stakes, he had to be on the list of weights.

We'd rate maybe ninety 2-year-old fillies, colts and geldings. The races were discontinued for the reason there were too many other 3-year-old races around the country."

In doing the current Jockey Club Experimental Handicap, Trotter said, "We have certain criteria. We look at horses finishing first through fourth in stakes races that aren't restricted (for example, races restricted to New York-breds). We'll work initially with printouts of between 1,500 to 2,000 2-year-olds. We get it down to 400 to 500, then we work from that."

When he's done, he compares notes with his compatriots in the Jockey Club Experimental Handicap, Bruce Lombardi, Racing Secretary for NYRA, and Keeneland Racing Secretary, Howard Battle. Their resulting list of 120 of the nation's top 2-year-old colts and fillies indicate the horses relative abilities by the weight they're assigned.

Most certainly, it's a reflection of the class they've demonstrated in their 2-year-old seasons.

Speed

8

I wanted to call this chapter "The Figs Do Lie," but I didn't want some nut from a date company suing me.

"The figs don't lie" is a colloquialism frequently heard in the press box from speed handicappers after one of their numbers wins. The figs mean the speed figures. The cliché means the horse with the highest speed figure always wins.

Not true.

The race, indeed, usually goes to the fastest. That does not mean the horse with the highest speed figure.

Speed is an element of handicapping, a very important one, yet one which is misused many times by speed handicappers as a panacea for all the problems presented by handicapping a race.

"If only one speed horse is in a race, he's dangerous, no matter how far the race is," jockey Angel Cordero, Jr., said.

Trainer Woody Stephens said, "I've been training horses a long time. You either use speed or you don't. It depends on the race. I study the *Form* before I send out any horse. Then I talk to my rider and tell him where I think he should be."

The implications of Cordero and Stephens reflect a true understanding of speed as a vital factor. It's not the only factor in handicapping.

Speed handicappers, who work many hours deriving their own figures instead of using the ones calculated for each horse by the *Form*, interpret their numbers as absolute evaluations of a horse's chances in a given race. If this were true, speed handicappers—assuming they didn't flunk fifth grade mathematics—would never be wrong. They are wrong, just as we all are when we handicap. The best way to use speed is as another important tool of handicapping.

Common sense dictates how we'll deal with evaluations of a horse's speed.

A problem with speed figures in the *Form* is their construction. The speed rating is a comparison of a horse's time with the track record for that distance set at a figure of 100. Each fifth of a second equals one point. If the track record for six furlongs is 1:08 and a horse runs the distance in 1:09 1/5, he is 6 points off the record and given a speed rating of 94, 100 minus 6. If he races in 1:07.4 to break the record by 1/5 of a second, he'd earn a figure of 101, 100 plus 1.

The *Form* also offers a second figure after the speed rating. This number is the track variant. It compares the average of all races run that day against the track record. For example, if nine races were run and the winning times were a combined total of 90 points off the track records for their distances, the average would be 10. Thus the track variant would be 10. This in itself smacks of unreliability. Common sense tells us a race card which is mediocre in the quality of its nine races would, under normal circumstances, produce slower winning times than a nine-race card of high quality. The track variant can't help but be influenced by the particular quality of horses racing on any given day.

Say two $40,000 claimers were entered on successive days at Santa Anita and ran the same distance in the exact same time. We'll say they each earned an 85 speed rating.

The first horse raced on a high-quality stakes card that produces a track variant of 10. The second horse raced on a card which included several claiming races, some of them cheap. Naturally, the average winning times were worse, producing a track variant of, let's say, 15.

When handicappers evaluate these horses' speed in their last race, they may give the second horse an advantage because he ran the same time despite a greater track variant. The track might not have changed one iota, yet one horse is being given better speed figures because of a track variant determined by the quality of the other races. That horse had nothing to do with the track variant.

Now let's consider the validity of the speed rating itself. Speed handicappers use their own numbers and establish expected norms of performance for horses of various levels. What these figures do is lull speed handicappers into a false sense of security. The speed numbers themselves have inherent inadequacies which fail to measure the vital element of speed itself: pace. Also, speed figures may not take into account changes in a track surface which can happen as a single afternoon of racing proceeds. The bias of the track—when the surface tends to favor one part of the racetrack and one type of horse, either speed horses or closers—can change from one day to the next, from one race to the next. Track biases at speed-favoring tracks such as Saratoga build up a front-running horse's figures.

In an effort to facilitate handicapping, the *Form* last October introduced a new line of information at the bottom of each horse's PPs. Titled a Speed Index, a number is given combining the speed rating and track variant. The Speed Index is designed to offer an easy-to-read indication of a horse's speed at a comparable distance and the same surface he is entered in today.

Distances are divided into two categories: short (less than one mile), and long (one mile and longer).

Dirt and turf figures are calculated separately.

The math is elementary. A horse with a speed rating of 80 who raced with a track variant of 26 gets a combined number of 106. This number is converted to the Speed Index as +6.0, showing the amount of points higher than 100.

Conversely, a horse with a speed rating of 80 who raced with a track variant of 11 gets a total figure of 91, 100 minus 9. Thus the Speed Index is –9.0.

If there isn't an applicable race, such as a horse who has raced on dirt but is making his turf debut, no number is given, which is shown by: Speed Index: Last Race (–).

Four Speed Indexes are given for each horse: last race at today's conditions; average of last three starts fitting today's conditions; average of all PPs fitting today's conditions, and an overall average of all PPs including all distances and surfaces.

Accompanying the Speed Index are welcome revisions of the *Form's* speed rating and track variant calculations.

Previously, speed ratings were based on the track record regardless of when it was set. Citing changes in many tracks' surfaces, the *Form* now computes speed ratings to the best time recorded at the distance in the last three calendar years.

Each January 1, the previous year's best times will become part of the three-year calculations while the fourth year back is dropped.

Revisions computing the track variant are twofold: 1) the track variant is the average of the number of points (one point being equivalent to one length) faster or slower than the three-year best time, and 2) separate track variants are computed for races under 1 mile and 1 mile and longer, both on dirt and turf. Within these categories, separate variants are calculated if there is a change in track condition during the day's racing.

Here are Slew The Knight's PPs as they appeared in the *Form* before his October 27 turf race at Aqueduct:

Slew The Knight — **B. c. 3(Apr), by Seattle Slew—Gueniviere, by Prince John**
Own.—Dileo P — **Br.—Seminole Syndicate (Ky)** — **Tr.—Hertler John O** — **118**

Lifetime	1989	6	3	2	0	$146,040
8 3 2 0	1988	2	M	0	0	$1,560
$147,600	Turf	4	2	1	0	$125,280

9Jly89- 8Bel	fm	1 1/16 Ⓣ	:45	1:10	1:41	Hill Prince	10	5	68½	51¾	2hd	1¾	Antley C W	121	10.90	91-11	SlwThKnght121¾OrngSnshn1173½ExpnsvDcson121¾ Blocked. drvg	10
9Jly89-Grade III																		
3Jun89- 9Mth	fm	1 [T]	:47⅕	1:10⅘	1:36⅗	Long Branch	2	4	42½	2hd	1hd	2¾	Samyn J L	120	*1.40	90-10	OrngeSunshine120¾SlewTheKnight1202½CurrentlyRd1131¾ Gamely	7
20May89- 8Bel	gd	1 Ⓣ	:46	1:10⅖	1:36	Saranac	5	2	1hd	1½	11½	1¾	Samyn J L	114	11.40	85-15	Slew The Knight 114¾ Verbatree 1143 Luge II 1235 Driving	8
20May89-Grade II; Run in divisions																		
10May89- 6Bel	my	1	:45⅗	1:09⅘	1:37⅕	3↑ Md Sp Wt	2	1	12½	12½	12	16	Cordero A Jr	115	*.70	79-19	Slew The Knight 1156 Mr. Carvel 115nk Gleneagles 11513 Driving	9
13Apr89- 7Aqu	fst	7f	:23	:46⅕	1:24	3↑ Md Sp Wt	5	2	1½	1½	2hd	21¼	Cordero A Jr	115	3.60	80-27	FestiveNob!1151¼SlwThKnight1151½LdingStyl!15½ Best of others	7
6Apr89- 7Aqu	my	7f	:22⅗	:46	1:24⅘	Md Sp Wt	6	2	3½	22	55½	46¾	Antley C W	122	9.90	70-21	Twice Iced 1222½ PrivateAction1221½SquareRuler1222¾ Weakened	8
28Oct88- 4Aqu	fm	1⅛ Ⓣ	:48⅘	1:14⅖	1:54⅕	Md Sp Wt	5	1	2½	53¼	56½	48	Vega A	118	2.70	56-36	Coosaragga 1183 Gold oftheIndies1183½AshGrove1181½ Weakened	10
19Oct88- 6Aqu	fst	6f	:22⅗	:46	1:10⅖	Md Sp Wt	10	7	64¼	912	917	914¾	Vega A	118	7.80	73-18	Guadalupe Peak 1182¾ Valid Carat 1181¾ Traskwood1183¾ Outrun	14

Speed Index: Last Race: +2.0 3–Race Avg.: +0.6 4–Race Avg.: –1.5 Overall Avg.: –2.3
LATEST WORKOUTS Oct 24 Bel 5f fst 1:00⅘ H Oct 14 Bel 6f fst 1:17⅕ B ●Oct 10 Bel 3f fst :35⅗ H Oct 5 Bel 5f fst 1:00⅕ H

His Last Race Speed Index is +2.0, determined by adding his speed rating (91) and the track variant (11) and comparing the sum to 100: 91 + 11 = 102. Thus the Speed Index is +2.0.

To calculate his 3-Race Speed Index Average, we first calculate the Speed Index of his previous two races over the same surface as today (all his turf PPs are classified the same distance, long, because all are one mile and over). These two Speed Indexes are each 0, because each sum is 100; 90 + 10, and 85 + 15. To average the three, we add 2.0 + 0 + 0 = 2.0. Divided by three, we get a 3-Race Speed Index Average of +0.6 (0.67 rounded off by the *Form* to 0.6).

To get the 4-Race Speed Index Average, we must go down to his PP of Oct. 28, 1988, because that's the next most recent turf race. The

Speed Index of that race is –8.0 (56 + 36 = 92; 100 – 92 = 8.0). That makes the 4-Race Average –1.5 (2.0 + 0 + 0 – 8.0 = –6.0; –6.0 divided by 4 = –1.5).

The Overall Speed Index Average is derived by taking the Speed Index of all eight of his PPs: +2.0; 0; 0; –2.0 (79 + 19 = 98; 100 – 98 = 2.0); +7.0 (80 + 27 = 107; 107 – 100 = 7.0); –9.0 (70 + 21 = 91; 100 – 91 = 9.0); –8.0, and –9.0 (73 + 18 = 91; 100 – 91 = 9.0). Adding the eight Speed Indexes produces a sum of –19. When divided by 8, the Overall Average is –2.3 (–2.37 rounded off by the *Form* to –2.3).

Washington Post columnist Andy Beyer has built a national reputation as one of the top speed handicappers anywhere. His well-written and widely read book about speed handicapping offers excellent insight. Yet Beyer, himself, in his subsequent book about trip handicapping, questioned the exclusivity of speed figures in handicapping winners.

One of the best pieces of speed handicapping I've ever seen was done by a long-time friend who handicapped three Saratoga seasons for my former paper, the *Times Union*. Bob Gersowitz believes in the importance of speed without spending hours daily to calculate speed figures. And through excellent speed handicapping, Bob made a betting coup at the 1983 Saratoga meeting. By pure coincidence, Beyer and myself were left alone in a corner of the press box in front of a TV monitor when the horses went to post for the ninth race, Sunday, August 21. While Bob was on his way to collecting more than $1,500 on the race, Beyer was standing in front of the TV set screaming at the horse in front, an easy wire-to-wire winner, to quit. She didn't come close to quitting.

Heartless, the wire-to-wire winner of the allowance race for non-winners of two, went off at 6 to 1. What made this a fine job of handicapping was that Heartless was a maiden filly in only her second start.

Most handicappers would have quickly dismissed Heartless' chances against winners. Bob's detailed handicapping caught her because of the blazing speed she had demonstrated in her only previous start, August 5. You didn't have to be a speed handicapper to see how impressive she was in that debut, in which she was well bet at 5 to 1. Breaking from post eight in a seven furlong maiden race for New York-bred fillies, 3-year-olds and up, Heartless streaked to the top for apprentice jockey Marjorie Clayton. Heartless was first at the start, first by one and a half lengths at the quarter in :22 4/5, first by a length after a half in :45 2/5, first at the head of the stretch, and then she tired. She finished seventh, beaten by five and a half lengths, after racing her first six furlongs in 1:11 2/5. The winning time of the race was 1:25, giving Heartless a time of 1:26 1/5.

Was her final time significant? No.

Now consider the eighth race that same day at the same track at the same distance. The race was the $54,400 Ballerina Stakes for fillies and mares, 3-year-olds and up. The winner, Ambassador of Luck, would finish the year undefeated and be named the Eclipse Champion Older Filly in the country.

In a field of just four in the Ballerina, Ambassador of Luck raced near front-running Triumphal early, then battled head-to-head with her to the half. She sprinted to a clear but small lead, and defeated Number by one length and Broom Dance by four and three-quarters. Her winning time of 1:22 1/5 produced a speed rating of 93. Heartless' speed rating was 71.

Look closer at the fractional times. The Ballerina field reached the first quarter in :23 and the half in :46 1/5. Keep in mind the race was just two hours after the one by Heartless on the same track. If Heartless was in the Ballerina field and ran the same fractions she had in the maiden race, she would have led after the first quarter by a length and at the half by an astounding four lengths.

This is not to say Heartless could have beaten Eclipse champion Ambassador of Luck. Nothing of the sort. What Heartless had done was clearly exhibit more early speed than Ambassador of Luck on the same surface on the same day.

When Heartless made her next start, she had the advantage of dropping in distance to six furlongs weighing against the negative factor of facing winners. The only other speed in the race belonged to Striking.

In Striking's last race, a seven furlong allowance for New York-bred fillies and mares at Saratoga, she rushed to the lead as the 2 to 1 second choice in a field of six. The favorite, Jazzercizer, broke second, then bolted to the extreme outside. Jockey Robbie Davis got Jazzerciser straightened out and went after Striking. After the first quarter, Striking led Jazzercizer by half a length. At the half, Striking was a head in front. Striking opened the lead to a length at the top of the stretch, but Jazzercizer beat her by a head in 1:25 4/5. The splits were :23 2/5, :47 2/5 and 1:12 4/5. The track was labeled muddy, but the race before, a seven furlong allowance, was won by Mugatea in 1:22 1/5 off fractions of :22 3/5, :44 4/5 and 1:09 4/5. The race after Jazzercizer's win was a six furlong maiden race won easily by Exit Five B. in 1:11, fractions of :22 2/5 and :46 1/5. We conclude, therefore, even with the benefit of Jazzercizer bolting, Striking couldn't get clear in extremely slow fractions. Striking did not have as much early speed as Heartless.

In their confrontation, Heartless bounced out to the lead and was never headed, a probability that common sense speed handicapping could have predicted.

Returning now to speed figures, the day Heartless made her debut, Pleasant Bid, a 4-year-old filly, won a $45,000 claiming race at the same seven furlong distance in 1:23 4/5, a speed figure of 85. Fanny's Fox took a seven furlong $25,000 claimer in 1:22 3/5 (91 speed rating). Directed Star won a six furlong $25,000 claimer in 1:10 1/5 (89 speed rating). High Street won a 2-year-old maiden race in 1:10 1/5 (89 speed rating). Remember: Heartless' speed rating was 71, and Ambassador of Luck's was 93.

The final speed figures of the winning horses in sprints that day made sense and were a realistic reflection of their abilities.

But look at the fractions at the half: Heartless, :45 2/5; Ambassador of Luck, :46 1/5; Pleasant Bid, :45 3/5; Fanny's Fox, :45; and High Street, :45 1/5. Ambassador of Luck's fractions can be called an aberration, but the plain fact is the speed of Heartless, a 3-year-old filly in her debut, compared favorably with older proven horses. Final speed figures didn't show that.

The point here is a vital one. Speed handicapping is wonderful if applied correctly within the limits of our framework. Speed is a valuable component, not the ultimate answer.

Now that we've settled that, we can go about using speed as a handicapping tool. It's importance will vary. Here are the basics: 1) cheap speed differs from class speed; 2) speed and pace are separate entities and should be treated as such; and 3) speed is more important in sprints than in distance races. And always remember the bottom line, the last and most important basic: speed is only important as it relates to the other horses in a given race.

Speed horses are defined as showing high early speed. How fast is fast? Use twelve seconds for each furlong (an eighth of a mile) as a guideline. Any rate faster than twelve seconds per furlong is sharp. A rate approaching eleven seconds per furlong is exceptional. The further the workout or race, the more impressive the speed. Most thoroughbreds are capable of running two furlongs in :24. Few can run two furlongs in :22. Fewer yet can run four furlongs at a rate of eleven seconds per furlong, :44 for half a mile.

When evaluating times, it's important to understand the relative speed of different racetracks. California tracks are invariably harder and thus faster than the tracks in the East. A six furlong race in 1:09 is common at Santa Anita or Hollywood Park. In New York, it's exceptional.

Before we examine speed in races, let's examine speed in workouts. Handicappers' evaluation of workouts span two extremes: 1) workouts in the *Form* are commonly inaccurate and thus worthless; and 2) workouts are accurate in the *Form* and extremely relevant indications of a horse's condition approaching a race. Some go as far as to adopt a system of "betting the bullet." This means betting horses in the *Form* who show bullet workouts, which are designated by a large black dot (a bullet) indicating it was the fastest workout of the day at that track at that distance. Though the *Form* fails to note how many horses worked the same distance as the horse with the bullet, a bullet workout is important, indicating a horse is primed to run well. Woody Stephens says of workouts: "They're everything. Horses usually run to their training."

Are workouts accurately reported by clockers in the *Form?* That's a question which is impossible to prove unless you have the time to clock hundreds of horses yourself every morning and compare. Inaccuracies are more likely to occur at tracks which have basement bottom racing. We'll assume workouts in the *Form* are accurate. We won't routinely bet the bullet. Instead—are you getting the idea yet?—we'll use workouts as another tool. When a horse pops in a good workout, we ask ourselves: does his trainer usually work his horses fast? Some trainers frequently do. Leroy Jolley is a prominent example. Fast-working Jolley 2-year-olds often get pounded at the betting windows with mixed results at best. Invariably, these horses are underlays, getting more action than they deserve and definitely not worth our interest. In 1987 and 1988 at Saratoga, Jolley was 0-for-13 with first-time starters, four of them bet down to 2 to 1 or lower off fast workouts.

Another question we'll ask about workouts is the nature of the horse. Speed horses usually exhibit speed in workouts. A bullet workout by a frontrunner means less than one by a decided come-from-behind horse. If the latter does work in bullet time, we'll interpret the move as a sign of fitness and react favorably as we go about our handicapping.

The most important question about workouts asks: has there been an equipment change? If there is for today's race, we'll assume the trainer used that change for the workout. If the change produced a dramatic change in the workout pattern of the horse, then it's worth assuming he reacted favorably to the change and will do so again in his race. For example, a horse shows four workouts, three ordinary ones before his last race: four furlongs in :48 4/5, three furlongs in :36 2/5 and three furlongs in :36 3/5. Say these workouts were followed by an uneventful performance in his last race, hypothetically:

"An Average Horse" 6 6 7^4 7^5 6^6 6^5

Then the horse shows a workout of five furlongs in :58 3/5, with or without a bullet. He's raced without blinkers in all his PPs and is wearing blinkers for today's race. We'll assume the blinker change is the reason for his rapid work and gives him every right to improve drastically. On the other hand, he could run a duplicate poor race. The blinker change may, and sometimes will, affect no change in performance or a negative change. Remember: no guarantees.

A note of caution: be sure to check that the workout you're examining wasn't before the horse's last race, a mistake made when handicapping in a hurry. Check the date of the workout.

Let's look at speed in races and the difference between class and cheap speed.

Quitters come in all different packages at various levels of racing. Some horses make a career of it. The cheap speed horse is important to identify in handicapping a race since that horse will still exhibit speed and be a factor, even though he seldom wins.

Speed horses are easy to identify when the *Form* shows all 1s at the first call throughout their PPs.

Compare two horses, each a 4-year-old-filly in 1983, and the speed of each.

What An Act was entered in a $26,500 allowance for New York-bred fillies and mares, at Aqueduct, November 20.

All ten of the races in What An Act's past performance lines

1 AQUEDUCT

6 FURLONGS
AQUEDUCT

6 FURLONGS. (1.08⅕) ALLOWANCE. Purse $26,500. Fillies and mares, 3-year-old and upward foaled in New York State and approved by the New York State-bred registry which have never won a race other than maiden, claiming or starter. Weights, 3-year-olds, 120 lbs. Older, 122 lbs. Non-winners of a race other than claiming since October 18 3 lbs. Of such a race since October 1, 5 lbs. (Purse reflects $5,500 from New York Breeding Fund enrichment.)

Sumac Sue

B. f. 3, by Restless Restless—Blanc De Chine, by Nashua
Br.—Waller Mrs T M (NY)
Tr.—Waller Thomas M
Own.—Tanrackin Farm
115
Lifetime 3 1 0 1 $15,840
1983 1 0 0 0
1982 2 1 0 1 $15,840

13Nov83- 5Aqu fst 6f :23⅘ :47 1:12⅘ 3↑ Ⓕ[S]Alw 28000 2 7 $5^{5½}$ 5^{8} 6^{8} $6^{8½}$ Davis R G 115 5.20 70-20 EmpireBeauty$115^{1½}$BrazenDane117^{nk}GentleGme115^{nk} Broke slow 7
28Jun82- 6Bel fst 5½f :23⅕ :47⅗ 1:07⅗ Ⓕ[S]Md Sp Wt 10 9 $4^{½}$ 1^{hd} 1^{2} $1^{1½}$ Fell J 117 5.30 79-17 Sumac Sue $117^{1½}$ Dehli's Gift 117^{2} April Miracle 117 Driving 10
17Jun82- 4Bel fst 5½f :23 :46⅘ 1:06 Ⓕ[S]Md Sp Wt 6 4 2½ $2^{1½}$ 2^{3} $3^{5¼}$ Fell J 117 6.10 80-20 Halo Dotty 117¾AprilMiracle$117^{2½}$SumacSue$117^{3¼}$ Drifted out, in 7
LATEST WORKOUTS Oct 31 Bel tr.t 5f fst 1:05 b Oct 26 Bel tr.t 5f fst 1:04 b Oct 22 Bel tr.t 6f fst 1:18⅗ h Oct 15 Bel tr.t 4f fst :50 b

Mrs. Goldberg

Ch. m. 5, by Nehoc's Bullet—Mrs Frog, by Social Hour
Br.—Lawrence J C (NY)
Tr.—Sciacca Gary J
Own.—Eggart K
117
Lifetime 35 1 5 3 $41,082
1983 8 0 2 0 $4,41
1982 16 0 1 1 $7,30

5Nov83- 6FL sly 5½f :22⅘ :47⅗ 1:09 3↑ ⒻAlw 5600 2 4 1^{1} $1^{1½}$ 1^{2} 2^{2} Saul D 116 3.60 69-37 Orkney 109^{2} Mrs. Goldberg 116^{3} Cosmo Girl 114^{5} Weakened
28Oct83- 7FL gd 6f :22⅘ :46⅗ 1:15⅘ 3↑ Ⓕ[S]Alw 9800 6 1 1^{hd} 2½ 2^{3} $6^{14¾}$ Saul D b 116 7.00 55-38 I'm A Tomboy 119^{5} Twilight Turkey $116^{1½}$ Orkney $116^{2½}$ Tired
18Oct83- 7FL fst 5½f :22⅘ :47⅖ 1:07⅖ 3↑ ⒻAlw 5000 3 7 5^{6} $5^{6½}$ $5^{7½}$ $6^{16¾}$ Saul D b 116 *2.50 62-23 Poker's Judge $113^{2½}$Birdseyeview113^{nk}CosmoGirl115^{4} Drifted out
25Apr83- 4Aqu my 6f :23 :47 1:10⅗ ⒻClm 25000 5 2 3^{2} 3^{4} 8^{14} $8^{15¼}$ Rogers K L 117 19.40 67-20 Break At Dawn $113^{2½}$ La Foresita 117^{nk} Run for Oscar 112½ Tired
30Mar83- 9Aqu fst 7f :23⅘ :47⅖ 1:25⅘ ⒻClm 20000 8 4 8^{4} $6^{3½}$$10^{6½}$ $9^{12¼}$ Rogers K L 117 7.60 59-24 La Foresita $113^{5½}$ Syncopating 113^{nk} Corlito 112^{nk} No factor
11Mar83- 5Aqu sly 6f ⊡:22⅘ :46⅖ 1:10⅘ ⒻClm 30000 5 4 3^{1} 4^{3} 3^{7} $5^{8¼}$ Rogers K L 113 5.30 81-11 Moody Day $119^{2½}$ Sharonna 117^{3} Vanities Bid 115^{3} Tired
4Mar83- 9Aqu fst 6f ⊡:23 :46⅗ 1:12⅕ ⒻClm 25000 2 8 $5^{3½}$ $3^{1½}$ 3^{2} 2^{nk} Rogers K L 117 13.70 83-19 Sharonna 117^{nk} Mrs. Goldberg 117½ Committ 108^{2} Gamely
29Jan83- 6Aqu fst 6f ⊡:22⅘ :46⅗ 1:13⅕ ⒻAlw 20000 5 6 5^{6} $6^{5½}$ $6^{5½}$ $6^{3½}$ Rogers K L 117 11.50 74-20 Loyal Diplomat 119^{1} Moody Day 112¾ Wailing Gail 117^{hd} Outrun
23Dec82- 7Aqu fst 1⅛ ⊡:50⅕ 1:14⅘ 1:54⅖ 3↑ Ⓕ[S]Alw 28000 1 3 2½ 3^{8} 6^{21} $7^{38½}$ Attanasio R 117 9.30 35-27 SwoonLke110^{11}Everylittlebreeze$115^{4½}$ReserveDecision120^{no} Tired
9Dec82- 7Aqu fst 6f ⊡:23⅗ :48⅕ 1:14⅘ 3↑ Ⓕ[S]Alw 26500 2 9 $12^{9½}$$10^{10}$ $8^{9½}$ $5^{7½}$ Attanasio R 117 13.00 62-30 SomCs$113^{1½}$WhtAnAct120^{no}RunTudorRn$117^{1½}$ Passed tired ones
LATEST WORKOUTS Nov 17 Aqu 3f fst :37 b ●Oct 15 FL 4f fst :49⅘ bg Oct 8 FL 3f fst :38⅕ b

Dr. Fager's Dream

Ch. f. 3, by Plastic Surgeon—Cast A Dream, by Cast Loose
Br.—Curpler Joy (NY)
Tr.—Cohn Marvin
Own.—Stevens G L
115
Lifetime 11 1 3 1 $34,480
1983 11 1 3 1 $34,48
1982 0 M 0 0

5Nov83- 5Aqu fst 6f :22⅘ :46⅖ 1:13⅗ 3↑ Ⓕ[S]Alw 26500 1 4 2^{8} 2^{9} 2^{4} $2^{1½}$ Bailey J D b 115 3.70 71-22 Tiki Singh $115^{1½}$ Dr. Fager's Dream 115¾ WhatAnAct117^{no} Rallied
28Oct83- 7Aqu fst 7f :22⅘ :46 1:25⅘ 3↑ Ⓕ[S]Alw 26500 1 10 4^{2} $4^{2½}$ $2^{1½}$ $5^{3¾}$ Bailey J D b 114 6.30 68-23 Rich N' Foolish 119^{2} Tara K.117^{nk}Raja'sDecision$109^{1½}$ Weakened
26Aug83- 2Bel fst 6f :22⅘ :46⅘ 1:11⅕ 3↑ Ⓕ[S]Md Sp Wt 2 9 $4^{2½}$ 2½ 1^{5} 1^{10} Bailey J D b 117 3.60 86-17 Dr.Fger'sDrem117^{10}MyLdiesSvge$117^{1½}$NoCshNow117^{3} Ridden out
18Aug83- 5Sar sly 1⅛ :48 1:13⅘ 1:55 3↑ Ⓕ[S]Md Sp Wt 7 5 $4^{6½}$ $2^{1½}$ 3^{7} $6^{20¾}$ Bailey J D b 117 3.30 39-27 Fantasia Agapi Mou $117^{2½}$ Jennifer Jill 117^{8} BernABit$112^{3½}$ Tired
5Aug83- 4Sar fst 7f :22⅘ :45⅖ 1:25 3↑ Ⓕ[S]Md Sp Wt 2 8 $2^{1½}$ 2^{1} 2½ $5^{4½}$ Smith A Jr b 117 4.10 72-14 Blasted Heath 117½ Social Season 117^{3} BernABit117^{nk} Weakened
14Jly83- 3Bel fst 6½f :23⅕ :47 1:19⅘ 3↑ Ⓕ[S]Md Sp Wt 10 13 8^{5} 6^{6} 4^{5} $2^{6½}$ Smith A Jr b 116 12.30 72-24 KeepThmSmiling$116^{6½}$Dr.Fgr'sDrm116½AprilMircl116^{nk} Slow start
24Jun83- 6Bel fst 7f :23 :46⅗ 1:25⅖ 3↑ Ⓕ[S]Md Sp Wt 10 8 $10^{7½}$ $7^{6½}$ $4^{7½}$ $3^{7¾}$ Smith A Jr b 114 5.60 67-20 SunSounds114^{7}KeepThemSmiling114¾Dr.Fager'sDrem114^{4} Rallied
6Jun83- 9Bel fst 6f :23 :46⅗ 1:12⅘ 3↑ Ⓕ[S]Md Sp Wt 6 7 $8^{8½}$ $6^{8½}$ 5^{9} $4^{7¾}$ Smith A Jr b 114 5.40 70-17 AltamontAnn109^{5}BlstedHeth$114^{2½}$Loudonville109½ Checked, wide
13May83- 4Aqu fst 6f :22⅘ :47⅕ 1:13⅘ 3↑ Ⓕ[S]Md Sp Wt 13 3 3^{nk} 2½ $8^{8½}$$13^{16½}$ Smith A Jr 113 *1.80 58-28 Conveyance 113½ Regal Lady 113¾ Rich N'Foolish 103^{2} Done early
29Apr83- 9Aqu fst 7f :23 :46⅗ 1:26 Ⓕ[S]Md Sp Wt 2 12 $12^{9½}$$10^{9}$ 8^{8} $5^{4¾}$ Thibeau R J^{5} 116 *2.40 66-26 ThreeDogNight$121^{1½}$Starbit$121^{1½}$SunSounds121½ Slow st.,blocked
LATEST WORKOUTS Oct 26 Bel tr.t 3f fst :36 b

What An Act

Ch. f. 4, by An Act—Warmed Bottom, by Hitting Away
Br.—Freeman W C (NY)
Tr.—Freeman Willard C
Own.—Freeman W C
117
Lifetime 13 1 4 4 $42,410
1983 8 0 2 3 $20,00
1982 5 1 2 1 $22,41

5Nov83- 5Aqu fst 6f :22⅘ :46⅖ 1:13⅗ 3↑ Ⓕ[S]Alw 26500 8 1 1^{8} 1^{9} 1^{4} $3^{2½}$ MacBeth D b 117 4.50 71-22 Tiki Singh $115^{1½}$Dr.Fager'sDream115¾WhatAnAct117^{no} Weakened
26Oct83- 7Aqu fst 6f :22⅘ :45⅘ 1:10⅘ 3↑ Ⓕ[S]Alw 28000 8 2 2^{hd} $4^{4½}$ $5^{9½}$ 7^{15} Murphy D J^{5} b 112 6.60 72-21 Nany $116^{2½}$ Empire Beauty 114^{nk} Heartless 115^{nk} Tired
30Sep83- 3Bel sly 6f :22⅗ :46 1:12 3↑ Ⓕ[S]Alw 26500 2 1 $1^{3½}$ 1^{3} 1^{hd} $2^{1¾}$ Murphy D J^{5} b 112 1.90 80-20 Nany $115^{1¾}$ What An Act 112^{nk} Raja's Decision 113^{nk} Gamely
3Sep83- 3Bel fst 6f :23⅕ :46⅗ 1:12⅖ 3↑ Ⓕ[S]Alw 26500 3 2 $1^{1½}$ $1^{1½}$ 2^{2} $3^{1½}$ Murphy D J^{5} b 112 *.60e 78-13 KeepThemSmiling113^{1}KyToThGold117½WhtAnAct112½ Lost whip
19Aug83- 1Sar my 6f :22⅖ :46 1:11⅘ 3↑ ⒻClm 35000 4 2 1^{1} 1^{1} 2^{hd} $4^{3½}$ MacBeth D b 113 4.50 78-19 [D]Corer 113^{1} Bono Shik $117^{2½}$ Run for Oscar 113^{hd} Bumped
19Aug83-Placed third through disqualification
6Jly83- 1Bel fst 6f :23⅕ :47 1:11⅗ ⒻClm 50000 2 3 1^{1} 2½ $4^{3½}$ $6^{9½}$ MacBeth D b 117 5.60 74-10 Bigger Enough $115^{1½}$ Slave Doll 110^{nk} Cognito 115^{6} Gave way
19Jan83- 6Aqu fst 6f ⊡:23⅕ :47⅗ 1:13⅗ ⒻAlw 21000 5 5 2½ $3^{2½}$ 6^{6} $8^{9¾}$ McCarron G b 117 4.40 66-24 Versailles$117^{1½}$IntentionalMove$117^{1½}$MajesticMam112¾ Gave way
6Jan83- 9Aqu fst 6f ⊡:23 :47 1:13⅕ Ⓕ[S]Alw 26500 2 2 $1^{1½}$ 1^{4} 1^{3} 2½ Migliore R b 119 *.80 77-16 Onyx Beauty 112½ What AnAct119^{5}LittleMissG.$117^{2½}$ Just missed
9Dec82- 7Aqu fst 6f ⊡:23⅗ :48⅕ 1:14⅘ 3↑ Ⓕ[S]Alw 26500 6 3 $1^{1½}$ 1^{2} 1^{1} $2^{1½}$ MacBeth D b 120 *1.80 69-30 Some Case $113^{1½}$ What An Act120^{no}RunTudorRun$117^{1½}$ Game try
21Nov82- 6Aqu fst 6f :22⅘ :46⅘ 1:12⅗ 3↑ ⒻMd Sp Wt 7 1 1^{2} $1^{3½}$ 1^{5} 1^{5} MacBeth D b 120 *.90 78-24 What An Act 120^{5} In Your Life 120¾ LoyalDiplomat120^{nk} Driving
LATEST WORKOUTS Oct 23 Bel 7f fst 1:28⅗ h Sep 25 Bel 4f fst :48⅕ h

Tara K.

Dk. b. or br. f. 4, by North Sea—Raise a Daisey, by Search for Gold
Br.—Lepden Stable Inc (NY)
Tr.—Levine Bruce N
Own.—Kreidman N
117
Lifetime 29 1 6 3 $56,377
1983 9 0 1 2 $13,54
1982 13 1 4 1 $37,61
Turf 6 0 1 0 $6,30

5Nov83- 5Aqu fst 6f :22⅘ :46⅖ 1:13⅗ 3↑ Ⓕ[S]Alw 26500 6 3 3^{9} 3^{11} $4^{6½}$ 6^{3} Maple E b 117 5.30 73-22 TikiSingh$115^{1½}$Dr.Fager'sDream115¾WhatAnAct117^{no} Raced wide
28Oct83- 7Aqu fst 7f :22⅘ :46 1:25⅘ 3↑ Ⓕ[S]Alw 26500 14 2 $5^{2½}$ 1^{hd} $1^{1½}$ 2^{2} Maple E b 117 5.80 70-23 Rich N' Foolish 119^{2} Tara K.117^{nk}Raja'sDecision$109^{1½}$ Weakened
30Sep83- 3Bel sly 6f :22⅗ :46 1:12 3↑ Ⓕ[S]Alw 26500 6 3 4^{4} 3^{6} 3^{3} $4^{2¾}$ Maple E b 117 8.60 80-20 Nany $115^{1¾}$ What An Act 112^{nk} Raja's Decision 113^{nk} Wide str.
16Sep83- 7Bel fm 1$\frac{1}{16}$ Ⓣ:46⅘ 1:11⅗ 1:45⅗ 3↑ Ⓕ[S]Alw 28000 3 4 $2^{1½}$ 5^{5} $7^{8¾}$ 6^{11} Maple E b 117 3.80 58-31 Everlovin Adelaide $113^{3¾}$ Baker's Bet113½SisterSunny$117^{1½}$ Tired
27Aug83- 7Bel fm 1$\frac{1}{16}$ [T]:47⅗ 1:11⅗ 1:43⅘ 3↑ Ⓕ[S]Alw 28000 2 2 3^{2} $3^{2½}$ $2^{1½}$ 6^{4} Maple E 117 4.80 78-19 Kittymouse 117^{3} Praise N' Reward 112¾ Sister Sunny 117no Tired
13Aug83- 3Sar my 7f :23⅗ :47⅖ 1:25⅘ 3↑ Ⓕ[S]Alw 25500 3 6 $4^{2½}$ 4^{2} 3^{4} $3^{5½}$ Maple E b 117 5.20 67-16 Jazzerciser 112^{hd} Striking $107^{5½}$ Tara K. $117^{1½}$ Wide, wknd
15Jly83- 7Bel fst 6f :22⅗ :46⅗ 1:11⅗ 3↑ Ⓕ[S]Alw 25500 7 6 $6^{6½}$ $6^{5½}$ $3^{7½}$ $5^{10¾}$ Vasquez J b 117 8.30 74-17 Sun Sounds $113^{6½}$ Jazzerciser 111^{3} Regal Lady 113^{nk} Tired
1Jun83- 5Bel fst 1 :46⅕ 1:11⅕ 1:37⅗ 3↑ Ⓕ[S]Alw 27000 8 8 $9^{7½}$$10^{8½}$ 8^{7} $7^{9½}$ Velasquez J 117 *2.30 58-12 Conveyance 111^{nk} La Samanna Lu 110^{2} Scones 110^{nk} Outrun
20May83- 6Bel gd 7f :23⅕ :46⅖ 1:23⅘ 3↑ Ⓕ[S]Alw 25500 11 10 $8^{5¾}$ $7^{4½}$ $3^{3½}$ $3^{4¾}$ Alvarado R Jr^{5} 114 9.70 78-13 Clover Miss $112^{2¾}$ Kittymouse 112^{2} Tara K. 114¾ Rallied
30Jun82- 1Bel gd 1¼ [T]:49⅕ 1:40⅕ 2:05⅘ 3↑ [S]Alw 26000 5 4 3^{1} $4^{½}$ $7^{4½}$ $7^{9½}$ Miranda J 106 4.60 55-26 Current Pride $114^{2¾}$ Commissioned $112^{2½}$ Nightly Act 109no Tired
LATEST WORKOUTS Nov 15 Aqu 4f fst :49 h Oct 23 Aqu 5f fst 1:01⅗ h

Miss Tentam

Dk. b. or br. f. 3, by Tentam—Quiet Queen, by Silent Screen
Br.—Wehle R G (NY)
Tr.—Barrera Oscar S

Own.—Gendney Farms

17Nov83- 7Aqu fst 1	:47¾ 1:13½ 1:40	3↑⑤Ⓖ Alw 28000	2 5 6⁴ 6⁵½ 7¹⁰ 7¹²½	Smith A Jr	115	8.70	54-29 Praise N' Reward 119ⁿᵈ Raja's Decision 115⁷ Ligner 119ⁿᵈ Outrun 9
5Nov83- 5Aqu fst 6f	:22¾ :46¾ 1:13½	3↑⑤Ⓖ Alw 26500	3 5 6¹³ 6¹⁴ 5⁸ 5²½	Smith A Jr	120	28.40	71-22 Tiki Singh 115¹¼ Dr.Fager'sDream115½WhatAnAct117ⁿᵒ No threat 8
27Oct83- 9Aqu fst 6f	:23½ :47½ 1:14½	3↑⑤Ⓖ Md Sp Wt	5 7 3⁴½ 2⁴ 2½ 1ⁿᵏ	Smith A Jr	119	2.30	70-24 MissTntm119ⁿᵏGlimpsofHvn114¹½MyLdsSvg119¼ Bore in, driving 10
13Oct83- 9Aqu gd 6f	:23½ :47 1:11¾	3↑⑤Ⓖ Md Sp Wt	7 11 9⁵½ 5⁴ 4⁶½ 3⁶½	Smith A Jr	119	41.50	75-20 CornishArt119²½LadyRealyExplode119⁴¼MissTentam119ⁿᵏ Bore in 12
26Sep83- 9Bel fst 1	:47½ 1:13 1:39¾	3↑⑤Ⓖ Md Sp Wt	1 7 6⁴¼ 7⁸¼ 8¹⁷ 8¹⁶¼	Lovato F Jr	b 118	43.00	52-18 AprilMiracle118ⁿᵒSocialSeson112½RichN'Foolish118½ No factor 11
15Sep83- 9Bel fst 6½f	:23 :46¾ 1:18	3↑⑤Ⓖ Md Sp Wt	11 11 11¹²½ 11¹³½ 11²¹ 11³⁰	Cruguet J	119	41.30	56-18 Nany 113⁷ Lady Realy Explode 118¹ April Miracle 118¹¼ Trailed 11
2 Jly83- 1Bel fst 1⅟₁₆	:48 1:14¾ 1:48½	3↑⑤Ⓖ Md Sp Wt	12 8 5⁴¾ 4⁴ 6⁵½ 6¹¹	Cruguet J	o 116	9.30f	57-20 Starbait116⁴¼FantasiaAgpiMou111½RonmurLssie113¹ No menace 12
3 Jly83- 1Bel fm 1 ① 1:49	1:13 1:44¼	3↑⑤Ⓖ Md Sp Wt	4 8 8¹¹ 7⁷½ 7⁹½ 7¹¹½	Douglas R R⁵	111	20.50	68-15 Empire Beauty 116¹½ Starbait 116¼ Priceless Miss 116² Outrun 8
16Jun83- 4Bel fst 1¼	:47¼ 1:13½ 1:45¾	3↑⑤Ⓖ Md Sp Wt	3 10 11¹² 9¹⁷ 8¹⁷ 8²⁰¼	Thibeau R J⁵	109	35.20f	56-22 RegILdy109ⁿᵒEmpirButy114²¼Wlkmilinmyshos105²¾ Broke slowly 12
2 Jun83- 3Bel fst 1	:47¾ 1:13¾ 1:38¾	3↑⑤Ⓖ Md Sp Wt	7 12 12⁸¼14¹⁷11²⁶10²⁴½	Thibeau R J⁵	109	64.70	47-20 Illusive Eyes 114¹½ EmpireBeauty114²½RichN'Foolish114³ Outrun 14

LATEST WORKOUTS Nov 15 Bel ⅜ fst :48 b   Nov 3 Bel tr.t ⅜ fst :50 b   Oct 26 Bel tr.t ⅜ fst :37¾ b   Oct 14 Bel tr.t ¼ fst :36 b

120   Lifetime   1983 11 1 0 1 $17,200
         11 1 0 1   1982   0 0 0 0
         $17,200   Turf 1 0 0 0

Regal Dowager

B. f. 3, by Regal Embrace—Dajarra, by Canonero II
Br.—Blue Sky Farm (NY)
Tr.—Thomas Richard

Own.—Buckley J E

9Oct83- 3Bel gd 1¼ ① 1:48½ 1:40¾ 2:06¾	3↑⑤Ⓖ Alw 28000	5 7 7¹¹ 8⁷ 7⁸ 7¹¹¾	Rivera M A	115	54.80	49-30 Mia Reale 117¹ Praise N' Reward114¾Ms.Mafalda117¾ No factor 9
26Sep83- 2Bel fst 6f	:23¾ :47¾ 1:18½	3↑⑤Ⓒ Clm 45000	3 8 11⁷½11⁸½12¹³12¹³½	MacBeth D	112	71.70	72-18 Crushem 113ⁿᵏ Ring On Doc 112½ Corer 112¾ Outrun 12
14Sep83- 1Bel fst 6f	:22¾ :46¾ 1:24¾	3↑⑤Ⓖ Alw 26500	7 5 4²½ 5³½ 7⁹½ 7¹⁰¾	MacBeth D	113	58.70	63-16 Empire Beauty 113ⁿᵒ Mia Reale 117¾ Talc Coating 113½ Tired 11
28Feb83- 6Aqu fst 1⅟₁₆ ⊡ :49¾ 1:15¼ 1:48½	⑤Ⓖ Alw 27000	5 6 6⁵ 6⁵½ 6⁸½ 6¹¹½	Gonzalez M A	115	23.00	58-25 Romalane 111¾ Monarch's Magic 111³ Tall 'N Tan 121³ No factor 9
20Feb83- 6Aqu fst 1⁷⁰ ⊡ :48 1:13½ 1:45¾	⑤Ⓖ Alw 74500	6 6 5⁷½ 5⁶½ 4⁴ 5³¾	Gonzalez M A	115	54.40	71-20 Cobitony 111½ Subversive Chick 111ⁿᵏ Energetica 113ⁿᵏ No rally 12
14Feb83- 9Aqu fst 6f ⊡ :23¾ :47½ 1:12¾	⑤Ⓖ Alw 75½0	3 8 8⁹½ 8¹⁰ 7⁹½ 8⁶½	Barnett W A⁷	109	73-13 SubversiveChick111¾AprilTarget111½Monarch'sMgic116¾ Outrun 9
2Feb83- 1Aqu fst 1⅟₁₆ ⊡ :48¾ 1:14 1:47¾	⑤Ⓖ Sag Harbor	4 7 8⁸ 7⁹½ 6¹³ 6¹⁵	Zuniga M	112	33.20	60-24 Halo Dotty 112½ Abraxis 112ⁿᵏ Subversive Chick 112¹⁰ Outrun 8
23Jan83- 5Aqu sly 6f ⊡ :23½ :47½ 1:13¾	⑤Ⓖ Clm 25500	8 6 6⁸ 6⁵½ 4⁶½ 3⁶½	Zuniga M	118	37.50	70-26 HaloDotty116⁵½SubversiveChick111²RegalDowger118⁴½ Mild rally 9
2Jan83- 6Aqu fst 1⁷⁰ ⊡ :49½ 1:15½ 1:46¾	⑤Ⓖ Alw 28000	9 6 6¹¹ 5⁷½ 6¹² 7¹⁴	Alvarado R Jr⁵	116	5.10	56-28 Energetica111⁵Killemwithkindness116ⁿᵒPopularByFr116² Outrun 9
17Dec82- 9Aqu fst 1⁷⁰ ⊡ :49¾ 1:16½ 1:47¾	⑤Ⓖ Md Sp Wt	2 5 4²½ 1³ 1⁹ 1⁵½	Alvarado R Jr⁵	112	2.60	64-25 Regal Dowager 112⁵½ MiracleMile117½PopularByFar117¹ Driving 9

LATEST WORKOUTS Oct 29 Sar tr.t 5f fst 1:03¾ b   Oct 8 Sar tr.t 4f fst :50 b   Sep 21 Sar tr.t 5f fst 1:04¾ b

105   Lifetime   1983 9 0 0 1 $3,06
       10 13 1½ 2   1982 1 1 1 1 $22,63
         $25,650   Turf 1 0 0 0

Scones

Dk. b. or br. f. 3, by Harvard Man—Teadate, by Verbatim
Br.—Elmendorf Farm (NY)
Tr.—Fernandez Floreano

Own.—Miron S E

3Nov83- 1Aqu fst 7f	:21¾ :45 1:25	⑦Ⓒ Clm 22500	7 5 6¹¹ 6¹³ 6¹¹ 8¹⁴	Cruguet	116	17.30	62-23 OurTrish113²CommnderNThief116²½HoldYourLughs107²¼ Outrun 9
20Oct83- 7Aqu gd 1	:47½ 1:12 1:37¾	3↑⑤Ⓖ Alw 28000	~1 3 2¹ 3⁷ 7¹⁵ 7¹⁸½	Murphy D J⁵	109	5.50	58-26 Brazen Dane 117³ Rich N' Foolish 114½¹Baker'sBet114ⁿᵏ Stopped 7
15Sep83- 8Bel fst 6f	:22¾ :45½ 1:12	⑦Ⓒ Clm 25000	1 5 4³½ 5⁴½ 8⁴½ 8ⁿᵏ	Smith A Jr	116	13.90	74-18 April Target 109¾ Dazzling Glory 114½ Our Trisha 114½ Fin. early 9
3Sep83- 8Bel fst 6f	:23½ :46¾ 1:12¾	3↑⑤Ⓖ Alw 26500	5 5 4³½ 3⁴½ 3³ 4²	Smith A Jr	113	8.90	78-13 KeepThemSmiling113¹KeyToTheGold117²WhtAnAct112¾ Bore in 7
31Jly83- 9Sar fst 7f	:22¾ :45½ 1:24½	3↑⑤Ⓖ Alw 25500	2 10 9⁸ 7⁵ 5⁵½ 7⁹	Cruguet J	111	12.00	69-12 Regal Lady 113¼ Striking 111² Tiki Singh 113ⁿᵒ No factor 11
4Jly83- 4Bel fm 1⅟₁₆ ① 1:47¾ 1:11¾ 1:44¾	3↑⑤Ⓖ Alw 25500	12 6 5⁴½ 5²½ 6⁴½ 6⁷	Cruguet J	111	7.80	67-14 Valid Gal 111½ Ms. Mafalda 117ⁿᵏ Baker's Bet 111¾ Off slowly 12
23Jun83- 9Bel fst 6f	:23¾ :46¾ 1:25½	3↑⑤Ⓖ Alw 25500	2 5 5²½ 2⁴ 2⁴ 4¹¹½	Cruguet J	109	5.20	64-22 Chaldea 109¹¹ Three Dog Night 109½ Tiki Singh 111ⁿᵏ Weakened 10
16Oct82- 9Bel fst 1¼	:48¾ 1:12¾ 1:51¾	3↑⑤Ⓖ Alw 27000	8 3 3½ 3½ 3²½ 4⁷½	Cruguet J	118	5.30	61-22 Genista 104⁴ Dehli's Gift 109½ Freckles Wish 112½ Weakened 10

115   Lifetime   1983 14 0 0 2 $9,600
       21 1 1 4   1982 7 0 0 1 $23,920
         $33,520   Turf 1 0 0 0

Copyright© by News America Publications Inc. Reprinted with permission of the copyright owner.

were six furlong sprints. Looking at the first call at the quarter in each race shows What An Act first eight of ten times and second within half a length of the leader in the other two. Here is a filly with consistently high early speed. But this filly also shows a lifetime record of 1-4-4 in thirteen career starts. Her one victory, the bottom PP, was in a maiden race a year earlier when she won by five lengths, wire-to-wire of course. In that race, she opened a two length lead after the first quarter and was never headed. When we examine her other races, we see other times she sprinted clear after the first quarter and packed it in anyway. Her two worst races are, not the least bit surprising, the ones when she couldn't get the lead after the first quarter. Then she quit badly, finishing eighth and seventh.

What An Act also quit other times, although not as badly. In her last race fifteen days earlier in the same class at Aqueduct, she opened an eight length lead after a quarter, was in front by nine lengths after a half, remained in front by four in the stretch, and finished third by two and a quarter lengths. Horses which stop in such a crushing manner frequently have breathing problems. They exert themselves greatly during the early part of a race and by the end are having trouble getting sufficient amounts of air to keep going. We'll stay away from horses such as What An Act. Just for your information, that day at Aqueduct, What An Act outdueled Sumac Sue for the early lead and won by seven lengths. This again demonstrates we can be wrong in a single race. But we'll never be completely wrong if we avoid such quitters. What An Act went off at 5 to 2, a horrid underlay for a proven quitter.

Jones Time Machine is at the other end of the spectrum of speed horses. This stakes-winning filly popped up at Saratoga, Aug. 7, 1983, in a $35,000 allowance race at six furlongs. Despite a two month layoff, Jones Time Machine was bet down to 3 to 5 and won easily on Saratoga's speed-favoring track.

7 **SARATOGA**

6 FURLONGS. (1.08) **ALLOWANCE.** Purse $35,000. Fillies and Mares. 3-year-olds an upward, which have not won two races of $10,800 since May 1. Weights, 3-year-olds, 11 lbs. Older, 122 lbs. Non-winners of a race of $15,000 since July 15, allowed 3 lbs. Of suc a race since May 1, 5 lbs. Of two such races since January 1, 7 lbs. (Maiden, claimin starter and state-bred races not considered.)

Coupled—Sprouted Rye and Viva Sec.

Jones Time Machine

Ch. f. 4, by Current Concept—Daunt's Girl, by Daunt
Br.—Jones Livestock (Utah)
Tr.—Parisella John
Own.—Sabarese T M

117

Lifetime				
24 12 5 3	1983	6 4 1 0		$130,56
$308,500	1982	13 4 4 3		$156,47
	Turf	4 3 0 0		$69,20

4Jun83- 7Bel	gd	6f		:22	:44⅗	1:08⅗	3↑ⒻAlw 35000	4	1	1^{1}	2^{hd}	2^{1}	$2^{4\frac{3}{4}}$	Cordero A Jr	122	*.80	94-08	AmbssdorofLck$117^{4\frac{3}{4}}$JonsTmMchn122^{11}Mrs.Rbrts$117^{4\frac{1}{4}}$	Game try	
8May83- 8Aqu	fst	7f		:22⅖	:45⅕	1:22⅘	3↑ⒻVagrancy H	5	3	$1^{1\frac{1}{2}}$	1^{1}	1^{1}	$4^{2\frac{3}{4}}$	Cordero A Jr	121	2.00	84-26	Broom Dance 121½ Syrianna 114¾ Sprouted Rye $115^{1\frac{1}{2}}$	Weakened	
19Mar83- 8Aqu	my	7f		:22⅖	:45⅗	1:23⅕	3↑ⒻDistaff H	1	1	$1^{1\frac{1}{2}}$	1^{1}	$1^{1\frac{1}{2}}$	$1^{1\frac{1}{4}}$	Cordero A Jr	122	*.80	85-21	Jones Time Machine $122^{1\frac{1}{4}}$ Fancy Naskra $113^{4\frac{3}{4}}$Adept111^{2}	Driving	
6Mar83- 8Aqu	fst	6f	⊡	:22⅖	:45⅗	1:10⅖	3↑ⒻCorrection H	6	2	1½	$1^{1\frac{1}{2}}$	1^{3}	1^{2}	Cordero A Jr	121	*.50	92-19	JonesTimeMachine121^{2}FancyNaskr112^{1}RosD'Argent$107^{2\frac{3}{4}}$	Driving	
5Feb83- 1Aqu	fst	6f	⊡	:23	:46⅘	1:11	ⒻAlw 35000	1	1	$1^{2\frac{1}{2}}$	$1^{2\frac{1}{2}}$	1^{8}	1^{10}	Buscemi S^{7}	112	*.20	89-20	JonesTimeMchin112^{10}Coprincss119^{2}WdingPowr$108^{7\frac{3}{4}}$	Ridden out	
8Jan83- 8Aqu	fst	6f	⊡	:22⅖	:45⅗	1:11	3↑ⒻInt'borugh H	2	3	$1^{2\frac{1}{2}}$	1^{4}	1^{8}	$1^{8\frac{1}{2}}$	Rivera M A	116	3.10	89-16	JonesTimeMachine$116^{8\frac{1}{2}}$Stellarette$112^{1\frac{1}{4}}$LadyLothrio$108^{3\frac{1}{2}}$	Easily	6
28Nov82- 8Aqu	fst	6f		:22⅕	:45⅖	1:11	3↑ⒻPetrify H	3	3	$1^{1\frac{1}{2}}$	1^{hd}	1^{hd}	$3^{2\frac{1}{4}}$	Cordero A Jr	113	*.80e	84-28	ChepSets$110^{2\frac{1}{4}}$WestportNtiv116^{no}JonsTimMchin$113^{1\frac{1}{2}}$	Weakened	7
20Nov82- 8Aqu	fst	6f		:22⅖	:45⅘	1:10	ⒻDark Mirage	1	2	$1^{2\frac{1}{2}}$	$1^{1\frac{1}{2}}$	2½	$2^{1\frac{3}{4}}$	Rivera M A	118	5.20	89-21	DnceNumber$116^{1\frac{3}{4}}$JonesTimeMchin118¾PrincssZn116^{2}	Weakened	7
13Oct82- 9SA	fm	*6½f	Ⓣ	:20⅘	:43	1:12⅘	Morvich H	3	2	1½	2^{1}	4^{4}	$5^{6\frac{3}{4}}$	Shoemaker W	115	6.60	88-05	Shanekite 115^{2} Remember John 120^{1} Smokite 117^{nk}	Tired	7
29Sep82- 9SA	fm	*6½f	Ⓣ	:21⅗	:44⅕	1:16	ⒻAut Days H	7	2	1½	$1^{1\frac{1}{2}}$	1^{2}	$1^{3\frac{1}{2}}$	Pincay L Jr	117	*1.70	79-20	Jones Time Machine$117^{3\frac{1}{2}}$RosyCloud115¾Manzanera117^{nk}	Handily	9

29Sep82-Run in Two Divisons 8th & 9th Races

Aminaun

B. m. 5, by Jacinto—Puddie Q, by Loom
Br.—Thompson Bros (Ky)
Tr.—Ludwig Jack D
Own.—Franks J

117

Lifetime				
40 17 3 4	1983	8 3 0 1		$50,870
$182,734	1982	14 8 1 1		$85,062
	Turf	1 0 0 0		$1,382

9Jly83- 7Key	fst	6½f	:22⅕	:45⅕	1:17⅖	3↑ⒻAlw 15000	2	5	$7^{4\frac{1}{2}}$	7^{11}	7^{15}	6^{18}	Vigllotti M J	122	3.40	68-19	Swift Attraction $122^{1\frac{1}{4}}$ Sunshine Sandal117^{1}MayBay$119^{4\frac{1}{2}}$	Outrun	7
18Jun83-10Det	fst	6f	:22⅕	:45⅖	1:10⅘	3↑ⒻQueen	1	7	3^{1}	$5^{6\frac{1}{2}}$	$8^{9\frac{1}{4}}$	$8^{9\frac{3}{4}}$	Perrodin E J	120	3.00	76-16	Miss Hyperion 115^{3} North Rustim 112^{2} TiffanyTam120^{1}	Steadied	11
28May83- 9LaD	fst	5½f	:22⅕	:45⅘	1:04⅗	3↑ⒻAlw 15000	2	3	2½	$2^{2\frac{1}{2}}$	1^{1}	1^{3}	Ardoin R	116	*.80	97-15	Aminaun 116^{3} Draconic's Lady 114^{2} Hail Tudor $114^{1\frac{1}{4}}$	Driving	6
22Apr83- 9LaD	fst	6f	:22	:45⅕	1:10	3↑ⒻSuthernAcnt	11	1	2½	2½	$4^{5\frac{1}{2}}$	7^{12}	Ardoin R	123	*.80e	81-16	Monique Rene 123^{2} All Sold Out $114^{2\frac{1}{4}}$ Florida Jig 123^{6}	Tired	11
13Mar83-10FG	fst	6f	:22⅖	:46	1:11⅕	ⒻMatchmaker	6	1	1½	$1^{1\frac{1}{2}}$	$1^{2\frac{1}{2}}$	$1^{1\frac{1}{2}}$	Ardoin R	119	*1.10e	89-20	Aminaun $119^{1\frac{1}{2}}$ Shining Bronze 113^{3} Heatherten 112¾	Ridden out	9
15Feb83- 9FG	fst	6f	:21⅘	:45⅖	1:11⅕	ⒻMardi Gras H	8	2	1^{2}	1^{2}	$1^{2\frac{1}{2}}$	1^{nk}	Ardoin R	117	4.20	89-19	Aminaun 117^{nk} Really Royal 110½ Mickey's Echo $115^{1\frac{1}{2}}$	Driving	13
23Jan83- 8FG	sl	6f	:22⅗	:46⅗	1:12⅘	ⒻAlw 12000	1	3	1^{1}	1^{2}	1^{3}	3¾	Ardoin R	117	3.00	80-34	Shining Bronze 121¾ Rose Judge 108^{hd} Aminaun 117¾		12
8Jan83- 9FG	fst	6f	:22⅖	:45⅘	1:11⅗	3↑ⒻPan Zareta	6	5	3^{2}	$4^{3\frac{1}{2}}$	$8^{7\frac{3}{4}}$	10^{10}	Delahoussaye D J	119	*.70e	77-20	Monique Rene $127^{2\frac{1}{2}}$ Mickey's Echo $115^{2\frac{1}{2}}$ Really Royal111¾	Tired	12
19Dec82- 9FG	fst	6f	:22⅕	:45⅘	1:11⅕	3↑ⒻChoucroute	5	4	$3^{3\frac{1}{2}}$	3^{2}	3^{3}	$5^{4\frac{1}{2}}$	Ardoin R	121	*.50e	84-23	Lila Jean 116^{1} Monique Rene 129^{3} Forty Watts 117^{hd}	Wide, tired	10
8Dec82- 9FG	fst	6f	:22⅕	:45⅗	1:11⅖	3↑ⒻAlw 12500	4	6	3½	2^{2}	1^{hd}	1¾	Ardoin R	118	*.70	88-20	Aminaun 118¾ Paris Rumor 112^{hd} Best of Peaches 111^{1}	Driving	10

LATEST WORKOUTS ●Jly 30 Mth 6f fst 1:13 h Jly 21 Mth 5f fst 1:01 h ●Jly 7 Mth 3f fst :35 h

Swift Attraction ✳

Own.—Lewis J F

Dk. b. or br. f. 4, by Lord Gaylord—Tudor Beauty, by Tudor Grey
Br.—Nichols Elizabeth W (Md)
Tr.—Boniface J William

1105

								Lifetime	1983	8	3	2	3	$3,455
								17 7 3 5	1982	9	4	1	2	$68,512
								$112,067	Turf	1	1	0	0	$9,600

27Jly83-	8Tim fst *6½f	:23	:46¾ 1:17¾	3 + ⓅPhoebe's Dky	2 5	2hd 1hd 1hd	22 Grove P	122	*1.20	90-09 CHessMove117²SwiftAttr/ction122³StephiGirl117nk Best of others 7
9Jly83-	7Key fst 6¼f	:22½	:45½ 1:17¾	3 + ⓅAlw 15000	3 3	3nk 1hd 2hd	11½ Pino M G	122	*1.70	86-19 Swift Attraction 122½ Sunshine Sandal117¾MayBay119¾ Driving 7
25Jun83-	8Bow fst 6f	:22¾	:45¾ 1:11	3 + ⓅTosmah H	1 2	2hd 1¹ 3¹½	Nicol P A Jr	114	3.00	84-20 Amanti114¹½KenwoodPrincess114noSwiftAttrction114½ Weakened 7
11Jun83-	7Pim fst 6f	:23¾	:46¾ 1:12	3 + ⓅAlw 20000	6 4	1hd 1hd 1¹	2hd McCauley W H	²22	2.30⒝	86-18 KnwoodPrncss122¹½⒝SwftAttrctin122½Jv'sLdy119¹½ Lugged in 6
11Jun83-Disqualified and placed third									
28May83-	8Pim fst 6f	:23½	:46½ 1:11¾	3 + ⑤Jameela H	7 2	1hd 2hd 2nd	33½ Passmore W ½	119	3.10	86-18 SweetChrissy113¹¼Jove'sLady116²SwiftAttrction119nk Weakened 9
14May83-	7Mth fst 6f	:22	:44½ 1:11½	3 + ⓅAlw 15000	3 2	3nk 1hd 1¹	1¹½ Rocco J	119	3.60	84-20 Swift Attraction 119¼ Al's Annie 115² Silver Valley 110⁴ Driving 9
4May83-	8Pim yl 6f	ⓉⒹ:22½	:46¾ :59	ⓅAlw 16000	6 3	1¹½ 1½	13 1¹ Passmore W J	114	*.90	91-10 Swift Attraction 114¹ Scherzo's Last 119²Ashbrittle114²½ Driving 9
23Apr83-	9Pim fst 6f	:23½	:46½ 1:12	ⓅAlw 16000	5 2	1hd 1½	1hd 2½ Passmore W J	114	*.90	85-18 SwetChrissy114²SwiftAttrction114noWgonDggon109¹½ Weakened 10
12Jun82-	8Lrl fst 1½	:46½ 1:11½ 1:45¾		ⓅⓈPearlNklace	5 2	2hd 3¹ 48¼	5¹² Tejeira J	116	5.80	69-21 Golden Wage 112nk Wise Colleen 112¼ Platinum Belle114⁵ Tired 8
29May82-	9Mth sly 6f	:22½	:45½ 1:12¾	ⓅMs Woodford	3 5	2hd 1hd 1½	34 Tejeira J	123	4.30	74-25 PlatinumBelle119²TalcShker119³½SwiftAttrction123nk Weakened 7

Hasty Damascene

Own.—Shapoff E L

B. f. 4, by Gold and Myrrh—Hasty Jane, by Hasty Road
Br.—Dowdy Dorothy W & T W (NY)
Tr.—Shapoff Stanley R

115

								Lifetime	1983	8	0	1	0	$10,620
								41 3 4 6	1982	22	2	1	4	$61,378
								$102,578	Turf	2	0	0	0	$1,650

31Mar83-	7Aqu fst 1	:45	1:09¾ 1:36¾	3 + ⓅAlw 27000	2 7	713 813 812	810 Clayton M D⁵	b 116	28.30	74-21 Regal Taheka 110½ Petit Ball 121hd SwiftAndSudden121³½ Outrun 9
16Mar83-	8Aqu fst 1	:47½	1:12 1:38¾	3 + ⑤Alw 41000	8 10	10¹⁰10¹³ 9¹³	714 Smith A Jr	b 121	5.80	58-27 Logic 121¹¼ Subversive Chick 102hd Dam Little 121¹¼ Outrun 10
5Mar83-	7Aqu sly 1½	⊡:47½	1:12¾ 1:43	ⓅAlw 27000	2 6	66½ 63½	33½ Smith A Jr	b 117	11.90	93-11 Foolish Spin 117⁴½ HastyDamascene117²¼Minor'sGift117²¼ Rallied 6
25Feb83-	7Aqu fst 170	⊡:48	1:13¾ 1:45¾	ⓅAlw 37000	3 7	714 7¹² 510	48 Kaenel J L	b 115	26.70	65-27 SoftMornng115²HostEmy'sFlg119⁶SwtLughtr110¹¾ No contender 7
20Feb83-	7Aqu fst 6f	⊡:22½	:46 1:12	ⓅAlw 35000	8 11	12¹⁴11¹³11¹⁰	86½ Kaenel J L	b 115	56.40	77-20 Bestowed 115¹ Aironlass 115½ Ebullient 110½ No factor 12
10Feb83-	8Aqu fst 6f	⊡:23	:46¾ 1:11¾	ⓅAlw 35000	4 7	78² 78⅜ 78⅛	57½ Kaenel J L	b 115	37.20	79-18 Hoist Emy's Flag 119¹½ Rosa D'Argent117¹¼Aironlass110² Outrun 7
19Jan83-	8Aqu fst 170	⊡:48½	1:14¾ 1:45¾	3 + ⑤BroadwayH	6 9	9¹²10¹¹ 8¹⁰	710 Molina V H	b 105	24.60	63-24 Soft Morning 115¹¼ Logic 113¹¼ Dam Little 120²¼ Outrun 7
2Jan83-	1Aqu fst 6f	⊡:23½	:47¾ 1:13	ⓅⓈAlw 41000	5 5	68½ 610 513	413 Molina V H	b 117	15.90	66-28 Belwood Deb 117⁸½ Stone of Blue 110no Czajka 115⁴½ outrun 6
24Dec82-	7Aqu fst 6f	⊡:23¾	:47¾ 1:13	3 + ⑤Handicap	2 5	69½ 69 57	35 Molina V H	b 105	13.60	74-27 Belwood Deb 122³ Czajka 118² Hasty Damascene 105¹½ Rallied 6
5Dec82-	8Aqu fst 1⅛	⊡:49¾	1:15 1:48½	3 + ⑤Tic'derogH	3 10	117½118¼ 97½	591 Molina V H	b 105	29.00	63-25 Dam Little 114³ Logic 109nk Wise 'N Willing 114²¼ Mild bid 11

LATEST WORKOUTS • Jly 31 Sar 6f fst 1:15¾ b • Jly 27 Sar 5f fst 1:01¾ b • Jly 22 Aqu ⊡ 3f fst :37 b

Viva Sec

Own.—Brennan R

Dk. b. or br. m. 5, by Secretariat—Viva La Vivi, by Royal Note
Br.—Malibu Stables (Ky)
Tr.—Nobles Reynaldo H

119

								Lifetime	1983	10	1	3	4	$70,162
								25 8 8 5	1982	9	3	4	0	$99,706
								$239,250	Turf	1	0	0	1	$4,440

20Jly83-	8Bel gd 7f	:23½	:46¾ 1:24¾	3 + ⓅImp'trice H	3 4	54½ 54½ 44	3² MacBeth D	112	5.00	76-25 Medieval Moon 108nk I'm In Time 112¹⅛ Viva Sec 112¹⅛ Rallied 5
11Jly83-	7Bel fst 6¼f	:23½	:46½ 1:17¾	3 + ⓅHandicap	3 6	43 42½ 2³	1no MacBeth D	117	2.30	87-21 Viva Sec 117no All Sold Out122³¾LizMatizz117no Wide str. driving 6
3Jly83-	6Bel fst 7f	:22¾	:45½ 1:23¼	3 + ⓅHandicap	4 6	64¾ 53¼ 2½	2⁴½ Vasquez J	117	3.40	80-20 I'm In Time 114½ Viva Sec 117nk Mochila 119³¼ Held place 6
1Jun83-	4Bel my 6f	:22½	:47¼ 1:11¾ 1:42¾	3 + ⓅCicada	6 3	41½ 2½ 21	26½ Cordero A Jr	117	2.70	81-14 May Day Eighty 117½ Viva Sec117½CleverGuest117½ Held gamely 9
10May83-	4Bel my 6f	:22½	:45½ 1:09¼	3 + ⓅAlw 35000	5 3	3³ 3¹½ 3¹½	3² Cordero A Jr	124	*2.00	94-11 Geraldine's Store 119¹⅛I'mInTime119²VivaSec124³ Mild response 7
2May83-	8Aqu fst 6f	:23¾	:46¾ 1:10¾	3 + ⓅHandicap	1 4	42½ 3½ 2²	2¹½ MacBeth D	117	2.80	87-20 Ambassador of Luck 122¹½ Viva Sec 117½ Mochila118¹⁰ 2nd Best 5
2May83-	8Aqu fst 1	ⓉⒹ:22½	:45½ 1:38¾	3 + ⓅHandicap	4 3	48½ 34½ 34½	34¼ MacBeth D	119	3.20	81-14 Doodle 119½ MajesticNorth119⁴½VivaSec119³½ Lacked a response 7
9Apr83-	8Aqu gd 1	:45½	1:10½ 1:35¾	3 + ⓅBed O'Roses	2 4	44½ 42 32½	33½ MacBeth D	112	5.00	85-18 Broom Dance 118³ Adept 109¼ Viva Sec 112⁶ Rallied 7
23Mar83-	9Hia fst 7f	:22¾	:45½ 1:23½	3 + ⓅPoinciana H	6 3	32 4¹ 45½	4¼ Fires E	114	*1.40e	83-16 Sprouted Rye 118½ Vany 113³ Tracie Elaine 118¼ Weakened 13
12Mar83-	8Hia fst 6f	:22¾	:45½ 1:10¾	ⓅMiami Beach H	8 5	44 52½ 4³	6¹¾ Fires E	116	*1.80	89-14 Chilling Thought 118nk Wendy's Ten119hdMrs.Roberts118nk Tired 8

LATEST WORKOUTS • Aug 2 Sar 5f sly :59¾ h Jun 25 Aqu ⊡ 5f fst 1:01¾ h

In her ten PPs, dating back to two races at Santa Anita the previous fall, Jones Time Machine showed nothing but ones after the first quarter. Throwing out the two turf races as irrelevant to today's race, we see Jones Time Machine's record in her last eight starts on dirt was 4-2-1 including a second by four and three-quarters lengths in her last race as the 4 to 5 favorite against Ambassador of Luck. Ambassador of Luck ran six furlongs in 1:08 3/5 at Belmont to beat her. One of Jones Time Machine's wins was by eight and a half lengths in the Interborough Handicap. Another of her wire-to-wire victories was by ten lengths.

None of the other four fillies facing Jones Time Machine at Saratoga matched her class, even though Viva Sec was a legitimate stakestough, hard hitter. Working against Jones Time Machine was her layoff. Better horses than her have lost off similar vacations.

But if she could gain the lead with little pressure, Jones Time Machine would be impossible to beat. We must determine if any of her four rivals had the early speed to press the pace.

Viva Sec and Hasty Damascene didn't show a single '1' at the first quarter call out of their combined twenty PPs. Obviously, they had little to do with our speed evaluation. The other two horses had shown speed. Aminaun, a shipper from Keystone, won a stakes race at the Fair Grounds in New Orleans wire-to-wire in 1:11 1/5 for the six furlongs. In her last four starts, however, Aminaun didn't make the lead at the first call. She won an allowance race three starts back, but in her last effort, a $15,000 allowance at six and a half furlongs at Keystone, she showed no speed at all and finished sixth by eighteen lengths to Swift Attraction, who is the final horse we'll evaluate for speed. After her allowance win, Swift Attraction raced second by two lengths as the 6 to 5 favorite in the six and a half furlong Phoebe's Donkey Stakes at Timonium. Going straight through her PPs at the first call (excluding the one turf race), we see Swift Attraction has either been a head in front or no more than a neck behind the leader after the first quarter. Excluding her lone distance race, she had the lead in each of the eight remaining races after a half mile. Her times at the half were, from her most recent race: :46 2/5, :45 1/5, :45 4/5, :46 3/5, :46 1/5, :44 4/5, :46 4/5 and :45 4/5. Compare the half mile times of Jones Time Machine, again from the most recent race: :44 3/5 (she was second by a head at that point against Ambassador of Luck), :45 1/5, :45 3/5, :45 3/5, :46 4/5, :45 3/5, :45 2/5 and :45 4/5. The median half-mile time of their last eight sprints was Swift Attraction :46; Jones Time Machine :45 3/5 against higher quality horses.

Is this a guarantee Jones Time Machine has higher speed? Compare their median first quarter times: Swift Attraction's is slightly faster than :22 4/5. Jones Time Machine's is slightly faster than :22 2/5. Keep in mind five of Jones Time Machine's lines are from winter racing in New York. Swift Attraction's are all from the spring and summer, when faster times are usually run.

A difficulty in comparing the two is the lack of a common racetrack. Jones Time Machine's eight lines are from Aqueduct and Belmont; Swift Attraction's are from five different tracks of varying speeds.

We'll conclude Jones Time Machine is the faster horse and certainly the classier of the two. Again, we won't bet her. It's a good race to watch as Jones Time Machine rockets to the lead virtually by herself and wins easily.

Not betting is the best strategy when confronted with an underlay we feel will win. Simply skip the race.

Speed is a measure of one horse's ability. Pace means determining the relationship between two, three or even more horses as we handicap. Horse A may be able to go a quarter in :22 and a half in :45. Will that allow him to control the pace of a six furlong sprint? Only if there isn't a Horse B or C, or both, who can go just as rapidly or almost as rapidly. If all three can, the pace will be guaranteed: too fast as a speed duel develops. Maybe you've heard the term "suicide speed duel." Any speed duel has the potential to be mutually suicidal for the combatants who are staging it. In any race, at any distance, a horse on the lead will normally expend less energy if allowed to set the pace by himself. When two horses run head-to-head, be it in a sprint or a distance race, they are liable to run each other into the ground if they match stride for stride for an extended period of time. Only an exceptional horse can take head-to-head pressure for an entire race and still have enough energy left to be there at the wire. Two notable examples are Triple Crown champion Affirmed and Alydar's historic 1978 Belmont Stakes duel and the 1962 Travers between Jaipur and Ridan. In each, two great horses were at each other's throat from the opening of the gate to the end of their battle, a mile and a half in the Belmont and a mile and a quarter in the Travers. Affirmed won by a head. Jaipur won by a nose.

We, of course, will be looking to avoid having a horse in a speed duel. Can you accurately handicap speed duels? Yes. Handicapping should point out whether any race has one or more speed horses. Barring scratches which would force us to re-handicap the race, we can determine how much early speed is logically indicated by past performance lines.

Sometimes, it's so simple it hurts. An excellent example occurred in the 1981 Hopeful at Saratoga. The Hopeful is a six and a half furlong stakes, the first time on dirt 2-year-olds are asked to go farther than six furlongs in a Grade I stakes. The hope is that a horse who takes to the added half furlong will respond well to the Triple Crown distances the following season as a 3-year-old. In fact, fourteen Hopeful winners have gone on to take the Belmont Stakes.

The 1981 edition of the Hopeful had three important members: undefeated Out of Hock, who shipped north from a victory in the Sapling Stakes at Monmouth Park; Mayanesian, the recent winner of the Sanford Stakes at Saratoga, and a New England invader named Timely Writer.

Mayanesian, who went on to modest success, and Out of Hock, who found his best stride in turf sprint racing, had one thing in common on Hopeful Day; each was a speed merchant. In their then brief careers, these two had shown exactly one style of running—straight to the lead taking no prisoners. The bettors on and off-track felt Out of Hock would win despite the presence of Mayanesian. Out of Hock went off the odds-on favorite and wound up another statistic in Saratoga's storied Graveyard of Favorites. Out of Hock raced the only way he knew how: for the lead. Mayanesian did the exact same thing, and they cooked each other in a blazing speed duel. Guess who was around to close and clean up? Timely Writer. The Hopeful marked his emergence as one of the best of his generation. And he would prove, with victories in the Florida Derby and the Flamingo before injuring himself, that he didn't need a speed duel in front of him to set him up. Yet, it certainly didn't hurt him that August afternoon at Saratoga.

Let's look at another race from Saratoga, Aug. 13, 1983. Eleven horses were entered in a six furlong $40,000 handicap for 3-year-olds and up. Scratches reduced the field to seven. One of them, coincidentally, was Mayanesian.

7 **SARATOGA** 6 FURLONGS SARATOGA

6 FURLONGS. (1.08) HANDICAP. Purse $40,000. 3-year-olds and upward. Weights, Wednesday, August 10. Declarations by 10:00 a.m., Thursday, August 11.

Explosive Bid — Ch. h. 5, by Explodent—Golden Way, by Diplomat Way
Br.—Greiner-Ocala STud Inc-Wilkerson (Fla)
Own.—Hawksworth Farm — Tr.—Delp Grover G
116 — Lifetime 38 9 11 5 $267,337 — 1983 6 2 3 0 $63,170 — 1982 16 4 4 3 $132,113 — Turf 11 3 3 2 $101,123

8Aug83- 5Sar fst 7f :21⅘ :43⅘ 1:22 3+Alw 35000 6 1 11½ 11½ 11½ 2hd Guerra W A 115 4.00 92-12 Stiff Sentence 119hd Explosive Bid 115¾ Copelan 1123½ Gamely 7
1Jun83-10LaD fst 6f :22⅗ :45⅕ 1:10⅗ 3+Alw 14500 4 1 12½ 1hd 1hd 1hd Franklin R J 117 2.00 90-14 Explosive Bid 117hd Sword Devil 1224 Silent Man 1191 Driving 6
0May83-10LaD fm 1⅟₁₆ (T):46⅗ 1:10⅗ 1:40⅘ 3+Barksdale 7 1 11½ 11½ 21 25 Franklin R J 114 2.40 96-04 PoliceInspector1245ExplosiveBid114hdCgeyCougr1141½ Game try 7
0Apr83- 9LaD fst 1⅛ :47⅖ 1:11⅕ 1:50⅕ 3+Arklatex 1 1 1½ 1hd 31½ 45½ Franklin R J 113 2.70 93-19 [D]Rivalero113½PoliceInspector1134½StgeReviewer113½ Weakened 7
0Feb83-10FG fm *1⅛ (T) 1:50⅗ F G Classic 12 2 21½ 21 12 2¾ Franklin R J 118 5.40 80-11 Listcapade 120¾ Explosive Bid 118¾CageyCougar1161½ Weakened 13
3Jan83- 9FG fm *1⅟₁₆ (T) 1:42⅖ Alw 12500 1 1 11½ 12 15 11½ Franklin R J 116 *2.00 103 — ExplosiveBid1161½Listcapade1155½OccasionalyMondy118¾ Driving 8
1Dec82- 9FG sly 6f :22⅘ :46⅕ 1:11⅖ 3+Alw 14000 7 3 1½ 1hd 12 2nk Franklin R J 116 *.80 88-22 Jayme G. 113nk Explosive Bid 1164½ Princely 114nk 9
5Nov82- 9FG fst 6f :21⅗ :44⅘ 1:10 3+Handicap 2 2 1hd 1hd 2hd 33 Franklin R J 119 *1.30 92-14 Cherokee Circle 114no Up Limit 1213 Explosive Bid 119½ 11
6Sep82- 7Pen yl 1⅟₁₆ (T) 1:43⅘ 3+Pa Gov Cup H 7 1 11 11½ 13 1nk Bracciale V Jr 115 8.60 71-29 Explosive Bid 115nk Uncle Jeff 1092½ Alhambra Joe 1115½ Driving 10
1Aug82- 9Mth fst 1⅛ :46⅗ 1:10⅕ 1:48⅕ 3+Mth Hcp 4 1 11½ 1½ 22 45¼ Fann B 115 38.60 89-14 Mehmet115¾PukkaPrincess1083¾SummerAdvocte117¾ Weakened 13
LATEST WORKOUTS ●Aug 5 Sar 4f fst :45⅘ h

With Caution — B. h. 5, by Raja Baba—Daring Step, by Prince Dare
Br.—Daring Step Partnership (Va)
Own.—Farish W S — Tr.—Carroll Del W II
113 — Lifetime 35 10 7 6 $157,123 — 1983 6 1 1 1 $27,228 — 1982 10 4 2 1 $67,407 — Turf 5 1 0 1 $8,700

4Jun83- 8CD fst 6f :21⅘ :44⅗ 1:09⅗ 3+Buckskin 1 6 32 42½ 65¼ 613 Allen K K 119 2.50 85-12 LuckyPoint122½PecefulSymmtric1226LbourPrty1192½ Brief speed 6
3Apr83- 5Kee gd 6f :22⅖ :45⅗ 1:11⅗ Alw 17700 2 5 2hd 11½ 15 15½ Sellers M S 118 *.80 84-21 With Caution 1185½RonnyTurcotte1122DoneWell1144½ Ridden out 6
3Mar83- 3Spt sly 6f :23⅕ :47 1:12⅖ Alw 20300 1 2 1½ 1½ 23 23¼ Guajardo A 120 1.40[D] 85-25 FullFlme1203½[D]WithCution120hdMr.Monsenor1201½ Ran out turn 6
18Mar83-Disqualified and placed fourth
4Feb83- 7Aqu fst 6f [•]:22⅘ :46⅕ 1:10⅘ Alw 35000 2 2 1½ 1hd 1hd 2no Hernandez R 119 4.20 90-13 Main Stem 110no With Caution 1192½ Mortgage Man 117hd Sharp 8
3Jan83- 8Key fst 6f :22⅖ :45⅕ 1:10⅕ 3+Bensalem H 5 2 31 31½ 32½ 43¼ Barrera C 123 *1.30 87-23 Swelegant 1161½ Hard Hit 1132 Cyane's Best 118no Weakened 6
8Jan83- 8Bow fst 6f :22⅖ :45⅗ 1:11⅖ 3+S Maryland H 1 3 2hd 2½ 2½ 31 Pino M G 118 *1.90 82-26 WhatAMichael117noPrinceValid1141WithCution1181½ Fin. Evenly 8
3Dec82- 8Aqu fst 6f [•]:23⅕ :46⅖ 1:11⅕ 3+Gravesend H 3 1 1½ 2hd 21½ 42½ Hernandez R 116 7.20 85-23 Chan Balum 1081 Maudlin 126½ In From Dixie 1201 Weakened 9
1Nov82- 8Key fst 6f :22⅖ :45⅖ 1:09⅗ 3+Al Hattab 3 2 11 11 12½ 13½ Agnello A 123 2.60 93-22 With Caution 1233½ Obgyn 1154½ Willy Wank 1152½ Driving 7
6Nov82- 6Lrl fst 6f :22 :45⅗ 1:10⅘ 3+Handicap 7 3 2hd 21 2½ 21 Terry J b 118 26.00 88-11 Top Avenger 1211 With Caution 118¾WhatAMichael1193½ Gamely 12
5Oct82- 8Key fst 7f :22⅖ :45⅘ 1:24 3+Quaker H 5 2 2½ 11 1hd 22 Terry J b 117 17.70 85-30 SupremeGlow1182WithCaution117¾DedictedRullh1196½ Weakened 8
LATEST WORKOUTS Aug 8 Sar tr.t 6f fst 1:15 b ●Aug 1 Sar 4f fst :46 h ●Jly 25 Sar tr.t 6f fst 1:13 h

Mayanesian — Ch. c. 4, by Bold Hour—Cozumel, by T V Lark
Br.—Madden Preston (Ky)
Own.—Gordonsdale Farm — Tr.—Zito Nicholas P
111 — Lifetime 33 5 5 4 $123,812 — 1983 15 2 2 2 $48,590 — 1982 7 0 1 0 $8,120 — Turf 3 0 2 0 $16,500

0Jly83- 7Sar fst 6f :22⅖ :45⅖ 1:10⅕ 3+Alw 35000 2 6 2½ 2hd 31½ 64¼ MacBeth D b 115 7.10 85-14 Guyana 1172 Vittorioso 117no Main Stem 112¾ Tired 6
3Jly83- 7Bel gd 6f (T):21⅘ :44⅘ 1:11⅖ 3+Alw 35000 3 4 31½ 53½ 56 68 Bailey J D b 117 6.00 78-12 HexgrevStr117nkCurrntHop1113¾OutOfHock1141¾ Loose bandage 6
4Jly83- 6Bel hd 6f (T):21⅕ :43⅖ 1:08 3+Alw 35000 1 2 11½ 1hd 23 24 Bailey J D b 122 4.10 99-05 Out Of Hock 1174 Mayanesian 1222 HexgreaveStar1174 Game try 6
3Jun83- 7Bel fst 6f :22⅖ :45⅘ 1:10⅖ 3+Alw 35000 4 2 12 1½ 23 38¼ Bailey J D b 119 5.00 82-18 Linkage 1178 Prosper 117nk Mayanesian 119¾ Weakened 8
1Jun83- 3Bel fm 6f (T):21⅘ :44⅗ 1:09⅕ 3+Alw 40000 9 1 14 14 12 21 Bailey J D b 117 20.90 96-06 Muttering 1221 Mayanesian 117no Ski Jump 114¾ Game try 11
0May83- 8Mth fst 6f :22⅕ :45 1:10 3+Handicap 3 2 11 2½ 31½ 43¾ Perret C b 115 7.50 86-12 Top Avenger 1232½ Bill Wheeler 118hd Laddie Dancer 1121½ Tired 5
2Apr83- 8Aqu fst 6f :22⅖ :45⅗ 1:09⅖ 3+Alw 35000 9 5 63½ 74½ 89 812 Hernandez R b 119 15.80 82-16 Fit to Fight 1211½ Star Gallant 1213½ Sepulveda 119nk No factor 11
4Apr83- 7Aqu fst 6f :22⅕ :45⅕ 1:09⅘ 3+Alw 35000 5 2 11½ 14 1½ 36 MacBeth D b 119 7.50 86-19 Willy Wank 1193 Kim's Chance 1193 Mayanesian1192¼ Weakened 6
4Mar83- 8Aqu fst 6f :22⅖ :45⅗ 1:10 Alw 35000 6 2 14 12½ 43 68 Smith A Jr b 115 9.50 83-21 Main Stem 112hd Maudlin 1123½ And More 117¾ Gave way 7
Mar83- 9GP fst 6f :22 :45⅗ 1:10⅘ Alw 30000 1 4 1hd 2hd 56 59 Fell J b 122 5.30 76-28 Sonofagov 1221½ Vittorioso 122hd Spanish Drums 1152½ Used up 6
LATEST WORKOUTS Jly 28 Sar tr.t 3f fst :37 b ●Jly 24 Sar 4f fst :46⅖ h Jun 30 Bel 4f fst :48 b

Storm Wave — B. g. 6, by Stage Director—Wild Water, by Windy City II
Br.—Davis Mrs D M Jr (Ky)
Own.—Marydel Farm — Tr.—Odom George P
111 — Lifetime 23 6 2 5 $116,062 — 1983 1 1 0 0 $15,600 — 1982 8 1 2 2 $46,702 — Turf 7 2 2 2 $56,[illegible]2

4Aug83- 3Sar my 6f :22⅖ :46 1:11⅕ 3+Clm 85000 3 4 1½ 14 14 12¾ Vasquez J 116 5.50 84-24 StormWv1162¾ThTimIsNow1226¾AccountRcivbl1221½ Ridden out 7
Sep82- 5Bel fm 6f (T):21⅗ :44⅖ 1:08⅗ 3+Alw 32000 4 6 610 69 45½ 44 Vasquez J 119 3.50 97-08 OutOfHock1061[D]Hrmonizer1171½OneNeverNose1191¾ No menace 7
18Sep82-Placed third through disqualification
2Sep82- 8Bel gd 6f (T):21⅘ :44⅘ 1:09⅖ 3+Chas Hatton 2 7 67 56 44½ 22¾ Vasquez J 117 3.80 94-03 One Never Nose 1172¾ StormWave117nk[D]Sepulveda1121½ Rallied 8
Aug82- 9Sar fm 1 [T]:47⅘ 1:11⅕ 1:36 3+Alw 35000 2 3 52½ 33½ 45 56 Vasquez J 119 2.60 90-16 Aristocratical 115½ Sportful 1151¾ Rivertot 1151¾ Weakened 10
Jly82- 8Bel gd 6f (T):22 :45⅗ 1:09⅘ 3+Alw 32000 2 6 77 87 56 22½ Vasquez J 122 2.40 92-14 SoldierBoy1152½StormWave122½SmartndShrp1112 Gained placed 11
Jly82- 7Bel fm 7f (T):22⅖ :44⅘ 1:21⅘ 3+Clm 300000 5 3 43½ 42½ 32 31¾ Vasquez J 118 3.10 93-13 Bottled Water 120no Aristocratical 1161¾StormWave118no Rallied 9
Jly82- 9Bel fm 6f (T):21⅘ :45 1:09⅗ 3+Alw 32000 3 5 86¼ 55½ 31½ 11½ Vasquez J 115 7.60 96-18 StormWve1151½Accomplishmnt112½Dosn'tEvryon115½ Drew clear 11
4Aug81- 8Sar fst 6f :21⅘ :45 1:10⅖ 3+Alw 32000 1 5 45½ 54 43½ 56 Vasquez J 115 *2.40 82-24 SpeedToSpare115¾CharmingNtive1151½ExplosiveBid1103¾ Evenly 7
Aug81- 7Sar fst 6f :21⅗ :44⅕ 1:09⅕ 3+Alw 32000 5 3 55 44½ 44½ 35¼ Vasquez J 115 11.10 89-11 Miswaki 1115 Face the Moment 112nk Storm Wave 115nk Wide 6
Jun81- 8Bel fst 6f :22⅕ :45⅖ 1:10⅕ 3+Alw 32000 5 3 31½ 53 49 515 Vasquez J 115 7.10 76-16 Bolductive 1154 Dr. McGuire 1128 Ribosom 1022¾ Tired 6
LATEST WORKOUTS Aug 8 Sar 4f fst :47 h Jly 31 Sar 3f fst :35 h Jly 26 Sar 3f fst :39 b

Shadowmar Ro. c. 4, by Pontoise—Cautious Fairy, by Neptune
Br.—Schoenborn Bros Farm (NY)
Own.—Schoenborn E F Tr.—Schoenborn Everett F
111 Lifetime 17 4 3 2 $103,360 1983 7 1 1 0 $34,93 1982 8 2 1 2 $49,34 Turf 1 0 0 0
29Jly83- 8Sar fst 6f :22⅘ :46 1:11⅕ 3↑[S]Elmira 1 3 3² 2² 2¹½ 1nk Velasquez J 117 3.00 84-12 Shadowmar 117nk Hamlet 111⁵ Elegant Life 116³¾ Driving
16Jly83- 7Bel fst 6½f :23⅕ :46⅕ 1:16⅘ 3↑Alw 35000 4 2 4³ 3¹½ 4³ 4⁴½ Venezia M 117 8.80 88-17 FatherDonJuan111²¾HerefordMan112¹½QuatiGold111no Weakened
6Jly83- 7Bel fst 6f :22⅗ :45⅖ 1:09⅗ 3↑Alw 35000 2 3 5⁴ 4⁴ 4⁶ 4⁵½ Venezia M 117 9.00 88-10 Warcry 119¾ Jan's Kinsman 112hd Prosper 117⁴¾ Evenly
30May83- 9FL fst 6f :22⅘ :46⅗ 1:11⅗ 3↑[S]Williamson 7 12 118¾ 85½ 44½ 2⁴½ Hanks M 115 6.10 86-19 Ask Muhammad 115⁴½ Shadowmar 115¹½ Chopito 115nk In tight
25May83- 9Bel fst 7f :22⅘ :45⅘ 1:23⅘ 3↑Alw 25000 4 6 87¾ 85¾ 65½ 64½ Venezia M 119 13.50 78-16 Mr. Badger 119hd Fortuis119³ChapterOne119¹ Lacked a response
13May83- 7Aqu fst 6f :22⅗ :46 1:10⅗ 3↑Alw 25000 3 7 6⁷ 78¼ 77¼ 41¾ Venezia M 121 55.70 86-28 StrikeGold112nkSpaceMountin116¹½Alchise110no Off slowly, wide
16Feb83- 8Aqu fst 6f [•]:23⅕ :46⅖ 1:10⅖ 3↑[S]H Hughes H 9 4 5⁴ 4⁴ 3⁶ 6¹⁰ Venezia M 117 10.20e 82-23 Master Digby 123⁷ Jan's Kinsman 120¾ Big Izzy 117hd Hung late
29Dec82- 8Aqu fst 1 1/16 [•]:48 1:12⅗ 1:46 3↑[S]Alex M Robb 2 3 3¹ 42¼ 57½ 46¾ Venezia M 114 6.80 76-24 MasterDigby116¹½FirstClassAct116½Jan'sKinsmn116⁴¾ Weakened
20Dec82- 7Aqu fst 6f [•]:23 :46⅘ 1:12⅕ 3↑Alw 23000 3 4 43½ 4² 11½ 1nk Venezia M 115 *1.30e 83-21 Shadowmar 115nk Riva'sMagic112²½SadTrombone115½ Hard drive
8Dec82- 8Aqu fst 6f [•]:22⅘ :46⅕ 1:11⅘ 3↑[S]Joe Palmer 3 7 64¼ 43½ 3² 2hd Venezia M 113 8.50e 85-21 Kim's Chance 122hd Shadowmar113½Jan'sKinsman117¾ Sharp try
LATEST WORKOUTS Aug 9 Sar 4f fst :50 b Jly 25 Sar 4f fst :47⅗ h Jly 1 Bel 5f fst 1:00⅗ h Jun 22 Bel 3f fst :37 h

Trenchant B. c. 4, by Naskra—Fairest Chant, by Shantung
Br.—Meadowhill (Fla)
Own.—Meadowhill Tr.—Johnson Philip G
114 Lifetime 14 5 2 0 $156,205 1983 4 0 0 0 $4,3 1982 10 5 2 0 $151,88 Turf 1 0 0 0
2Jun83- 6Bel yl 1 ①:47⅕ 1:13 1:39⅘ 3↑Alw 37000 10 5 64¾ 6⁸ 69¾ 6¹¹ Samyn J L 119 4.60 55-34 Red Brigade 117¹ Mr. Dreamer 117hd Current Hope 109⁶ Outrun
15May83- 1Aqu fst 1 :46 1:09⅘ 1:35 3↑Handicap 2 2 2¹ 33½ 3⁵ 44½ Samyn J L 114 1.80e 86-18 West On Broad 109²½ Star Choice 115¹¾ Otter Slide 113nk Tired
1May83- 7Aqu fst 7f :23 :46 1:23 3↑Alw 35000 7 1 6⁴ 64½ 76½ 55¼ Davis R G⁵ 114 *.60e 81-21 Satan's Charger 101¾ Acaroid 109¹¾ Otter Slide 124¾ Outrun
22Apr83- 8Aqu fst 6f :22⅖ :45⅗ 1:09⅖ 3↑Alw 35000 10 10 9⁷ 85½ 6⁵ 4⁵ Davis R G⁵ 116 3.80e 89-16 Fit to Fight 121¹½ Star Gallant 121³½ Sepulveda 119nk Mild bid
25Nov82- 8Aqu fst 1 3/16 :48 1:12⅗ 1:58⅕ 3↑Queens Co H 1 3 3⁸ 42½ 5⁹ 5¹² Samyn J L 113 *1.80 59-26 Bar Dexter 112³¾ Castle Knight 111hd Nice Pirate 110⁵½ Tired
6Nov82- 8Aqu fst 1⅛ :50 1:14 1:50⅘ Discovery H 2 2 2½ 1hd 1hd 1¾ Samyn J L 113 *1.40 81-17 Trenchant 113¾ Dew Line 113¾ Exclusive Era 112¹½ Driving
9Oct82- 8Bow fst 1⅛ :47⅖ 1:11⅗ 1:50⅗ Gov's Cup H 3 3 35½ 33½ 1hd 1nk Samyn J L 108 3.50 92-17 Trenchant 108nk Semaj 106nk Royal Roberto 118¹ Driving
25Sep82- 5Bel fst 1 1/16 :48⅕ 1:12⅖ 1:42⅖ 3↑Alw 21000 1 1 1¹ 1¹ 1hd 1¾ Samyn J L 118 *.70 90-15 Trenchant 118¾ Faces Up 113⁵ Skin Dancer 113¹ Driving
15Sep82- 3Bel fst 1⅛ :46 1:10⅖ 1:48⅖ 3↑Alw 20000 1 4 32½ 2hd 1³ 14¾ Samyn J L 113 *1.20 85-14 Trenchant 113⁴¾ ChapterOne117³½ConditionRed105³½ Ridden out
18Aug82- 4Sar fst 7f :22⅘ :45⅘ 1:23⅕ 3↑Md Sp Wt 9 2 85¼ 56¼ 2³ 11½ Samyn J L 117 *.80 86-15 Trenchant 117¹½ My Liphard 117⁶¾ Mi Negro 117³¾ Driving
LATEST WORKOUTS ●Aug 11 Sar tr.t 3f fst :35⅕ h ●Aug 6 Sar tr.t 4f fst :47⅕ h ●Aug 1 Sar tr.t 5f fst :59⅕ h Jly 20 Bel tr.t 3f gd :35⅘ h

Roughcast B. h. 5, by Noholme II—Bold Empress, by Bold Ruler
Br.—Mabee Mr-Mrs J C (Ky)
Own.—Douglass R F Tr.—Freeman Willard C
109 Lifetime 16 4 4 2 $75,380 1983 2 0 0 0 $1,67 1982 10 4 4 1 [illegible] Turf 2 0 0 0 $1,08
29Jly83- 1Sar fst 6f :21⅗ :44 1:08⅗ 3↑Alw 27000 1 5 3² 45½ 46½ 49¾ Migliore R 117 20.50 87-12 Shimatoree 117²¾ Strike Gold 113⁴ Delay of Game117³ Early foot
27Jun83- 8Bel fst 6f :22⅘ :46⅕ 1:10⅗ 3↑Alw 35000 4 6 54¼ 63½ 57½ 7¹⁷ Migliore R 117 9.10 72-19 In From Dixie 117½ World Appeal 113⁶ Starbinia 117¹½ Off slowly
5Dec82- 7Aqu gd 6f [•]:22⅖ :45⅘ 1:11 3↑Alw 37000 2 3 2² 3nk 1hd 31½ Migliore R 119 3.20 87-16 GoodbyeStarter122¹½Havagretdte119nkRoughcst119hd Weakened
6Nov82- 7Aqu fst 6f :22⅕ :45⅗ 1:10⅖ 3↑Alw 25000 7 1 2hd 1hd 1½ 1hd Migliore R 117 *2.00 89-17 Roughcast 117hd King Naskra 112²½ Hail Emperor 117nk Driving
8Oct82- 7Bel fst 6f :22⅖ :45⅗ 1:10⅖ 3↑Alw 23000 5 3 4² 2² 2⁵ 2¹⁰ Migliore R 119 2.40 80-25 Sepulveda 114¹⁰ Roughcast 119¹½ Suzanne's Star117⁵½ Weakened
11Sep82- 5Bel fst 6f :22⅘ :45⅗ 1:10⅖ 3↑Alw 20000 5 1 1¹ 1hd 11½ 11¼ Migliore R 122 2.10 90-12 Roughcast 122¹½ Citius 118¹¾ Faces Up 113²½ Driving
1Sep82- 4Bel fst 6f :23⅕ :46 1:10 3↑Alw 19000 7 1 2hd 2hd 1½ 1hd Migliore R 117 2.70 92-13 Roughcast 117hd King Naskra 106¹½ Tory Willow 113¹¾ Driving
17Jly82- 9Bel fst 6f :23 :46⅗ 1:11⅖ 3↑Alw 19000 6 3 2½ 1hd 2¹ 2³ Migliore R 117 10.20 82-21 ChanBalum112³Roughcast117¹½HowNowDow111²¾ Best of others
29Jun82- 5Bel fst 6f :22⅖ :45⅕ 1:09⅘ 3↑Alw 19000 6 2 5⁵ 6⁷ 69½ 68¼ Migliore R 117 3.50 85-10 Shifty Sheik 113hd Citius 113⁴½ King Naskra 109¾ Outrun
12Jun82- 6Bel fst 6f :22⅘ :45⅗ 1:10⅕ 3↑Alw 19000 7 1 1¹ 1¹ 1¹ 2nk Migliore R 117 2.80 91-14 Muskoka Wyck114nkRoughcast117¹¾ToryWillow111⁴¾ Drifted out
LATEST WORKOUTS Jly 21 Bel 4f fst :48⅘ b Jly 9 Bel 5f fst 1:00⅗ h Jun 23 Bel 5f fst 1:02 h Jun 18 Bel 4f fst :47⅘ h

Bud Delp-trained Explosive Bid went off as a 4 to 5 favorite. This 5-year-old showed six starts in 1983 with two wins and three seconds, including a second by a head finish in his last start at Saratoga. That seven furlong sprint, as in the other three sprints on his past performance lines, showed him in front after a quarter and after a half. But of the four sprints, he won only one, a $14,500 allowance race at Louisiana Downs. In his previous start at Saratoga, Explosive Bid zipped the quarter in :21 4/5 and the half in :43 4/5. He raced the seven furlongs in 1:22, just getting caught at the wire by Stiff Sentence.

Certainly this was a high-speed horse. He also had lots of class, having won $267,337 in thirty-eight lifetime starts. And he was coming off a super race over the same track in what was his first start in two months.

Those were the credentials which bettors used to make him the heavy chalk.

Going against his chances was an abundance of early speed to soften him up. In his last race, Explosive Bid had been clear by a length and a half both after the quarter and after the half. He had set those fast fractions by himself. He wouldn't be by himself today.

First, there was Mayanesian, whose one-run style has already been documented. As a 4-year-old, Mayanesian wasn't getting the early lead in every race, but he was coming awfully close. In his seven sprints on dirt (all at six furlongs), he was first after the quarter in five of them, second by half a length in one, and uncharacteristically sixth when overmatched in April against Fit To Fight, Star Gallant and Sepulveda. Mayanesian's last race was a six furlong allowance at Saratoga when he was second by a half length in a :22 2/5 opening quarter and second by a head in a :45 2/5 half. On the turf three races back, he forged the lead with a half mile in :43 2/5. Mayanesian might not figure to last against Explosive Bid, yet he sure figured to be with the favorite early.

Right inside of Mayanesian was With Caution, another fast horse. With Caution showed ten sprints and was first four times, second by a head three times, second by a half once, and third twice, including his last performance in an out-of-town stakes, the Buckskin, at Churchill Downs, June 24. He showed a quarter as fast as :22 and a half as fast as :45 2/5. His layoff might prevent him from maintaining that speed, but his workouts, including two bullets of six furlongs in 1:13 on Saratoga's notoriously slow training track, and four furlongs in :46 on the main track, gave every indication he, too, would dispute the early lead.

Of the other four who started, Roughcast showed some speed, first or a close second in five of ten sprints. The other three horses: Trenchant, Storm Wave and Shadowmar, usually raced from off the pace. Storm Wave and Shadowmar had each won their last race, each a six furlong sprint at Saratoga.

If we proceed with the idea there would be a definite speed duel on the front end, the idea of betting against Explosive Bid at odds of 4 to 5 made sense. If we dismissed Explosive Bid, Mayanesian, With Caution and even Roughcast as certain victims on the front end, our betting choices would be Storm Wave at 5 to 2, Trenchant at 8 to 1 and Shadowmar at 21 to 1.

What happened? Exactly what we handicapped would happen. Explosive Bid, Mayanesian and With Caution raced heads apart through a first quarter in :21 4/5. Explosive Bid was done by the half (:45 2/5), while With Caution and Mayanesian battled neck and neck the rest of the way. For fourth place.

Shadowmar, Trenchant and Storm Wave each rolled past the tired pacesetters. Shadowmar paid $45.80 to win, and the exacta of him and Trenchant returned $399.20. The cost of boxing the three closers in the exacta was $12. Storm Wave finished third, half a length and a head behind Shadowmar and three and three-quarters lengths in front of With Caution, who edged Mayanesian by a neck for fourth.

SEVENTH RACE
Saratoga
AUGUST 13, 1983

6 FURLONGS. (1.08) HANDICAP. Purse $40,000. 3-year-olds and upward. Weights, Wednesday, August 10. Declarations by 10:00 a.m., Thursday, August 11.

Value of race $40,000, value to winner $24,000, second $8,800, third $4,800, fourth $2,400. Mutuel pool $325,479, OTB pool $162,445. Exacta Pool $241,040. OTB Exacta Pool $272,645.

Last Raced	Horse	Eqt. A. Wt. PP St	1/4	1/2	Str	Fin	Jockey	r	Odds $1
29Jly83 8Sar 1	Shadowmar	4 111 5 6	6-8	3-1	1 ½	1 ½	Lovato F Jr		21.90
2Jun83 6Bel 6	Trenchant	4 114 6 2	7	7	5-2	2hd	Samyn J L		8.50
1Aug83 3Sar 1	Storm Wave	6 114 4 5	4-1½	4 ½	3-3½	3hd	Vasquez J		2.50
24Jun83 8CD 6	With Caution	5 114 2 3	2hd	2 ½	2hd	4nk	Maple E		8.20
30Jly83 7Sar 6	Mayanesian	b 4 113 3 1	3-6	1 ½	3-1	5-5½	Bailey J D		12.90
29Jly83 1Sar 4	Roughcast	5 109 7 7	5hd	6-3	7	6-3	Davis R G		20.50
8Aug83 5Sar 2	Explosive Bid	5 117 1 4	1hd	5-3	6 ½	7	Pincay L Jr		.80

OFF AT 4:57 Start good, Won driving. Time, :21 4/5, :45 2/5, 1:10 4/5 Track good.

$ 2 Mutuel Prices:	8- SHADOWMAR	45.80	16.80	5.40
	10- TRENCHANT		9.20	5.00
	7- STORM WAVE			3.20

$2 EXACTA 8-10 PAID $399.20.

Ro. c, by Pontoise–Cautious Fairy, by Neptune. Trainer Schoenborn Everett F. Bred by Schoenborn Bros Farm (NY).

SHADOWMAR came out to loom a threat nearing the stretch and after reaching the front, was all out to last while lugging in slightly. TRENCHANT, outrun for a half, finished full of run while racing wide. STORM WAVE raced wide into the stretch while rallying, loomed boldly leaving the furlong grounds but wasn't good enough. WITH CAUTION raced between horses while showing speed to the stretch and weakened. MAYANESIAN prominent to the stretch while racing well out in the track, drifted out slightly while tiring. ROUGHCAST was always outrun. EXPLOSIVE BID showed speed for three furlongs and tired badly.

Owners– 1, Schoenborn E F; 2, Meadowhill; 3, Marydel Farm; 4, Farish W S; 5, Gordonsdale Farm; 6, Douglass R F; 7, Hawksworth Farm.

Trainers– 1, Schoenborn Everett F; 2, Johnson Philip G; 3, Odom George P; 4, Carroll Del W II; 5, Zito Nicholas P; 6, Freeman Willard C; 7, Delp Grover G.

Overweight: Storm Wave 3 pounds; With Caution 1; Mayanesian 2; Explosive Bid 1.

Scratched– Prosper(3Aug83 7Sar 1); Warcry(6Jly83 7Bel 1); Cast Party(14Feb83 9GP 1); Main Stem(8Aug83 5Sar 5).

Now let's look at a race that was run in 1988 at Saratoga. Twelve 3-year-old fillies went to post in the ninth race, August 21, a six furlong sprint for $25,000 claimers.

The field is chock-full of early speed. Six of the twelve fillies showed racing on the lead in at least one sprint. Several showed more than one.

Saucy Voyage made the lead at the quarter in her last six starts, all sprints, with fractions as fast as :22 in one race and :45 1/5 from her last race when she tired to finish fourth in a $45,000 claimer.

9 SARATOGA

6 FURLONGS. (1.08) CLAIMING. Purse $18,000. Fillies 3-year-old weights, 121 lbs. Non-winners of two races since August 1, allowed 3 lbs. Of a race sine then 5 lbs. Claiming price $25,000 for each $2,500 to $20,000 2 lbs. Races when entered to be claimed for $18,000 for less not considered.

Coupled—Saucy Voyage and Fair and Frosty.

Cracking Good

B. f. 3, by Grey Dawn II—Heavy Sugar, by What Luck
$25,000 Br.—Beler C P (Ky)
Tr.—Dutrow Richard E
Own.—Beler C P

116

Lifetime	1988	12	1	2	0 $21,250
12 1 2 0	1987	0	M	0	0
$21,250	Turf	1	0	0	0

14Aug88- 4Sar	fst	6f	:22⅘	:45⅕	1:10⅗	ⒻClm 35000	4	2	32½	33½	67	613¾	Day P	b 116	5.40	73-12	SummerBlossom1121¾Koluctoo'sBetty1152½MedivlMrin112¾	Tired 7
8Aug88- 5Sar	fst	6f	:22⅕	:45⅕	1:11⅗	ⒻClm 47500	8	1	52	1014	1016	—	Cordero A Jr	b 114	8.00	— —	Moving Appeal 116no Air Star 1141¾ You'llbesurprised116¾	Eased 10
24Jly88- 4Bel	my	7f	:23	:46⅖	1:25⅘	ⒻClm 50000	1	5	2hd	1hd	1½	4¾	Romero R P	b 116	*2.70e	72-24	Neatly Arranged116noGinBuzz114hdBlackjackLady116¾	Weakened 10
26Jun88- 4Bel	my	7f	:23⅗	:47	1:25⅖	3↑ⒻMd 50000	4	3	11	12	16	16½	Cordero A Jr	b 114	*.60	75-16	Cracking Good 1146½ Maja Flo 110½ Loving Embrace1143	Driving 6
15Jun88- 6Bel	fst	7f	:23⅕	:46⅘	1:25⅖	ⒻMd Sp Wt	4	4	21½	21½	67	69¾	Cordero A Jr	b 121	*1.90e	65-17	Olatha 1213¼ Saratoga Warning 1212¼ Onamia 1211½	Tired 11
30May88- 4Bel	fm	1 1/16	Ⓣ:46⅕	1:10⅘	1:42⅘	3↑ⒻMd Sp Wt	12	1	2hd	2hd	1017	1024¼	Santos J A	b 115	7.10	58-17	Curlew 1153½ A Great Princess 1151½NaturalForest115no	Stopped 12
25May88- 3Bel	my	7f	:23	:46⅗	1:26	ⒻMd Sp Wt	3	3	21	2½	2½	21¾	Antley C W	b 121	3.40	70-23	Al Dam 1211¾ Cracking Good 1214½MaloneWater1214½	Held place 6
14Apr88- 4Aqu	fst	7f	:23	:46	1:25⅖	ⒻMd Sp Wt	7	1	1hd	1½	2hd	21¼	Antley C W	b 121	26.20	73-21	LovYoubyHrt1211¼CrckingGood1212¾ScondLnding1211¼	2nd best 9
23Mar88- 2Aqu	fst	7f	:22⅘	:46⅕	1:26⅕	ⒻMd Sp Wt	9	5	96½	105¾	85¾	88½	Santagata N	b 121	123.10	61-24	[D]Gilly Callum 121nk GreenSum1213½FaintGlow121nk	Awkward st. 13
13Mar88- 5Aqu	fst	6f	⊡:22⅗	:46	1:12⅗	ⒻMd Sp Wt	9	5	119½	89¾	1020	1020¼	Santagata N	b 121	18.30e	61-18	Pretiola 1211¼ American Dance 1215 Lee's Tsakus 121¾	Steadied 12

LATEST WORKOUTS Jly 8 Aqu 5f fst 1:00⅘ h

Saucy Voyage

B. f. 3, by Sauce Boat—Little Gaylord, by Lord Gaylord
$25,000 Br.—Reynolds David P (Ky)
Tr.—Lake Robert P
Own.—Evans R M

116

Lifetime	1988	12	3	0	1 $42,360
19 4 1 4	1987	7	1	1	3 $12,835
$55,195					

8Aug88- 5Sar	fst	6f	:22⅕	:45⅕	1:11⅗	ⒻClm 45000	2	3	1hd	11	11½	42½	Day P	b 112	8.30	79-14	MovingAppeal116noAirStar1141¾You'llbesurprised116¾	Weakened 10
18Jly88- 5Bel	fst	6½f	:22⅘	:46⅗	1:19	ⒻClm c-35000	7	1	11	1½	54½	510	Peck B D5	b 111	*1.90	70-19	Koluctoo's Betty 1141 She'sFreezing1121HerWay1162½	Weakened 8
9Jly88- 6Bel	fst	6f	:22⅖	:45⅘	1:10⅘	3↑ⒻAlw 27000	7	2	1½	1hd	1hd	65½	Peck B D5	b 107	4.90	79-21	Platinum Halo 1112½ Olatha 1131¾ Toll Fee 112¾	Tired 8
26Jun88- 5Bel	my	6f	:22⅖	:45⅖	1:09	ⒻClm 25000	3	1	12	12	14	18¾	Peck B D5	b 111	*2.20	94-16	Saucy Voyage 1118¾ Newbury Street 1163 Feverish 1141¼	Driving 12
18Jun88- 9Bel	fst	6f	:22	:45⅖	1:11⅘	ⒻClm 45000	2	1	12	2hd	24	56½	Pezua J M	b 112	9.00	73-16	Big Jalc 1123 Crafty Alexas 1161 Trin 1162	Tired 9
6Jun88- 3Bel	fst	6f	:22⅕	:46	1:12⅖	ⒻClm 35000	7	3	1hd	1½	11	32¾	Correa C J5	b 111	*2.10[D]	74-27	Festive Lady 1132¼ Her Way116½[D]SaucyVoyage111hd	Drifted out 11
6Jun88-Disqualified and placed seventh																		
6Apr88- 1Aqu	fst	6f	:22⅖	:46⅕	1:12⅕	ⒻClm 45000	6	1	2½	11	14	1nk	Peck B D5	b 107	2.80	79-25	SucyVoyg107nkHonysucklQun1121¾CrftyAlxs1084	Drifted, driving 7
18Mar88- 5Aqu	fst	6f	:21⅘	:45⅕	1:10⅗	ⒻClm 45000	4	2	3½	32	36	614	Migliore R	b 112	*2.60	73-22	Judy's Halo 1116½ Dusty Donna 1163½ Rocketai 1161	Tired 10
11Mar88- 6Aqu	fst	6f	⊡:23	:46⅘	1:13	ⒻClm c-35000	7	1	22	21	12	1nk	Maple E	b 116	5.40	79-31	SaucyVoyage116nkGoldenSweethert1113¾Nskr'sSong1163	Driving 8
24Feb88- 3GP	fst	6f	:22⅗	:46⅗	1:13	ⒻClm 50000	4	6	2hd	11	1hd	32	Lee M A	b 116	17.20	72-25	Whisper Love 1161½ Hi Maudie 116½ Saucy Voyage 1162	Tired 9

LATEST WORKOUTS ●Jly 31 Aqu ⊡ 4f fst :47⅖ h   Jly 6 Bel tr.t 4f fst :47⅕ h

Travellingknightly

Ch. f. 3, by Travelling Music—David's Neill, by Final Ruling
$25,000 Br.—Benson Caroline T (Md)
Tr.—Salzman John E
Own.—Benson Caroline

116

Lifetime	1988	10	0	2	1 $9,500
12 1 2 1	1987	2	1	0	0 $4,260
$13,760	Turf	1	0	0	0

6Aug88- 9Sar	sly	7f	:21⅘	:45⅗	1:24⅖	ⒻClm 25000	3	9	99	79	47½	47	Bracciale V Jr	b 116	33.20	73-12	FrAwyLssie1163½HppyDpple1141½SummerBlossom1162	Very wide 11
21Jly88-10Pim	my	1 1/16	:46⅗	1:12	1:45⅘	3↑ⒻAlw 18000	8	3	23½	34½	79	714¼	Nicol P A Jr	b 110	17.00	61-16	What's On the Menu 1102¾MiamiWives1141Pop'sCoco1125½	Tired 9
1Jly88- 9Pim	fm	1 1/16	Ⓣ:47⅕	1:12⅕	1:44⅕	3↑ⒻAlw 18000	2	10	1012	88¾	810	719¼	Douglas F G	b 112	24.00	63-18	Marilyn Glen 110hd Kerfoot 1105 Pop'sCoco112nk	Pinched bk. st. 10
2Jun88- 7Pim	fst	1 1/16	:47⅗	1:13⅕	1:47	3↑ⒻAlw 18000	1	5	43	41½	1½	31¼	Douglas F G	b 113	39.70	68-22	PotomacRock108¾DoodleBop114½Trvellingknightly1131½	Bumped 10
7May88- 8Del	my	6f	:23⅗	:48⅕	1:14	ⒻAlw 7000	4	7	4nk	32½	33	57¼	Intelisano GPJr	b 116	4.50	64-31	Midnight Trout 1223 Eugenicist 1163¾ Biggest Bustle 116½	Tired 8
4Apr88- 9Pim	fst	1 1/16	:48	1:12⅗	1:44	Ⓕ[S]Caesr'sWsh	5	3	42¼	55½	516	532¾	Stacy A T	b 113	34.80	51-22	WillaontheMove1191¼FatandFoxy11318SunnyRobert1144½	Outrun 6
14Mar88- 4Pim	fst	1 1/16	:47	1:12⅘	1:47	ⒻClm 18500	1	6	512	46	33½	25	Stacy A T	114	8.50	64-29	CleverMother1155Travellingknightly114¾BlackMondy114½	Rallied 6
27Feb88- 9Lrl	fst	6½f	:23⅗	:48⅕	1:20⅖	ⒻClm 18500	4	6	76¼	89¾	59¼	47	Johnson W C7	112	9.90	72-25	McTavish Avenue 112hd Tanith 1145 Clever Mother 1152	Rallied 9
29Jan88- 8Lrl	fst	6½f	:22⅗	:46	1:18⅕	ⒻAlw 14000	8	8	88¼	78	711	712	Baboolal J	114	14.20	78-18	A Joyful Try 1152¼ Saucy Gaylord 1171¼ Hag's Nag 117¾	Outrun 8
10Jan88- 2Lrl	fst	6f	:23⅖	:47⅘	1:13⅖	ⒻClm 18500	5	7	810	810	54½	2½	Chavez S N	114	19.00	75-12	Puzzllino119½Trvllingknghtly114nkDwnsALdy1141	Stumbled break 8

LATEST WORKOUTS ●Jun 25 Tim 5f fst 1:02⅖ b

Auntie Gosh

B. f. 3, by Cormorant—Jimminy Gosh, by Jim J
$20,000 Br.—Kinderhill Corp-General Partner (NY)
Tr.—Garren Murray M
Own.—Garren M M

102[10]

Lifetime	1988	21	0	3	1 $14,400
23 1 3 2	1987	2	1	0	1 $4,480
$18,880					

6Aug88- 9Sar	sly	7f	:21⅘	:45⅗	1:24⅖	ⒻClm 20000	1	5	11	11	921	—	Soto R10	102	29.20	— —	FarAwayLassie1163½HappyDpple1141½SummerBlossom1162	Eased 11
22Jly88- 4Bel	my	6f	:22⅖	:46⅗	1:12⅗	ⒻClm 15500	4	1	2hd	21½	611	718	Pezua J M	112	9.70	58-25	Affy 1141¼ Savage Nite 1161¾ Feverish 1113½	Tired 10
8Jly88- 1Bel	fst	6f	:22⅘	:46⅘	1:13⅕	ⒻClm 15500	2	1	11½	2hd	31	21¼	Pezua J M	112	9.50	72-25	Int'l Guest 1121¼ Auntie Gosh 1121 Provelvet 118hd	Gamely 7
3Jly88- 2Bel	fst	1	:47	1:13⅖	1:40⅖	ⒻClm 15500	12	1	12	11½	1215	1217¼	Pezua J M	112	9.50f	46-25	Skate'n Kate 116hd Crystalero 1072 Perjurer 116hd	Used up 14
22Jun88- 9Bel	fst	1 1/16	:47	1:13⅕	1:47	ⒻClm 15500	11	1	11½	52¾	1119	1137¼	Venezia M	b 112	18.10	30-19	Devastated 1121¼ Hollywood Barb 1122¼ PromisetoYou1164	Tired 12
10Jun88- 5Bel	fst	6f	:22	:45⅖	1:11⅖	3↑Ⓕ[S]Alw 27000	2	1	21½	34	713	914¼	Pezua J M	b 109	20.80	68-20	BigMamLiz112¾BesttoBeLucky1111¾YingN'Yng114nk	Early speed 13
4Jun88- 7Bel	fst	1 1/16	:45⅗	1:11⅗	1:45⅖	3↑Ⓕ[S]Alw 29000	8	1	14½	12½	42	57¾	Pezua J M	b 109	38.40	67-13	Black Beaver 1101 Aljadam 117nk Home bySeven1096	Drifted out 14
26May88- 9Bel	fst	6f	:23	:47	1:13	ⒻClm 16500	7	3	21	2hd	1½	22½	Romero R P	b 114	12.10	71-16	Dancing Socks 1162½ Auntie Gosh 114¾ Miss Sherby 107½	Gamely 8
15May88- 9Bel	fst	6f	:21⅘	:45⅗	1:12⅘	3↑Ⓕ[S]Alw 27000	4	2	2½	31½	97½	911¼	Romero R P	b 112	21.50	64-15	Talc Two 114¾ Big Mama Liz 1121 Konnies Joy 121½	Used up 11
4May88- 2Aqu	fst	6f	:22	:45⅖	1:11⅗	ⒻClm 20000	10	3	43	65	52¼	45¾	Bermudez J E5	b 108	25.10	76-19	JessicaPie111nkSplitMoment1165ChangeableQueen116½	Wide str. 10

LATEST WORKOUTS Aug 3 Sar 3f fst :38⅘ b   Jun 29 Bel 4f fst :48⅖ bg

Crafty Ville — B. f. 3, by Crafty Prospector—Pattyville, by Crazier
Own.—Landsberg D C — $22,500 — Br.—Iselin & Lippert (NJ) — Tr.—Jacobs J Sterling — 114
Lifetime 9 1 1 0 $14,440 — 1988 7 0 0 0 $940 — 1987 2 1 1 0 $13,500 — Turf 1 0 0 0 $87

13Aug88- 5Sar fst 1⅛ :46⅘ 1:11⅕ 1:52⅘ ⒻClm 25000 5 2 2½ 22 79 610½ Davis R G 116 7.60 62-12 Cooling Point 1122 Guarded Wings 1161½MegaGal1144 Weakened 10
7Aug88- 3Sar my 6f :22⅘ :45⅕ 1:10⅕ 3+ⒻClm 35000 2 4 52½ 56 57½ 67½ Lovato F Jr 116 67.30 81-12 Rajiste 1172 Henna Girl 1132½ Star Brilliant 117nk Outrun 10
6Jly88- 9Atl fm *1 1/16 Ⓣ:49⅕ 1:15 1:48⅗ 3+ⒻAlw 8700 5 4 31½ 5½ 99¾ 1018½ Intelisano G P Jr 108 8.30 56-23 Withallmyluv1165RacingRagmo1162½WtchMyMgic112no Fell back 10
25Jun88- 9Atl fst 6f :21⅗ :44⅕ 1:09⅘ 3+ⒻNorthfield H 1 5 55 58 512 516 Torso M A 102 39.30 77-22 Just Smashing 1204 Creme Royale 115½ SpeedyJane11210 Trailed 5
15Jun88- 7Mth fst 6f :21⅘ :44⅕ 1:11 3+Ⓕ[S]Alw 18700 6 6 79¾ 714 714 811¼ Diaz L F 110 22.40 74-17 KlassyBriefcase112½PrincessLuis116nkOneMnorDrive1136 In tight 11
2May88- 9GS fst 1 :48⅗ 1:14 1:41⅗ 3+ Alw 12000 4 4 74 817 — — Cabrera S b 108 16.50 — — DoneBefor111nkDoctorTony114noFlightCommndr1161½ Distanced 8
20Mar88- 8Aqu fst 1⅛ :47 1:11⅘ 1:50⅘ ⒻRuthless 5 4 712 736 — — Baird E T b 112 61.80 — — Aptostar 112hd Sham Say 1185 Joe's Tammie 11810¾ Eased 7
5Nov87- 8Med fst 6f :22⅗ :46⅗ 1:13⅕ ⒻAlw 15000 1 6 65¼ 46 36 22½ Nuesch D5 112 8.80 73-29 Las Manitas 1172½ Crafty Ville 1125FlawlessMelody117¾ 2nd best 6
30Oct87- 1Med sly 6f :23 :47 1:14⅕ Ⓕ[S]Md Sp Wt 6 6 43½ 37½ 35 1¾ Gavidia W 117 *1.10 71-21 Crafty Ville 117¾ Flawless Melody 1174½ Dame Amy1172½ Driving 9
LATEST WORKOUTS Jly 30 Sar 3f fst :36 bg — Jly 4 Atl 3f fst :37 b

Crafty Alexas — Dk. b. or br. f. 3, by Crafty Prospector—Blake's Twin, by Blakeney
Own.—Donnelly F — $25,000 — Br.—Hendricks Venture Farms Ltd (Fla) — Tr.—Galluscio Dominick — 111[5]
Lifetime 12 3 2 1 $52,000 — 1988 12 3 2 1 $52,000 — 1987 0 M 0 0

14Aug88- 2Sar fst 6f :22 :45 1:11⅕ ⒻClm 35000 8 5 45½ 43½ 54 74½ Peck B D5 b 111 8.70 79-12 WellPersonified1141½CstilinRose115nkMxDonnell116½ Raced wide 10
2Jly88- 5Bel fst 7f :22⅘ :46⅗ 1:24 ⒻClm 50000 8 1 55½ 44 58½ 613¾ Velasquez J b 116 5.50 68-20 You'llbesurprised 1165½ Big Jalc 114¾ In Focus II 1163½ Wide 8
18Jun88- 9Bel fst 6f :22 :45⅗ 1:11⅘ ⒻClm 50000 9 6 59 58 34½ 23 Velasquez J b 116 5.60 77-16 Big Jalc 1123 Crafty Alexas 1161 Trin 1162 Wide turn 9
22May88- 7Bel fst 7f :22⅘ :45⅕ 1:24 ⒻAlw 27000 5 6 84¾ 77½ 85¾ 97¼ Velasquez J b 116 21.10 75-19 Starofanera 1163½ Fairest College118hdDanceinaVeil1211¾ Outrun 10
25Apr88- 3Aqu fst 6f :23 :47⅗ 1:13 ⒻClm 50000 6 6 52½ 51½ 1½ 13 Velasquez J b 116 2.10 75-24 Crafty Alexas 1163 Cute Move 1121½ Yellowtail 116nk Drew clear 6
6Apr88- 1Aqu fst 6f :22⅘ :46⅕ 1:12⅕ ⒻClm 45000 4 4 67 34 35 32 Bermudez J E5 b 108 4.40 77-25 SaucyVoyge107nkHoneysuckleQueen1121¾CrftyAlexs1084 Blocked 7
28Mar88- 3Aqu fst 7f :23⅗ :47⅘ 1:26 ⒻClm 50000 7 4 41 1hd 23 57 Pezua J M b 116 7.10 64-30 Dusty Donna 1154 Koluctoo's Betty 118nk Proud Flirt 1122 Tired 9
17Mar88- 7Aqu fst 7f :23 :46⅗ 1:24⅘ ⒻAlw 30000 3 6 53 87 1012 1018¾ Peck B D5 b 111 51.50 60-27 Our Gallamar 1166 EmpressofLove118nkMyCaravann116nk Outrun 11
29Feb88- 1Aqu fst 6f [•]:22 :45⅘ 1:13 ⒻClm 50000 1 8 23½ 32½ 1½ 1¾ Peck B D5 b 111 6.90 79-25 Crafty Alexas 111¾ Dusty Donna 116½ Smart n' Irish 116¾ Driving 8
18Feb88- 3Aqu fst 6f [•]:22⅗ :46⅘ 1:12⅘ ⒻClm 45000 4 6 53¼ 54½ 35½ 27 Peck B D5 107 28.40 75-23 Links of Gold 1127 Crafty Alexas 1071 Rajab's Tune115nk Gamely 8
LATEST WORKOUTS Aug 11 Sar Ⓣ 3f fm :39 b

Parole the Lady — Dk. b. or br. f. 3, by Stiff Sentence—On a Shoestring, by Quadrangle
Own.—Morrell S F — $20,000 — Br.—International Thbrd Breeders Inc (NJ) — Tr.—Curtis William Jr — 112
Lifetime 5 1 0 0 $7,725 — 1988 4 1 0 0 $7,725 — 1987 1 M 0 0

6Aug88- 9Sar sly 7f :21⅘ :45⅗ 1:24⅘ ⒻClm 22500 4 6 21 914 1128 1034 Velasquez J b 114 10.30 46-12 FrAwyLssie1163½HppyDpple1141½SummrBlossom1162 Brief speed 11
21Jly88- 7Mth fst 6f :22 :44⅘ 1:11 3+Ⓕ[S]Alw 20000 3 5 52½ 57½ 715 719¼ Ferrer J C b 111 30.00 66-18 Luvinherisluv' 1144 One Manor Drive 1135 Jo'sJem114¾ No factor 7
13Jly88- 2Bel fst 6f :22⅗ :46⅗ 1:12⅗ 3+ⒻMd 30000 6 2 11½ 11½ 12 13 Peck B D5 b 107 8.30 76-20 Parole the Lady 1073 Hill Music 116nk Happy June 1124½ Driving 13
23Jun88- 7Mth fst 6f :22⅘ :46⅕ 1:12⅕ 3+Ⓕ[S]Md Sp Wt 4 6 31½ 34 48 510 Tejeira J b 115 120.70 69-24 Rock'nRollMadam1151Luvinherisluv'1151Mosquer1154 Weakened 11
13Nov87- 1Med fst 6f :22 :46⅕ 1:12⅘ ⒻMd 20000 4 2 33½ 43½ 58 710¾ Castaneda K 117 29.10 68-16 Mogumby 117nk Mary Morey 1173½ Cookie Maker 113no Tired 10
LATEST WORKOUTS ●Aug 4 Sar 3f fst :34⅘ h — Jly 19 Bel 3f fst :36 h — Jly 10 Bel 3f fst :38⅘ b — Jly 1 Bel 4f fst :50 b

Private Conscience — Dk. b. or br. f. 3, by Guilty Conscience—Private Show, by T V Commercial
Own.—Farone L J — $25,000 — Br.—Farone Louis J (NY) — Tr.—Collins Karen — 106[10]
Lifetime 2 0 0 0 — 1988 1 M 0 0 — 1987 1 M 0 0

14Aug88- 4Sar fst 6f :22⅘ :45⅕ 1:10⅗ ⒻClm 35000 2 5 79 714 712 717¾ Soto R10 106 47.30 69-12 SummerBlossom1121¾Koluctoo'sBtty1152½MdivlMrin112¾ Trailed 7
23Oct87- 6Aqu fst 6f :22⅘ :46 1:12⅕ Ⓕ[S]Md Sp Wt 6 8 1325 1334 1224 1221½ Venezia M 117 54.60 58-18 GrecianDancer1176¾YingN'Yng117nkChngebleQueen1172½ Outrun 13
LATEST WORKOUTS Aug 13 Sar 3f fst :38⅘ b — Aug 6 Sar 4f fst :49 hg — Jun 28 Sar tr.t 4f fst :52⅘ b — Jun 21 Sar tr.t 5f fst 1:05⅗ b

She's Freezing — Dk. b. or br. f. 3, by Quadratic—She's So Cold, by Hagley
Own.—Davis A — $25,000 — Br.—Greyhound Stas Inc-Silversmith Inv (Ky) — Tr.—Moschera Gasper S — 111[5]
Lifetime 17 1 6 0 $33.305 — 1988 8 0 2 0 $9,240 — 1987 9 1 4 0 $24,065

14Aug88- 4Sar fst 6f :22⅘ :45⅕ 1:10⅗ ⒻClm 35000 3 1 2½ 1½ 42½ 58¼ Samyn J L 116 6.60 79-12 SummrBlossom1121¾Koluctoo'sBtty1152½MdivlMrin112¾ Used up 7
8Aug88- 5Sar fst 6f :22⅕ :45⅕ 1:11⅗ ⒻClm 45000 3 5 74 914 97½ 98¾ Antley C W 112 17.10 73-14 Moving Appeal 116no Air Star 1141¾You'llbesurprised116¾ Outrun 10
18Jly88- 5Bel fst 6½f :22⅘ :46⅗ 1:19 ⒻClm 30000 8 2 21 2½ 1½ 21 Samyn J L 112 21.00 79-19 Koluctoo's Betty 1141 She's Freezing1121HerWay1162½ Held well 8
29Jun88- 9Bel fst 7f :23⅗ :46⅗ 1:25⅕ ⒻClm 35000 6 1 1½ 1½ 53¾ 711¾ Samyn J L 116 6.70 64-22 Mia Casa 1072HoneysuckleQueen1163½SummerBlossom1142 Tired 11
18Jun88- 9Bel fst 6f :22 :45⅗ 1:11⅘ ⒻClm 50000 6 2 22 34 611 79¾ Cordero A Jr 116 3.50 70-16 Big Jalc 1123 Crafty Alexas 1161 Trin 1162 Tired 9
12May88- 5Bel my 6f :22 :45⅕ 1:10⅕ ⒻClm 50000 9 1 12 1½ 2hd 2½ Cordero A Jr 116 5.10 87-14 CuteMove112½She'sFreezing116nkRajab'sTune1112 Gain the place 12
21Apr88- 5Aqu fst 6f :22⅘ :46⅘ 1:11⅕ ⒻAlw 30000 1 4 43½ 56 59 516½ Romero R P 116 12.20 67-26 Redding Ridge 1167½ Judy's Halo 1162¾ Rocketai 1164¾ Even try 8
6Apr88- 1Aqu fst 6f :22⅘ :46⅕ 1:12⅕ ⒻClm c-50000 2 6 1½ 21 24 56 Krone J A 116 *1.70 73-25 SucyVoyge107nkHoneysuckleQueen1121¾CrftyAlxs1084 Weakened 7
27Oct87- 3Kee fst 6f :22⅘ :45⅕ 1:12 ⒻAlw 17300 7 1 11 11 2½ 21¾ Melancon L 115 4.60 80-12 Miss Threesum 1151¾ She's Freezing 115nk Dear Dusty 115hd 7
16Oct87- 3Kee fst 7f :22⅗ :45 1:23⅘ ⒻAlw 17300 1 6 2hd 2hd 33 57½ Day P 115 2.30 79-09 Loveswept 1152½ Strada 1152½ Dear Dusty 115nk 9

Loveswept — Dk. b. or br. f. 3, by Clever Trick—Sarl's Tobin, by Tobin Bronze
Own.—Klein E V — $25,000 — Br.—Bauer Mr-Mrs J M (Ky) — Tr.—Lukas D Wayne — 116
Lifetime 11 2 1 1 $28,140 — 1988 5 0 1 0 $6,220 — 1987 6 2 0 1 $21,920

14Aug88- 2Sar fst 6f :22 :45 1:11⅕ ⒻClm 35000 3 2 2hd 2hd 2hd 64½ Bailey J D b 116 *2.30 80-12 WellPersonified1141½CastilianRose115nkMaxDonnell116½ Used up 10
18Jly88- 5Bel fst 6½f :22⅘ :46⅗ 1:19 ⒻClm 35000 3 3 42½ 41½ 33 44½ Bailey J D 116 3.90 75-19 Koluctoo's Betty 1141 She's Freezing 1121HerWay1162½ Steadied 8
8Apr88-10OP fst 6f :22 :45⅗ 1:10⅘ ⒻAlw 15000 6 1 2hd 21 34 55 Ardoin R 114 3.40e 81-18 Deep RiverWoman114hdRaisedInSong1203½PopPopB.B.Gun120no 7
23Feb88- 8OP fst 6f :22⅕ :46⅕ 1:11⅗ ⒻAlw 17000 6 1 11 1½ 1hd 22 Ardoin R 114 5.30 80-24 Ofelia Girl 1142 Loveswept 1141½ Deep River Woman 1148 6
5Feb88- 6OP fst 6f :22⅕ :46⅕ 1:12⅕ ⒻAlw 17000 2 3 2½ 3½ 44 48¾ Ardoin R 117 3.80 70-24 Georgica's Gal 117nk Ofelia Girl 1143½ Deep River Woman 1145 8
22Nov87- 3CD fst 6f :21⅗ :45⅘ 1:12 ⒻAlw 30250 2 2 32 43 33½ 35 Smith M E 118 5.60 78-17 Irish Nymph 1152½ Miss Threesum 1152½ Loveswept 118¾ 6
8Nov87- 8CD fst 1 :45⅕ 1:11⅗ 1:38⅕ ⒻPocahontas 8 3 44½ 33½ 918 929½ Smith M E 116 7.90e 48-19 Epitome 1142½ Darien Miss 120 Cushion Cut 120 9
16Oct87- 3Kee fst 7f :22⅗ :45 1:23⅘ ⒻAlw 17300 8 1 3nk 3nk 11½ 12¼ Smith M E 115 5.30 87-09 Loveswept 1152½ Strada 1152½ Dear Dusty 115nk 9
7Sep87- 7AP gd 7f :23 :46⅗ 1:25⅘ ⒻAlw 13000 3 7 56½ 34 41 52½ Vasquez J 118 5.80 71-23 Gemella 1122 She's Freezing 118no Undermythum 118hd 7
5Jly87- 2AP fst 5½f :22⅘ :46⅘ 1:05⅘ ⒻMd Sp Wt 3 1 1hd 1hd 1hd 1no Frazier R L 117 3.10 86-25 Loveswept 117no Reverance 1122 Liloy's Girl 1173 7
LATEST WORKOUTS Aug 8 Mth 4f fst :49 bg — Jly 31 Mth 4f fst :51 b — Jly 14 Mth 3f fst :35⅘ hg — Jun 29 Mth 4f fst :48 h

Brooklyn Bred	B. f. 3, by Breezing On—Miss Leatherneck, by Lt Stevens					Lifetime	1988	6	1	1	0	$12,060

Brooklyn Bred
Own.—Schwartz B K
$25,000
Br.—Stonewall Farm (NY)
Tr.—Alexander Frank A
116
Lifetime 6 1 1 0
1988 6 1 1 0 $12,060
1987 0 M 0 0

5Aug88- 9Sar sly 7f	:21¾ :45¾ 1:24¾	ⓕClm 25000	7 4 76¾11181025 928	Maple E	b 116	6.00	52-12 FarAwayLassie116³¼HppyDpple114¼SummerBlossom116² Outrun 11
3Jly88- 4Bel my 7f	:23 :46¾ 1:25¾	ⓕClm 50000	5 7 54¼ 57¼ 7⁷ 69¼	Hernandez R	b 116	16.60	64-24 Neatly Arranged 116ⁿᵒGinBuzz114ᵐBlackjackLady116¼ No factor 10
2Jun88- 2Bel sly 7f	:23¾ :47 1:25¾	3+ⓕMd 50000	1 4 3¹ 3¹ 1½ 1²	Maple E	b 114	*1.50	73-16 Brooklyn Bred 114² Nashira 110⁴ Suzanne Spector 118⁵ Driving 8
7May88- 5Bel fst 6f	:22¾ :46½ 1:12¾	3+ⓕMd 35000	13 7 4¹¼ 2½ 2½ 2³	Velasquez J	b 114	5.70	74-22 WirdCombinton114³BrooklynBrd114⁴¼LovngEmprss114³ 2nd best 14
20May88- 5Bel gd 6f	:22¾ :46½ 1:11¾	3+ⓕMd Sp Wt	5 3 3² 44¾ 56½ 510	Vasquez J	b 115	2.30	71-17 Estates Jewel 115⁷ Overrule 119ⁿᵏ Rum Go 115¾ Tired 13
7Jan88- 4Aqu fst 6f	⊡:23¾ :47¾ 1:14¾	3+ⓕMd 50000	9 2 2¹½ 2⁴ 3⁸ 48	Migliore R	121	7.80	63-30 Crafty Alexas 112¹ Dusty Donna 121⁵ D'or Etoile 117² Weakened 9

LATEST WORKOUTS Aug 16 Sar 4f fst :48⅗ h • Aug 2 Sar 4f fst :49½ b • Jly 21 Bel 4f sly :52 b

O. K. Rose	B. f. 3, by D'Accord—Roses for the Lady, by Buffalo Lark					Lifetime	1988	9	1	1	0	$22,580

O. K. Rose
Own.—Manhasset Stable
$25,000
Br.—Mettinger J (NY)
Tr.—Zito Nicholas P
116
Lifetime 9 1 1 0
1988 9 1 1 0 $22,580
1987 0 M 0 0

13Aug88- 5Sar fst 1	:46¾ 1:11½ 1:52¾	ⓕClm 25000	10 9 9¹⁵ 8⁹ 47¼ 7¹¹	Antley C W	116	13.00	61-12 Cooling Point 112² Guarded Wings 116¹¼ Mega Gal 114⁴ Wide 10
22Jly88- 7Bel my 1	:46½ 1:11½ 1:38¾	3+ⓕⓢAlw 29000	8 11 9¹¹ 9¹² 8¹¹ 610¾	Thibeau R J	111	11.60	60-25 Ying N' Yang 111⁵¼ C'est Marron 117¼ Fini La Guerre106²¼ Wide 11
5Jun88- 7Bel fst 7f	:22¾ :45¾ 1:26	3+ⓕⓢAlw 27000	2 12 9¹⁴ 8¹⁴ 6¹⁰ 66½	Pezua J M	109	8.50	65-21 Fiocroft 111¼ Noble Preview 117¼ What a Femme 117ⁿᵈ Outrun 12
25Jun88- 8Bel fst 1	:45¾ 1:11 1:36¾	3+ⓕⓢHydePark H	4 10 10¹¹10⁸¼10¹⁵10²⁰¼	Correa C J	108	24.60	61-17 Grecian Flight 124¹⁰¼ Unsanctioned 111¹ Spring Leaf10⁹² Outrun 10
10Jun88- 8Bel fst 6f	:22 :45¾ 1:11¾	3+ⓕⓢAlw 27000	9 13 13¹⁶10¹¹ 5⁹ 5⁴	Correa C J⁵	b 108	25.40	78-20 Big Mama Liz 112¾BesttoBeLucky111¹¾YingN'Yang114ⁿᵏ Slow st. 13
1Jun88- 7Bel fst 1¼	:45¾ 1:11¾ 1:45¾	3+ⓕⓢAlw 29000	13 13 1224¹09¼108½10¹¹¼	Romero R P	111	*2.20e	63-13 Black Beaver 110¹ Aljadam 117ⁿᵏ Home by Seven 109⁶ Outrun 14
19May88- 7Bel my 1¼	:45¾ 1:11¾ 1:46½	3+ⓕⓢAlw 29000	7 12 9¹⁵ 75¼ 4³ 2²	Krone J A	112	8.70	69-18 FamilyFraud1120.K.Rose112ⁿᵈPatinadora121¾ Pnchd strt.chcked 13
6Apr88- 9Aqu fst 1	:46½ 1:12¾ 1:39¾	3+ⓕⓢAlw 31000	4 10 10¹⁴ 7⁷ 66¼ 77¼	Maple E	112	6.90	60-21 Planchette 112ⁿᵒ Squawter 113² Havana Express 112²¾ Outrun 10
25Apr88- 4Aqu fst 7f	:23¾ :47 1:27	3+ⓕⓢMd Sp Wt	10 13 12¹¹ 6⁷ 2⁴ 11¾	Maple E	115	9.60	66-23 O. K. Rose 115¹¾ Story's First Tri 115²OverFlo'sLady124¾ Driving 14

LATEST WORKOUTS Aug 8 Sar tr.t 4f fst :51½ b • Jly 18 Bel 4f my :51 b • Jly 11 Bel 4f fst :49¾ b

Auntie Gosh made the lead at the quarter in two of her last three sprints, the last with fractions of :21 4/5 and :45 3/5 on a sloppy track at seven furlongs. But she stopped so badly she was eased. She is an excellent example of cheap speed, evidenced by her lifetime record of one win in twenty-three starts. Auntie Gosh wouldn't win this race, but she'd likely make sure any early speed horse testing her wouldn't win either.

Loveswept raced with blinkers added in her last start. She raced a head off the lead in :22 and :45 before fading to sixth. Before the addition of blinkers she made the lead in a sprint in :22 1/5.

She's Freezing was first at the quarter four times and second four more in eight of her last ten sprints. Her last start was at Saratoga when she dueled for the lead through a :22 2/5 quarter. She made the front after a half in :45 1/5 before tiring to fifth.

Cracking Good made the lead twice and was second by a head once at the quarter in three of her last seven sprints, although she hadn't made the lead in her last two. In her last nine losses, she never moved forward from the last call to the finish. Never.

Three of the frontrunners, Saucy Voyage, Loveswept and She's Freezing, went off 9 to 5, 7 to 2 and 9 to 1.

They created overlays all over the board.

Of the other seven fillies, four showed horrible form. Parole the Lady, Private Conscience, O.K. Rose and Brooklyn Bred had lost their last tiffs by thirty-four, seventeen and three-quarters, eleven and twenty-eight lengths, respectively. A fifth, Crafty Ville, hadn't been closer than fifth in her last seven starts.

That left two fillies, Travellingknightly and Crafty Alexas, at odds of 11 to 1 and 3 to 1.

There were no surprises. Auntie Gosh pushed Saucy Voyage through a :22 2/5 quarter and :45 4/5 half. Loveswept, fourth by three at the quarter, joined the leaders at the half; battled past them, and held second as Travellingknightly blew by for a seven length win, paying $24.80.

NINTH RACE

Saratoga

AUGUST 21, 1988

6 FURLONGS. (1.08) CLAIMING. Purse $18,000. Fillies 3-year-old weights, 121 lbs. Non-winners of two races since August 1, allowed 3 lbs. Of a race sine then 5 lbs. Claiming price $25,000 for each $2,500 to $20,000 2 lbs. Races when entered to be claimed for $18,000 for less not considered.

Value of race $18,000; value to winner $10,800; second $3,960; third $2,160; fourth $1,080. Mutuel pool $308,599. Exacta Pool $333,157. Triple Pool $839,429.

Last Raced	Horse	Eqt.A.Wt PP St	¼	½	Str	Fin	Jockey	Cl'g Pr	Odds $1
6Aug88 9Sar4	Travellingknightly	b 3 116 3 11	8½	8½	1½	17	Bracciale V Jr	25000	11.40
14Aug88 2Sar6	Loveswept	b 3 116 10 5	43	3 1½	2½	2¾	Cordero A Jr	25000	3.50
13Aug88 5Sar6	Crafty Ville	3 114 5 6	62½	51	4hd	3nk	Goossens L	22500	17.30
14Aug88 4Sar5	She's Freezing	3 116 9 4	3hd	4 1½	51	4¾	Pezua J M	25000	9.60
14Aug88 2Sar7	Crafty Alexas	b 3 111 6 7	72	62	61	5 1½	Peck B D5	25000	3.30
8Aug88 5Sar4	Saucy Voyage	b 3 116 2 2	1½	1hd	3 1½	6½	Day P	25000	1.90
14Aug88 4Sar6	Cracking Good	b 3 116 1 9	10 1½	9½	73	73½	Antley C W	25000	19.90
13Aug88 5Sar7	O. K. Rose	3 116 12 12	94	104	81½	81¾	Santagata N	25000	22.10
6Aug88 9Sar10	Parole the Lady	b 3 112 7 1	5hd	7hd	10½	9no	Venezia M	20000	40.20
6Aug88 9Sar	Auntie Gosh	3 102 4 3	22	2½	91	10no	Soto R10	20000	32.60
6Aug88 9Sar9	Brooklyn Bred	b 3 116 11 8	113	11½	11 1½	113	Maple E	25000	27.80
14Aug88 4Sar7	Private Conscience	3 106 8 10	12	12	12	12	Carr D10	25000	106.00

OFF AT 6:11. Start good, Won driving. Time, :22⅖, :45⅘, 1:11 Track fast.

$2 Mutuel Prices:

3-(E)-TRAVELLINGKNIGHTLY	....	24.80	11.20	6.80
10-(M)-LOVESWEPT	....		6.40	4.60
5-(G)-CRAFTY VILLE	....			10.60

$2 EXACTA 3-10 PAID $146.20. $2 TRIPLE 3-10-5 PAID $2,126.00.

Ch. f, by Travelling Music—David's Neill, by Final Ruling. Trainer Salzman John E. Bred by Benson Caroline T (Md).

TRAVELLINGKNIGHTLY saved ground into the stretch while rallying, came out near final furlong to continue his bid and drew off under good handling. LOVESWEPT made a run from the outside leaving the turn, was vying for the lead between horses when her rider lost the whip a furlong out and continued on with good energy to gain the place. CRAFTY VILLE made a run from the outside leaving the turn but wasn't good enough. SHE'S FREEZING never far back, was checked between horses near midstretch. CRAFTY ALEXAS raced wide into the stretch while moving but failed to sustain her bid. SAUCY VOYAGE saved ground showing speed to midstretch and gave way. CRACKING GOOD off slowly, rallied approaching midstretch but lacked a late response. O.K. ROSE raced wide. PAROLE THE LADY tired. AUNTIE GOSH was used up vying for the lead.

Let's look at two intriguing, high-profile races, the 1985 Kentucky Derby and the $1 million Breeders' Cup Sprint in 1987.

The importance of the Derby is obvious. Every trainer's dream is to win the Run for the Roses. Different trainers take different routes.

The field of thirteen which entered the 111th running of the Derby in 1985 was led by the 1984 juvenile (2-year-old) champion Chief's Crown. His principal opponents included Spend A Buck, Proud Truth, Skywalker, Tank's Prospect and Stephan's Odyssey. The considerable depth of quality of this group would be demonstrated well after the Derby. Proud Truth and Skywalker won successive runnings of the $3 million Breeders' Cup Classic in 1985 and 1986. Tank's Prospect set a track record in winning the Preakness. Chief's Crown gave Cordero his first win in the Travers, then beat older horses in the Marlboro Cup. Stephan's Odyssey ran second in the Belmont Stakes to stablemate Creme Fraiche.

8 CHURCHILL

1 ¼ MILES. (1.59⅖) 111th Running KENTUCKY DERBY (Grade I). $250,000 Added. The race to be run for 3-year-olds with a subscription fee of $200 each; an entry fee of $10,000 each and a starting fee of $10,000 each. All fees to be paid to the winner, $250,000 shall be paid by Churchill Downs Incorporated (the Association) as the Added Purse. Second place shall receive $100,000, third place shall receive $50,000 and fourth place shall receive $25,000 from the Added Purse. (The added purse and fees to be divided equally in the event of a dead heat.) Starters shall be named through the entry box on Thursday, May 2, 1985, at the usual time of closing. The maximum number of starters shall be limited to twenty and each shall carry a weight of 126 lbs. In the event that more than twenty entries pass through the entry box at the time of closing, the starters shall be determined at that time with preference given to those horses that have accumulated the highest earnings, excluding earnings won in a restricted race. For purposes of this preference, a restricted race shall mean a state bred restricted race (a race where entries are restricted to horses qualifying under state breeding programs), a sales restricted race (a race were entries are restricted by the origin of purchase), and a restricted sweepstakes (a race where entries are restricted by money previously earned, sweepstakes previously won, sweepstakes won at varying distances or sweepstakes won within period of time preceding race.) The owner of the winner shall receive a gold trophy. No supplementary nominations shall be accepted. Closed Friday, February 15, 1985 with 359 nominations.

Coupled—Rhoman Rule and Eternal Prince.

Irish Fighter

Own.—Proler I

Ch. c. 3, by Irish River—Go On Dreaming, by Dewan
Br.—Seven Hill Corp (Ky)
Tr.—Borders Billy S

126 Lifetime 6 2 0 3 $94,625 — **1985 6 2 0 3 $94,625** — **1984 0 M 0 0**

20Apr85- 9OP	fst	1⅛	:46⅗ 1:11 1:48⅖	Ark Derby	6	4	55¾	51¼	34½	37½	Hernandez C	115	37.20	84-18 Tank's Prospect 1236½ Encolure 1261 IrishFighter1151½	Bid, hung	9
20Apr85-Grade I																
31Mar85-11FG	fst	1⅛	:47 1:12 1:50⅕	La Derby	1	2	32½	32	22	32	Hernandez C	113	39.50	91-21 Violado 115no Creme Fraiche 1202 Irish Fighter 1134	Evenly	11
31Mar85-Grade III																
16Mar85-10FG	sl	1 1/16	:47⅘ 1:13⅕ 1:45⅘	Spec'l Wt	4	3	34½	21	2hd	32	Hernandez C	116	3.00	81-20 Mischiefinmind117noNordicScndl1162IrishFightr1162	Good effort	6
23Feb85-10FG	fst	1 1/16	:47⅖ 1:12⅘ 1:45⅘	Lecomte H	6	7	86¼	97¼	69	69¼	Walker B J Jr	115	7.60	74-24 Encolure 1141 Northern Bid 1193 Ten Times Ten 1165	Outrun	11
30Jan85- 9FG	gd	6f	:22⅖ :46⅘ 1:12	Alw 9000	5	8	41¾	31	13	13	Walker B J Jr	119	*.70	85-18 Irish Fighter 1193 Single Bid 1193¾ Delierio1191½	Lugged in, clear	8
10Jan85- 4FG	fst	6f	:22⅗ :46⅗ 1:12	Md Sp Wt	9	12	1hd	12½	14	15	Walker B J Jr	119	*.80	85-20 IrishFighter1195PocketOfMircles1191½Slloum'sJewel1192	Handily	12

LATEST WORKOUTS Apr 14 Kee 7f fst 1:28 b — Apr 9 Kee 5f fst 1:01⅖ b — Mar 25 FG 7f fst 1:26⅖ h — Mar 10 FG 7f fst 1:26⅕ b

Chief's Crown *

Own.—Star Crown Stable

B. c. 3, by Danzig—Six Crowns, by Secretariat
Br.—Rosen C (Ky)
Tr.—Laurin Roger

126 Lifetime 12 9 2 0 $1,229,422 — **1985 3 3 0 0 $308,532** — **1984 9 6 2 0 $920,890**

25Apr85- 7Kee	fst	1⅛	:48⅖ 1:12 1:47⅗	Blue Grass	2	1	11½	11	13	15½	MacBeth D	121	*.30	99-16 Chief'sCrown1215½FlotingReserve121hdBnnerBob12111	Hand ride	4
25Apr85-Grade I																
30Mar85-11Hia	fst	1⅛	:48⅘ 1:12⅖ 1:48⅖	Flamingo	5	1	1hd	11	12½	11	MacBeth D	122	1.30 [D]	90-12 [D]Chf'sCrown1221ProudTrth122nkStphn'sOdyssy1223½	Drifted out	8
30Mar85-Grade I. Disq., placed 2d; reversed by Fla. board 9Apr85, awarded 1st money																
2Mar85-10GP	fst	7f	:22⅗ :45⅕ 1:22⅖	Swale	9	2	2hd	2hd	11	13¼	MacBeth D	122	*.30	92-15 Chief'sCrown1223¼CremeFriche1173½CherokeFst113nk	Ridden out	9
10Nov84- 1Hol	fst	1	:45 1:10 1:36⅕	Br Cp Juv	5	6	64¾	32½	21	1¾	MacBeth D	122	*.70	— — Chief's Crown 122¾Tank'sProspect122¾SpendABuck1226½	Driving	10
10Nov84-Grade I																
27Oct84- 8SA	fst	1 1/16	:46⅗ 1:10⅘ 1:42⅖	Norfolk	6	2	2½	1hd	1hd	11½	MacBeth D	118	*.30	89-13 Chief's Crown 1181½ MatthewT.Parker1189VivaMaxi118hd	Driving	6
27Oct84-Grade I																
6Oct84- 8Bel	fst	1	:45⅖ 1:10⅗ 1:36⅗	Cowdin	4	4	21	12	13	16	MacBeth D	122	*.50	82-17 Chief's Crown 1226BionicLight12212½ScriptOhio1221¼	Ridden out	5
6Oct84-Grade I																
15Sep84- 5Bel	sly	7f	:22⅘ :46 1:23⅕	Futurity	5	2	68	64	34	21	MacBeth D	122	*.70	85-18 SpectculrLove1221Chif'sCrown1223¼Mugzy'sRullh1222¾	Wide str	8
15Sep84-Grade I																
26Aug84- 8Sar	fst	6½f	:21⅘ :44⅘ 1:16	Hopeful	3	4	33½	3½	1½	13¾	MacBeth D	122	*1.10	92-15 Chief'sCrown1223¾TiffanyIce1223¾Mugzy'sRullah122½	Ridden out	9
26Aug84-Grade I																
3Aug84- 8Sar	fst	6f	:22⅗ :46 1:10⅕	Sar Spec'l	4	3	33	2hd	1hd	12¾	MacBeth D	117	*2.10	89-19 Chief'sCrown1172¾DoItAginDn117hdSkyCommnd122¾	Ridden [illegible]	[illegible]
3Aug84-Grade II																
5Jly84- 6Bel	fst	5½f	:22⅖ :45⅘ 1:04⅖	Md Sp Wt	5	1	1hd	2hd	11	15	MacBeth D	118	*1.10	93-15 Chief's Crown 1185 Desert War 1182¼TigerBidder1184	Ridden out	9
22Jun84- 4Bel	fst	5½f	:22⅕ :46⅕ 1:05⅗	Md Sp Wt	1	1	43½	46½	34½	21	MacBeth D	118	5.20	86-21 Secretary General 1181 Chief's Crown1181¼TiffanyIce1189	Rallied	10
13Jun84- 4Bel	fst	5f	:22⅘ :46⅖ :58⅘	Md Sp Wt	8	8	46½	613	513	411½	Cordero A Jr	118	3.10	81-18 Don'tFoolWithMe1188Attribute118nkMountRlity1183¼	Carried out	8

LATEST WORKOUTS May 1 CD 4f sly :47⅗ b — Apr 22 Kee 4f fst :49⅗ b — ● Apr 17 Kee 5f fst :58⅘ h — ● Apr 6 GP 4f fst :48⅕ b

Rhoman Rule

B. c. 3, by Stop The Music—Morning Bird, by Swaps — Br.—Ledyard L C (Pa) — Tr.—Penna Angel Jr

Own.—Combs B II — 126 — Lifetime 8 3 1 2 $193,928 — 1985 3 2 0 1 $120,480 — 1984 5 1 1 1 $73,448

20Apr85- 8Aqu gd 1⅛ :48 1:11⅗ 1:48⅘ Wood Mem 1 4 35 34 24 35 Vasquez J 126 2.90 86-10 EternalPrince1262¾ProudTruth1262½RhomanRule1263½ Weakened 6

20Apr85-Grade I

16Mar85-10Hia fst 1⅛ :48⅘ 1:12 1:47⅘ Everglades 6 1 12 12½ 15 18 Vasquez J 112 1.30 93-13 Rhoman Rule 1128 Creme Fraiche 1176 IrishSur119hd Ridden out 8

16Mar85-Grade II

2Mar85- 1GP fst 7f :22⅕ :44⅘ 1:22 Alw 16000 1 7 42 2hd 13 110 Vasquez J 117 *1.50 94-15 Rhoman Rule 11710 J. O.'s Best 1224 Magloire 1192 Ridden out 9

18Oct84- 8Med fst 1 1/16 :46 1:11⅕ 1:45 Yng America 8 6 611 44 44½ 43 Hernandez R 119 7.60 81-22 ScriptOhio119¾SpendABuck122nkTank'sProspect1192 Drifted out 11

18Oct84-Grade I

6Oct84- 8Lrl fst 1 1/16 :46⅘ 1:12⅘ 1:43 Laurel Fty 12 8 84¾ 53 2½ 32½ Hernandez R 122 32.50 90-15 MightyAppealing1222½CutlassReality122hdRhomnRule12210 Wide 12

6Oct84-Grade I

8Sep84- 5Bel fst 7f :22⅘ :45⅗ 1:24 Alw 20000 8 7 75½ 54 35½ 24 Hernandez R 119 12.80 78-17 Herat 1224 Rhoman Rule 1193½ Stone White 112¾ Wide 8

8Aug84- 4Sar fst 7f :22⅘ :46⅖ 1:25 Md Sp Wt 11 2 31 2½ 13 13½ Hernandez R 118 3.90f 77-16 RhomnRule1183½CoyoteDncer1183½FbulousMov1181½ Ridden out 13

26Jly84- 6Bel fst 6f :22⅗ :46⅕ 1:11⅗ Md Sp Wt 9 10 85½ 66½ 913 817¼ Samyn J L 118 13.40 66-17 Salem Drive 118¾ Anconeus 1181½ Haberdasher1184 Broke slowly 10

LATEST WORKOUTS May 3 CD 3f gd :36⅖ b Apr 29 CD 6f fst 1:14⅘ h Apr 19 Bel 3f fst :36 b Apr 15 Bel 6f fst 1:14 b

Tank's Prospect

B. c. 3, by Mr Prospector—Midnight Pumpkin, by Pretense — Br.—Seltzer E A (Ky) — Tr.—Lukas D Wayne

Own.—Klein Mr-Mrs E V — 126 — Lifetime 11 4 2 2 $932,445 — 1985 4 3 0 0 $513,850 — 1984 7 1 2 2 $418,595

20Apr85- 9OP fst 1⅛ :46⅗ 1:11 1:48⅖ Ark Derby 9 5 45½ 4¾ 11 16½ Stevens G L b 123 3.10 92-18 Tank's Prospect1236½Encolure1261IrishFighter1151½ Steady drive 9

20Apr85-Grade I

6Apr85- 8SA fst 1⅛ :46⅗ 1:10⅗ 1:48⅖ S A Derby 7 4 42 83¾ 812 911¼ Velasquez J b 122 3.20 76-10 Skywalker122noFastAccount1222½Nostalgia'sStr122¾ Fin. after 5f 9

6Apr85-Grade I

3Feb85- 8BM fst 1 1/16 :45⅗ 1:09⅗ 1:41 Camino Real 4 5 31½ 4¾ 1hd 1½ Velasquez J b 120 2.40 87-13 Tnk'sProspct120½RightCon120½[D]Skywlkr1201 Lugged in, driving 9

3Feb85-Grade III

6Jan85- 4SA fst 1 :45⅖ 1:10⅕ 1:36 Alw 24000 1 1 1½ 13 12½ 1¾ Delahoussaye E b 115 *.30 88-06 Tank's Prospect115¾ProtectYourself1188FutureFable1183 Driving 6

16Dec84- 8Hol gd 1 1/16 :45⅗ 1:10⅗ 1:43⅖ Hol Futy 4 9 96½ 85 42½ 42½ Velasquez J b 121 3.30 — — Stephan's Odyssey 1211 First Norman1211½RightCon121hd Rallied 13

16Dec84-Grade I

10Nov84- 1Hol fst 1 :45 1:10 1:36⅕ Br Cp Juv 4 7 76½ 45 32½ 2¾ Velasquez J b 122 25.60 — — Chief's Crown 122¾ Tank'sProspect122¾SpendABuck1226½ Rallied 10

10Nov84-Grade I

27Oct84- 8Aqu my 1⅛ :48⅕ 1:12⅕ 1:49⅕ Champagne 2 5 45½ 43½ 45½ 34 Velasquez J 122 3.00 85-16 ForCrtnDoc122noMghtyApplng1224Tnk'sProspct122nk Came over 6

27Oct84-Grade I

18Oct84- 8Med fst 1 1/16 :46 1:11⅕ 1:45 Yng America 9 9 714 77½ 56 31 MacBeth D 119 16.00 83-22 Script Ohio 119¾ Spend ABuck122nkTank'sProspect1192 Fin. well 11

18Oct84-Grade I

5Oct84- 6SA fst 6f :22⅖ :45⅗ 1:10⅗ Md Sp Wt 6 7 67¾ 66½ 32 13½ Delahoussaye E 117 4.80 85-16 Tank'sProspect1173½Chieftain'sClass1171½QualityJet117½ Handily 9

11Jly84- 4Hol fst 6f :22⅗ :46 1:11⅕ Md Sp Wt 6 6 63½ 43½ 43 22½ Valenzuela P A 116 8.20 78-16 Metronomic 1162½ Tank'sProspect116noRoyalOlympia116½ Rallied 9

1Jly84- 6Hol fst 5½f :22⅘ :45⅕ 1:04⅗ Md Sp Wt 3 8 76½ 68½ 69½ 56¾ Valenzuela P A 116 13.80 81-16 Lomax 1164 Royal Olympia 116¾ Michadilla 1161½ No threat 8

LATEST WORKOUTS Apr 28 Hol 5f fst 1:02⅕ h Apr 14 SA 5f fst 1:01⅘ h Apr 1 SA 6f fst 1:13⅗ h ●Mar 27 Hol 1 sly 1:44⅖ h

Eternal Prince

B. c. 3, by Majestic Prince—Eternal Queen, by Fleet Nasrullah — Br.—Kinsman Stud Farm (Fla) — Tr.—Lenzini John J Jr

Own.—Hurst-Steinbrenner et al — 126 — Lifetime 8 4 2 0 $389,362 — 1985 5 4 0 0 $379,740 — 1984 3 M 2 0 $9,622

20Apr85- 8Aqu gd 1⅛ :48 1:11⅗ 1:48⅘ Wood Mem 5 1 11 12½ 14 12¾ Migliore R b 126 2.50 91-10 Eternal Prince 1262¾ Proud Truth1262½RhomanRule1263½ Driving 6

20Apr85-Grade I

6Apr85- 8Aqu fst 1 :44⅕ 1:08⅗ 1:34⅗ Gotham 7 1 11½ 11½ 12 15 Migliore R b 114 18.40 94-21 Eternal Prince 1145 Pancho Villa 121½ ElBasco1141½ Brisk urging 7

6Apr85-Grade II

23Mar85- 8Aqu fst 7f :22⅘ :45⅗ 1:22⅕ Bay Shore 6 1 21 3nk 55½ 68¾ Migliore R b 114 3.70 81-23 Pancho Villa 1143¾ El Basco 1141¾ Spend A Buck 1232 Gave way 9

23Mar85-Grade II

13Mar85- 7Aqu fst 7f :23⅕ :46⅘ 1:25⅕ Alw 25000 6 1 1½ 11 14 16¾ Migliore R b 122 *.80 75-28 Eternal Prince 1226¾ Super Scope 1172 Verbascum 1176 Easily 7

4Mar85- 6Aqu fst 6f [•]:23 :46⅖ 1:11⅗ Md Sp Wt 5 1 11½ 12 16 18 Migliore R b 122 *1.00 87-22 Eternal Prince 1228 ChangeTheLock122nkAlex'sGame122no Easily 10

31Jly84- 9Mth fst 5½f :22⅕ :45 1:04 Tyro 8 9 108 710 79 413 Delgado A b 113 30.10 82-15 Doubly Clear 1223 Ziggy'sBoy1167Whatever'sRight1223 No threat 11

16Jly84- 6Bel fst 6f :22⅗ :46 1:11⅗ Md Sp Wt 1 1 2hd 2hd 2hd 24 Cordero A Jr b 118 14.10 81-24 Nickel Back 1184 Eternal Prince 118no Anconeus 1181 No match 13

27Jun84- 4Bel fst 5½f :23 :47⅕ 1:06⅗ Md 40000 5 3 1hd 1½ 11½ 21¼ Migliore R 118 2.60 81-17 BernaCgney1111¼EternlPrince1181½WesternChmp1164 Weakened 9

LATEST WORKOUTS ●Apr 29 CD 5f fst 1:00⅗ h Apr 15 Aqu 5f fst 1:02 b Apr 2 GS 5f fst :57⅖ b ●Mar 20 Aqu 4f fst :46⅖ h

Stephan's Odyssey

Dk. b. or br. c. 3, by Danzig—Kennelot, by Gallant Man — Br.—Kennelot Stables Ltd (Ky) — Tr.—Stephens Woodford C

Own.—DeKwiatkowski H — 126 — Lifetime 8 4 1 1 $739,635 — 1985 4 1 1 1 $88,535 — 1984 4 3 0 0 $651,100

16Apr85- 7Kee fst 1 1/16 :47⅗ 1:11⅕ 1:42⅗ Lexington 4 6 46 54½ 31½ 11½ Pincay L Jr 118 *.50 93-16 Stephan'sOdyssey1181½Tajawa1121½NorthernBid1121¾ Ridden out 7

30Mar85-11Hia fst 1⅛ :48⅘ 1:12⅖ 1:48⅖ Flamingo 4 4 42 42½ 32½ 31½ Maple E 122 3.50 89-12 [D]Chf'sCrown1221ProudTrth122nkStphn'sOdyssy1223½ Forced out 8

30Mar85-Grade I

2Mar85-11GP fst 1⅛ :47⅗ 1:11⅗ 1:50 Fla Derby 1 3 53¼ 42 55 64½ Maple E 122 *1.10 78-15 Proud Truth 122nk Irish Sur 1221 Do ItAgainDan1221½ Weakened 11

2Mar85-Grade I

18Feb85-10GP fst 1 1/16 :46⅗ 1:11⅕ 1:43⅗ Ftn Youth 11 11 1112 96½ 5½ 2nk Maple E 122 2.70 83-22 ProudTruth112nkStphn'sOdyssy1224DoItAginDn1124½ Just missed 14

18Feb85-Grade II

16Dec84- 8Hol gd 1 1/16 :45⅗ 1:10⅗ 1:43⅖ Hol Futy 8 12 109 42½ 11½ 11 Maple E 121 11.20 — — Stephan's Odyssey 1211 FirstNorman1211½RightCon121hd Driving 13

16Dec84-Grade I

2Dec84- 3Hol fst 6f :22 :45⅗ 1:09⅗ Alw 22000 1 6 65½ 31½ 2hd 1no Pincay L Jr 118 3.90 101-05 Stephn'sOdyssey118noImgeofGretness1185ProBowlr1183½ Driving 6

28Oct84- 6Aqu gd 7f :22⅕ :45 1:22⅗ Alw 20000 3 6 53¾ 31½ 32 43½ McCarron G 122 *1.90 84-14 Another Reef 117½ Secretary General 1172¾SkipTrial117nk Drifted 7

21Oct84- 6Bel fst 6f :22⅘ :46⅖ 1:12 Md Sp Wt 4 7 43 32½ 2½ 11½ Day P 118 *.70 82-21 Stphn'sOdyssy1181½RllngMnstrl1185¾DmscsSm1182 Bumped,clear 11

LATEST WORKOUTS ●May 2 CD 4f my :48 h Apr 28 CD 1 my 1:46⅖ b Apr 24 Kee 5f fst 1:01⅘ b ●Apr 11 Hia 6f fst 1:13⅕ b

Encolure

B. c. 3, by Riva Ridge—Jabot, by Bold Ruler
Br.—Claiborne Farm (Ky)
Tr.—Morgan Tom T
Own.—Porter Margaret
126
Lifetime 11 4 4 0 $281,824
1985 6 2 2 0 $213,600
1984 5 2 2 0 $68,224

20Apr85- 9OP fst 1⅛ :46⅗ 1:11 1:48⅖ Ark Derby 5 2 2hd 2hd 21 26½ Ardoin R 126 50.30 85-18 Tank's Prospect 1236½ Encolure 1261IrishFighter1151½ Weakened 9
20Apr85-Grade I
31Mar85-11FG fst 1⅛ :47 1:12 1:50⅕ La Derby 8 7 86¾ 74¾ 814 812¾ Ardoin R 123 10.40 80-21 Violado 115no Creme Fraiche 1202 IrishFighter1134 Nvr prominet 11
31Mar85-Grade III
23Mar85-10FG fst 1$\frac{1}{16}$:46⅘ 1:12⅘ 1:45⅖ Hits P Dby 9 3 38 35½ 14 11 Ardoin R 123 *1.20 85-19 Encolure 1231 Under Orders 1172½ Dusty'sDynamite1151½ Driving 10
14Mar85-10FG sly 1$\frac{1}{16}$:47⅘ 1:13⅕ 1:46⅖ Spec'l Wt 8 3 3½ 1hd 12½ 22 Ardoin R 123 *.90 78-21 Under Orders 1122 Encolure 1231½ Flashy Diamond 1152 2nd best 10
Feb85-10FG fst 1$\frac{1}{16}$:47⅖ 1:12⅘ 1:45⅘ Lecomte H 3 2 22 21 11½ 11 Ardoin R 114 40.70 83-24 Encolure 1141 Northern Bid 1193 Ten Times Ten 1165 Driving 11
Jan85-10FG fst 6f :22⅕ :46⅕ 1:11 Master Dby H 7 1 53 84¾ 35 47 Faul J H 116 5.00 83-19 Marshua'sEchelon1134½TenTimesTen1141½MsterCll1131 Bid, hung 8
15Dec84-10FG fst 6f :22 :46⅕ 1:11⅖ Hits Pde Fty 10 1 63¾ 21½ 11½ 14½ Ardoin R 115 8.90 88-17 Encolure 1154½ Under Orders 117nk Kama Sutra 1173 Ridden out 13
6Dec84-11FG gd 6f :22⅗ :47⅖ 1:14⅖ [R]Fut Trl 9 6 64¾ 57 25 24 Ardoin R 115 2.90 69-32 Kama Sutra 1154 Encolure 1153½ Bashful Angel 1101½ 2nd best 11
6Dec84-Run in three divisions, 7th, 9th and 11th races
15Nov84-10LaD fst 6f :22⅗ :46⅕ 1:11⅘ Alw 7400 8 2 43½ 42½ 33 48¾ Ardoin R 122 *.80 75-26 MsterCll1176JunglePilgrim116nkNtiveCrwmn1222½ Lacked a rally 9
8Nov84- 4LaD fst 7f :23 :46⅗ 1:25⅖ Md Sp Wt 9 5 2hd 2hd 13 15 Ardoin R 120 *1.30 97-21 Encolure 1205 Oceail's Pride 12010 Rivaten 1201½ Handily 12
8Jun84- 4LaD gd 5f :23 :47⅖ 1:00⅖ Md Sp Wt 7 9 44 46 38 210 Frazier R L 120 2.10 79-23 Politariat 11710 Encolure 120½ Two Cheers 1205 Brk sluggishly 10
LATEST WORKOUTS Apr 30 CD 5f fst 1:01⅗ b ●Apr 16 OP 5f fst :59⅘ b Mar 28 FG 5f sly 1:05⅘ b Mar 20 FG 5f fst 1:02⅗ b

I Am The Game *

B. c. 3, by Lord Gaylord—Kitchen Window, by Dead Ahead
Br.—Jones W L Jr (Md)
Tr.—Leatherbury King T
Own.—Leatherbury & Mandjuris
126
Lifetime 8 4 2 1 $212,183
1985 7 3 2 1 $200,183
1984 1 1 0 0 $12,000

20Apr85- 8GS fst 1⅛ :45⅗ 1:09⅖ 1:45⅘ Garden State 1 4 48 44½ 26 29½ Antley C W b 117 17.10 — — SpndABuck1229½IAmThGm1175½DoItAginDn115nk Best of others 9
6Apr85- 8GS fst 1 :45⅖ 1:10 1:35⅖ Ch'y Hill H 3 14 1421 1316 712 210½ Antley C W b 115 12.40 — — Spend A Buck 12210½ I Am TheGame115¾KingBabar1161¼ Rallied 14
23Mar85- 8Aqu fst 7f :22⅘ :45⅗ 1:22⅕ Bay Shore 9 3 53 51¾ 78½ 79¼ Vasquez J 117 5.60 81-23 PanchoVill1143¾ElBsco1141¾SpendABuck1232 Wide,flattened out 9
23Mar85-Grade II
9Mar85- 8Lrl fst 1 :46⅕ 1:11⅗ 1:38 [S]St De Naskra 2 1 2hd 1½ 13½ 13¼ Delgado A 112 *.40 82-27 I Am The Game1123¼JoyfullJohn112hdLittleBoldJohn1126 Driving 5
Feb85- 8Lrl fst 1 :46⅕ 1:11⅘ 1:37⅗ Gen George 6 1 3½ 2hd 2½ 36 Delgado A 119 *.40 78-20 Roo Art 1222 Joyfull John 1124 I Am The Game 1191¼ Wide 8
Feb85- 8Lrl sly 7f :23⅕ :46⅗ 1:24⅕ F. Scott Key 2 1 11 12 11½ 15½ Delgado A 122 *1.20 90-28 I Am The Game 1225½ Sparrowvon 110nkJoyfullJohn112hd Driving 10
Jan85- 8Lrl fst 6f :22⅖ :45⅘ 1:10⅘ W P Burch 1 2 21½ 2hd 1hd 11 Delgado A 113 *.30 89-14 I Am The Game1131JayBryan119noAlongCameJones115nk Driving 6
Dec84- 7Aqu fst 6f [•]:23 :46⅘ 1:11⅖ Md Sp Wt 8 4 1½ 1½ 14 14 Cordero A Jr 118 2.60 87-15 IAmThGm1184FirstConqust1131¼HistoryRsponds118½ Ridden out 11
LATEST WORKOUTS Apr 30 CD 5f fst 1:01⅗ b ●Apr 17 Lrl 4f fst :47⅕ h ●Apr 3 Lrl 3f fst :35 bg Mar 20 Lrl 3f fst :36⅗ b

Floating Reserve

B. c. 3, by Olden Times—Tick Tock, by Quack
Br.—Hibbert R E (Ky)
Tr.—Manzi Joseph
Own.—Hibbert R E
126
Lifetime 7 2 1 0 $121,295
1985 6 1 1 0 $110,295
1984 1 1 0 0 $11,000

25Apr85- 7Kee fst 1⅛ :48⅖ 1:12 1:47⅗ Blue Grass 1 3 31½ 32 34 25½ Hawley S 121 13.30 93-16 Chief'sCrown1215½FlotingResrv121hdBnnrBob12111 Saved ground 4
25Apr85-Grade I
6Apr85- 8SA fst 1⅛ :46⅗ 1:10⅗ 1:48⅖ S A Derby 4 8 73¾ 53 52¾ 43¼ Hawley S 122 10.50 84-10 Skywalker 122no FastAccount1222½Nostalgia'sStar122¾ Hung late 9
6Apr85-Grade I
17Mar85- 8SA fst 1$\frac{1}{16}$:44⅘ 1:10 1:43⅕ S Felipe H 3 8 814 86½ 65½ 54 Maple E b 120 6.40 81-15 ImageofGreatness120noSkywalker1201Nostalgi'sStr117¾ Late bid 9
17Mar85-Grade I
23Feb85- 8SA fst 1 :45⅘ 1:10⅕ 1:36⅕ San Rafael 5 7 75 56 44½ 63¼ Pincay L Jr 122 2.20 84-13 Smarten Up 1221¼FastAccount122½Stan'sBower118no Drifted out 9
23Feb85-Grade II
6Feb85- 8SA fst 1$\frac{1}{16}$:46⅗ 1:10⅘ 1:42⅗ [R]S'nta Catlna 9 5 54 63¾ 32½ 1¾ Pincay L Jr 117 3.30 88-15 FlotngRsrv117¾BrconsChrg1172½BldrThnBld1141 Bumped, driving 11
19Jan85- 4SA fst 6½f :21⅘ :44⅖ 1:15⅘ Alw 24000 4 6 54¼ 54½ 44½ 45½ Delahoussaye E 120 *.80 85-16 Lucky NGreen1153½PerfecTravel1202Infantryman114no Lugged in 6
26Dec84- 6SA fst 6f :22⅕ :45⅖ 1:10⅗ Md Sp Wt 1 4 3½ 31 1½ 14 Hawley S 118 10.40 85-15 FlotingRsrv1184[D]EvrBrillint1181CptnVgors118¹¾ Bmpd st., easily 8
LATEST WORKOUTS ●Apr 22 Kee 4f fst :46⅘ h Apr 17 Kee 1 fst 1:40⅘ h ●Mar 31 SA 6f fst 1:10⅕ h Mar 13 SA 5f fst :59⅘ h

Spend A Buck

B. c. 3, by Buckaroo—Belle De Jour, by Speak John
Br.—Harper & Irish Hill Farm (Ky)
Tr.—Gambolati Cam
Own.—Hunter Farm
126
Lifetime 11 7 2 2 $991,709
1985 3 2 0 1 $323,724
1984 8 5 2 1 $667,985

20Apr85- 8GS fst 1⅛ :45⅗ 1:09⅖ 1:45⅘ Garden State 2 1 13½ 13 16 19½ Cordero A Jr 122 *.40 — — SpendABuck1229½IAmTheGme1175½DoItAginDn115nk Ridden out 9
6Apr85- 8GS fst 1 :45⅖ 1:10 1:35⅖ Ch'y Hill H 7 1 12½ 12 16 110½ Cordero A Jr 122 1.70 — — Spend ABuck12210½IAmTheGame115¾KingBabar1161¼ Ridden out 14
23Mar85- 8Aqu fst 7f :22⅘ :45⅗ 1:22⅕ Bay Shore 1 6 31 41¼ 34½ 35½ Cordero A Jr 123 *1.40 84-23 PnchoVill1143¾ElBsco1141¾SpendABuck1232 Wknd under impost 9
23Mar85-Grade II
10Nov84- 1Hol fst 1 :45 1:10 1:36⅕ Br Cp Juv 3 1 1hd 12½ 11 31½ Cordero A Jr 122 6.40 — — Chief'sCrown122¾Tnk'sProspect122¾SpndABuck1226½ Weakened 10
10Nov84-Grade I
18Oct84- 8Med fst 1$\frac{1}{16}$:46 1:11⅕ 1:45 Yng America 4 1 11½ 11 1½ 2¾ Cordero A Jr 122 *1.00 83-22 Script Ohio 119¾ Spend A Buck 122nkTank'sProspect1192 Gamely 11
18Oct84-Grade I
22Sep84- 9AP fst 1 :44⅘ 1:10 1:38 Arl Was Fut 6 3 21 2hd 1½ 1½ Hussey C 122 2.90 71-24 Spend A Buck 122½ Dusty's Darby 1222½ Viva Maxi 1221¾ All out 7
22Sep84-Grade I
2Sep84-11RD fst 1$\frac{1}{16}$:47⅗ 1:12 1:45⅘ Cradle 6 2 11 14 18 115 Hussey C 120 *1.20 80-18 Spend A Buck 12015 Grand Native 1206 Alex's Game 120nk Easily 13
16Aug84- 7Crc fst 6f :22⅗ :46⅕ 1:12⅘ Alw 15000 1 1 11½ 14 16 19½ Hussey C 112 *.50 87-23 Spend A Buck 1129½ Secret Goal 1128½Mr.Introienne1143 Handily 5
4Aug84- 9Crc fst 5½f :22⅗ :47 1:07 Criterium 4 2 23 22 22½ 22½ Hussey C 116 *.60 87-21 Smile 1142½ Spend A Buck 116hd Cherokee Fast 1164½ Held place 7
4Aug84-Run In Divisions
25Jly84- 8Crc fst 5½f :22⅗ :46⅗ 1:06 Alw 11000 3 1 1½ 11½ 13 14 Hussey C 113 2.40 95-20 SpendABuck1134Mr.Introinn1161½PlyingPolitics1144½ Ridden out 8
14Jly84- 2Crc fst 5½f :23 :47 1:07⅕ Md Sp Wt 6 3 11½ 1hd 12 1nk Hussey C 116 5.50 89-19 SpendABuck116nkHickoryHillFlyer1163SuperbAnswr1163½ Driving 12
LATEST WORKOUTS ●May 1 CD 4f sly :47 h ●Apr 17 GS 4f fst :45⅖ h ●Apr 3 GS 4f fst :45⅖ h ●Mar 22 Aqu 3f fst :35⅖ h

Proud Truth — **Ch. c. 3, by Graustark—Wake Robin, by Summer Tan** — **Br.—Galbreath Mrs J W (Ky)** — **Tr.—Veitch John M** — **Own.—Darby Dan Farm** — **126** — Lifetime 8 5 2 0 $453,927 — 1985 6 3 2 0 $435,927 — 1984 2 2 0 0 $18,000

20Apr85- 8Aqu gd 1⅛ :48 1:11⅗ 1:48⅘ Wood Mem 4 3 4^7 4^6 3^6 $2^{2¾}$ Velasquez J 126 *1.60 88–10 Eternal Prince $126^{2¾}$ Proud Truth $126^{2¼}$RhomanRule$126^{3½}$ Rallied 6
20Apr85-Grade I

30Mar85-11Hia fst 1⅛ :48⅘ 1:12⅖ 1:48⅖ Flamingo 7 2 2^{hd} 3^1 $2^{2½}$ 2^1 Velasquez J 122 *1.20 89–12 [D]Chif'sCrown122^1ProudTruth122^{nk}Stphn'sOdyssy$122^{3½}$ Impeded 8
30Mar85-Grade I; Placed 1st thru. disq.; reversed by Fla. board 9Apr85, awarded 2d money

2Mar85-11GP fst 1⅛ :47⅗ 1:11⅗ 1:50 Fla Derby 7 6 $6^{6¼}$ $6^{5¼}$ $3^{3½}$ 1^{nk} Velasquez J 122 2.00 82–15 ProudTruth122^{nk}IrishSur122^1DoItAgainDn$122^{1½}$ Steadied, driving 11
2Mar85-Grade I

18Feb85-10GP fst 1 1/16 :46⅗ 1:11⅕ 1:43⅗ Ftn Youth 9 10 9^{10} $8^{6¼}$ 3^{nk} 1^{nk} Velasquez J 112 *1.90 83–22 ProudTruth112^{nk}Stephan'sOdyssey122^4DoItAgainDn$112^{4½}$ Driving 14
18Feb85-Grade II

4Feb85- 8GP fst 1 1/16 :46⅗ 1:11⅗ 1:44⅖ Alw 16000 2 5 $6^{3½}$ $4^{1¾}$ 1^1 1^6 Velasquez J 117 *.80 79–18 ProudTruth117^6CrowningHonors$117^{1¼}$ScrtryGnrl$117^{½}$ Ridden out 10

5Jan85- 9Crc fst 1 1/16 :48⅕ 1:13 1:46⅗ Trop Pk Dby 15 11 13^{16} 9^{15} 6^8 $4^{2¾}$ Velasquez J 121 *1.60 83–14 Irish Sur $121^{1½}$ Artillerist $121^{½}$ Banner Bob $121^{¾}$ Rallied 16
5Jan85-Grade II

26Dec84- 8Crc fst 7f :22⅖ :45⅘ 1:25⅕ Alw 10000 1 12 $7^{7¼}$ 5^8 $5^{2¼}$ 1^3 Velasquez J 119 *1.10 90–22 ProudTruth119^3Bowladrome114^2ReglBrek113^{hd} BrkeInTangle,Clr 12

2Dec84- 6Aqu fst 6f :22⅘ :47 1:12⅘ Md Sp Wt 2 7 $8^{4½}$ $7^{6¾}$ 3^1 $1^{2¾}$ Velasquez J 118 2.10e 79–24 Proud Truth $118^{2¾}$ Take Control $118^{1½}$ Buckner 118^3 Handily 10

LATEST WORKOUTS May 3 CD 3f gd :37 b Apr 28 CD 5f my 1:02⅘ b Apr 19 Bel 3f fst :35⅗ b ●Apr 14 Bel 6f fst 1:13⅕ h

Skywalker * — **Dk. b. or br. c. 3, by Relaunch—Bold Captive, by Boldnesian** — **Br.—Oak Cliff Tbds Ltd (Ky)** — **Tr.—Whittingham Michael** — **Own.—Oak Cliff Stable** — **126** — Lifetime 6 3 1 0 $330,700 — 1985 4 2 1 0 $291,200 — 1984 2 1 0 0 $39,500

6Apr85- 8SA fst 1⅛ :46⅗ 1:10⅗ 1:48⅖ S A Derby 9 3 $3^{½}$ $3^{½}$ 2^{hd} 1no Pincay L Jr 122 *1.30 87–10 Skywalker 122no Fast Account $122^{2½}$ Nostalgia'sStar$122^{¾}$ Just up 9
6Apr85-Grade I

17Mar85- 8SA fst 1 1/16 :44⅘ 1:10 1:43⅕ S Felipe H 5 6 6^{11} 3^2 $2^{½}$ 2no Day P 120 *2.20 85–15 ImageofGretness120^{no}Skywlker120^1Nostlgi'sStr$117^{¾}$ Just missed 9
17Mar85-Grade I

3Feb85- 8BM fst 1 1/16 :45⅗ 1:09⅗ 1:41 Camino Real 6 7 $6^{4¼}$ $5^{2¾}$ 4^1 3^1 Day P 120 *1.30[D] 86–13 Tnk'sProspect$120^{½}$RightCon$120^{½}$[D]Skywlker120^1 Caused bumping 9
3Feb85-Grade III; Disqualified and placed fourth

13Jan85- 4SA fst 1 1/16 :46⅖ 1:11⅖ 1:42 Alw 24000 2 2 $2^{½}$ 2^{hd} $1^{½}$ $1^{2½}$ Day P 118 *1.20 91–13 Skywalker $118^{2½}$ Turkoman 114^6 Royal Olympia $115^{½}$ Drew clear 7

16Dec84- 8Hol gd 1 1/16 :45⅗ 1:10⅗ 1:43⅖ Hol Futy 6 11 13^{11} $6^{3¾}$ 6^7 5^4 Day P 121 9.70 — — Stephan's Odyssey 121^1 FirstNorman$121^{1¼}$RightCon121^{hd} Outrun 13
16Dec84-Grade I

24Nov84- 6Hol sly 1 :46⅕ 1:11⅕ 1:36⅕ Md Sp Wt 4 8 7^{10} $5^{3¼}$ 2^2 1no Delahoussaye E 118 6.70 94–07 Skywlker118^{no}FstAccount$118^{6½}$ExclusiveDrling$118^{1½}$ Slow st., up 8

LATEST WORKOUTS ●Apr 30 CD 5f fst 1:00⅖ h ●Apr 24 CD 1 fst 1:37⅖ h Apr 18 CD 1 fst 1:39 h

Fast Account * — **Dk. b. or br. c. 3, by Private Account—Fast Beauty, by Fleet Nasrullah** — **Br.—Hawn W R (Ky)** — **Tr.—Johnson Patricia L** — **Own.—Hawn W R** — **126** — Lifetime 12 2 6 1 $144,330 — 1985 4 0 3 0 $91,780 — 1984 8 2 3 1 $52,550

27Apr85- 9CD sly 1 :45⅖ 1:11⅖ 1:37⅗ Derby Trial 6 5 $5^{3¼}$ $1^{½}$ 1^{hd} $2^{½}$ McCarron C J b 122 2.40 80–26 Creme Fraiche $119^{½}$ Fast Account122^3NordicScandal113^2 Gamely 11
27Apr85-Grade III

6Apr85- 8SA fst 1⅛ :46⅗ 1:10⅗ 1:48⅖ S A Derby 3 5 $5^{2¼}$ $4^{1½}$ 1^{hd} 2no Stevens G L b 122 25.00 87–10 Skywalker 122^{no}FastAccount$122^{2½}$Nostalgia'sStar$122^{¾}$ Just failed 9
6Apr85-Grade I

17Mar85- 8SA fst 1 1/16 :44⅘ 1:10 1:43⅕ S Felipe H 9 7 7^{14} 9^8 $8^{7¼}$ 6^4 Stevens G L b 119 6.00 81–15 ImgeofGretnss120^{no}Skywlkr120^1Nostlgi'sStr$117^{¾}$ Brk slwly, wide 9
17Mar85-Grade I

23Feb85- 8SA fst 1 :45⅘ 1:10⅕ 1:36⅕ San Rafael 2 5 $6^{3½}$ $6^{6¼}$ $5^{4¾}$ $2^{1¼}$ Stevens G L b 122 3.10e 86–13 Smarten Up $122^{1¼}$ Fast Account $122^{½}$ Stan'sBower118^{no} Brushed 9
23Feb85-Grade II

24Dec84- 7Hol fst 1 :46 1:10⅗ 1:36⅖ [R]Kennedy Rd 7 5 $5^{1¼}$ 4^5 $1^{2½}$ $1^{3½}$ McCarron C J b 115 4.40 93–13 Fast Account $115^{3½}$ Air Alert $115^{½}$ Protect Yourself $115^{¾}$ Driving 9

9Dec84- 6Hol fst 1 :46⅗ 1:11⅘ 1:37⅘ Md Sp Wt 7 1 2^{hd} 1^{hd} 1^{hd} 1^1 McCarron C J b 118 *.80 86–10 Fast Account 118^1 Bonham $118^{7½}$ Be A Hawaiian 118^{nk} Driving 12

24Nov84- 6Hol sly 1 :46⅕ 1:11⅕ 1:36⅕ Md Sp Wt 7 4 3^{nk} 1^{hd} 1^2 2no McCarron C J b 118 *2.10 94–07 Skywalker118^{no}FstAccount$118^{6½}$ExclusiveDrling$118^{1½}$ Just failed 8

7Nov84- 6Hol fst 1 :46 1:11⅘ 1:37⅗ Md Sp Wt 5 4 $4^{1½}$ 3^2 $4^{¾}$ 3^1 McCarron C J 118 *.50e — — ProtectYourself118^1BayShoreDrive118^{no}FastAccount118^4 Rallied 8

17Oct84- 8SA fst 7f :22⅘ :45⅗ 1:23⅘ Sunny Slope 1 11 $10^{5½}$ 10^7 $9^{7¼}$ 6^5 McCarron C J 114 15.00 76–18 Matthew T. Parker117^1PrivateJungle117^{nk}Dan'sDiablo$124^{1¾}$ Wide 11

3Oct84- 6SA fst 6f :22 :45⅗ 1:11⅗ Md Sp Wt 1 10 6^8 5^7 4^5 2no Valenzuela P A 117 3.10 80–18 Dr. Riva 117no Fast Account $117^{1½}$ Just the Facts 117^{nk} Rallied 12

8Sep84- 6Dmr fst 6f :22⅖ :45⅖ 1:10⅕ Md Sp Wt 7 7 4^2 $3^{2½}$ $2^{2½}$ 2^2 McCarron C J 117 9.90 85–12 Carload 117^1 Fast Account 117^8 Southern Show 112^2 Rallied 12

27Aug84- 6Dmr fst 6f :22⅗ :45⅘ 1:10⅘ Md Sp Wt 4 6 $7^{4¾}$ $6^{9½}$ 5^{11} $5^{6¾}$ Lipham T 117 37.30 77–19 Proudest Doon 117^{nk} Carload 117^3 Pro Bowler $112^{½}$ No mishap 8

LATEST WORKOUTS May 3 CD 3f gd :37 b Apr 26 CD 3f fst :36 b Apr 21 SA 5f fst 1:02⅖ h Apr 16 SA 4f fst :51⅗ h

A year before in the 1984 Derby, ill-fated Swale had won with an early move to the lead. Could Spend A Buck take it one step further and go wire-to-wire?

He certainly had a chance to do it.

The speed Spend A Buck had shown in the past was extraordinary. Despite that; stakes wins in his last two starts by ten and a half and nine and a half lengths; the presence of Cordero as his jockey, and well-documented class, Spend A Buck went off at 4 to 1.

Let's analyze how Spend A Buck came up to the Derby.

Spend A Buck won four of his first five races as a 2-year-old before entering the Grade I Arlington Washington Futurity. With jockey

Charlie Hussey aboard, Spend A Buck gutted out a half length victory termed "All out" in the *Form*'s comment. He'd pressed the leader through an extremely fast :44 4/5 opening half, then held on past the three-quarters in 1:10 and finished the one mile stakes in a moderate 1:38. Harness horses can pace a final quarter as fast as Spend A Buck's :28.

Trainer Cam Gambolati made a key decision before Spend A Buck's next start in the Grade I Young America at The Meadowlands. He put Cordero aboard.

Sent off at even-money, Spend A Buck raced on the lead, weakening late and finishing second by three-quarters of a length to Script Ohio. Tank's Prospect was another neck back in third in the 1¹/₁₆ mile stakes.

Spend A Buck's final race as a 2-year-old was an historic one, the $1 million, one mile Breeders' Cup Juvenile, Nov. 10, 1984, the first race of the inaugural Breeders' Cup Day at Hollywood Park.

The classy Chief's Crown went off the 7 to 10 favorite. Impeccably bred, Chief's Crown was a son of the now red-hot sire, Danzig, undefeated in his lone three starts before injury forced his retirement. Chief's Crown's dam was Six Crowns, whose name was derived by the unique mating of two Triple Crown champions, Secretariat and Chris Evert. Chief's Crown, ridden by Don MacBeth for trainer Roger Laurin (whose father, Lucien, trained Secretariat) would cap off his championship 2-year-old season by making the Breeders' Cup Juvenile his sixth victory in nine starts. He was second two other times.

A field of ten contested the first Breeders' Cup race. Spectacular Love, the 5 to 1 second choice, finished a distant eighth. Tank's Prospect lost to Chief's Crown by three-quarters of a length at odds of 25 to 1. Spend A Buck, the third choice at 6 to 1, finished third, beaten one and a half lengths by Chief's Crown. He finished six and a half lengths ahead of Script Ohio in fourth.

When top-of-the-line horses lose, as they invariably all do, their performances occasionally reveal more than many of their wins. Do they give up completely when beaten? Do they keep battling to be second or third? Great horses keep trying despite being beaten.

Whether or not Spend A Buck was a great horse (his career record was 15-10-3-2) is debatable. Unquestionably, though, this loss would reveal the secret of correctly handicapping the Kentucky Derby the following year.

As he did in most of his starts, Spend A Buck raced on the lead in the Juvenile, dueling with 33 to 1 longshot Proudest Hour. Spend A Buck put him away, opened a two and a half length lead, then got passed by Chief's Crown and Tank's Prospect.

Take a quick look at the chart, and you might make a quick conclusion of Spend A Buck's effort: tired to third, no big deal. However, when we place Spend A Buck's speed in context, we uncover just how startling his performance was. The final time for the mile, 1:36 1/5, wasn't special. What was special were Spend A Buck's fractions of :22 2/5, :45, and 1:10.

In the other four Breeders' Cup races held on the dirt that day, no horse ran fractions as fast as Spend A Buck in the Juvenile. That Spend A Buck's fractions were faster than the Juvenile Filly race isn't surprising. Nor is it shocking that the Distaff and the Classic, both 1 1/4-mile races, would produce slower fractions than the eight furlong Juvenile. But the proof of Spend A Buck's performance came when a field of eleven speedsters, all 3-year-olds and up, raced in the Sprint.

The race was won by the favorite, Eillo (that's Ollie spelled backwards; his breeder was Ollie A. Cohen), wire-to-wire. His fractions were :22 2/5, :45 3/5 and 1:10 1/5. Keep in mind this is the best collection of sprinters in the world, and they went those fractions on the same track on the same day as Spend A Buck just an hour earlier.

Spend A Buck's fractions were :22 2/5, :45, and 1:10. How big was his speed figure? He'd have been ahead of every single high-quality horse that raced that same day. Think of it! His three-quarters time was faster than the winner of the Sprint!

There were no speed figures put out that day because Hollywood Park's track had been restructured to lengthen the stretch run. That was perfectly fine. Spend A Buck showed his superior speed to those who spent enough time handicapping that race.

Spend A Buck had also checked in highly in terms of courage. When beaten, he didn't collapse. He held on for a strong third.

The following May 4th at Churchill Downs, there was no reason to believe he couldn't go wire-to-wire in the Derby. His breeding, reflected by his dosage index (a subject discussed later in the book), gave every indication he had the stamina to make a mile and a quarter. And his form was tremendous.

The lone question was whether or not the speedy Eternal Prince, wire-to-wire winner of the Gotham Stakes and Wood Memorial in his last two starts, would force Spend A Buck into maniacal fractions.

The lack of speed in the race outside those two was incredible.

Examining the last three races of the other eleven horses, a total of thirty-three PPs, revealed a total of three lines where a horse led at the first call of his race. Two starts back, Rhoman Rule went wire-to-wire in the 1^1/$_8$ mile Everglades, strolling to the half in :48 4/5 and the three-quarters in 1:12. Chief's Crown, who usually rated off the pace, had also gone wire-to-wire in his last two races, both at 1^1/$_8$ miles, the Flamingo and Blue Grass Stakes. In each, he was in front with slow fractions, :48 4/5 and 1:12 2/5 in the Flamingo and :48 2/5 and 1:12 against just three rivals in the Blue Grass.

Spend A Buck was a horse lacking speed figures in the *Form*. Besides the Breeders' Cup Juvenile, Spend A Buck didn't have speed figs in either of his last two races at Garden State because of track renovations. His time at the half and three-quarters in his easy victories against weak opposition was :45 2/5 and 1:10 on the way to a ten and a half length win in the Cherry Hill and :45 3/5 and 1:09 2/5 in the Garden State.

How about Eternal Prince? He'd had just eight races in his life. He was on the lead in five of them, second by a head in one, second by a length in one and tenth in a poor 2-year-old performance. The lines which mattered were the five PPs of his 3-year-old season, all of them at Aqueduct.

Incredibly, he was in a maiden race exactly two months earlier when he went wire-to-wire in his fourth career start, a six furlong romp by eight in 1:11 2/5 off fractions of :23 and :46 2/5. Next, he went wire-to-wire in a six and three-quarters length allowance win, seven furlongs in 1:25 1/5 after a quarter in :23 1/5 and a half in :46 4/5.

In the seven furlong Bay Shore Stakes, Eternal Prince pressed the pace before tiring to sixth after fractions of :22 4/5 and :45 3/5.

In the one mile Gotham, Eternal Prince was an 18 to 1 longshot who destroyed the field wire-to-wire for jockey Richard Migliore in 1:34 2/5 off a half in :44 1/5 and the three-quarters in 1:08 2/5.

Finally, in the 1^1/$_8$ mile Wood Memorial, Eternal Prince again led from start to finish, winning by two and three-quarters in 1:48 4/5, a so-so final time off decidedly slower fractions: :48 and 1:11 3/5.

The *Form* gave Eternal Prince speed ratings of 94 in the Gotham and 91 in the Wood. Of Spend A Buck's last nine races, three were without speed ratings. Of the six which were, none were higher than an 87.

Fortunately, we knew how fast he was from not only the fast fractions at Garden State, but of much greater significance, how much speed he had shown that afternoon in the Breeders' Cup Juvenile.

There was one other strong factor in comparing Spend A Buck and Eternal Prince. Cordero was on Spend A Buck. Migliore, a sensation as an apprentice earlier in his career and highly successful in New York afterwards, was making his first start in the pressure-packed Derby.

We handicapped Spend A Buck to be faster than Eternal Prince. He sure was out of the gate. Eternal Prince got off poorly, while Cordero shot Spend A Buck to an uncontested lead. The Derby was no contest. Spend A Buck rolled wire-to-wire by himself, winning by five and a quarter lengths in 2:00 1/5, the third fastest Kentucky Derby in the 111 runnings. He paid $10.20.

EIGHTH RACE
Churchill
MAY 4, 1985

1¼ MILES. (1.59⅖) 111th Running KENTUCKY DERBY STAKES SCALE WEIGHT (Grade I). $250,000 Added. 3–year–olds. With a subscription fee of $200 each, an entry fee of $10,000 each and a starting fee of $10,000 each. All fees to be paid to the winner. $250,000 shall be paid by Churchill Downs Incorporated (the "Association") as the added purse. Second place shall receive $100,000, third place shall receive $50,000 and fourth place shall receive $25,000 from the added purse. (The added purse and fees to be divided equally in the event of a dead heat.) Starters shall be named through the entry box on Thursday, May 2, 1985, at the usual time of closing. The maximum number of starters shall be limited to twenty and each shall carry a weight of 126 lbs. In the event that more than twenty entries pass through the entry box at the time of closing, the starters shall be determined at that time with preference given to those horses that have acccumulated the highest earnings, excluding earnings won in a restricted race. For purposes of this preference, a "restricted race" shall mean a state bred restricted race (a race where entries are restricted to horses qualifying under state breeding programs), a sales restricted race (a race where entries are restricted by the origin of purchase), and a restricted sweepstakes (a race where entries are restricted by money previously earned, sweepstakes previously won, sweepstakes won at varying distances or sweepstakes won within periods of time preceeding race.) The owner of the winner shall receive a gold trophy. No supplementary nominations shall be accepted. (Closed with 359 nominations.) Value of race $581,800; value to winner $406,800; second $100,000; third $50,000; fourth $25,000. Mutuel pool $5,105,694. Exacta pool, $664,380.

Last Raced	Horse	Eqt.	A.Wt	PP	¼	½	¾	1	Str	Fin	Jockey	Odds $1
20Apr85 ^{8}GS^1	Spend A Buck		3 126	10	$1^{1\frac{1}{2}}$	1^6	1^6	1^6	1^5	$1^{5\frac{1}{4}}$	Cordero A Jr	4.10
16Apr85 ^{7}Kee^1	Stephan's Odyssey		3 126	6	13	13	$10^{\frac{1}{2}}$	5^1	3^{hd}	$2^{\frac{1}{2}}$	Pincay L Jr	13.40
25Apr85 ^{7}Kee^1	Chief's Crown		3 126	2	$2^{\frac{1}{2}}$	$2^{1\frac{1}{2}}$	2^{hd}	$2^{2\frac{1}{2}}$	2^1	3^{nk}	MacBeth D	1.20
27Apr85 ^{9}CD^2	Fast Account	b	3 126	13	11^1	$10^{\frac{1}{2}}$	8^1	4^1	4^4	4^2	McCarron C J	92.80
20Apr85 ^{8}Aqu^2	Proud Truth		3 126	11	12^1	$12^{\frac{1}{2}}$	11^1	$9^{\frac{1}{2}}$	$5^{1\frac{1}{2}}$	5^3	Velasquez J	4.90
6Apr85 ^{8}SA^1	Skywalker		3 126	12	$6^{\frac{1}{2}}$	7^{hd}	$9^{1\frac{1}{2}}$	8^{hd}	7^1	6no	Delahoussaye E	17.70
20Apr85 ^{9}OP^1	Tank's Prospect	b	3 126	4	7^1	$8^{1\frac{1}{2}}$	$3^{\frac{1}{2}}$	$3^{\frac{1}{2}}$	$6^{\frac{1}{2}}$	7^2	Stevens G L	11.30
25Apr85 ^{7}Kee^2	Floating Reserve		3 126	9	$8^{\frac{1}{2}}$	$9^{\frac{1}{2}}$	12^2	11^5	8^5	$8^{6\frac{1}{2}}$	Hawley S	134.80
20Apr85 ^{8}Aqu^3	Rhoman Rule		3 126	3	$9^{1\frac{1}{2}}$	$6^{\frac{1}{2}}$	6^1	$10^{\frac{1}{2}}$	10^3	$9^{\frac{3}{4}}$	Vasquez J	a-7.50
20Apr85 ^{9}OP^2	Encolure		3 126	7	3^{hd}	4^{hd}	5^{hd}	$7^{\frac{1}{2}}$	9^1	10^4	Ardoin R	103.50
20Apr85 ^{9}OP^3	Irish Fighter		3 126	1	$4^{\frac{1}{2}}$	3^{hd}	$4^{1\frac{1}{2}}$	6^{hd}	$11^{1\frac{1}{2}}$	$11^{\frac{3}{4}}$	Day P	40.90
20Apr85 ^{8}Aqu^1	Eternal Prince	b	3 126	5	5^1	$5^{1\frac{1}{2}}$	$7^{\frac{1}{2}}$	$12^{\frac{1}{2}}$	12^2	$12^{3\frac{1}{2}}$	Migliore R	a-7.50
20Apr85 ^{8}GS^2	I Am The Game	b	3 126	8	$10^{\frac{1}{2}}$	11^3	13	13	13	13	McHargue D G	101.30

a–Coupled: Rhoman Rule and Eternal Prince.

OFF AT 5:39. Start good. Won driving. Time, :23, :45⅘, 1:09⅗, 1:34⅘, 2:00⅕ Track fast.

$2 Mutuel Prices:

9–SPEND A BUCK	10.20	5.40	3.40
5–STEPHAN'S ODYSSEY		10.20	5.00
3–CHIEF'S CROWN			5.00

$2 EXACTA (9–5) PAID $118.20.

B. c, by Buckaroo—Belle De Jour, by Speak John. Trainer Gambolati Cam. Bred by Harper Roe (Ky).

SPEND A BUCK quickly sprinted to the front, jumped a path just inside the sixteenth pole after opening a clear lead, then drew off quickly while remaining well out from the rail into the backstretch. He continued well out from the rail while maintaining his advantage to the upper stretch and was under left-handed urging to hold sway. STEPHAN'S ODYSSEY, outrun into the backstretch, commenced to rally along the inside nearing the far turn, came out between horses for the drive bumping with TANK'S PROSPECT and FAST ACCOUNT, then finished with good courage to wear down CHIEF'S CROWN for the place. The latter, prominent from the outset, raced well out in the track while prompting the pace to the stretch but lacked a rally. FAST ACCOUNT moved through along the inside nearing the end of the backstretch, came out to continue his bid approaching the stretch, bumped with STEPHAN'S ODYSSEY and failed to sustain his rally. PROUD TRUTH, outrun early, moved up outside horses leaving the far turn but failed to be a serious factor. SKYWALKER failed to seriously menace while racing wide. TANK'S PROSPECT, steadied between horses approaching the first turn, made a run along the inside on the backstretch, but was finished soon after going seven furlongs and drifted out into STEPHAN'S ODYSSEY during the drive. FLOATING RESERVE was always outrun. RHOMA RULE worked his way outside entering the backstretch, made a run racing into the far turn but was finished before reaching the distance to the far turn and gave way. IRISH FIGHTER, well placed to the far turn while saving fround, tired badly. ETERNAL PRINCE, failed to break alertly, was steadied along looking for room between horses approaching the first turn and was finished before reaching the far turn. I AM THE GAME, eased back between horses approaching the first turn, failed to be a serious factor.

In 1987, the Breeders' Cup returned to Hollywood Park. The opening race was the $1 million, six furlong Sprint. Fourteen horses entered, offering a dazzling array of speed.

The favorite would be Groovy, who had won all six of his 1987 starts at odds of 1 to 1, 1 to 5, 1 to 20, 3 to 5, 3 to 5 and 3 to 10. His last victory was by three-quarters of a length in the Grade I seven furlong Vosburgh Stakes at Belmont Park. Cutting back to six furlongs seemed to make Groovy even tougher to beat.

Seemed to. Could we shoot holes in Groovy's PPs? Yes.

1 HOLLYWOOD — START — 6 FURLONGS HOLLYWOOD PARK — FINISH

6 FURLONGS. (1.08⅘) 4th Running of THE BREEDERS' CUP SPRINT (Grade I). Purse $1,000,000. 3-year-olds and upward. Weight, 3-year-olds, 124 lbs. Older 126 lbs. Fillies and mares allowed 3 lbs. Value of a race $1,000,000. Value to winner $450,000, second $225,000, third, $108,000, fourth $70,000, fifth $50,000, sixth $10,000. Nominator Awards: Stallion, winner $25,000, second $12,500, third, $6,000; Foal winner $25,000, second $12,500, third $6,000. Stallion awards will be paid only to the nominators of fully eligible stallions. Owners who supplement horses to Breeders' Cup Day races will be eligible for the Foal Nominator's Award in the case of a 12 per cent supplementary nomination or both the Foal Nominator's Award and the Stallion Nominator's Awards in the case of a 20 per cent supplementary nomination. In accordance with the Breeders, Cup/European Breeders' Fund cross-registration agreement, nominator's award will not be paid to horses eligible through the E. B. F. All unpaid nominator's awards will remain the property of Breeders' Cup Limited.

Mutuel field— Governor General, Sharp Romance, Sylvan Express.

Sabona — **B. h. 5, by Exclusive Native—Hail Maggie, by Hail To Reason**
Br.—North Ridge Farm (Ky)
Tr.—Gosden John H M
Own.—Harrison Sir E

126

Lifetime								
13 5 2 1	1987	5	2	1	1	$100,650
$215,029	1986	4	2	1	0	$108,250
	Turf	6	3	0	0	$69,779

21Oct87- 8SA fm *6½f Ⓣ:21⅕ :44⅘ 1:14⅘ Morvich H 7 4 74¼ 52½ 41½ 1hd McCarron C J 117 *2.90 85–15 Sabona 117hd Aberuschka 117½ Deputy Governor 118nk Driving 8

8Oct87- 8SA fm *6½f Ⓣ:22 :44⅘ 1:15⅖ 3↑Alw 45000 1 8 51¾ 33 32½ 1hd McCarron C J 115 2.40 82–18 Sabona 115hd Lord Ruckus 117no Pokare 1121¼ Driving 9

~~7Jun87- 8Hol fst 1⅛ :46⅘ 1:10⅘ 1:48⅕ 3↑Californian 6 4 43 42 43½ 68¾ McCarron C J 115 10.90 88–17 Judge Angelucci 1181 Iron Eyes 115no Snow Chief 1262¾ Tired 8~~

7Jun87-Grade I

25May87- 8Hol fst 1 :45 1:09⅗ 1:34⅘ 3↑M Le Roy H 1 4 41¾ 31½ 32 33¾ McCarron C J 114 3.00 85–15 Zabaleta 1171¾ Nostalgia's Star 1162 Sabona 114nk Evenly 7

25May87-Grade II

3May87- 7Hol fst 6f :22⅕ :45⅕ 1:09⅖ Alw 35000 5 6 43 32½ 21½ 21 McCarron C J 118 *.70 95–15 Lincoln Park 1151 Sabona 1182 Captain Vigors 1102½ Rallied 6

1Jun86- 8Hol fst 1 :44⅕ 1:08⅖ 1:33⅗ 3↑Californian 6 7 68 67 69 611¾ Delahoussaye E 115 6.20 83–14 Precisionist 126½ Super Diamond 1173½ Skywalker 1212½ Outrun 7

1Jun86-Grade I

18May86- 8Hol fst 7f :21⅕ :43⅘ 1:21 3↑Trpl Bnd H 6 4 44½ 41¾ 2½ 11¾ McCarron C J 114 *.50 99–08 Sabona 1141¾ Innamorato 1131¼ Michadilla 1151¾ Driving 6

27Apr86- 8Hol fst 1 :44⅗ 1:09⅕ 1:34⅘ 3↑M Le Roy H 8 3 1hd 2hd 3nk 22½ McCarron C J 113 3.80 86–15 Skywalker 1172½ Sabona 1131½ Al Mamoon 120¾ Held place 8

27Apr86-Grade II

11Apr86- 7SA fst 6½f :22⅘ :45⅗ 1:15⅗ Alw 32000 1 6 51½ 5¾ 1hd 12½ McCarron C J 115 5.80 92–17 Sabona 1152½ Pride Of Ours 1174 Michadilla 1172¾ Off slowly 6

LATEST WORKOUTS Nov 15 Hol 6f fst 1:14⅘ h Nov 10 Hol 5f fst 1:00⅖ h Nov 4 Hol 3f fst :36⅗ h Oct 18 SA 4f fst :48 h

Groovy * Ch. c. 4, by Norcliffe—Tinnitus, by Restless Wind
Br.—Robinson Marshall T (Tex)
Own.—Prestonwood Farm Inc Tr.—Martin Jose
126 Lifetime 25 12 3 1 $1,121,956 1987 6 6 0 0 $539,250 1986 14 5 1 1 $445,906
10Oct87- 7Bel fst 7f :22⅘ :45⅕ 1:22⅘ 3↑Vosburgh 8 1 11 12½ 15 1¾ Cordero A Jr 126 *.30 89-22 Groovy 126¾ Moment Of Hope 1263 Sun Master 1261½ Driving 8
10Oct87-Grade I
23Aug87- 8Sar fst 7f :22 :44⅕ 1:21⅘ 3↑Forego H 5 1 11½ 11½ 12½ 11¾ Cordero A Jr 132 *.60 93-14 Groovy 1321¾ Purple Mountain 1131¾ Sun Master 1182 Driving 6
23Aug87-Grade II
18Jly87- 8Bel fst 7f :23⅕ :45⅘ 1:22⅘ 3↑Tom Fool 5 1 12 11½ 14½ 16½ Cordero A Jr 128 *.60 90-20 Groovy 1286½ Sun Master 121nk Moment Of Hope 1193 Driving 6
18Jly87-Grade II
5Jly87- 9FL fst 6f :22⅕ :44⅘ 1:09⅖ 3↑Bud Brds Cup 3 3 1½ 1hd 1½ 1hd Pezua J M 122 *.05 102-11 Groovy 122hd Purple Mountain 1192½ Vinnie theViper1197 Driving 7
21Jun87- 8Bel my 6f :22 :44 1:07⅘ 3↑Tru Nrth H 1 1 11½ 14 15 15¾ Cordero A Jr 123 *.20 101-10 Groovy 1235¾ King's Swan 120nk Sun Master 117no Ridden out 4
21Jun87-Grade II
6Jun87- 1Bel fst 6f :21⅗ :44 1:08⅖ 3↑Roseben H 1 1 12½ 14 14½ 14½ Cordero A Jr 119 *1.10 98-15 Groovy 1194½ Love That Mac 1182 King's Swan 1213½ Drew clear 6
6Jun87-Grade III
15Nov86- 8Aqu fst 6f :21⅗ :44⅕ 1:08⅘ 3↑Sprt Page H 4 1 1½ 1hd 3½ 46½ Cordero A Jr 122 *.50 90-22 Best By Test 1125 King's Swan 118hd SunMaster1171½ Weakened 7
15Nov86-Grade III
1Nov86- 3SA fst 6f :21⅕ :43⅗ 1:08⅖ 3↑Br Cp Sprnt 9 2 31 31½ 32 44½ Santos J A 124 *.40 92-13 Smile 1261½ Pine Tree Lane1231¾BedsidePromise1261½ Weakened 9
1Nov86-Grade I
15Oct86- 8SA fst 6f :21⅗ :43⅘ 1:08⅕ 3↑Anct Tle H 5 1 11½ 13 12½ 12 Santos J A 123 *.40 97-18 Groovy 1232 Rosie's K. T. 1171 Sun Master 114½ Driving 8
1Sep86- 8Bel fst 1 :44 1:08⅖ 1:34 Jerome H 4 1 18 13½ 2½ 45½ Velasquez J 124 2.50 90-14 Ogygian 126hd Mogambo 1192 Moment Of Hope 1113½ Tired 5
1Sep86-Grade I
LATEST WORKOUTS Nov 18 Hol 3f fst :34⅕ b ●Nov 11 Hol 5f fst :58⅘ h Nov 5 Hol 5f gd 1:02⅘ h ●Oct 28 Bel 4f gd :46 b

Slyly Gifted B. g. 4, by On the Sly—Fig's Pride, by Figonero
Br.—Sovereignty Farm (Ky)
Own.—Franks John Tr.—Hronec Philip
126 Lifetime 16 6 1 1 $386,239 1987 8 2 1 1 $124,714 1986 8 4 0 0 $261,525 Turf 2 0 0 0 $15,750
7Nov87- 6Haw fst 1¼ :48 1:36⅗ 2:02 3↑Gold Cup H 3 3 42 33 41½ 42¾ Frazier R L 113 28.10 81-16 Nostalgia's Star 1171½ Savings 1141½ Minneapple 117no Evenly 9
7Nov87-Grade II
30Oct87- 7Kee fst 7f :22⅘ :45⅗ 1:21⅘ 3↑Alw 28800 4 4 75½ 78 31 12½ Day P 121 *1.40 97-18 Slyly Gifted 1212½ Tribute to Royalty112noVarennes1152½ Driving 7
26Sep87-10LaD fm 1⅜ Ⓣ:48⅖ 1:38 2:13⅘ 3↑La Downs H 10 4 45 42 43 46½ Romero R P 114 21.10 90-10 Iades 1151½ Ifrad 1173¾ Great Communicator 1131 No rally 12
23Aug87-10Lga fst 1 :45⅗ 1:09⅗ 1:34⅕ 3↑Lga Mile H 8 6 63½ 54 34 34¾ Lamance C 117 7.80 93-18 Judge Angelucci 1214 Leading Hour 111¾ Slyly Gifted1171 Evenly 8
23Aug87-Grade II
19Jly87- 7Hol fst 1 :45 1:09⅖ 1:34⅘ Alw 45000 4 3 32 31 1hd 12 McCarron C J 115 *1.30 89-07 Slyly Gifted 1152 Triple Sec 1151 Lincoln Park 1152¾ Driving 6
28Jun87- 8Hol fst 1¼ :46 1:34⅗ 2:00⅗ 3↑Gold Cup H 1 4 53 99½ 913 1018½ Meza R Q 114 14.50 70-12 Ferdinand 1241½ DH Judge Angelucci 118 DH Tasso 1154 Tired 11
28Jun87-Grade I
4Jun87- 8Hol fst 1 :44⅘ 1:09⅗ 1:34⅗ Alw 45000 1 4 45 43 22 2no Delahoussaye E 117 4.60 90-13 Late Request 115no Slyly Gifted 1172 Sperry 1155 Bumped st 5
17Jan87- 8BM fst 1 :46⅗ 1:10⅗ 1:34⅘ W P Kyne H 5 2 31 31½ 45½ 57½ Sibille R 118 7.60 87-19 BedsidePromise1236HopefulWord121½GrandExchange116hd Tired 6
26Dec86- 8SA fst 7f :22⅖ :44⅘ 1:21⅗ Malibu 6 6 52½ 52½ 63¾ 46¾ Sibille R 123 34.60 85-13 Ferdinand 1231½ Snow Chief 1261½ Don B. Blue 1144 No rally 12
26Dec86-Grade II
20Sep86-10LaD fst 1¼ :47⅖ 1:37⅘ 2:04 Super Dby 7 4 42 53 55 55 Hansen R D 126 4.20 76-16 WiseTimes126½DHSouthernHalo126DHCheapskte1264½ Wide turn 7
20Sep86-Grade I
LATEST WORKOUTS Nov 18 Hol 3f fst :36⅖ h Oct 20 CD 5f fst 1:03⅘ b Sep 23 LaD Ⓣ 4f fm :49⅘ b (d)

Zany Tactics Dk. b. or br. g. 6, by Zanthe—Escort's Lady, by Escort
Br.—Forth Brenda & S (Cal)
Own.—Brunette Vera C Tr.—Heap Blake
126 Lifetime 31 15 7 3 $573,664 1987 10 5 1 1 $311,898 1986 13 5 3 2 $187,260 Turf 8 4 1 2 $126,850
4Nov87- 8SA sly 6f :21⅘ :44 1:09 3↑Anct Title H 1 1 1½ 1½ 11½ 1½ Kaenel J L 123 *.90 93-26 Zany Tactics 123½ On The Line 1163½ Carload 117 Driving 3
20Sep87-10LaD fst 7f :22⅘ :45⅗ 1:23 3↑Isl Whirl H 9 2 1½ 1hd 21½ 41 Kaenel J L 124 *.70 92-19 Savings 114nk Big Sturgeon 116hd Who Doctor Who 121¾ Tired 10
22Aug87- 8Dmr fst 7f :22⅖ :44⅘ 1:21⅕ 3↑P O' Brn H 4 1 2hd 2hd 1½ 1nk Kaenel J L 123 *1.70 96-15 ZanyTctics123nkBoldSmoocher1141½BolderThnBold1203½ Driving 7
2Aug87- 8Dmr fst 6f :21⅗ :44⅖ 1:09 3↑B Crosby H 8 4 31 3½ 3nk 1nk Kaenel J L 120 *1.30 93-12 ZnyTctics120nkBolderThnBold118nkMyFvoriteMomnt115½ Driving 8
2Aug87-Grade III
2May87- 8Aqu fst 7f :21⅗ :44 1:21⅕ 3↑Carter H 1 2 22½ 22 24 34 Kaenel J L 119 *.70 91-19 PineTreeLne1192½King'sSwn1231½ZnyTctics119½ Lacked response 6
2May87-Grade II
11Apr87- 8Aqu fst 6f :21⅗ :44 1:09 3↑Bold Ruler 2 3 22 22 32 44½ Kaenel J L 121 2.60 91-23 PineTreeLane1181½LoveThatMc123nkPlyTheKing1212¾ Weakened 7
11Apr87-Grade III
8Mar87-11TuP fst 6f :21⅕ :43 1:06⅘ 3↑Phx Gld Cp 9 4 2½ 21½ 2½ 11 Kaenel J L 126 1.90 102-15 Zany Tactics 1261 Faro 1159 Zabaleta 1241 Driving 9
8Mar87-Grade III
22Feb87- 8SA fst 1⅛ :46 1:10 1:47⅕ S Antonio H 3 4 42½ 4¾ 51¾ 42¾ Kaenel J L 116 10.90 90-14 Bedside Promise 1211½ Hopeful Word 1181½Bruiser114nk No rally 9
22Feb87-Grade I
11Feb87- 8SA fst 6½f :21⅘ :44⅕ 1:15 Ptro Grnd H 2 1 2hd 1hd 1½ 2hd Kaenel J L 120 2.70 95-17 Zabaleta 117hd Zany Tactics 120hd Bedside Promise 1255½ Failed 4
10Jan87- 8SA gd 7f :22⅕ :44⅘ 1:22⅖ S Carlos H 8 3 1hd 2½ 1hd 1½ Kaenel J L 118 2.40 88-20 Zany Tactics 118½ Bolder Than Bold 1162¾ Epidaurus115½ Driving 8
10Jan87-Grade II
LATEST WORKOUTS Nov 14 Hol 6f fst 1:14⅖ h ●Oct 28 SA 6f fst 1:11⅗ h Oct 21 SA 6f fst 1:16⅘ h Oct 14 SA 5f fst 1:01⅘ h

On The Line Ch. c. 3, by Mehmet—Male Strike, by Speak John
Br.—International Thbrd Breeders Inc (Fla)
Own.—Klein E V Tr.—Lukas D Wayne
124 Lifetime 18 4 5 0 $202,380 1987 14 3 4 0 $182,980 1986 4 1 1 0 $19,400 Turf 4 0 0 0 $10,625
4Nov87- 8SA sly 6f :21⅘ :44 1:09 3↑Anct Title H 2 2 2½ 2½ 21½ 2½ Stevens G L b 116 2.80 92-26 Zany Tactics 123½ On The Line 1163½ Carload 117 Bumped start 3
23Oct87- 8SA sly 7f :22 :44⅗ 1:21⅘ 3↑Alw 48000 1 3 22 1hd 12 2¾ Stevens G L b 114 1.70 90-21 Skywalker 122¾ On The Line 1148 Hot Sauce Baby 115hd Gamely 5
12Oct87- 8SA fst 1⅛ :45⅘ 1:09⅗ 1:40⅘ 3↑Ynkee Vlr H 5 2 2½ 2hd 31½ 43½ McCarron C J b 113 5.30 93-15 Super Diamond 125¾ Stop The Fighting1162½Infinidad116nk Tired 5
27Sep87- 9Cby fst 1 :46 1:09⅕ 1:35⅕ 3↑Bud Brd Cp H 2 1 11½ 1½ 2½ 2½ Perret C b 116 *1.10 104-09 Minneapple 121½ On The Line 1168 Arctic Dream 115¾ Gamely 9
9Aug87- 8Dmr fm 1⅛ Ⓣ:47⅗ 1:11⅕ 1:42⅕ La Jolla H 10 3 51½ 31½ 42½ 62¾ Valenzuela P A b 117 10.40 86-12 The Medic 116½ Something Lucky 120nk SavonaTower117nk Rank 11
9Aug87-Grade III
26Jly87- 9Hol fst 1¼ :45 1:34⅖ 2:02⅕ Swaps 3 1 2hd 22½ 23½ 46 Valenzuela P A b 120 5.00 75-12 Temperate Sil 1231 Candi's Gold 1232 Pledge Card 1153 Tired 6
26Jly87-Grade I
3Jly87- 8Hol fst 1⅛ :46 1:09⅘ 1:47⅗ Slvr Scrn H 1 1 1½ 1hd 11½ 2nk Valenzuela P A b 116 6.80 99-09 Candi's Gold 116nk On The Line 11610 The Medic 1164 Gamely 6
3Jly87-Grade II
21Jun87- 8Hol fm 1⅛ Ⓣ:44⅗ 1:09 1:46⅘ Cinema H 1 1 17 15 32 56 Valenzuela P A b 118 7.40 88-06 Something Lucky 1192½ The Medic1172½SavonaTower1151½ Tired 8
21Jun87-Grade II
7Jun87- 3Hol fst 1⅛ :46⅕ 1:10⅘ 1:43⅗ Handicap 1 1 12 13 13 12½ Stevens G L b 117 *1.30 90-17 On The Line 1172½ The Medic 119nk Davids Smile 1209 Driving 5
23May87- 8Hol fm 1⅛ Ⓣ:46⅗ 1:11⅕ 1:43 Wl Rgrs H 5 2 11 1hd 2½ 43½ McCarron C J b 117 7.70 75-21 Something Lucky 1171 The Medic 1151½ Persevered 119½ Tired 9
23May87-Grade III
LATEST WORKOUTS Nov 17 Hol 4f fst :48⅖ h Oct 7 SA 5f fst :59⅕ h Sep 23 SA 4f fst :48⅖ h

***Governor General** B. c. 4, by Dominion—Law and Impulse, by Roan Rocket
Br.—Skinner Mrs B (Eng)
Own.—Richards R Tr.—Elsworth D
126 Lifetime 16 4 3 1 $92,296 | 1987 7 1 3 1 $62,694 | 1986 6 2 0 0 $26,118 | Turf 16 4 3 1 $92,296

17Oct87♦5Newmarket(Eng) gd 5f 1:02⅘ Ⓣ Bentinck Stakes 21½ Carson W 126 3.00 — — Perion 1261½ Governor General 1261 Cragside 1223 Prom,led 11
26Sep87♦5Ascot(Eng) gd 6f 1:14⅗ Ⓣ Diadem Stakes(Gr3) 21 Carson W 128 16.00 — — Dowsing 1241 Gov General 1282½ Serve N' Volley 1211½ Led 5f 17
5Sep87♦4Haydock(Eng) gd 6f 1:14⅘ Ⓣ VernonsSprintCup(Gr2) 68 Cook P 128 25.00 — — Ajdal 1262 SharpRomance 128¾ HandsomeSailor 128¾ Led 3f 8
19Jun87♦4Ascot(Eng) sf 5f 1:05⅕ Ⓣ King'sStandStakes(Gr1) 911 Cochrane $ 129 14.00 — — Bluebird 1214 Perion 1291½ Orient 1261½ Prominent 3f 12
30May87♦3Lingfield(Eng) fm 6f 1:09 Ⓣ ToteLeisure Stakes 2no Asmussen C 131 *1.75 — — Mistermjestic115no GovrnorGnrl131nk SingingStvn1152 Prom,led 11
14May87♦2York(Eng) gd 6f 1:12⅖ Ⓣ Duke of YorkStks(Gr3) 32¾ Rouse B 126 6.00 — — Handsome Sailor 1262 Hallgate 134nk Gov General 126½ Led 5f 9
14Apr87♦4Newmarket(Eng) gd 6f 1:15⅕ Ⓣ Abernant Stakes 13 Rouse B 132 7.00 — — GovernorGenerl1323 QuSymptic1292 HndsomSilor1321 Led fnl 2f 12
29Sep86♦4Goodwood(Eng) gd 7f 1:27⅗ Ⓣ Harroways Stakes 916 Reid J 119 16.00 — — Sarab 127hd BollinKnight 1243 VerdantBoy 1161½ Led 4f 10
LATEST WORKOUTS Nov 20 Hol 3f fst :38⅗ h

Pine Tree Lane * B. m. 5, by Apalachee—Carealot, by Sebring II
Br.—Wood & Woodhaven Farm (Ky)
Own.—Young W T Tr.—Lukas D Wayne
123 Lifetime 32 17 3 3 $1,035,536 | 1987 12 7 0 2 $548,689 | 1986 15 5 3 1 $410,647

31Oct87- 7Aqu fst 6f :22⅘ :45⅘ 1:09⅘ 3↑ⒻBarn Swallow 4 1 11½ 13 15 16 Antley C W 117 *.30 92-20 Pine Tree Lane 1176 LeftCourt115nkAroundback1151½ Ridden out 5
26Sep87- 9Med fst 6f :22 :45 1:10 3↑ⒻBud Brdrs H 4 2 1½ 11 11 41¼ Cordero A Jr 123 2.00 91-20 StormndSunshin118noGrlPowdr116noJustSmshng1161½ Weakened 6
5Sep87- 6Bel fst 6f :22 :45 1:09⅕ 3↑Boojum H 5 1 11½ 11½ 43 65½ Cordero A Jr 119 *.60e 87-15 Sun Master 117no Banker's Jet 115nk Play The King 1223¾ Tired 7
5Sep87-Grade III
14Aug87- 8Sar fst 7f :21⅗ :44 1:22⅗ 3↑ⒻBallerina 5 1 1½ 11½ 2hd 33¾ Cordero A Jr 122 *.80e 85-21 I'mSweets119¾StormandSunshine1163PineTreeLne122nk Brushed 5
14Aug87-Grade II
4Jun87- 8Bel sly 6f :22⅘ :45⅗ 1:10⅕ 3↑ⒻGenuine Rsk 1 1 13 16 17 17¼ Cordero A Jr 122 *.30 89-21 Pine Tree Lane 1227¼ Silent Account 1173 Royal Tali 117½ Easily 4
4Jun87-Grade III
25May87- 8Bel fst 1 :44⅖ 1:09⅕ 1:34⅘ 3↑Metropltn H 5 1 15 13 77¼ 811¼ Romero R P 119 2.80 80-16 Gulch 110nk King's Swan 121½ Broad Brush 1282 Gave way 9
25May87-Grade I
2May87- 8Aqu fst 7f :21⅗ :44 1:21⅕ 3↑Carter H 6 1 12½ 12 14 12½ Romero R P 119 *1.10 95-19 Pine Tree Lane 1192½ King's Swan 1231½ZanyTactics119½ Driving 6
2May87-Grade II
11Apr87- 8Aqu fst 6f :21⅗ :44 1:09 3↑Bold Ruler 5 1 12 12 12 11½ Cordero A Jr 118 2.10 96-23 Pine TreeLane1181½LoveThatMac123nkPlayTheKing1212¾ Driving 7
11Apr87-Grade II
14Mar87- 8Aqu fst 7f :22⅖ :45 1:22⅖ 3↑ⒻDistaff H 2 3 12 14 14 13¾ Cordero A Jr 125 *1.20e 89-28 PineTreeLane1253¾SpringBeauty1176¾Gene'sLady1175 Ridden out 7
14Mar87-Grade III
15Feb87- 9Lrl fst 7f :22⅖ :46⅕ 1:25⅖ 3↑ⒻFritchie H 10 5 1hd 1hd 31 33½ Cordero A Jr 126 *.80 80-28 SpringBeuty1151¾NotchesTrce1101¾PineTrLn126¾ Weakened late 12
15Feb87-Grade III
LATEST WORKOUTS ●Oct 17 Bel 4f fst :47⅗ h Sep 22 Bel 4f fst :50 b

Zabaleta B. c. 4, by Shecky Greene—Winver, by Vertex
Br.—Parr E Q (Ky)
Own.—Holmes M H R & Court Tr.—Gosden John H M
126 Lifetime 14 5 5 2 $425,675 | 1987 8 3 3 1 $229,225 | 1986 6 2 2 1 $196,450

8Nov87-10BM fst 6f :22⅕ :44⅗ 1:09 3↑Handicap 2 2 1hd 11½ 11½ 2no McHargue D G 123 *1.20 94-14 Bold Smoocher 116no Zabaleta 1231½ Just In Case 1111 Sharp 10
~~27Jun87- 8Hol fst 6f :21⅘ :44⅗ 1:08⅖ 3↑L Angeles H 3 5 1hd 2hd 2hd 44 Pincay L Jr b 118 *1.10 97-09 BedsidePromise1261¾BolderThanBold1171½LincolnPark115½ Tired 5~~
~~27Jun87-Grade III~~
25May87- 8Hol fst 1 :45 1:09⅗ 1:34⅘ 3↑M Le Roy H 6 1 2hd 1hd 1½ 11¾ Pincay L Jr b 117 *2.30 89-15 Zabaleta 1171¾ Nostalgia's Star 1162 Sabona 114nk Driving 7
25May87-Grade II
2May87- 8Hol fst 7f :21⅗ :43⅘ 1:21 3↑Trple Bnd H 1 3 12 11½ 2hd 22 McHargue D G b 118 2.90 97-13 Bedside Promise 1242 Zabaleta1181¾BolderThanBold1182 Held pl 5
8Mar87-11TuP fst 6f :21⅕ :43 1:06⅘ 3↑Phx Gld Cp 8 1 51½ 53¼ 44½ 310 McHargue D G b 124 *1.40 92-15 Zany Tactics 1261 Faro 1159 Zabaleta 1241 No rally 9
8Mar87-Grade III
11Feb87- 8SA fst 6½f :21⅘ :44⅕ 1:15 Ptro Grnd H 4 3 1hd 2hd 2½ 1hd Pincay L Jr 117 3.20 95-17 Zabaleta 117hd Zany Tactics 120hd Bedside Promise1255½ Driving 4
16Jan87- 7SA fst 6½f :21⅘ :44⅗ 1:16⅖ Alw 33000 3 6 21 31½ 31½ 2hd Stevens G L 118 *.90 88-18 Grand Allegiance117hdZabaleta118½PaisanoPete1211½ Bore in str. 7
3Jan87- 3SA fst 6f :21⅘ :44⅕ 1:09⅘ Alw 29000 1 3 31½ 31½ 3nk 1hd Stevens G L 116 *1.10 89-16 Zabaleta 116hd Salt Dome 1183½ Northern Policy 116¾ Checked 7
3May86- 8CD fst 1¼ :45⅕ 1:37 2:02⅘ Ky Derby 15 2 21 85½ 1214 1219¾ McHargue D G b 126 16.00f 63-10 Ferdinand 1262¼BoldArrangement126¾BroadBrush126nk Bothered 16
3May86-Grade I
19Apr86- 9GS fst 1⅛ :46⅖ 1:11⅗ 1:51 Garden State 8 1 1hd 2hd 2hd 2½ McHargue D G 117 *1.30 73-21 FobbyForbes115½Zabalet1171½MircleWood117¾ Ducked out,brshd 10
LATEST WORKOUTS Nov 18 Hol 3f fst :35⅖ h ●Nov 5 Hol 3f gd :35⅕ h Oct 27 SA 6f fst 1:12⅗ h ●Oct 22 SA 5f fst :59⅖ h

Sharp Romance Ch. h. 5, by Sharpen Up—Sir Ivor's Favour, by Sir Ivor
Br.—Little W P (Ky)
Own.—Sheikh Mohammed al Sabah Tr.—Mellor Stanley T
126 Lifetime 50 2 4 5 $110,815 | 1987 14 0 1 1 $51,266 | 1986 15 0 1 2 $9,033 | Turf 46 2 4 5 $109,915

25Oct87♦4Longchamp(Fra) sf*7f 1:25⅘ Ⓣ Prix de la Foret(Gr1) 12 Wigham M 138 95.00 — — Soviet Star 1371 HighestHonor138¾ TurkishRuler138¾ On pace 6f 14
4Oct87♦4Longchamp(Fra) fm*5f :56⅗ Ⓣ Prix de l'Abbaye(Gr1) 99 Wigham M 137 46.00 — — Polonia1331 LaGrndeEpoque133no TenuedeSoiree133½ Poor start 9
26Sep87♦5Ascot(Eng) gd 6f 1:14⅗ Ⓣ Diadem Stakes(Gr3) 1310 Wigham M 128 12.00 — — Dowsing 1241 Gov General 1282½ Serve N' Volley1211½ No threat 17
5Sep87♦4Haydock(Eng) gd 6f 1:14⅘ Ⓣ VernonsSprintCup(Gr2) 22 Wigham M 128 20.00 — — Ajdal 1262 SharpRomance 128¾ HandsomeSailor 128¾ Fin. well 8
19Aug87♦4Deauville(Fra) gd*6f 1:11⅗ Ⓣ Prix de Meautry(Gr3) 99 McGlone A 123 34.00 — — CricketBall 1231½ SakuraReiko1211 ShyPrincess116¾ Prom, wknd 10
30Jly87♦1Goodwood(Eng) gd 5f :58⅗ Ⓣ KingGeorgeStks(Gr3) 53¼ Asmussen C 126 12.00 — — SingingSteven125hd CrolsTresure120nk TresureKy1341½ Impeded 9
17Jly87♦4Newbury(Eng) gd 6f 1:12⅗ Ⓣ Hackwood Stakes 36¾ Wigham M 129 25.00 — — Interval 117¾ Print 1206 SharpRomance 1293 Bid then evenly 10
9Jly87♦3Newmarket(Eng) gd 6f 1:11 Ⓣ July Cup(Gr1) 97 Starkey G 132 66.00 — — Ajdal 123hd Gayane 1201 Bluebird 1233 No factor 11
19Jun87♦4Ascot(Eng) sf 5f 1:05⅕ Ⓣ King'sStandStakes(Gr1) 47 Cook P 129 50.00 — — Bluebird 1214 Perion 1291½ Orient 1261½ Stride late 12
12Jun87♦3York(Eng) gd 6f 1:13 Ⓣ InnovativeMarketingHcp 13 Lynch B 135 10.00 — — Father Time 1101½ Royal Fan 1052 ChaplinsClub 1141½ No threat 15
LATEST WORKOUTS Nov 17 Hol 5f fst 1:00⅖ h

***Sylvan Express** B. c. 4, by Baptism—Folle Remont, by Prince Tenderfoot
Br.—Lodge Park Stud (Ire)
Own.—Johnson Mrs R A Tr.—Mitchell Philip
126 Lifetime 25 6 2 2 $130,133 | 1987 10 2 0 1 $65,601 | 1986 7 2 0 0 $36,314 | Turf 25 6 2 2 $130,133

31Oct87♦1Newmarket(Eng) gd 1 1:42⅕ Ⓣ FlurocarbonMarshallStks 45½ Starkey G 133 20.00 — — Shady Heights 1261½ Azyaa 1174 Cresta Auction 130hd Bid, wknd 9
11Oct87♦6Munich(Ger) gd*6½f 1:18 Ⓣ GrosserSprintPreis 1½ Starkey G 129 *1.80 — — Sylvan Express 129½ Bel Byou127nk HomePlease1292 Bid, up late 14
4Sep87- 8AP gd 1 Ⓣ:50 1:14⅘ 1:37⅖ 3↑Bud Brd Cup 4 3 31½ 32 42 56¼ Eddery P 121 7.70 82-23 Persian Mews 1183 Mister C. 1143 Vernon Castle 114hd Tired 7
27Jly87♦4Newcastle(Eng) gd 7f 1:29⅕ Ⓣ Beeswing Stakes(Gr3) 813 Eddery P A 133 33.00 — — Farajullah 127hd Midyan 124½ Noble Minstrel 1213 No threat 8
4Jly87♦7Hamburg(Ger) gd*7f 1:22⅖ Ⓣ AmericanExpressPreis(Gr3) 3½ Matthias J 132 *1.00 — — Home Please 128½ Kellytalk 130hd SylvanExpress132 Closed well 9
17Jun87♦3Ascot(Eng) sf 1 1:46⅖ Ⓣ RoyalHuntCupHcp 17 Swinburn W R 122 16.00 — — Vague Shot131½ Granny'sBank113nk GoldProspect1181 No factor 25
28May87♦4Longchamp(Fra) sf*7f 1:24⅕ Ⓣ Prix duPalaisRoyal(Gr3) 11 Swinburn W R 137 7.75 — — Turkish Ruler 1305 Mercadah 127¾ Whakilyric 121nk No factor 13
16May87♦3Curragh(Ire) gd 6f 1:10⅖ Ⓣ Greenlands Stakes(Gr3) 1nk Swinburn W R 136 14.00 — — Sylvan Express 136nk ⒹFlawless Image 116½ Orient 1271 Up late 11
29Apr87♦3Ascot(Eng) gd 7f 1:28 Ⓣ InsulapkVictoriaCupHcp 65¾ Carter G 116 7.50 — — Fusilier 107hd Saker 1234 Kick The Habit 112¾ Bid,wknd 20
14Apr87♦4Newmarket(Eng) gd 6f 1:15⅕ Ⓣ Abernant Stakes 98 Starkey G 138 20.00 — — GovernorGeneral1323 QueSymptic1292 HndsomeSilor1321 Spd 3f 12

Exclusive Enough

B. c. 3, by Exclusive Native—One Is Enough, by Three Martinis
Br.—Mandysland Farm (Ky)
Tr.—Van Berg Jack C
Own.—Scharbauer Dorothy

124 Lifetime 9 4 0 1 $174,660 — 1987 5 2 0 0 $114,760 — 1986 4 2 0 1 $59,900

16Oct87- 8Kee fst 6f :22 :43⅖ 1:08⅖ 3↑Cmweath Brd 6 6 2hd 11 12 1½ Smith M E 111 17.70 100-09 Exclusive Enough 111½ Lazer Show 1205 High Brite 1202 Driving 8

3Sep87- 7Dmr fst 6f :21⅖ :44⅕ 1:09⅕ 3↑Alw 25000 5 4 45 42 22 11 Baze G 115 8.20 92-18 ExclusvEnogh1151AsInEgls116nkOlympcProspct1171¼ Bumped st. 7

20Jun87- 7Hol fst 7f :22 :44⅖ 1:22⅘ 3↑Alw 25000 6 6 51¾ 12 32 610 Stevens G L b 112 6.80 80-11 Tommy The Hawk 114hd Fleet Sudan 1121 Don Diege 1195 Tired 8

24May87- 7Hol fst 6f :21⅘ :45 1:10 Alw 25000 2 6 821 814 813 — Shoemaker W 114 6.00 — — W. D. Jacks 1202½ Captain Valid 1141¾ Thunder Cat 1161½ Eased 8

22Apr87- 8Hol fst 7f :21⅘ :44⅖ 1:22⅕ Debonair 6 3 42 41½ 78½ 718¼ McCarron C J 119 6.40 75-18 Jamoke 1171 Persevered 122no Honky Tonk Dancer 1173½ Wide 7

14Dec86- 8Hol fst 1 :44⅘ 1:09⅗ 1:36⅕ Hol Fut'y 2 10 85 75½ 1012 1016¾ Snyder L 121 6.60e 65-18 TemperateSil121nkAlysheba121nkMasterfulAdvocate1212¼ Outrun 12
14Dec86-Grade I

15Nov86- 8Hol fst 7f :22 :44⅘ 1:23 Hol Prvue 3 4 11½ 11½ 12 1½ Shoemaker W 112 13.50 89-14 Exclusive Enough 112½ Persevered 1223GoldOnGreen116½ Erratic 8
15Nov86-Grade III

2Nov86- 6SA fst 6f :21⅖ :44⅖ 1:10⅖ Md Sp Wt 1 2 23½ 2½ 12 14 Day P 118 *1.50 86-10 ExclusiveEnough1184BrigantineDancer118nkCalvinist1185½ Easily 8

11Oct86- 6SA fst 6½f :21⅘ :44⅘ 1:17⅖ Md Sp Wt 3 3 11½ 2½ 2hd 33¾ Solis A 117 5.70 79-17 Just Bobby 1171¼ Barb's Relic 1172½ ExclusiveEnough117no Tired 12

LATEST WORKOUTS Nov 16 Hol 5f fst 1:01⅗ h — Nov 10 SA 5f fst 1:02⅕ h — Oct 27 SA tr.t 3f fst :36⅖ h — Oct 10 SA 4f fst :48⅗ b

Very Subtle *

Ch. f. 3, by Hoist the Silver—Never Scheme, by Never Bend
Br.—King J Howard (Ky)
Tr.—Stute Melvin F
Own.—Rochelle B

121 Lifetime 15 9 2 2 $824,860 — 1987 11 5 2 2 $497,135 — 1986 4 4 0 0 $327,725

31Aug87- 9AP fst 7f :22 :44⅖ 1:22⅘ 3↑ⒻBud Brd CpH 1 5 31 3nk 22 23½ Solis A 120 *.40 84-27 Lazer Show1233½VerySubtle120nkMoonbeamMcQueen1111½ Tired 6

6Aug87- 8Sar fst 7f :21⅗ :43⅗ 1:21 ⒻTest 6 4 2½ 1hd 14 15¼ Valenzuela P A 121 3.60 97-14 Very Subtle 1215¼UptheApalachee1213½SilentTurn121hd Drew off 14
6Aug87-Grade II

12Jly87- 8Hol fst 1⅛ :46⅕ 1:10⅕ 1:48⅗ ⒻHol Oaks 2 1 2hd 1hd 31½ 47½ McCarron C J 121 1.70 86-09 Perchance To Dream 121½ Sacahuista 1215PenBalLady1212 Tired 6
12Jly87-Grade I

20Jun87- 8Hol fst 1 1/16 :45⅗ 1:10⅕ 1:43 ⒻPrincess 6 3 3½ 41½ 33½ 31½ Shoemaker W 122 *.90 92-11 Ransomed Captive 116nkSacahuista1221¼VerySubtle1222 Mild bid 6
20Jun87-Grade II

6Jun87- 8Hol fst 7f :22 :44⅗ 1:22⅗ ⒻRailbird 2 3 31 2½ 1½ 15½ Shoemaker W 122 *.60 91-17 Very Subtle 1225½ Joey The Trip 1171 Sacahuista 122 Off slowly 4
6Jun87-Grade III

1May87- 9CD fst 1⅛ :46⅖ 1:10⅘ 1:50⅖ ⒻKy Oaks 4 4 47 43¾ 66½ 612 McCarron C J 121 4.60 78-12 Buryyourbelief 1212¾ HometownQueen1212SuperCook1211¾ Tired 8
1May87-Grade I

11Apr87- 9OP fst 1 1/16 :46⅕ 1:10⅕ 1:42⅖ ⒻFantasy 3 2 22½ 22 21½ 22½ McCarron C J 121 5.00 86-16 ⒹUptheAplchee1212½VerySubtle1211½HomtownQun1161 Impeded 7
11Apr87-Grade I; Placed first thorugh disqualification

15Mar87- 8SA fst 1 1/16 :46⅗ 1:11 1:43⅗ ⒻS A Oaks 3 1 11½ 11 1½ 33¼ Valenzuela P A b 117 *.50 80-20 Timely Assertion 1171¾Buryyourbelief1171½VerySubtle1175¼ Tired 7
15Mar87-Grade I

21Feb87- 8SA fst 1 :45⅘ 1:10 1:36⅘ ⒻLs Vrgnes 5 2 1hd 1hd 1½ 2nk Valenzuela P A 121 *.70 84-14 TimelyAssertion114nkVerySubtle1211MyTurbulentBu1141 Gamely 5
21Feb87-Grade II

31Jan87- 8SA fst 7f :22⅘ :45⅘ 1:22⅗ ⒻSta Ynez 1 1 1½ 11 12 14½ Shoemaker W 122 *.30 87-15 Very Subtle 1224½ Chic Shirine 1191¾ Young Flyer1221½ Drew out 5
31Jan87-Grade III

LATEST WORKOUTS ●Nov 19 Hol 4f fst :46 hg — ●Nov 14 Hol 5f fst :58⅗ h — Nov 8 Hol 6f fst 1:14⅕ h — Nov 1 Hol 6f sly 1:13 h

Taylor's Special *

B. h. 6, by Hawkin's Special—Bette's Gold, by Espea
Br.—Foley Dravo (Ky)
Tr.—Mott William I
Own.—Lucas W F

126 Lifetime 40 21 7 2 $1,055,805 — 1987 6 3 1 0 $121,535 — 1986 9 4 3 0 $267,738

16Oct87- 8Kee fst 6f :22 :43⅖ 1:08⅖ 3↑Cmweath Brd 2 5 74¼ 76¼ 79 58¼ Romero R P 126 *1.30 92-09 Exclusive Enough 111½ Lazer Show 1205 High Brite 1202 Dull try 8

23Aug87- 8Sar fst 7f :22 :44⅕ 1:21⅘ 3↑Forego H 4 6 64½ 57 — — Day P 123 2.40 — — Groovy 1121¾ Purple Mountain 1131¾ Sun Master 1182 Pulled up 6
23Aug87-Grade II

9Aug87- 8AP sly 1⅛ :46⅗ 1:11 1:51⅗ 3↑Wash Park H 2 1 12 13½ 15 12¼ Lively J b 118 *.70 73-30 Taylor's Special 1182¼ Blue Buckaroo 1201½ Fuzzy 1143¼ Easily 6
9Aug87-Grade II

19Jly87- 9AP fst 1 :45⅕ 1:09⅕ 1:34⅕ 3↑Equpose M H 5 1 1½ 12 12 2½ Day P 127 *.30 89-21 RedAttack116½Taylor'sSpecil1274¾ComeSummer1141¼ No excuse 5
19Jly87-Grade III

27Jun87- 8AP fst 7f :22⅖ :44⅘ 1:22 3↑I Murphy H 4 1 11 13½ 15 15½ Day P 123 *.20 92-21 Taylor's Special 1235½ Irish Freeze 115½ Rivotious 1175½ Easily 4

6Jun87- 8AP fst 7f :22⅖ :45 1:22⅖ Alw 19000 2 2 21½ 21 15 12½ Lively J 118 *.50 90-19 Taylor's Special 1182½ Rivotious 1214 Proud Dhabi 121nk Driving 7

29Nov86- 8CD fst 1⅛ :47 1:11⅘ 1:49⅘ 3↑Clark H 6 1 1hd 1hd 2½ 21 Smith M E 126 *.40e 92-20 Come Summer 1121 Taylor's Special 1263 Sumptious 1205 Failed 9

16Nov86- 8CD fst 1 :46⅕ 1:11⅕ 1:36⅕ 3↑Rvr City 5 1 11 11 11½ 12½ Day P 123 *.30 88-19 Taylor's Special 1232½ Doonesbear 1162½ Sumptious121hd Driving 8

1Nov86- 3SA fst 6f :21⅕ :43⅗ 1:08⅖ 3↑Br Cp Sprnt 3 6 64½ 45 44½ 56¾ Romero R P 126 11.80 89-13 Smile1261¼PineTreeLne1231¾BdsidPromis1261¼ Needed response 9
1Nov86-Grade I

20Sep86- 9LaD fst 6f :21⅘ :44⅘ 1:10 3↑Bud Brd Cup 4 1 2hd 1½ 12 13½ Day P 118 *.20 92-16 Taylor's Special 1183½ Aggies Best 120hdSharperThan1142½ Easily 5

LATEST WORKOUTS Nov 17 Hol 4f fst :47⅖ h — ●Nov 12 Hol 5f fst :59⅖ h — ●Oct 9 CD 5f fst :59⅘ h

High Brite

B. c. 3, by Best Turn—Spray, by Forli
Br.—Allen J (Ky)
Tr.—Lukas D Wayne
Own.—Allen Joseph

124 Lifetime 21 5 7 3 $414,496 — 1987 15 3 6 1 $377,408 — 1986 6 2 1 2 $37,088

31Oct87- 9Pha fst 7f :22⅕ :44⅘ 1:21⅗ 3↑Bud Brds Cup 6 2 2½ 1hd 2hd 13½ Kaenel J L 116 6.40 99-19 High Brite 1163½ Vinnie the Viper 1154 Foligno 115½ Drew clear 8

16Oct87- 8Kee fst 6f :22 :43⅖ 1:08⅖ 3↑Cmweath Brd 5 8 86¼ 86¼ 46½ 35¼ Vasquez J 120 5.80 94-09 Exclusive Enough 111½ Lazer Show 1205 High Brite1202 Mild bid 8

2Oct87- 8Bel fst 7f :22⅕ :45⅖ 1:23⅖ 3↑Handicap 4 1 1hd 1hd 25 24¾ Santos J A 115 3.50 80-24 Omar Khayyam 1104¾ High Brite1151¾WindChill1148 Second best 5

13Sep87- 9Pim sly 6f :23 :46⅗ 1:11⅘ War Admiral 2 3 11 1½ 12 13 Bracciale V Jr 122 *1.20Ⓓ 87-20 ⒹHigh Brite 1223 Cardiff 117hd Radicchio 11716¼ Bore out 5
13Sep87-Disqualified and placed second

22Aug87- 7Sar sly 7f :22⅖ :45⅕ 1:23 King Bishop 3 3 52¾ 89¼ 814 829 Cordero A Jr 122 *2.30e 58-16 Templar Hill 119nk Mister S. M. 1195 Homebuilder 115nk Outrun 8
22Aug87-Grade III

12Jly87- 9Pim fst 1 1/16 :46⅕ 1:11 1:43⅕ Survivor 5 2 22 21½ 43½ 48¼ Perret C 122 *.70 80-20 Landyap 1222½ Green Book 1223 Harriman 1222¾ Tired 6

27Jun87-10Lrl fst 1⅛ :47⅘ 1:12 1:49⅗ Govrn's Cp H 1 1 1½ 11 1½ 11¼ Perret C 116 *1.40 98-16 High Brite 1161¼ Homebuilder 1141¾ Green Book 1152½ Driving 6

6Jun87- 5Bel fst 7f :22⅖ :45⅖ 1:22⅖ Riva Ridge 3 2 11½ 1½ 24 28 Cordero A Jr 119 2.10e 82-15 Jazzing Around 1158[DH]HighBrite119[DH]PolishNavy1221½ 2nd best 7
6Jun87-Dead heat

24May87- 8Bel fst 1⅛ :46⅘ 1:10⅖ 1:48 Peter Pan 4 2 2½ 1½ 32½ 54¼ Cordero A Jr 117 4.30 83-16 Leo Castelli 114½ Gone West 1261½ Shawklit Won 1141½ Tired 9
24May87-Grade II

6May87- 8Bel gd 1 :46⅖ 1:10⅖ 1:36⅖ Withers 1 2 31½ 33½ 22½ 2½ Cordero A Jr 126 8.20 82-23 Gone West 126½ High Brite 126¾ Mister S. M. 1269½ Gamely 6
6May87-Grade II

LATEST WORKOUTS Nov 17 Hol 4f fst :48 h — Nov 10 Hol 4f fst :47⅖ h — Oct 26 Bel 4f fst :48⅕ h — Oct 11 Bel 5f fst 1:02 h

As a 3-year-old in 1986, Groovy had been poorly managed. His connections wouldn't concede Groovy was incapable of lasting at longer distances than seven furlongs. Their final attempt to stretch Groovy out ended Sept. 1, 1986, when he opened an eight length lead but finished fourth by five and a quarter to Ogygian in the Grade I one mile Jerome Handicap at Belmont.

Finally, after his sixteenth start, Groovy was allowed to develop into the outstanding sprinter he was meant to be. He tuned up for the 1986 Breeders' Cup Sprint with a two length win in the Ancient Title Handicap at Santa Anita, which was the site of the 1986 Breeders' Cup. Groovy was the 2 to 5 favorite in the Breeders' Cup Sprint and never made the lead. His other nine PPs were a straight row of ones at the first point of call. Except in the biggest race of his life. Groovy didn't make the lead because Pine Tree Lane was quicker out of the gate, carving out incredible fractions of :21 1/5 and :43 3/5. Pine Tree Lane hung on to finish second by one and a quarter to Smile, who won in 1:08 2/5. Groovy finished fourth by four and a quarter. Groovy knew only one way to race, and that was in front. It's difficult for a horse to do something he's never done. We understand that Groovy always raced on the lead. He would not rate behind a horse, and thus when he wasn't leading, he did not pass horses.

After the Breeders' Cup loss, Groovy threw in another clunker, finishing fourth by six and a half to Best By Test in the Grade III Sporting Page Handicap at Aqueduct. Groovy was likely feeling the fatigue from his poorly managed season when he'd been asked to repeatedly run too far and, evidenced by the Sporting Page Handicap, too often.

Groovy's owners were determined in 1987 to establish Groovy as the nation's best sprinter. He certainly played the part, winning all six of his starts before the Breeders' Cup. How can you argue against such a report card? Let's look a little closer at the PPs.

In the summer of 1987, Groovy was awesome. He won the Grade III Roseben by four and a quarter, earning a speed rating of 98 with his 1:08 2/5 clocking for the six furlongs. He was even better in his next start, the Grade II True North, winning by five and three-quarters and setting a track record of 1:07 4/5 over a track listed as "muddy" at Belmont Park. Groovy shipped to Finger Lakes in upstate New York and was life and death to hold on for a head victory in the Budweiser

Breeders' Stakes over Purple Mountain, hardly a top stakes-caliber horse. But the time was sensational. For the second consecutive time, Groovy set a track record (1:09 2/5) for six furlongs at a notoriously slow track.

Groovy followed with easy and impressive victories in the Tom Fool at Belmont and the Forego Handicap at Saratoga carrying 128 and 132 pounds, respectively. But his final victory in the Vosburgh was by a diminishing three-quarters of a length against Moment Of Hope, an ordinary horse. And he and Groovy carried the same weight, 126.

We conclude Groovy was much sharper in the summer than he seemed to be for a race he had lost a year before. There were no ordinary horses in this race. Groovy couldn't win if he wasn't at his best. His narrow six furlong victory against Purple Mountain and the close decision against Moment Of Hope in the seven furlong Vosburgh demanded our attention and suggested he just might get beaten in the Breeders' Cup Sprint again. Another negative was that despite his glittering record, Groovy's PPs showed just three appearances in Grade I stakes, the 1986 Jerome and Breeders' Cup and the Vosburgh.

An even stronger consideration was that the same horse who outsprinted Groovy to the lead in the 1986 Sprint could do it again this time: the brilliantly fast mare Pine Tree Lane. Going up and down her PPs for the first and second points of call, there was only a single number: one. Pine Tree Lane always made the lead. In three of her last ten races, she zipped the opening quarter in :21 3/5 and the half in :44. She also had oodles of class, seventeen wins in thirty-two starts and earnings of more than $1 million. She uncharacteristically had a three race losing streak in stakes at Saratoga, Belmont and The Meadowlands. In her last start in a minor stakes at Aqueduct, she whipped four filly rivals by six lengths in 1:09 4/5 for six furlongs. One of Pine Tree Lane's losses was in the Boojum Handicap when she was sixth by five and a half to Sun Master, a horse Groovy had beaten conclusively three straight times. Does this mean Pine Tree Lane couldn't beat Groovy? Probably, yes. Did it mean Groovy would win? No.

Handicapping the race, we examine the race dynamics, how we think the race will be run. We had reached two conclusions so far: 1) Groovy might not be as sharp as he was in the summer, and 2) Groovy would likely beat Pine Tree Lane.

But it's a third conclusion that is vital: Pine Tree Lane might not win, but she sure figured to be on the lead, which equated with Groovy's defeat. Groovy can't win any way except wire-to-wire, and Pine Tree Lane always makes the lead. That was the exact scenario the year before in the Breeders' Cup. Why wouldn't it happen again?

We conclude that it will. Groovy, therefore, will be an extremely large underlay, with his jockey, Cordero, further lowering the odds.

Who were the candidates to upset Groovy? Governor General, Sharp Romance and Sylvan Express comprised the field (two or three horses grouped together as a single betting interest because most tote boards can only accommodate twelve horses). A field has the same principle as an entry, bet one and you get them all. You needed them all. Two of the three European invaders had *never* run on dirt. The other, Sharp Romance, was 0-for-29 the last two years. They could properly be labeled ridiculous longshots.

Our handicapping determines six other horses who are weak and have little chance of winning: Slyly Gifted, On The Line, Exclusive Enough, Taylor's Special, High Brite and Sabona. Slyly Gifted had last raced in the 1 1/4 mile Gold Cup Handicap and showed only two sprints, each at seven furlongs, in his PPs. The last was a two and a quarter length victory in an allowance race at Keeneland. On The Line had an eight race losing streak. Exclusive Enough was a 3-year-old off two six furlong wins in an allowance at Delmar and the ungraded Commonwealth Breeders Stakes at Keeneland. He tied the track record in the second, but he'd yet to compete against top sprinters and was picking up thirteen pounds. Taylor's Special was fifth by eight and a quarter against Exclusive Enough in the Commonwealth Breeders his last start. High Brite had a spotty sprint record of two wins in six tries against weaker opposition. Sabona had won his last two sprints, an allowance and ungraded stakes, but they were on turf. Previously, he'd sprinted on dirt three times, winning a six and a half furlong allowance, winning a seven furlong ungraded stakes and finishing second in an allowance at Hollywood Park. He seemed overmatched.

There were three horses left.

Zany Tactics and Zabaleta had more in common than the first letter of their name. They both were high quality sprinters who had met twice previously in 1987. In an ungraded six and a half furlong stakes at Santa Anita, February 11, Zabaleta and Zany Tactics alternated leads in a bitter battle. Zabaleta led Zany Tactics by a head after an opening quarter in :21 4/5. At the half, in :44 1/5, Zany Tactics put a head in front. At the top of the stretch, Zany Tactics regained a half length lead, but Zabaleta rallied again and beat Zany Tactics by a head in 1:15, an excellent time for six and a half furlongs.

Zany Tactics beat Zabaleta by ten lengths in the rematch, setting a world record of 1:06 4/5 for six furlongs in the Grade III Phoenix Gold Cup at Turf Paradise. But Zany Tactics followed with two fairly substantial losses to Pine Tree Lane, fourth by four and a half and third by four in the Bold Ruler and Carter Handicap at Aqueduct.

Given three months off, Zany Tactics responded with three wins in four races, including a half length victory in the slop in an un-graded stakes at Santa Anita his last start. The 6-year-old gelding beat On The Line in that race while giving him seven pounds. He'd give him two in the Breeders' Cup.

Careful scrutiny of his PPs showed after the first quarter, he was on the lead or within a length of the leader in the sprints he won. In his two sprint losses to Pine Tree Lane, he was two and two and a half lengths off Pine Tree Lane at the quarter and lost both. Facing Pine Tree Lane again, what reason was there for him to be closer? A subtle point yet one worth thinking about. Certainly his career record, 15-7-3 in thirty-one starts, reflected his tenacity.

Zabaleta, a son of crack sprinter Shecky Greene, was versatile enough to finish second by half a length in the 1 1/8 mile Garden State Stakes in 1986. Off that race, his connections pulled a Groovy, asking their sprinter to go 1 1/4 miles in the 1986 Kentucky Derby. Zabaleta was second early, ran into traffic problems and tired badly to finish twelfth to Ferdinand. Zabaleta didn't return to the races for eight months.

Zabaleta was the 7 to 5 favorite (Zany Tactics was 9 to 5) in Zany Tactic's world record performance in the Phoenix Gold Cup. In his next three races, he was second, first by one and three-quarters in the Grade II one mile Mervyn LeRoy Handicap, and fourth by four in the Grade III Los Angeles Handicap. Trainer John Gosden then gave the 4-year-old four months off before prepping him for the Breeders' Cup. In an overnight handicap at Balmoral, Zabaleta was second by a nose. It was a game performance, one typical of a horse with a record of 5-5-2 in fourteen starts. Yet it also was Zabaleta's fourth consecutive loss in a sprint.

There were many legitimate questions about Very Subtle. For openers, she was a 3-year-old filly not only racing against colts for the first time in her career, but also older colts. It's rare to see a 3-year-old filly attempt such a difficult assignment. However, we need to look no farther than Pine Tree Lane's PPs to see a filly can handle colts in graded stakes. Pine Tree Lane was five when she beat colts in consecutive Grade II stakes, the Bold Ruler and the Carter Handicap. Genuine Risk, Lady's Secret, Personal Ensign, Winning Colors, Miesque and Pebbles proved in the 1980s that a filly can beat colts if she has the talent.

How much did Very Subtle possess? Her career record, 15-9-2-2 with earnings of $824,860 spoke well. Subtract two losses in Grade I $1^1/8$ miles stakes, and she'd been in the money in all her starts. Subtract three more defeats (in the money each time, though) at $1^1/16$ miles and her record is 10-9-1-0. In fact, she'd been beaten just once in sprints. That happened in her last start when she was second by three and a half as the 2 to 5 favorite in a Budweiser Breeders' seven furlong sprint at Arlington Park, August 31.

Her line generated two additional concerns. All the sprints in her PPs were at seven furlongs. Plus, she hadn't raced in more than two months. The first concern is answered by analyzing her style of racing: close to the pace but not on the lead in her last three sprints. Her tactical speed would suffer no disadvantage at six furlongs instead of seven.

The layoff of eleven weeks was irksome. It wasn't intolerable given four contingencies:

1. She had to show she ran well fresh. Her PPs showed one race off a five week layoff, when she won the Grade III Railbird Stakes by five and a half lengths at odds of 3 to 5 at Hollywood Park. Five weeks aren't eleven, but they do constitute a layoff.

2. Receiving only a semi-satisfactory answer about the layoff, we must have confidence in the trainer's tactics in bringing her up to this demanding race off workouts. Mel Stute is a highly-respected California trainer whose brightest star was Snow Chief. He had pointed Very Subtle to this race, the Sprint, instead of the longer ($1^1/4$ mile) Breeders' Cup Distaff against fillies.

3. Her workouts better be impressive and recent. They were. Very Subtle worked six furlongs in the slop in 1:13, November 1; six furlongs in 1:14 1/5, November 8; a bullet five furlongs in :58 3/5, November 14, and a bullet four furlongs in :46, November 19, eight days before the race. All the workouts were at Hollywood Park.

4. She must have shown an extraordinary sprint. She did. Stute raced Very Subtle in the 1¹/₈ mile, Grade I Hollywood Oaks, July 12. She was a tiring fourth in a field of six, beaten by seven and a half lengths by Perchance To Dream. Off that effort, Stute shipped her cross-country to run in the seven furlong, Grade II Test Stakes at Saratoga, August 6. The Test is the traditional prep for the 1¹/₄ mile Alabama Stakes. Stute had the good sense not to ask his talented sprinter to go 1¹/₄ miles despite a performance in the Test which was unreal. In a highly competitive field of fourteen, Very Subtle zoomed to battle for the lead in a :21 3/5 opening quarter. She got a head in front after the fastest half mile I've ever seen in fifteen years of daily attendance at Saratoga's twenty-four day meet: :43 3/5. Instead of packing it in after suicidal fractions, Very Subtle simply drew away from the entire field, winning by five and a quarter lengths in a stakes record 1:21, three-fifths of a second off the track record. It was a performance to savor and remember. There would be no better time to remember than Breeders' Cup Day.

Groovy went off 4 to 5; Zany Tactics 3 to 1; Zabaleta 7 to 1; Pine Tree Lane 9 to 1, and Very Subtle 16 to 1. Our handicapping revealed legitimate concerns regarding Very Subtle. She wasn't the top contender, yet she was truly a contender. At 16 to 1, she was an obvious overlay.

Very Subtle broke alertly and fought to a half-length advantage over Pine Tree Lane—with Groovy just a head farther back—in a sizzling opening quarter of :21 1/5. When Very Subtle tacked on a second quarter in :22 4/5, she was clear by one and a half lengths at the half, run in :44. Groovy held well to finish second as Very Subtle, mirroring her performance in the Test, raced to a four length win in 1:08 4/5. She paid $34.80.

FIRST RACE
Hollywood
NOVEMBER 21, 1987

6 FURLONGS. (1.08⅘) 4th Running of THE BREEDERS' CUP SPRINT (Grade I). Purse $1,000,000. 3-year-olds and upward. Weight, 3-year-olds, 124 lbs. Older 126 lbs. Fillies and mares allowed 3 lbs. Value of a race $1,000,000. Value to winner $450,000, second $225,000, third, $108,000, fourth $70,000, fifth $50,000, sixth $10,000. Nominator Awards:

Total purse $1,000,000. Value of race $913,000; value to winner $450,000; second $225,000; third $108,000; fourth $70,000; fifth $50,000; sixth $10,000. $87,000 in Foal and Stallion Nominator Awards. Mutuel pool $848,204.

Last Raced	Horse	Eqt.	A.	Wt	PP	St	¼	½	Str	Fin	Jockey	Odds $1
31Aug87 ^{9}AP^{2}	Very Subtle		3	121	11	2	$1^{\frac{1}{2}}$	$1^{1\frac{1}{2}}$	$1^{3\frac{1}{2}}$	1^{4}	Valenzuela P A	16.40
10Oct87 ^{7}Bel^{1}	Groovy		4	126	1	3	$3^{2\frac{1}{2}}$	2^{2}	$2^{1\frac{1}{2}}$	$2^{1\frac{3}{4}}$	Cordero A Jr	.80
16Oct87 ^{8}Kee^{1}	Exclusive Enough		3	124	10	6	$6^{\frac{1}{2}}$	$4^{\frac{1}{2}}$	$4^{1\frac{1}{2}}$	3^{1}	Day P	25.10
8Nov87 ^{10}BM^{2}	(S)Zabaleta	b	4	126	7	7	$7^{1\frac{1}{2}}$	5^{1}	3^{hd}	4^{1}	Pincay L Jr	7.90
31Oct87 ^{9}Pha^{1}	High Brite		3	124	13	4	4^{1}	6^{1}	$6^{\frac{1}{2}}$	$5^{1\frac{1}{4}}$	Santos J A	97.10
15Oct87 ^{8}Kee^{5}	Taylor's Special		6	126	12	8	$8^{2\frac{1}{2}}$	8^{2}	8^{1}	6^{nk}	Vasquez J	71.30
7Nov87 ^{6}Haw^{4}	Slyly Gifted		4	126	2	9	12	$9^{\frac{1}{2}}$	9^{1}	7no	Meza R Q	111.70
31Oct87 ^{1}Eng^{4}	Sylvan Express		4	126	9	11	$10^{2\frac{1}{2}}$	11^{5}	$10^{1\frac{1}{2}}$	$8^{1\frac{3}{4}}$	Cauthen S	f-66.70
4Nov87 ^{8}SA^{1}	(S)Zany Tactics		6	126	3	5	5^{hd}	$7^{1\frac{1}{2}}$	7^{hd}	9^{nk}	Kaenel J L	3.00
4Nov87 ^{8}SA^{2}	On The Line	b	3	124	4	13	9^{hd}	10^{hd}	11^{5}	$10^{\frac{1}{2}}$	Romero R P	26.40
31Oct87 ^{7}Aqu^{1}	Pine Tree Lane		5	123	6	1	2^{hd}	$3^{1\frac{1}{2}}$	$5^{\frac{1}{2}}$	11^{7}	McCarron C J	9.30
25Oct87 ^{4}Fra^{12}	Sharp Romance		5	126	8	12	13	$12^{2\frac{1}{2}}$	12^{5}	12^{6}	Wigham M	f-66.70
17Oct87 ^{5}Eng^{2}	Governor General		4	126	5	10	11^{hd}	13	13	13	Eddery P	f-66.70

f—Mutuel field.
(S) Supplementary nomination.

OFF AT 11:18 Start good, Won driving. Time, :21⅕, :44, :55⅗, 1:08⅘ Track fast.

Official Program Numbers↘

$2 Mutuel Prices:

9-VERY SUBTLE	**34.80**	**8.80**	**5.00**
2-GROOVY		**3.20**	**2.60**
8-EXCLUSIVE ENOUGH			**7.80**

Ch. f, by Hoist the Silver—Never Scheme, by Never Bend. Trainer Stute Melvin F. Bred by King J Howard (Ky).

VERY SUBTLE sprinted to the front before going a quarter after getting away in alert fashion, quickly drew away in the upper stretch and remained well clear through the final furlong while under a drive. GROOVY pressed the early pace from along the inner rail after a good start, could not keep pace with VERY SUBTLE in the drive but held on well enough to gain the place. EXCLUSIVE ENOUGH, never far back, came into the stretch four wide and could not gain the necessary ground in the drive. ZABALETA, outrun early after veering out and being jostled and checked in the initial strides, mildly menaced from the inside early in the drive but flattened out. HIGH BRITE, in close contention early, lacked the needed response in the last quarter. TAYLOR'S SPECIAL was wide down the backstretch and six wide into the stretch. SYLVAN EXPRESS, devoid of early speed after breaking slowly and being jostled and shuffled back in the opening strides, found his best stride too late. ZANY TACTICS, outrun early, entered the stretch five wide and lacked the needed response when called upon. ON THE LINE bobbled at the start to get away slowly. PINE TREE LANE, off alertly and prominent early, gave way. SHARP ROMANCE broke slowly and was jostled and shuffled back in the initial strides. GOVERNOR GENERAL broke a bit awkwardly and was six wide into the stretch. SABONA (1) WAS WITHDRAWN. ALL WAGERS ON HIM IN THE REGULAR AND DAILY DOUBLE POOLS WERE ORDERED REFUNDED AND ALL OF HIS PICK NINE SELECTIONS WERE SWITCHED TO THE FAVORITE, GROOVY (2).

Owners— 1, Rochelle B; 2, Prestonwood Farm Inc; 3, Scharbauer Dorothy; 4, Holmes M H R & Court; 5, Allen Joseph; 6, Lucas W F; 7, Franks John; 8, Johnson Mrs R A; 9, Brunette Vera C; 10, Klein E V; 11, Young W T; 12, Sheikh Mohammed al Sabah; 13, Richards R.

Trainers— 1, Stute Melvin F; 2, Martin Jose; 3, Van Berg Jack C; 4, Gosden John H M; 5, Lukas D Wayne; 6, Mott William I; 7, Hronec Philip; 8, Mitchell Philip; 9, Heap Blake; 10, Lukas D Wayne; 11, Lukas D Wayne; 12, Mellor Stanley T; 13, Elsworth D.

Scratched—Sabona (21Oct87 ^{8}SA^{1}).

Inside with Angel Cordero, Jr.

CHAPTER 9

Jockey Angel Cordero, Jr., flagged by the stewards for a disqualification the day before, offered a succinct summary of his career: "I was born in trouble and I'll die in trouble."

He made this assessment last August on the eve of capturing his thirteenth Saratoga riding title in fourteen years. Only Jose Santos, who edged Cordero in 1987, has derailed Cordero during his uncanny domination of the nation's premier thoroughbred meeting. "Records are made to be broken, but I'll probably be retired and dead when this one's broken," Cordero said. "Saratoga gives me great self-satisfaction. I look forward to going to Saratoga every year and being the leading rider. The rest of the year when I ride in New York [at Belmont Park and Aqueduct], I try to win, but I don't worry about being the leading rider. If I feel I can take a day off, I'll just do it. In the mornings, I go whenever I feel like riding workouts. But when I'm at Saratoga, I go every morning. I want to ride a lot of horses that can win."

So he rides every morning, searching for live mounts. Then he rides every afternoon. When he gets home, he watches replays of that day's races, figuring out which horses he wants to ride back in their next starts. He talks to his agent about upcoming races, then picks up the next day's *Racing Form* and handicaps his races long into the night. "I don't think I could take that routine for a whole year," he said.

On August 11, 1988, the same day his wife Marjorie gave birth to a daughter, Cordero was elected to the Hall of Fame. He's forever enshrined in the minds of racing fans, who frequently proffer ambivalent feelings toward Cordero. Many disparage his penchant for pushing every limit in the rules of racing, yet admire his courage when he shoots a horse through a narrow opening other jockeys wouldn't dare attempt to go through. And they'd want no other jockey in the world riding the horse they bet in a close, driving finish. "I say trouble follows me all the time," Cordero said. "I laugh when I say that, but it's true. Controversy happens. Controversy seems like it's always there for me. Most of the time, I know when it's coming."

He certainly knew after the 1980 Preakness when he guided Codex to victory, crowding Kentucky Derby winner Genuine Risk on the turn for home. Stewards conducted an inquiry, but let the finish stand, a striking example of Cordero's ability to skirt the fringes of racing rules without breaking them.

From the late 1960s through the 1980s, only two jockeys, Laffit Pincay, Jr., and Bill Shoemaker, performed at Cordero's level. Now, Cordero and Pincay are joined by Santos, with Pat Day and Chris McCarron real close.

Cordero is the only rider to surpass $5 million in earnings in a single season twelve straight years, one of only three jockeys to win more than $100 million, and one of just four to ever win 6,000 races. He's been the leading rider in New York seven times, led the nation in earnings three times, and won two Eclipse Awards as the nation's leading jockey. In 1988, he won back-to-back Breeders' Cup races on Gulch and Open Mind. He's won five races in one day eight times and once won six. Cordero had more wins in 1989 Grade I stakes (sixteen) than any jockey in the country.

He's also one of the few jockeys with a grandchild (Amanda). Cordero, forty-seven, became a grandfather June 12, 1986, exactly twenty-six years after he rode his first race in his native Puerto Rico. Cordero's father was a jockey and a trainer at El Commandante racetrack. Having groomed his father's horses as a child, Cordero was well-prepped for his livelihood.

Only nineteen, and in just his second year of riding, Cordero was the leading rider at El Commandante with 124 wins. A year later, he won his first race in New York on Counterate.

If a single race demonstrates Cordero's brilliant career, it is the 1976 Belmont Stakes. Bold Forbes, who won the 1976 Derby with Cordero aboard, was a speed horse who got burned in a speed duel in the Preakness with Honest Pleasure. People wondered if Bold Forbes could win the 1½ mile Belmont even with the service of Cordero and Hall of Fame trainer Laz Barrera. Barrera did a masterful job and Cordero followed with an outstanding ride, nursing Bold Forbes on the lead and driving him relentlessly in the stretch. Bold Forbes bore out late as he tired, yet Cordero kept him going straight enough to withstand late charges from McKenzie Bridge and Great Contractor. Bold Forbes had a six length lead at the top of the stretch. At the wire he was a neck in front. "If you ride a horse that wins by fifteen lengths, you haven't accomplished anything yourself," Cordero said. "Anybody can win that. It's when you win a race that you contributed to winning, that makes you feel good. On horses that, if you don't give them a good ride, they don't win. That makes you happy."

108th RUNNING—1976—BOLD FORBES

SEVENTH RACE
Bel
June 5, 1976

1½ MILES. (2:24). One-hundred and eighth running BELMONT. SCALE WEIGHTS. $150,000 added. 3-year-olds. By subscription of $100 each to accompany the nomination; $250 to pass the entry box; $1,000 to start. A supplementary nomination may be made of $2,500 on June 2 plus an additional $10,000 to start with $150,000 added, of which 60% to the winner, 22% to second, 12% to third and 6% to fourth. Colts and geldings. 126 lbs.; fillies, 121 lbs. The winning owner will be presented with the August Belmont Memorial Cup to be retained for one year, as well as a trophy for permanent possession and trophies will be presented to the winning trainer and jockey. Closed with 210 original nominations and one supplementary nomination

Value of race $195,000. Value to winner $117,000; second, $42,900; third, $23,400; fourth, $11,700.
Mutuel Pool, $775,764. Off-track betting, $1,063.504. Exacta Pool, $462,153. Off-track betting Exacta Pool, $824,680.

Last Raced	Horse	EqtAWt	PP	¼	½	¾	1	Str	Fin	Jockeys	Owners	Odds to $1
15 May76 ^{8}Pim^{3}	Bold Forbes	b3 126	8	1^{2}	1^{6}	$1^{1\frac{1}{2}}$	1^{6}	1^{6}	1^{nk}	ACorderoJr	E R Tizol	.90
24 May76 ^{7}Bel^{1}	McKenzie Bridge	3 126	2	$8^{1\frac{1}{2}}$	9^{2}	9^{5}	$7^{\frac{1}{2}}$	3^{4}	2^{nk}	DMcHargue	Mrs D Carver	6.60
23 May76 ^{8}Bel^{6}	Great Contractor	b3 126	7	10	8^{1}	5^{3}	$3^{1\frac{1}{2}}$	$2^{1\frac{1}{2}}$	$3^{8\frac{1}{2}}$	JVasquez	H P Wilson	5.40
15 May76 ^{8}GS^{1}	Majestic Light	3 126	6	5^{1}	6^{3}	6^{1}	5^{h}	$4^{\frac{1}{2}}$	4^{nk}	JVelasquez	O M Phipps	14.40
27 May76 ^{7}Bel^{1}	Aeronaut	3 126	1	$3^{\frac{1}{2}}$	4^{1}	4^{2}	6^{2}	$7^{1\frac{1}{2}}$	5^{nk}	RTurcotte	O Wilson Jr	22.90
15 May76 ^{8}Pim^{2}	Play the Red	b3 126	4	6^{2}	$3^{\frac{1}{2}}$	3^{2}	$4^{1\frac{1}{2}}$	$5^{\frac{1}{2}}$	6^{h}	JCruguet	Elmendorf	4.10
2 Jun76 ^{7}Bel^{2}	Mullineaux	b3 126	3	$9^{1\frac{1}{2}}$	10	8^{h}	8^{12}	6^{2}	7^{7}	MARivera	Darby Dan Farm	33.40
23 May76 ^{8}Bel^{4}	Best Laid Plans	3 126	9	2^{2}	2^{4}	2^{6}	$2^{\frac{1}{2}}$	8^{20}	8^{26}	PDay	Christiana Stable	28.80
24 May76 ^{6}Pim^{5}	Close to Noon	3 126	5	7^{h}	7^{2}	10	10	10	9^{1}	MVenezia	Mrs P Hofmann	46.40
30 May76 ^{8}Bel^{3}	Quick Card	3 126	10	4^{1}	5^{4}	7^{4}	9^{8}	9^{4}	10	MSolomone	J M Schiff	46.40

(s) Supplementary nomination.

OFF AT 5:38½ EDT. Start good. Won driving. Time. :23⅗, :47, 1:11⅕, 1:36, 2:01⅗. 2:29. Track fast.

$2 Mutuel Prices:

8-BOLD FORBES	3.80	3.40	2.80
2-McKENZIE BRIDGE		5.00	3.80
7-GREAT CONTRACTOR			3.80
$2 EXACTA (8-2) PAID $23.40.			

Dk. b. or br. c, by Irish Castle—Comely Nell, by Commodore M. Trainer, Lazaro S. Barrera. Bred by Eaton Farm Inc. and Red Bull Stable (Ky.).

BOLD FORBES sprinted right to the front, drew off quickly while remaining well out in the track on the first turn, made the pace under good handling, put BEST LAID PLANS away when ready approaching the stretch, settled into the stretch with a good lead and lasted while bearing out under pressure just before the finish. McKENZIE BRIDGE, outrun for a mile, angled out while moving leaving the far turn and finished strongly from the outside. GREAT CONTRACTOR, unhurried early, moved fast from the outside approaching the stretch and continued on gamely while finishing between the top pair. MAJESTIC LIGHT failed to be a serious factor. AERONAUT saved ground to no avail. PLAY THE RED rallied racing into the far turn but had nothing left for the drive. MULLINEAUX was never close. BEST LAID PLANS raced in closest attendance to BOLD FORBES. went after that rival approaching the end of the backstretch but was finished leaving the far turn. CLOSE TO NOON showed nothing. QUICK CARD was finished early.

Scratched—Charleston.

Nowhere is Cordero happier than at Saratoga. Unbelievably, until his eleven consecutive riding titles began in 1976, he was the leading rider there just once in eleven years, and that was in 1967.

Cordero's string of Saratoga riding titles is hard-earned. His aggressive riding, combined with his intimate knowledge of the track and its frequently changing bias, gives Cordero an edge. "The atmosphere at Saratoga really helps your attitude," Cordero said. "All year in New York, I go from my house to the track and from the track to my house. And like a horse, you get kind of sour. When you move to Saratoga, it inspires you and you work a little harder. In Saratoga, people know I know the track and I ride a lot of winners there. So even people who don't ride me at Belmont give me a mount there."

Riding every morning gives Cordero vital clues when the track may be changing. Saratoga has an unusual surface, one that is only used for one month a year in August. Significantly speed favoring in most of the past fifteen years, Saratoga's $1 1/8$ mile main track can change instantly when rain comes during thunderstorms which occasionally are torrential. "I've been coming to Saratoga since 1965," he said. "That has to be an advantage. Saratoga is a good track, but it's a funny track. I remember from 1965 to 1970, the rail was very heavy. Nobody wanted to be near it. Then it changed. The track looks one way in the morning, a different way in the afternoon. When it rains, you have to guess what part of the track is good."

Cordero doesn't guess. Year after year, he seems to be the first jockey to know if the rail is alive or dead, if speed is holding up or dying in sprints.

He supplements his knowledge of the track by spending as many as four hours handicapping races he's in the next day. "It's like doing my homework," Cordero said. "Sometimes I'm up until two or three in the morning. I go home at night, put checks by the horses I have to beat. I mark speed horses. I check workouts. I figure out what I have to do the next day. I check out the trainers and jockeys on horses that I have to beat."

Then he does his damnedest to beat them.

Before a race, Cordero exudes serenity. Frequently, he chats with another jockey in the walking ring, many times in Spanish. He croons to his horse to relax him. After a win, he doesn't simply dismount, he tosses his whip to his valet as if he was spearing a fish. He leaps skyward, raises clenched fists and lands with the precision of a gymnast.

While writing his Saratoga success story, Cordero is still in pursuit of Manny Ycaza's 1959 record of forty-one winners in the twenty-four day meet. Cordero's best total was thirty-six in 1967 and 1988. "It's a tough record," Cordero said. "I don't know how the hell he did it."

Fans watch Cordero August after August and say the same thing. Eleven straight years! Incredibly, the closer he got to losing the streak, the better he rode.

In 1982, Cordero and Eddie Maple were tied going into the Seneca Handicap, the next-to-last race on the final day of the meet. Maple, who won the seventh race that day to move into a tie, was riding Native Courier in the Seneca. Native Courier won the $1^5/8$ mile turf stakes two years earlier. Cordero rode Great Neck, who'd won the Seneca the previous year.

With both Cordero and Maple having longshot mounts in the ninth (neither finished in the money), Cordero's quest for a sixth straight title was to be decided in the Seneca. In the post parade, another horse, Wicked Will, reared and kicked Cordero. "It hurt like hell," Cordero said. "But no way I was getting off this horse."

Maple went for the lead and tried going wire-to-wire on Native Courier, the 7 to 2 second choice. Cordero waited with Great Neck, sent off the 6 to 5 favorite. When they hit the final turn, Native Courier increased his lead from half a length to a length. "I didn't think I was going to win at the head of the stretch," Cordero said. "I thought, 'What a way to lose. I'm going to wind up empty.'"

He didn't. Great Neck, carrying six more pounds than Native Courier, merely needed time to get rolling. He cruised by Native Courier at the sixteenth pole and won by three lengths.

Cordero continued his Saratoga streak despite twice losing days because of suspension. He survived twice getting dumped when a horse he was riding on the lead swerved suddenly, breaking through the hedges on the inner turf course.

But the year Cordero never should have won was 1984. A year earlier, Cordero won the Jim Dandy Stakes, the traditional prep race for the Travers, aboard A Phenomenon. A Phenomenon returned to Saratoga in 1984 and was sent off the 2 to 5 favorite in the Forego Handicap. In the lead midway on the final turn, A Phenomenon broke down and had to be destroyed. Cordero was flung to the track in the immediate path of two horses. "I looked at the film," Cordero said. "I couldn't believe it. When I went down, I thought I was gone. I thought both horses were going to hit me. Somebody up there must like me. Not too many do."

Only one of the two horses hit Cordero, leaving him with a badly bruised back as a memento from his brush with death.

Cordero was back riding the next day. "I've been riding for twenty-four years," Cordero said at the time. "When you get hurt, your muscles are sore. It doesn't do you any good to sit home. I'm used to pain. It's nothing new to me. As long as nothing is broken...eight out of ten athletes have pain."

While the physical pain diminished, the mental pain continued for Cordero. Mired in a horrid slump before the injury, the slump grew into one of Cordero's worst ever. He lost twenty-one straight races and forty-five of forty-seven, yet he recovered from a two-win deficit to Eddie Maple in the final four days, clinching his ninth straight title by winning the Spinaway Stakes for 2-year-old fillies, again the next-to-last race of the meet (the Seneca was moved to an earlier date). Five years later, he did it again, eliminating Santos by winning the Spinaway with Lukas-trained Stella Madrid last August.

Cordero is no stranger to injury. His worst accident was at Aqueduct, March 8, 1986, when his mount, Highfalutin, clipped heels with another horse. Cordero endured four and a half hours of surgery to repair a lacerated liver and a fractured tibia. He missed more than four months of racing, but returned with a flair, winning on his only two mounts, I'm Your Boy and Gulch, his first day back. Two years later, Cordero rode Gulch to victory in the Breeders' Cup Sprint.

These days, Cordero is still bet inordinately high in many of his races, especially at Saratoga in August. "People bet a lot of horses that

I ride," he said. That frequently transfers into underlays, situations we desperately want to avoid. Remember, unhealthy underlays create overlays on other horses.

"People will bet my horses, even if they don't know anything about my horse, even if the horse is a first-time starter," Cordero said. "Somebody goes around saying they hear the horse can fly and they make him 3 to 2 or 3 to 5. Maidens. Also New York-bred races. Claiming races. It's very hard to make a horse a big favorite because there's a lot of inconsistency in those kinds of races. The only horses you can really make a big favorite are horses like Easy Goer or Open Mind. These are good horses that run regularly. You follow the workouts. The claiming horse, you're never in contact with. Sometimes, they don't run in a month and you don't see a workout. You don't know if he's sore. You don't know if he's doing good or bad."

Usually, the horse with Cordero up doesn't do badly.

Probably the best time to find a Cordero overlay is on the turf, where his immense skill is occasionally overlooked. Ten Below's 1981 maiden grass win ($20.40) at Saratoga pops into mind as a classic. Ten Below went on to become a major grass stakes winner. A more recent example is Second Court, who won twice on the Saratoga turf last August. She paid a juicy $12.60 the first time despite showing a close fifth as the 9 to 10 favorite with Jean-Luc Samyn in her previous race at a moderately lower claiming level ($45,000 vs. $35,000). Fifteen days later at the same claiming level, she and Cordero won again at odds of 5 to 2.

Cordero, whose 248 career suspensions are nearly three times as many as any other active jockey, speaks of someday retiring and becoming a trainer. During his recovery from his 1986 spill, Cordero began helping his fiancee, former jockey Marjorie Clayton, train a small stable on the backstretch. "It's a whole different world," Cordero said. "Trainers are like doctors—everybody has different methods.

"I always wanted to train. I wanted to do it since I was a kid. People will knock me. Everything you want to do new in life, people say you can't do it."

Except riding. Nobody's ever said Cordero can't ride.

Form

CHAPTER 10 Form is the most widely used school of handicapping, the simplest to understand, and yet one that always must be placed in the proper perspective. The favorite in most races will be the most formful horse, that is the horse showing the best recent form. Bettors have little trouble identifying such horses, and the general population likes betting horses with all ones or twos in their past performance lines. The supposition is Horse A raced well in his last start, and, therefore, will race well again today. If it was that easy, though, favorites would win more than the 30 to 40 percent they annually do across the nation.

Any novice handicapper can point to a horse which won its last race by five lengths, is in the same company today, and has no apparent reason not to win again, and say, "This is the horse to beat." What of a race with none of the horses showing a win in their last start, or one horse showing a win four starts ago and then mixed results?

The problem of form handicapping is the dangerous assumption of consistency. Too many times, it's assumed a horse will automatically run back to its last race or last few races. If he has shown promising form, he will race well today. That's not necessarily true.

Consistency is the measure which separates claimers from allowance horses, allowance horses from stakes horses, and stakes horses from champions. The true thoroughbred champion not only has great talent, he or she shows it and proves it time after time after time. Great horses have the rare ability to maintain high quality for several weeks or months. A large majority of horses do not repeat their best efforts consistently. Some get good for a while, then tail off. Others are good until they get tested by better quality horses. Claimers are good some times and bad others. Frequently it's hard to gauge when they will suddenly change directions in their performances. Remember the tenet of handicapping: never ask a horse to do something he hasn't previously done. In other words, don't expect a $25,000 claimer to jump up and beat $50,000 claimers if he's shown in the past a lack of success at that level. Form players would argue the exact opposite if that horse has won his last two starts impressively. They reason he's good now, and will stay good, and may be good enough to win at a much higher level. There is no hard, black-and-white line of demarcation here. Rather, there are generalities, often true but sometimes broken. Generally, horses older than four don't suddenly improve to a new level of performance. Exceptions do happen. Trainer Oscar Barrera's entire 1983 season was a documentation of exceptions as he unseated Frank Martin, perennial New York leading trainer, by claiming several horses, jumping them way up, and winning, then running them back on two or three days rest instead of the accepted norm of one or two weeks. Many of Barrera's horses won again. How he accomplished his unprecedented success is still a matter of debate, with his detractors insisting illegal drugs had to be involved. Such a charge was never proven, even though Barrera was under considerable scrutiny by racing officials that year. His subsequent lack of success makes his 1983 season even more mysterious.

We will emphasize that such exceptions are not the norm. Our guidelines for form will be: 1) we'll expect young or inexperienced horses to show improvement; 2) we'll be open to the notion of relatively inexperienced horses improving in ability when moving upwards in class; 3) we'll acknowledge equipment changes, distance changes, changes in racing surface (be it from turf to dirt or from one track to another), trainer changes, and/or jockey changes may improve a horse; 4) we'll tend to evaluate form qualitatively based on our knowledge of class, and 5) our guiding light many times in handicapping form will be a theory I call "The Sign of Life," a sudden clue of impending improvement.

Form was the dominant factor in handicapping the 1983 running of the Travers at Saratoga, August 13. The mile and a quarter, $200,000-added Travers, America's oldest continual stakes, matches 3-year-olds after they've had a chance to mature and after the leaders in the division have clearly emerged.

Although Kentucky Derby winner Sunny's Halo didn't make the race as planned because of injury, the 1983 Travers was an intriguing matchup pitting Play Fellow, winner of the Arlington Classic and American Derby in his last two starts, against Slew O' Gold, the runner-up in the Belmont Stakes; Preakness and Haskell winner Deputed Testamony; Hyperborean, an easy winner of the Swaps in his last race; and three longshots: Timeless Native, Exile King and Head of the House.

All carried scale weight of 126.

8 **SARATOGA**

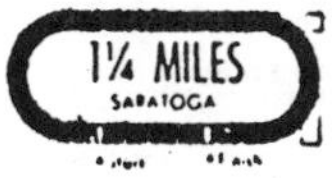

1¼ MILES. (2.00) 114th Running THE TRAVERS (Grade I). $200,000 added. 3-year-olds. Weight, 126 lbs. By subscription of $500 each, which should accompany the nomination; $1,500 to pass the entry box, with $200,000 added. The added money and all fees to be divided 60% to the winner, 22% to second, 12% to third and 6% to fourth. Starters to be named at the closing time of entries. The winner shall have its name inscribed on the Man o'War Cup and a gold-plated replica will be presented to the owner. Trophies will also be presented to the winning trainer and jockey. Closed Wednesday, July 27, 1983 with 29 nominations.

Slew O' Gold — B. c. 3, by Seattle Slew—Alluvial, by Buckpasser
Br.—Claiborne Farm (Ky)
Tr.—Watters Sidney Jr
Own.—Equusequity Stable
126 — Lifetime 11 5 2 1 $287,190 — 1983 8 3 2 1 $264,990 — 1982 3 2 0 0 $22,200

30Jly83- 9Mth fst 1⅛ :46⅗ 1:10⅖ 1:49⅕ Haskell H 5 8 8^{7} 4^{4} $5^{1\frac{1}{2}}$ 6^{4} Cordero A Jr 124 *1.00 85-17 DeputedTestamony124^{nk}BetBig116^{2}Prfitement116½ Lacked room 10

11Jun83- 8Bel fst 1½ :47⅗ 1:59⅘ 2:27⅘ Belmont 1 3 $2^{1\frac{1}{2}}$ 1½ 2^{1} $2^{3\frac{1}{2}}$ Cordero A Jr 126 *2.50 77-14 Caveat 126$^{3\frac{1}{2}}$ Slew O' Gold 126$^{1\frac{3}{4}}$ Barberstown 126no Led, wknd 15

29May83- 8Bel fst 1⅛ :45⅗ 1:09⅕ 1:46⅘ Peter Pan 5 4 2½ $1^{2\frac{1}{2}}$ 1^{8} 1^{12} Cordero A Jr 126 *.80 93-11 Slew O' Gold 126^{12} Enclose 123$^{3\frac{3}{4}}$ Foyt 117^{6} Ridden out 5

7May83- 8CD fst 1¼ :47⅕ 1:36⅘ 2:02⅕ Ky Derby 1 7 7^{8} $7^{5\frac{1}{2}}$ 3^{3} $4^{3\frac{1}{2}}$ Cordero A Jr 126 10.10 83-10 Sunny's Halo 126^{2} Desert Wine 126^{nk} Caveat 126^{1} Bothered start 20

23Apr83- 8Aqu fst 1⅛ :48⅕ 1:12⅕ 1:51 Wood Mem 1 6 5^{2} $4^{1\frac{1}{2}}$ 1^{hd} 1^{nk} Maple E 126 *1.30 80-24 Slew O' Gold 126^{nk} Parfaitement 126½ High Honors 126$^{3\frac{3}{4}}$ Driving 7

23Apr83-Run in two divisions 7th & 8th races

13Apr83- 1Aqu fst 1⅛ :48⅗ 1:12⅗ 1:50⅘ Alw 23000 4 2 1^{hd} 1^{1} 1^{6} $1^{7\frac{3}{4}}$ Cordero A Jr 117 *1.00 81-19 Slew O' Gold 117$^{7\frac{3}{4}}$ Law Talk 117$^{1\frac{1}{2}}$ El Cubano 117¾ Ridden out 6

19Mar83-10Tam fst 1$\frac{1}{16}$:48 1:13 1:47⅕ Tampa Dby 2 5 $4^{2\frac{1}{2}}$ $4^{3\frac{1}{2}}$ 2^{3} 2¾ Rivera H Jr 118 2.30 82-21 Morgnmrgnmrgn118¾SlwO'Gld118¾QckDp118^{6} Steadied, checked 14

5Mar83-10Tam fst 1$\frac{1}{16}$:47⅘ 1:13⅗ 1:47⅗ Sam F Davis 4 7 $8^{6\frac{3}{4}}$ 4^{3} $3^{2\frac{1}{2}}$ $3^{3\frac{3}{4}}$ Molina V H 118 *.40 78-23 Saverton 118$^{1\frac{3}{4}}$ Two Turns Home 120^{2} Slew O'Gold118$^{1\frac{1}{2}}$ Mild bid 8

13Nov82- 8Aqu gd 1⅛ :48⅖ 1:12⅘ 1:50⅕ Remsen 11 4 $5^{2\frac{1}{2}}$ 5^{3} 6^{10} 6^{12} Lovato F Jr 115 *1.80e 72-20 Pax In Bello 113$^{1\frac{3}{4}}$ Chumming 115^{8} PrimitivePleasure113^{hd} Tired 11

23Oct82- 9Aqu fst 1 :47 1:12⅕ 1:37⅗ Alw 20000 8 2 2½ 1^{hd} $1^{1\frac{1}{2}}$ $1^{1\frac{3}{4}}$ Lovato F Jr 117 3.70 79-21 Slew O' Gold 117$^{1\frac{3}{4}}$ Last Turn 117$^{2\frac{3}{4}}$ Chumming 122$^{2\frac{3}{4}}$ Ridden out 9

LATEST WORKOUTS Aug 11 Sar 4f fst :47⅕ b Jly 28 Mth 4f fst :47⅘ b ●Jly 23 Bel 5f fst :59⅗ h ●Jly 18 Bel 1 fst 1:38⅗ h

Head of the House — Ch. g. 3, by Mr Leader—Chez Go, by Bold Commander
Br.—Cook R J (Ky)
Tr.—Sheppard Jonathan E
Own.—Augustin Stable
126 — Lifetime 10 2 3 2 $37,191 — 1983 6 1 1 2 $23,006 — 1982 4 1 2 0 $14,185 — Turf 3 0 1 1 $8,996

31Jly83- 8Sar fst 1⅛ :46⅘ 1:10⅘ 1:49⅖ Jim Dandy 3 8 $8^{9\frac{1}{2}}$ 7^{9} 7^{6} 3½ Cruguet J b 114 30.40 87-12 APhenomenon114^{hd}TimelessNtive126½HedoftheHous114^{nk} Rallied 8

13Jly83- 8Bel fm 1¼ Ⓣ:47 1:35⅗ 2:00⅗ Lexington 8 6 6^{11} 4^{5} $5^{5\frac{1}{2}}$ 5^{4} Vasquez J b 114 7.60 87-12 Kilauea 114^{hd} Fortnightly 126$^{3\frac{1}{2}}$ Top Competitor 114^{hd} Evenly 10

2Jly83- 9Mth fm 1$\frac{1}{16}$ Ⓣ:48 1:11⅗ 1:42⅗ Lamplighter 6 7 $7^{4\frac{1}{2}}$ $2^{1\frac{1}{2}}$ $3^{2\frac{1}{2}}$ 3¾ Walford J b 111 6.70 87-20 ToughMickey115¾Domynsky120^{hd}HedoftheHouse111$^{1\frac{1}{2}}$ Weakened 11

13Jun83- 8Mth fm 1 Ⓣ:46⅕ 1:10⅖ 1:35⅗ 3↑ Alw 12500 5 8 7^{5} $4^{2\frac{1}{2}}$ $2^{2\frac{1}{2}}$ 2^{hd} Vigliotti M J b 112 4.90 97-03 Settimino118^{hd}HeadoftheHouse112^{3}MagnaMark113^{4} Just missed 10

30May83- 6Key gd 170 :46⅗ 1:11⅗ 1:42⅘ 3↑ Alw 11500 5 5 $5^{6\frac{1}{2}}$ $4^{5\frac{1}{2}}$ $4^{5\frac{1}{2}}$ 1no Vigliotti M J 108 *1.20 86-13 Head of the House 108no Molasses 99¾ Kvell 113$^{1\frac{3}{4}}$ Driving 7

14May83- 6Key fst 6f :21⅘ :44⅘ 1:11 Alw 11000 5 10 9^{13} 8^{16} 8^{16} 5^{9} Walford J 116 3.40 77-20 Gin Gimlet 109$^{1\frac{1}{2}}$ Hail to Leader 116^{hd} Norway 116^{7} Outrun 10

18Dec82- 8Med fr 1 :47⅖ 1:11⅗ 1:36⅕ Play Palace 5 5 4^{3} 5^{6} $3^{5\frac{1}{2}}$ 2^{4} Vigliotti M J 112 6.00 97-07 DputdTstmony114^{4}HdofthHos112$^{1\frac{1}{2}}$OpnonLdr114¾ Best of others 6

9Dec82- 9Med fst 170 :47⅖ 1:13⅕ 1:44⅘ Alw 13000 1 4 $5^{7\frac{1}{2}}$ 5^{7} 3^{7} 2^{nk} Dufton E 120 2.60 77-23 CaseBck114^{nk}HedoftheHouse120$^{3\frac{1}{2}}$Kevin'sTurn109$^{3\frac{1}{2}}$ Just missed 6

1Dec82- 7Med sly 1$\frac{1}{16}$:47⅗ 1:12⅗ 1:47⅕ Md Sp Wt 3 7 $7^{9\frac{1}{2}}$ $5^{8\frac{1}{2}}$ 3^{6} 1½ Dufton E 118 4.90 73-20 Head oftheHouse118½ApacheCompany118^{5}J.R.Collins118¾ Driving 8

25Nov82- 4Key fst 6f :23⅕ :47⅗ 1:14⅕ Md Sp Wt 1 8 $7^{4\frac{3}{4}}$ $6^{5\frac{3}{4}}$ $9^{8\frac{1}{2}}$ 5^{6} Dufton E 120 3.30 64-29 Rodi's Ruler 120^{nk} Mountain Freeze 120^{nk} Norway120^{4} No factor 11

LATEST WORKOUTS Aug 10 Sar 5f fst 1:00⅕ b Jly 30 Key 4f fst :50⅕ b ●Jun 28 Key 5f fst :59 h Jun 24 Key 4f fst :47⅕ h

Exile King — Ch. c. 3, by Exclusive Native—Inca Queen, by Hail to Reason
Br.—Whitney C V (Ky)
Own.—Whitney C V — Tr.—Burch William E
126 — Lifetime 5 3 0 1 $65,690 — 1983 5 3 0 1 $65,690 — 1982 0 M 0 0

31Jly83- 8Sar fst 1⅛	:46⅘ 1:10⅘ 1:49⅖	Jim Dandy	2 7 75¼ 66 54 61¼	Samyn J L	117	2.60	86-12 APhenomenon114hdTimelessNtiv126½HdofthHous114nk	No threat	8
16Apr83- 9OP fst 1⅛	:46⅖ 1:11⅗ 1:49⅖	Ark Derby	2 8 1014 811 55½ 35¼	Day P	117	4.00	91-19 Sunny's Halo 1264 Caveat 1201½ Exile King 1171½	Altered course	14
6Apr83- 9OP fst 1₁⁄₁₆	:48⅖ 1:14⅕ 1:45	Alw 30000	4 5 54½ 53 3½ 1hd	Day P	113	*1.30	83-26 Exile King 113hd Caveat 1162¾ Sligh Jet 1133½	Driving	5
22Mar83-10OP fst 1₁⁄₁₆	:48⅖ 1:13⅖ 1:45	3↑Alw 17500	9 4 62¾ 4nk 1hd 13½	Snyder L	112	4.50	83-20 Exile King 1123½ Lesion 1062 Clev Er Creek 1105½	Driving	11
5Feb83- 6GP fst 6f	:22⅗ :46 1:12	Md Sp Wt	1 8 65½ 56 1hd 1½	Samyn J L	122	5.20	79-21 Exile King 122½ Names 122nk Cold Remark 1225	Driving	12

LATEST WORKOUTS ●Aug 11 Sar 4f fst :46⅕ h — Aug 7 Sar 6f fst 1:12 h — Aug 6 Sar 3f fst :39 b — Jly 28 Sar 5f fst :59⅗ h

Deputed Testamony * — B. c. 3, by Traffic Cop—Proof Requested, by Prove It
Br.—Bonita Farm (Md)
Own.—Palev Stable — Tr.—Boniface J William
126 — Lifetime 15 9 3 0 $588,654 — 1983 8 5 1 0 $533,800 — 1982 7 4 2 0 $54,854

30Jly83- 9Mth fst 1⅛	:46⅗ 1:10⅖ 1:49⅕	Haskell H	6 10 109 54 3nk 1nk	McCauley W H	124	3.80e	89-17 Deputed Testamony 124nk Bet Big 1162Parfaitement116½	Driving	10
16Jly83- 8Bow fst 1⅛	:48⅖ 1:12⅘ 1:50⅖	Gov's Cup H	4 5 53½ 53½ 2hd 1nk	McCauley W H	124	*1.00	93-17 DeputedTestmony124nkCountryPine1195BtBig1173¾	Steadied, dr.	5
11Jun83- 8Bel fst 1½	:47⅖ 1:59⅘ 2:27⅘	Belmont	14 2 32½ 67 75¾ 65¾	Miller D A Jr	126	9.80	75-14 Caveat 1263½ Slew O' Gold 1261½ Barberstown126no	Drift'd, wknd	15
21May83- 8Pim sly 1³⁄₁₆	:46⅘ 1:10⅗ 1:55⅖	Preakness	3 4 54 64 1½ 12¾	Miller D A Jr	126	14.50e	93-11 DeputedTestmony1262¾DsrtWin1264HighHonors1261½	Ridden out	12
14May83- 8Key fst 170	:47 1:12⅕ 1:42⅖	Keystone	2 3 4¾ 1½ 1½ 14½	McCauley W H	122	*.90	88-20 DptdTstmony1224½ClsscStd115noTwoDvds1194½	Stumbled st.clear	10
28Apr83- 7Kee sly 1⅛	:46⅘ 1:11 1:49⅖	Blue Grass	9 7 710 79 78¼ 615	Hawley S	121	13.40	75-16 Play Fellow 121no ⓓMarfa 1217½ Desert Wine 1211	Outrun	12
16Apr83- 8Pim fst 1₁⁄₁₆	:47⅗ 1:12 1:42⅘	ⓈFedrco Tesio	7 5 54½ 3½ 11 12¼	McCauley W H	116	*1.60e	91-17 DeputedTestamony1162¼DixielandBnd122½IslndChmp1101	Driving	8
4Apr83- 8Key fst 6½f	:22⅗ :45⅘ 1:17⅕	Alw 17000	4 4 43 3½ 21½ 21½	McCauley W H	113	4.30	85-26 TwoDvids1141½DeputedTestmony1131¾DixielndBnd1136¾	Bobbled	6
18Dec82- 8Med fr 1	:47⅖ 1:11⅖ 1:36⅕	Play Palace	4 3 21½ 11 13 14	McCauley W H	114	*1.10	101-07 DeputdTstmony1144HdofthHous1121½OpinionLdr114¾	Ridden out	6
27Nov82- 8Lrl fst 1₁⁄₁₆	:47⅘ 1:13⅘ 1:45⅕	ⓈMaryland Juv	2 6 63½ 54 42½ 2no	Miller D A Jr	122	9.10	82-26 Dixieland Band 122no Deputed Testamony1221½Caveat1223½	Wide	9

LATEST WORKOUTS Aug 8 Sar 1 fst 1:44⅘ b — Jly 8 Pim 1 fst 1:43 h

Hyperborean — Gr. c. 3, by Icecapade—La Queenie, by Prince John
Br.—Crescent Farm & Gainesway Farm (Ky)
Own.—Singer C B — Tr.—Fanning Jerry
126 — Lifetime 13 3 2 2 $160,700 — 1983 11 2 2 2 $151,350 — 1982 2 1 0 0 $9,350 — Turf 3 0 1 0 $10,000

24Jly83- 8Hol fst 1¼	:46⅗ 1:35⅕ 2:01	Swaps	8 1 11 13 13½ 13	Toro F	b 115	9.70	86-14 Hyperborean 1153 My Habitony 120hd TanksBrigade1203½	Driving	9
3Jly83- 8Hol fst 1⅛	:46 1:10 1:48⅗	Sil Screen H	1 2 21½ 1hd 2hd 31	Toro F	b 115	7.50	85-16 My Habitony115nkTanksBrigade119¾Hyperborean115nk	Weakened	6
26Jun83- 7Hol fst 6½f	:22 :44⅘ 1:15⅘	3↑Alw 22000	4 6 52½ 53 56½ 54¾	Lipham T	b 113	*2.20	86-09 Son Of Song 112½ Record Catch 113¾ LeonLeon1153½	Bumped st.	7
19Jun83- 7Hol fst 7f	:22⅖ :45⅗ 1:21⅗	3↑Alw 22000	7 — — — — —	Lipham T	b 113	2.50	— — Run OfDiamonds117noLeonLeon1151½Can'tBeBeat1162	Lost rider	7
11Jun83- 8Hol fm 1₁⁄₁₆	Ⓣ:48 1:13⅗ 1:43	Cinema H	4 3 41½ 31 3½ 74½	Sibille R	115	27.10	79-16 Baron O'Dublin 115¾ Tanks Brigade 119hd Re Ack 1162	Tired	9
21May83- 8Hol fm 1₁⁄₁₆	Ⓣ:46⅕ 1:10⅖ 1:41⅖	W Rogers H	9 1 2½ 2hd 1½ 64½	Valenzuela P A	116	13.90	87-10 Barberstown 1161 Lover Boy Leslie 117½TanksBrigade1201½	Tired	13
8May83- 8Hol fm 1	Ⓣ:47⅖ 1:11⅕ 1:36	Spotlight H	1 1 1½ 1½ 2½ 2no	Lipham T	b 114	4.00	88-10 TnksBrigde119noHyperboren114½BuriedTresure1151½	Drifted late	7
8May83-Run in two divisions 6th & 8th races;									
3Apr83- 3SA fst 6f	:22 :45 1:10⅘	Alw 24000	2 6 1hd 21½ 42½ 52	Lipham T	b 120	*.90	82-16 Kona Hills 120nk Grenoble 120hd American Legion 1201½	Tired	7
16Mar83- 8SA fst 1₁⁄₁₆	:46⅕ 1:10⅘ 1:42⅗	S Catalina	6 4 52½ 31 33 22½	Hansen R D	114	11.30	85-17 FstPssge1162½Hyperboren114hdMyHbitony1143	Bumped aft start	8

LATEST WORKOUTS Jly 19 Hol 6f fst 1:15 h — Jly 13 Hol 6f fst 1:15 h — ●Jun 21 Hol 5f fst :58⅕ h

Play Fellow * — B. c. 3, by On The Sly—Play For Keeps, by Run For Nurse
Br.—Bakewell Mr-Mrs P III (Ky)
Own.—Vanier Nancy & Lauer & Victor — Tr.—Vanier Harvey L
126 — Lifetime 14 6 4 1 $297,288 — 1983 10 5 1 1 $284,068 — 1982 4 1 3 0 $13,220

17Jly83- 8AP fst 1¼	:48⅕ 1:38⅗ 2:04⅖	Amer Derby	4 4 54½ 2hd 11 13½	Day P	b 123	*.30	75-22 Play Fellow 1233½ Le Cou Cou114noBrother1142	Wide, ridden out	8
12Jun83- 8AP fst 1⅛	:46⅘ 1:10⅘ 1:49	Arl Classic	2 8 67 53¾ 1½ 13	Day P	b 123	4.80	86-27 Play Fellow 1233 Bet Big 1143½ Passing Base 114½	Ridden out	9
21May83- 8Pim sly 1³⁄₁₆	:46⅘ 1:10⅗ 1:55⅖	Preakness	1 7 75½ 86½ 76½ 58½	Cruguet J	b 126	8.30	84-11 DeputedTestmony1262¾DesrtWin1264HighHonors1261½	Bid, hung	12
7May83- 8CD fst 1¼	:47⅕ 1:36⅘ 2:02⅕	Ky Derby	2 11 1012 64½ 54½ 64½	Cruguet J	b 126	10.90	81-10 Sunny's Halo 1262 Desert Wine 126nk Caveat 1261	Well up, hung	20
28Apr83- 7Kee sly 1⅛	:46⅘ 1:11 1:49⅖	Blue Grass	3 12 812 45½ 1hd 1no	Cruguet J	b 121	19.40	90-16 Play Fellow 121no ⓓMarfa 1217½ Desert Wine 1211	Driving	12
2Apr83-10Hia fst 1⅛	:47⅕ 1:11⅕ 1:49⅖	Flamingo	1 9 139½128½117 103¾	Cruguet J	b 118	4.70	81-18 CurrntHop122nkChumming118½Gn'lPrctitionr1221½	Wide, brushed	14
19Mar83-10Hia fst 1⅛	:45⅗ 1:09⅗ 1:48⅘	Everglades	9 10 108¾ 68 55 3½	Cruguet J	b 112	*1.30	87-18 Gen'lPractitioner112hdOhMyWindland112½PlayFellow112½	Rallied	12
28Feb83- 7GP fst 7f	:22⅖ :45 1:23⅖	Alw 21000	5 5 67 67 31½ 15½	Cruguet J	b 122	*1.10	87-24 Play Fellow 1225½ Smart Style 1171½GunCarriage1171	Ridden out	8
9Feb83- 8GP fst 7f	:22 :44⅘ 1:23⅗	Alw 14000	9 9 109 99½ 3nk 12	Cruguet J	b 119	*1.60	86-24 Play Fellow 1192 Tarmoud 1171 High Honors 117nk	Handily	12
26Jan83- 8GP fst 6f	:22 :45 1:09⅘	Alw 14000	2 6 95½ 66 24 22½	Cruguet J	b 119	6.40	87-20 Justice Sanders 1172½ Play Fellow 1198 El Perico 1172	2nd best	10

LATEST WORKOUTS Aug 9 Sar 5f fst 1:00⅕ b — ●Aug 4 Sar 1 fst 1:41⅘ b

Timeless Native — Ch. c. 3, by Timeless Moment—Head Off, by Executioner
Br.—Clay J E (Ky)
Own.—Hawksworth Farm — Tr.—Delp Grover G
126 — Lifetime 6 4 1 0 $136,782 — 1983 5 3 1 0 $132,882 — 1982 1 1 0 0 $3,900

31Jly83- 8Sar fst 1⅛	:46⅘ 1:10⅘ 1:49⅖	Jim Dandy	5 5 31½ 32 21 2hd	Graell A	126	6.20	88-12 APhenomenon114hdTimelessNtive126½HedoftheHous114nk	Sharp	8
2Jly83- 9Aks fst 1₁⁄₁₆	:46 1:10⅕ 1:43⅗	Gold Cup H	12 2 21 11 15 14½	Franklin R J	114	4.90	85-18 Timeless Native 1144½ Shamtastic 1203 Anticipative114nk	Driving	12
18Jun83- 9Aks sl 1₁⁄₁₆	:50⅖ 1:16 1:52⅗	Four H	7 6 68½ 34 2½ 44	Franklin R J	115	*1.40	36-49 Shamtastic 1183 Anticipative 111½LuckySalvation118½	Weakened	7
29May83- 9LaD fst 6½f	:23 :46 1:16⅗	Airline	6 3 31½ 11 13½ 17	Franklin R J	115	*.70	92-14 Timeless Native 1157NeedAQuarter1172½ProudEnvoy1151	Handily	6
22Apr83- 3LaD fst 6f	:22⅘ :46 1:10⅖	Alw 12000	5 3 2½ 2hd 11½ 16½	Franklin R J	114	*2.10	91-16 Timeless Native 1146½ JayBarToughie1124AndyCary114nk	Driving	8
10Jly82- 3Atl fst 5f	:22⅖ :46 :58⅘	Md Sp Wt	8 6 21½ 2hd 12 12	Tejeira J	120	*.90	93-19 TimelessNative1202AlwaysPolite1204FirstSpeaker1207	Drew clear	8

LATEST WORKOUTS Aug 11 Sar 4f fst :51 b — Jun 16 Aks 3f sly :37⅗ b

With the benefit of hindsight, from his two victories and loss by a neck in the Jockey Gold Cup, Woodward and Marlboro, respectively, Slew O' Gold was a 3-year-old of exceptional quality. But he wasn't my selection in the Travers. Or my bet. Play Fellow was.

Slew O' Gold, who was fourth by three and a quarter lengths in the Kentucky Derby, came into his own with a twelve length laugher in the Peter Pan Stakes at Belmont. He then was second in the Belmont Stakes by three and a half lengths to Caveat before running a dull sixth by four lengths versus Deputed Testamony in the Haskell at Monmouth Park. The comment in the *Form* for Slew O' Gold in the Haskell was "lacked room," but even his jockey, Cordero, admitted his horse didn't fire when Cordero asked him.

On Saratoga's speed-favoring strip, Slew O' Gold's early speed was dangerous. It would've been more dangerous without the presence of Hyperborean, who won the rich, 1¼ mile Swaps at Hollywood Park wire-to-wire by three lengths. He was picking up eleven pounds from the race, and his connections' late decision to enter the Travers gave him precious little time to get used to the track. But Hyperborean still figured as a factor on or near the lead.

With two proven speed horses in the race, Play Fellow figured to have a good chance at getting his race: coming off a legitimate pace.

Play Fellow's form was impeccable. He had followed his nose victory in the Blue Grass with mediocre performances in the Kentucky Derby (sixth by four and a half) and Preakness (fifth by eight and a half). But then at Arlington Park in Chicago, Play Fellow had blossomed, winning the 1⅛ mile Arlington Classic by three lengths (soundly beating Sunny's Halo in the process) and the 1¼ mile American Derby by three and a quarter as the 3 to 10 favorite.

Play Fellow was clearly at the top of his game.

Deputed Testamony was too, having won four of five races around a sixth place finish by five and three-quarters lengths in the Belmont Stakes. His performance in the Belmont Stakes, the 1½ mile final leg of the Triple Crown, forced me to question the distance ability of this overachiever despite his win in the 1³⁄₁₆ mile Preakness. The comment from his race in the Belmont Stakes in the *Form* was "drifted, weakened."

In the Travers, a sixteenth of a mile longer than the Preakness, he wasn't a factor.

Slew O' Gold stalked and eventually ran down Hyperborean, but couldn't sustain Play Fellow's strong charge in the middle of the track under Pay Day's guidance. At 5 to 2, Play Fellow paid $7.60 for the one and three-quarters length win. Play Fellow probably should have been 3 to 2 off his last two easy victories. We will play 5 to 2 horses when we think they're overlays.

EIGHTH RACE
Saratoga
AUGUST 13, 1983

1 1/4 MILES. (2.00) 114th Running THE TRAVERS (Grade I). $200,000 added. 3-year-olds. Weight, 126 lbs. By subscription of $500 each, which should accompany the nomination; $1,500 to pass the entry box, with $200,000 added. The added money and all fees to be divided 60% to the winner, 22% to second, 12% to third and 6% to fourth. Starters to be named at the closing time of entries. The winner shall have its name inscribed on the Man o'War Cup and a gold-plated replica will be presented to the owner. Trophies will also be presented to the winning trainer and jockey. Closed Wednesday, July 27, 1983 with 29 nominations.

Value of race $225,000, value to winner $135,000, second $49,500, third $27,000, fourth $13,500.   Mutuel pool $590,166, OTB pool $669,062.

Last Raced	Horse	Eqt.	A.	Wt.	PP	1/4	1/2	3/4	1	Str	Fin	Jockey	r	Odds $1
17Jly83 8AP 1	Play Fellow	b	3	126	6	5-1	5-3	5-1½	3 ½	3-2½	1-1¾	Day P		2.80
30Jly83 9Mth 6	Slew O' Gold		3	126	1	2-1½	2-5	1hd	2-3	2-1	2-2½	Cordero A Jr		2.40
24Jly83 8Hol 1	Hyperborean	b	3	126	5	1-1½	1 ½	2-7	1hd	1hd	3-2½	Toro F		19.80
30Jly83 9Mth 1	Deputed Testamony		3	126	4	4-1	4-1½	3 ½	4-1½	4-1½	4-1¾	McCauley W H		2.90
31Jly83 8Sar 6	Exile King		3	126	3	7	6 ½	6-3	5-6	5-6	5-7¾	Maple E		3.20
31Jly83 8Sar 3	Head of the House	b	3	126	2	6hd	7	7	6-2	6-8	6	Vasquez J		12.70
31Jly83 8Sar 2	Timeless Native		3	126	7	3-1½	3-1	4hd	7	7	—	Pincay L Jr		4.60

Timeless Native, Eased.
OFF AT 5:40. Start good, Won driving. Time, :23, :46 4/5, 1:10 1/5, 1:35 2/5, 2:01 Track good.

6- PLAY FELLOW..	7.60	3.80	3.40
1- SLEW O' GOLD..		3.80	3.00
5- HYPERBOREAN...			5.00

$ 2 Mutuel Prices:

B. c, by On The Sly-Play For Keeps, by Run For Nurse. Trainer Vanier Harvey L. Bred by Bakewell Mr-Mrs P III (Ky).
    PLAY FELLOW, reserved for six furlongs, rallied while racing well out from the rail approaching the stretch, caught the leaders from the outside nearing the final sixteenth and drew clear under brisk urging. SLEW O'GOLD moved to the outside of HYPERBOREAN racing into the first turn, prompted the pace into the backstretch, caught that rival nearing the far turn, raced forwardly to the final sixteenth and drifted out some while weakening. DEPUTED TESTAMONY moved with play fellow while racing outside that rival approaching the stretch but tired during the drive. EXILE KING movd within striking distance leaving the far turn but lacked a further response. HEAD OF THE HOUSE was always outrun. TIMELESS RIDE, finished approaching the end of the backstretch, was eased during the late states. DEPUTED TESTAMONY raced with mud caulks.
    Owners- 1, Lauer C; 2, Equusequity Stable; 3, Singer C B; 4, Palev Stable; 5, Whitney C V; 6, Augustin Stable; 7, Hawksworth Farm.
    Trainers- 1, Vanier Harvey L; 2, Watters Sidney Jr; 3, Fanning Jerry; 4, Boniface J William; 5, Burch William E; 6, Sheppard Jonathan E; 7, Delp Grover G.

From a top stakes race, let's go to humbler beginnings.

A lot of handicappers dislike maiden races. I've always done well with them, and I would argue they are often easier to handicap. Maidens with only two or three past performance lines are just beginning their careers, and are more apt to either try their hardest or not try at all for several of their initial starts as they learn what they are doing. If we maintain a perspective of looking for a young or inexperienced horse to improve as he makes his first few starts, we will be very careful when we gauge the form the horse has shown in prior races. Often, their lines show an indication of improvement which may not be readily seen by evaluating the finish alone. Thus a horse can have two lifetime starts, each a sixth place finish, but show significant improvement in the second start, improvement which likely will be built upon in the next start, perhaps at a juicy overlay. Consider our mythical Horse A, and her two race career:

6/24 Bel fst 6f :23 :46 4/5 1:11 3/5 MdnSpWt 3 4 2$^{1/2}$ 3^1 3^2 6^5 12-1 tired

6/5 Bel fst 6f :23 :46 2/5 1:13 MdnSpWt 8 8 6[5] 6[6] 6[6] 6[10] 6-1 outrun

A quick glance at these two lines would prompt a bettor to pass on Horse A. Closer examination would reveal improvement, and point out she received action at the windows for her debut, going off at 6 to 1. She must have done something in her workouts preparing for her first start that suggested she has some ability. She ran poorly, losing by ten lengths and running six furlongs in 1:15. Ignored at 12 to 1 her next start, she suddenly showed a desire to get in front of horses, moving up to second by half a length at the quarter call, remaining a length within the leader after a half and then tiring in the stretch. In doing so, she still raced the same six furlong distance in 1:12 3/5 (let's assume for our example the track variant was constant for the two races). I would expect Horse A to show continued improvement in her third start. She might not win, but she should be a good value at what would have to be a generous price off a pair of sixth place finishes. Keep in mind if she didn't show the poor first race and only the second one, she'd likely be bet much heavier, say to 4 to 1, in her next start. Because of her initial poor race, you could get 6 to 1 or 8 to 1, and you're getting the advantage of having already seen her improve once. A horse such as this one isn't a lock, yet could compare favorably with other horses in her next race who will be bet more.

Let's do a real race.

This 1983 race at Saratoga was an $18,000, seven furlong maiden special weight for fillies and mares, 3-year-olds and up. Seven scratches still left a bulky field of thirteen.

4 SARATOGA

7 FURLONGS. (1.20⅘) MAIDEN SPECIAL WEIGHT. Purse $18,000. Fillies and Mares. 3-year-olds and up. Weights: 3-year-olds, 117 lbs.; older, 122 lbs.

Coupled—Crystal Key and Eyeliner.

Keys 'N' Keys — B. f. 3, by Key To The Kingdom—Empress Erin, by Gentle Art
Own.—Humphrey G W Jr — Br.—Owens C & N D & P T (Ky) — Tr.—Kay Michael — **117**
Lifetime 3 0 3 0 $12,100 — 1983 3 M 3 0 $12,100 — 1982 0 M 0 0

22Jly83- 6Bel fst 1 :47⅘ 1:13⅖ 1:39 3+ⒻMd pwt 6 6 6⁷½ 6⁵ 4⁶½ 2⁶ McCarron G 116 2.60 64-26 Nonchalance 116⁶ Keys 'N'Keys116¾Neopolitan116¾ Gained place 8
3Jly83- 6Bel fst 6½f :22⅗ :46⅗ 1:19⅖ 3+ⒻMd Sp Wt 10 9 9⁸ 6⁸½ 4⁴½ 2³½ McCarron G 116 *2.10 75-18 It's Fine 116³½ Keys 'N' Keys 116²½ Toute Suite Lil 116² Rallied 12
3Jun83- 4Bel fst 6f :22⅗ :46⅕ 1:12 ⒻMd Sp Wt 13 9 11¹² 9¹¹ 6⁶½ 2³ McCarron G 121 5.50e 79-18 SauceOfLife121³Keys'N'Keys121hdDee'sDilem121²½ Wide stretch 14
LATEST WORKOUTS Jly 4 Bel 5f fst 1:01 h — Jun 15 Bel 3f fst :35⅘ hg — Jun 9 Bel 6f fst 1:15⅕ h

Last Word Susie — B. f. 3, by Dance Spell—Access Time, by Gallant Man
Own.—Schwartz B K — Br.—Jones R B Jr (Pa) — Tr.—Trovato Joseph A — **117**
Lifetime 1 0 0 0 — 1983 1 M 0 0 — 1982 0 M 0 0

May83- 6Bel my 6f :22⅕ :45⅗ 1:11⅘ ⒻMd Sp Wt 3 4 10¹¹ 8⁸¾ 7⁷½ 5²¾ Venezia M 121 *2.90 81-11 Smuggled 121hd Parisian Print 121¹¾ Sauce Of Life 121¾ Rallied 13
LATEST WORKOUTS ●Jly 14 Aqu Ⓣ 4f fm :50 b (d) — Jun 17 Aqu ⊡ 4f fst :48 h — ●Jun 12 Aqu ⊡ 4f fst :48⅕ h — Jun 6 Aqu ⊡ 4f fst :51⅘ b

Toute Suite Lil — B. f. 3, by Exclusive Native—Gala Lil, by Sprin Double
Br.—Rutherford M G (Ky) | Tr.—Jolley Leroy | Own.—Rutherford M G | 117
Lifetime 2 0 0 2 $3,660 | 1983 2 M 0 2 $3,660 | 1982 0 M 0 0

8Jly83- 6Bel fst 6½f :22⅘ :46⅘ 1:19⅘ 3+ⒻMd Sp Wt 6 4 32½ 32 23 35¾ Cruguet J 116 3.00 73-18 It's Fine 1163½ Keys 'N' Keys 1162½ ToutesuiteLil1162 Weakened 12
25Feb83- 4GP fst 6f :23 :47⅘ 1:12 ⒻMd Sp Wt 11 4 1½ 11 23 313 Fell J 121 2.00 66-19 Menteuse11613YouWon'tBeSorry121noToutSuitLil1211 Weakened 12
LATEST WORKOUTS Jly 29 Sar 5f fst 1:00⅘ h Jly 21 Bel 7f fst 1:29 b Jly 16 Bel 6f fst 1:16⅕ b ●Jly 7 Bel 3f fst :35 h

Elevator Girl — Ch. f. 3, by Raise A Native—Unconclous Doll, by Unconscious
Br.—Green C C (Ky) | Tr.—DiMauro Stephen | Own.—Dogwood Stable | 117
Lifetime 6 0 2 0 $8,570 | 1983 6 M 2 0 $8,570 | 1982 0 M 0 0

25Jly83- 2Bel my 6f :22⅘ :45⅘ 1:12⅘ 3+ⒻMd Sp Wt 9 2 32½ 43½ 33 2¾ Santagata N b 116 3.20 78-19 Nutmeg 111¾ Elevator Girl 1163 Foolish Clover 1162¾ Wide 10
30Jun83- 5Bel fst 6f :22⅘ :46⅕ 1:11⅘ 3+ⒻMd Sp Wt 3 2 43 33 23½ 22¼ Santagata N b 114 34.00 81-23 Wild Beat 1222¼ Elevator Girl 114¾ Down Stage 1143 Game try 14
12Jun83- 6Bel fst 6½f :22⅘ :45⅘ 1:18⅘ 3+ⒻMd Sp Wt 13 1 32 32 43½ 76¾ Santagata N b 114 20.90f 77-13 Bonne Bouche 114¾ Dink 1072½ Gold Heist 1142¾ Tired 13
30May83- 6Bel my 6f :22⅕ :45⅘ 1:11⅘ ⒻMd Sp Wt 7 2 1hd 1hd 32½ 95¾ MacBeth D b 121 9.10f 78-11 Smuggled 121hd Parisian Print 1211¼ Sauce OfLife121¾ Gave way 13
27Jan83- 4GP fst 6f :22 :45⅘ 1:11⅘ ⒻMd Sp Wt 2 6 33½ 46 610 89½ Hernandez C 121 19.60 70-23 Carom 121no Stewpendus Stew 1212½OutstandingJade121nk Tired 12
13Jan83- 6GP fst 6f :22⅘ :46⅘ 1:12 ⒻMd Sp Wt 1 11 42½ 42½ 43 48 Hernandez C 121 10.60 71-21 Idle Gossip 1213 Laurel Dell 1214 Kouklamou 1211 Tired 12
LATEST WORKOUTS Jly 23 Bel tr.t 3f fst :37⅘ b Jly 12 Bel tr.t 5f fst 1:02 b Jly 7 Bel tr.t 4f fst :52 b Jun 23 Bel tr.t 4f fst :49⅕ b

Dink — B. f. 3, by Proudest Roman—Come Ashore, by Tudor Way
Br.—Stephens Lucille E (Ky) | Tr.—Stephens Woodford C | Own.—Stephens Lucille E | 112⁵
Lifetime 6 0 3 1 $14,040 | 1983 4 M 2 1 $10,300 | 1982 2 M 1 0 $3,740 | Turf 2 0 1 0 $4,180

25Jly83- 9Bel sf 1⅛ Ⓣ:47⅘ 1:13⅘ 1:48⅘ 3+ⒻMd Sp Wt 2 8 78½ 42 11½ 2¾ Maple E 116 3.00 52-43 Strewth 116¾ Dink 1163½ I'm Tard 1163¾ Gamely 11
10Jly83- 9Bel fm 1⅛ Ⓣ:47 1:11⅘ 1:42⅘ 3+Md Sp Wt 8 1 11 1½ 2½ 69¾ Maple E 111 6.30 75-20 Antigua 1111½ Penzance 1165 Makarios 122½ Used up 12
22Jun83- 5Bel fst 7f :23⅘ :46⅘ 1:25⅕ 3+ⒻMd Sp Wt 1 3 11 2hd 2hd 34¾ Maple E 114 *1.30 71-22 Irish Liberal 1093 Magaro 1141¾ Dink 1143 Weakened 8
12Jun83- 6Bel fst 6½f :22⅘ :45⅘ 1:18⅘ 3+ⒻMd Sp Wt 11 2 42 42½ 31½ 2¾ Shelton R L7 107 4.00 82-13 Bonne Bouche 114¾ Dink 1072½ Gold Heist 1142¾ Rallied 13
8Aug82- 6Sar fst 6f :22⅕ :46 1:12⅕ ⒻMd Sp Wt 6 7 32 2½ 52¾ 66½ Maple E 117 *2.30 72-14 Rob's Lady 117¾ Spit Curl 1171¼ Blond Bomber 1171 Gave way 12
31Jly82- 6Bel fst 5½f :23 :46⅘ 1:05⅘ ⒻMd Sp Wt 3 3 3½ 2hd 22 24¾ Maple E 117 2.90 81-15 Lee Vista 1174¾ Dink 1171½ Lady Sauce Boat 1173¾ Drifted out 9
LATEST WORKOUTS Aug 1 Sar 4f fst :48 h Jly 23 Bel 4f fst :51⅕ b Jly 19 Bel 5f sly 1:05⅘ b Jly 9 Bel 3f fst :36 b

Charlottetown — B. f. 3, by Ambernash—Kenilworth Gal, by Pretense
Br.—Miller Mr-Mrs W J (Md) | Tr.—Watters Eric | Own.—Waters E | 122
Lifetime 1 0 0 0 | 1983 1 M 0 0 | 1982 0 M 0 0

14May83- 5Aqu fst 6f :22⅘ :46⅘ 1:11⅘ ⒻMd Sp Wt 8 7 44½ 54½ 47½ 314 Clayton M D5 116 22.70Ⓓ 70-20 Gnash 1216¾ Sauce Of Life 1167 ⒹCharlottetown 116¾ Came over 8
14May83-Disqualified and placed seventh

Precious Perfect — Dk. b. or br. f. 4, by Proudest Roman—Devon Lang, by Bold Favorit
Br.—Owens & Shaw (Ky) | Tr.—Gillen Christina E | Own.—Ocean Summit Stable | 112⁵
Lifetime 21 0 2 3 $6,800 | 1983 3 M 0 0 | 1982 17 M 2 3 $6,800 | Turf 2 0 0 0 $1,080

7Feb83- 4Aqu my 6f ⊡:23⅘ :47⅕ 1:13 ⒻMd Sp Wt 7 6 54½ 56½ 56¾ 57¾ Santagata N b 122 25.40 71-17 A Little Princess122noGail'sWish1223EeMyMy1221 Lacked a rally 8
28Jan83- 6Aqu fst 6f ⊡:24⅕ :48⅘ 1:14⅕ ⒻMd Sp Wt 2 13 115 1111 812 88¾ Clayton M D7 b 115 21.20 65-25 Lost Crown 1223½ Ee My My 122nk Bandy's Miss 122¾ No factor 14
6Jan83- 2Aqu fst 170 ⊡:49 1:15 1:45⅘ ⒻMd Sp Wt 5 2 21½ 43 711 613 Alvarado R Jr5 b 117 *1.60 62-16 Mia Reale 1227 Enthraller 122¾ Q. T. Lady 117nk Steadied 7
18Dec82- 3Aqu fst 6f ⊡:24 :48⅘ 1:12⅘ 3+ⒻMd Sp Wt 3 3 63 65½ 56¾ 35 Alvarado R Jr5 b 115 13.00 75-20 Svarga 1205 Stylography 120nk Precious Perfect 115no Railied 7
25Nov82- 1Aqu sf 1⅛ Ⓣ:49⅘ 1:15⅘ 1:54⅘ 3+Md Sp Wt 2 2 34½ 31 510 513 Migliore R b 117 23.90 58-28 Lovely Duckling 114noJeffersWest1204¾TroopShip120nk Gave way 7
10Nov82- 1Aqu fm 1⅛ Ⓣ:49⅘ 1:14⅘ 1:46 3+ⒻMd Sp Wt 6 3 21½ 32½ 35 47½ Migliore R b 120 36.90 68-25 PolitcsNTrcks1204¾LovlyDuckling1222¾SvnYrltch120no Weakened 8
31Oct82- 7Aqu fst 6f :22⅘ :46⅕ 1:11 3+ⒻMd Sp Wt 6 6 811 814 713 713 Bailey J D b 119 28.20 73-18 Je'Da Qua 1193¾ What An Act 1194 LoyalDiplomat119¾ No Speed 8
1Aug82- 6RD fst 6f :22⅘ :46⅘ 1:13⅕ 3+ⒻMd Sp Wt 2 6 66 58½ 48 25 Headley O b 117 2.70 72-27 I See Spring 1075 Precious Perfect 1172Silk'nFleece122nk Rallied 7
18Jly82- 3RD fst 6f :22⅘ :47⅕ 1:13⅘ 3+ⒻMd Sp Wt 4 10 1110 89½ 63½ 43 Headley O b 115 4.30 73-27 Miss Self 115¾ Seal's Lullaby 106nk Rise To Glory 1092 Late foot 11
10Jly82- 5EIP fst 1 :47⅕ 1:12⅕ 1:39⅘ 3+ⒻMd Sp Wt 5 4 52½ 62½ 76 611 Bealmear B L b 113 8.80 74-09 Straight Bad Girl 113hdMyJaneEllen1131¾ReinFree107¾ No threat 9
LATEST WORKOUTS Jly 31 Sar tr.t 3f fst :38⅘ b Jly 25 Sar Ⓣ 5f fm 1:01⅘ h Jly 20 Sar 5f fst 1:03 b Jly 15 Sar tr.t 4f fst :53 b

That Satin Doll — B. f. 3, by Hagley—Bundle Of Love, by Tudorka
Br.—Watters S Jr (Md) | Tr.—Watters Sidney Jr | Own.—Watters S Jr | 117
Lifetime 4 0 0 0 $1,140 | 1983 4 M 0 0 $1,140 | 1982 0 M 0 0 | Turf 3 0 0 0 $1,140

25Jly83- 9Bel sf 1⅛ Ⓣ:47⅘ 1:13⅘ 1:48⅘ 3+ⒻMd Sp Wt 8 3 1hd 1½ 21½ 58¾ Clayton M D5 111 13.80 44-43 Strewth 116¾ Dink 1163½ I'm Tard 1163¾ Gave way 11
8Jun83- 4Bel fm 1¼ Ⓣ:49 1:39⅘ 2:05 3+ⒻMd Sp Wt 5 3 36 23 23 73¼ Clayton M D5 109 40.30 66-22 Belwood Jule 1221¼ Rolfe's Ruby 114¾ Jelsomina 1141 Tired 12
28May83- 5Bel yl 1⅛ Ⓣ:48⅘ 1:15⅘ 1:49⅘ 3+ⒻMd Sp Wt 10 4 54½ 65½ 56 48¼ Clayton M D5 108 42.00 42-49 Infinite 1144 Countess Cork 117nk Betty's Bullet 1144 Evenly 12
22May83- 6Bel my 6f :22⅘ :46 1:11 3+ⒻMd Sp Wt 4 6 914 915 919 921 Miranda J 113 6.10 66-14 Chic Belle 1062¾ Beneficence 1132¾ Sauce Of Life1082¾ No speed 10
LATEST WORKOUTS Jly 13 Bel 6f fst 1:15⅘ b Jly 1 Bel 5f fst 1:00⅘ h Jun 22 Bel 5f fst 1:01⅘ h Jun 16 Bel 4f fst :49 b

Parisian Print — Dk. b. or br. f. 3, by Fire Dancer—Wannigan, by Besomer
Br.—Newchance Farm (Fla) | Tr.—Marcus Alan B | Own.—Chalk Phyllis P | 117
Lifetime 3 0 1 0 $3,960 | 1983 3 M 1 0 $3,960 | 1982 0 M 0 0

30Jun83- 5Bel fst 6f :22⅘ :46⅕ 1:11⅘ 3+ⒻMd Sp Wt 11 6 32 43½ 913 1215 Smith A Jr b 114 10.00 69-23 Wild Beat 1222¼ Elevator Girl 114¾ Down Stage 1143 Tired 14
12Jun83- 6Bel fst 6½f :22⅘ :45⅘ 1:18⅘ 3+ⒻMd Sp Wt 1 13 52½ 55 1113 1216 Smith A Jr b 114 *1.40 67-13 Bonne Bouche 114¾ Dink 1072½ Gold Heist 1142¾ Broke slowly 13
30May83- 6Bel my 6f :22⅕ :45⅘ 1:11⅘ ⒻMd Sp Wt 11 10 33 2hd 12 2hd Smith A Jr b 121 37.50 84-11 Smuggled 121hd Parisian Print 1211¼ SauceOfLife121¾ Just failed 13
LATEST WORKOUTS Jun 27 Bel tr.t 4f fst :51 b ●Jun 8 Bel tr.t 5f fst :59⅘ h

Vandy's Joy — Dk. b. or br. f. 3, by Good Counsel—Vandy Girl, by Prince John
Br.—Phillips Mr-Mrs J W (Ky) | Tr.—Rondinello Thomas L | Own.—Phillips J W | 117
Lifetime 2 0 0 0 $1,210 | 1983 2 M 0 0 $1,210 | 1982 0 M 0 0

25Jly83- 2Bel my 6f :22⅘ :45⅘ 1:12⅘ 3+ⒻMd Sp Wt 7 5 76½ 67¾ 47 46½ Beitia E b 116 9.00e 72-19 Nutmeg 111¾ Elevator Girl 1163 Foolish Clover 1162¾ No menace 10
21Jan83- 4GP my 6f :21⅘ :46 1:12⅕ ⒻMd Sp Wt 9 9 89 97 86½ 87 Solomone M b 121 24.10 71-19 Runski 121¾ Virginia Reel 1211 Clover Miss 121½ Reared at start 12
LATEST WORKOUTS Jly 31 Sar 5f fst 1:06 b Jly 29 Sar 4f fst :50⅘ b Jly 23 Bel 4f fst :51⅕ b Jly 18 Bel 3f fst :36⅘ hg

Swift Gal — Ch. f. 3, by Little Current—Wenona, by Larkspur
Br.—Heyward J H (Va) | Tr.—Tesher Howard M | Own.—Brody J | 112⁵
Lifetime 0 0 0 0 | 1983 0 M 0 0 | 1982 0 M 0 0
LATEST WORKOUTS Jly 31 Sar 3f fst :37 b Jly 14 Aqu ⊡ 4f fst :52 bg Jun 30 Aqu ⊡ 6f fst 1:17 b Jun 27 Aqu ⊡ 4f fst :48⅘ h

Acquiescence B. f. 3, by Gallant Man—Stinger Mist, by Misty Day Lifetime 1983 1 M 0 0
Br.—Evans & Evans & Co (Va) **117** 1 0 0 0 1982 0 M 0 0
Own.—Evans E P Tr.—Kelley Thomas J
8Jly83- 6Bel fst 6½f :22⅘ :46⅘ 1:19⅘ 3↑ Ⓕ Md Sp Wt 5 12 10^{10} 11^{16} 9^{16} 9^{19} Douglas R R7 b 109 51.20 60–18 It's Fine $116^{3\frac{1}{2}}$ Keys 'N' Keys $116^{2\frac{1}{2}}$ ToutеSuiteLil 116^{2} Broke slow 12
LATEST WORKOUTS Jly 28 Sar 5f fst 1:03⅘ b Jly 21 Bel 5f fst 1:06 b Jly 14 Bel 3f fst :38 b Jly 1 Bel 4f fst :49⅘ hg

Equine Rights Dk. b. or br. f. 3, by Verbatim—Alan's Princess, by Distinctive Lifetime 1983 2 M 0 0
Br.—Floyd-Ginter-Jelsam-Isaacs (Ky) **117** 2 0 0 0 1982 0 M 0 0
Own.—Zanker E Tr.—Conway John P
6Jly83- 3Bel fst 7f :23⅘ :46⅘ 1:25 3↑ Ⓕ Md Sp Wt 6 6 $4^{3\frac{1}{2}}$ $5^{6\frac{1}{2}}$ 6^{11} 6^{16} Graell A 116 40.10 61-17 Down Stage 116^{5} Never Twist 116^{9} Grande Finis 116^{hd} Tired 10
0Jun83- 5Bel fst 6f :22⅘ :46⅕ 1:11⅘ 3↑ Ⓕ Md Sp Wt 7 14 13^{13} 13^{15} 11^{15} 10^{15} Graell A 114 75.10 69-23 Wild Beat $122^{2\frac{1}{2}}$ Elevator Girl $1^{1\frac{1}{2}}$ Down Stage 114^{3} Slow start 14
LATEST WORKOUTS Jly 26 Sar 4f fst :49 b ● Jly 13 Bel 3f fst :35⅕ h Jly 6 Bel 4f fst :49 b Jun 19 Bel 3f fst :36⅘ hg

The favorite at 2 to 1 was Dink, a Woody Stephens' filly who had started six times and finished second thrice and third once. Her last two races, however, were on the turf, including her best effort to date in her last start when she was second by three-quarters of a length. Of her four races on dirt, she showed a second by half a length at six and a half furlongs, then a tiring third by four and three-quarters lengths at seven furlongs. She appeared to be a logical contender, but already in her career had failed twice as the favorite, once at 6 to 5 and once at 2 to 1. A 2 to 1 price on her, again, today, returning from the turf to dirt, was of questionable value.

Of Dink's twelve rivals, Last Word Suzie had closed for a well-bet fifth in her lone start. She and Elevator Girl, second in each of her last two starts, would both go off at 3 to 1.

The horse which interests us is Toute Suite Lil. The daughter of Exclusive Native had two starts in her life. She was bet down to 2 to 1 in her debut, February 25, at Gulfstream Park in Florida, when she showed early speed and tired to finish a distant third by thirteen lengths. Trainer Leroy Jolley then laid her off until July 8, when she went off at 3 to 1 in a six and a half furlong race (her first start was at six furlongs). Toute Suite Lil didn't get the lead as she had in her first start, but she raced better, going from second by three lengths in the stretch to third by five and three-quarters at the finish. Her speed figure was seven points higher on a track variant which was only a point less. Her last race was obviously an improvement at a longer sprint. She had lost ten lengths in the stretch in her six furlong debut and two and three-quarters in her six and a half furlong second start in a faster time.

Why wasn't she bet this time? I have no idea, but at a closing price of 14 to 1, Toute Suite Lil was certainly an overlay. She raced well, stalked the early pacesetter, took over the lead at the head of the stretch and couldn't hold off a 12 to 1 first time starter, Swift Gal.

Toute Suite Lil did hold second by three and a quarter lengths and returned $14.80 to place and $9.20 to show. Dink was tenth by sixteen lengths.

FOURTH RACE
Saratoga
AUGUST 3, 1983

7 FURLONGS. (1.20 2/5) MAIDEN SPECIAL WEIGHT. Purse $18,000. Fillies and Mares. 3-year-olds and up.Weights: 3-year-olds, 117 lbs.; older, 122 lbs.

Value of race $18,000, value to winner $10,800, second $3,960, third $2,160, fourth $1,080. Mutuel pool $139,768, OTB pool $130,856. Quinella Pool $144,594. OTB Quinella Pool $171,024.

Last Raced		Horse	Eqt.	A.	Wt.	PP	St	1/4	1/2	Str	Fin	Jockey	r	Odds $1
		Swift Gal		3	117	10	10	11-6	5-3	3 ½	1-2½	Davis R G+		12.90
8Jly83	6Bel 3	Toute Suite Lil		3	117	3	5	2-1½	2hd	1 ½	2-3¼	Cruguet J		14.40
25Jly83	9Bel 5	That Satin Doll		3	117	8	2	7 ½	8-2	5-1	3hd	Bailey J D		19.70
25Jly83	2Bel 2	Elevator Girl	b	3	117	4	6	3-1	3-1½	2hd	4-1¾	Santagata N		3.30
30May83	6Bel 5	dh-Last Word Susie	b	3	117	2	12	10 ½	10-4	7hd	5	Hernandez R		3.40
30Jun83	5Bel12	dh-Parisian Print	b	3	117	9	4	1-1	1-1½	4-4	5nk	Smith A Jr		56.50
22Jly83	6Bel 2	Keys 'N' Keys		3	117	1	11	9hd	9-1	8-1	7-7¼	McCarron G		6.40
14May83	5Aqu 7	Charlottetown		3	112	6	7	5-1½	6hd	9-1½	8no	Clayton M D-5		40.50
7Feb83	4Aqu 5	Precious Perfect		4	122	7	3	12 ½	13	11-1½	9 ½	Murphy D J-5	f-	24.20
25Jly83	9Bel 2	Dink		3	117	5	8	4 ½	4-3	6 ½	10-1	Maple E+		2.40
25Jly83	2Bel 4	Vandy's Joy	b	3	117	13	1	6-1½	7hd	10-3	11-3	Beitia E		29.40
16Jly83	3Bel 6	Equine Rights	b	3	117	12	9	8 ½	11 ½	12-4	12	Graell A	f-	24.20
8Jly83	6Bel 9	Acquiescence	b	3	112	11	13	13	12-1½	13	-	Douglas R R-5		74.80

Acquiescence, Lost Irons.
dh-Dead heat.
f-Mutuel field.
OFF AT 3:13. Start good, Won ridden out. Time, :22 1/5, :45 1/5, 1:11 1/5, 1:24 3/5 Track fast.

$ 2 Mutuel Prices:				
9-	SWIFT GAL	27.80	18.80	14.00
3-	TOUTE SUITE LIL		14.80	9.20
7-	THAT SATIN DOLL			9.80

$2 QUINELLA 3-9 PAID $237.20.

Form doesn't necessarily entail placing great emphasis on a horse's last race. A horse can still have good form without an impressive last PP if there was an excuse or if that race had little to do with the one he is entered in today. Again, I emphasize a horse's form on dirt and on turf are two separate entities, many times without any relationship at all.

Now let's handicap this 1983 race at Saratoga. A field of eight New York-bred fillies and mares entered the 1¹/8 mile allowance on the main track, a non-winners of three (two races other than maiden claiming or starter handicap). In evaluating distance races, it's always wise to find a horse who can make the distance.

Romalane, who went off 54 to 1 and finished seventh by nineteen lengths in her last start, is such a filly. Romalane's embarrassing last race was a sprint at six and a half furlongs, and her first start in three and a half months. In going through her other PPs, we see three of nine were at a distance of more than a mile. On January 31 at Aqueduct, she raced in a 1¹/8 mile maiden race for New York-bred fillies. Similar to her appearance at Saratoga, Romalane was coming off a

1 SARATOGA

1⅛ MILES
SARATOGA
Start • Finish

1 ⅛ MILES. (1.47) ALLOWANCE. Purse $28,500. Fillies and Mares, 3-year-old and upward foaled in New York state and approved by the New York State-Bred Registry which have never won two races other than maiden, claiming or starter. Weights, 3-year-olds, 117 lbs. Older, 122 lbs. Non-winners of a race other than maiden or cliaming over a mile since August 1, allowed 3 lbs. Of such a race since July 15, 5 lbs. (Purse reflects $5,500 from New York Breeding Fund enrichment).

Coupled—Tiki Singh and Ever Higher.

Sally The Shiek

Ch. f. 3, by Little Miracle—Dixie Deeny, by Prince Blessed
Br.—Mistretta C (NY)
Own.—Fertile Acres Stable **Tr.—Ortiz Paulino O**
107⁵ Lifetime 9 1 0 0 $7,920 | 1983 9 1 0 0 $7,920 | 1982 0 M 0 0 | Turf 2 0 0 0 $1,620

2Aug83- 2Sar sly 1⅛ :47⅗ 1:13 1:54⅕ 3↑Ⓕ[S]Alw 27000 7 7 96½ 911 919 929 Samyn J L 112 14.50 35-23 Gentle Game 107¾ Mia Reale 117no Tiki Singh 1132½ Outrun 9
1Jly83- 9Sar fst 7f :22⅖ :45⅘ 1:24⅘ 3↑Ⓕ[S]Alw 25500 4 7 88 88 76¾ 55½ Samyn J L 111 11.90 72-12 Regal Lady 1131½ Striking 1112 Tiki Singh 113nk No threat 11
7Jly83- 4Bel fm 1 1/16 Ⓣ:47⅖ 1:11⅗ 1:44⅖ 3↑Ⓕ[S]Alw 27000 7 1 11 1½ 31 55¼ Samyn J L 111 5.30 68-14 Valid Gal 1173¼ Ms. Mafalda 117hd Baker's Bet 1111¾ Weakened 12
1Jly83- 7Bel hd 1¼ [T]:49⅘ 1:39⅗ 2:05 3↑Ⓕ[S]Alw 27000 6 5 3½ 21 31½ 42¾ Thibeau R J5 106 19.60 66-16 Belwood Jule 119¾ Truth Shall Out 106nk ValidGal1171¾ Weakened 12
5Jun83- 3Bel fst 1 1/16 :48 1:13⅖ 1:47⅕ 3↑ⒻMd 35000 4 1 11 11½ 14 11¾ Thibeau R J5 109 43.60 66-20 Sally The Shiek 1091¾ HatchRose1142½PricelessMiss110hd Driving 9
3May83- 3Bel my 7f :22⅗ :45⅘ 1:24⅘ 3↑Ⓕ[S]Md Sp Wt 10 2 107¼ 1213 1113 1019 Santiago A 113 56.90 59-16 Genista 1066 Empire Beauty 1132¾ Timeless Anna 113nk Outrun 13
3May83- 4Aqu fst 6f :22⅗ :47⅕ 1:13⅖ 3↑Ⓕ[S]Md Sp Wt 10 7 1110 1215 912 89 Hernandez C 113 40.80 65-28 Conveyance 113½ Regal Lady 113¾ Rich N' Foolish 1032 Outrun 14
5May83- 9Aqu fst 6f :22⅕ :45⅘ 1:11⅗ ⒻMd Sp Wt 4 9 1215 1219 1117 1122 Hernandez C 121 43.40 61-18 Temper The Wind 1215 Dee's Dilema 121nk Gnash 1211½ Outrun 12
3Jan83- 2Aqu fst 6f ⊡:23⅗ :48 1:13⅗ Ⓕ[S]Md Sp Wt 8 12 1313 1217 1225 1229 Davis R G5 116 23.80 47-25 Second Notice 116¾ Precipitate 1146¾ Mobile Miss 1211 Outrun 14

LATEST WORKOUTS Aug 8 Sar tr.t 4f fst :51⅘ b | Jly 29 Sar 4f fst :48 h | Jly 14 Bel Ⓣ 3f fm :38 b (d) | Jly 11 Bel tr.t 4f fst :50⅘ b

Hail to France

Dk. b. or br. f. 4, by Hail the Pirates—Meggenhorn, by Dan Cupid
Br.—Blue Sky Farm (NY)
Own.—Kevmar Stable **Tr.—Thomas Richard**
117 Lifetime 34 2 3 2 $57,770 | 1983 9 0 1 0 $11,340 | 1982 13 2 1 1 $35,570 | Turf 12 1 0 1 $20,100

4Aug83- 3Sar fm 1 1/16 [T]:49 1:13⅕ 1:45⅕ 3↑ⒻClm 45000 4 6 96¾ 910 99½ 911 Cruguet J 113 21.20 68-20 Funny Tumbler 1081 Lavendulane 113½ Liz's Babe 1121½ Outrun 9
Jly83- 1Bel fm 1 1/16 [T]:47⅗ 1:12⅕ 1:44⅖ 3↑Ⓕ[S]Alw 28500 1 7 719 717 617 514 Douglas R R5 112 5.70 65-18 April Target 1065 Ghia Marie 1173 You're All Heart 117nk Outrun 7
Jun83- 6Bel fm 1¼ [T]:51⅖ 1:41⅖ 2:06 3↑[S]Alw 28500 4 7 67½ 77 712 712 Graell A 112 22.00 52-27 Danderoo 117no KnuckleheadSmith1121WimborneSky1024 Outrun 9
2Jun83- 1Bel fst 1 :45⅘ 1:10⅘ 1:37⅘ 3↑Ⓕ[S]Alw 28500 7 7 723 715 59½ 43 Douglas R R5 112 32.20 73-20 Restless Gerry 104hd Wimborne Sky1101¾Genista1131½ Stride late 7
3May83- 1Bel fm 1¼ [T]:49⅖ 1:38⅘ 2:04⅕ ⒻClm 75000 1 10 1014 1013 1011 1015 Thibeau R J5 107 47.90 58-24 Singleton II 116no Lovely Duckling 1163 Bedazzle 114no Trailed 10
3Apr83- 1Aqu my 1 :46⅘ 1:11⅕ 1:37⅖ 3↑Ⓕ[S]Alw 28500 2 6 59½ 712 59½ 69 Graell A 121 13.80 70-17 Swoon Lake 1161½ Kiss Appeal 1091¾ Romalane 1061½ No factor 8
3Mar83- 7Aqu fst 1⅛ :47⅖ 1:13⅗ 1:53⅕ ⒻAlw 23000 7 8 814 811 718 725 Cordero A Jr 117 13.30 44-28 For Pleasure 1174 Pipparoo 117½ Ring On Doc 1121½ Outrun 8
5Feb83- 3Aqu fst 1 1/16 ⊡:48⅖ 1:14⅕ 1:48 Ⓕ[S]Alw 28500 6 8 713 77 45 22½ Cordero A Jr 117 2.60e 70-22 Onyx Beauty 1122½ Hail to France 1171¾ SwoonLake1121½ Rallied 10
3Jan83- 8Aqu fst 170 ⊡:48⅕ 1:14⅖ 1:45⅘ 3↑Ⓕ[S]BroadwyH 11 12 1013 78 55½ 45 Davis R G 107 33.10e 68-24 Soft Morning 1151½ Logic 1131½ Dam Little 1202½ No factor 12
0Dec82- 3Aqu fst 1 1/16 ⊡:49⅘ 1:15⅕ 1:48⅗ 3↑Ⓕ[S]Alw 29500 6 3 32 43 75¼ 86¾ Graell A 115 8.60e 63-24 Logic 1152 Everylittlebreeze 115¾ Stone of Blue 1151½ Tired 8

LATEST WORKOUTS Aug 14 Aqu 4f gd :51⅗ b | Jly 28 Aqu ⊡ 6f fst 1:16⅖ b | Jly 12 Sar tr.t 4f fst :49 h | Jun 25 Aqu ⊡ 1 fst 1:44⅘ b

Starbait

B. f. 3, by Bailjumper—Ms Superstar, by Vertex
Br.—Woodside Stud Inc (NY)
Own.—Chasrigg Stable **Tr.—DeBonis Robert**
114 Lifetime 13 2 4 0 $54,500 | 1983 10 2 4 0 $53,180 | 1982 3 M 0 0 $1,320 | Turf 1 0 1 0 $5,390

Aug83- 5Sar my 1⅛ :47⅗ 1:13 1:55⅗ 3↑Ⓕ[S]Alw 27000 5 6 58 38½ 35 1nk Cordero A Jr 117 *1.60 57-24 Starbait 117nk Truth Shall Out 1074 Key ToTheGold112hd Driving 7
Jly83- 1Bel fst 1 1/16 :48 1:14⅗ 1:48⅘ 3↑Ⓕ[S]Md Sp Wt 7 10 85¾ 56 11 14½ Cordero A Jr 116 *1.80 58-26 Starbait1164½FantasiaAgpiMou1111½RonmurLssie1113 Ridden out 13
Jly83- 1Bel fm 1 1/16 [T]:49 1:13 1:44⅖ 3↑Ⓕ[S]Md Sp Wt 5 4 21 2hd 2½ 21¾ Cordero A Jr 116 4.30 77-15 Empire Beauty 1161¾ Starbait 116½ Priceless Miss 1162 Gamely 8
Jun83- 4Bel fst 1 1/16 :47⅖ 1:12⅖ 1:45⅖ 3↑Ⓕ[S]Md Sp Wt 11 6 33 3½ 44 58½ Murphy D J5 109 7.60 67-22 ReglLdy109nkEmpireBeuty1142¾Wlkmileinmyshos1093¾ Gave way 12
May83- 3Bel my 7f :22⅗ :45⅘ 1:24⅘ 3↑Ⓕ[S]Md Sp Wt 13 5 86¼ 1011 1214 1121 Smith A Jr 113 4.20 57-16 Genista 1066 Empire Beauty 1132¾ TimelessAnna113nk No excuse 13
Apr83- 3Aqu fst 7f :23 :46⅗ 1:26 Ⓕ[S]Md Sp Wt 9 6 97¾ 76½ 76 21½ Smith A Jr 121 6.00 69-26 Three Dog Night 1211½ Starbait 1211½ Sun Sounds 121½ Wide 12
Mar83- 4Aqu fst 6f :23⅕ :47⅗ 1:13⅖ Ⓕ[S]Md Sp Wt 2 11 116¾ 108½ 46 41¾ Smith A Jr 121 7.50 72-24 Precipitate 1161 Flip's Pleasure 121no Talcum Blue 121¾ Rallied 13
Feb83- 9Aqu fst 1 1/16 ⊡:50 1:15⅗ 1:49⅘ Ⓕ[S]Md Sp Wt 5 9 74¾ 76¾ 56½ 63¾ Migliore R 121 *2.30 60-22 Tall'NTn121¾I'mATomboy116¾MircleMile1211½ Lacked a response 12
Jan83- 6Aqu fst 1⅛ ⊡:48⅘ 1:14⅗ 1:54⅕ Ⓕ[S]Md Sp Wt 5 6 54½ 22 3½ 21¾ Migliore R 121 *1.40 73-15 Romalane 1141¾ Starbait1213½Walkamileinmyshoes116¾ Game try 10
Jan83- 6Aqu fst 6f ⊡:23⅘ :48⅗ 1:14 Ⓕ[S]Md Sp Wt 10 7 73½ 63¾ 33 2¾ Migliore R 121 13.60 73-24 Monarch's Magic 116¾ Starbait 121hd PraiseN'Reward1212 Bore in 14

LATEST WORKOUTS Aug 10 Sar 3f fst :35⅘ h | Jly 30 Sar 3f fst :37⅘ b | Jly 17 Bel tr.t 5f fst 1:04⅕ b | Jly 10 Bel 3f fst :37⅗ b

Tiki Singh

Ch. f. 3, by Singh—Tiki Minx, by Gate Smasher
Br.—Wooden Horse Investments (NY)
Own.—Singin Frog Stable **Tr.—Alvarez Harold G**
112 Lifetime 21 1 1 7 $31,850 | 1983 11 0 0 4 $13,050 | 1982 10 1 1 3 $18,800

Entered 20Aug83- 9 SAR

2Aug83- 2Sar sly 1⅛ :47⅗ 1:13 1:54⅕ 3↑Ⓕ[S]Alw 27000 9 6 31 21½ 2hd 3¾ Vergara O b 113 11.00 63-23 Gentle Game 107¾ Mia Reale 117no Tiki Singh 1132½ Weakened 9
Jly83- 9Sar fst 7f :22⅖ :45⅘ 1:24⅘ 3↑Ⓕ[S]Alw 25500 7 8 55 54 33 33½ Vergara O b 113 24.90 75-12 Regal Lady 1131½ Striking 1112 Tiki Singh 113nk Rallied 11
Jly83- 7Bel fst 6f :22⅖ :46⅖ 1:11⅖ 3↑Ⓕ[S]Alw 25500 10 9 810 89 811 49½ Vergara O b 111 65.30 75-17 Sun Sounds 1136½ Jazzerciser 1113 Regal Lady 113nk Mild bid 10
Jun83- 9Bel fst 7f :23⅖ :46⅘ 1:25⅕ 3↑Ⓕ[S]Alw 25500 9 8 97½ 98½ 515 312 Vergara O b 111 87.00 64-22 Chaldea 10911 Three Dog Night 109½ Tiki Singh 111nk Rallied 10
Jun83- 9Bel fst 6f :22⅖ :46⅕ 1:11⅖ 3↑Ⓕ[S]Alw 27000 8 10 911 911 711 712 Vergara O b 114 68.10 73-20 Flip'sPleasure1101SubversiveChick104¾RadcliffeGirl1111½ Outrun 10
Apr83- 5Aqu fst 1 :48⅘ 1:15⅗ 1:41⅘ ⒻClm 20000 6 7 75½ 77¾ 711 515 Samyn J L b 112 14.90 42-30 SweetIrish11611ChillyChaCh118nkMrvelousMontuk1161 No factor 7
Mar83- 9Aqu fst 1 1/16 ⊡:48⅘ 1:15 1:49⅕ ⒻClm 25000 10 6 65½ 912 1012 1014 Santagata N b 116 13.30 53-21 Old Values 116nk Annie Sullivan 1161¾ Game Replay 111¾ Outrun 11
Feb83- 5Aqu fst 1 1/16 ⊡:49⅕ 1:15⅕ 1:48⅘ ⒻClm 40000 7 9 913 911 913 916 Asmussen S M5 b 111 22.10 53-27 Tarpis 105¾ Cenerentola 1163 Champ Nasrubold 112nk Outrun 11
Feb83- 9Aqu fst 6f ⊡:23⅖ :47⅖ 1:12⅗ Ⓕ[S]Alw 25500 5 6 75¾ 68 69¼ 57¾ Samyn J L b 116 13.90 73-13 SubversiveChick111½AprilTarget111¾Monarch'sMgic1163½ Outrun 9
Jan83- 6Aqu fst 170 ⊡:48⅘ 1:15⅗ 1:46⅗ ⒻClm 40000 8 9 94¾ 76½ 54 35 Asmussen S M7 b 110 11.20 64-23 Lady D. 1112½ Gold Plated 1132¾ Tiki Singh 1103 Rallied 10

Ever Higher

B. f. 4, by Take Your Place—Lady Everest, by Fathers Image
Br.—Mountan P C (NY)
Own.—Bellrose Farm **Tr.—Alvarez Harold G**
117 Lifetime 30 2 4 4 $38,847 | 1983 11 1 1 0 $13,305 | 1982 19 1 3 4 $25,542 | Turf 2 0 0 0

Entered 20Aug83- 9 SAR

Aug83- 3Sar my 7f :23⅗ :47⅖ 1:25⅘ 3↑Ⓕ[S]Alw 25500 5 3 65½ 66½ 69 612 Miranda J b 117 32.80 61-16 Jazzerciser 112hd Striking 1075½ Tara K. 1171¾ Trailed 6
Jly83- 5Bel fm 1 1/16 Ⓣ:47 1:10⅘ 1:42⅗ 3↑ⒻAlw 21000 10 12 1211 1216 1223 1125 Pompay T10 b 107 108.60 58-18 BoltFromTheBlu1161½FuturFun1112ExplosivPrincss111hd Outrun 12
Jun83- 3Bel fst 1 1/16 :48⅗ 1:13⅖ 1:46⅗ ⒻClm 18000 4 3 41¾ 55 79½ 814 Vergara O b 114 13.20 55-22 Double Dacquare 113nk Root Fore108nkNoMoreTearsII108¾ Tired 8
Jun83- 5Bel fst 1 :46⅕ 1:11 1:37⅘ 3↑[S]Alw 27000 1 13 1316 1318 1318 1215 Vergara O b 114 73.40 61-20 Jordn'sGry1091¾WrghtSkppr112hdBhndClosdoors1111½ Poor start 13
May83- 6Bel gd 7f :23⅕ :46⅖ 1:23⅘ 3↑Ⓕ[S]Alw 25500 2 13 1211 97½ 99 911 Vergara O 119 29.90 72-13 Clover Miss 1122¾ Kittymouse 1122 Tara K. 114¾ Broke sluggish 13
Apr83- 9Aqu fst 1 :47 1:12⅗ 1:39⅖ 3↑Ⓕ[S]Alw 27000 3 8 84½ 67 89 89½ Vergara O 121 8.00 59-25 Monrch'sMgic113¾KissAppl113nkTll'NTn1092½ Lacked a response 10
Apr83- 9Aqu fst 6½f :23⅕ :46⅖ 1:17⅘ 3↑Ⓕ[S]Alw 25500 6 8 1013 910 611 47½ Davis R G5 116Δ 6.30 79-25 Second Notice 1045 Monarch's Magic 1121¾ Dehli'sGift104½ Wide 10
7Apr83-Dead heat
Mar83- 5Aqu fst 1 :47⅖ 1:14 1:41 Ⓕ[S]Alw 27000 6 9 1010 63½ 3½ 2no Miranda J b 117 19.20 61-28 LittleMissG.117noEverHigher1173VoygToDmscus1174 Forced out 10
Mar83- 9Aqu sly 1 1/16 ⊡:47⅘ 1:13⅗ 1:48⅖ ⒻClm 10000 8 9 917 49 23 1¾ Graell A b 117 20.10 71-17 Ever Higher 117¾ Diamond Shamrock 1133Quisqueya113¾ Driving 10
Feb83- 7Aqu fst 6f ⊡:22⅘ :46 1:12⅕ [S]Alw 25500 8 12 1217 1221 1219 1116 Graell A b 112 69.80 67-25 StgeGossip1173WrightSkipper117hdPositivlyFrnch112¾ No factor 12

LATEST WORKOUTS Jly 22 Sar tr.t 3f fst :36⅘ h

Romalane — Ro. f. 3, by Kirby Lane—Turoma, by Tumiga
Own.—Milange Farm · Br.—Chianelli A (NY) · Tr.—Bradley John M
1075 · Lifetime 13 2 0 1 $37,950 · 1983 7 2 0 1 $36,0 · 1982 6 M 0 0 $1,9

22Jly83- 7Bel	fst	6½f		:23	:46⅖	1:18⅕	3↑ⒻⓈAlw 27000	5	5	611	813	818	719	Thibeau R J	b 116	54.00	66-26 Chaldea 1084¾ Clover Miss 1125¾RapidProspector117nk	No factor
8Apr83- 1Aqu	my	1		:46⅘	1:11⅕	1:37⅖	3↑ⒻⓈAlw 28500	8	4	46½	44½	43½	33	Thibeau R J7	b 106	4.80	76-17 Swoon Lake 1161¼ KissAppeal1091¾Romalane1061¼	Lacked a rally
28Feb83- 6Aqu	fst	1 1/16	⊡	:49⅗	1:15⅕	1:48⅗	ⒻⓈAlw 27000	2	5	75	41¾	32	1¾	Thibeau R J7	b 111	*2.10	70-25 Romalane 111¾ Monarch's Magic 1113 Tall 'N Tan 1212	Driving
20Feb83- 5Aqu	fst	170	⊡	:48	1:13⅖	1:45⅖	ⒻⓈAlw 28500	2	10	1014	713	57½	42¼	Thibeau R J7	b 109	33.80	73-20 Cobitony1111¾SubversiveChick111nkEnergetica113nk	Broke in air
31Jan83- 6Aqu	fst	1⅛	⊡	:48⅘	1:14⅗	1:54⅕	ⒻⓈMd Sp Wt	1	7	78¾	85¼	1½	11¾	Thibeau R J7	b 114	14.90	75-15 Romalane1141¾Starbait1213½Walkamileinmyshoes116¾	Drew clear
28Jan83- 2Aqu	fst	6f	⊡	:23⅘	:48	1:13⅗	ⒻⓈMd Sp Wt	11	14	1413	1419	919	616	Thibeau R J7	b 114	15.10f	60-25 SecondNotice116¾Precipitte1146¾MobilMiss1211	P'ssd tired ones
5Jan83- 6Aqu	fst	6f	⊡	:23⅖	:47⅖	1:13⅕	ⒻⓈMd Sp Wt	7	11	1112	1118	713	614	Thibeau R J7	b 114	57.40	64-24 Mrs.Lwrence1217¾SecondNotice1161¾Monrch'sMgic116hd	Outrun
17Nov82- 4Aqu	fst	1		:47⅖	1:13	1:38	ⒻⓈMd Sp Wt	1	8	88	69	511	511	Thibeau R J7	b 110	19.50	65-18 RadcliffeGirl1128ReglDowger1172½Monrch'sMgic117hd	No factor
29Oct82- 6Aqu	fst	7f		:23	:46⅖	1:25⅗	ⒻⓈMd Sp Wt	8	12	1411	1111	710	75¾	Martens G	b 117	10.00	67-23 Dncer'sHbitt1171¾RdcliffeGirl112nkPriseN'Rewrd117¾	No menace
25Oct82- 4Aqu	my	6f		:23⅘	:48⅘	1:14⅗	ⒻMd 25000	11	12	1212	1213	69½	46½	Thibeau R Jr7	b 110	3.80	61-33 Final Stroke 117½ WhiskeyAndEggs1174IWasOpen1082	Very wide

LATEST WORKOUTS Aug 15 Bel 7f fst 1:28 h ●Aug 6 Bel tr.t 6f fst 1:13⅘ h Jly 30 Bel tr.t 1 fst 1:44⅗ b Jly 16 Bel 6f fst 1:16 b

Regal Lady — B. f. 3, by Buck Private—Regalment, by What A Pleasure
Own.—Mangurian H T Jr · Br.—Mangurian H T Jr (NY) · Tr.—Root Richard R
112 · Lifetime 8 2 2 1 $41,480 · 1983 6 2 2 1 $41,3 · 1982 2 M 0 0 $1

31Jly83- 9Sar	fst	7f		:22⅖	:45⅘	1:24⅘	3↑ⒻⓈAlw 25500	3	9	76½	43½	1hd	11¼	Velasquez J	113	2.60	78-12 Regal Lady 1131¼ Striking 1112 Tiki Singh 113nk	Driving
15Jly83- 7Bel	fst	6f		:22⅖	:46⅖	1:11⅖	3↑ⒻⓈAlw 25500	9	8	76¼	45	26	39¼	Velasquez J	113	4.10	76-17 Sun Sounds 1136¼ Jazzerciser 1113 Regal Lady 113nk	Wide str.
16Jun83- 4Bel	fst	1 1/16		:47⅖	1:12⅖	1:45⅖	3↑ⒻⓈMd Sp Wt	12	3	21½	2hd	12	1nk	Douglas R R5	109	10.90	75-22 RegalLdy109nkEmpireBeuty1142¾Wlkmileinmyshoes1093¾	Driving
13May83- 4Aqu	fst	6f		:22⅗	:47⅕	1:13⅖	3↑ⒻⓈMd Sp Wt	4	4	65¾	45	31½	2½	Velasquez J	113	6.70	73-28 Conveyance 113½ Regal Lady 113¾ Rich N' Foolish 1032	Gamely
29Apr83- 9Aqu	fst	7f		:23	:46⅗	1:26	ⒻⓈMd Sp Wt	12	2	77	53	53	43½	Santagata N	121	10.00	67-26 Three Dog Night 1211½ Starbait 1211½ SunSounds121½	No excuse
21Mar83- 3Hia	fst	6f		:22⅖	:46⅗	1:13	ⒻMd Sp Wt	3	8	67½	66	2hd	2½	Cardone E	119	18.70	77-20 Gourmet Lori 114½RegalLady1191½MemoriesWeShare1193	Rallied
30Jun82- 5Crc	fst	5½f		:22⅗	:46⅘	1:06	ⒻMd Sp Wt	5	4	22	22	46½	517	Long J S	115	48.00	78-15 Crystal Rail 10810 Marie V. 1153½ Over Burden 1151½	Tired
19Jun82- 3Crc	sly	5f		:23	:48	1:01⅗	ⒻMd Sp Wt	3	7	98¼	913	914	912	Long J S	115	15.20	73-21 Rest To Romeo 115¾HeavenlyMystery1151½RecksBid1061½	Outrun

LATEST WORKOUTS Aug 14 Sar tr.t 6f fst 1:14⅖ h Aug 9 Sar tr.t 4f fst :49 b Jly 29 Sar 3f fst :36 h Jly 23 Bel tr.t 4f fst :49⅖ h

Energetica — Ro. f. 3, by Energy Crisis—Full Delivery, by Irish Ruler
Own.—Wohl A · Br.—Power J F (NY) · Tr.—Nickerson Victor J
1075 · Lifetime 17 4 1 3 $66,526 · 1983 13 3 0 3 $53,4 · 1982 4 1 1 0 $13,0

4Aug83- 1Sar	fst	6f		:22⅖	:45⅘	1:11⅗	3↑ⒻClm 35000	4	3	21	3½	32	32¾	Vasquez J	114	6.40	79-16 BellaMoneta117½HoldYourLaughs1032½Energetic114hd	Weakened
9Jly83- 2Bel	fst	1⅛		:47⅖	1:12⅖	1:53	ⒻClm 25000	3	1	11½	12	13½	1½	Cordero A Jr	116	5.20	62-23 Energetica 116½ Toast To Zookie 118¾ History Belle 118½	All out
26Jun83- 1Bel	fst	1 1/16		:46⅗	1:12⅗	1:48	ⒻClm 25000	3	2	2½	1½	13	33¾	Murphy D J5	111	3.20	58-24 History Belle 1161¾ Gold Plated 1092 Energetica 111½	Weakened
15Jun83- 9Bel	fst	6f		:22⅖	:46⅕	1:11⅖	3↑ⒻⓈAlw 27000	1	3	1½	42	814	1018	Thibeau R J5	104	11.10	67-20 Flip's Pleasure 1101 SubversiveChick104¾RadcliffeGirl1111½	Tired
2Jun83- 1Bel	fst	1		:45⅘	1:10⅘	1:37⅘	3↑ⒻⓈAlw 28500	1	1	11	24	714	723	Davis R G	109	10.90	53-20 Restless Gerry 104hd Wimborne Sky 1101¾ Genista 1131¼	Used up
29May83- 9FL	fst	6f		:22⅖	:45⅗	1:11⅘	ⒻⓈNiagara	6	6	63¼	45	713	815	Vergara O	117	13.50	75-20 Zipperoo 123¾ Clover Miss 1175 Terminal Miss 1142	Tired
8Apr83- 1Aqu	my	1		:46⅘	1:11⅕	1:37⅖	3↑ⒻⓈAlw 28500	4	1	1½	2hd	2½	44¼	Davis R G5	108	*1.30e	75-17 Swoon Lake 1161¼ Kiss Appeal 1091¾ Romalane 1061¼	Weakened
10Mar83- 5Aqu	sly	6f	⊡	:22⅖	:46⅗	1:12⅕	ⒻClm 50000	4	3	22½	21½	41¾	58¼	Cordero A Jr	116	*1.40	75-17 So Called Judge 1141½DonnaJ.1076¾RamFever116hd	Fin. enter str.
20Feb83- 5Aqu	fst	170	⊡	:48	1:13⅖	1:45⅖	ⒻⓈAlw 28500	7	1	11½	1hd	2hd	32	Davis R G5	113	5.40	73-20 Cobitony 1111¾ SubversiveChick111nkEnergetica113nk	Weakened
2Feb83- 8Aqu	fst	1 1/16	⊡	:48⅘	1:14	1:47⅗	ⒻⓈSag Harbor	5	1	11½	2hd	44½	411	Davis R G	112	11.90	64-24 Halo Dotty 112½ Abraxis 112nk Subversive Chick 11210	Weakened

LATEST WORKOUTS ●Aug 17 Aqu 3f fst :35⅘ h ●Jly 30 Aqu ⊡ 4f fst :47 b ●Jly 25 Aqu ⊡ 4f sly :46⅕ h (d)

horrible previous race, a sixth by sixteen lengths in a six furlong sprint. At a mile and an eighth, though, Romalane won at Aqueduct by one and three-quarters lengths at odds of 14 to 1, beating one of the top contenders in today's race at Saratoga, Starbait.

Romalane then ran in an allowance race at one mile and seventy yards. At odds of 33 to 1, Romalane closed ten and three-quarters lengths to finish fourth by two and a quarter, beaten by a neck for third by another of her competitors today, Energetica. The *Form*'s comment was "broke in air," meaning Romalane was unprepared for the start and came out of the gate poorly. When that happens, a horse spots the rest of the field several lengths, making her fourth place finish look even better.

Romalane had two more starts in allowance company at Aqueduct before being laid off. She won a 1 1/16 mile race by three-quarters of a length as the 2 to 1 favorite. Then, at a mile, which may be too short for her, she rallied mildly to finish third by three lengths.

Thus, all of Romalane's distance races were solid performances.

Romalane had shown a distinct preference for route races, and we'll assume trainer John Bradley used her last start, the seventh place finish in the sprint at Belmont, as a tightener. She followed that race with three workouts, one a bullet six furlongs in 1:13 4/5 on the Belmont training track, a very sharp move for a come-from-behind horse.

We handicap Romalane as a legitimate challenger here and one almost certain to be an overlay because of her last race. Of her competition, she has already beaten Starbait and was a neck off Energetica.

The other logical horse in the field was Regal Lady, who had won two of her last three races but had never been farther than 1¹/₁₆ miles in eight lifetime starts.

Our handicapping proved to be correct. And very painful to watch. The final price on Romalane was 9 to 2. She collared the leaders in mid-stretch and seemed a sure winner for apprentice jockey Robert Thibeau. But another apprentice, Eclipse Award winner Delcan Murphy, shot longshot Sally The Shiek through along the rail while Thibeau let Romalane weave the final steps as he applied the pressure with the whip. It was a photo finish with a large gap back to third place. Sally The Shiek, who herself had finished ninth by twenty-nine lengths in her last start, won by half a head. Romalane paid $6.20 to place and $4.40 to show. That's part of the game, too. We'll stick with our convictions and our handicapping principles and take shots with live 9 to 2 horses anytime we can find them, although Romalane's odds were not a huge overlay.

One of the principles mentioned earlier in this chapter is expecting young or inexperienced horses to improve; that they can improve enough to win as they ascend in company against more difficult opposition. Every horse from Secretariat on down either goes into claimers or works his or her way up the maiden-allowance-stakes ladder. Certain horses do it faster and more impressively than others. Certain trainers are more adept at conditioning their horses into peak form when they make the move up in company.

In such cases, we'll have to interweave our opinions of form and class, specifically focusing on the class shown by the other horses in the field when we're interested in an inexperienced horse taking the jump up in competition.

The Count Fleet Stakes, a $60,000-added, one mile and seventy yards race for 3-year-olds, attracted a field of nine, Jan. 28, 1984, at Aqueduct.

Take an in-depth look at the field and see whether or not we can make a case for Empravatar, a son of Avatar who had only raced twice, winning a maiden and a first step allowance race.

8 AQUEDUCT

1 MILE 70 YDS
INNER DIRT TRACK
AQUEDUCT
START FINISH

1 MILE 70 YARDS. (INNER-DIRT). (1.40) 9th Running THE COUNT FLEET. Purse $60,000 added. 3-year-olds. Weights, 126 lbs. By subscription of $100 each, which should accompany the nomination; $1,000 to pass the entry box, with $60,000 added. The added money and all fees to be divided 60% to the winner. 22% to second. 12% to third and 6% to fourth. Non-winners of two races of $35,000 at any distance since November 1 allowed 3 lbs. Of a race of $25,000 at a mile or over since October 1, 5 lbs. Of such a race of $15,000 since August 15, 7 lbs. Of two races other than Maiden or Claiming 9 lbs. Starters to be named at the closing time of entries. A trophy will be presented to the winning owner. Closed with 31 nominations Wednesday, January 11, 1984.

Coupled—Crude Ways and Wind Flyer.

Empravatar

Ch. c. 3, by Avatar—Floral Empress, by Irish Ruler
Br.—Frinsand & Globerman (Ky)
Tr.—O'Connell Richard
Own.—Arcady Stable
117 — Lifetime 2 2 0 0 $24,600 — 1984 1 1 0 0 $13,200 — 1983 1 ' 0 0 $11,400

19Jan84- 7Aqu fst 170 [•]:49⅖ 1:15⅖ 1:47⅕ Alw 22000 2 1 1½ 1½ 13 16 Velasquez J 117 2.60 65-32 Empravatar 1176 Meal Ticket 117- Striking Rich 1175 Easily 6
28Dec83- 6Aqu sly 6f [•]:22⅘ :47⅗ 1:14 Md Sp Wt 8 11 5½ 62½ 4¾ 1nk Miranda J 118 6.60 74-29 Empravatar 118nk MilitaryOrder118hdSteppinBattler1182¾ Driving 12
LATEST WORKOUTS Jan 15 Bel tr.t 4f fst :49⅘ b Jan 10 Bel tr.t 5f fst 1:04⅗ b Dec 24 Bel tr.t 5f fst 1:02 h Dec 18 Bel tr.t 5f fst 1:00⅕ h

Meal Ticket

Ch. c. 3, by Bombay Duck—Bold Becky, by Bold Monarch
Br.—Petigrow C (Ky)
Tr.—Campo John P
Own.—Petigrow C
117 — Lifetime 8 1 2 3 $44,420 — 1984 1 0 1 0 $4,840 — 1983 7 1 1 3 $39,580

19Jan84- 7Aqu fst 170 [•]:49⅖ 1:15⅖ 1:47⅕ Alw 22000 6 6 56½ 42½ 33½ 26 McCarron G b 117 11.60 59-32 Empravatar 1176 MealTicket1172StrikingRich1175 Best of others 6
18Dec83- 7Aqu fst 1 1/16 [•]:48⅗ 1:14 1:47⅖ Alw 22000 5 2 2hd 31 710 717½ Velasquez J b 122 9.90 57-25 IsYourPleasure1173Cooper'sHawk1173RovingMinstrel1171½ Tired 9
3Dec83- 6Aqu gd 1⅛ :47⅘ 1:13 1:51⅗ Md Sp Wt 2 2 2½ 1½ 1hd 1hd Velasquez J b 118 *2.50 77-20 Meal Ticket 118hdVigumand 1182 Crowning118nk Drifted out, dr. 9
24Nov83- 6Aqu fst 1 :46⅘ 1:12⅖ 1:39 Md Sp Wt 1 2 1½ 1hd 32 49 Skinner K b 118 4.30 62-24 CertainTret1185½RmblingRector1183ExclusiveRed118½ Weakened 14
29Oct83- 9Crc fst 1 1/16 :47⅗ 1:14 1:48⅕ Fla Stallion 1 5 512 33 34½ 35¾ Solis A 120 10.30 72-18 Rexson's Hope 1205½ Upper Star 120nkMealTicket120no Mild rally 11
29Oct83-In Reality Div. Run in two div. 7th & 9th races
16Oct83- 2Bel fst 1 1/16 :48⅕ 1:12⅕ 1:43⅗ Md Sp Wt 1 1 2½ 35 312 214 Velasquez J 118 2.00 70-14 Is YourPleasure11814MealTicket118½IceBucket1183 Gained place 8
7Oct83- 5Med fst 1 :47⅗ 1:13⅖ 1:40⅕ Md Sp Wt 6 7 42½ 44½ 47 36½ Lovato F Jr 118 *1.30 73-19 Snowcot 1182 Ferrari 1184½ Meal Ticket 1183¾ Rallied 7
29Sep83- 4Bel fst 6f :22⅘ :46⅕ 1:11⅖ Md Sp Wt 6 4 41½ 42¼ 34½ 37¼ Lovato F Jr 118 20.10 78-17 Country Manor 1182¾ Loud And Clear1185MealTicket118¾ Rallied 13
LATEST WORKOUTS Jan 26 Bel tr.t 4f fst :49 b Jan 14 Bel tr.t 5f fst 1:03 b ● Jan 6 Bel tr.t 1 fst 1:47 b Dec 31 Bel tr.t 4f fst :48⅕ hg

S. S. Hot Sauce

B. c. 3, by Sauce Boat—Electric Blanket, by Le Fabuleux
Br.—Honey Acres Farm & Kline (Md)
Tr.—Kousin Jack
Own.—Kline A S
123 — Lifetime 7 2 2 2 $76,000 — 1984 1 0 1 0 $6,750 — 1983 6 2 1 2 $69,250

7Jan84- 8Bow fst 7f :22⅘ :45⅘ 1:25⅖ [S]E P Heagerty 5 2 66¼ 65½ 48 24½ Kaenel J L 122 3.70 70-34 Jyp 1154½ S. S. Hot Sauce 122½ Rambler Red 115½ Gamely 9
26Nov83- 8Lrl fst 1 1/16 :47⅖ 1:12⅖ 1:44⅘ [S]Maryland Juv 8 4 44 41 1hd 1½ Kaenel J L 122 12.90 84-16 S.S.HotSuce122½PidA'Tirr1221½MDrlinAnnB.1192 Bumped, driving 8
15Nov83- 7Lrl sly 1 :46⅘ 1:13 1:39⅘ Alw 9500 6 7 77 64¼ 43½ 32 Kaenel J L 117 *1.90 71-19 Dixie's Island108½AccompanyMe1101½S.S.HotSauce117nk Bumped 9
7Nov83- 7Lrl fst 1 :47⅕ 1:12 1:37⅘ Alw 9500 6 3 68 44½ 43¾ 32¼ Miller D A Jr 119 5.60 81-18 RamblerRed117¾GmblingGreenie1191½S.S.HotSuce119hd Mild bid 6
22Oct83- 3Lrl fst 6f :23 :47 1:12⅕ Md Sp Wt 3 1 2hd 1½ 12 13½ Kaenel J L 118 5.80 82-15 S. S. HotSauce1183½TakeTurns1181Jane'sDilemma1182½ Drew off 9
4Oct83- 6Lrl fst 6f :22⅖ :46⅕ 1:11⅘ Md Sp Wt 1 2 22 35 36½ 210 Kaenel J L 118 18.30 74-19 Fourmtt11810S.S.HotSuce1182½D'sBrightBoy1181½ Best of others 9
24Sep83- 9Lrl fst 6f :23 :47 1:12⅕ Md Sp Wt 12 1 2hd 48 613 718¾ Kaenel J L 118 7.90 63-17 Daring Assault 1183½ Baby Chile 1183 Take Turns 1186 Tired 12
LATEST WORKOUTS Jan 17 Lrl 1 fst 1:39⅘ b ● Jan 2 Lrl 5f fst :59⅗ h Dec 20 Lrl 7f fst 1:27 h

Crude Ways

Ch. c. 3, by Victory Stride—Lady Milldale, by Nade
Br.—Walker T R (Okla)
Tr.—Dickey Charles L
Own.—Sons of Val Stable
119 — Lifetime 12 4 2 1 $132,514 — 1984 1 1 0 0 $42,660 — 1983 11 3 2 1 $89,854

7Jan84- 8Aqu fst 6f [•]:22⅗ :46⅗ 1:11⅘ Rockaway 1 1 1hd 12½ 16 17 Santagata N 121 3.60e 85-24 Crude Ways 1217 Whitebrush 1173 Wind Flyer 1211½ Handily 9
3Dec83- 8Med fst 170 :47 1:11⅘ 1:42⅖ Trenton 7 1 1½ 1hd 1hd 2nk Thornburg B 121 19.40 89-16 Homecoming Game 114nk Crude Ways 1214 Mr.Radius114½ Sharp 8
25Nov83- 6Med sly 6f :22⅗ :46⅕ 1:12⅖ Playpalace 3 5 3½ 2hd 11½ 11¼ Bailey J D 121 12.70 81-22 Crude Ways 1211¼ Attaway To Go 121¾ Agile Jet 1171 Driving 6
5Nov83- 8Med fst 1 1/16 :46⅕ 1:11⅖ 1:45⅕ Yng America 15 9 1113 1320 1429 1433¼ Whited D E 119 17.20f 50-20 Swale 122no Disastrous Night 1193 Dr. Carter 1196 No factor 16
25Oct83- 8Med fst 1 :47 1:12⅘ 1:39 Alw 14000 3 2 25 22½ 34½ 35¼ Whited D E 117 9.70 81-19 Attaway To Go 114½ Hai Andrew1174¾CrudeWays1177¼ Weakened 6
14Oct83- 6Med fst 1 :46⅗ 1:11⅕ 1:37⅗ Montclair 1 5 510 411 513 518¼ Whited D E 118 37.50 74-18 Shuttle Jet 1135 Loft 1125 Arabian Gift 113½ Outrun 6
28Sep83- 8Bel fst 7f :22⅗ :45⅕ 1:21⅖ Cowdin 1 7 911 914 828 825¾ Whited D E 122 42.20e 69-19 Devil's Bag 1153 Dr. Carter 1153 Exit Five B. 1153 Outrun 9
11Sep83-10LaD fst 6½f :22⅘ :46⅘ 1:19⅘ Lad Futy 11 3 61½ 4¾ 14 14 Pettinger D 115 8.80 76-20 Crude Ways 1154 Quick Justice 114½ Cir Lobo 1152 Drew clear 11
24Aug83- 4LaD fst 6½f :22⅗ :46⅖ 1:19⅘ [S]Alw 9000 8 8 63¼ 52½ 2½ 43 Pettinger D 115 3.80 73-20 Quick Justice 1141½ Cir Lobo 1141½ Big James 115hd 10
10Aug83- 5Aks fst 6f :22⅖ :45⅖ 1:12⅘ Md Sp Wt 8 1 23 23 1hd 1¾ Pettinger D 118 3.40 73-28 Crude Ways 118¾ Hawkin's Trick 1182½ Jo Jo's Crocodile 118nk 9
LATEST WORKOUTS Jan 27 Bel tr.t 3f fst :38 b ● Jan 21 Bel tr.t 6f fst 1:16⅗ b Jan 16 Bel tr.t 4f fst :50⅘ b Jan 6 Bel tr.t 3f fst :38 b

Wind Flyer

B. c. 3, by Full Pocket—Demure Miss, by Cyane
Br.—Glencrest Farm-Greathouse D & Jr (Ky)
Tr.—Dickey Charles L
Own.—Masterson R E
119 — Lifetime 11 3 2 3 $66,570 — 1984 1 0 0 1 $8,532 — 1983 10 3 2 2 $58,038

7Jan84- 8Aqu fst 6f [•]:22⅗ :46⅗ 1:11⅘ Rockaway 7 6 66¾ 67½ 56¾ 310 Samyn J L 121 3.60e 75-24 Crude Ways 1217 Whitebrush 1173 Wind Flyer 1211½ Rallied 9
30Dec83- 6Med fr 170 :45⅗ 1:10 1:39⅘ For'r Castin 8 6 53½ 32 21 2no Murphy D J 118 13.30 102-10 RovingMinstrel113noWindFlyer1187Donn'sTime1181½ Just missed 8
8Dec83- 8Med fst 6f :22⅖ :45 1:10⅗ Morven 1 5 1½ 21½ 24 35 Bailey J D 118 16.10 85-21 Fortunate Prospect 1184 Shuttle Jet 1141 Wind Flyer 1182 Tired 7
26Nov83- 8Aqu gd 1 :44⅘ 1:11 1:38⅖ Nashua 9 8 79½ 78 77 610¼ Hernandez R 117 8.10 64-24 Don Rickles 1141½ Arabian Gift 1142½ Raja's Shark 1144 Far back 9
12Nov83- 8Med gd 6f :22⅗ :46⅕ 1:11⅕ Morristown 3 6 66¾ 25 21½ 12 Perret C 119 9.30 87-25 Wind Flyer 1192 Mickey Mall 1147½NorthernFortress1156 Driving 6
28Sep83- 8Bel fst 7f :22⅗ :45⅕ 1:21⅗ Cowdin 4 6 32 46 722 720¾ MacBeth D 119 42.20e 74-19 Devil's Bag 1153 Dr. Carter 1153 Exit Five B. 1153 Tired 9
27Aug83- 8AP sly 7f :22⅘ :46 1:27 Arlwash Fty 9 15 1411 711 811 912 Kutz D 122 50.20 55-36 All Fired Up 1221½ Holme On Top122noSmartNSlick1221 Far back 17
13Aug83- 9Aks fst 6f :22⅗ :45⅖ 1:11⅗ Juvenile 5 8 74 53¼ 34 32 Kutz D 122 3.50 77-22 All Fired Up 110hd Rene's Rainbow 1222 Wind Flyer 1222½ Rallied 8
29Jly83- 8Aks fst 5½f :21⅕ :46 1:06⅖ Freshman 12 8 76½ 2½ 11½ 12 Kutz D 113 8.80 78-29 WindFlyer1132Dan'sBumperKing113hdRene'sRinbow1226½ Driving 13
13Jly83- 3Aks fst 5½f :22⅕ :46 1:06 Md Sp Wt 3 5 34½ 43 11 16½ Kutz D 118 3.70 80-26 Wind Flyer 1186½ O'Prospect 1181½ One Bold Stride 118nk 12
LATEST WORKOUTS Jan 27 Bel tr.t 3f fst :38⅗ b Jan 22 Bel tr.t 6f fst 1:17⅘ b Jan 17 Bel tr.t 4f fst :51⅗ b Dec 29 Med 3f my :39⅗ b

Lt. Flag *　B. c. 3, by Delta Flag—Stevens Stream, by Lt Stevens　Br.—Shropshire Mrs J S (Ky)　Tr.—Amos L Douglas
Own.—Cedar Copse Stable　**117**　Lifetime 13 7 1 2 $55,517　1984 2 1 1 0 $21,560　1983 11 6 0 2 $33,957

14Jan84- 6Aqu fst 170	[•]:49⅕ 1:14⅕ 1:42⅗	...dicap	3 1 1hd 2hd 21½ 22¾	Davis R G	112	3.10	85-17 ColdAndCloudy1122¾Lt.Flg11210NorthernFortress1141¼	Game try	7
7Jan84- 5Aqu fst 1 1/16	[•]:49 1:15 1:48	Alw 22000	1 1 11½ 1½ 12 16	McHargue D G	117	0.60	72-24 Lt. Flag 1176Vanlandingham1177½Cooper'sHawk1172½	Ridden out	7
5Dec83- 1Grd sly 6½f	:24 :48 1:20⅘	Clm 37500	5 6 44 21½ 1½ 12½	Hosang G	114	2.80	83-29 Lt. Flag 1142½ Group Of Seven 1112½ Long Song1161½	Drew clear	6
15Nov83- 1Grd my 7f	:22⅘ :47⅕ 1:27⅖	Clm c-20000	3 3 22½ 21½ 11 13	Attard L	122	*1.75	78-31 Lt. Flag 1223 Nova Bluff 1112½ Michael John 1142	Handily	5
4Nov83- 1Grd my 7f	:23⅖ :47⅗ 1:27⅘	Clm c-16000	3 2 31½ 32 22 12	Swatuk B	122	2.55	76-28 Lt. Flag 1222 Battle Dust 1176 Winfired 114¾	Handily	8
21Oct83- 7WO fst 6½f	:23⅕ :47⅗ 1:20⅗	Clm 20000	10 1 41¾ 33½ 25 35½	Attard L	122	*1.50e	65-32 Bald Admiral 1222½ Michael John 1142¾ Lt. Flag 1222½		10
9Oct83- 1WO gd 6½f	:23 :46⅘ 1:19⅘	Clm 15000	6 4 2hd 1½ 13 14¼	Attard L	120	3.40e	74-23 Lt. Flag 1204¼ Winfired 116¾ Praise The Prince 1142½	Handily	8
30Sep83- 6WO fst 6f	:22⅘ :47 1:14	Clm 12500	4 4 1½ 2hd 1hd 11½	Attard L	119	*1.35	73-26 Lt. Flag 1191½ Winfired 112¾ Prehysterical Guy 1141½		10
14Sep83- 1WO fst 6f	:22⅗ :46⅗ 1:13⅕	Clm 16000	6 3 2½ 21½ 34½ 39	Attard L	b 119	*1.65	68-28 [D]Opal Fire 1221½ Praise The Prince 1147½ Lt. Flag 1192½		8
11Sep83- 7WO fst 6f	:22⅕ :46 1:13⅘	Clm 24000	6 2 2hd 2hd 44½ 75½	Swatuk B	b 114	7.40	68-24 Season Premiere 119no Internie Look 115no GoGoDeMarco1161½		9

LATEST WORKOUTS　Jan 23 Bel tr.t 5f fst 1:04 b　Jan 2 Bel tr.t 4f fst :48 h　Dec 24 Bel tr.t 3f fst :38⅘ b　Dec 20 Bel tr.t 4f fst :53 b

Full Confidence　·R c. 3, by Full Partner—Cold Trick, by Northern Dancer　Br.—Evans T M (Va)　Tr.—Pearce Ross R
Own.—Buckland Farm　**117**　Lifetime 7 2 1 0 $15,011　1984 1 1 0 0 $6,900　1983 6 1 1 0 $8,111

14Jan84- 7Key fst 170	:46 1:12 1:43⅗	Alw 11500	3 3 32 31½ 21 12½	Lloyd J S	b 114	2.80	83-20 FullConfidence1142½SeeItThrough1127PecTricks1181½	Drew clear	7
30Dec83- 6Med fr 170	:45⅖ 1:10 1:39⅘	For'r Castin	7 7 87½ 612 613 615½	Santagata N	b 112	38.40	86-10 Roving Minstrel 113noWindFlyer1187Donna'sTime1181½	No factor	8
26Nov83- 8Aqu gd 1	:44⅘ 1:11 1:38⅖	Nashua	3 7 913 919 928 939	McCarron G	b 114	39.30	35-24 Don Rickles 1144½ Arabian Gift 1142½ Raja's Shark 1144	Far back	9
23Aug83- 6Mth fst 6f	:23⅖ :46⅘ 1:12⅖	Alw 12500	1 4 1½ 11½ 12 21	Terry J	b 115	5.60	77-22 Revere Paul 1171 Full Confidence 1154RightAndRegal1171	Failed	9
2Aug83- 9Mth fst 5½f	:23 :46⅕ 1:05	Tyro	3 6 53½ 55½ 45½ 49¾	Terry J	116	9.80	80-21 Smart N Slick116nkWillardScott1169StarChampion116½	No threat	8
10Jly83- 8Bel fst 6f	:22 :45⅕ 1:10⅖	Tremont	9 7 910 913 715 514¾	Terry J	115	10.90	75-15 Track Barron 1152 Tonto 1153½ Supporting Cast 1153¾	Outrun	9
13Jun83- 3Atl fst 4½f	:23⅕ :46⅖ :52⅗	Md Sp Wt	1 4 1½ 14 18½	Terry J	118	11.00	98-02 FullConfidence1188½PrivatelyProud1183½FlightJudge1182	Handily	6

LATEST WORKOUTS　Jan 27 Aqu [•] 3f fst :39⅘ b　Jan 24 Key 5f fst 1:02 b　Jan 13 Del 3f fst :37⅖ b　Jan 9 Del 5f fst 1:03 b

Cold And Cloudy　Ch. rig. 3, by Nordic Prince—Little Cloudy, by Hagley　Br.—Noonan & Runnymede Farm (Ky)　Tr.—Garcia Carlos J
Own.—Bigelow J W　**119**　Lifetime 4 3 1 0 $50,600　1984 1 1 0 0 $22,800　1983 3 2 1 0 $27,800

14Jan84- 6Aqu fst 170	[•]:49⅕ 1:14⅕ 1:42⅗	Handicap	2 4 41½ 31½ 11½ 12¾	Santiago A	112	*1.00	88-17 ColdAndCloudy1122¾Lt.Flg11210NorthernFortrss1141¼	Drew clear	7
31Dec83- 7Aqu fst 6f	[•]:22⅗ :46 1:10⅗	Alw 20000	3 5 42½ 21 2hd 11¼	Santiago A	122	*1.20	91-21 Cold And Cloudy 1221¼ It's Frigid 1175½ A Gift 1176¾	Driving	7
17Dec83- 4Aqu fst 6f	[•]:22⅘ :46⅘ 1:11⅗	Md Sp Wt	1 3 1hd 1hd 13 18¾	Santiago A	118	2.80	86-19 ColdAndCloudy1188¼RunnngBold1113¾CrclRond118nk	Ridden out	12
28Nov83- 6Aqu my 6f	:23⅕ :47 1:12⅘	Md Sp Wt	8 5 31½ 21½ 22½ 2hd	Santiago A	118	9.40	77-30 Pure Rascality 118hd Cold And Cloudy 1183 NileRiver1187¼	Sharp	13

LATEST WORKOUTS　Jan 10 Bel tr.t 5f fst 1:04 b　Dec 27 Bel tr.t 4f fst :50⅗ b　Dec 8 Bel tr.t 3f fst :36⅖ h

Whitebrush　B. c. 3, by Far North—Bronze Figurine, by Tobin Bronze　Br.—Backer J W (Ky)　Tr.—McGaughey Claude III
Own.—Loblolly Stable　**117**　Lifetime 8 2 4 2 $40,172　1984 1 0 1 0 $15,642　1983 7 2 3 2 $24,530

7Jan84- 8Aqu fst 6f	[•]:22⅗ :46⅗ 1:11⅘	Rockaway	3 7 76¾ 56½ 36 27	Lovato F Jr	117	4.50	78-24 Crude Ways 1217 Whitebrush 1173 Wind Flyer 1211½	Gamely	9
6Nov83- 7CD sly 6f	:22⅖ :46 1:12⅘	Alw 10625	3 5 65½ 63 22 2½	Day P	118	*.60	81-34 At The Threshold 115½ Whitebrush 1183 Textile 1151		7
2Nov83- 7CD sly 6½f	:23 :46⅘ 1:20	Alw 11200	4 9 86½ 32 2½ 14	Day P	118	*.60	80-25 Whitebrush 1184 BigPistol1183½SeamanTeelo112¾	Steadied, clear	11
3Sep83- 9CD fst 7f	:23⅕ :46⅕ 1:24⅘	Perryville	1 8 32½ 32 31 3nk	Allen K K	113	2.10	83-15 BiloxiIndian116nkTylor'sSpecil116hdWhitebrush1136	Lacked room	8
1Aug83- 3CD fst 6f	:22⅖ :46 1:10⅘	Md Sp Wt	5 1 22 13 16 18	Allen K K	118	*.50	92-13 Whitebrush 1188 Katie's Bidder 1186 Exclusive Greer 118½	Easily	7
3Aug83- 1CD gd 6f	:22⅖ :46⅕ 1:12⅕	Md Sp Wt	5 5 41¾ 33 2½ 22¼	Allen K K	119	3.60	83-19 Flying Finish 1192¼ Whitebrush 1193 Blush Of Fame 1196		8
1Jly83- 2CD fst 5½f	:22⅘ :46 1:05	Md Sp Wt	2 7 41 31 2hd 2nk	Allen K K	117	2.00	96-14 Lucky Larry 117nk Whitebrush 1173 Flying Finish 1176		8
1Jun83- 1CD fst 5½f	:23⅕ :46⅕ 1:05⅗	Md Sp Wt	8 8 85¾ 54½ 32 34	Day P	118	4.60	90-18 Nice Try 118hd Blind Man's Bluff 1184 Whitebrush 1182		9

LATEST WORKOUTS　Jan 16 Bel tr.t 4f fst :54 b　Jan 1 Bel tr.t 4f fst :47⅘ h　Dec 27 Bel tr.t 3f fst :49⅗ b　Dec 17 Bel tr.t 4f fst :50 b

Empravatar—There's no questioning the form of Empravatar. In his first start in a maiden race at 6 to 1, he broke eleventh in a field of twelve yet rallied to win the six furlong test by a neck. His time on a sloppy track, 1:14, was extremely slow, but of little meaning considering the time of year and condition of the track. Plus, he won by overcoming a dreadful start, an imposing achievement in itself for a first-time starter at six furlongs. In his next start, a $22,000 allowance at Aqueduct at a mile and seventy yards, Empravatar was an easy winner at 5 to 2, this time racing on the lead and increasing his margin from three to six lengths in the stretch. He will go off today at 9 to 1.

Meal Ticket—Was second by six lengths to Empravatar in his last start. Enough said.

S.S. Hot Sauce—Shows a record of 2-2-2 in seven lifetime starts, but it's hard to gauge his class. After taking three races to break his maiden, he was twice third in open allowance company at Laurel (purse of $9,500), then was twice entered in a stakes race restricted to Maryland-breds. S.S. Hot Sauce won the Maryland Juvenile by half a length despite being bumped, an impressive effort at $1^1/16$ miles. Then in the seven furlong E P Heagerty Stakes at Bowie in Maryland, he was second by four and a half lengths to Jyp while spotting him seven pounds. S.S. Hot Sauce certainly is in good form, but his class is unproven in relation to a New York stakes race. He spots Empravatar six pounds.

Crude Ways—Coupled in the wagering with Wind Flyer, Crude Ways is off the best race of his career, a seven length win at Aqueduct in the six furlong Rockaway Stakes. His two previous races were a second by a neck in the Trenton Stakes at a mile and seventy yards at The Meadowlands and a first by one and a quarter in a six furlong Meadowlands stakes, the Playpalace. This, too, is a fairly inexperienced horse who has gotten a lot better. What can we say about his class? Four consecutive races from the late fall of 1983 give an indication. After winning a stakes race at Louisiana Downs by four lengths, Crude Ways was entered against Devil's Bag in the seven furlong Cowdin Stakes at Belmont. Crude Ways finished eighth by twenty-five and three-quarters lengths. In his next start, the one mile Montclair at The Meadowlands, he lost to Shuttle Jet, finishing fifth by eighteen and a half lengths. Crude Ways then finished third by five and a quarter lengths in a $14,000 allowance at one mile at The Meadowlands before finishing fourteenth by thirty-three and a quarter lengths in the Young America at The Meadowlands won by Swale. In fairness to Crude Ways, he beat Shuttle Jet in the Rockaway. Actually, he crushed him as Shuttle Jet ran out of the money. We can take that to mean two things: 1) Crude Ways has improved some twenty-five lengths, or 2) Shuttle Jet was overrated and is, indeed as he's shown, an inconsistent horse. The huge margins Crude Ways was beaten in other stakes suggest he doesn't have the class to be competitive with the best of his generation or to even be close. In the Rockaway, he shook free on the lead and romped. We don't question the class he demonstrated in that stakes, rather we ask if he has a distinct class edge here. He does not, and at 8 to 5 is not a good investment.

Wind Flyer—Crude Way's stablemate is 3-2-3 in eleven starts with several interesting PPs. In his last start, Wind Flyer was third by ten against Crude Ways in the Rockaway. Previously, Wind Flyer won two stakes races, one at Ak-Sar-Ben in Nebraska (Ak-Sar-Ben is Nebraska spelled backwards) and one at The Meadowlands. Against proven top horses, however, Wind Flyer was also lacking. He was seventh by twenty and three-quarters lengths to Devil's Bag in the Cowdin and sixth by ten and a quarter to Don Rickles—the horse not the comedian—in the Nashua at one mile at Aqueduct. He followed the Nashua with a third and a second in two Meadowlands stakes before running third in the Rockaway. In the Morven, he was third by five against Fortunate Prospect and one length off Shuttle Jet while giving him four pounds. He and Crude Ways each give Empravatar two pounds.

Lt. Flag—He shows several lines in claimers, including a victory in a $12,500 claimer at Woodbine in Canada. Lt. Flag was claimed in consecutive races for $16,000 and $20,000 at Greenwood in Canada, each an easy win, then beat a $37,500 claiming field. Trainer Douglas Amos shipped Lt. Flag to Aqueduct, and on January 7, he won a $22,000 allowance at $1^1/_{16}$ miles by six lengths. In his last start, a handicap at Aqueduct at a mile and seventy yards, Lt. Flag was second by two and three-quarters to today's favorite, Cold And Cloudy. Of note is the ten length gap to the horse in third. That race gave Lt. Flag a record of six wins, one second and one third in his last eight starts, each without blinkers. Handicappers might be prone to take one look at Lt. Flag's cheap claiming races and throw him out of consideration. Form-wise, however, Lt. Flag gets a high ranking. He should be considered off his reasonably close second to Cold And Cloudy. In that race, they were weighted equally at 112. Today, Lt. Flag races at 117, getting 2 pounds from the favorite. Normally, cheap claimers don't make dents in stakes races, but we have yet to see demonstrative top class in this field. Keeping an open mind about horses improving, we'll conclude Lt. Flag is much improved.

Full Confidence—Beaten by fifteen and a half lengths by Wind Flyer two starts back at The Meadowlands.

Cold And Cloudy—The 8 to 5 co-favorite has four lifetime races. After finishing second by a head in his debut, Cold And Cloudy broke his maiden at Aqueduct by eight and a quarter lengths. He then won a $20,000 six furlong allowance by one and a quarter lengths. In his first try at a distance, he won a one mile and seventy yards handicap by two and three-quarters lengths against Lt. Flag. He picks up seven pounds from that race. Obviously, Cold And Cloudy is in excellent form. Has he proven class? Hardly. This is his first stakes race, too, just as it is for Empravatar.

Whitebrush—He's never been farther than seven furlongs and was beaten by seven lengths by Crude Ways in the Rockaway. But his lifetime record in eight starts is 2-4-2. The fact he beat Wind Flyer by three lengths in the Rockaway forces us to label him a contender.

What do we do here? Several of the horses have fine form, and one of them is Empravatar. None of the horses have proven a significant class edge with the possible exception of Crude Ways. We must make a conclusion about Crude Ways before we can consider betting against him, which—at his price—is something we'd like to do. If Crude Ways showed one bad race in stakes company last year, it'd be easier to make an excuse for his 2-year-old form. Three races, however, suggest he is not at a significantly higher class level than the other horses entered in the Count Fleet. Put another way, just being in a stakes race against better company doesn't magically transform a horse's ability. Empravatar and others in this race could have accomplished what Crude Ways did: get killed against better horses.

The odds on the board dictate one horse to bet: Empravatar. Worth noting is that jockey Jorge Velasquez rode Empravatar in his allowance victory, but today is riding Lt. Flag for the first time. People who would automatically use this to dismiss Empravatar's chances would be drawing a dangerous conclusion because Velasquez was not listed originally to ride Empravatar today and thus did not make a late choice between the two. Even if he had, jockeys intermittently pick the wrong horse when they have a choice of horses. Asked how often he chooses the right mount when he is listed for two horses in the same race, Cordero said, "I guess it's about even. My agent does the choosing unless I rode both horses the last time. Then he asks me."

We will go with Empravatar at the generous overlay. He receives a horrid ride from Jimmy Miranda, who manages to shut him off twice trying to move up on the inside.

Empravatar finished second to Lt. Flag, who went off at 6 to 1 combining with him for a $159.60 exacta.

Using our overlay horse, or Lt. Flag as the other overlay, was the right move.

Empravatar certainly didn't figure to be dismissed by the betting public at 9 to 1. The betting public, however, sometimes gets deep-rooted perceptions about a specific horse and is reluctant to alter that opinion. That's why you'll occasionally see horses winning three in a row and still going off at 3 to 1 or 4 to 1 for the third win. Simply, they are Rodney Dangerfield horses, ones which get no respect. When that happens, we're sure to get overlays.

Handicapping can entail learning an easy lesson, even if you weren't clever enough to learn it the first time. Horses are creatures of habit. Different horses perform well at certain tracks. They are aptly called Horses for Courses.

Handicappers have varying opinions of the validity of Horses for Courses, but Saratoga is famous for them. We'll use Horses for Courses to identify overlays. Let the disbelievers explain horses such as Love Sign, winner of the Alabama; Fio Rito, a New York-bred shipper from Finger Lakes who won the Whitney, and Quick Call.

Trainer Sidney Watters, Jr. brought Quick Call to Saratoga in 1987 during his 3-year-old season. Quick Call is one of a very few horses to ever cram four races into Saratoga's twenty-four day season. Watters' scheduling was validated by Quick Call's performances: three wins and one fourth (in a Grade III stakes, the King's Bishop) in four Saratoga starts. I had none of his victories, which produced surprisingly good mutuels of $18.20, $12.60 and $6.80. However, I did learn this simple lesson: Quick Call loved Saratoga.

When Quick Call returned as a 4-year-old in 1988, this conclusion led us to play him in his first start, a handicap against tough but not terrific sprinters. Only five other horses were in the race. Prospector's Halo was bet down to 6 to 5 favoritism despite a layoff of nearly two months. The second choice at 2 to 1 was Mom's Ruler, coming off an out-of-town victory at Pimlico. Amazingly, despite good form (a win, a sixth and a third in his last three races) and his documented fondness for Saratoga, Quick Call went off at 5 to 2. He gamely wore down Prospector's Halo in the final yards for a neck victory in a rapid 1:09 3/5 with an excellent final quarter mile in :23 2/5.

Final quarter time is widely used in harness racing handicapping. An interesting book applying this principle to thoroughbred racing, *Investing at the Race Track*, was written a few years ago. It endorsed handicapping by comparing final fractions, termed "ability times." I can't endorse it as an ultimate answer in thoroughbred handicapping, yet I'd suggest any serious handicapper could do worse than figuring out ability times for contenders in a race.

Quick Call's ability time produced a $7.40 payoff and reinforced the simple lesson learned: bet him at Saratoga.

Actually, it was hard to check the enthusiasm waiting for his next start. The bettors at Saratoga could be divided into two camps about Quick Call, those who bet him and those who bet against him. Only a year earlier, I was one of many muttering "I can't believe he won again." Now I was in the other camp saying "Of course he won again. He was at Saratoga."

I had no difficulty believing he'd win his next start at Saratoga, too. The pertinent question was: Would he again be an overlay?

Quick Call was entered nine days later in another handicap with the exact same purse, $41,000. In fact, one of his four rivals was Mr. Classic, who was fifth versus Quick Call the first time around.

Of the other three, My Prince Charming and Harriman came out of the same race at Pimlico, having finished sixth and eighth, respectively. Each went off at 5 to 1.

Clearly the horse to beat was one of D. Wayne Lukas' top sprinters, Jazzing Around, a ho-hum fourth in a New York-bred, one mile stakes at Belmont in his last start. Jazzing Around went off 4 to 5. Quick Call again, incredibly, was 5 to 2. Why? I have no idea. But I was certain about this: Quick Call was again a generous overlay. He won by three and a quarter lengths and paid $7.20 in a blazing 1:21 1/5 performance, just four-fifths off Saratoga's track record for seven furlongs.

Truly remarkable. The only thing that would make it even better was if Quick Call got in another race at Saratoga.

Voila. Eight days later, Quick Call went to post in the seven furlong Forego Handicap, a Grade III $114,200 stakes. Again, Quick Call faced a small field. There were only five horses and one of them was Mr. Classic, who had done worse against Quick Call the second time, finishing last by eight and a quarter lengths.

Of the others, Mawsuff was an interesting horse, a shipper from England who found a new career racing on dirt as a strong closing sprinter. In England, Mawsuff, of course, raced on turf. Interestingly, he had raced on the lead in his last two starts abroad, winning one of

8 SARATOGA

7 FURLONGS
SARATOGA

7 FURLONGS. (1.20⅖) 9th running THE FOREGO HANDICAP (Grade III). Purse $100,000 Added. 3-year-olds and upward. By subscription of $200 each, which should accompany the nomination; $800 to pass the entry box; $800 to start, with $100,000 added. The added money and all fees to be divided 60% to the winner, 22% to second, 12% to third and 6% to fourth. Weights Tuesday, August 16. Starters to be named at the closing time of entries. Trophies will be presented to the winning owner, trainer and jockey. Nominations Closed Wednesday, August 3 with 23 nominations.

Shadowmar

Ro. h. 9, by Pontoise—Cautious Fairy, by Neptune
Br.—Schoenborn Bros Farm (NY)
Tr.—Schoenborn Everett F
Own.—Schoenborn E F
109
Lifetime 40 8 6 5 $261,120 | 1988 2 0 0 1 $4,920 | 1987 2 0 0 0 $2,520 | Turf 1 0 0 0

13Jly88- 7Bel fst 7f :22⅗ :46 1:23⅗ 3+Alw 41000 7 2 65 54 55½ 69 Venezia M 115 7.50 75-20 ScottishMonk1154½Embrc'sSybling1103Smrknd115no Raced wide 9
12Jun88- 6Bel fst 6f :22⅗ :46 1:10⅕ 3+Alw 41000 7 3 62¾ 32 22 32¼ Maple E 117 33.10 86-17 Seattle Knight 1221¼ Scottish Monk 1171 Shadowmar 1173¼ Wide 8
9Oct87- 7Bel fst 6f :22⅕ :46 1:11 3+Alw 42000 7 8 84¾ 72½ 42½ 44 Davis R G 115 12.40 80-29 Mugatea 115noRaja'sShark1154Cullendale115no Lckd finished bid 8
23Sep87- 8Bel fst 6f :22⅗ :44⅘ 1:09 3+Handicap 1 6 69 69½ 611 611 Davis R G 112 9.20 83-16 Sunny Feet 121½ Omar Khayyam 111¾ Why Not Try 1153¾ Trailed 6
10Dec86- 8Aqu gd 6f ⊡:22⅕ :45⅕ 1:09⅘ 3+ⓈJ Palmer 12 1 107½106½1012 911½ Lovato F Jr 119 6.70 83-08 H. T. Willis 1192 Maelstrom 117¾ LandingPlot120¹¾ Wide into str. 13
22Aug86- 8Sar fst 6f :22 :45⅖ 1:10⅖ 3+Crnsh Prince 1 4 48 22 12½ 11 Davis R G 115 9.00 87-17 Shadowmar 1151 Cost Conscious 115nk Cullendale 1153½ Driving 6
7Aug86- 5Sar fst 7f :22⅗ :45⅕ 1:23 3+Alw 36000 1 2 24 26 2½ 1½ Davis R G 115 6.30 87-17 Shadowmar 115½ E. K. Spatz 113nk Up Pops Awinner115¾ Driving 7
28Aug86- 5Sar fst 6f :21⅗ :44⅖ 1:09⅕ 3+A Phenomenon 7 7 710 68 56½ 56 Davis R G 115 18.90 88-10 Cognizant 117nk Royal Pennant 112¹½ Cullendale 1153¾ No factor 7
LATEST WORKOUTS Aug 18 Sar 3f fst :35⅕ h Aug 13 Sar 5f fst 1:01 h Jly 28 Sar 5f fst 1:02⅘ b ●Jly 8 Bel 6f fst 1:14⅗ h

High Brite

B. c. 4, by Best Turn—Spray, by Forli
Br.—Allen Joseph (Ky)
Tr.—Lukas D Wayne
Own.—Allen Joseph
122
Lifetime 34 12 7 5 $917,911 | 1988 10 6 0 2 $388,415 | 1987 18 4 6 1 $492,408

6Aug88- 1Sar sly 6f :21⅘ :44⅘ 1:10⅕ 3+A Phenomenon 4 4 2½ 1½ 13½ 11¾ Cordero A Jr 122 *.40 89-12 High Brite 122¹¾ Abject 1157½ Uncle Ho 115 Driving 4
2Jly88- 9FL fst 6f :22 :44⅘ 1:09⅗ 3+Bud Brdr Cup 7 2 2½ 1½ 11½ 15 Cordero A Jr 122 *.40 98-18 High Brite 1225 Highland Ruckus115hdLoveThatMac113no Driving 8
19Jun88- 8Bel fst 6f :22⅗ :45⅗ 1:10 3+True Nrth H 4 1 11½ 11 2hd 1nk Cordero A Jr 120 *1.00e 89-21 High Brite 120nk Irish Open 115½ King's Swan 122nk Driving 6
19Jun88-Grade II
4Jun88- 8Bel fst 6f :22⅕ :45 1:08⅗ 3+Roseben H 8 8 11 11 1hd 1no Cordero A Jr 119 *.80e 96-13 High Brite 119no Jazzing Around 1133½ Irish Open 116¹½ Driving 8
4Jun88-Grade III
21May88- 7Pim gd 6f :23 :46 1:10⅗ 3+Bud Brds Cup 2 6 2½ 21 33 34 Stevens G L 121 *1.70 89-11 Fire Plug 116¹½ Harriman 1172½ High Brite 121²½ Weakened 6
21Apr88- 9OP fst 6f :21⅗ :44⅕ 1:08⅗ C Fleet H 7 6 33½ 34½ 67½ 68 Stevens G L 123 *1.10 89-17 Salt Dome 1163 Pewter 1131 Bold Pac Man 1123 9
21Apr88-Grade II
6Mar88- 3SA fst 7f :22 :44⅖ 1:21⅗ 3+Vkng Spt H 1 2 11½ 11 11½ 11½ Stevens G L 121 *1.30 92-13 High Brite 121¹½ Earn Your Stripes 118hd My GallantGame112hd 7
13Feb88- 8SA fst 5½f :22 :45⅕ 1:03⅘ El Conejo H 1 8 21½ 21½ 21 3nk Stevens G L 120 4.30 92-22 Sylvan Express 119hd Carload 117nk High Brite 120¹¾ 8
30Jan88- 3SA fst 1 :47 1:11⅗ 1:36⅘ Alw 60000 3 1 11 11 11½ 1¾ Stevens G L 116 *2.90 84-20 High Brite 116¾ Sabona 1152¾ Lord Grundy 1143 7
9Jan88- 8SA fst 7f :22⅕ :44⅕ 1:22 S Carlos H 4 1 42 45½ 57 53½ Stevens G L 118 2.80 86-17 Epidaurus 117no Super Diamond 125nk Lord Ruckus 1182 7
9Jan88-Grade II
LATEST WORKOUTS Aug 17 Sar tr.t 4f fst :49 b Aug 1 Bel 5f fst 1:00⅘ b Jly 26 Bel 5f fst 1:02⅘ b

*Mawsuff

B. h. 5, by Known Fact—Last Request, by Dancer's Image
Br.—Hamdan Al Maktoum (Eng)
Tr.—Skiffington Thomas J
Own.—Shadwell Farm
110
Lifetime 18 5 2 3 $91,013 | 1988 6 3 0 1 $65,260 | 1987 5 1 0 1 $16,342 | Turf 11 2 2 1 $21,913

20Jly88- 8Mth fst 1⅛ :47⅘ 1:11⅕ 1:42⅕ 3+Alw 25000 6 5 54½ 42¾ 43 43½ Johnson P A 119 *1.90 91-16 Fast Forward 115hdToweringStar115²½Bowladrome115¾ No threat 7
25Jun88- 6Bel fst 7f :23⅕ :46⅗ 1:23⅕ 3+Handicap 3 8 74¾ 76½ 63½ 4¾ Santos J A 114 *1.00 85-21 Omar Khayyam 109no Abject 111½ Conquer 120nk Wide 8
9Jun88- 3Bel fst 1 :46⅕ 1:10⅖ 1:35⅘ 3+Alw 47000 7 5 46½ 33 11 13¾ Day P 117 2.10 88-13 Mawsuff 1173¾ Pledge Card 117nk Fourstardave 110nk Driving 7
23May88- 7Bel fst 7f :22⅗ :45⅗ 1:22⅘ 3+Alw 30000 10 1 43 23 11½ 13½ Day P 121 *1.50 88-23 Mawsuff 121³½RonStevens121nkConquilot121¹½ Wide, going away 10
22Apr88- 7Kee fst 6½f :23⅗ :45⅘ 1:17 Alw 23100 3 5 52½ 62¾ 44 32½ Velasquez J 121 2.00 89-22 Passing Ships 118no Irish Freeze 1152½ Mawsuff 121¾ 7
8Apr88- 6Kee fst 7f :23 :45⅗ 1:23⅗ Alw 22000 5 6 43½ 32 11 16 Perret C 114 5.90 88-21 Mawsuff 1146 Willowick 112¾ Measurement 112no 12
17Dec87- 7Aqu fst 6f ⊡:23⅕ :47 1:11⅘ 3+Alw 32000 6 4 42½ 21½ 33 34 Maple E 117 10.10 84-21 Hibernation 1172¾ Real Account 112¹½ Mawsuff 1173½ Weakened 9
22Jun87♦4Brighton(Eng) gd 1 1:38⅗ Ⓣ BrightonMileChallengeHcp 7 Hills R b 137 4.00 — — Prince Merandi 107¹½ Fouz 127¹½ Sit This One Out 1342½ Led 5f 7
3Jun87♦6Epsom(Eng) gd*7f 1:21 Ⓣ Craven Hcp 1¾ Hills R b 129 25.00 — — Mawsuff 129¾ Haber 131¹½ Shmaireekh 136hd Led thruout 11
5May87♦2Chester(Eng) fm*7½f 1:32⅘ Ⓣ HolstenDiatPilsHcp 10 Hills R 137 12.00 — — ComeOnTheBlues127nk RindrWlk115²½ KnightsScrt117hd Outrun 14
LATEST WORKOUTS Aug 9 Sar tr.t 4f fst :49 b Aug 2 Sar tr.t 5f fst 1:02⅗ b Jly 19 Bel 3f fst :37⅘ b Jly 12 Bel 5f fst 1:00⅘ b

Quick Call *

B. g. 4, by Quack—Sadie Mae, by Sadair
Br.—Jones W I Jr & Greathouse D L Jr (Ky)
Tr.—Watters Sidney Jr
Own.—Stokes Lynda
110
Lifetime 30 8 3 4 $211,386 | 1988 7 3 0 1 $81,180 | 1987 18 4 3 2 $114,126 | Turf 3 0 0 0

13Aug88- 1Sar fst 7f :22⅗ :44⅖ 1:21⅘ 3+Handicap 5 1 3½ 2½ 2½ 13½ Day P b 108 2.60 96-12 QuickCall108³½ⒹHarriman113½JzzingAround1162 Strong handling 5
4Aug88- 5Sar fst 6f :22⅗ :46⅕ 1:09⅗ 3+Handicap 5 1 42½ 31 1hd 1nk Day P b 107 2.70 92-11 QuickCall107nkProspector'sHlo115²½Seeker'sJourney108nk Lasted 6
25Jly88- 8Bel fst 6f :23⅕ :46⅗ 1:10⅘ 3+Handicap 5 1 2hd 1½ 31½ 34½ Day P b 108 3.70 80-27 Abject 1124½ Conquer 120no Quick Call 1083½ Weakened 5
25Jun88- 6Bel fst 7f :23⅕ :46⅗ 1:23⅕ 3+Handicap 4 6 31 21 52½ 66¾ Cruguet J b 109 15.70 79-21 Omar Khayyam 109no Abject 111½ Conquer 120nk Tired 8
11Jun88- 3Bel fst 6f :22⅗ :45⅗ 1:09⅗ 3+Handicap 2 2 21 2hd 2hd 1nk Day P b 107 *1.50 91-13 Quick Call 107nk Peppy Le Pew 109nk Royal Value 1102¾ Driving 7
23May88- 8Bel fst 6f :22⅗ :46 1:09⅘ 3+Handicap 7 3 2hd 3nk 52½ 75 Day P b 108 13.10 85-23 Irish Open 1142¾ Prospector's Halo 1152 Its Acedemic111no Wide 9
15May88- 6Bel fst 6f :22 :45 1:10⅕ 3+Alw 41000 8 2 2hd 2hd 2hd 41½ Santos J A b 121 16.90 87-15 Abject 124no Gay Rights 1121 Hibernation 124nk Faltered 8
22Nov87- 8Aqu fst 6f :22⅗ :46⅕ 1:10⅖ 3+Sprt Pge H 1 8 84¾ 83¾ 76¾ 79¾ Davis R G b 110 26.20 79-32 Vinnie the Viper 115¹½ King's Swan 123½Banker'sJet118²½ Outrun 10
22Nov87-Grade III
15Nov87- 5Aqu fst 6f :21⅘ :44⅕ 1:08⅘ 3+Handicap 5 2 31½ 31½ 42 2½ Davis R G b 110 6.10 96-10 Banker's Jet 122½ Quick Call 110¹¾ Why Not Try 1132 Gamely 6
30Oct87- 8Aqu fst 6f :22⅗ :45 1:09⅗ 3+Alw 42000 5 2 31½ 3½ 32 32½ Vasquez J b 119 9.10 91-25 Matthews Keep 1191 Pinecutter 119¹½ Quick Call 1194 Weakened 6
LATEST WORKOUTS Aug 19 Sar 3f fst :38 b Jly 31 Sar 4f fst :49⅘ b Jly 15 Bel 4f fst :47⅘ h Jly 8 Bel 4f fst :47 h

No Points

Ch. c. 4, by Miswaki—Take a Stand, by Amerigo
Br.—Humphrey Louise I (Ky)
Tr.—Frankel Robert
Own.—Clover Racing Stable
113
Lifetime 9 5 1 0 $64,520 | 1988 5 1 1 0 $30,320 | 1987 4 4 0 0 $34,200 | Turf 1 0 0 0

11Aug88- 7Sar fst 7f :22 :44⅗ 1:21⅕ 3+Alw 41000 6 3 35½ 43½ 2½ 1no Day P 115 3.90 96-10 No Points 115no Claramount 1154 Conquilot 1153 Driving 10
29Jun88- 8Hol fst 1 :45 1:09⅗ 1:34⅗ Alw 55000 3 2 31 68 614 621¼ Baze R A 115 13.50 68-14 Epidaurus 1151 Red Attack 117nk Midwest King 116¹½ 7
6Mar88- 3SA fst 7f :22 :44⅖ 1:21⅗ 3+Vkng Spt H 6 1 35 45½ 67 64¾ Pincay L Jr 117 6.80 87-13 High Brite 121¹½ Earn Your Stripes 118hd My GallantGame112hd 7
19Feb88- 8SA fm 1 Ⓣ:47⅗ 1:11⅗ 1:36 Alw 50000 9 1 1hd 2hd 64 88¼ Gryder A T5 109 4.60 87-05 Putting 115nk Neshad 1151 Motley 114½ Bmpd,steadied 9
2Jan88- 6Hia fst 7f :23⅗ :46⅗ 1:22⅘ Key West 8 1 31 3½ 21½ 21½ Perret C 114 *.80 87-14 Prospctor'sHlo114¹½NPnts114hdⒹⒽBldsk'sStr117 Between horses 8
17Dec87- 8Hia fst 7f :23⅗ :46 1:22⅘ 3+Alw 14000 2 3 11 1½ 11½ 13 Perret C 114 *2.30 89-24 No Points 1143 Villa Bright 114hd Cliff Flower 116no Ridden out 11
8Jly87- 8Mth sly 6f :22 :44⅗ 1:10⅘ 3+Alw 16000 5 4 31 1hd 1½ 14½ Perret C 114 *.70 86-22 No Points114⁴½Can'tStandStill116²½Exuberation116hd Ridden out 6
18Jun87- 8Mth fst 6f :22⅘ :45⅕ 1:10⅕ 3+Alw 14000 7 2 2hd 1hd 12 13½ Perret C 114 *1.50 89-14 No Points 1143½ Limited Access 1112 Toll Key 116½ Handily 9
1Feb87- 7Hia fst 6f :22⅕ :45⅗ 1:10⅗ Md Sp Wt 10 2 45½ 44½ 31 1no Perret C 121 *3.00 87-19 NoPoints121noDiamondKnight121³½JustaProspector121³½ Driving 12
LATEST WORKOUTS Aug 18 Sar tr.t 4f fst :49⅕ b Aug 8 Sar tr.t 4f fst :49 b ●Aug 3 Sar tr.t 6f fst 1:15⅘ b Jly 26 Bel 5f fst 1:01 h

Mr. Classic						**Dk. b. or br. h. 5, by Mr Prospector—Classic Dance, by Board Marker**										Lifetime	1988 20 0 2 0	$49,440
						Br.—Regal Oak Farm (Fla)									**105**	64 5 9 4	1987 13 3 1 1	$81,460
Own.—Garren M M						**Tr.—Garren Murray M**										$384,698	**Turf** 2 0 0 0	
Entered 20Aug88- 7 SAR																		
13Aug88- 1Sar	fst	7f	:22⅗	:44⅖	1:21⅕	3♦Handicap	2	5	517	519	59½	58¼	Venezia M		108	12.90	88-12 QuickCall1083¼[D]Harriman113½JazzingAround1162 Without speed	5
4Aug88- 5Sar	fst	6f	:22⅗	:46⅕	1:09⅗	3♦Handicap	6	4	615	65½	56¼	55¼	Venezia M		108	17.00	87-11 QuckCll107nkProspctor'sHlo1152¼Skr'sJorny108nk Without speed	6
23Jly88- 3Bel	gd	7f	:22⅘	:45⅗	1:23	3♦Alw 41000	3	6	611	69	55	45	Hernandez R		117	10.30	82-24 Uncle Ho 115hd Forest Fair 1153¼ I Rejoice 1151¾ No factor	6
3Jly88- 5Bel	fst	6f	:23	:46	1:10⅗	3♦Alw 41000	1	3	516	516	514	49¼	Antley C W		117	13.30	77-25 JzzingAround1224¼IrishOpn1223Embrc'sSyblng1102 Saved ground	5
25Jun88- 6Bel	fst	7f	:23⅕	:46⅖	1:23⅕	3♦Handicap	2	3	89¾	814	818	814¾	Venezia M		107	23.40	71-21 Omar Khayyam 109no Abject 111½ Conquer 120nk Outrun	8
11Jun88- 3Bel	fst	6f	:22⅘	:45⅘	1:09⅗	3♦Handicap	4	5	711	79¾	712	77½	Venezia M		107	8.50	84-13 Quick Call 107nk Peppy Le Pew 109nk Royal Value 1102¾ Outrun	7
4Jun88- 8Bel	fst	6f	:22⅕	:45	1:08⅗	3♦Roseben H	5	3	610	810	89¾	67¾	Day P	b	106	19.20	88-13 High Brite 119no Jazzing Around 1133½ Irish Open 1161½ Outrun	8
4Jun88-Grade III																		
26May88- 8Bel	fst	1 1/16	:46	1:10⅘	1:42⅖	3♦Alw 47000	2	2	1hd	2½	68½	717¾	Venezia M	b	121	8.70	72-16 My Prince Charming 121½ Fuzzy 124¾ JackOfClubs1213½ Stopped	7
23May88- 8Bel	fst	6f	:22⅘	:46	1:09⅘	3♦Handicap	8	1	74½	95¼	86½	87½	Venezia M		106	25.40	82-23 Irish Open 1142¾ Prospector's Halo1152ItsAcedemic111no Outrun	9
12May88- 8Bel	my	7f	:22⅕	:44⅖	1:21⅕	3♦Handicap	2	4	610	611	57	26½	Venezia M		107	13.80	89-14 JzzingAround1136½Mr.Clssic107hdRj'sShrk115hd Gained the place	6
LATEST WORKOUTS						**Aug 11 Sar 3f fst :35⅗ h**							**Jly 30 Bel 4f fst :48⅕ h**				**●Jly 18 Bel tr.t 5f my 1:01 h**	**Jly 11 Bel tr.t 4f fst :48⅘ b**

them at 25 to 1. In America, he finished third in his debut, was given nearly four months off and raced well in 1988 with three wins, a third and two fourths in six starts. His last two efforts were fourth place finishes as the favorite at 1 to 1 at Belmont and at 9 to 5 in a 1¹⁄₁₆ mile allowance at Monmouth Park.

No Points shipped in from California to win his last start at Saratoga, a $41,000 allowance. Three starts back, he finished sixth by four and three-quarters in a minor stakes at Hollywood Park won by High Brite, who happened to be racing in the Forego. High Brite, the latest sprint star Wayne Lukas sent in to battle Quick Call, had won his last four races, the final two at odds of 2 to 5.

In ten 1988 starts, High Brite had six wins and two thirds.

Did Quick Call figure to beat him?

It's fortunate we begin our examination of PPs from the bottom line and work our way up to each horse's most recent race. Otherwise, we might have missed this riveting line: in the Budweiser Breeders' Cup Sprint at Pimlico, High Brite finished third by four lengths. Harriman beat him by two and a quarter lengths to finish second. Yes, that's the same Harriman that Quick Call had beaten by three and a quarter in his last start.

After that loss, High Brite began his four race win streak. Casual handicappers glancing just at his most recent races saw a bunch of ones. There was more to see.

The final horse opposing Quick Call in the Forego was symbolic. Shadowmar, a 9-year-old, hadn't won a race in two years and managed just four starts. Before that, though, he had been the ultimate Horse For Course at Saratoga. He had won at least one race at Saratoga every year from 1983, when he won an open handicap paying $45.80, through 1986, when he won an allowance and the Cornish Prince Stakes, paying $14.60 and $20.00.

Shadowmar was well past his prime. But his presence in the Forego passed the torch of Saratoga Horses For Courses to Quick Call, a horse many bettors at Saratoga just would not believe.

That's right. Quick Call not only wasn't bet into favoritism, he was gauged at 2 to 1. High Brite was odds-on, 9 to 10, and No Points 3 to 1. High Brite, ridden by Cordero, set torrid fractions of :22 2/5 and :44 3/5 with Quick Call and jockey Pat Day stalking him relentlessly on his flank. When the two raced past the three-quarters in 1:08 2/5—two-fifths of a second off Spanish Riddle's six furlong track record which has held up for seventeen years—Quick Call gained a narrow lead as Mawsuff continued a menacing rally.

It was too late. Quick Call held Mawsuff safe by three-quarters of a length with High Brite another three-quarters of a length back. Quick Call paid $6.60, setting a stakes record of 1:21.

EIGHTH RACE
Saratoga
AUGUST 21, 1988

7 FURLONGS. (1.20⅘) 9th running THE FOREGO HANDICAP (Grade II). Purse $100,000 Added. 3-year-olds and upward. By subscription of $200 each, which should accompany the nomination; $800 to pass the entry box; $800 to start, with $100,000 added. The added money and all fees to be divided 60% to the winner, 22% to second, 12% to third and 6% to fourth. Weights Tuesday, August 16. Starters to be named at the closing time of entries. Trophies will be presented to the winning owner, trainer and jockey. Nominations Closed Wednesday, August 3 with 23 nominations.
Value of race $114,200; value to winner $68,520; second $25,124; third $13,704; fourth $6,852. Mutuel pool $405,602. Exacta Pool $481,043.

Last Raced	Horse	Eqt.A.Wt	PP	St	¼	½	Str	Fin	Jockey	Odds $1
13Aug88 ¹Sar¹	Quick Call	b 4 110	4	1	$2^{1\frac{1}{2}}$	2^5	$2^{2\frac{1}{2}}$	$1^{\frac{3}{4}}$	Day P	2.30
20Jly88 ⁸Mth⁴	Mawsuff	5 110	3	6	5^5	5^8	$3^{\frac{1}{2}}$	$2^{\frac{1}{4}}$	Davis R G	9.10
6Aug88 ¹Sar¹	High Brite	4 122	2	4	1^1	$1^{\frac{1}{2}}$	1^{hd}	3^1	Cordero A Jr	.90
11Aug88 ⁷Sar¹	No Points	4 113	5	2	4^1	$3^{2\frac{1}{2}}$	4^5	4^7	Santos J A	3.70
13Aug88 ¹Sar⁵	Mr. Classic	5 105	6	5	6	6	6	$5^{1\frac{3}{4}}$	Belmonte J F	35.20
13Jly88 ⁷Bel⁶	Shadowmar	9 109	1	3	$3^{\frac{1}{2}}$	$4^{\frac{1}{2}}$	5^3	6	Venezia M	15.40

OFF AT 5:38 Start good, Won driving. Time, :22⅖, :44⅗, 1:08⅖, 1:21 Track fast.

$2 Mutuel Prices:

4–(D)–QUICK CALL	6.60	4.00	2.40
3–(C)–MAWSUFF		8.40	3.20
2–(B)–HIGH BRITE			2.20

$2 EXACTA 4–3 PAID $53.20.

B. g, by Quack—Sadie Mae, by Sadair. Trainer Watters Sidney Jr. Bred by Jones W I Jr & Greathouse D L Jr (Ky).

QUICK CALL prompted the pace while racing outside HIGH BRITE, caught that one nearing the stretch, dueled for the lead until near the final sixteenth and proved best under good handling. MAWSUFF rallied along the inside leaving the turn, came out for the drive and finished strongly. HIGH BRITE saved ground while making the pace, held on well until near the final sixteenth and weakened. NO POINTS rallied from the outside entering the stretch but lacked the needed late response. MR. CLASSIC was always outrun. SHADOWMAR was finished while saving ground.

Quick Call returned to Saratoga in 1989; finished second and first in his first two starts, and then, in a field of five, was once again virtually ignored in the tenth running of The Forego Handicap. Quick

Call went off as the 9 to 5 third choice, won the race wire-to-wire, and improved his Saratoga record to 8-1-0 in ten starts. Incredibly, he was the favorite just once in his eight victories.

EIGHTH RACE
Saratoga
AUGUST 20, 1989

7 FURLONGS. (1.20⅖) 10th Running THE FOREGO HANDICAP. (Grade II). $100,000 Added. 3-year-olds and upward. By subscription of $200 each, which should accompany the nomination; $800 to pass the entry bo; $800 to start, with $100,000 added. The added money and all fees to be divided 60% to the winner, 22% to start, 12% to third and 6% to fourth. Weights Tuesday, August 15. Starters to be named at the closing time of entries. Trophies will be presented to the winning, owner, trainer and jockey. Closed Wednesday, August 2, 1989 with 22 nominations.

Value of race $108,196; value to winner $62,920; second $24,900; third $13,584; fourth $6,792. Mutuel pool $518,176.

Last Raced	Horse	Eqt.	A.	Wt	PP	St	¼	½	Str	Fin	Jockey	Odds $1
12Aug89 ^{7}Sar^1	Quick Call	b	5	116	3	1	1^1	1^2	$1\frac{1}{2}$	1^{nk}	Day P	1.90
13Aug89 ^{8}Sar^7	Dancing Spree	b	4	117	4	3	5	4^6	$2^{2\frac{1}{2}}$	$2^{4\frac{3}{4}}$	Cordero A Jr	1.50
15Jly89 ^{8}Bel^1	Sewickley		4	119	2	5	$3^{2\frac{1}{2}}$	$3^{1\frac{1}{2}}$	$3^{1\frac{1}{2}}$	$3^{1\frac{3}{4}}$	Romero R P	1.90
14Aug89 ^{7}Sar^1	Crusader Sword	b	4	113	1	4	$2^{1\frac{1}{2}}$	$2^{2\frac{1}{2}}$	4^{12}	4^{13}	Bailey J D	8.10
31Jly89 ^{8}Bel^4	Landing Plot		6	110	5	2	$4\frac{1}{2}$	5	5	5	Samyn J L	41.40

OFF AT 5:38. Start good. Won driving. Time, :23⅘, :46⅕, 1:10⅕, 1:21⅘ Track fast.

$2 Mutuel Prices:			
3-(C)-QUICK CALL	5.80	3.00	2.20
4-(D)-DANCING SPREE		2.80	2.10
2-(B)-SEWICKLEY			2.20

B. g, by Quack—Sadie Mae, by Sadair. Trainer Watters Sidney Jr. Bred by Jones W I Jr & Greathouse D L Jr (Ky).

QUICK CALL, allowed to get away with an easy lead while racing well out from the rail, increased his advantage around the turn, was roused when challenged with a furlong remaining and turned back DANCING SPREE under good handling. The latter, outrun early, moved boldly along the inside leaving the turn, continued his bid to midstretch but wasn't good enough in a game effort. SEWICKLEY rallied from the outside leaving the turn but weakened during the drive. CRUSADER SWORD, close up early while saving ground, eased out when unable to stay with quick call nearing the turn and tired under pressure. LANDING PLOT wasn't able to keep pace.

The split divisions of the 1983 Bernard Baruch Handicap, a $50,000 turf stakes at Saratoga, offered two additional vivid examples of Horses for Courses.

Ten Below, a 4-year-old stakes-winning son of Avatar, first came to Saratoga as a 2-year-old maiden in 1981 making only the second start of his life. Conditioned at the time by the accomplished horseman, Edward Kelly, a trainer particularly adept at winning races on the turf, Ten Below had been an okay yet unspectacular fourth in his career debut at Belmont. At Saratoga, he was somehow allowed to go off at 9 to 1 in a maiden turf race despite the presence of perennial Saratoga riding champion Cordero. Ten Below won, and would go on to accumulate more than $300,000 in earnings in his lifetime.

Ten Below returned to Saratoga to win a turf race in 1982 and was claimed by Mrs. Viola Sommer for $75,000. Trainer Frank Martin promptly saddled him to win the Grade II Lawrence Realization at

Belmont. As a 4-year-old in 1983, Ten Below had been given a near four month layoff by Martin, who brought him back to the races in late April.

Ten Below's summer performances before Saratoga were a victory in a handicap, then a fifth, a third and a second. Obviously, he was in good form.

He and seven others would challenge the 4 to 5 favorite, Tantalizing, in the first division of the Bernard Baruch.

6 **SARATOGA**

TURF COURSE
1 1-8 MILES
SARATOGA
START FINISH

1 ⅛ MILES. (TURF). (1.45⅖) 25th Running THE BERNARD BARUCH HANDICAP (Grade II). Purse $50,000 Added. (1st Division). 3-year-olds and upward. By subscription of $100 each, which should accompany the nomination; $400 to pass the entry box, with $50,000 added. The added money and all fees to be divided 60% to the winner, 22% to second, 12% to third, and 6% to fourth. Weights, Tuesday, August 2. Starters to be named at the closing time of entries. A trophy will be presented to the winning owner. The New York Racing Association reserves the right to transfer this race to the main course. Closed Wednesday, July 20, 1983 with 58 nominations.

```
*Sun and Shine            Gr. c. 4, by African Sky—Ica, by Great Nephew              Lifetime      1983  9  ?  1  1   $77,339
                          Br.—Bunting & Hine Mmes (Eng)                       114   19  6  4  1   1982  5  2  1  0   $17,900
  Own.—DuPont Anne A      Tr.—Pugh Peter D                                               $113,663   Turf 17  6  3  1  $109,263
9Jly83- 9Mth fm 1⅛ (T):47⅖ 1:11⅗ 1:43⅖ 3+Oceanport H  11 12 1116 97 45 54 Terry J   117  5.10  80-17 Fray Star 1141½ Domynsky 1121½ And More 1171½  Rallied 12
Jly83- 8Atl fm 1⅜ (T):47 1:10⅗ 1:53⅖ 3+U Nations H  12 13 107¾ 74¾ 77½ 77½ Terry J  116  29.60  89-08 Acaroid 113½ Trevita 1162½ Majesty's Prince 120no  Outrun 13
Jun83- 9Mth fm 1 (T):47⅖ 1:11⅕ 1:36⅗ 3+Red Bank H  1 10 109½ 85½ 32 1½ Terry J  115  7.50  92-21 SunandShine115½St.Brendn116noMr.Dremer1135  Brushed, driving 11
May83- 8Pim fm 1½ (T):49⅖ 2:04 2:28⅗ 3+Dixie H  8 5 56 31 99½ 916 Saumell L  115  4.50  78-10 Khatango 1142¾ London Times 1083 Super Sunrise 1141½  Wide 10
30Apr83- 8Pim yl 1⅛ (T):48⅗ 1:13⅗ 1:46⅗ 3+Riggs H  2 6 57½ 34 1hd 11 Wright D R  113  8.80  78-23 Sun and Shine 1131 McCann 116½ ThirtyEightPaces1162½  Driving 8
23Apr83- 6Pim fst 1⅛ :48⅕ 1:12⅖ 1:44⅕  Alw 20000  3 6 54½ 42½ 1hd 2nk Bracciale V Jr  114  12.10  84-18 Count Disco 114nk Sun and Shine 114hd A MagicSpray1146  Sharp 6
20Feb83-10FG fm *1⅛ (T)  1:50⅗  F G Classic  13 8 811 75¾ 54½ 96¾ Saumell L  114  17.20  75-11 Listcapade 120¾ Explosive Bid 118¾ Cagey Cougar 1161½  Outrun 13
23Jan83- 9FG fm *1⅛ (T)  1:44  Handicap  7 7 73¾ 42½ 1hd 3nk Saumell L  114  5.20  95-10 Listcapade 116nk Rapid Rebound 115hd Sun and Shine 114¾  8
9Jan83- 7FG fm *7½f (T):21⅗  1:31⅕  Alw 10200  10 10 910 76½ 11½ 1½ Saumell L  116  3.20  93-07 Sun and Shine 116½ Davrick 1131 Truetoo 114½  Driving 10
11Nov82- 7Lrl fm 1⅛ (T):48⅕ 1:14 1:45⅖ 3+Alw 10500  3 7 62½ 1hd 1nk 1nk Saumell L  117  *.90  76-27 Sun and Shine117nkEurodancer1156BuckJump116no  Ret. bleeding 9
  LATEST WORKOUTS   Aug 3 Sar 4f gd :49 h   Jly 27 Atl 4f fst :52 b   Jun 29 Atl (T) 4f sf :53 b   ●Jun 15 Atl (T) 4f fm :51 b (d)

Disco Count               Dk. b. or br. g. 7, by Dancing Count—Grecian Coin, by Royal Coinage   Lifetime      1983  6  3  1  0   $68,120
                          Br.—Weymouth Mrs E E (Pa)                            112   69 10 16 10   1982 21  5  4  3  $118,257
  Own.—MacMillen W C Jr   Tr.—Watters Sidney Jr                                           $267,984   Turf 24  7  7  3  $173,883
27Jly83- 6Sar fm 1⅛ [T]:48 1:11⅕ 1:42⅕ 3+Alw 37000  5 1 17 13 11½ 1½ Maple E  119  *1.40  94-11 Disco Count 119½ Fray Star 1191½ Erin's Tiger 119nk  Driving 7
17Jly83- 7Bel fm 1 (T):45 1:08⅖ 1:34 3+Handicap  2 1 16 14 14 13¾ Maple E  111  2.90  95-14 Disco Count 1113¾ Ten Below 1135½ AskClarence1093  Ridden out 8
2Jly83- 3Bel fm 7f (T):23 :45⅖ 1:23⅕  Clm 100000  5 2 2hd 2½ 1½ 2nk Maple E  122  *1.30  88-11 Mr. Badger 113nk Disco Count 1221¾ Ten Bore 1122  Sharp try 11
17Jun83- 8Bel fm 1⅛ (T):46⅖ 1:11 1:42⅗ 3+Alw 37000  6 2 21½ 2½ 22½ 64½ Maple E  117  2.70  78-12 Lamerok 1193 Red Brigade 119nk Half Iced 117hd  Gave way 8
10Jun83- 6Bel fm 1⅛ [T]:47⅘ 1:11⅕ 1:42⅕  Clm 175000  5 1 11 11½ 12 12½ Maple E  112  5.90  90-17 Disco Count 1122½ Fray Star 1222½ Red Brigade 112no  Ridden out 8
25May83- 8Bel gd 1⅛ [T]:48 1:12⅖ 1:44⅗ 3+Handicap  7 2 21½ 2hd 66 711 Maple E  116  12.00  67-32 Ten Below 117½ Santo's Joe 1152½ Campus Capers 113¾  Stopped 8
22Nov82- 9Aqu fst 1 :45⅘ 1:10⅕ 1:35⅕ 3+Handicap  2 4 42 66 815 817 Molina V H  112  12.50  73-23 Winter's Tale 1225 Goodbye Starter 113nk Citius 113nk  Tired 8
28Oct82- 8Med yl 1⅛ (T):49 1:13⅕ 1:44⅗ 3+Cliff Hngr H  4 2 1hd 1hd 32 45 Bailey J D  115  1.90  74-22 Acaroid 1143½ North Course114½ThirtyEightPaces1161  Weakened 7
     28Oct82-Run in Two Divisions: 6th & 8th Races
8Oct82- 8Bel fm 1 (T):45⅘ 1:09⅗ 1:33⅘ 3+Alw 35000  4 1 1½ 11 12½ 12¼ Bailey J D  122  4.50  96-13 Disco Count 1222¼ War of Words 115hd Erin's Tiger1198¼  Driving 7
30Sep82- 5Bel fm 1 (T):45⅖ 1:09 1:34⅗ 3+Clm 80000  6 2 2hd 1hd 11 1½ Bailey J D  114  2.30  92-15 Disco Count 114½ No Neck 1121½ Gauguin Native 1164¾  Driving 7
  LATEST WORKOUTS   Aug 5 Sar 4f fst :47⅕ b   Jly 16 Bel 3f fst :36⅘ h   Jly 10 Bel 4f fst :51 b   Jun 28 Bel 4f fst :49⅖ h

Pride Of Satan            Ch. c. 4, by Crimson Satan—Pretty Pride, by Kentucky Pride   Lifetime      1983  6  2  0  0   $22,800
                          Br.—Crimson King Farm (Ky)                           101   11  3  2  1   1982  5  1  2  1   $13,610
  Own.—Paparo I           Tr.—Coladonato Eugene J                                          $36,410   Turf  7  2  2  0   $22,500
1Aug83- 2Sar my 7f :22⅘ :46 1:25 3+Clm 45000  4 3 2hd 11½ 14 16½ Miranda J  b 113  17.40  77-24 Pride Of Satan 1136½ Ack Attack 110¾ Starbinia 1082  Ridden out 8
9Jly83- 6Bel fm 1⅛ [T]:48⅕ 1:12⅖ 1:43 3+Alw 23000  2 2 21½ 32 710 713 McCarron G  b 117  30.30  73-12 Stoney Lonesome 1111¾ A Real Leader 1172 J.R.Collins1121  Tired 8
3Jly83- 7Bel fm 1⅛ (T):46⅕ 1:10⅖ 1:42⅖ 3+Alw 21000  11 1 21 31 76 86½ Davis R G  b 117  25.00  77-15 Jeffers West 117hd Chica's Prince 111hd Hypertee 113nk  Tired 12
22Jun83- 4Bel fm 1¼ [T]:47⅗ 1:37⅘ 2:02⅘  Clm 35000  10 5 54½ 12 12 1no Davis R G  b 117  3.90  80-14 PrideOfSatn117noBeuBidder117hdRichButterfly112½  Bore out, dr. 11
13Jun83- 2Bel hd 1 (T):45⅘ 1:08⅖ 1:33⅗  Clm 75000  8 3 3½ 23 58½ 710 Davis R G  112  24.60  87-08 King's Glory 1223¾ Deedee'sDeal116¾FabulousFur1131¾  Gave way 11
9Jun83- 1Bel fst 6f :22⅗ :45⅘ 1:10⅘  Clm 35000  4 7 87 87 75 76¾ Davis R G  117  25.80  81-17 Colonel Law 1083½ Jeffery C. 1172 Harmonizer 117hd  Outrun 9
22Nov82- 1Aqu yl 1⅛ (T):49 1:15 1:54⅗  Clm c-50000  5 6 56¼ 64¾ 23 2¾ Fell J  117  5.60  70-27 Whale's Eye 113¾ Pride Of Satan 1171½ Flatterer 114nk  Rallied 7
15Jly82- 4Mth fm *1⅛ (T):49⅘ 1:14⅖ 1:45⅘ 3+Md Sp Wt  6 1 11½ 12½ 18 15½ Tejeira J  115  *1.50  90-11 Pride Of Satan 1155½ Outpost 1155 Goldmania 118½  Ridden out 10
26Jun82- 5Mth fm *1⅛ (T):47⅗ 1:12⅘ 1:46 3+Md Sp Wt  8 3 28 31½ 4nk 2¾ Tejeira J  114  5.00  88-05 Governorship 114¾ Pride Of Satan 114½ K. C.'sRelic115nk  In tight 8
29May82-10Mth sly 6f :22⅖ :45⅘ 1:12⅖ 3+Md Sp Wt  4 6 661 39 39 46 Tejeira J  115  7.10  72-25 Northern Magus 1153¾IronGladiator1151Sandsaw1151¾  Weakened 11
  LATEST WORKOUTS   Jly 28 Sar 6f fst 1:14⅘ b

Native Raid *             Gr. c. 3, by Native Aid—High Scoring, by Sea-Bird            Lifetime      1983 17  6  4  2   $84,100
                          Br.—Iandoli Mr-Mrs L E (Fla)                         106   26  6  6  5   1982  9  M  2  3    $6,900
  Own.—Cohen R B          Tr.—Shapoff Stanley R                                            $91,000   Turf  4  2  2  0   $30,820
25Jly83- 5Bel sf 1¼ [T]:48⅖ 1:39⅖ 2:06⅘ 3+Alw 21000  1 1 14 2hd 12½ 1nk McCarron G  b 112  2.50  60-43 Native Raid 112nk Twelve Tone 1122¼ Antigua 1161½  Driving 7
15Jly83- 8Bel hd 1⅜ [T]:11 2:01 2:14 3+Alw 21000  8 1 15 13 11½ 2hd McCarron G  b 112  *2.90  87-15 New Discovery117hdNativeRaid112nkTampaTown1133¾  Weakened 9
1Jly83- 5Bel hd 1⅛ (T):45 1:09 1:40⅗  Clm 45000  8 1 12½ 12 14 13½ McCarron G  b 113  8.70  93-16 Native Raid 1133½ Speier's Luck 1132 Lutyens 1142¾  Drew clear 10
11Jun83- 1Bel fst 1 :46⅖ 1:11⅗ 1:36⅖ 3+Alw 21000  2 2 3½ 810 1022 1026 Bailey J D  b 112  9.00  57-14 DaringGroom1043½CathedralAisle1142¾BrodwyHrry1123½  Used up 10
1Jun83- 7Bel fst 1⅛ :47 1:11⅕ 1:49⅗ 3+Alw 21000  1 2 2½ 1hd 32 87¾ Bailey J D  b 112  4.60  71-12 Held Blameless 112nc Norclin 1103¾ Asticou 1121¼  Gave way 9
16May83- 4Aqu sly 1⅛ :47⅖ 1:13⅕ 1:52⅘  Clm c-45000  3 1 14 13 21½ 23 Davis R G5  b 110  *.90  66-28 Olden Pocket 1133NativeRaid1102½SuperbMissile1152¾  Lost whip 9
4May83- 3Aqu my 1⅛ :47⅖ 1:11⅖ 1:51⅕  Clm 50000  4 3 1hd 1hd 12½ 11¼ Cordero A Jr  b 117  *.70  79-18 Native Raid 1171¼ Coast Range 1171½ Billy Bailey 1062  Driving 7
28Apr83- 9Aqu fst 7f :22 :45 1:22⅕  Clm 50000  6 5 44 3nk 2½ 25½ Smith A Jr  b 117  *2.20  84-16 Brooder's Tip1155½NativeRaid1172¼KingBilly1105½  Best of others 10
24Apr83- 5Aqu sly 1 :46 1:11 1:36⅕  Clm c-35000  2 3 32 1½ 14 110 Vasquez J  b 117  *1.80  85-19 Native Raid 11710 Dashido1121¾SirPrizeBirthday1151¾  Ridden out 10
11Apr83- 6Aqu my 6½f :22⅘ :46⅕ 1:17⅗  Clm 35000  5 2 63½ 54 32½ 1hd Smith A Jr  b 117  3.50  87-23 Native Raid 117hd Dashido 1102¾ Brooder's Tip 1145  Driving 8
  LATEST WORKOUTS   Aug 4 Sar 4f fst :48 h   Jly 9 Bel 4f fst :48 h   Jun 25 Bel 6f fst 1:14⅘ h   Jun 19 Bel tr.t 5f fst 1:02 b
```

Fit to Fight B. c. 4, by Chieftain—Hasty Queen II, by One Count
Br.—Congleton & Courtney (Ky)
Own.—Rokeby Stable Tr.—Miller Mack
112
Lifetime 15 7 1 3 $261,435
1983 9 1 1 2 $88,979
1982 6 4 0 1 $173,436

30Jly83- 8Sar fst 1⅛ :46⅘ 1:10⅘ 1:48⅖ 3↑Whitney H 9 4 31 3½ 42 42¾ Bailey J D 114 19.60 90-14 Island Whirl 123no Bold Style 114½ Sunny's Halo 1162 Weakened 9
30Jly83-Dead heat
17Jly83- 8Bel fst 7f :22⅘ :45⅗ 1:22⅕ 3↑Tom Fool 7 6 74 64½ 54½ 24¾ Maple E 119 6.50 86-13 Deputy Minister 1264¾ Fit to Fight 119no Muscatin 126hd Rallied 8
26Jun83- 8Bel fst 6f :22⅖ :45⅕ 1:10⅖ 3↑True North H 5 8 66 56½ 45 33½ Bailey J D 113 5.30 86-24 Gold Beauty 1212½ Singh Tu 1111½ Fit to Fight 1132 Wide str. 8
30May83- 8Bel my 1 :44⅖ 1:08⅕ 1:33⅘ 3↑Metroplt'n H 9 7 65 69 89¾ 89½ Bailey J D 115 *1.50 86-11 StrChoic1131½ToughCritc1103¾John'sGold1112 Lacked a response 1?
7May83- 8Aqu fst 7f :22⅘ :44⅗ 1:22⅘ 3↑Carter H 2 8 73¾ 64½ 71¾ 33 McCarron G 116 *1.50 84-19 Vittorioso 113nk Sing Sing 1222¾ Fit to Fight 116¾ Blocked 9
22Apr83- 8Aqu fst 6f :22⅖ :45⅗ 1:09⅖ 3↑Alw 35000 4 9 43 42½ 1hd 11½ Bailey J D 121 4.40 94-16 Fit to Fight 1211½ Star Gallant 1213¾ Sepulveda 119nk Drew clear 1?
30Oct82- 8Aqu fst 1⅛ :47⅘ 1:11⅗ 1:49⅗ 3↑Stuyvesant H 3 2 2½ 21 33½ 34 Bailey J D 118 2.40 83-16 Engine One 1232 Bar Dexter 1122 Fit to Fight 1182 Weakened 6
30Sep82- 6Med fst 1⅛ :47⅗ 1:11⅖ 1:49 Pegasus H 1 2 31½ 33 68½ 48½ Bailey J D 118 *1.30 80-15 Fast Gold 1103½ Muttering 1202 Exclusive One 1163 Weakened 6
6Sep82- 8Bel fst 1 :45⅘ 1:10⅕ 1:35⅖ Jerome H 1 2 1hd 1½ 13½ 16 Bailey J D 112 1.60 88-17 Fit to Fight 1126 John's Gold 1152¾ Lord Lister 1071 Ridden out 6
19Aug82- 7Sar fst 6f :22 :45 1:09⅖ 3↑Alw 32000 1 4 45 32 21½ 1¾ Fell J 117 *1.60 93-17 Fit to Fight 117¾ Hat Room 1151½ Ring of Light 1191 Driving 5
LATEST WORKOUTS ●Aug 5 Sar Ⓣ 3f fm :36⅖ h Jly 27 Sar 5f fst 1:01 h Jly 9 Bel 6f fst 1:14 b ●Jun 20 Bel 6f gd 1:12⅘ h

***Domynsky** Ch. c. 3, by Dominion—My Therape, by Jimmy Reppin
Br.—Webster C A (Eng)
Own.—Dogwood Stable Tr.—Curtis William Jr
110
Lifetime 18 7 7 1 $108,586
1983 8 2 2 1 $79,750
1982 10 5 5 0 $28,836
Turf 16 7 7 1 $108,446

9Jly83- 9Mth fm 1⅟₁₆ Ⓣ:47⅖ 1:11⅗ 1:43⅖ 3↑Oceanport H 3 6 68½ 64 33½ 21½ Rocco J 112 3.50 83-17 Fray Star 1141½ Domynsky 1121½ And More 1171½ Angled out 12
2Jly83- 9Mth fm 1⅟₁₆ Ⓣ:48 1:11⅗ 1:42⅗ Lamplighter 4 3 21 11½ 11 2¾ Perret C 120 4.20 87-20 Tough Mickey 115¾Domynsky120hdHeadoftheHouse1111½ Gamely 11
5Jun83- 8Bel sf 1 Ⓣ:48 1:13⅖ 1:39⅗ Saranac 2 2 21½ 21½ 23 36½ Bailey J D 123 4.50 61-40 Sabin 1136 Fortnightly 117nk Domynsky 1231 Weakened 10
22May83- 8Bel sf 1⅟₁₆ Ⓣ:48⅘ 1:14⅘ 1:48⅘ Hill Prince 6 2 1hd 1½ 2hd 11½ Bailey J D 114 6.50 52-41 Domynsky 1141½ White Birch 1144½ Macho Duck 114nk Driving 11
7May83- 8Pim fm 1 Ⓣ:48⅗ 1:13 1:39 Woodlawn 5 5 53½ 42½ 51½ 41¾ Bracciale V Jr 116 2.80 62-10 Disrco'sRib110nkNow'sTheTime1161AustinC.112½ Steadied at str. 11
16Apr83- 4Hia fm *1⅛ Ⓣ 1:41 Alw 15000 6 2 22 32 1½ 13 Cruguet J 112 5.40 94-07 Domynsky 1123 Intransic Sailor 115no GloryO.So1121½ Drew clear 7
9Mar83- 9Hia fst 7f :23 :46 1:23⅖ Alw 14000 2 1 11 3½ 715 718 Brumfield D 114 31.00 68-22 Hamlet 114hd Justice Sanders 1142½ El Cubano 1142½ Fell back 7
14Feb83- 7GP fst 7f :23 :46⅕ 1:24⅕ Golden Grass 1 7 63¾ 54½ 714 719 Brumfield D 115 14.40 64-21 Thalassocrat 1136 Alchise 1175 Very Funny 114hd No factor 8
14Feb83-Run in two division 7th & 9th races
9Oct82♦4York(Eng) gd 6f 1:17⅗ Ⓣ Marston Moor Stakes 12 Birch M 127 2.00 — — Domynsky1272 BoyTrumpeter1234 AldernStrem1246 Well pl drvg 4
18Sep82♦3Catterick(Eng) fm 7f 1:24 Ⓣ London&NorthernNrsyHcp 2nk Taylor B 134 1.75 — — LindasFantasy123nk Domynsky1347 VIndication1051½ Well up,led 5
LATEST WORKOUTS ●Aug 2 Mth 6f my 1:13⅖ h (d) Jly 23 Mth 5f fst 1:02⅘ b ●Jun 28 Mth 4f fst :47 h ●Jun 23 Mth 6f fst 1:13 h

Ten Below B. c. 4, by Avatar—Out Cold, by Cloman
Br.—Bwamazon Farm (Ky)
Own.—Sommer Viola Tr.—Martin Frank
110
Lifetime 23 6 6 1 $180,551
1983 8 2 1 1 $53,980
1982 13 3 5 0 $115,771
Turf 18 6 6 1 $179,231

17Jly83- 7Bel fm 1 Ⓣ:45 1:08⅖ 1:34 3↑Handicap 4 6 26 24 24 23¾ Fell J b 113 4.00 91-14 Disco Count 1113¾ Ten Below 1135½ Ask Clarence 1093 Went well 8
2Jly83- 7Bel fm 1 Ⓣ:47⅕ 1:11⅕ 1:35⅘ 3↑Handicap 1 2 1hd 2½ 32 33 Fell J b 115 *.90e 83-11 RedBrigade1121½ProtectionRcket1221½TenBelow1151½ Weakened 6
11Jun83- 5Bel fm 1½ Ⓣ:47⅖ 2:00⅘ 2:25⅖ 3↑Handicap 1 4 44 2hd 32 54½ Fell J b 116 7.70 93-06 Field Cat 116no Tantalizing 113nk Highland Blade 1264 Weakened 12
25May83- 8Bel gd 1⅟₁₆ Ⓣ:48 1:12⅖ 1:44⅗ 3↑Handicap 8 5 54½ 42 21 1½ Fell J b 117 4.20 78-32 Ten Below 117½ Santo's Joe 1152½ Campus Capers 113¾ Driving 8
16May83- 8Aqu sf 1⅟₁₆ Ⓣ:49 1:14⅘ 1:47⅖ 3↑Fort Marcy H 4 5 63¾ 55½ 48 513 Fell J b 113 6.90 55-32 John's Gold 1085½ Acaroid 1153¾ Beagle 105¾ No response 8
8May83- 7Aqu fm 1⅟₁₆ Ⓣ:49⅗ 1:13 1:44⅗ 3↑Alw 32000 5 5 63¾ 53¾ 22½ 1hd Fell J b 121 3.20 81-19 Ten Below 121hd Forkali 1212¾ KeyCount1212 Lacked room st.,dr 9
29Apr83- 8Aqu fst 1⅛ :46⅘ 1:11⅗ 1:50⅖ 3↑Alw 27000 2 2 25 45 59 513 Fell J b 121 *1.40e 70-26 ⓓChapter One 121hdNathanDetroit1217MainTop1211¾ Tired badly 5
9Jan83- 9Aqu fst 170 ▣:48⅕ 1:12⅗ 1:42 Alw 29000 5 4 43 1010 1015 1016 Kaenel J L b 117 9.80 76-17 Tarberry 112hd Grand Felice 1171½ Climbing High 1191½ Stopped 10
13Dec82- 8Aqu fst 1⅛ ▣:49⅘ 1:14⅘ 1:52⅘ 3↑Alw 29000 2 1 1½ 2½ 54 78¼ Kaenel J L b 115 3.40e 74-22 Our Escapade 1102½ Skin Dancer 115hd Airbus 1171½ Tired 7
20Nov82- 6Aqu gd 1⅟₁₆ Ⓣ:49 1:14⅖ 1:48⅖ 3↑Alw 25000 1 4 2hd 2hd 53 65¾ Cordero A Jr b 115 *1.10 57-32 Bexar 1131½ Haunted Lad 115nk Main Top 115hd Tired 6
LATEST WORKOUTS ●Aug 1 Sar 6f fst 1:11 h Jly 26 Sar 5f fst 1:00 h Jly 10 Bel 5f fst 1:01⅗ h ●Jun 26 Bel tr.t 5f fst 1:00 h

Tantalizing B. c. 4, by Tom Rolfe—Lady Love, by Dr Fager
Br.—Phipps O M (Ky)
Own.—Phipps O M Tr.—Penna Angel
115
Lifetime 5 4 1 0 $150,920
1983 5 4 1 0 $150,920
1982 0 M 0 0
Turf 3 2 1 0 $132,320

19Jun83- 8Bel fm 1⅜ ⓣ:48⅗ 1:37⅖ 2:14⅘ 3↑Bwlg Green H 7 4 46 32 43½ 1¾ Vasquez J 113 *1.80 83-25 Tantalizing 113¾ Sprink 1131 Majesty'sPrince122¾ Brushed, drvng 7
11Jun83- 5Bel fm 1½ Ⓣ:47⅖ 2:00⅘ 2:25⅖ 3↑Handicap 7 6 67 1hd 11½ 2no Bailey J D 113 *1.50 97-06 Field Cat 116no Tantalizing 113nk Highland Blade 1264 Just failed 12
26May83- 7Bel gd 1¼ ⓣ:49 1:39 2:04⅖ 3↑Alw 27000 8 4 312 1½ 14 17¾ Bailey J D 121 3.80 72-33 Tantalizing 1217¾ Silver Ring 1193¾ Groomed 119½ Ridden out 8
12May83- 5Aqu fst 1 :46⅖ 1:12⅗ 1:38⅖ 3↑Alw 21000 3 5 49 44½ 2½ 1nk Bailey J D 121 *.90 74-20 Tantalizing 121nk Nepal 1102½ Starhitch 1162¾ Raced Greenly,Dr 7
29Mar83- 4Hia fst 7f :23⅕ :46⅗ 1:24⅕ Md Sp Wt 7 10 85¾ 33 12 17 Bailey J D 122 *.80 82-19 Tantalizing 1227 Rexson's Rock 1221½ Hazard Man 1225 Handily 11
LATEST WORKOUTS ●Aug 5 Sar Ⓣ 4f fm :47 h ●Jly 30 Sar tr.t 5f fst 1:01⅗ b Jly 18 Bel 6f fst 1:14⅗ h Jly 12 Bel 5f fst 1:00⅘ h

Acaroid Dk. b. or br. h. 5, by Big Spruce—Arachne, by Intentionally
Br.—Tartan Farms (Fla)
Own.—Tartan Stable Tr.—Nerud Jan H
115
Lifetime 22 8 4 4 $341,699
1983 4 1 2 0 $111,120
1982 8 2 1 3 $94,887
Turf 17 8 2 3 $325,819

2Jly83- 8Atl fm 1⅜ Ⓣ:47 1:10⅗ 1:53⅖ 3↑U Nations H 4 5 31 3nk 2hd 1½ Cordero A Jr b 113 13.40 97-08 Acaroid 113½ Trevita 1162½ Majesty's Prince 120no Driving 13
4Jun83- 8Bel sf 1¼ ⓣ:48⅗ 1:41 2:06⅖ 3↑Red Smith H 3 3 45½ 21½ 34½ 511 Cordero A Jr b 114 8.00 51-39 Thunder Puddles 1171½ John's Gold 1122½ Open Call 1245½ Tired 7
4Jun83-Run in two divisions, 6th & 8th races
16May83- 8Aqu sf 1⅟₁₆ Ⓣ:49 1:14⅘ 1:47⅖ 3↑Fort Marcy H 8 6 43 22½ 24 25½ Cordero A Jr b 115 2.20e 62-32 John's Gold 1085½ Acaroid 1153½ Beagle 105¾ Off slowly 8
1May83- 7Aqu fst 7f :23 :46 1:23 3↑Alw 35000 6 2 42 42½ 32½ 2¾ BernhrdtEJJr10 b 109 13.50 85-21 Satan's Charger 101¾ Acaroid 1091¾ Otter Slide 124¾ Wide str. 7
4Dec82- 7Aqu gd 1⅟₁₆ ▣:47 1:11⅗ 1:44⅗ 3↑Handicap 5 5 32 2hd 43½ 44½ Miranda J b 119 2.00e 85-15 Castle Knight 117¾ Faces Up 1132 John Casey 1121½ Weakened 7
28Oct82- 8Med yl 1⅟₁₆ Ⓣ:49 1:13⅕ 1:44⅗ 3↑Cliff Hngr H 6 4 41¾ 2hd 11½ 13½ Cordero A Jr b 114 *1.70 79-22 Acaroid 1143½ North Course 114½ Thirty Eight Paces1161 Driving 7
28Oct82-Run in Two Divisions: 6th & 8th Races
17Oct82- 7Aqu fm 1 Ⓣ:46 1:10⅖ 1:35⅘ 3↑Alw 35000 6 3 31½ 2hd 1hd 31½ Bailey J D b 115 *1.20 98-01 Santo's Joe 114½ Ten Below 116¾ Acaroid 115hd Off Slowly 6
1Sep82- 8Bel fm 1⅟₁₆ Ⓣ:45⅖ 1:09⅖ 1:41 3↑Brtn Beach H 7 3 14 12 11 3¾ Cordero A Jr b 113 2.00 90-27 Sprink 112no Erin's Tiger 112¾ Acaroid 1136 Weakened 10
15Aug82- 8Sar fm 1⅛ Ⓣ:47⅕ 1:11 1:47⅘ 3↑B Baruch H 7 5 53 21 32½ 66¾ Cordero A Jr b 114 *1.60 81-07 Pair of Deuces 115¾ Native Courier 117½ McCann112nk Gave way 11
31Jly82- 8Atl fm 1⅜ Ⓣ:48⅘ 1:12⅗ 1:55⅗ 3↑U. N. Hcp 9 2 2½ 1hd 2hd 25 Cordero A Jr b 115 *2.40 81-25 Naskra's Breeze 1175 Acaroid 1151 Don Roberto 116hd Game try 10
LATEST WORKOUTS Aug 1 Sar 5f fst 1:01 b Jly 27 Sar 5f fst 1:00 h Jly 17 Bel 5f fst 1:05 b Jly 11 Bel 4f fst :51⅗ b

Tantalizing, a 4-year-old colt trained by Angel Penna for Ogden Mills Phipps, had won four of five races lifetime, two of them on turf. His only loss was by a nose to Field Cat. Tantalizing had beaten Majesty's Prince, a multi-stakes winner, in his last start when he won the Bowling Green Handicap at Belmont Park.

Ten Below had faced Tantalizing in the 1½ mile turf race won by Field Cat. Ten Below finished fifth by four and a quarter lengths in the handicap while giving Tantalizing three pounds. Today, he would receive five, an important shift of eight pounds.

The Baruch distance of 1⅛ miles would also help Ten Below, who seemed best suited to middle distances.

If we can be presumptuous enough to disregard the others in the race—Acaroid was easily the best of the rest and he had run sixth by six and three-quarters lengths in the 1982 Bernard Baruch—can we logically endorse Ten Below against an odds-on horse he has already lost to, Tantalizing?

We can if we believe Ten Below will run a superior race because he is at his favorite track, Saratoga's turf course. He had already won races at Saratoga the last two years, but even more important was the workout he showed once he got to Saratoga. A steady yet certainly unspectacular worker throughout his career, Ten Below had two workouts at Saratoga, a decent five furlongs on the main track in 1:00, then a fantastic move on the main track: six furlongs in a bullet 1:11. Realizing Ten Below is a turf specialist and not a dirt horse, and realizing he's not a flashy worker, we have every reason to believe Ten Below is at his absolute peak for this race, a belief which fits well into Ten Below's proven history of success on the Saratoga turf.

Tantalizing may hold a class edge, but Tantalizing is 4 to 5. Ten Below is an astonishing 11 to 1, a price hard to understand for anyone familiar with his previous record at Saratoga.

Ridden atrociously by Jeff Fell—the charts tell you Ten Below was "steadied"—he nonetheless boldly moved through the pack to grab a short lead over Acaroid and Tantalizing in the stretch. Then lugging in towards the hedge badly, Ten Below was passed by Tantalizing, finishing second by three-quarters of a length. The replays showed Ten Below actually skimmed the hedge just before the wire as Fell failed to maintain a straight course with his horse. Acaroid finished third, a neck behind Ten Below, who paid $5.80 to place and $3.60 to show, teaming with the 4 to 5 favorite for a quinella worth $32.40.

SIXTH RACE
Saratoga
AUGUST 7, 1983

$1\frac{1}{8}$ MILES.(turf). (1:45$\frac{3}{5}$) 25th Running THE BERNARD BARUCH HANDICAP (Grade II). Purse $50,000 Added. (1st Division). 3-year-olds and upward. By subscription of $100 each, which should accompany the nomination; $400 to pass the entry box, with $50,000 added. The added money and all fees to be divided 60% to the winner, 22% to second, 12% to third, and 6% to fourth. Weights, Tuesday, August 2. Starters to be named at the closing time of entries. A trophy will be presented to the winning owner. The New York Racing Association reserves the right to transfer this race to the main course. Closed Wednesday, July 20, 1983 with 58 nominations. Value of race $56,900, value to winner $34,140, second $12,518, third $6,828, fourth $3,414. Mutuel pool $181,500, OTB pool $163,340. Quinella Pool $169,430. OTB Quinella Pool $191,136.

Last Raced	Horse	Eqt.A.Wt	PP	St	¼	½	¾	Str	Fin	Jockey	Odds $1
19Jun83 [8]Bel[1]	Tantalizing	4 115	8	9	8^{3}	$8^{1\frac{1}{2}}$	6^{1}	2^{2}	$1^{\frac{3}{4}}$	Bailey J D	.80
17Jly83 [7]Bel[2]	Ten Below	b 4 114	7	8	7^{hd}	$7^{\frac{1}{2}}$	8^{2}	3^{2}	2^{nk}	Fell J	11.00
2Jly83 [8]Atl[1]	Acaroid	b 5 115	9	7	3^{1}	3^{1}	$2^{1\frac{1}{2}}$	1^{hd}	$3^{8\frac{1}{4}}$	Cordero A Jr	4.00
9Jly83 [9]Mth[2]	Domynsky	3 110	6	6	6^{2}	$5^{\frac{1}{2}}$	$4^{1\frac{1}{2}}$	$4^{\frac{1}{2}}$	4^{4}	Samyn J L	12.90
25Jly83 [5]Bel[1]	Native Raid	b 3 107	4	4	2^{4}	$2^{1\frac{1}{2}}$	1^{1}	5^{1}	5^{nk}	Davis R G	39.20
9Jly83 [9]Mth[5]	Sun and Shine	4 114	1	3	9	9	$7^{\frac{1}{2}}$	6^{hd}	$6^{3\frac{3}{4}}$	McCarron G	47.20
27Jly83 [6]Sar[1]	Disco Count	7 112	2	1	$5^{\frac{1}{2}}$	4^{hd}	5^{hd}	7^{5}	$7^{4\frac{3}{4}}$	Cruguet J	6.20
30Jly83 [8]Sar[4]	Fit to Fight	4 112	5	5	4^{2}	$6^{1\frac{1}{2}}$	9	8^{12}	8^{18}	MacBeth D	6.90
1Aug83 [2]Sar[1]	Pride Of Satan	b 4 101	3	2	$1^{1\frac{1}{2}}$	1^{1}	$3^{\frac{1}{2}}$	9	9	Murphy D J	67.50

OFF AT 4:13 Start good, Won driving. Time, :22$\frac{3}{5}$, :46$\frac{3}{5}$, 1:11, 1:35$\frac{4}{5}$, 1:48$\frac{4}{5}$ Course firm.

$2 Mutuel Prices:			
8-(I)-TANTALIZING	3.60	3.00	2.60
7-(H)-TEN BELOW		5.80	3.60
9-(J)-ACAROID			3.00

$2 QUINELLA 7–8 PAID $32.40.

B. c, by Tom Rolfe—Lady Love, by Dr Fager. Trainer Penna Angel. Bred by Phipps O M (Ky).

TANTALIZING outrun early, rallied from the outside leaving the far turn, was carried out slightly by ACAROID after catching that rival near the final furlong and was strongly handled to turn back TEN BELOW The latter steadied along for room along the inside at the far turn, moved around horses approaching the stretch, loomed boldly while lugging in leaving the furlong grounds but wasn't good enough. ACAROID well placed early, moved to the fore from the outside nearing the stretch, drifted out some into TANTALIZING near midstretch and weakened slightly. DOMYNSKY rallied approaching the stretch but gave way under pressure. NATIVE RAID prompted the pace, took over nearing the far turn but lacked a further response. DISCO COUNT reserved early, raced within striking distance to the stretch and gave way. FIT TO FIGHT tired badly. PRIDE OF SATAN stopped suddenly after showing speed to the far turn.

After two scratches, a field of nine was left to contest the second division of the Baruch.

By sheer coincidence, Ten Below's half-brother (that means the same dam, different sire), Fortnightly, was entered in the second division. The 3-year-old son of Dance Spell went off as the 5 to 2 second favorite despite the fact he was facing older horses.

The even-money favorite was Nijinsky's Secret, a multi-stakes winner who still had two PPs from the previous year at Saratoga in his charts. In the 1982 Bernard Baruch, Nijinsky's Secret rallied to finish fourth by one and a half lengths. Then, as the 2 to 1 favorite in the $1\frac{5}{8}$ mile Seneca Handicap, Nijinsky's Secret ran a very dull fifth by five and a quarter lengths. Nijinsky's Secret was even money because of his last three races, each a stakes victory. But he had two things going against him besides a proven poor record on the Saratoga turf: 1) he hadn't raced since June 19, and 2) as the starting highweight of 123 pounds, he was spotting his opponents from 7 to 20 pounds, significant concessions.

Nijinsky's Secret was easy to bet against in the Baruch. The problem was finding the right overlay.

8 **SARATOGA**

TURF COURSE
1 1-8 MILES
SARATOGA
START FINISH

1 1/8 MILES. (TURF). (1.45⅗) 25th Running THE BERNARD BARUCH HANDICAP (Grade II). Purse $50,000 Added. (2nd Division). 3-year-olds and upward. By subscription of $100 each, which should accompany the nomination; $400 to pass the entry box, with $50,000 added. The added money and all fees to be divided 60% to the winner, 22% to second, 12% to third, and 6% to fourth. Weights, Tuesday, August 2. Starters to be named at the closing time of entries. A trophy will be presented to the winning owner. The New York Racing Association reserves the right to transfer this race to the main course. Closed Wednesday, July 20, 1983 with 58 nominations.

Erin's Tiger — Ch. h. 5, by Terrible Tiger—Irish Exchange, by Swaps
Br.—Humphrey Pamela S (Ky)
Tr.—Nieminski Richard
Own.—Kluesener Mrs Dennis
112 — Lifetime 35 8 4 10 $195,646 — 1983 4 2 0 1 $38,640 — 1982 15 4 2 5 $113,988 — Turf 29 8 4 9 $193,488

27Jly83- 6Sar fm 1 1/16 [T]:48 1:11⅕ 1:42⅕ 3↑Alw 37000 1 4 511 68½ 35½ 31¾ Velasquez J b 119 2.70 92-11 Disco Count 119½ Fray Star 1191¼ Erin's Tiger 113nk Rallied 7
14Jly83- 8Bel fm 1¼ [T]:49⅕ 1:37⅘ 2:01⅘ 3↑Handicap 5 3 35 2no 12½ 1nk Velasquez J b 122 *1.80 85-18 Erin's Tiger 122nk Four Bases 1132 Kentucky River 114½ Driving 7
28Jun83- 9Mth fm 1 1/16 (T):49⅗ 1:13⅘ 1:44⅕ 3↑Alw 20000 1 7 52¾ 53½ 1hd 14 Velasquez J b 115 *1.30 80-19 Erin's Tiger 1154 Her Pal 1141 Fray Star 117¾ Driving 7
17Jun83- 8Bel fm 1 1/16 (T):46⅖ 1:11 1:42⅗ 3↑Alw 37000 3 6 56½ 43½ 42¾ 54¼ Velasquez J b 117 9.50 79-12 Lamerok 1193 Red Brigade119nkHalfIced117hd Lacked a response 8
2Nov82- 6Aqu gd 1⅜ (T):50 1:39⅕ 2:18⅕ 3↑Knickbckr H 3 2 21 21½ 11 34 Velasquez J b 113 3.20 76-23 Half Iced 1143½ No Neck 109½ Erin's Tiger 1131½ Weakened 8
2Nov82-Run in Two Divisions 6th & 8th Races
28Oct82- 6Med yl 1 1/16 (T):48⅕ 1:12⅘ 1:44⅘ 3↑Cliff Hngr H 8 4 33 3nk 12½ 12½ Velasquez J b 114 *1.80 79-22 Erin's Tiger 1142½ Santo's Joe 1161 Dew Line 1146 Driving 8
28Oct82-Run in Two Divisions: 6th & 8th Races
8Oct82- 8Bel fm 1 (T):45⅘ 1:09⅗ 1:33⅘ 3↑Alw 35000 5 4 45½ 43½ 22½ 32¼ Velasquez J b 119 *3.10 94-13 DscoCont1222¼WrofWords115hdErn'sTgr1198¼ Lacked a response 7
1Sep82- 8Bel fm 1 1/16 (T):45⅖ 1:09⅖ 1:41 3↑Brtn Beach H 3 10 911 65 32½ 2no Velasquez J b 112 7.80 91-27 Sprink 112no Erin's Tiger 112¾ Acaroid 1136 Brushed 10
15Aug82- 8Sar fm 1⅛ (T):47⅕ 1:11 1:47⅘ 3↑B Baruch H 8 9 89 53 43 810 Skinner K b 114 29.90 78-07 Pair of Deuces 115¾ Native Courier 117½ McCann 112nk Bid, tired 11
LATEST WORKOUTS Jly 11 Bel tr.t 4f fst :52 b — Jun 10 Bel tr.t 4f fst :52⅗ b

Who's For Dinner — Dk. b. or br. c. 4, by Native Charger—Expectancy, by Intentionally
Br.—Tartan Farms (Fla)
Tr.—Nerud Jan H
Own.—Tartan Stable
109 — Lifetime 22 4 5 5 $120,519 — 1983 6 0 2 0 $30,660 — 1982 10 3 2 3 $71,559 — Turf 17 4 5 5 $119,499

4Jly83- 8AP sf 1 1/16 (T):49⅗ 1:15 1:48⅘ 3↑Strstripe H 5 5 52¼ 42 2½ 2½ Migliore R b 110 19.20 64-35 Rossi Gold 122½ Who's For Dinner 1103 Lucence 1151 Wide 7
19Jun83- 8Bel fm 1⅜ [T]:48⅗ 1:37⅖ 2:14⅘ 3↑Bwlg Green H 4 2 2½ 42 54 62¾ Migliore R b 110 20.50 80-25 Tantalizing 113¾ Sprink 1131 Majesty's Prince 122¾ Brushed 7
9Jun83- 8Bel fm 1 (T):45⅗ 1:09⅘ 1:34⅘ 3↑Alw 32000 3 2 23 2½ 2hd 2½ Cordero A Jr b 117 *2.10 90-16 Four Bases 122½ Who's For Dinner 1174½Arcd'Or117½ Raced wide 6
16May83- 8Aqu sf 1 1/16 (T):49 1:14⅘ 1:47⅖ 3↑Fort Marcy H 1 4 53½ 77½ 612 615 Migliore R b 109 2.20e 53-32 John's Gold 1085½ Acaroid 1153¾ Beagle 105¾ Fell back 8
1May83- 6Aqu fst 1⅛ :49⅖ 1:13⅖ 1:51⅗ 3↑Alw 37000 6 6 76½ 812 818 824 Cordero A Jr b 119 10.50 53-21 LrkOscilltion119½AccountRecivbl119nkWstOnBrod1135¾ Fell Back 8
8Apr83- 8Aqu my 6f :22⅗ :45⅖ 1:09⅘ 3↑Alw 37000 1 6 56½ 511 57½ 65¼ BernhrdtEJJr10 b 109 7.70e 87-17 Vittorioso 1212¾ Northern Magus119¾ToughCritic1191¼ No factor 7
11Dec82- 7Aqu fst 170 [•]:46⅘ 1:12⅕ 1:43 3↑Alw 40000 8 8 817 811 712 713 Cordero A Jr b 115 8.70 74-20 Stiff Sentence1222¾Waj.Jr.1102½AccountReceivable1152 No speed 8
11Nov82- 7Aqu fm 1⅛ (T):51⅖ 1:14⅘ 1:53⅕ 3↑Alw 25000 2 1 1½ 2hd 2hd 1hd Cordero A Jr b 117 2.40 78-22 Who's For Dinner 117hd TenBelow115hdKingNeptune1172 Driving 6
9Oct82- 4Bel fm 1 1/16 [T]:49 1:12⅖ 1:42⅗ 3↑Alw 21000 1 3 32 1hd 12½ 13¼ Cordero A Jr b 114 *.80 88-17 Who's For Dinner 1143¼ Nihoa 1192 Lord Lister 1142 Ridden out 7
25Sep82- 8Bel fm 1½ (T):49⅗ 2:02⅕ 2:26⅖ Lwrnce Rlztn 2 2 45 22 46 57½ Cordero A Jr 114 5.30 84-12 Ten Below 114½ Majesty's Prince 1235¼ Khatango121no Gave way 8
LATEST WORKOUTS Aug 1 Sar 5f fst 1:03 b — Jly 18 Bel tr.t 4f fst :50⅕ b — Jly 12 Bel 4f fst :50⅖ b

Fortnightly — B. c. 3, by Dance Spell—Out Cold, by Etonian
Br.—Bwamazon Farm (Ky)
Tr.—Basile Anthony
Own.—Bwamazon Farm
113 — Lifetime 11 3 5 0 $152,991 — 1983 4 1 2 0 $45,923 — 1982 7 2 3 0 $107,068 — Turf 10 3 5 0 $152,991

13Jly83- 8Bel fm 1¼ [T]:47 1:35⅖ 2:00⅗ Lexington 2 4 38 33½ 23 2hd Velasquez J b 126 4.40 91-12 Kilaue114hdFortnightly1263¼TopCompetitor114hd Steadied,lug in 10
2Jly83- 9Mth fm 1 1/16 (T):48 1:11⅗ 1:42⅗ Lamplighter 8 10 95¾ 52¼ 44 42¼ Velasquez J b 118 *1.50 86-20 Tough Mickey115¾Domynsky120hdHeadoftheHouse1111½ Mild bid 11
16Jun83- 7Bel fm 1⅜ [T]:51 1:39 2:14⅘ 3↑Alw 27000 4 2 21 1½ 11½ 1¾ Velasquez J b 111 *1.20 83-14 Fortnightly 111¾ Saronic 1171½ Arc d'Or 1176 Tried lug in; drv 8
5Jun83- 8Bel sf 1 (T):48 1:13⅖ 1:39⅗ Saranac 3 7 76¼ 44½ 33½ 26 Velasquez J b 117 3.10 61-40 Sabin 1136 Fortnightly 117nk Domynsky 1231 Lugged in 10
13Nov82- 8Aqu gd 1⅛ :48⅖ 1:12⅘ 1:50⅕ Remsen 4 11 1118 1120 1130 1132 Shoemaker W b 122 7.80 52-20 Pax In Bello 1131¾ Chumming1158PrimitivePleasure113hd Trailed 11
25Oct82- 8Aqu sf 1⅛ (T):50⅖ 1:16⅖ 1:57⅗ Pilgrim 7 4 43 2½ 1hd 1hd Cordero A Jr b 122 1.90 56-56 Fortnightly122hdCvt1224½DomintingDooly1131¼ Bumped, stiff dr. 8
7Oct82- 8Bel fm 1 1/16 (T):47⅘ 1:11⅗ 1:42 Prince John 7 7 75 42½ 32½ 22 Cordero A Jr b 122 *1.30 84-14 Caveat 1172 Fortnightly 1221½ Nivernay 1132½ Wide 7
20Sep82- 8Bel fm 1 (T):46⅘ 1:10⅘ 1:36 Cascade 6 7 77 42½ 1hd 14 Cordero A Jr b 113 2.80 85-19 Fortnightly1134LovrBoyLsli113nkElCubnso113hd Wide, ridden out 9
9Sep82- 4Bel fm 1 1/16 (T):47⅕ 1:12⅕ 1:43⅖ Md Sp Wt 9 7 73¾ 31 1½ 12 Maple E b 118 *.70[D] 79-16 [D]Fortnightly1182UpperCourt118hdDomintingDooly118½ Broke in 12
9Sep82-Disqualified and placed fourth
27Aug82- 4Sar fm 1 1/16 [T]:47⅖ 1:12 1:44 Md Sp Wt 9 7 712 56 33 2no Fell J 118 *1.20 90-11 Bright Secretary 118noFortnightly1184SoIntent1184¾ Just missed 10
LATEST WORKOUTS Aug 3 Sar tr.t 5f fst 1:02⅘ b — Jly 21 Bel 4f fst :51⅗ b — Jly 9 Bel 6f fst 1:15⅖ b — Jun 27 Bel 6f fst 1:15⅗ h

Beldale Concorde — B. c. 3, by Super Concorde—My Gal Lucky, by Gallant Man
Br.—Bent Tree Farm Inc (Fla)
Tr.—Maxwell Adrian J
Own.—Maxwell A J
103 — Lifetime 10 2 3 1 $58,298 — 1983 4 1 1 0 $32,694 — 1982 6 1 2 1 $24,604 — Turf 10 2 3 1 $58,298

5Jun83♦6Milan(Italy) gd*1 1:35⅖ (T)Premio Emilio Turati(Gr1) 7 Cook P 119 4.60 — — Bold Run 129no Drumalis 119nk Bate; 1292 Bid,tired 9
8May83♦2Rome(Italy) gd*1 1:37⅘ (T)Premio Nearco(Gr.3) 12 Eddery P 119 *.70 — — BldlConcord1192 OkyForSnd1191 CmmndRspct119nk Going away 8
10Apr83♦4Rome(Italy) gd*1 1:39⅖ (T)Premio Parioli(Gr.1) 21 Cauthen S 128 6.10 — — Drumalis1281 BeldaleConcorde1281½ BenjaminBaker1281 Fin.well 9
28Mar83♦4Leicester(Eng) sf 7f 1:32⅗ (T)Burton Overy Stakes 44½ Piggott L 127 10.00 — — Proclaim 1271½ Drumalis 127hd Able Albert 1273 Bid,wknd 6
23Oct82♦4Doncaster(Eng) gd 1 1:44 (T)W.HillFuturityStks(Gr1) 53 Cauthen S 126 14.00 — — Dunbeath 1261½ Cock Robin126no LyphardsSpecial1261½ In close 8
10Oct82♦4Milan(Italy) sf*1 1:43⅖ (T)Gran Criterium(Gr.1) 22 Piggott L 123 1.00 — — Anguillo 1232 Beldale Concorde 1235 My Top 1231½ Fin.well 8
3Sep82♦3Haydock(Eng) gd 140 1:43⅗ (T)New Grandstand Stakes 21½ Eddery P 127 11.00 — — TheNoblePlyer1271½ BeldleConcord1278 Montrvi116½ Well pl,led 8
10Aug82♦4Newcastle(Eng) gd 7f 1:30 (T)Seaton Delaval Stk(Gr3) 412 Eddery P 123 3.50 — — AllsystemsGo 126½ Cause Celebre 1231½ Shearwalk 12310 Led 5f 5
21Jly82♦2Sandown(Eng) gd 7f 1:29 (T)Trident Debut Stakes 16 Piggott L 123 *2.00 — — BeldlConcord1236 Accusd1194 FlyingCorps119nk Prom,led fnl 2f 16
29May82♦6Haydock(Eng) fm 5f 1:01⅖ (T)Skelmersdale Stakes(Mdn) 32½ Eddery P 126 4.50 — — Ayman126½ SheriffMuir1261½ BeldleConcorde1268 Prom thruout 9
LATEST WORKOUTS Aug 4 Sar 6f fst 1:13⅘ hg — Aug 1 Sar 5f fst 1:01⅘ h — Jly 25 Sar 3f fst :36⅘ h

Sprink

B. g. 5, by Canadian Gil—Sprinkle Power, by Balance of Power
Br.—Edwards R L (Wash)
Tr.—Coladonato Eugene J

Own.—Paparo I

112 — Lifetime 43 7 9 6 $240,921 | 1983 7 0 1 0 $40,944 | 1982 25 5 5 5 $185,827 | Turf 16 3 5 2 $199,861

27Jly83- 8Bel sf 1½ Ⓣ:50⅖ 2:08 2:34⅘ 3↑Sword Dancer 5 1 16 67¼ 919 921 Miranda J 112 17.20 31-48 Mjesty'sPrince1201ⒹHushDer118hdThunderPuddles118¾ Stopped 9

2Jly83- 8Atl fm 1 3/16 Ⓣ:47 1:10⅗ 1:53⅖ 3↑U Nations H 10 7 2hd 2hd 1014 1013 Vasquez J b 113 5.90 84-08 Acaroid 113½ Trevita 1162½ Majesty's Prince 120no Tired 13

19Jun83- 8Bel fm 1⅜ Ⓣ:48⅗ 1:37⅖ 2:14⅘ 3↑Bwlg Green H 6 1 1½ 1½ 13 2¾ MacBeth D b 113 7.60 82-25 Tantalizing 113¾ Sprink 1131 Majesty's Prince 122¾ Gamely 7

11Jun83- 3Bel fm 6f Ⓣ:21⅘ :44⅗ 1:09⅕ 3↑Alw 40000 8 11 912 811 86½ 41¾ Miranda J b 117 4.90 95-06 Muttering 1221 Mayanesian 117no Ski Jump 114¾ Wide 11

16May83- 8Aqu sf 1 1/16 Ⓣ:49 1:14⅘ 1:47⅖ 3↑Fort Marcy H 3 2 1½ 34½ 712 817 Miranda J b 115 5.70 51-32 John's Gold 1085½ Acaroid 1153¾ Beagle 105¾ Used early 8

1May83- 6Aqu fst 1⅛ :49⅖ 1:13⅖ 1:51⅗ 3↑Alw 37000 8 1 11½ 2½ 45½ 67¼ Miranda J b 119 5.20 70-21 LarkOscilltion119½AccountReceivble119nkWestOnBrod1195¾ Tired 8

8Apr83- 8Aqu my 6f :22⅗ :45⅖ 1:09⅘ 3↑Alw 37000 4 5 66¾ 611 68 55 Miranda J 121 8.40 87-17 Vittorioso 1212¾ Northern Magus119¾ToughCritic1191¼ No factor 7

6Nov82- 8Lrl yl 1½ Ⓣ:48⅗ 2:07 2:31 3↑D C Intern'l 6 1 18 42½ 711 726 Miranda J b 127 47.10 38-36 AprilRun1246½Mjesty'sPrince1204½ThundrPuddls1201½ Used early 10

23Oct82- 8Aqu fm 1½ Ⓣ:50⅕ 2:05⅖ 2:29⅘ 3↑Turf Classic 1 2 2½ 32 57½ 519 Miranda J b 126 5.00 73-08 AprilRun1236½Naskra'sBreeze1263¼BottledWter1264¼ Speed, tired 7

3Oct82- 8Bel fm 1⅜ Ⓣ:46⅖ 1:34⅕ 2:13 3↑Man O' War 5 1 110 16 12 2hd Miranda J b 126 4.50 97-07 Naskra's Breeze 126hdSprink1265¼ThunderPuddles1211 Weakened 9

LATEST WORKOUTS Aug 4 Sar 5f fst 1:00⅖ b Jly 22 Bel 4f sly :47⅗ h ●Jly 16 Bel 1 fst 1:39⅗ h Jly 12 Bel tr.t 5f fst 1:02⅕ b

Nijinsky's Secret

Ch. h. 5, by Nijinsky II—Secret Beauty, by Raise a Native
Br.—Oxford Stable (Ky)
Tr.—Stirling Kent H

Own.—McDouglad Mrs J A

123 — Lifetime 23 8 1 0 $300,697 | 1983 3 3 0 0 $188,610 | 1982 12 3 1 0 $79,000 | Turf 22 8 1 0 $299,437

19Jun83- 9WO fm 1⅛ Ⓣ:46⅕ 1:10 1:46⅖ 3↑King Ed H 11 2 31 1½ 13 12½ Velez J A Jr 126 *1.20 100-03 Nijinsky'sSecret1262½Determinant1172¼Wayover114nk Ridden out 11

23Apr83-10Hia fm 1½ Ⓣ 2:26⅗ 3↑Hia Turf Cup 10 1 1½ 1½ 11½ 1½ Velez J A Jr 119 4.00 97-08 Nijinsky's Secret 119½ Discovered 114½ Tonzarun 1141½ Driving 11

9Apr83- 8Hia fm 1 3/16 Ⓣ 1:52⅘ 3↑Bouganvle H 4 3 35 42¼ 1½ 11¼ Velez J A Jr 115 36.30 93-10 Nijinsky'sSecret1151¼DataSwp116noSuperSunrise117½ Drew clear 13

9Apr83-Run in two divisions 8th & 10th races

18Dec82- 8Crc fm *1⅛ Ⓣ 1:46⅖ 3↑Alw 16000 8 11 1116 1010 1215 1214 Smith A Jr 119 *1.90 77-05 RoylPrunr114nkRsnThundr119noCommndAttnton1142¾ Dull effort 12

4Dec82- 7Crc fm *1 1/16 Ⓣ 1:43⅘ 3↑Alw 15000 3 4 57 611 56 42 Rivera M A 117 2.80 94-11 Royal Pruner 112½ Parcel 119hd Cesario 1141½ Rallied 7

17Oct82- 8WO yl 1⅝ Ⓣ:52⅕ 2:09⅗ 2:49⅖ 3↑Rothmans Int 4 9 810 97 811 715 Grubb R 126 30.05 38-38 Majesty's Prince 1182ThunderPuddles1182¾Paradise115nk Outrun 12

3Oct82- 9WO yl 1¼ Ⓣ:47⅗ 1:40⅗ 2:08⅕ 3↑Jky Club H 5 6 69 54 32½ 21¼ Grubb R 119 3.55e 65-34 FrostKing1311¼Nijinsky'sSecret119hdCurrentCharge1163½ Gamely 9

25Sep82- 8WO sly 1⅛ :49 1:13⅕ 1:52⅖ 3↑Alw 21000 4 4 46½ 49½ 417 419 Grubb R 123 2.50 59-28 Total Respect 1199 Nalee's Tyson 1079½ Mr Showbiz 117nk 4

30Aug82- 8Sar fm 1⅝ Ⓣ:50 2:02⅖ 2:39⅕ 3↑Seneca H 5 6 78 74¾ 56 55¼ Fell J 115 *2.20 84-09 Khatango 1131¼ Johnny Dance 114½ Field Cat 110nk Mild bid 11

15Aug82- 8Sar fm 1⅛ Ⓣ:47⅕ 1:11 1:47⅘ 3↑B Baruch H 6 10 911 74½ 53½ 41½ Fell J 116 4.10 86-07 Pair of Deuces 115¾ Native Courier 117½ McCann 112nk Wide str. 11

LATEST WORKOUTS ●Aug 1 Sar Ⓣ 6f fm 1:12⅖ h ●Jly 16 WO Tr.Ⓣ 7f fm 1:29⅘ b Jly 9 WO Tr.Ⓣ 5f fm 1:03⅘ b (d) Jly 2 WO Tr.Ⓣ 5f fm 1:03 b

McCann

B. h. 5, by Forli—Tusi Bella, by Better Bee
Br.—King Mr-Mrs J Howard (Ky)
Tr.—DiMauro Stephen

Own.—Penn-Field Stable

115 — Lifetime 30 6 6 2 $219,037 | 1983 10 2 2 0 $101,996 | 1982 7 1 2 2 $57,557 | Turf 26 6 6 2 $218,537

23Jly83- 8AP fm 1 3/16 Ⓣ:53⅕ 1:18 2:01 3↑Swoons Son H 1 5 55½ 64¾ 63½ 65¼ Fires E 115 4.90 57-26 Dom Cimarosa 1131 Lucence 1141¾ Rossi Gold 114¾ 7

2Jly83- 8Atl fm 1 3/16 Ⓣ:47 1:10⅗ 1:53⅖ 3↑U Nations H 9 6 86¼ 85¼ 87¾ 98¾ Santagata N b 116 27.90 88-08 Acaroid 113½ Trevita 1162½ Majesty's Prince 120no Outrun 13

18Jun83- 9Mth fm 1 Ⓣ:47⅖ 1:11⅕ 1:36⅗ 3↑Red Bank H 3 5 43½ 44 44 45½ Santagata N b 118 *2.10 86-21 Sun and Shine 115½ St. Brendan 116no Mr. Dreamer 1135 Evenly 11

30May83- 7AP sf 1⅛ Ⓣ:51⅖ 1:17 1:56⅘ 3↑L. Armour H 2 5 64½ 42½ 21 1nk Santagata N b 115 5.90 53-47 McCann 115nk Lucence 112¾ Rossi Gold 1231 Steadied, dr. 12

30Apr83- 8Pim yl 1 1/16 Ⓣ:48⅗ 1:13⅗ 1:46⅗ 3↑Riggs H 7 5 67¾ 46 33 21 Velez R I b 116 2.90 77-23 Sun and Shine 1131 McCann 116½ Thirty EightPaces1162½ Rallied 8

21Mar83- 7Hia fm 1 1/16 Ⓣ 1:41 3↑Royal Palm H 5 8 85¼ 87 32½ 12¼ Bailey J D b 113 13.60 93-14 McCann 1132¼ Fray Star 112nk Gleaming Channel1147 Drew clear 11

21Mar83-Run in two divisions 7th & 9th races

7Mar83- 7GP gd 1 1/16 Ⓣ:48 1:12 1:43⅕ Alw 20000 6 9 910 84¾ 45 25½ Fell J b 117 4.90 79-20 Discovered 1195½ McCann 1172 Forkali 117¾ Best of others 11

20Feb83-10FG fm *1⅛ Ⓣ 1:50⅗ F G Classic 11 12 913 85¾ 1010 107¼ Fell J b 115 8.90 74-11 Listcapade 120¾ Explosive Bid 118¾CageyCougar1161½ Came over 13

5Feb83-10GP yl *1 1/16 Ⓣ 1:46⅗ 3↑Can Turf H 3 5 54½ 32 1hd 46½ Fell J b 115 7.70 66-30 SuperSunrise1126SummerAdvocate118½PinPuller112hd Weakened 10

5Feb83-Run in two divisions, 8th & 10th races

29Jan83- 8GP yl 1 1/16 Ⓣ:49 1:14 1:45⅘ Alw 18000 10 2 21½ 2hd 2½ 75½ Fell J b 117 6.00 66-32 Reimbursement122¾DomDonizetti1171SuperSunris117¾ Gave Way 11

LATEST WORKOUTS Aug 5 Sar 4f fst :47⅗ h Aug 1 Bel tr.t 4f gd :49 h Jly 14 Bel tr.t 6f fst 1:18 b Jly 9 Bel tr.t 4f fst :49 b

*Fray Star

B. h. 5, by Frari—Stanza, by Cardington King
Br.—Haras Parque (Arg)
Tr.—Parisella John

Own.—Sabarese T M

114 — Lifetime 27 6 8 4 $132,668 | 1983 12 3 4 1 $103,275 | 1982 13 2 4 3 $27,955 | Turf 19 5 8 2 $127,205

27Jly83- 6Sar fm 1 1/16 Ⓣ:48 1:11⅕ 1:42⅕ 3↑Alw 37000 4 3 38 23 21½ 2½ Vergara O 119 6.20 93-11 Disco Count 119½ Fray Star 1191¼ Erin's Tiger 119nk Gamely 7

9Jly83- 9Mth fm 1 1/16 Ⓣ:47⅖ 1:11⅗ 1:43⅖ 3↑Oceanport H 4 8 89¼ 31½ 12½ 11¼ Vergara O 114 10.40 84-17 Fray Star 1141¼ Domynsky 1121½ And More 1171½ Driving 12

26Jun83- 9Mth fm 1 1/16 Ⓣ:49⅗ 1:13⅘ 1:44⅕ 3↑Alw 20000 2 1 1hd 1½ 3nk 35 Smith A Jr 117 *1.30 75-19 Erin's Tiger 1154 Her Pal 1141 Fray Star 117¾ Weakened 7

10Jun83- 6Bel fm 1 1/16 Ⓣ:47⅘ 1:11⅕ 1:42⅕ Clm 200000 4 3 31½ 21½ 22 22¼ Smith A Jr 122 *2.30 88-17 Disco Count 1122¼ Fray Star 1222¼ Red Brigade 112no 2nd best 8

23Apr83-10Hia fm 1½ Ⓣ 2:26⅗ 3↑Hia Turf Cup 6 2 2½ 2½ 45 65 Smith A Jr 114 10.80 92-08 Nijinsky's Secret 119½ Discovered 114½ Tonzarun 1141½ Tired 11

9Apr83-10Hia fm 1 3/16 Ⓣ 1:53 3↑Bouganvle H 11 5 46 42 33½ 21 Santiago J A 112 25.90 91-10 Lamerok 1181 Fray Star 1122¼ Tonzarun 110hd Rallied 14

9Apr83-Run in two divisions 8th & 10th races

21Mar83- 7Hia fm 1 1/16 Ⓣ 1:41 3↑Royal Palm H 4 1 2½ 2½ 2hd 22¼ Santiago J A 112 9.00 91-14 McCann 1132¼ Fray Star 112nk Gleaming Channel1147 Held place 11

21Mar83-Run in two divisions 7th & 9th races

7Mar83- 9GP gd 1½ Ⓣ:50 2:04⅘ 2:29⅕ 3↑Pan Amer'n H 10 1 11 2½ 23 411 Lynch H D 110 27.40 67-20 Highland Blade 1216½ Tonzarun 1082 Dhausli 1132¼ Weakened 10

7Mar83-Run in two divisions 9th & 10th races

LATEST WORKOUTS Jly 22 Sar 6f fst 1:13⅘ h Jly 8 Bel tr.t 3f fst :39 b Jun 19 Bel tr.t 5f fst 1:04⅗ b

Pair of Deuces

Ch. h. 5, by Nodouble—Rosy Alibhai, by Your Alibhai
Br.—Hartigan J H (Fla)
Tr.—Barrera Luis

Own.—Happy Valley Farm

116 — Lifetime 30 14 1 5 $369,143 | 1983 5 1 0 0 $12,319 | 1982 12 7 0 1 $267,970 | Turf 8 4 0 0 $170,895

30Jly83- 9Aks my 1⅛ :48 1:12⅖ 1:53⅕ 3↑Cornhusker H 2 2 34 815 1128 1137 Jones K 117 9.80 34-33 Win Stat 1112½ Bersid 1165 Aspro 1213 Tired 11

10Jly83- 8AP fst 7f :22⅕ :44⅗ 1:23 Alw 17200 1 6 11½ 12 13½ 1nk Fires E 115 3.90 87-15 Pair of Deuces 115nk Recusant 1222½ Maha Baba 1156½ Driving 8

16Apr83- 7Kee gd 1⅛ :47⅖ 1:11⅕ 1:49⅗ 3↑Ben Ali H 5 5 56½ 44½ 813 825 Gallitano G 118 12.00 64-25 Aspro 1152½ Thirty Eight Paces 115nk Rivalero 1215½ Tired 8

21Mar83- 9Hia fm 1 1/16 Ⓣ 1:41⅘ 3↑Royal Palm H 9 1 1hd 1hd 1hd 65¼ Vasquez J 120 2.60 84-14 Discovered 1131¼ⒹReimbursement1101½Santo'sJoe109no Stopped 11

21Mar83-Run in two divisions 7th & 9th races

12Mar83-10Hia fst 1⅛ :45⅘ 1:10⅕ 1:47⅗ 3↑Seminole H 2 4 48½ 44½ 57½ 59¾ Fires E 119 6.40 84-14 Spanish Drums 1201¼ Rivalero 1191½ Withholding 1086 No factor 7

6Nov82- 8Lrl yl 1½ Ⓣ:48⅗ 2:07 2:31 3↑D C Intern'l 3 2 28 88¾ 814 826 Day P 127 32.10 38-36 AprilRun1246½Mjesty'sPrince1204½ThunderPuddls1201½ Fell back 10

16Oct82- 6Med fst 1⅛ :46 1:11 1:49⅘ 3↑Paterson H 3 3 36½ 1016 1024 1025 Velasquez J 118 *1.80 59-15 Fast Gold 111½ Exclusive One 1121¾ French Cut 110½ Stopped 13

3Oct82- 9LaD fm 1⅜ Ⓣ:48 1:37⅕ 2:15⅕ 3↑Lad Downs H 2 1 1½ 1hd 11½ 11¼ Gallitano G 122 *1.90 92-10 Pair of Deuces 1221¼ Domd'Albignac1151Stop'mCold1141 Driving 11

3Oct82-Run in two divisions 9th & 10th races

18Sep82- 8Bel fst 1¼ :47⅗ 1:36 2:01 3↑Mrlbro Cup H 1 1 11 21 25 39½ Maple E 116 28.60 83-17 Lemhi Gold 1158¾ SilverSupreme117¾PairofDeuces1169 Gave way 8

Fortnightly, a 3-year-old taking on older horses, was no bargain at 5 to 2. Several of the others in the field had credentials, including Pair of Deuces, who beat Nijinsky's Secret in last year's Baruch while getting one pound. Today, he got seven. Yet he went off at 18 to 1 despite having won the exact same race the previous year. Pair of Deuces' last three races were on dirt, the last when he finished eleventh by thirty-seven lengths in the Cornhusker Handicap at Ak-Sar-Ben. Pair of Deuces hadn't raced on the turf since March 21, a definite drawback.

Another horse worth a look was Fray Star. Back on April 23, at Hialeah, Fray Star had finished sixth by five lengths to Nijinsky's Secret in the Hialeah Turf Cup. That race was at 1 1/2 miles, not Fray Star's best distance. He showed another tiring race, a fourth by eleven in the Pan American Handicap, March 7, at that distance. After getting a rest from April 23 to June 10, Fray Star had been sharp with a second, a third, a one and a quarter length victory and a second by half a length in his last four starts, all on turf. Today, he was getting nine pounds from Nijinsky's Secret, four more than he received in the Hialeah Turf Cup.

Fray Star showed two races with split results against another contender in today's Baruch, Erin's Tiger.

Erin's Tiger went off at 7 to 1. Fray Star, with a lifetime turf record of 5-8-2 in nineteen starts—throw out the two races at 1 1/2 miles and his record is fifteen of seventeen in the money—went off at 13 to 1 in the Baruch.

Fray Star was not the most logical contender, yet he deserved consideration. So did the other overlays.

Fray Star won the race by a nose against Fortnightly, returning $29 to win. Nijinsky's Secret, repeating his previous form at Saratoga, was a soundly beaten fifth by five and a half lengths, although he and several others in the race had to endure a bump-filled stretch drive. A foul claim against Fray Star, lodged by jockey Miranda on fourth place finisher Sprink, was disallowed by the stewards.

Sign of Life

11 An intriguing element of form handicapping—and potentially the most rewarding—is what I call "The Sign of Life" theory. The thinking behind it is simple. The vast majority of horses in racing won't consistently be at their peak level of performance. Rather, they'll reach a top level for a limited amount of time. If we can handicap when they'll reach their best form, at whatever level of racing they fit in, we'll invariably discover overlays. Our assumption is when a horse shows several poor races and then, perhaps because of a change in equipment or other reasons, shows a prolonged move in a race indicating improvement, we'll interpret that as a signal for greater improvement and possibly a win in his next start.

The old veteran Wimpfybell, an 8-year-old claimer in 1984, will demonstrate the point. Wimpfybell showed up at Aqueduct, Jan. 7, 1984, off some miserable past performances. After being rested from Feb. 5 to Oct. 29, 1983, the old gelding, with ten wins in eighty-five lifetime starts and earnings of more than $120,000, had been plainly uncompetitive in $10,000 claimers, the same price he was entered for this day at Aqueduct. All of his PPs were miserable, except for his last race. After losing the previous four races by a total of sixty-five lengths, Wimpfybell suddenly threw in a good race, finishing second by a head in the same company at 42 to 1.

Wimpfybell had shown an obvious sign of life. He was bet at Aqueduct and went off at 6 to 1. Is it an overlay? In this case, yes. Wimpfybell showed as much as the other contenders in the race. He won by two and three-quarters lengths and paid $14.40.

Here's a more recent and even more rewarding example.

Road To Ponder has been racing in $20,000-$25,000 claimers for what seems to be a decade. He's the prototype of a claimer; the type of horse who gets good for a while, looks like he'll dominate his claiming level forever, and instead suddenly and dramatically loses his form.

Road To Ponder surely wasn't in good form the summer of 1988. On June 20, at Belmont, he finished seventh. He didn't start again until July 24, when, despite a proven record of racing well on off tracks, he finished seventh by fourteen and three-quarters lengths in a 1 1/8 mile $25,000 claimer in the slop. He was 6 to 1. The *Form* said "Showed nothing."

When Road To Ponder resurfaced in Saratoga, August 3, it was in his familiar trappings, $25,000 claimers going 1 1/8 miles. Bettors dismissed him at odds of 19 to 1. Target X, a 9 to 2 choice in the field of eleven, won by seven lengths on a fast track. Road To Ponder finished a distant fourth by nine and three-quarters lengths. He might have been closer had he not encountered traffic problems duly noted in the chart of the race in the *Form*: "Checked attempting to split horses."

NINTH RACE

Saratoga
AUGUST 3, 1988

1 1/8 MILES. (1.47) CLAIMING. Purse $20,000. 3-year-olds and upward. Weight, 3-year-olds, 117 lbs., Older, 122 lbs., Non-winners of two races at a mile or over since July 1, allwoed 3 lbs., Of such a race since then, 5 lbs. Claiming Price $25,000; for each $2,500 to $20,000, 2 lbs. (Races when entered to be claimed for $18,000 or less not considered).

Value of race $20,000; value to winner $12,000; second $4,400; third $2,400; fourth $1,200. Mutuel pool $292,920. Exacta Pool $281,463. Triple Pool $681,567.

Last Raced	Horse	Eqt.A.Wt PP St	1/4	1/2	3/4	Str	Fin	Jockey	Cl'g Pr	Odds $1
28Jly88 1Bel1	Target X.	b 4 115 10 7	5½	51	1hd	16	17	Hernandez R	22500	4.90
27Jly88 6Bel3	Starting Gun	4 117 11 5	7½	83	6½	31	2nk	Day P	25000	5.80
22Jly88 8Suf1	Speedometer	b 4 119 2 6	63	6hd	51½	2hd	32½	Romero R P	25000	5.90
24Jly88 2Bel7	Road To Ponder	b 5 115 3 8	84	71	74	41	41½	Samyn J L	22500	19.40
24Jly88 2Bel3	It's About Seven	b 5 117 4 10	105	10½	91	6hd	52¾	Venezia M	25000	10.60
13Jly88 5FL1	Barber Izzy	b 6 117 1 3	12½	11	2hd	53	63	Pezua J M	25000	13.00
24Jly88 2Bel8	Louisiana Jones	4 117 8 1	21	21	3½	71½	71	Santagata N	25000	3.60
23Jly88 5Bel3	Sunrise Service	b 4 115 5 4	41	3hd	43	86	89	Davis R G	22500	4.20
27Jly88 3Bel4	Pershing Pach	4 113 9 9	11	11	11	92½	92½	Santos J A	20000	15.90
23Jly88 7Bel11	Just Two Four One	b 4 113 6 2	3½	41½	105	10	10	Thibeau R J	20000	57.30
8Jly88 5Bel6	Road Game Johnny	4 117 7 11	91	9½	8hd	—	—	Cruguet J	25000	16.50

Road Game Johnny, Eased.

OFF AT 5:53 Start good, Won ridden out. Time, :23⅗, :47⅘, 1:12⅕, 1:36⅗, 1:49 Track fast.

$2 Mutuel Prices:

10–(K)–TARGET X.	11.80 6.80 5.80
11–(L)–STARTING GUN	7.60 5.20
2–(C)–SPEEDOMETER	4.40

$2 EXACTA 10–11 PAID $62.80. $2 TRIPLE 10–11–2 PAID $284.00.

B. c, by Exclusive Native—Target Practice, by Gunflint. Trainer LaBoccetta Frank. Bred by Gailyndel Farms (Ky).

TARGET X. moved to the fore from the outside on the far turn and drew off quickly. STARTING GUN, unhurried while outrun early, split horses near midstretch and outgamed SPEEDOMETER for the placé. SPEEDOMETER came out to make a run approaching the stretch but lacked the needed late response. ROAD TO PONDER was checked attempting to split horses at the far turn. IT'S ABOUT SEVEN passed tired horses. BARBER IZZY tired badly from his early efforts. LOUISIANA JONES prompted the pace, made a bid between horses at the far turn but was finished entering the stretch. SUNRISE SERVICE made a run at the leaders on the far turn and stopped badly. JUST TWO FOUR ONE gave way soon after going a half. ROAD GAME JOHNNY, off slowly, was eased during the drive.

If he'd finished a close third, bettors would have paid more attention. Think about his race, though. Target X won by seven. Road To Ponder lost second by two and three-quarters lengths despite being checked. It was a sign of improvement, a wake-up call, a sign of life.

Road To Ponder returned August 15 in the same old race, $25,000 claimers going 1 1/8 miles. This day, the track was sloppy. Though he'd lost in the slop at Belmont earlier in the summer, anyone who'd seen Road To Ponder in previous races on a wet track knew he loved it.

Target X was made the even-money favorite. He ran seventh by twelve and a quarter. Road To Ponder won by two lengths and returned $23.20. To show it wasn't a fluke, he won on a sloppy track at Saratoga again, August 24, in the same 1 1/8 mile $25,000 claimer. He paid $4.20. The overlay was his first win, after his first sign of life. After the second sign, his victory on August 15, everybody knew he was back.

SECOND RACE

Saratoga

AUGUST 15, 1988

1 1/8 MILES. (1.47) CLAIMING. Purse $20,000. 3–year–olds and upward. Weight, 3–year–olds, 117 lbs., Older, 122 lbs., Non–winners of two races since July 15, allowed 3 lbs., Of a race since then, 5 lbs. Claiming Price $25,000; for each $2,500 to $20,000, 2 lbs. (Races when entered to be claimed for $18,000 or less not considered).

Value of race $20,000; value to winner $12,000; second $4,400; third $2,400; fourth $1,200. Mutuel pool $252,615. Exacta Pool $410,446. Quinella Pool $166,625.

Last Raced	Horse	Eqt.A.Wt	PP	St	1/4	1/2	3/4	Str	Fin	Jockey	Cl'g Pr	Odds $1
3Aug88 9Sar4	Road To Ponder	b 5 117	6	6	4½	4½	4³	1¹	1²	Antley C W	25000	10.60
7Aug88 5Sar5	Filial Duty	4 117	2	9	8¹	7½	7¹½	2hd	2¹	Venezia M	25000	3.80
29Jly88 7Bel9	Royal Court	3 108	8	3	22½	2¹	1hd	3³	32½	Goossens L	20000	39.10
3Aug88 9Sar5	It's About Seven	b 5 117	7	1	6²	6¹½	6½	5¹½	42¾	Murphy D J	25000	7.80
29Jly88 8BE7	Stop Light	b 5 103	3	7	7no	8²	8⁶	6½	5⁴	Soto R¹⁰	20000	40.20
3Aug88 Sar2	Starting Gun	b 4 117	5	5	5³	5²½	5¹	7⁶	6nk	Day P	25000	5.90
3Aug88 9Sar1	Target X	b 4 117	4	4	3¹½	3¹½	3¹	4²	7¹⁰]	Hernandez R	22500	1 00
28Jly88 7Bel3	Turbo Charger II	6 113	9	2	1¹	1²	2¹½	8⁶	8³	Santos J A	20000	10.30
29Apr88 7Aqu9	Mr. J. V.	b 4 113	1	8	9	9	9	9	9	Belmonte J F	20000	29.60

OFF AT 2:03 Start good, Won driving. Time, :23⅗, :47⅗, 1:12, 1:37⅘, 1:50⅖ Track sloppy.

$2 Mutuel Prices:				
	6-(H)-ROAD TO PONDER	23.20	9.60	5.60
	2-(A)-FILIAL DUTY		5.80	4.40
	8-(J)-ROYAL COURT			9.20

$2 EXACTA 6–2 PAID $137.20. $2 QUINELLA 2–6 PAID $54.40.

Ch. g, by Kennedy Road—Sentimental Notion, by Honest Pleasure. Trainer Moschera Gasper S. Bred by Tudor Ridge Farm (Alb-C).

ROAD TO PONDER moved up along the inside nearing the far turn, came out to continue his rally into the stretch and proved clearly best. FILIAL DUTY loomed boldly along the inside nearing midstretch and bested the others. ROYAL COURT prompted the pace, headed TURBO CHARGER after going six furlongs but weakened during the drive. IT'S ABOUT SEVEN failed to seriously menace while racing wide. STOP LIGHT lost too much ground. STARTING GUN bled. TARGET X., never far back, made a run from the outside midway of the far turn and flattened out. TURBO CHARGER was used up making the pace.

Now let's take the Sign of Life Theory to a higher level of racing. The scratch of Erin Bright left a field of eight to contest the $125,000, 1¼ mile Excelsior Handicap for 3-year-olds and up on a sloppy track at Aqueduct, April 14, 1984.

Let's go over the field. Weight follows the horse's name.

8 **AQUEDUCT** 1¼ MILES INNER DIRT TRACK AQUEDUCT START FINISH

1 ¼ MILES. (INNER-DIRT). (2.03⅗) 76th Running THE EXCELSIOR HANDICAP (Grade II). Purse $125,000 added. (Plus $25,000 Breeders' Cup Premium Awards) 3-year-olds and upward. By subscription of $250 each, which should accompany the nomination; $2,000 to pass the entry box, with $125,000 added. The added mmoney and all fees to be divided 60% to the winner, 22% to second, 12% to third and 6% to fourth. Weights, Monday, April 9. Starters to be named at the closing time of entries. Trophies will be presented to the winning owner, trainer and jockey. Closed with 19 nominations Wednesday, March 28, 1984.

Coupled—In the Ruff and Moro.

Canadian Calm — **B. c. 4, by Wajima—Lost Majorette, by Majestic Prince**
Br.—Gardiner Farms Ltd (Ky)
Own.—Oak Manor Farm — **Tr.—Sedlacek Michael C**
108 — Lifetime 11 2 1 4 $42,280 — 1984 7 2 1 2 $36,400 — 1983 4 M 0 2 $5,880

23Mar84- 8Aqu fst 1 70 [•]:48 1:13⅖ 1:43⅖ Alw 21000 6 2 1½ 12½ 16 110 Murphy D J5 b 112 *2.30 83-24 Canadian Calm 11210 Mi Te Syd 112no Vaguely Bold 117nk Easily 7
10Mar84- 3Aqu fst 1 70 [•]:47⅘ 1:13⅕ 1:43⅗ Clm c-50000 6 7 74½ 44 36½ 310 Lovato F Jr b 117 10.30 73-17 British Gunner 1138¼ Full Deck 1171¾ CanadianCalm1171½ Rallied 8
3Feb84- 1Aqu fst 1⅛ [•]:48⅘ 1:13 1:51⅗ Clm 75000 8 4 21 32½ 46½ 58½ Lovato F Jr b 117 18.00 78-18 Mr. Badger 1135 Blue Quadrant 113½ Last Turn 117½ Weakened 10
28Jan84- 7Aqu fst 1 1/16 [•]:47⅕ 1:12⅖ 1:45⅘ Alw 22000 1 10 64½ 32 31½ 33 Lovato F Jr b 119 3.00e 80-20 Fast John 117no Righteous Anger 1103 CanadianCalm1192 Rallied 11
19Jan84- 5Aqu fst 1⅛ [•]:48⅗ 1:14⅘ 1:55⅖ Alw 22000 4 4 55 53½ 53¾ 34½ Lovato F Jr b 122 7.40 63-32 [D]PuttingGreen1172¼ColonelLaw1122¼CanadianClm122¾ Steadied 10
19Jan84-Placed second through disqualification
11Jan84- 6Aqu fst 1⅛ [•]:48⅘ 1:15⅗ 1:56⅖ Md Sp Wt 2 4 87 52½ 2hd 11½ Lovato F Jr b 122 *1.60 63-28 Canadian Calm 1221½ Sir Star 1221¾ Bon Etoile 110½ Driving 9
8Jan84- 4Aqu fst 6f [•]:23 :46⅗ 1:11 Md Sp Wt 7 1 55½ 44½ 37½ 411¼ Lovato F Jr b 122 5.70 78-21 Minstrel Glory 1227¾ Wandering Feet1153IrishOre112½ Wide early 9
19Dec83- 6Aqu fst 6f [•]:23⅖ :48⅕ 1:13⅗ 3+ Md Sp Wt 5 4 61¾ 84¾ 65¾ 35¾ Lovato F Jr b 120 *2.80 70-26 I'mAHappyOne1201HowieofWinloc1204¾CanadinClm120nk Rallied 9
10Dec83- 4Aqu fst 6f [•]:22⅘ :46⅖ 1:12⅗ 3+ Md Sp Wt 6 7 43½ 32 22½ 33 Bailey J D b 120 3.70 78-17 GameTable1201¼HowieofWinloc1201¾CanadinClm120no Weakened 10
23Nov83- 5Aqu fst 6f :23⅕ :47 1:11⅘ 3+ Md Sp Wt 2 5 54¼ 64½ 53¼ 57¼ Molina V H 120 *2.30 75-27 Puntivo 1206¼ Pepe Vilar 120nk Oyster 120nk Outrun 8
LATEST WORKOUTS Apr 9 Aqu [•] 5f fst 1:00⅘ h Mar 2 Bel tr.t 4f fst :48⅗ h Feb 23 Bel tr.t 4f fst :48⅕ h

In the Ruff — **Ch. c. 4, by Prove Out—Fairway Flight, by Tom Fool**
Br.—Floyd William (Fla)
Own.—Davis A — **Tr.—Moschera Gasper S**
116 — Lifetime 19 7 3 2 $160,198 — 1984 7 1 1 1 $38,458 — 1983 12 6 2 1 $121,740

Entered 13Apr84- 8 AQU
4Apr84- 7Aqu fst 1⅛ [•]:47⅘ 1:12 1:50⅖ 3+ Alw 36000 7 3 44 56½ 612 618 Muino M M7 117 4.80 72-20 Luv A Libra 121hd Reinvested 119nd Startop's Ace 1218¼ Tired 8
16Mar84- 8Aqu fst 1½ [•]:50⅘ 2:08⅘ 2:34⅖ Handicap 5 3 2hd 12 13½ 13 Cordero A Jr 120 *1.50e 76-28 In the Ruff 1203 Fleet Pirate 118nk Erin Bright 119nk Driving 8
7Mar84- 6Aqu fst 1 70 [•]:48⅕ 1:13⅗ 1:43⅗ Alw 25000 8 4 42 21 1hd 2½ Cordero A Jr 117 *1.50 81-22 Luv A Libra 117½ In the Ruff 1176¼ Special Care 1172 Game try 8
10Mar84- 8Bow fst 1¼ :48⅖ 1:38⅗ 2:04⅖ 3+ J B Camp'l H 7 3 43½ 53¾ 86¾ 86½ Edwards J W 116 6.70 88-20 Island Champ 115no Forceful Intent 1161LuxuriantMan1113 Tired 10
18Feb84-10Hia fst 1¼ :47⅘ 1:35⅕ 1:59⅘ 3+ Widener H 2 4 46 610 919 928¼ Maple E 117 13.10 71-11 Mat Boy 1153½ Indian Lei 110½ World Appeal 1203½ Tired 9
29Jan84- 8Aqu fst 1 1/16 [•]:47⅘ 1:12⅕ 1:43⅖ 3+ Aqueduct H 2 1 2hd 41¼ 54¾ 69½ Davis R G 124 *1.80e 85-15 Moro 120¾ Jacksboro 1202 Ask Muhammad 1172 Tired 9
14Jan84- 8Aqu fst 1⅛ [•]:47⅘ 1:12 1:50⅕ 3+ Assault H 6 6 64 64 4¾ 3¾ McHargue D G 117 3.40e 93-17 Megaturn 115hd Moro 111¾ In the Ruff 1171¾ Rallied 11
14Dec83- 8Aqu fst 2¼ [•]:52⅕ 3:29⅘ 3:55⅖ 3+ Display H 3 2 67 31½ 13 11¼ Davis R G 115 4.80 82-21 In the Ruff 1151¼ Nice Pirate 1163¾ Bolden Raja 1121 Driving 9
4Dec83- 7Aqu fst 1⅛ [•]:50 1:15⅘ 1:56⅗ 3+ Alw 24000 7 3 2½ 11 32½ 35¼ Cordero A Jr 120 *1.30 56-43 Alec George 117nk Tampa Town 1155¼ IntheRuff1205¼ Weakened 8
1Dec83- 7Aqu fst 1¼ [•]:48⅗ 1:39⅘ 2:05⅖ 3+ Alw 24000 4 2 31½ 12½ 15 111 Davis R G 115 2.70 91-27 In the Ruff 11511 Hunter's Dawn 1152 Mangione 1151¼ Easily 10
LATEST WORKOUTS Apr 11 Bel tr.t 5f fst 1:01⅘ b Mar 16 Bel tr.t 3f fst :37 b Mar 7 Bel tr.t 5f fst 1:01⅗ h Feb 27 Bel tr.t 4f fst :48⅖ h

Luv A Libra

B. c. 4, by Diplomat Way—Lip Talk, by Assagai
Br.—Farnsworth Farm (Fla)
Tr.—Martin Jose
Own.—Old Glory Stable
117
Lifetime 34 5 9 6 $311,578
1984 4 2 0 0 $38,100
1983 15 1 4 3 $59,840

4Apr84- 7Aqu fst 1⅛ [•]:47⅘ 1:12 1:50⅗ 3+ Alw 36000 2 4 32 2hd 1hd 1hd Miceli M 121 13.20 90-20 LuvALibra121hdReinvested119hdStrtop'sAce1218¼ Bumped, drvng 8
17Mar84- 6Aqu fst 170 [•]:48⅕ 1:13⅗ 1:43⅗ Alw 25000 7 1 11 11 2hd 1½ Miceli M 117 5.60 82-22 Luv A Libra 117½ In the Ruff 1176¼ Special Care 1172 Came gain 8
10Mar84- 4Aqu fst 6f [•]:23⅕ :46⅗ 1:11⅖ Alw 25000 6 2 41½ 31½ 42¾ 43½ Miceli M 117 7.20 84-17 Bold Target 114¾ Big McCoy 117½ Special Care 1192 Weakened 7
1Mar84- 8Aqu fst 6f [•]:22⅘ :46 1:11⅗ Alw 35000 4 4 31 52½ 52½ 54¼ Miceli M 115 9.70 83-23 Havagreatdate 117½ North Glade 117½ Startop's Ace 115nk Tired 6
4Nov83- 8Aqu fst 1 :46⅖ 1:11⅗ 1:38⅕ 3+ Alw 35000 3 3 41½ 33½ 34½ 44¾ Miceli M 115 3.00 70-27 BtWhoKnows1153½Hgly'sRwrd115hdSdTrombon1171½ Raced wide 6
29Oct83- 9Aqu fst 1 :47⅕ 1:12⅗ 1:38⅘ 3+ Alw 30000 10 5 42 33 42¾ 43½ Miceli M 114 *3.20 68-28 Eskimo 1141½ Thalassocrat 1142 Unmistaken 114nk Hung 12
30Sep83- 8Bel sly 1 1/16 :48 1:12⅖ 1:44 3+ Alw 30000 1 1 1½ 11 1½ 2¾ Miceli M 115 6.10 81-20 El Perico 113¾ Luv A Libra 1153 Turkey Shoot 1152¾ Gamely 6
21Sep83- 7Bel fst 1 :45⅗ 1:10⅖ 1:36⅕ 3+ Alw 26000 2 4 32 31½ 2½ 1nk Miceli M 113 3.30 84-17 Luv A Libra 113nk Moment of Joy 113hd Intention 1132½ Driving 7
8Sep83- 8Bel fst 1⅛ :46⅕ 1:11⅕ 1:49⅗ 3+ Alw 26000 1 3 31½ 2hd 3nk 43 Miceli M 113 4.30e 76-19 Turkey Shoot 113¾ Act It Out 117no Moon Spirit1142¼ Weakened 7
20Aug83- 1Sar fst 1⅛ :47⅕ 1:11 1:50 3+ Alw 23000 5 2 21 1hd 11½ 31¾ Miceli M 112 4.80 83-16 Waitlist 1191¾ Kleiglight 117no Luv A Libra 1121¾ Weakened 7

LATEST WORKOUTS ●Apr 11 Bel tr.t 5f fst 1:00 h Apr 2 Bel tr.t 4f fst :47 h Mar 25 Bel tr.t 5f fst 1:00 h Mar 8 Bel tr.t 4f fst :48 h

Morning Review

Gr. h. 5, by Grey Dawn II—Arlene Francis, by Sword Dancer
Br.—Pen-Y-Bryn Farm (Ky)
Tr.—Nadler Herbert
Own.—Best Friends Stable
109
Lifetime 30 3 8 7 $83,764
1984 8 2 3 2 $55,834
1983 18 1 5 4 $26,130
Turf 2 0 0 0

25Mar84- 7Aqu fst 1⅛ [•]:48⅗ 1:13 1:51⅘ Alw 22000 1 4 54 42 22½ 2hd Venezia M b 119 *1.90 85-16 ShareTheRisk117hdMorningReview11910LstTurn117¾ Just missed 7
10Mar84- 8Aqu fst 1⅛ [•]:47⅘ 1:12⅗ 1:51⅗ 3+ Grey Lag H 5 6 613 65½ 24 24½ Venezia M 109 10.90 82-17 Moro 1224½ Morning Review 109nk To Erin 107nk Broke in air 6
4Mar84- 6Aqu fst 170 [•]:48 1:12⅗ 1:43 Alw 24000 1 5 52¾ 32 32½ 35¾ Vergara O b 122 3.20 80-21 Minbchr117noTmpTown1175¾MorningReview1222¼ Lacked fin bid 7
18Feb84- 7Aqu fst 1⅛ [•]:46⅕ 1:10⅗ 1:49⅗ Alw 22000 3 8 46 23½ 13½ 16¾ Vergara O b 117 16.10 98-12 MorningReview1176¾PuttingGren117nkMinstrlGlory1171½ Handily 9
10Feb84- 3Aqu fst 1 3/16 [•]:50⅗ 1:15 2:00⅗ Clm 25000 6 6 43 41¾ 2hd 1hd Cordero A Jr b 117 *2.80 75-20 Morning Review 117hdLeadTheWay1124½Exuberance117hd Driving 9
30Jan84- 3Aqu fst 1 1/16 [•]:48⅘ 1:14 1:47⅕ Clm 25000 1 5 62½ 42½ 3½ 31 Cordero A Jr b 117 5.50 75-25 Colonel Law 114½SwapforPower119½MorningReview1171¾ Rallied 12
18Jan84- 2Aqu fst 170 [•]:49 1:15 1:45⅗ Clm 25000 5 5 — — 24 29¾ Cordero A Jr b 117 *2.30 63-35 Haunted Lad1109¾MorningReview1172Eldag'sProspect1131 Snow 10
9Jan84- 9Aqu fst 6f [•]:23 :46⅗ 1:12⅘ Clm 20000 1 1 54½ 43½ 5¾ 72 Cordero A Jr b 117 5.40 78-25 Ruschenberg117½Eldg'sProspct113nkFlyingGnrl114no Checked str 12
22Dec83- 3Aqu sly 1 1/16 [•]:49 1:14 1:47 3+ Clm 20000 1 5 53 32 21 32 Vergara O b 117 4.80 75-25 Dnderoo1171¾FeelingTooMuch110nkMorningReviw1177¼ Bid,wknd 8
19Dec83- 9Aqu fst 6f [•]:23⅗ :47⅘ 1:13⅕ 3+ Clm c-16000 4 7 64½ 63½ 64¾ 33¾ Miranda J b 119 4.40 74-26 Rauschenberg 1171¼StageGossip1082½MorningReview119½ Rallied 9

LATEST WORKOUTS Apr 11 Aqu [•] 5f fst 1:00⅗ h Apr 7 Aqu [•] 1 fst 1:43 b Apr 2 Aqu [•] 5f fst :59⅘ h ●Mar 22 Aqu [•] 5f fst 1:00⅖ h

Canadian Factor

Dk. b. or br. c. 4, by Sinister Purpose—Tico's Donna, by Bosun
Br.—Beechwood Farm Ltd (Ont-C)
Tr.—Gross Mel W
Own.—Stronach F
117
Lifetime 20 6 2 4 $199,887
1984 3 0 0 0 $2,160
1983 17 6 2 4 $197,727
Turf 7 1 2 2 $86,375

26Mar84- 8Aqu fst 1½ [•]:50⅘ 2:08⅕ 2:34⅕ Handicap 6 4 3½ 42½ 44½ 43½ Velasquez J b 122 6.50 72-28 In the Ruff 1203 Fleet Pirate 118nk Erin Bright 119nk Weakened 8
10Mar84- 8Bow fst 1¼ :48⅖ 1:38⅗ 2:04⅗ 3+ J B Camp'l H 10 9 912 75¼ 76½ 76 Bracciale V Jr 119 *2.50 89-20 Island Champ 115noForcefullntent1161LuxuriantMan1113 Outrun 10
18Feb84- 8Aqu fst 1⅛ [•]:47⅕ 1:11 1:48⅗ 3+ Stymie H 11 13 1314119¾ 78¾ 610½ Velasquez J 122 18.70 93-12 Gen'l Practitioner 119hd Jacque's Tip 113nk Puntivo1154¾ Outrun 14
26Nov83 ♦9Tokyo(Japan) fm*1½ 2:27⅗ Ⓣ Japan Cup(Gr.1) 1513 Stahlbaum G 121 52.80 — — Stanerra 121hd KyoeiPromise 126hd Esprit deNord121½ No factor 16
2Nov83- 8Grd sly 1 :47⅘ 1:13⅗ 1:40⅕ [R]Sir Barton 4 9 912 57½ 31½ 35¾ Stahlbaum G 126 5.40 73-29 GoneToRoylty124noFrenchRegency1155½CndinFctor1265½ Rallied 9
22Oct83- 9WO fm 1 Ⓣ:47⅖ 1:13 1:37⅗ 3+ Bnty Lawless 7 5 54½ 66½ 57 57 Stahlbaum G 128 5.40 72-19 Cool Tania 1231½ Artic Briar 113nk Frost King 132¾ No factor 7
9Oct83- 9WO fst 1 1/16 :47⅘ 1:12 1:58⅗ Mclaughlin H 7 7 67 54½ 1hd 1nk Stahlbaum G 124 *1.45 86-23 CandinFctor124nkBgO'Bucks1134½GoneToRoylty120nk Ridden out 7
17Sep83- 9WO yl 1¼ Ⓣ:48⅗ 1:39⅕ 2:06 3+ [S]Seagram H 7 7 87½ 88½ 53½ 21½ Stahlbaum G 115 3.50 75-23 BridlePath1181½CanadianFctor115noFiddleDncerBoy1171½ Rallied 10
3Sep83- 9WO fm 1½ Ⓣ:49⅕ 2:05⅗ 2:32⅘ [S]Breeders 6 7 811 45 44½ 3½ Stahlbaum G 126 1.65e 75-24 Kingsbridge 126no Val Du Nord 126½ Canadian Factor126¾ Rallied 9
20Aug83- 9FE fm 1⅛ Ⓣ:46⅗ 1:11⅕ 1:43⅗ Inter Hcp 11 7 98¾ 87½ 95 1no Stahlbaum G 122 4.00 93-08 CndinFctor122noVictoriousEmperor116hdFeuD'enfer118hd Driving 11

LATEST WORKOUTS Apr 12 Bel tr.t 4f fst :48 b Apr 8 Bel tr.t 1 fst 1:43 b Mar 20 Bel tr.t 6f fst 1:13 h Mar 7 Bow 5f gd 1:03⅗ b

Moro

Dk. b. or br. h. 5, by Full Out—Winking Aye, by Mito
Br.—Frizzell Bunny & Tackett (Ky)
Tr.—Moschera Gasper S
Own.—Davis A
126
Lifetime 44 13 9 8 $353,699
1984 7 3 2 0 $148,223
1983 18 7 2 5 $141,400
Turf 3 0 0 2 $6,960

Entered 13Apr84- 8 AQU

25Mar84- 8Aqu fst 170 [•]:47⅗ 1:12 1:41⅘ 3+ Westchstr H 3 8 78½ 55¾ 42½ 52½ Samyn J L 124 2.90 89-16 Jacque's Tip114nkMinstrelGlory107½Havagreatdate1111½ Steadied 8
10Mar84- 8Aqu fst 1⅛ [•]:47⅘ 1:12⅗ 1:51⅗ 3+ Grey Lag H 3 3 3½ 3½ 14 14½ Samyn J L 122 3.50 87-17 Moro 1224½ Morning Review 109nk To Erin 107nk Drew clear 6
18Feb84- 8Aqu fst 1⅛ [•]:47⅕ 1:11 1:48⅗ 3+ Stymie H 10 11 107¾ 97½ 46½ 59 Samyn J L 126 7.50 94-12 Gen'l Practitioner 119hd Jacque'sTip113nkPuntivo1154¾ No factor 14
29Jan84- 8Aqu fst 1⅛ [•]:47⅘ 1:12⅕ 1:43⅗ 3+ Aqueduct H 4 4 51½ 51¾ 3½ 1¾ Samyn J L 120 *1.80e 95-15 Moro 120¾ Jacksboro 1202 Ask Muhammad 1172 Driving 9
22Jan84- 6Aqu fst 1⅛ [•]:49⅕ 1:14⅕ 1:52⅘ Alw 38000 4 2 2hd 2hd 2hd 2no Davis R G 115 *.80 83-25 Galaxy Guide 114no Moro 1155 Determined Bidder 1155 Game try 6
14Jan84- 8Aqu fst 1⅛ [•]:47⅘ 1:12 1:50⅕ 3+ Assault H 3 9 86½ 52½ 1hd 2hd Davis R G 111 3.40e 94-17 Megaturn 115hd Moro 111¾ In the Ruff 1171½ Sharp 11
7Jan84- 7Aqu fst 6f [•]:23⅗ :48 1:12⅘ Alw 35000 7 4 53½ 3½ 11½ 14 Davis R G 115 *.90 80-24 Moro 1154 Forgot the Ring 115½ Sixth of May 1105½ Drew clear 7
31Dec83- 5Aqu fst 170 [•]:47⅕ 1:12⅕ 1:41⅘ 3+ Clm 100000 6 6 56 31½ 2½ 1no Messina R5 117 3.60 92-21 Moro 117no Mortgage Man 117nk Deedee's Deal 1166¾ Driving 8
23Dec83- 8Aqu gd 170 [•]:47⅗ 1:13 1:43⅘ 3+ Alw 27000 1 3 1hd 1½ 3½ 53 Cordero A Jr 117 *.90 79-21 North Glade 115no Huckster 1151¾ Tarantara 1121½ Faltered 9
17Dec83- 7Aqu fst 6f [•]:22⅗ :46 1:10⅗ 3+ Alw 35000 6 4 64½ 55 45½ 24¾ Cordero A Jr 115 2.20 87-19 Hagley's Reward 1134¾ Moro 1151½ Special Care 1174 Slow early 8

LATEST WORKOUTS ●Apr 8 Bel tr.t 6f fst 1:12 h ●Apr 3 Bel tr.t 4f fst :46⅗ h Mar 22 Bel tr.t 4f gd :47 h Mar 17 Bel tr.t 4f fst :47⅗ h

Reinvested

Ch. h. 5, by Irish Castle—Crafty Alice, by Crafty Admiral
Br.—Regal Oak Farm (Fla)
Tr.—Martin Frank
Own.—Harbor View Farm
114
Lifetime 32 7 7 5 $569,389
1984 5 0 2 0 $25,500
1983 9 1 1 3 $54,340
Turf 7 2 2 0 $67,510

4Apr84- 7Aqu fst 1⅛ [•]:47⅘ 1:12 1:50⅗ 3+ Alw 36000 3 7 64½ 32 2hd 2hd Cordero A Jr 119 *1.30 90-20 Luv A Libra 121hd Reinvested 119hd Startop's Ace 1218¼ Bumped 8
10Mar84- 9GP fst 1⅛ :46⅘ 1:10⅘ 1:49 3+ Donn H 7 6 59 45½ 55 56¾ Bailey J D 113 11.40 80-16 PlyFellow122½CourteousMjsty1111JckSld1145 Bumped st.bore in 8
18Feb84- 10Hia fst 1¼ :47⅘ 1:35⅕ 1:59⅘ 3+ Widener H 1 2 22 45 46½ 47¼ Bailey J D 112 7.90 91-11 Mat Boy 1153¼ Indian Lei 110½ World Appeal 1203½ Tired 8
6Feb84- 9Hia fst 7f :23⅗ :46⅕ 1:22⅕ 3+ [S]Roman Bro H 2 5 47 37½ 33 43¼ Bailey J D 116 1.80 88-16 SpnishDrums1151½CenterCut1182½BntheBlus114no Lacked fin bid 8
26Jan84- 9Hia fst 7f :23⅕ :45⅗ 1:22⅗ Alw 20000 8 9 83½ 72¾ 24 23 Bailey J D 119 2.90 87-16 Center Cut 1173 Reinvested 1192¼ Gallant Prelude 1151½ Bore in 10
5Nov83- 8Aqu fst 1⅛ :47⅘ 1:11⅕ 1:49 3+ Stuyvesant H 7 3 31 53 58½ 511½ Velasquez J 112 3.70 79-22 Fit to Fight 1171½ Deputy Minister 119nd Sing Sing 1154 Bore in 7
29Oct83- 7Aqu fst 1⅛ :47⅗ 1:12⅘ 1:52 3+ Sham 4 2 11½ 12 15 16 Velasquez J 115 *2.10 75-28 Reinvested 1156 Lark Oscillation 115¾OtterSlide1172¼ Ridden out 6
15Oct83- 8Bel fst 1½ :48 2:01 2:26⅕ 3+ J C Gold Cup 6 8 74¾ 8231029 1034¾ Maple E 126 36.30 54-14 Slew O' Gold1213HighlandBlade126nkBoundingBasque1211½ Rank 10
6Oct83- 1Bel fst 1¼ :47⅗ 1:37 2:02⅗ 3+ Alw 40000 2 5 57 21½ 1hd 3hd Maple E 117 *.80 86-22 Otter Slide 119no SilverSupreme117noReinvested1174 Taken back 6
28Sep83- 7Bel fst 1 :45⅘ 1:09⅗ 1:34⅗ 3+ Alw 40000 1 4 42 53 44 22 Maple E 115 16.30 91-19 Fit to Fight 1192 Reinvested 115nk Deputy Minister 1152 Rallied 6

LATEST WORKOUTS ●Apr 11 Bel tr.t 6f fst 1:11⅘ h Apr 1 Bel tr.t 5f fst :58⅘ h Mar 25 Hia 5f fst 1:02⅗ b Mar 4 Hia 7f fst 1:25 h

Mr. Badger — B. h. 5, by Mr Leader—Pago Dancer, by Pago Pago

Own.—Barrera O S — Br.—Whitney T P (Ky) — Tr.—Barrera Oscar S

112 — Lifetime 27 10 2 2 $160,952 — 1984 11 6 1 0 $103,970 — 1983 8 3 0 1 $42,880 — Turf 10 2 1 1 $29,702

7Apr84- 3Aqu	fst	1⅛	⊡:46⅘	1:11⅘	1:51⅕	Clm 72500	7	7	6^{4}	$3^{1½}$	1^{3}	1^{2}	Cordero A Jr	b 117	*1.00	86-16 Mr. Badger 117^{2} Inner Circuit 113^{4} Lutyens 115½	Ridden out	8
28Mar84- 5Aqu	fst	1 70	⊡:48⅗	1:13⅗	1:43	Clm 70000	3	5	3^{1}	3^{nk}	1nd	$2^{1½}$	Cordero A Jr	b 115	*.80e	83-22 Fleet Receiver $117^{1½}$ Mr. Badger 115^{hd} Gauley 108^{nk}	Gamely	9
25Mar84- 6Aqu	fst	6f	⊡:22⅕	:45⅕	1:09⅗	Handicap	6	4	5^{4}	$4^{2½}$	$5^{5½}$	$5^{3¾}$	MacBeth D	b 116	3.40	93-16 Shadowmar113^{no}CannonShell$114^{1¼}$AgileShoebill$113^{1¾}$	No menace	6
17Mar84- 7Aqu	fst	1 70	⊡:49	1:13⅘	1:43	Alw 36000	4	3	$2^{1½}$	2^{1}	$1^{½}$	$1^{1½}$	Cordero A Jr	b 115	*1.60	85-22 Mr. Badger$115^{1½}$MortgageMan112^{3}Havagreatdate115^{4}	Drew clear	7
8Mar84- 8Aqu	fst	6f	⊡:22⅘	:46⅕	1:10⅘	Alw 35000	1	5	5^{4}	6^{3}	$4^{¾}$	1no	Cordero A Jr	b 115	*.90	90-24 Mr.Badger115^{no}Shadowmr115^{hd}NorthernIce115^{3}	Blocked, driving	7
5Mar84- 5Aqu	fst	6f	⊡:22⅕	:45⅕	1:10⅕	Clm 70000	2	5	5^{6}	5^{5}	4^{3}	1^{3}	MacBeth D	b 118	5.80	93-22 Mr. Badger 118^{3} Cutter Sark 113no Big McCoy 117½	Drew clear	9
24Feb84- 8Aqu	sly	1 70	⊡:47⅕	1:11⅗	1:41	Alw 38000	4	4	4^{4}	4^{3}	$6^{2¾}$	$5^{6¼}$	MacBeth D	b 115	2.40	90-16 ClassHero115^{nk}ShreTheRisk110^{2}FeelingTooMuch115^{hd}	No threat	8
13Feb84- 1Aqu	fst	1⅛	⊡:48⅘	1:13	1:51⅗	Clm 70000	6	2	$3^{1½}$	$2^{½}$	$1^{2½}$	1^{5}	MacBeth D	b 113	*1.30	87-18 Mr. Badger 113^{5} Blue Quadrant 113½ Last Turn 117½	Drew clear	10
9Feb84- 5Aqu	fst	6f	⊡:22⅗	:45⅗	1:10⅗	Clm 70000	3	9	7^{5}	$6^{4¾}$	2^{4}	1^{nk}	MacBeth D	b 113	*1.30	91-18 Mr. Badger 113^{nk} Citius $117^{3¾}$ Cutter Sark 108^{1}	Slow early, drvg	9
2Feb84- 2Aqu	fst	1 70	⊡:49	1:13⅕	1:43⅕	Clm c-35000	6	8	$10^{6½}$	8^{8}	6^{6}	$4^{2¾}$	Davis R G	117	3.80	82-22 Surf Club 117¾ Big Izzy 117½ Full Concert $113^{1½}$	Rallied	10

LATEST WORKOUTS Apr 13 Bel tr.t 3f fst :38 b — Apr 3 Bel tr.t 3f fst :37 b — Mar 23 Bel tr.t 4f fst :49⅕ b — Mar 4 Bel tr.t 3f fst :36⅘ h

Canadian Calm—108—This well-bred 4-year-old was claimed for $50,000 by Mike Sedlacek and won his last start, an allowance race, by ten lengths. He makes his debut in stakes company and is unproven at the 1¼ mile distance. He also doesn't show a past performance line on an off track. Pass.

In The Ruff—116—He's coupled with high weight Moro as the 2 to 1 favorite. He was sixth by eighteen lengths vs. Luv A Libra in his last start, a 1⅛ mile allowance. Enough said.

Luv A Libra—117—A game winner by a head against Reinvested in an allowance race, he also showed a good second in the slop. But he's never done it in stakes company.

Morning Review—109—Claimed for $16,000 in December, he's improved greatly for trainer Herbert Nadler. He showed good distance races, one good race in the slop, and a second by four and a half lengths to Moro after a bad start in the 1⅛ mile Grey Lag Handicap, getting thirteen pounds. He gets seventeen from Moro today.

Canadian Factor—117—This 4-year-old was unraced at two and impressive at three, going 6-2-4 in seventeen starts and earning $197,727, a little more than half of it on dirt. Last year in Canada, he won the 1³⁄₁₆ mile McLaughlin Handicap by a neck as the 7 to 5 favorite, carrying 124 pounds and spotting the second place horse 11. His race in the slop in a restricted stakes (indicated by an 'R' enclosed in a box in that PP) at one mile was an okay third by five and a half lengths carrying 126 pounds.

Two turf stakes, producing a third by a half a length and a second by a length and a half, gave further proof of his ability to handle a distance. The turf races were at $1^1/_2$ and $1^1/_4$ miles, respectively.

For his last start of 1983, Canadian Factor had been shipped to the Japan Cup in Tokyo. He ran horribly in the turf stakes, finishing fifteenth, but a lot of horses, including John Henry, have done poorly in that race.

Following a twelve week layoff, trainer Mel Gross chose a difficult spot for Canadian Factor's 4-year-old debut, the Stymie Handicap at Aqueduct, February 18, carrying 122 pounds and spotting the top two finishers, General Practitioner and Jacque's Tip, 3 and 9 pounds, respectively. Canadian Factor was sixth by ten and a quarter lengths in the field of fourteen.

Gross then tried Canadian Factor in the John B. Campbell Handicap at Bowie. Spotting the winner 4 pounds, Canadian Factor was never a factor, running seventh by six lengths as the 5 to 2 favorite.

In his last race, a mile and a half handicap at Aqueduct, Gross made an equipment change: blinkers on. Canadian Factor responded with a sign of life: fourth by three and a half lengths in the field of eight, giving two pounds to winner In The Ruff.

Canadian Factor followed the improved race with two breezing workouts, one mile in 1:43 and four furlongs in :48 on the Belmont training track, always slower than the main track.

With loads of back class and an arrow of improvement showing he was ready, Canadian Factor seemed to have significant advantages against a less than imposing stakes group.

Moro—126—Trainer Gasper Moschera deserved a medal for improving this former claimer to a stakes winner. But Moro was picking up two pounds off a fifth place finish by two and a quarter lengths to Jacque's Tip in his last race, the one mile and seventy yards Westchester Handicap. Moro had an excuse that race: he was steadied. However, the longest race in his PPs was a mile and an eighth, and he was conceding a lot of weight. A shift of Jean-Luc Samyn to Cordero and a pair of bullet workouts created a lot of support for Moro at the betting windows. Yet he hadn't demonstrated more class and a better ability to make the distance than Canadian Factor. He was also spotting him nine pounds. He also didn't show a race in the slop.

Reinvested—114—Second by a head versus Luv A Libra in a $1^1/_8$

mile allowance as the 6 to 5 favorite, he was inconsistent. But he has shown he can handle the distance and has won more than $560,000 in his career.

Mr. Badger—112—The 5-year-old ex-claimer was untested in stakes and distance. Pass.

The entry of Moro-In The Ruff went off at 2 to 1. So did Reinvested. Canadian Factor was a hard-to-believe 9 to 1. He won going away by one and one-half lengths and returned $21.60.

EIGHTH RACE
Aqueduct
APRIL 14, 1984

1 ¼ MILES.(INNER DIRT). (2.03⅗) 76th Running THE EXCELSIOR HANDICAP (Grade II). Purse $125,000 added. (Plus $25,000 Breeders' Cup Premium Awards) 3-year-olds and upward. By subscription of $250 each, which should accompany the nomination; $2,000 to pass the entry box, with $125,000 added. The added mmoney and all fees to be divided 60% to the winner, 22% to second, 12% to third and 6% to fourth. Weights, Monday, April 9. Starters to be named at the closing time of entries. Trophies will be presented to the winning owner, trainer and jockey. Closed with 19 nominations Wednesday, March 28, 1984. Breeders' Cup Fund Award to Canadian Factor.

Total purse $162,750. Value of race $161,250, value to winner $102,150, second $32,505, third $17,730, fourth $8,865. Nominator Award $1,500. Mutuel pool $177,861, OTB pool $231,381. Exacta Pool $170,011. OTB Exacta Pool $192,443.

Last Raced	Horse	Eqt.A.Wt	PP	¼	½	¾	1	Str	Fin	Jockey	Odds $1
25Mar84 ^{8}Aqu^{4}	Canadian Factor	b 4 117	5	7^{2}	$7^{2\frac{1}{2}}$	$7^{2\frac{1}{2}}$	4^{4}	$3^{1\frac{1}{2}}$	$1^{1\frac{1}{2}}$	Velasquez J	9.80
4Apr84 ^{7}Aqu^{1}	Luv A Libra	4 117	3	3^{3}	3^{3}	2^{1}	1^{hd}	1^{hd}	$2^{1\frac{1}{2}}$	Miceli M	4.10
23Mar84 ^{8}Aqu^{1}	Canadian Calm	b 4 108	1	$1^{1\frac{1}{2}}$	$1^{1\frac{1}{2}}$	1^{hd}	2^{1}	2^{1}	$3^{\frac{1}{2}}$	Graell A	21.00
25Mar84 ^{8}Aqu^{5}	Moro	5 126	6	5^{4}	4^{3}	$4^{1\frac{1}{2}}$	$3^{\frac{1}{2}}$	4^{5}	$4^{7\frac{1}{2}}$	Cordero A Jr	a-2.10
4Apr84 ^{7}Aqu^{2}	Reinvested	5 114	7	$6^{\frac{1}{2}}$	$6^{2\frac{1}{2}}$	5^{1}	5^{4}	5^{7}	$5^{4\frac{1}{2}}$	Cruguet J	2.00
25Mar84 ^{7}Aqu^{2}	Morning Review	b 5 109	4	8	8	8	8	7^{hd}	$6^{\frac{1}{2}}$	Venezia M	6.60
7Apr84 ^{3}Aqu^{1}	Mr. Badger	b 5 112	8	4^{hd}	5^{hd}	6^{1}	7^{hd}	8	$7^{3\frac{1}{2}}$	Davis R G	9.20
4Apr84 ^{7}Aqu^{6}	In the Ruff	4 116	2	2^{1}	2^{hd}	$3^{1\frac{1}{2}}$	6^{1}	6^{hd}	8	MacBeth D	a-2.10

a-Coupled: Moro and In the Ruff.

OFF AT 4:45 Start good, Won driving. Time, :23⅗, :47⅕, 1:12⅕, 1:37⅘, 2:03 Track sloppy.

(New Track Record)

$2 Mutuel Prices:

5-(E)-CANADIAN FACTOR	21.60	9.20	5.40
3-(C)-LUV A LIBRA		5.80	4.20
2-(A)-CANADIAN CALM			6.00

$2 EXACTA 5–3 PAID $145.40.

Dk. b. or br. c, by Sinister Purpose—Tico's Donna, by Bosun. Trainer Gross Mel W. Bred by Beechwood Farm Ltd (Ont-C).

CANADIAN FACTOR commenced to rally approaching the end of the backstretch, raced wide into the stretch and proved clearly best after catching the leader inside the final furlong. LUV A LIBRA, close up early, went up after CANADIAN CALM nearing the end of the backstretch, dueled for the lead to the final sixteenth and wasn't good enough. CANADIAN CALM saved ground while showing speed, held on well midstretch and weakened. MORO reserved early, made a run between horses nearing the stretch but lacked the needed late response. REINVESTED moved with easy striking distance along the inside nearing the end of the backstretch but lacked a further response. MORNING REVIEW was never close. MR. BADGER had no apparent excuse. IN THE RUFF raced forwardly to the far turn and had nothing left.

Inside with Woody Stephens

CHAPTER 12 From humble beginnings, Woodward Cefis "Woody" Stephens fashioned his Hall of Fame training career. His greatest accomplishment is five consecutive victories in the Belmont Stakes, the final leg of the Triple Crown. Even entering a horse in the demanding mile and a half "Test of the Champion" five successive years would be commendable. Winning five straight defies common sense. But that's exactly what Stephens did from 1982 to 1986 with 1982 Horse of the Year Conquistador Cielo, Caveat, Swale, Creme Fraiche and Danzig Connection. Associated Press named Stephens Trainer of the Decade for the 1980s.

His list of champions includes Forty Niner, Miss Oceana, Sabin, Bald Eagle, Never Bend, Smart Angle, Heavenly Cause and Devil's Bag, whose undefeated 2-year-old season was considered by many to be one of the finest ever. Devil's Bag was syndicated for $36 million following his 2-year-old season, injured his knee at three, and was retired. Another Stephens' star, Danzig, was also injured and retired in 1980 after winning his only three races. Through 1989, Danzig ranks as the second leading active sire behind Alydar, according to *The Blood-Horse* Magazine. "There's no telling what kind of horse Danzig might have been," Stephens said.

Stephens, born in Stanton, Kentucky, Sept. 1, 1913, envisioned a career in racing at an early age—as a jockey. "One of my biggest disappointments in racing is that I didn't do better as a rider," Stephens said.

Stephens began his racing career when he was thirteen, breaking yearlings for a banker in Midway, Kentucky. He rode his first winner at the age of eighteen. When he grew too big to ride—he is 5-foot-8 and 155 pounds—Stephens continued in racing by becoming assistant trainer for John S. Ward, whose son, Sherrill saddled three-time Horse of the Year Forego. "Sherrill Ward's father told me that I had a career in racing, but it wasn't as a jockey," Stephens said. "He was right, and I wish he was still around today to see how right he was. I've never had a bad year training horses."

His first training win was with Bronze Bugle in a race at Keeneland in 1940. Stephens came to New York in 1943 and has been a fixture in racing ever since. In 1945, he saddled Saguaro, a horse he claimed for $2,500 two years earlier, to win the Excelsior Handicap, Stephens' first stakes victory.

More than 200 stakes victories have followed. His career highlights include his election into the Hall of Fame in 1976; a street in Midway being named in his honor, and the publication of his autobiography, entitled *Guess I'm Lucky* in 1985.

Stephens has continued his training magic through the 1980s, conceding little to his age while circumventing an assortment of infirmities which would have stopped most his age. In 1984, Stephens outfought double pneumonia—compounded by bruised ribs he suffered when he slipped stepping out of the shower—and had a banner year typified by a string of stakes wins in May and early June. Swale, who would die eight days after his Belmont Stakes win from an apparent heart attack, gave Stephens his second Kentucky Derby. Sabin ripped off five straight stakes victories on turf. Miss Oceana won the Acorn Stakes at Belmont Park, the first leg of the filly Triple Crown. Two days later, Morning Bob won the Pennsylvania Derby.

"That was like medicine for him," Stephens' wife, Lucille, said. Woody said, "I had pneumonia. It took some time to get over."

No way did Stephens ponder retirement. "I'm going to slow down a little," he said. "I know I've always said that, but I guess there's a time when I'll have to." Having 2-year-olds such as Danzig's Beauty, an impressive winner of her first three starts, including the $200,000

Gardenia Stakes last fall; Yonder, winner of the World Appeal Stakes and the Grade II Remsen; and De La Devil, who won the Grade II Golden Rod Stakes the same day Yonder took the Remsen, make it difficult for Stephens to retire.

In a mid-September 1989 interview, Stephens, freshly turned seventy-six and still training, discussed the impact of handicapping on his storied career. "Handicapping has helped me all the way through my career," Stephens said. "I came to New York in 1943 and began training here. I was claiming horses. I studied the sheets [*Daily Racing Form*] very hard to see who's the speed and who's the class in a race. It helped me learn to place a horse. If I have a real good speed horse and he's the only speed in the race, I'll use him [on the lead]. If there's other speed in the race, I might tell my rider to hold the horse back a little first, try to conserve as much energy as possible. If a horse only runs one way and that is as a speed horse, you're going to get in trouble. If he's a speed horse, there will almost always be somebody who can run with you."

A notable exception was Stephens' brilliant speed horse Conquistador Cielo. The son of Mr. Prospector, given ample time to recover from a saucer fracture, defeated older horses by daylight in the 1982 Metropolitan Handicap, winning the Grade I stakes race in a track record 1:33 for the mile. When Stephens wheeled Conquistador Cielo back in the Belmont Stakes five days later, most everybody thought Stephens was losing a grasp on reality. Horses, even top stakes horses, rarely race with less than a week's rest. To do so in Grade I stakes company is difficult enough. Besides that, Stephens was asking a son of Mr. Prospector, a horse solidly entrenched as a speed sire, to stretch out to one and a half miles.

Stephens, however, had a distinct edge: he knew his horse. "There's a lot of people who think they're handicappers, but they're not," Stephens said. "I've spent sixty years with horses, all kinds of them, great ones, cheap ones. If I have been around a horse, I pretty much know about him. People said I was taking a gamble with Conquistador because I'd never won a Belmont. But he was sharp enough, and I knew he loved the mud."

Conquistador Cielo justified Stephens' judgment in one of the most impressive performances in Triple Crown history, going wire-to-wire on a sloppy track to win the Belmont Stakes by fourteen lengths, the largest margin since Secretariat's thirty-one length win in 1973.

In doing so, Conquistador Cielo also demonstrated two of Stephens' strongest attributes, pointing a horse to a specific race and showing patience despite temptations. Of Stephens' five consecutive Belmont Stakes, the winners showed a total of just one win in the earlier two legs of the Triple Crown: Swale in the 1984 Kentucky Derby. Stephens brought all five to a peak in the Belmont. Conquistador Cielo, injured earlier in his 3-year-old season, recovered completely. An important element of his recovery was Stephens' patience and ability to live with the fact that rushing his horse into the Kentucky Derby or the Preakness was not in the horse's best interest. Too often, especially with the Triple Crown, trainers compromise their horses' long-term careers by rushing into the Kentucky Derby without the proper preparation. Frequently, these horses overextend themselves in the Derby and never recover. Recent runnings of the Derby are rife with examples including D. Wayne Lukas-trained Capote, Winning Colors and, to a lesser extent, Houston.

The philosophy espoused by another Hall of Fame trainer, Horatio Luro, is "Don't squeeze the lemon dry." In other words, don't ask your horse to do too much, a philosophy summarized by the racetrack adage, "Take care of the horse, and the horse will take care of you."

By ignoring the Derby and especially the Preakness, Stephens allowed Conquistador Cielo enough time to completely recover. Stephens' reward was his Belmont Stakes victory, one which began his remarkable five straight. "I don't think young trainers learn the right way of doing things overnight," Stephens said. "So many people make a mistake running a horse over his head. Then, when they do run him in the right spot, he might not be right that day, and he might get beat."

To help identify the right spot for his horses, Stephens still spends as much as a half hour handicapping one race that his horse is in. "It's hard to go past the *Form*," he said. "It tells you the facts. I'll spend whatever time I have. I may try to study in my office, at the barn, in my home or at the track before my race. After I handicap, I have more confidence. Say I run a horse at a mile and a quarter and use him in the pace. Then I'll drop him back to seven furlongs. Then he'll have a kick, a big kick. If you want to stretch him out, you'd reverse the order. I do it both ways, and it's paid off for me all my life. But nothing gives you guaranteed winners. You can give a rider just so many instructions. It doesn't always turn out the way you think it will. The race changes when the horses step onto the track. Many times, a horse loses because the race doesn't shape up right. An edge I have is knowing my horse, how sound he is, if he gets keyed up in the paddock."

Two handicapping edges Stephens offers are the importance of class and a dislike of horses racing after a layoff. "Class will always show," Stephens said. "A class horse will run either way, on the pace or off. A class horse is the one to beat."

Not so for layoff horses. "I don't bet on any horse who's been away too long," he said. "If he's a quick training horse, I might like him a little. I never like a horse off three or four months. Say I might have a horse who's been away two, three months. He might need a race."

That's why it's important to recognize if a horse you're handicapping today is nominated to a stakes race one to two weeks later. Nominations are summarized regularly in the *Form*. Remember, information is an ally. Try to garner as much as possible, an extension of the strategy of handicapping each horse's PPs from the bottom to the top. Get the complete picture.

Now enjoy Stephens' insights on two of his major stakes wins.

"I think studying the *Form* keeps me better educated about other people's horses, who'll be in front, who has the speed," Stephens said. "Then I look at how far a horse could come from out of it. When I won the Belmont with Caveat, I told him [jockey Laffit Pincay, Jr.] when you've got this horse back where you think he should be, take him back another three or four lengths. I thought there was a lot of speed on the front end. This way, when my horse did come, he came hard. He rolled right by everyone. He came from way back."

Indeed, Caveat benefited from a lively pace as Slew O' Gold pressured Au Point. Caveat was eleventh, eighteen lengths behind, when Pincay asked him to move with a mile left. Caveat responded by flying along the inside to close the gap. Around the final turn, Pincay rushed Caveat to the inside of Au Point, ridden by Gregg McCarron, and Slew O' Gold, ridden by Angel Cordero, Jr. In a truly frightening moment, Slew O' Gold bore in on Au Point, pushing him into Caveat in a chain reaction which nearly sent Pincay over the rail. Pincay's boot actually scraped the rail, yet Pincay was cool enough to keep riding his horse, maintaining their momentum as they cruised to a three

115th RUNNING—1983—CAVEAT

EIGHTH RACE
Belmont
JUNE 11, 1983

1 ½ MILES. (2.24) 115th Running THE BELMONT (Grade I). $250,000 Added. 3-year-olds. Colts and Geldings, 126 lbs.; Fillies 121 lbs. By subscription of $100 each to accompany the nomination; $2,000 to pass the entry box, $3,000 to start. A supplementary nomination of $5,000 may be made on Wednesday, June 8 with an additional $20,000 to start, with $250,000 added of which 60% to the winner, 22% to second, 12% to third and 6% to fourth. Starters to be named at the closing time of entries. The winning owner will be presented with the August Belmont Memorial Cup to be retained for one year, as well as a trophy for permanent possession and trophies will be presented to the winning trainer and jockey. Nominations closed Tuesday, February 15, 1983 with 335 nominations. Value of race $358,500, value to winner $215,100, second $78,870, third $43,020, fourth $21,510. Mutuel pool $1,530,010, OTB pool $2,194,445.

Last Raced	Horse	Eqt.	A.	Wt	PP	¼	½	1	1¼	Str	Fin	Jockey	Odds $1
30May83 5Bel1	Caveat	b	3	126	7	$11^{1\frac{1}{2}}$	11^{hd}	8^1	$3^{1\frac{1}{2}}$	1^1	$1^{3\frac{1}{2}}$	Pincay L Jr	2.60
29May83 8Bel1	Slew O' Gold		3	126	1	3^1	2^1	2^2	$1\frac{1}{2}$	2^2	$2^{1\frac{3}{4}}$	Cordero A Jr	2.50
21May83 8Hol1	Barberstown		3	126	5	6^1	$6^{2\frac{1}{2}}$	5^1	5^4	3^{hd}	3no	Toro F	9.10
30May83 9Key6	Megaturn		3	126	2	13^2	12^1	$10^{2\frac{1}{2}}$	$7\frac{1}{2}$	6^{hd}	4^{hd}	Hernandez R	13.70
21May83 8Pim3	High Honors	b	3	126	8	$4\frac{1}{2}$	4^3	3^2	4^{hd}	$4^{1\frac{1}{2}}$	$5\frac{1}{2}$	Velasquez J	4.80
21May83 8Pim1	Deputed Testamony		3	126	14	$2\frac{1}{2}$	$3\frac{1}{2}$	4^1	6^1	7^4	6^5	Miller D A Jr	9.80
3Jun83 8WO1	Canadian Factor		3	126	12	9^1	10^2	12^1	$10\frac{1}{2}$	8^{hd}	$7\frac{3}{4}$	Stahlbaum G	f-23.30
30May83 9Mth1	Princilian		3	126	10	$8\frac{1}{2}$	$7\frac{1}{2}$	$9\frac{1}{2}$	11^2	10^4	8no	Maple E	59.70
2Jun83 6Bel3	Current Hope		3	126	9	$7\frac{1}{2}$	$8^{1\frac{1}{2}}$	13^1	9^{hd}	9^{hd}	$9\frac{1}{2}$	Solis A	16.60
2Jun83 8Bel4	Au Point		3	126	15	1^4	$1^{1\frac{1}{2}}$	1^1	2^1	5^1	$10^{4\frac{1}{4}}$	McCarron G	37.60
25May83 7Bel2	Law Talk	b	3	126	13	10^1	$9\frac{1}{2}$	$6^{1\frac{1}{2}}$	8^2	11^6	$11^{6\frac{1}{2}}$	Samyn J L	f-23.30
21May83 8Hol4	Balboa Native		3	126	3	$14^{1\frac{1}{2}}$	$14\frac{1}{2}$	14^6	$12\frac{1}{2}$	$12^{1\frac{1}{2}}$	$12^{2\frac{1}{4}}$	Hawley S	38.20
5Jun83 8Bel5	White Birch	b	3	126	4	12^2	13^4	$11\frac{1}{2}$	13^2	$13^{1\frac{1}{2}}$	13^{nk}	Cruguet J	f-23.30
30May83 9Key1	Dixieland Band	b	3	126	11	5^2	5^5	$7\frac{1}{2}$	14^8	14	14	Passmore W J	41.70
22May83 8Bel7	El Cubanaso	b	3	126	6	15	15	15	15	—	—	Graell A	f-23.30

El Cubanaso, Broke down.
f—Mutuel field.

OFF AT 5:44 Start good, Won driving. Time, :23⅗, :47⅘, 1:11⅗, 1:36⅖, 1:59⅘, 2:27⅘, Track fast.

$2 Mutuel Prices:				
	5-(G)-CAVEAT	7.20	3.60	3.40
	1-(A)-SLEW O' GOLD		4.60	4.00
	4-(E)-BARBERSTOWN			4.80

Dk. b. or br. c, by Cannonade—Cold Hearted, by The Axe II. Trainer Stephens Woodford C. Bred by Ryehill Farm (Md).

CAVEAT, outrun into the backstretch, moved to the inside while beginning to advance racing into the far turn, drove through inside the leaders bouncing off AU POINT and into the rail leaving the far turn, wrested command inside the final three sixteenths and drew away under left-handed urging. SLEW O' GOLD, sent up along the inside early, eased out nearing the backstretch while moving closest to AU POINT, reached the front nearing the stretch but was no match for the winner during the drive. BARBERSTOWN, never far back, came out between horses while rallying approaching the stretch but wasn't good enough. MEGATURN, outrun to the stretch, came out for the drive and finished with good energy. HIGH HONORS, never far back while racing well out in the track, rallied while continuing wide racing into the far turn, remained a factor into the stretch and weakened. DEPUTED TESTAMONY raced forwardly until near the far turn and drifted out while weakening. CANADIAN FACTOR raced wide. PRINCILIAN was always outrun. CURRENT HOPE saved ground to no avail. AU POINT sprinted to the front from the outside racing to the first turn, remained well out from the rail while making the pace, came over slightly bumping with CAVEAT leaving the far turn and had nothing left. LAW TALK raced wide. BALBOA NATIVE was never close. WHITE BIRCH was always outrun. DIXIELAND BAND was finished nearing the far turn. EL CUBANASO, never close, broke down after entering the stretch. There was a stewards inquiry involving the run leaving the far turn before the result was made official.

and a half length victory. The "Inquiry" sign came on immediately after the race, but the stewards left Slew O' Gold second.

Stephens has won just about every major stakes race in the country, yet until 1988 he had never won the Grade I Travers Stakes at Saratoga, the oldest major stakes race for 3-year-olds in America. First run in 1864, the Travers is known as the Mid-summer Derby. It's the same classic 1¼ mile distance as the Kentucky Derby and an excellent gauge of 3-year-olds who've had the summer to develop. For a variety of reasons, injury, poor racing luck or untapped ability, a horse may miss the Derby or perform poorly in it. Such horses can nonetheless establish themselves among the leaders of the 3-year-old division in the late summer and fall. Other horses who've been prominent earlier in their 3-year-old season can solidify their standing. Forty Niner was one such 3-year-old.

Voted 2-year-old champion of 1987, Forty Niner entered his sophomore season as the early favorite for the Kentucky Derby. He was a dead-game second to Winning Colors in the Derby then a poor and controversial seventh in the Preakness. Stephens was wrongly vilified when jockey Pat Day pushed Forty Niner into an ill-conceived speed duel with Winning Colors, who finished third, two and a half lengths behind Risen Star. Forty Niner was blamed by many for racing the talented filly into defeat and giving her a rough trip. Yet the simple truth is Winning Colors' jockey, Gary Stevens, chose to push for the lead. If he had taken back, even slightly, she could've avoided Forty Niner early and possibly bettered her game but debilitating finish.

The paths chosen by Lukas and Stephens offer an interesting contrast reflective of each trainer's philosophy.

A novice racing fan could have interpreted Winning Colors' performance in the Preakness. She had clearly fought courageously to finish as well as she did. Following her victory in the Derby—when she became just the third filly to win the race in 115 years—Winning Colors clearly deserved a rest. Lukas, instead, put her in the Belmont Stakes, a 1½ mile endurance test vs. colts. She led early only to finish last in a field of six by forty-four and three-quarters lengths. The toll? She won one race, an allowance at Saratoga, in her next ten starts. In the $1 million 1989 Breeders' Cup Distaff, she finished ninth by twenty-four lengths in a field of ten.

Stephens, realizing Forty Niner paid a price in the Preakness, too, chose to give him a rest. He returned to action in an easy spot, a one mile allowance race at Monmouth Park. Forty Niner won by seven and a quarter lengths, blazing a track record of 1:33 4/5. He then eked out an extremely tough nose win against Seeking The Gold in the $500,000 Haskell Invitational at Monmouth.

They'd meet again in the Travers, where they encountered Brian's Time, an impresssive five and a half length winner of the Jim Dandy Stakes at Saratoga in his last start.

Just three other horses entered the Travers, making a compact field of six. Strategy, based on flexibility, would decide this $1 million race.

Brian's Time, a one-run closer, would go off the slight favorite and run third by three-quarters of a length, a hapless victim of a crawling pace: 1:13 for the first six furlongs.

Forty Niner and Seeking The Gold would again finish a nose apart in the same order as the Haskell.

Forty Niner saved ground on the inside and held off Seeking The Gold in a desperate, all-out sprint to the wire. Forty Niner benefited from a superb ride by Chris McCarron, who flew in from California for the mount.

"McCarron had never ridden Forty Niner," Stephens said. "He came to the track that morning and I told him this horse races best when he's asked to run at the five-sixteenths pole. I told Chris, 'When you hit that pole, put him on the lead because he has a big kick. When you turn the corner, shut the gate. Don't let anybody on the inside of you.'"

Forty Niner surged to a two length lead at the five-sixteenths pole, then had enough left to hold off Seeking The Gold and Brian's Time. Stephens' strategy worked. "I've had a lifetime experience on it. If I don't know it by now, I'll never know," Stephens said.

Stephens rarely uses jockey Angel Cordero, Jr. Eddie Maple has been Stephens' regular rider, followed by Pincay and McCarron. Stephens was openly critical of Cordero's ride on Slew O' Gold in Caveat's Belmont. He is one of many who have criticized Cordero's aggressiveness.

Cordero himself was surprised to learn of Stephens' opinion of one of the few times Cordero rode a Stephens' horse.

The 100th running of the Kentucky Derby in 1974 attracted a mammoth field of twenty-three. Unlike the previous year when Secretariat won the Triple Crown, there were no standouts in the spring of 1974. That induced the overflow of entries. In 1975, the maximum number of Derby starters was set at twenty based on lifetime earnings in nonrestricted graded stakes.

Stephens saddled a two-horse entry, Judger and Cannonade.

Judger, considered the stronger of the two, was ridden by Pincay. They finished eighth. "Things didn't break for him in the 1974 Derby," Stephens said. "Judger had the No. 22 post and got in trouble."

Cannonade won. "I never saw a horse get a better ride," Stephens said. "There's twenty-three horses. He [Cordero] kept sneaking through horses, outside and inside. Then, just before they turned for home, he switched to the outside because he thought if there was a challenge, it'd be from the outside. He wanted to be sure my horse would see another horse if a challenge came, but at the quarter pole he opened up three lengths and won easily.

"I thought that day, Cordero rode that horse as good as any I've ever seen."

Cordero, informed of Stephens' remark in a September 1989 phone interview, was silent for a second, then said, "That's a great compliment coming from him."

Turf

13 Turf racing, a sprawling green puzzle to some, is my favorite game, awarding those with an understanding of turf breeding, grass racing and jockeys' abilities an edge which frequently can be transformed into overlays.

The first step to understanding grass racing is realizing some horses race well on the turf and others don't. The idea sounds painfully simple, yet it's a vital point not picked up by many bettors. Horses will appear in turf races with proven records of no success on grass and still receive an inordinate measure of support from the betting public.

A race at Saratoga in 1981 is a perfect example. Carded as the first race of the day, a handicap on the grass matched a field of just six. The two favorites were Temperence Hill and The Liberal Member, each a fine horse in his own element. That element was dirt, the main track, where Temperence Hill won the Belmont Stakes and Travers; where The Liberal Member won the Brooklyn Handicap. Clearly that element had never been, nor would it be, the turf. They had poor turf form—Temperence Hill showed one third place finish in three turf races; The Liberal Member had one win in eight grass starts—yet they were bet heavily. The amount of action each of those horses received—The Liberal Member was the 3 to 2 favorite in a field of six; Temperence Hill was 5 to 2—created overlays for the other four horses in the race. Manguin, a turf specialist who went off at 4 to 1, won by a nose over longshot Scythian Gold. Neither Temperance Hill nor The Liberal Member were factors.

Grass is physically an easier surface for horses to race on than dirt because grass is a safer cushion for the horses' feet. Some horses just prefer the grassy surface. Another theory as to why a horse will take to grass is that some horses dislike getting hit in the face by dirt when they're running behind other horses on the main track.

Breeding is vitally important in determining whether a horse will do well on the turf if he's never raced on it. Yet breeding can't help a horse if he has demonstrated repeatedly that he hasn't performed well on grass.

Turf racing is invariably different from racing on dirt just from the physical nature of the course itself. Because the turf course is located inside the perimeter of the main track, grass courses are shorter in circumference with less width to them and have tighter, harder to negotiate turns. From that alone, turf courses consistently give an advantage to the horse and rider who can save ground on the turns. An inside post position on a turf course is a clear advantage, doubly so if it's the inner of two turf courses, such as at Belmont and Saratoga. The outside post position is a distinct disadvantage, particularly if there is a relatively short run into the first turn. Trainer Phil Johnson points out an interesting and little known exception: "I love to save ground on the turn when the turf is firm. But when the turf is soft, it tends to dry out slower on the inside, so the inside gets chopped up. On a softer course, an outside post position can be an advantage."

The difference between a firm turf course and one labeled soft or yielding is considerable. Many horses who perform well on grass don't run well on a soft course. When evaluating PPs in a turf race, we note such poor performances.

Graceful Darby, a daughter of Darby Creek Road out of a mare by His Majesty, had won just one of nine lifetime starts when trainer John Veitch entered the 3-year-old filly in a 1987 turf race at Belmont for her grass debut.

She won impressively; won again in allowance company by five and three-quarters lengths, then won again in the Tanya Stakes by five and a quarter lengths. Graceful Darby took her perfect turf record into the Grade II Sheepshead Bay Handicap. The course was soft, and she finished third by six and three-quarters lengths at odds of 9 to 10. Veitch wheeled her back in another stakes at Belmont, the Sweet Tooth, and she encountered a yielding course. She again finished a distant third, seven lengths behind Doubles Partner as the 9 to 10 favorite. Doubles Partner won by five as the 2 to 1 second choice.

The two met again in the Grade III Nijana Stakes at Saratoga, Aug. 12, 1987. This time, the turf was firm.

Doubles Partner was coupled in the wagering with Spectacular Bev, who won her last start out of town. Doubles Partner had raced at Saratoga in the Test Stakes on dirt in her last race and run eleventh. The race on dirt was meaningless. Bettors made the entry the 1 to 2 favorite in the field of seven.

Graceful Darby still hadn't been beaten on a firm (fast) turf course. If we count her last two performances as anomalies, we are thrilled to see her settle at 7 to 2 on the tote board. Graceful Darby beat Spectacular Bev by two lengths and returned $9.60. To catch her, all you had to do was throw out the two races on a far different turf surface.

EIGHTH RACE
Saratoga
AUGUST 12, 1987

1 $\frac{1}{16}$ MILES.(Turf). (1.39⅖) 14th Running THE NIJANA (GRADE III). Purse $75,000 Added. Fillies. 3-year-olds. By subscription of $150 each, which should accompny the nomination; $300 to pass the entry box; $300 to start, with $75,000 added. The added money and all fees to be divided 60% to the winner, 22% to second, 12% to third and 6% to fourth. 121 lbs. Non-winners of a race of $50,000 at a mile or over since May 1, allowed 3 lbs., Of such a race since January 1, 5 lbs., Of such a race of $35,000 in 1986-87, 7 lbs. (Maiden, cliaming, starter and restricted races not considered). Starters to be named at the closing time of entries. A trophy will be presented to the winning owner. The New York Racing Association reserves the right to transfer this race to the Main Course. Closed Wednesday, July 29, 1987 with 32 nominations.

Value of race $84,600; value to winner $50,760; second $18,612; third $10,152; fourth $5,076. Mutuel pool $153,321, OTB pool $71,815. Exacta Pool $124,912 OTB Exacta Pool $161,176.

Last Raced	Horse	Eqt.A.Wt	PP	St	¼	½	¾	Str	Fin	Jockey	Odds $1
11Jly87 7Bel3	Graceful Darby	3 116	2	2	5¹	6¹½	4¹½	1½	1²	Bailey J D	3.80
11Jly87 8Pim1	Spectacular Bev	3 114	5	5	6¹	5hd	5½	4²	2¹	Santos J A	a- 50
13Jun87 9Crc5	Token Gift	3 114	3	3	11½	11	11½	2¹	32½	Maple E	14.40
6Aug87 8Sar11	Doubles Partner	3 114	1	1	2²	2½	2³	3½	4nk	Cordero A Jr	a-.50
1Aug87 3Bel1	Miss Unnameable	b 3 114	4	4	3hd	4³	3¹	5⁴	511½	Cruguet J	11.50
30Jly87 6Bel1	Moms Birthday	3 114	6	6	7	7	6³	6⁶	6⁴	Antley C W	4.50
25Jly87 3Mth3	Pour Me Out	b 3 114	7	7	4⁴	3¹½	7	7	7	Samyn J L	22.70

a-Coupled: Spectacular Bev and Doubles Partner.

OFF AT 5:22. Start good, Won driving. Time, :24, :47⅖, 1:11, 1:35, 1:41⅖ Course firm.

$2 Mutuel Prices:

3-(B)-GRACEFUL DARBY	9.60	3.20	2.60
1-(F)-SPECTACULAR BEV (a-entry)		2.20	2.10
5-(D)-TOKEN GIFT			2.60

$2 EXACTA 3-1 PAID $18.40.

B. f, by Darby Creek Road—Graceful Touch, by His Majesty. Trainer Veitch John M. Bred by Phillips Mr-Mrs J W (Ky).

Many times, we can throw out, or at least qualify, grass performances from difficult outside posts. Consider this table:

POST POSITION ANALYSIS OF 1989 MAIN TURF COURSE RACES

Track	Meet	*Number of Outside Posts	Outside Posts' Combined Record
Laurel	Summer	3	1-33
Laurel	Winter	3	1-16
Monmouth	Summer	4	1-19
Aqueduct	Spring	3	0-17
Aqueduct	Winter	4	1-30
Belmont	Summer	1	1-24
Belmont	Fall	2	1-34
Saratoga	Summer	4	1-25
Atlantic City	Summer	5	0-30
Philadelphia	Summer	5	0-28
Calder	Winter	3	1-20
		TOTAL	8-276

*—e.g. 3 outside posts means post positions 10, 11 and 12 if the course's most outside post position is No. 12

Remember: 8-for-276

When a horse shows a strong effort but tires from a disadvantageous outside post on the turf, it's frequently overlooked, creating overlays.

A lovely example popped up May 29, 1989, in a one mile turf race for maidens.

5 **BELMONT**

1 MILE. (Turf). (1.33) MAIDEN SPECIAL WEIGHT. Purse $26,000. 3-year-olds and upward. Weights, 3-year-olds, 115 lbs.; older, 124 lbs.

Square Ruler — **Ch. c. 3, by Majesty's Prince—Four Angles, by Quadrangle**
Own.—Cantey J B Jr — **Br.—Cantey & Cress (Ky)** — **Tr.—Peitz Dan C** — **115**
Lifetime 7 0 0 4 $11,040 — 1989 2 M 0 2 $5,400 — 1988 5 M 0 2 $5,640

6Apr89- 7Aqu my	7f	:22⅗	:46	1:24⅘	Md Sp Wt	2	6	57½	32	22½	34	Santagata N	122	25.00	73-21	Twice Iced 1222½ PrivateAction1221½SquareRuler1222¾	Weakened
9Jan89- 6Aqu fst	6f	⊡:23	:47⅕	1:12⅗	Md Sp Wt	3	2	95¼	72¾	55	36¾	Lovato F Jr	122	5.40	74-21	Fuzziano 1226 Dauntsey 122¾ Square Ruler 122no	Wide trip
22Dec88- 5Aqu fst	6f	⊡:23⅕	:47⅖	1:12	Md Sp Wt	1	5	62¾	52¼	44½	34½	Lovato F Jr	118	32.70	79-15	One Easy Step 1183 Talking Point 1181½SquareRuler118nk	Rallied
8Dec88- 4Aqu fst	1⅛	⊡:49⅕	1:15	1:54⅖	Md Sp Wt	5	6	54½	54½	69¾	716	Lovato F Jr	118	6.60	54-21	Rock Point 1182½ Earnhardt 118hd Bell Bottom Blues1188	Outrun
24Nov88- 7Aqu fst	1⅛	:49	1:14⅘	1:54	Md Sp Wt	8	2	21½	31	2½	56¾	Lovato F Jr	118	11.60	58-26	Reaffirming 1181½ PremierDanseur1181¼BestAuthority118no	Tired
7Nov88- 4Aqu fst	1⅛	:48⅕	1:13⅕	1:54⅘	Md Sp Wt	5	2	1hd	2½	1hd	32½	Lovato F Jr	118	17.70	58-27	[D]Earnhrdt118½OnceOverKnightly1182SqureRuler1181¾	Weakened
19Oct88- 6Aqu fst	6f	:22⅗	:46	1:10⅖	Md Sp Wt	8	11	119¼	89½	813	812¾	Fox W I Jr	118	83.80	75-18	Guadalupe Peak 1182¾ Valid Carat 1181¾ Traskwood1183¾	Outrun

LATEST WORKOUTS May 20 Bel 5f fst 1:00 H — May 13 Bel 5f fst 1:01 H — May 4 Bel 5f fst 1:01⅕ H — Apr 27 Bel 4f fst :50 B

Road Eagle B. c. 4, by His Majesty—Quarrel Over, by One for All
Br.—Bwamazon Farm Div of Whitaker Fms (Ky)
Own.—Anchel E Tr.—LaBoccetta Frank
124 Lifetime 16 0 1 2 $8,900 | 1989 6 M 0 1 $1,800 | 1988 10 M 1 1 $7,100 | Turf 5 0 0 0 $1,560

1May89- 6Aqu gd 1⅜ Ⓣ:49⅘ 1:43⅘ 2:22 3↑Md Sp Wt 12 1 2¹ 1hd 3⁴ 5⁴ Hernandez R b 124 12.60 57–34 GoldenTwist117nkSocilScurity1153½BundlofMony115nk Weakened 12
1Apr89- 2Aqu fst 1⅛ :50⅕ 1:14⅘ 1:54⅖ 3↑Md 30000 3 4 4¹ 5⁴ 6¹² 615¾ LaboccettFJr10 b 110 19.80 47–23 Smooth Combination1159MusogeeMan115hdMr.Carvel1132¾ Tired 9
7Mar89- 2Aqu fst 1 :46⅘ 1:12⅗ 1:38⅗ Md 30000 2 9 9⁷ 74½ 6⁸ 515¼ Hernandez R b 118 10.70 58–21 Talc's Exemption 1185 Percifal1185¾TransBanner1183 Bumped st. 14
5Mar89- 2Aqu fst 1⅛ :49⅖ 1:14⅘ 1:54⅘ Md 30000 10 4 3² 65¼ 7¹² 717¼ LaboccettFJr10 b 108 5.30 44–27 Telephoto 118nk Nashville Hoedown 118¾ H. J.'s Babe1188¼ Tired 10
2Mar89- 1Aqu fst 1⅛ ⊡:50⅖ 1:16⅕ 1:56⅘ Md 45000 3 5 5⁵ 53¼ 4⁴ 38¼ Hernandez R b 118 6.10 50–28 Jr. Diplomask 1182¾ Telephoto1185½RoadEagle118¾ Evenly inside 9
2Feb89- 7Aqu fst 1 1/16 ⊡:47⅘ 1:14 1:49 Md Sp Wt 1 3 2⁵ 3⁶ 4⁵ 5⁹ Hernandez R b 122 6.60 55–28 Key Haze 117no Center Span 1157 Kanduit's Pride1221 Weakened 7
5Dec88- 9Aqu fst 1⅛ ⊡:49⅖ 1:15 1:56⅖ 3↑Md 35000 1 3 1½ 11½ 2hd 2¹ McCauley W H b 120 4.20 59–27 Karaine Hoist 1161 Road Eagle 1205 Oval Office1207 Gave way lt. 12
7Dec88- 9Aqu fst 1 1/16 ⊡:49⅗ 1:15⅘ 1:50 3↑Md 35000 12 3 31½ 6⁴ 64¼ 54¾ McCauley W H b 120 3.10 54–32 Spruce Street 1164 Senor 111hd Retroienne 116nk Tired 12
8Nov88- 3Aqu fst 1 :47⅕ 1:12⅕ 1:38 3↑Md Sp Wt 5 1 21½ 66¾ 6¹¹ 7¹⁴ McCauley W H b 120 19.40 62–23 Tumble Too 1201¾ Daily Review 1206 Oval Office 120½ Stopped 7
20Oct88- 2Aqu gd 1⅜ :50⅖ 1:40⅖ 2:20 3↑Md Sp Wt 5 1 11½ 1² 3½ 35½ Vega A b 119 6.50 73–18 Sayaret 119no Amuse The Minister1195½RoadEagle1198½ Steadied 9
LATEST WORKOUTS May 26 Aqu 5f gd 1:02⅘ B May 19 Aqu 4f fst :50 B Apr 11 Aqu 4f fst :50⅖ B

Pescadero B. c. 3, by The Bart—Hoist The Colors, by Hoist the Flag
Br.—Sea Spray Farm (Ky)
Own.—Whaling City Farms Tr.—Moschera Gasper S
115 Lifetime 1 0 0 0 | 1989 1 M 0 0 | 1988 0 M 0 0

0Apr89- 5Aqu fst 6f :23⅖ :47⅖ 1:12⅗ 3↑Md 72500 6 3 5⁴ 6⁵ 6¹¹ 616½ Castillo R E5 108 14.40 60–26 Congressman 1153¼ Goldlover 1157 Cymbidium 113hd Wide 6
LATEST WORKOUTS May 22 Bel tr.t 4f fst :49 B May 9 Bel 4f fst :49 H Apr 18 Bel tr.t 3f fst :39⅕ B Apr 13 Bel tr.t 4f fst :49⅘ B

Sweet Neck Ch. g. 3, by Great Neck—Arrow Canas, by Gun Bow
Br.—Delley & Farish III (NY)
Own.—Farish W S III Tr.—Watters Sidney Jr
115 Lifetime 1 0 0 0 | 1989 1 M 0 0 | 1988 0 M 0 0

2May89- 6Bel fst 7f :22⅗ :47 1:25⅖ 3↑ⓢMd Sp Wt 4 13 14¹¹ 11¹⁸ 9¹⁷ 919½ Maple E 115 27.20 55–24 Cavangh'sBeu1153¾RockvilleCentre1156WeAgree1151½ Brk slowly 14
LATEST WORKOUTS May 20 Bel 4f fst :48⅗ H May 15 Bel 5f fst 1:01⅗ H May 10 Bel 4f gd :49⅗ B May 5 Bel 5f fst 1:02 Hg

Petracella Dk. b. or br. c. 3, by Triocala—Cold Teepee, by American Native
Br.—Indian Head Stable (NY)
Own.—Indian Head Stable Tr.—Baeza Braulio
108⁷ Lifetime 7 0 0 0 | 1989 7 M 0 0 | 1988 0 M 0 0 | Turf 1 0 0 0

2May89- 6Bel fst 7f :22⅗ :47 1:25⅖ 3↑ⓢMd Sp Wt 8 8 128¼ 12²⁰ 13²¹ 1228¾ DeJesus I7 108 103.60 46–24 Cavanagh's Beau 1153¾RockvilleCentre1156WeAgree1151½ Outrun 14
5May89- 7Aqu gd 1⅛ :48⅘ 1:14⅘ 1:54⅕ 3↑Md Sp Wt 3 5 6¹¹ 8²⁴ 8²⁷ 842½ DeJesus I7 b 108 60.40 — — Prince Rain 1151 Almost Humble 1151²½ Grasstime 110¾ Outrun 8
3Apr89- 6Aqu fm 1 1/16 Ⓣ:49⅘ 1:14⅕ 1:47⅕ 3↑Md Sp Wt 7 1 2½ 7⁵ 9¹⁴ 1025¼ DeJesus I7 b 108 101.70 44–24 Heavenly Dance 115nk All Nite Soldier 115½ Biddemup 115½ Tired 10
9Mar89- 9Aqu fst 1⅛ :50⅖ 1:16⅕ 1:56⅗ 3↑Md 32500 12 10 11¹⁷ 12²⁵ 12²⁹ 12³¹ DeJesus I7 b 108 91.40 — — H. J.'s Babe 120½ Jolly Yosi 112nk Upgrading 112¾ Outrun 12
3Mar89- 9Aqu fst 6f :22⅗ :46⅗ 1:13⅗ Md 35000 9 1 11¹⁴ 11¹⁴ 10¹⁴ 1018¼ DeJesus I7 b 115 101.00 54–26 InquisitiveNick1184Cloudy'sCstle118½WveringMoon1182¾ Outrun 11
3Mar89- 9Aqu fst 6f ⊡:22⅖ :47⅕ 1:13⅖ ⓢMd Sp Wt 5 10 11²² 11²⁷ 11²⁷ 1137½ Lovato F Jr b 122 78.70 39–28 Sir Albert 1223¾ Uncle Hugo 1222¼ Bold Dutchman 1221¾ Trailed 11
3Jan89- 4Aqu fst 6f ⊡:23 :46 1:12 Md 35000 9 10 11¹⁵ 11²¹ 11²⁶ 1131¾ Lovato F Jr 122 30.50 52–16 Screen Legend 1182¼ CraftyArt1153CircleMarxASpot1223 Outrun 12
LATEST WORKOUTS May 20 Bel tr.t 3f fst :36 H Apr 9 Bel tr.t 4f gd :49⅘ B

It's Our Time B. g. 4, by Lejoli—Speed Delight, by Rheingold
Br.—Empire I (NY)
Own.—Petto Rosalie Tr.—Bolton Amos E
117⁷ Lifetime 11 0 0 0 | 1988 11 M 0 0 | 1987 0 M 0 0 | Turf 4 0 0 0

4Nov88- 3Aqu fst 7f :23⅕ :47⅕ 1:25⅗ 3↑Md 30000 2 11 95¼ 11¹¹ 13¹⁸ 13²³ Carr D5 b 111 23.00f 50–26 TivoliStar116nkSonnyTheRed1207¼NshvilleHoedown120nk Outrun [illegible]
4Nov88- 4Aqu my 1 :46⅕ 1:11⅕ 1:38⅕ 3↑Md Sp Wt 5 8 8¹² 8²⁰ 8²³ 8⁴⁷ Imparato J 120 70.80 28–25 Certain Circles 1203¾ Tafara 1203 Sands of Gold 12012 Outrun 8
2Nov88- 4Aqu my 1⅛ :48⅕ 1:13⅗ 1:54⅗ 3↑ⓢMd Sp Wt 11 8 6⁵ 8¹² 9¹⁹ 836¾ Cayo D J 120 113.10 25–26 Hammocking 120no Allies Boy 1158½ Air Piracy 1154¼ Outrun 11
0Oct88- 6Bel fm 1 1/16 Ⓣ:48⅕ 1:13⅕ 1:45 3↑ⓢMd Sp Wt 3 2 1hd 3nk 62½ 8⁹ Goossens L 119 27.70 67–22 Sa Marche 1163 Charmin Cliff 119¾ Wisdom Tree 1191¾ Tired 10
3Sep88- 6Bel fm 1 Ⓣ:47⅕ 1:11⅖ 1:37 3↑Md Sp Wt 11 6 74½ 86¼ 86½ 813½ Goossens L 118 140.30 66–20 Block Trader 118nk Tina's World 1183½ Treasury 118nk Outrun 12
1Sep88- 9Bel fst 7f :22⅗ :46⅕ 1:24⅕ 3↑ⓢMd Sp Wt 5 7 97¾ 10¹⁶ 9²⁰ 923¾ Goossens L 118 77.90 57–16 Herr von Kaninchen 1187¾ Ogle 1181 Tivoli Star 1183 Outrun 11
8Sep88- 9Bel fm 1 1/16 Ⓣ:48 1:12⅗ 1:44⅘ 3↑ⓢAlw 29000 11 3 4¾ 85½ 9¹² 8¹⁶ Goossens L b 113 100.80 56–21 Mr. Walter K. 1131¼ Clifford 114hd Drums in theNight1132½ Tired 11
2Sep88- 3Bel fst 1 :47⅘ 1:13⅕ 1:39⅕ 3↑Md 45000 3 7 87½ 8¹¹ 8²⁰ 824¼ Goossens L b 114 48.40 45–27 ⒹSparkO'Dan114noMinZaman11811½Hammocking1141¾ Slow start 9
1Aug88- 7Bel gd 1 1/16 Ⓣ:47⅗ 1:12⅘ 1:45 3↑Md Sp Wt 4 1 1½ 11¹² 12³³ 1244½ Cruguet J b 117 60.40 26–22 Clifford 117½ Mastyl 1172 High Anticipation 1172¾ Stopped 12
3Jly88- 9Bel fst 1 1/16 :46⅗ 1:12⅖ 1:46 3↑ⓢMd Sp Wt 7 4 5⁷ 10¹⁸ 10²⁹ 1039¼ Lovato F Jr 116 82.20 33–19 Classi Whip 1165¼ YonkelYonkel11610½TrickyBusiness1221½ Tired 11
LATEST WORKOUTS May 21 Aqu 4f fst :50⅖ B May 14 Aqu 4f fst :49 B Apr 27 Aqu 5f fst 1:03⅖ B ●Apr 21 Aqu 3f fst :35⅘ H

Lurking Dk. b. or br. c. 3, by Alleged—Careful Glance, by Roberto
Br.—Firestone Mr-Mrs B R (Va)
Own.—Firestone B R Tr.—Mott William I
115 Lifetime 0 0 0 0 | 1989 0 M 0 0 | 1988 0 M 0 0
LATEST WORKOUTS May 22 Bel 5f fst 1:00⅕ Hg May 15 Bel 6f fst 1:17 Bg Apr 28 CD 5f fst 1:02 B

In Motion Dk. b. or br. g. 6, by No Bend--Ina Clare, by Neptune
Br.—Schoenborn Bros Farm (NY)
Own.—Schoenborn E F Tr.—Schoenborn Everett F
114¹⁰ Lifetime 11 0 1 1 $12,660 | 1989 1 M 0 0 | 1986 10 M 1 1 $12,660
Entered 27May89- 9 BEL

0Mar89- 3Aqu fst 6f ⊡:23⅕ :47⅖ 1:13 Md 45000 6 5 52¾ 4³ 65½ 56½ LaboccettFJr10 b 108 30.40 72–24 Ra Kish 118nk Mister Points 118nk Joint Verdict 1135¾ No factor 7
6Nov86- 9Aqu sly 7f :22⅗ :45⅘ 1:25⅖ 3↑ⓢMd Sp Wt 4 7 6⁴ 6⁴ 5⁵ 512¼ Rydowski S R b 120 6.80 62–19 King Ralph 1201¾ Doctor Inglis 1206¾ Sword Zone 122¾ Even try 11
0Nov86- 6Aqu fst 1 :46⅗ 1:11⅖ 1:38⅕ 3↑ⓢMd Sp Wt 11 5 66½ 48½ 5⁶ 58¾ Rydowski S R b 120 5.90 66–20 Calatrava 1207¾ Uncle Buddy 120nk Crobosity 120hd Weakened 14
5Oct86- 7Bel gd 1 1/16 :46⅘ 1:12⅘ 1:46 3↑ⓢMd Sp Wt 14 7 34½ 2½ 42½ 45¼ Rydowski S R b 119 3.40 67–20 Bomb The Tote 119nkTitledPass1143ThisTimeTina1192 Weakened 14
0Oct86- 9Bel fst 6f :23 :46⅕ 1:12 3↑ⓢMd Sp Wt 7 6 62¼ 4⁵ 46½ 32½ Rydowski S R b 119 7.10 79–20 Wonderous Wise 119½ Hallen 1192 In Motion 119no Rallied 12
2Sep86- 9Bel fst 7f :23⅕ :47⅕ 1:25⅖ 3↑ⓢMd Sp Wt 6 3 2hd 1½ 2hd 2¹ Rydowski S R b 118 4.90 74–20 Favored Monarch 1181 In Motion 118¾ She's Blase 1153¼ Gamely 10
1Aug86- 9Bel fst 1 :46⅕ 1:11⅗ 1:36⅖ 3↑ⓢMd Sp Wt 9 6 4² 2⁴ 4¹⁰ 414¼ Rydowski S R b 117 12.00 69–11 Skate To Music 11710 Van's Boy 1174 EasyNDirty117nk Bid, tired 12
0Aug86- 9Sar 4 5 4⁶ 45½ 3⁹ 44½ Rydowski S R b 117 55.30 75 — No excuse 0
LATEST WORKOUTS May 19 Bel 5f fst 1:00⅘ H May 10 Bel 4f gd :50⅕ B May 5 Bel 3f fst :37⅖ B

Sibling Sword Ch. c. 3, by Sharpen Up--Soeur D'Arthur, by Mon Fils
Br.—Amerivest & Seltzerlky
Own.—Amerivest Stable Tr.—Skiffington Thomas J
115 Lifetime 0 0 0 0 | 1989 0 M 0 0 | 1988 0 M 0 0
LATEST WORKOUTS May 25 Fai wc 6f fm 1:17⅕ B May 20 Fai wc 5f fm 1:02⅖ B May 13 Fai wc 5f fm 1:02⅕ B May 8 Fai wc 4f fm :49⅕ B

Panorama — Dk. b. or br. c. 3, by Damascus—Bonnie Blink, by Buckpasser — Lifetime 2 0 0 0 $765 — 1989 2 M 0 0 $765 — 1988 0 M 0 0
Own.—Phipps O M — Br.—Phipps O (Ky) — Tr.—McGaughey Claude III — **115**

5Feb89- 2GP fst 1 1/16 :48 1:13 1:47 3/5 Md Sp Wt 7 9 9^{18} 8^{18} 6^{10} $5^{8\frac{1}{4}}$ Romero R P 122 *1.10 55-25 Cougar Island 122^{6} Eulogize 122^{1} ⒹLaser One 122no Late. ft. 11
8Jan89- 4GP fst 7f :22 3/5 :46 1:24 3/5 Md Sp Wt 2 7 4^{4} $5^{5\frac{1}{2}}$ 4^{11} $4^{8\frac{3}{4}}$ Romero R P 122 *1.20 72-27 RulersCrown122^{4}SathwanBayta$117^{4\frac{1}{2}}$RamprtRod122^{nk} No excuse 12
LATEST WORKOUTS May 25 Bel 5f my 1:01 H May 10 Bel 5f gd 1:00 3/5 H Apr 30 Hia 3f fst :36 2/5 B Apr 25 Bel 5f fst 1:01 2/5 H

Eulogize — B. c. 3, by Roberto—Euphrosyne, by Judger — Lifetime 9 0 2 0 $5,860 — 1989 5 M 2 0 $5,860 — 1988 4 M 0 0 — Turf 4 0 1 0 $2,520
Own.—Dogwood Stable — Br.—Kentucky Select Bloodstock (Ky) — Tr.—DiMauro Stephen — **115**

1May89- 6Aqu gd 1 3/8 Ⓣ:49 4/5 1:43 4/5 2:22 3↑Md Sp Wt 1 5 9^{11} $7^{4\frac{3}{4}}$ 7^{14} $6^{8\frac{1}{4}}$ Santos J A b 115 *1.10 53-34 GoldenTwist117^{nk}SocilScurity$115^{3\frac{1}{4}}$BundlofMony115^{nk} No threat 12
10Mar89-10Hia fm *1 1/8 Ⓣ 1:54 4/5 Md Sp Wt 9 6 $7^{3\frac{3}{4}}$ $7^{5\frac{1}{2}}$ $4^{4\frac{1}{2}}$ 2^{1} Samyn J L b 120 *1.80 56-40 Lord Summing120^{1}Eulogize120^{hd}DancingSkies120^{1} Shuffled back 12
4Mar89- 1GP fst 1 1/16 :48 1/5 1:12 4/5 1:45 3/5 Md Sp Wt 2 6 6^{7} 6^{7} 6^{11} $6^{13\frac{3}{4}}$ Samyn J L b 122 8.80 59-18 Aloetta 122^{3} Captain Savy 122^{nk} Iroquois Drive 122^{2} Outrun 12
5Feb89- 2GP fst 1 1/16 :48 1:13 1:47 3/5 Md Sp Wt 2 8 7^{15} 5^{16} $5^{9\frac{1}{2}}$ 2^{6} Samyn J L b 122 7.70 57-25 Cougar Island 122^{6} Eulogize 122^{1} ⒹLaser One 122no Best others 11
28Jan89- 4GP fst 7f :22 3/5 :45 2/5 1:24 1/5 Md Sp Wt 1 12 11^{11} 10^{14} 7^{13} $6^{13\frac{1}{2}}$ Samyn J L b 122 44.70 69-22 Kerosene $122^{9\frac{1}{2}}$HighThrone$122^{1\frac{1}{2}}$AncientWorld122^{nk} Broke slowly 12
16Oct88- 6Bel fm 1 1/16 Ⓣ:47 1/5 1:12 1:44 Md Sp Wt 1 10 9^{13} 8^{14} 7^{19} 7^{22} Lovato F Jr b 118 7.30 54-23 Whiskey a GoGo$118^{9\frac{3}{4}}$Reaffirming118^{nk}Congressman$118^{2\frac{1}{4}}$ Outrun 12
30Sep88- 6Bel fm 1 1/16 Ⓣ:47 1/5 1:12 1:44 Md Sp Wt 5 5 5^{6} 7^{8} $8^{8\frac{1}{2}}$ $7^{6\frac{1}{2}}$ Santagata N b 118 3.50 69-18 In the Groove $118^{\frac{3}{4}}$ Mawi Maka $118^{\frac{1}{2}}$ Summ Truly Do $118^{\frac{3}{4}}$ Tired 12
19Aug88- 5Sar fst 7f :22 4/5 :45 3/5 1:22 3/5 Md Sp Wt 1 8 $6^{4\frac{1}{2}}$ 6^{10} $5^{8\frac{3}{4}}$ 5^{15} Santagata N 118 57.50 74-19 Easy Goer $118^{2\frac{1}{2}}$ Is It True 118^{8} Magic Eagle $118^{3\frac{3}{4}}$ No factor 8
3Aug88- 6Sar fst 5f :22 3/5 :46 :58 3/5 Md Sp Wt 9 10 10^{19} 10^{16} 8^{14} $8^{12\frac{3}{4}}$ Davis R G 118 20.30 80-09 Even Faster $118^{\frac{3}{4}}$ Skyflash $118^{1\frac{1}{4}}$ Is It True $118^{1\frac{3}{4}}$ Slow start 10
LATEST WORKOUTS May 26 Bel 4f fst :50 3/5 B May 20 Bel 5f fst 1:04 B May 13 Bel 4f fst :51 B Apr 12 GP 4f fst :51 B

Busted Dancer — B. g. 3, by Noble Dancer—Miss Lilian, by Sandford Lad — Lifetime 2 0 0 0 $1,560 — 1989 2 M 0 0 $1,560 — 1988 0 M 0 0
Own.—Morton Stable — Br.—Frethelm H P (Fla) — Tr.—Martin Jose — **115**

21May89- 2Bel fst 1 :46 1/5 1:12 2/5 1:39 3↑Md 35000 2 4 9^{10} 12^{12} 13^{19} $12^{29\frac{3}{4}}$ Rojas C b 115 7.40 40-19 Mr. Carvel $113^{2\frac{1}{2}}$HailTheBrave115^{2}StageProspect$112^{2\frac{1}{4}}$ Brief foot 13
10May89- 6Bel my 1 :45 3/5 1:09 4/5 1:37 1/5 3↑Md Sp Wt 8 2 $2^{2\frac{1}{2}}$ 5^{5} $5^{7\frac{1}{2}}$ $4^{19\frac{1}{4}}$ Rojas C b 115 10.90 60-19 SlewTheKnight115^{6}Mr.Crvel115^{nk}Glenegles115^{13} Used early pace 9
LATEST WORKOUTS May 5 Bel tr.t 5f fst 1:03 B Apr 29 Bel tr.t 4f fst :49 1/5 H Apr 22 Bel tr.t 4f fst :48 4/5 B Apr 15 Bel 5f fst 1:01 Hg

Sassy Note — Dk. b. or br. c. 3, by I Enclose—Sassy Cyane, by Cyane — Lifetime 3 0 0 0 $840 — 1989 1 M 0 0 $840 — 1988 2 M 0 0
Own.—Rand Adele L — Br.—Rand Adele L (Ky) — Tr.—Kelly Michael J — **115**

15May89- 2Bel fst 6f :22 1/5 :45 2/5 1:10 1/5 3↑Md 50000 7 7 9^{8} 7^{7} 5^{12} $4^{17\frac{1}{2}}$ McCauley W H b 115 6.10 70-14 Ten Be Six 115^{7} Keep Calm $114^{5\frac{1}{4}}$ Oil Patch Kid $107^{5\frac{1}{4}}$ No factor 9
9Oct88- 5Bel my 7f :23 :46 3/5 1:24 Md 75000 5 3 5^{3} 6^{7} 5^{14} $5^{18\frac{1}{4}}$ McCauley W H b 118 6.60 64-24 Free Getaway $118^{\frac{1}{2}}$ Gab $118^{7\frac{3}{4}}$ Mr. Carvel $118^{4\frac{1}{2}}$ No factor 10
26Sep88- 4Bel fst 6f :22 4/5 :46 1/5 1:10 4/5 Md Sp Wt 1 4 5^{4} 4^{4} $5^{9\frac{1}{2}}$ $5^{11\frac{3}{4}}$ McCauley W H b 118 23.90 73-20 Twombly $118^{1\frac{1}{2}}$ Plentyofit $118^{4\frac{1}{2}}$ Fraternity $118^{1\frac{3}{4}}$ Outrun 8
LATEST WORKOUTS May 13 Bel 3f fst :37 2/5 B May 4 Bel 5f fst 1:02 3/5 B Mar 31 Hia 5f fst 1:05 B

The horse of interest is Road Eagle, who might be thrown out of consideration at a quick glance because of his awful overall record, 0-for-16. We've gone on record saying 0-for-10 is a good point to say goodbye to maidens, but Road Eagle had only five tries on turf. He finished in the money in none of them. Since he shows $1,560 in earnings on turf, we can deduce he finished fourth in one of the four turf starts not in his PPs because purses in New York, where his trainer, Frank LaBoccetta is based, divides purses only among the top four finishers.

Road Eagle's career included three extremely poor efforts in $30,000 maiden claimers. But they were on dirt and irrelevant.

Our key line is Road Eagle's last race, when he was returned to the turf and drew the outside No. 12 post in a 1 3/8 mile maiden race.

With Ruben Hernandez, a consistently underrated rider in New York, Road Eagle got away second early, moved to a head in front, tired to third by four, and finished fifth by four. Still, it was the first time in ten races Road Eagle didn't lose ground on the leader in the stretch.

Understanding the difficulty of the outside post in turf races is the key to seeing Road Eagle's substantially improved effort.

In this race, he'd drawn inside, the No. 2 post, and was dropping back from 1 3/8 miles to 1 mile, which also would help.

Road Eagle was ignored at the betting windows, sent off at 11 to 1. Eight of his eleven opponents were making their first grass start. We pinpoint four bred to perform well on turf: Square Ruler, Pescadero, Sweet Neck and Sassy Note, colts by Majesty's Prince, The Bart, Great Neck and I Enclose, respectively. Road Eagle won by one and a half lengths with Pescadero a clear second. Road Eagle paid $24.20 to win, and the exacta paid $359.40.

Exactly two months later at Belmont, we found another 11 to 1 overlay on the turf, Trin, who showed up in a one mile grass allowance for fillies and mares.

In her previous three starts in 1989, Trin had the misfortune to draw the No. 9, 10 and 10 posts, finishing fourth (despite being checked), eighth and fifth. The filly added blinkers in her last start, raced toward the lead and weakened, losing by five and three-quarters lengths.

7 BELMONT

1 MILE. (Turf). (1.33) ALLOWANCE. Purse $31,000. 3-year-olds and upward. Fillies and mares which have never won two races other than Maiden, Claiming or Starter. Weights, 3-year-olds 116 lbs. Older 122 lbs. Non-winners of a race other than Maiden or Claiming at a mile or over since July 1 allowed 3 lbs. Of such race since June 15, 5 lbs.

Coupled—Sister Margery and Gottagetitdone.

Trin — B. f. 4, by Cure the Blues—Rumah, by Habitat — Br.—Bricken & McMillan (Ky) — Tr.—Bush Thomas M — Own.—Jan-Ali Stable — **117**

Lifetime 21 2 2 5 $68,720 | 1989 3 0 0 1 $3,480 | 1988 16 2 2 4 $62,360 | Turf 10 1 1 3 $38,900

Entered 29Jly89- 5 BEL

21Jun89- 2Bel gd 1 1/16 Ⓣ:46⅘ 1:10⅘ 1:43⅕ ⒻClm 75000 10 5 52½ 31½ 54 55¾ Maple E b 112 15.50 74-18 Far East 118hd Dance in a Veil 1161 Pia's Baby 1121¼ Tired 11
1Jun89- 5Bel fm 1 1/16 [T]:48⅖ 1:11⅘ 1:42 ⒻClm 75000 10 6 63¼ 86½ 811 813¾ Maple E 112 5.30 77-13 Kemolina 113nk Dance in a Veil 1162¼ EnergySquare1141¾ Outrun 10
21May89- 5Bel gd 1 1/16 [T]:47⅘ 1:12⅗ 1:44⅘ ⒻClm 75000 9 7 712 45½ 33 46¼ Maple E 117 9.30 71-20 Native Candy 1132¼ [D]Pia's Baby 1132¾Kemolina1131¼ Checked st 10
21May89-Placed third through disqualification
24Dec88- 6Aqu sly 6f [•]:22⅕ :45⅕ 1:10⅗ 3↑ⒻAlw 24000 6 6 611 711 712 711¼ Martinez J R Jr7 108 24.20 80-18 NaturalElegance1156¾MaggieTonight117½MyCarvnn1151¾ Outrun 7
6Nov88- 6Aqu fst 1⅛ :48⅕ 1:13⅕ 1:53⅗ 3↑ⒻAlw 31000 6 4 59½ 612 59¼ 615¾ Samyn J L 115 4.40 51-26 Laugh and Be Merry 1155[D]BlackBeaver115nkFineza1151¾ Outrun 6
20Oct88- 8Aqu fm 1 1/16 Ⓣ:48⅕ 1:12⅗ 1:45 3↑ⒻAlw 31000 8 8 89¼ 75¼ 33 31¼ Sarvis D A 114 3.00 79-18 Dangerous Type 115¾ Fairest College 114½ Trin 114nk Rallied 8
30Sep88- 7Bel fm 1 1/16 [T]:47⅕ 1:10⅗ 1:42 ⒻClm 85000 6 9 98¼ 75¾ 43½ 35¾ Samyn J L 115 6.40e 85-18 Highland Penny 1174¼ Mia Casa 1111½ Trin 1154 L'ckd late resp. 9
17Sep88- 9Med gd 1 1/16 :47⅘ 1:11⅖ 1:43⅕ ⒻBoilg Spg H 4 6 63¾ 58 66½ 610 Samyn J L 111 27.40 77-12 Siggebo 119nk Flashy Runner 1152 Lusty Lady 1131¾ Outrun 7
17Sep88-Grade III
28Aug88- 4Sar fm 1 1/16 Ⓣ:47⅖ 1:11⅗ 1:44 3↑ⒻAlw 29000 7 4 38 24 2½ 1½ Maple E 112 17.90 77-20 Trin 112½ Wooing 1172½ Ionian Odyssey 1171½ Driving 10
20Aug88- 2Sar fm 1 [T]:47⅗ 1:12 1:36 3↑ⒻAlw 29000 3 8 86¾ 88¼ 58½ 410¼ Lovato F Jr 114 39.00 86-07 SummrRun112nkDnzig'sBrid1124Brry'sChptr1176 Pas'd tired ones 10
LATEST WORKOUTS Jly 23 Bel 5f fst 1:04⅗ B Jly 15 Bel 3f fst :36⅖ H Jly 8 Bel 6f fst 1:16 B

Sister Margery — Dk. b. or br. f. 4, by Darby Creek Road—Sacred Journey, by King's Bishop — Br.—Stonewall Farm (Ky) — Tr.—Alexander Frank A — Own.—Schwartz B K — **117**

Lifetime 14 2 2 5 $59,520 | 1989 4 0 0 2 $7,080 | 1988 7 1 2 2 $35,880 | Turf 4 1 0 1 $21,120

15Jly89- 6Bel gd 1 1/16 [T]:48 1:12⅘ 1:44⅖ 3↑ⒻAlw 31000 2 8 76½ 54 54½ 65½ Vasquez J b 117 5.90 73-22 Vanities 1132¼ River of Time 1171¾ Steady State 117nk No factor 10
1Jly89- 3Bel fm 1 Ⓣ:46⅖ 1:10⅕ 1:35⅕ 3↑ⒻAlw 31000 2 5 52½ 63¼ 34 31¾ Vasquez J b 117 6.10 87-15 Kemolina 117nk River of Time 1171½ SisterMargery1171¼ Fin. well 9
12May89- 3Bel gd 7f :22 :44⅖ 1:22⅕ 3↑ⒻAlw 28000 2 3 54 52½ 32 35¼ Vasquez J b 119 12.60 86-13 Wow 113nk Yen For Gold 1135 Sister Margery 1193 Lacked a bid 5
12Jan89- 5Aqu gd 170 [•]:48⅗ 1:13⅕ 1:44⅖ ⒻAlw 27000 3 4 53¾ 55½ 48½ 58½ Cordero A Jr b 117 *2.00 69-18 AWnkAndANod1172Dmonstrton1174½GldnT.Dncr1172 No menace 8
23Dec88- 8Aqu sly 1⅛ [•]:48⅖ 1:12⅗ 1:51⅕ 3↑ⒻAlw 27000 3 6 610 58½ 35 36 Cordero A Jr b 115 *1.50 80-10 LurJons1173½StockngFnd1172½SstrMrgry1152½ L'kd further resp. 7
14Dec88- 8Aqu fst 1 1/16 [•]:48⅗ 1:13⅘ 1:46⅕ 3↑ⒻAlw 27000 2 5 41¼ 32 2½ 2¾ Cordero A Jr b 115 6.70 77-25 MrinneThers110¾SistrMrgry115¾FirstCollg1154 Steadied,boxed in 6
26Nov88- 5Aqu fst 7f :22⅖ :45⅕ 1:23⅗ 3↑ⒻAlw 28000 6 6 710 57½ 68 511¼ Romero J A b 117 7.70 72-22 BodaciousTatas1151¾MarianneTheres1156¾TopNews1172 L'kd bid 7
14Nov88- 5Aqu my 7f :22 :44⅘ 1:23⅖ 3↑ⒻAlw 28000 5 1 611 610 613 36¾ Romero J A b 117 9.50 77-25 Haiati 1156½ Bodacious Tatas 115nk Sister Margery1171¼ Mild bid 6
29Oct88- 5Aqu fm 1 1/16 Ⓣ:49⅕ 1:14⅗ 1:47⅘ 3↑ⒻAlw 29000 5 3 31½ 1½ 1½ 1hd Romero J A b 114 2.80 66-33 Sister Margery 114hd Newhalem 114¾ Mia Casa 1143 Driving 8
24Sep88- 6Bel fm 1 1/16 Ⓣ:47 1:10⅗ 1:42⅕ 3↑ⒻAlw 29000 8 4 42¼ 32 32 51¼ Vasquez J b 114 6.90 84-15 DanceinaVeil113½[DH]Anorada117[DH]Bnker'sLdy118no Finished well 11
LATEST WORKOUTS Jly 25 Bel 4f fst :52⅗ B Jun 19 Bel 5f fst 1:04⅗ B Jun 3 Bel 4f fst :50⅗ B

Fairest College Ch. f. 4, by Super Concorde—Lady Donna, by Graustark
Own.—Unadilla Stable Br.—Galbreath Daniel M (Ky) Tr.—Van Berg Jack C
117 Lifetime 14 2 2 2 $63,940 1989 4 0 0 0 $5,160 1988 10 2 2 2 $58,780 Turf 4 0 1 1 $10,540
5Jun89- 8Bel fm 1⅜ Ⓣ:48⅘ 1:38⅗ 2:16⅗ 3+ⒻAlw 31000 9 1 17 2½ 69¼ 69¾ Rojas R I 117 7.60 69-18 Thor Baby 117¾ Balsa 117nk Dearness 113¾ Weakened 9
11May89- 7Bel my 1⅛ :45⅖ 1:10⅕ 1:42⅗ 3+ⒻAlw 31000 6 3 42 54½ 68½ 416½ Rojas R I b 119 3.90 74-14 Fineza 1196¾ Buzz Me Miss Blue 1142½ Oystercatcher 1137 Tired 7
22Apr89- 3Aqu fst 6f :23⅕ :48 1:14⅕ 3+ⒻAlw 28000 3 6 31 44 42 42½ Rojas R I b 119 3.10 66-29 DrlingDutch1141½AspenAlley1141½ToweringSuccess119hd Slow st. 6
2Jan89- 8Aqu fst 1⅛ ⊡:49 1:14 1:46⅘ ⒻAlw 27000 3 2 21 41½ 44½ 45½ Cordero A Jr 117 *1.40 69-27 NoBttr117½GoldnT.Dncr1173AWnkAndANod1172 Steadied far trn 6
14Dec88- 8Aqu fst 1⅛ ⊡:48⅘ 1:13⅘ 1:46⅕ 3+ⒻAlw 27000 3 2 31 21 31 31½ Santos J A 115 2.70 76-25 MrinneTheres110¾SistrMrgry115¾FirstCollg1154 Steadied 1st turn 6
28Oct88- 1Aqu fm 1⅜ Ⓣ:50⅕ 1:41⅘ 2:20⅖ 3+ⒻAlw 31000 8 1 2hd 1hd 33 34½ Imparato J 114 4.40 65-36 TimelyBusiness1143½FaintGlow109¾FairestCollege114½ Weakened 8
20Oct88- 8Aqu fm 1⅛ Ⓣ:48⅕ 1:12⅘ 1:45 3+ⒻAlw 31000 7 3 34½ 52¾ 43½ 2¾ Vega A 114 8.10 79-18 Dangerous Type 115¾ Fairest College 114½ Trin 114nk Gamely 8
23Sep88- 1Bel fst 1⅛ :46⅖ 1:11⅕ 1:43 3+ⒻAlw 31000 5 2 31½ 42 45½ 47 Velasquez J 114 11.40 80-19 Rythmical 113½ Neatly Arranged 1144½ For Kicks 1152 Gave way 7
31Aug88- 5Bel fst 1⅛ :47⅕ 1:12⅘ 1:45⅘ 3+ⒻAlw 31000 4 3 41 41½ 48½ 410½ Bailey J D 112 10.50 62-25 Stoneleigh'sHope112⁴JckieMcG1121½TisMichll1135½ Fin. near str. 7
7Jly88- 5Bel fst 1⅛ :47⅘ 1:12 1:43⅗ 3+ⒻAlw 29000 4 2 21 32 1½ 1hd Santos J A 112 2.40 84-20 Fairest College 112hd Abidjan 1178¾ Prince ofaLady1175½ Driving 7
LATEST WORKOUTS Jly 23 Bel tr.t 5f fst 1:06 B Jly 18 Bel 5f fst 1:01⅗ H Jly 15 Bel 5f fst 1:07 B ●May 31 Bel 5f fst :59 H

If At First B. m. 5, by Relaunch—Roses for the Lady, by Buffalo Lark
Own.—Aldila Farm Br.—Hettinger John (NY) Tr.—Quinn Brian
Entered 29Jly89- 3 BEL
117 Lifetime 12 2 2 4 $60,800 1989 1 0 0 0 1988 1 0 0 0
15Jly89- 9Bel fst 6f :22⅘ :46⅘ 1:12⅗ 3+ⒻⓈAlw 28000 5 6 99½1011 1114 1218½ Santiago A 117 32.30 58-20 Heathers Arrest 1171¾ SuperAppeal1161HappyDapple117½ Outrun 13
30Jan88- 7Aqu fst 1⅛ ⊡:48⅗ 1:13⅕ 1:47⅗ ⒻⓈAlw 33000 7 7 86½ 75 64 53½ Antley C W 117 4.60 67-17 OhHowWeDnced1171½ThRitChmistry1221½LdyIronsid117½ Outrun 9
14Dec87- 7Aqu fst 1⅛ ⊡:49 1:14⅘ 1:48⅕ 3+ⒻⓈAlw 35000 2 10 104 92½ 64½ 3¾ Davis R G 115 *1.90 67-20 GeneralCondition117½SixRedRoses117nkIfAtFirst1153 Belated bid 11
26Nov87- 7Aqu fst 7f :23⅘ :47⅖ 1:26⅗ 3+ⒻⓈAlw 34000 2 8 129¼1311 98¾ 99½ Davis R G 115 *2.80 58-33 FemmeGendarme1155¾Anchorgram1171½FoundJewel115nk Outrun 13
29Oct87- 7Aqu fst 1⅛ :49⅕ 1:13⅘ 1:54 3+ⒻⓈAlw 35000 8 4 43½ 43 32 2nk Davis R G 114 *2.40 65-28 Pass The Candy 117nk If AtFirst1144DeviousDutchess119nk Sharp 8
14Sep87- 7Bel gd 1⅛ :46⅘ 1:11⅘ 1:44⅕ 3+ⒻⓈAlw 31500 5 7 75 64 2½ 11 Davis R G 113 2.60 81-13 If At First 1131 Ingrid 1153½ Violet Who 1135½ Driving 11
6Sep87- 7Bel fst 7f :23 :46⅘ 1:24⅘ 3+ⒻⓈAlw 30000 2 10 54½ 42½ 38 310½ Davis R G 113 4.70 69-19 Rosie's Dancer 1177¾ Book Of Joy 1132¾ If At First 1135 Evenly 12
15Apr87- 7Aqu fst 7f :22⅘ :45⅕ 1:22⅘ 3+ⒻAlw 26000 1 6 55½ 58½ 59½ 514½ Nuesch D5 102 5.70 72-19 Hedgeabout 1122¾ Steady Gaze 1195½ Consecrated 1122¾ OUtrun 7
2Apr87- 5Aqu fst 1 :45⅘ 1:09⅘ 1:37⅘ 3+ⒻAlw 27000 4 3 35 2hd 2hd 32¾ Badamo J J5 102 4.90 74-24 May Be Bold 119no Dawn Break 1142¾ If At First1022½ Weakened 7
14Mar87- 7Aqu fst 6f :22⅘ :46⅘ 1:13⅘ ⒻⓈAlw 27000 6 8 85¾ 87 52½ 22¾ Nuesch D5 111 2.70 72-28 Peggy's Dream 1162¾ If At First 1112¾ Adanna Dear 111½ Gamely 14
LATEST WORKOUTS Jly 23 Bel tr.t 5f fst 1:04 B Jly 12 Bel tr.t 5f fst 1:03⅕ B Jly 5 Bel tr.t 5f fst 1:01⅖ H Jun 30 Bel 5f fst 1:03⅖ B

Bounty Search B. f. 3(Mar), by Stiff Sentence—Scenery, by Reviewer
Own.—Manorwood Stables Br.—Fleming Pat Trichter (Fla) Tr.—Gullo Thomas J
116 Lifetime 10 2 2 2 $33,860 1989 6 2 0 2 $27,480 1988 4 M 2 0 $6,380
21Jly89- 7Bel gd 1 :45⅗ 1:12 1:39⅘ 3+ⒻAlw 29000 2 5 44½ 1½ 12½ 14½ Rojas R I 111 24.10 66-28 Bounty Search 1114½FirstGrade1112¾Iron'sAdvance1118 Drew off 10
7Jly89- 2Bel fst 7f :22⅘ :46⅗ 1:25 3+ⒻMd 30000 9 1 21 21 13½ 110 Rojas R I 112 5.00 77-23 BountySerch11210HrComsBunny113½BrzilinQun1162¾ Going away 11
1Jly89- 6Bel fst 6f :22⅕ :46⅕ 1:13⅘ 3+ⒻMd 30000 4 5 59½ 816 510 32¾ Rojas R I 112 22.70 67-27 CrossandDrums1161BrazilinQueen1161¾BountySerch112nk Rallied 8
19Jun89- 2Bel fst 6f :22⅘ :47⅗ 1:12⅘ 3+ⒻMd 30000 13 5 51½ 64 65 68½ Antley C W 113 12.70 66-25 Gold Green 1104½ Split 1132 Dashing Jen 1051 No factor 14
29May89- 9Bel fst 7f :22⅗ :45⅘ 1:25⅘ 3+ⒻMd 30000 10 5 65¾1011 1326 1341½ Rojas R I 111 3.20 32-16 Woburn 1134½ Rabbit Hollow 115½ Split 1151½ Tired 13
20May89-10Bel fst 6f :22⅗ :46⅗ 1:13 3+ⒻMd 30000 8 8 54 43 56 43½ Rojas R I 111 3.60 71-17 ⒹWhirlwindDelight120hdZipdod1131½PrincssMhm1152 Wide turn 11
20May89-Placed third through disqualification
15Dec88- 4Aqu fst 1⅛ ⊡:48⅗ 1:14⅖ 1:49⅗ ⒻMd Sp Wt 4 3 53¾ 89 817 820 Romero J A 117 9.30 42-27 ⒹⒽLike Springtime 1122 ⒹⒽPigment 1172 Nofear 117nk Tired 9
26Nov88- 9Aqu fst 7f :22⅘ :46⅕ 1:26⅘ ⒻMd 70000 7 3 96¾ 911 58½ 22½ Romero J A 113 26.90 66-22 Windy Surf 1142½BountySearch113noKeyFlight117nk Up for place 10
8Nov88- 3Aqu fst 6f :22⅗ :46⅗ 1:13⅕ ⒻMd 35000 10 10 1415 1315 811 28 Romero J A 117 5.40 66-25 Farseeva 1178 Bounty Search 1172½ MedievalGlory113nk 2nd best 14
23Oct88- 4Aqu fst 6f :22⅗ :46⅘ 1:12⅘ ⒻMd 35000 8 2 75¾ 714 58½ 57½ Vazquez J J5 112 *2.40e 69-23 Angora Socks 1171½ Banded 1173 My Frances 117no Outrun 14
LATEST WORKOUTS Jly 14 Bel tr.t 4f gd :50 B Jun 26 Bel tr.t 4f fst :49⅘ H Jun 11 Bel tr.t 4f fst :49 B

Interested Party Ro. f. 4, by Top Command—Imarebel, by His Majesty
Own.—Brookfield Farms Br.—Isaacs Harry Z (Ky) Tr.—Kelly Edward I
117 Lifetime 6 1 0 0 $17,460 1989 1 0 0 0 1988 5 1 0 0 $17,460 Turf 1 0 0 0
1Jly89- 9Bel fm 1⅛ Ⓣ:46⅘ 1:10⅘ 1:42 3+ⒻAlw 29000 10 5 52½ 44½ 76 87½ Antley C W b 117 38.30 79-15 Turkish Coffee 1175 Yestday's Kisses 113hd Tremolos 113nk Wide 12
28Dec88- 5Aqu fst 1⅛ ⊡:49 1:14 1:47⅗ 3+ⒻAlw 25000 6 5 74¾ 67½ 512 512½ Santos J A b 115 *2.40 58-21 Holiday Pond 1103 D'or Etoile 1152 Al Dam 1153¾ Outrun 7
27Nov88- 7Aqu fst 7f :22⅘ :45⅗ 1:24⅘ 3+ⒻAlw 27000 7 8 89¾ 89 66 44 Baird E T b 115 38.80 75-23 SpcFntsy115½AWinkAndANod115noGottgltldon1153½ Belated bid 8
3Sep88- 6Bel fst 7f :23 :47⅕ 1:25⅗ 3+ⒻAlw 27000 7 4 43½ 87½ 822 831 Antley C W b 113 5.60 43-27 Lambros 1156½ Swiss Excellence 113nkConsecrated1174 Fell back 8
31Jly88- 6Bel fst 7f :22⅘ :46 1:26⅕ ⒻMd Sp Wt 6 6 44 23 3nk 1½ Antley C W b 121 *2.20 71-22 Interested Party121½AspenAlley121¾Stately1213¾ Lost whip, drvg 9
8Jly88- 3Bel fst 7f :22⅘ :46⅕ 1:25⅖ ⒻMd Sp Wt 2 7 812 68 45 45½ Davis R G b 121 5.40 69-25 Whiffling 121¾ Homepride 1211½ Tricky Miss 1213½ Mild gain 9
LATEST WORKOUTS Jly 27 Bel Ⓣ 5f fm 1:01⅖ B (d) Jly 20 Bel 3f fst :38 B Jly 16 Bel 4f fst :52 B Jly 13 Bel 6f fst 1:18 B

Piggy Wiggy Ro. f. 4, by Peace Corps—Piggy Bank, by Prove Out
Own.—Hobeau Farm Br.—Hobeau Farm Inc (Fla) Tr.—Jerkens H Allen
107[10] Lifetime 10 2 1 1 $29,520 1989 10 2 1 1 $29,520 1988 0 M 0 0 Turf 4 1 0 0 $17,400
15Jly89- 6Bel gd 1⅛ Ⓣ:48 1:12⅘ 1:44⅘ 3+ⒻAlw 31000 5 9 87 64½ 910 911 Samyn J L 119 *2.30e 68-22 Vanities 1132½ River of Time 1171¾ Steady State 117nk Outrun 10
28Jun89- 7Bel fm 1⅛ Ⓣ:49 1:13⅘ 1:45⅘ 3+ⒻAlw 33000 8 6 611 37½ 46½ 68 Samyn J L 119 12.00 64-28 Highland Penny 117¾ Eau Forte 1121¾ GreenSum1174¾ Weakened 9
21Jun89- 6Bel gd 1¼ Ⓣ:47⅘ 1:36⅘ 2:03 3+ⒻAlw 31000 9 8 612 66 512 514½ Samyn J L 117 8.50 64-18 Rose Diamond 1115½ Balsa 117¾ Majawas 117½ Outrun 10
4Jun89- 7Bel gd 1 Ⓣ:46⅗ 1:11⅘ 1:37⅕ 3+ⒻAlw 29000 4 10 63½ 31 1hd 11½ Samyn J L 117 10.70 79-22 Piggy Wiggy1171½MissyValentine1122¾TurkishCoffee1171 Driving 12
1May89- 3Aqu fst 7f :22⅘ :46⅗ 1:24⅗ 3+ⒻMd 30000 9 2 44½ 22½ 17 18½ Singh D10 110 *1.40 79-23 Piggy Wiggy 1108½ Dorado Flyer 1132¾ Swaizie 1068½ Ridden out 9
14Apr89- 1Aqu fst 6f :22⅘ :46⅗ 1:13 3+ⒻMd 30000 2 4 56 48 34½ 32½ Hernandez R 120 2.80 73-31 Spanish Serenade 106¾ Tija Ro 1111½ Piggy Wiggy 1206¾ Rallied 7
9Apr89- 5Aqu fst 6f :22⅗ :46 1:12 3+ⒻMd 30000 2 6 43 31 41 22 Singh D10 110 4.40 78-17 Impulsive Babe 1202 Piggy Wiggy 110hd Boston Miss113¾ Rallied 9
3Apr89- 4Aqu my 6f :22⅗ :46⅗ 1:13⅗ 3+ⒻMd 30000 1 8 63½ 44 35 66 Singh D10 110 8.60 66-23 SettleStorm113nkSpnishSerende1133½Repetitious110½ Drifted out 9
22Mar89- 3Aqu fst 1⅛ :48⅖ 1:13⅘ 1:55⅗ ⒻMd 30000 7 2 2hd 1½ 58½ 615¾ Hernandez R b 118 1.70 41-22 Dayzac 1182½ Masters Time 1226 Impulsive Babe 118nk Tired 7
17Mar89- 4Aqu fst 6f :22⅘ :46⅘ 1:14⅕ ⒻMd 45000 7 6 44½ 45 46½ 49½ Hernandez R 118 2.00 59-29 Quickster 1181½ Locust Lady 1183¾ Our Mimi 1184½ Evenly 7
LATEST WORKOUTS Jly 5 Bel tr.t 3f fst :36⅖ B Jun 17 Bel tr.t 1 sly 1:45 B Jun 13 Bel 7f gd 1:33 B May 31 Bel 4f fst :47⅕ H

Imago — B. f. 3(Apr), by Diamond Shoal—Tense Moment, by Torsion
Br.—New Hose Partnership (Ky)
Own.—Johnson Joan C — Tr.—Jolley Leroy
111 — Lifetime 10 2 1 1 $42,605 — 1989 6 1 0 1 $21,725 — 1988 4 1 1 0 $20,880 — Turf 8 2 0 1 $35,225

28Jun89- 7Bel fm 1 1/16 [T]:49 1:13 4/5 1:45 4/5 3↑ⒻAlw 33000 3 8 712 810 713 716½ Santos J A 112 5.80 55-28 Highland Penny 117¾ Eau Forte 1121¾ GreenSum1174¾ Slow start 9
20Apr89- 8Kee fm 1⅛ Ⓣ:48 1/5 1:13 3/5 1:51 2/5 ⒻPalisades 3 5 63¾ 4¾ 44¼ 411½ Perret C 114 1.80e 73-15 Key Flyer 113½ To The Lighthouse 1228 She's Scrumptious 1173 7
2Apr89-10Hia fm 1⅛ Ⓣ 1:48 4/5 ⒻPoinsettia 11 11 116 117 912 69¾ Cruguet J 111 5.70 78-12 Coolawin1132½PrincessMora118nkKeyFlyer1123 Failed to respond 15
2Apr89-Grade III
28Feb89- 9GP fst 1 1/16 :48 1/5 1:12 3/5 1:44 4/5 ⒻAlw 35000 1 4 55¾ 58½ 413 425¼ Santos J A 118 *1.20 52-25 Demonry 1148¼ Feliness 11412 Down South 1145 Stumbled start 5
15Feb89- 9GP fm 1 1/16 Ⓣ:46 2/5 1:10 4/5 1:42 4/5 ⒻHercomsbride 4 7 78 65 32 31½ Bailey J D 112 6.10 84-17 Darby Shuffle 121nk Seattle Meteor 1211¼ Imago 1122 Alt. course 8
24Jan89- 8GP fm *1 1/16 Ⓣ 1:44 ⒻAlw 18000 2 5 65¼ 56½ 24 12¼ Valiente D 118 4.30 86-14 Imago 1182¼ Forladiesonly 1166 LemonSoup1181 Driving steadied 11
5Nov88- 8Aqu sf 1⅛ Ⓣ:50 1/5 1:16 4/5 1:59 1/5 ⒻMiss Grillo 7 1 11 1½ 59 620¼ Maple E 114 48.70 – – Darby's Daughter 1213 Lyfestar 1142¾ Le Famo 1151¾ Tired 11
5Nov88-Grade II; Run in Divisions
22Oct88- 7Lrl fm 1 1/16 Ⓣ:47 1/5 1:11 3/5 1:44 4/5 ⒻSelima 12 7 87¼ 1114 1220 1224¾ Santos J A 119 29.10 48-28 Capades 1193¼ Darby Shuffle 1192 Money Movers 119nk Outrun 13
22Oct88-Grade I
1Oct88- 6Bel fm 1 1/16 Ⓣ:47 3/5 1:12 1/5 1:43 4/5 ⒻMd Sp Wt 3 10 96¼ 55½ 34 1nk Santos J A 117 3.50 77-16 Imago 117nk Predicting 117nk Shine Up 1175½ Driving 12
11Sep88- 3Bel fst 6f :23 1/5 :47 1:12 4/5 ⒻMd Sp Wt 2 7 1½ 12½ 2½ 21¾ Cordero A Jr 117 3.50 73-21 Bold Costa 1171¾ Imago 1174 Greek Porche 117nk Steadied 7
LATEST WORKOUTS Jly 9 Bel 5f fst 1:02 B — Jun 19 Bel 5f fst 1:00 1/5 H — ●Jun 11 Bel 3f fst :34 1/5 H — Jun 5 Bel 5f fst 1:01 1/5 B

Gottagetitdone — Gr. f. 4, by Kohoutek—Bombilonga, by Best Joy
Br.—Alexander & Martin Jr (Fla)
Own.—Schwartz B K — Tr.—Alexander Frank A
117 — Lifetime 11 2 3 2 $52,859 — 1989 4 1 2 0 $29,000 — 1988 7 1 1 2 $23,859 — Turf 3 1 0 0 $11,969

19Jly89- 7Bel fst 7f :22 4/5 :46 1:24 3/5 3↑ⒻAlw 28000 2 4 53½ 4¾ 47½ 417 McCauley W H b 117 19.00 62-25 Fantastic Find 1134½ Hot Account 1068½Alstroemeria1114 Outrun 5
3Mar89- 8Aqu fst 1 1/16 [•]:49 1/5 1:14 4/5 1:48 1/5 ⒻAlw 31000 7 4 43 32 22½ 24 McCauley W H b 119 3.90 64-28 Travenita 1174Gottagetitdone1191¼GoldenT.Dancer117nk 2nd best 8
5Feb89- 5Aqu fst 1 1/16 [•]:49 1:14 1/5 1:46 ⒻAlw 25000 2 3 3½ 12 15 17 McCauley W H b 117 *1.80 79-18 Gottagetitdone1177SocialSecret1172¼Julia'sMgic1171 Ridden out 9
16Jan89- 6Aqu gd 1 1/16 [•]:46 4/5 1:11 4/5 1:43 4/5 ⒻAlw 25000 3 2 1hd 11½ 11 22¼ Cordero A Jr b 117 *2.10 88-10 D'or Etoile 1172¼ Gottagetitdone1175¾ScaryLaugh117¾ No match 10
21Dec88- 8Aqu gd 1 1/16 [•]:50 4/5 1:15 1/5 1:45 4/5 3↑ⒻAlw 25000 4 2 21 21 35½ 38½ Cordero A Jr 115 *.70 71-19 AWinkAndANod1155D'orEtoile1153½Gottgetitdon1154¾ Weakened 6
7Dec88- 7Aqu fst 1 1/16 [•]:49 2/5 1:14 3/5 1:48 2/5 3↑ⒻAlw 25000 7 6 53 42 1½ 21¼ Cordero A Jr 115 3.20 66-32 MissEmbssy1171¼Gottgetitdone1154BrvestAngl112hd Gave way lt. 8
27Nov88- 7Aqu fst 7f :22 2/5 :45 2/5 1:24 2/5 3↑ⒻAlw 27000 6 5 62¾ 42 31 3½ Vasquez J 115 31.60 78-23 SpceFntsy115½AWinkAndANod115noGottgetitdone1153½ Willingly 8
8May88- 7Aqu gd 1⅛ Ⓣ:50 4/5 1:16 2/5 1:53 3/5 3↑ⒻAlw 31000 2 2 2½ 52½ 1019 1033¾ Perret C 114 2.10 33-33 BlossomingBeuty1158½CompletAccord1151¾Anord1212¾ Fin. early 10
3Apr88-10Crc fm *1⅛ Ⓣ 1:47 1/5 ⒻTrp Pk Oaks 3 3 31 32 52¼ 59½ Pezua J M 112 11.10 74-14 Aquaba 1156½ Pounding Mills 113hd Leave It Be 1182½ Weakened 10
3Apr88-Run in Divisions
1Mar88- 5GP hd *1 1/16 Ⓣ 1:46 1/5 ⒻMd Sp Wt 1 2 21 2½ 1½ 1½ Perret C 121 2.60 75-14 Gottgttdon121½BMyConqustdor1214½ShdowofDoubt121nk Driving 10
LATEST WORKOUTS Jly 15 Bel 4f fst :52 B — Jly 8 Bel 5f fst :59 3/5 H — Jly 1 Bel 5f fst 1:04 4/5 B — Jun 25 Bel 4f fst :49 4/5 B

Sultry Secret — B. f. 3(Apr), by Nijinsky II—Sultry Sun, by Buckfinder
Br.—Live Oak Plantation (Fla)
Own.—Live Oak Plantation — Tr.—Kelly Patrick J
111 — Lifetime 2 1 0 0 $15,600 — 1989 2 1 0 0 $15,600 — 1988 0 M 0 0 — Turf 1 1 0 0 $15,600

21Jly89- 7Bel gd 1 :45 3/5 1:12 1:39 4/5 3↑ⒻAlw 29000 8 6 913 815 822 829 Samyn J L 113 3.10 37-28 BountySearch1114½FirstGrade1112¾Iron'sAdvance1118 No excuse 10
26Jun89- 7Bel gd 1 Ⓣ:47 1/5 1:12 1:37 2/5 3↑ⒻMd Sp Wt 10 9 86¼ 66½ 22½ 11½ Samyn J L 114 *2.20e 78-24 Sultry Secret 1141½ Love Is Love 1142 Liz's Axe 1142½ Driving 12
LATEST WORKOUTS Jly 18 Bel tr.t 3f fst :36 4/5 H — Jly 13 Bel [T] 4f fm :52 B (d) — Jly 8 Bel tr.t 3f fst :37 3/5 B — Jly 3 Bel tr.t 3f fst :37 2/5 B

Before those three races, Trin's lifetime turf record was 1-1-3 in seven starts. Since we realize the disadvantages of outside posts in turf racing, we know moving inside to the rail has to help Trin. At 11 to 1, she was certainly an overlay if we cushion the impact of her last three PPs.

Trin stumbled out of the starting gate; raced seventh in the field of eight on the backstretch, then was forced to go five-wide on the turn to get around a wall of horses. She seemed a certain winner until the 9 to 10 favorite, Sister Margery, got through along the inside hedge. Trin and Sister Margery dueled the final sixteenth of a mile, bobbing heads as they crossed the finish line together in a swift 1:34 3/5.

Trin lost by half an inch. Win bets were out the window. She would have paid $25.60. Instead, there was a paltry $28.60 exacta with the favorite.

SEVENTH RACE

Belmont

JULY 30, 1989

1 MILE.(Turf). (1.33) ALLOWANCE. Purse $31,000. 3–year–olds and upward. Fillies and mares which have never won two races other than Maiden, Claiming or Starter. Weights, 3–year–olds 116 lbs. Older 122 lbs. Non–winners of a race other than Maiden or Claiming at a mile or over since July 1 allowed 3 lbs. Of such race since June 15, 5 lbs.

Value of race $31,000; value to winner $18,600; second $6,820; third $3,720; fourth $1,860. Mutuel pool $271,389. Exacta Pool $522,886.

Last Raced	Horse	Eqt.A.Wt	PP	St	$\frac{1}{4}$	$\frac{1}{2}$	$\frac{3}{4}$	Str	Fin	Jockey	Odds $1
15Jly89 6Bel6	Sister Margery	b 4 117	2	5	4½	3hd	5½	1hd	1no	Bailey J D	a-.90
21Jun89 2Bel5	Trin	b 4 117	1	8	73	77	78	21½	25	Maple E	11.80
21Jly89 7Bel8	Sultry Secret	3 111	8	3	61	6½	4hd	3hd	3½	Samyn J L	2.90
1Jly89 9Bel8	Interested Party	b 4 117	5	6	3hd	51½	3hd	42	41¾	Antley C W	10.60
19Jly89 7Bel4	Gottagetitdone	b 4 117	7	7	51½	4hd	61	78	54¼	McCauley W H	a-.90
5Jun89 8Bel6	Fairest College	b 4 117	3	2	1½	1½	1hd	5½	6nk	Migliore R	15.00
21Jly89 7Bel1	Bounty Search	3 116	4	1	2½	21	21	6½	712	Rojas R I	8.30
28Jun89 7Bel7	Imago	3 113	6	4	8	8	8	8	8	Santos J A	7.40

a–Coupled: Sister Margery and Gottagetitdone.

OFF AT 4:12 Start good, Won driving. Time, :23⅕, :46⅖, 1:10⅗, 1:34⅗ Course hard.

$2 Mutuel Prices:

1-(B)-SISTER MARGERY (a–entry)	3.80	2.60	2.40
2-(A)-TRIN		5.80	4.00
7-(J)-SULTRY SECRET			3.40

$2 EXACTA 1-2 PAID $28.60.

Dk. b. or br. f, by Darby Creek Road—Sacred Journey, by King's Bishop. Trainer Alexander Frank A. Bred by Stonewall Farm (Ky).

SISTER MARGERY, close up while saving ground, was steadied along approaching the stretch, got through to take over nearing the final furlong and lasted over TRIM after being bumped by that one. TRI raced six wide into the stretch while moving fast, angled over bumping SISTER MARGERY inside the final furlong and just missed. SULTRY SECRET moved up outside horses on the turn, remained a factor to midstretch and weakened. INTERESTED PARTY, never far back, lugged in while moving between horses after entering the stretch and gave way. GOTTAGETITDONE steadied along looking for room between horses around the turn and into the stetch, swung out after dropping back and lacked a further resonse. FAIREST COLLEGE was used up making the pace. BOUNTY SEARCH, prominent to the upper stretch, tired. IMAGO was always outrun.

Win with Road Eagle; lose with Trin. They don't all win. Our solace is having two lucrative, live overlays we recognized because of our understanding of turf racing.

Certainly, the right jockey on grass can be a decided advantage because of frequent crowding, especially on the turns. There are jockeys who consistently do better on dirt than turf: Randy Romero, Chris Antley, Jorge Velasquez, Frank Lovato, Nick Santagata and Eddie Maple. Others excel on turf: Jean-Luc Samyn and Jean Cruguet. Cordero excels on turf and dirt. Two underrated turf riders are Jerry Bailey and Robbie Davis.

A two month sample of turf races at Belmont and Saratoga in 1988 revealed abysmal numbers by Santagata (0-31); Romero (2-38); Lovato (2-31); Antley (5-60).

Johnson shared his thoughts about jockeys on turf: "I think you've got to move a few of them up. Cordero is very good. Velasquez is not good because he's not an inside rider. He doesn't stay in there.

Samyn is an absolute standout. So is Cruguet because of his European experience. Samyn—he waits. It's hard to make big moves on turf courses. At Aqueduct and Saratoga, you have to save ground."

Johnson rates Mack Miller and Angel Penna as his top contemporary turf trainers in New York. I would add Edward Kelly to the list of trainers who do inordinately well at switching horses from dirt to grass.

The first time horses are asked to switch from dirt to grass, or if they're asked to start their careers on grass, is the time a knowledge of breeding will provide an appreciable edge. A less-experienced handicapper might balk at the idea of becoming familiar enough with breeding to use it as an edge in turf races. It doesn't have to work that way. Slight knowledge of turf breeding is an edge over no knowledge whatsoever. Just going to the races and observing turf races will increase a novice's breeding knowledge. The least we can do for you here is provide a foundation. After you realize even a limited knowledge of grass sires will help your handicapping the rest is up to you. It will take a veteran handicapper to realize second-generation turf breeding, information not contained in the *Form*. For example, Prince John, one of the leading broodmare sires (the sire of the dam of a horse), is at the top of my list for turf breeding. That hardly makes me unique. Prince John's progeny's proven success on grass makes his bloodline a popular one with turf handicappers. It takes a more experienced or more knowledgeable observer to know Prince John's bloodline is there when one of his sons is listed as the sire of a horse. The *Form* will tell you each horse's sire, his dam, and the sire of the dam. But unless you knew Speak John is a son of Prince John, you might be surprised at his offspring's proficiency on turf. This is not to say each successful turf horse has a solid turf pedigree. There are turf winners with obscure, non-grass breeding who win on grass, just as there are horses who win big on the main track with little breeding. Some even become champions. John Henry immediately comes to mind as an example on turf; ill-fated Timely Writer was a fine example on dirt.

We're interested in seeing if we can discern which horses will do well on turf based on their breeding. Time after time, such knowledge can be used to pick overlays.

The most advantageous turf breeding is a horse with turf bloodlines on both sides of his pedigree, meaning his sire and his dam. If a horse has one side and not the other, we will place more importance on the dam's side. We'll look for those horses whose broodmare sires are highly regarded on turf.

First you have to know who's on first when it comes to grass racing. Through Nov. 15, 1989, the seasonal leading turf sires in North America were reported by *The Blood-Horse*.

LEADING TURF SIRES

For stallions represented by a runner in North America in 1989, the leaders are arranged by earnings in North American grass races through Nov. 15, 1989.

Rank, Stallion (Foreign foaled), Year, Sire	Runners All/Turf	Winners All/Turf	Stakes Wnrs All/Turf	Turf Earnings	% of Erngs
1. Caro (Ire), 1967-89, Fortino	53/29	34/8	5/2	$1,686,900	56
2. Habitat, 1966-87, Sir Gaylord	7/4	2/2	1/1	$1,570,230	100
3. Northern Fling, 1970-89, Northern Dancer	24/8	12/2	2/1	$1,256,450	84
4. Nijinsky II, 1967, Northern Dancer	44/32	23/13	8/5	$1,203,230	40
5. Silver Hawk, 1979, Roberto	45/19	23/6	4/3	$1,200,190	62
6. Vigors, 1973, Grey Dawn	102/41	65/12	4/3	$1,080,200	48
7. Explosive Bid, 1978, Explodent	55/19	26/6	2/2	$1,048,480	76
8. Kris S., 1977, Roberto	65/16	37/4	6/1	$1,007,010	35
9. Nodouble, 1965, Noholme II	97/43	55/13	8/4	$923,154	38
10. Darby Creek Road, 1975-88, Roberto	99/36	47/12	5/4	$918,471	50
11. Valdez, 1976-85, Exclusive Native	62/28	40/6	4/2	$842,347	57
12. Nureyev, 1977, Northern Dancer	23/20	9/6	4/3	$823,039	72
13. Pleasant Colony, 1978, His Majesty	79/39	48/6	10/3	$780,997	28
14. Majestic Light, 1973, Majestic Prince	85/40	39/11	5/3	$759,402	41
15. Petrone (Fr), 1964, Prince Taj	59/13	31/2	3/1	$704,925	64
16. Cure the Blues, 1978, Stop the Music	16/8	10/4	3/2	$695,537	77
17. Explodent, 1969, Nearctic	95/32	50/8	6/3	$689,711	31
18. What a Guest, 1979, Be My Guest	4/3	3/2	1/1	$678,015	95
19. Naskra, 1967-89, Nasram	132/43	73/10	11/5	$628,773	22
20. Overskate, 1975, Nodouble	87/32	50/8	3/1	$609,969	36
21. Seattle Slew, 1974, Bold Reasoning	72/29	38/7	10/3	$582,115	19
22. Northern Jove, 1968, Northern Dancer	106/35	59/8	4/2	$573,311	37
23. Roberto, 1969-88, Hail to Reason	53/31	28/13	2/1	$568,230	38
24. Val de l'Orne (Fr), 1972, Val de Loir	61/27	33/11	1/1	$566,470	56
25. His Majesty, 1968, Ribot	61/20	37/11	3/2	$564,087	53
26. Sharpen Up (GB), 1969, Atan	57/29	31/11	6/3	$562,651	48
27. Cipayo, 1974, Lacydon	6/4	3/2	2/2	$529,565	72
28. Northern Baby, 1976, Northern Dancer	62/38	29/12	2/1	$519,538	50
29. Perrault (GB), 1977, Djakao	58/22	26/4	1/1	$502,506	56
30. Caveat, 1980, Cannonade	79/27	37/11	5/3	$500,787	37
31. Alleged, 1974, Hoist the Flag	56/36	30/12	3/1	$499,871	52
32. Key to the Kingdom, 1970, Bold Ruler	80/14	39/3	2/1	$483,430	54
33. Lypheor (GB), 1975-86, Lyphard	48/24	25/8	3/1	$481,622	41
34. Vice Regent, 1967, Northern Dancer	77/25	45/9	5/2	$474,737	22
35. Mill Reef, 1968-86, Never Bend	5/5	2/2	0/0	$466,605	100
36. Don Roberto, 1977, Roberto	4/3	2/0	0/0	$450,000	92
37. Green Dancer, 1972, Nijinsky II	95/42	42/14	4/1	$442,523	29
38. Miswaki, 1978, Mr. Prospector	97/37	59/8	9/3	$435,806	19
39. Affirmed, 1975, Exclusive Native	74/34	30/6	8/2	$433,087	25
40. General Assembly, 1976, Secretariat	28/11	17/3	2/2	$431,852	62
41. Assert (Ire), 1979, Be My Guest	46/25	21/10	0/0	$428,156	71
42. Mr. Prospector, 1970, Raise a Native	79/25	43/3	11/3	$421,726	14
43. Northfields, 1968, Northern Dancer	8/2	5/1	1/1	$406,811	88
44. Danzig, 1977, Northern Dancer	59/26	36/6	6/2	$403,457	17
45. Mummy's Pet, 1968-86, Sing Sing	6/3	4/3	1/1	$394,906	95
46. Lyphard's Wish (Fr), 1976, Lyphard	102/51	51/14	4/2	$383,801	39
47. Grey Dawn (Fr), 1962, Herbager	70/34	36/6	3/1	$381,605	25
48. Irish River (Fr), 1976, Riverman	45/26	21/7	3/2	$379,392	45
49. Exclusive Native, 1965-83, Raise a Native	16/8	7/3	1/0	$372,662	47
50. Great Neck, 1976, Tentam	37/16	19/6	2/2	$367,759	61

Rank, Stallion (Foreign foaled), Year, Sire	Runners All/Turf	Winners All/Turf	Stakes Wnrs All/Turf	Turf Earnings	% of Erngs
51. Baldski, 1974, Nijinsky II	144/45	80/7	3/0	$362,927	16
52. Smarten, 1976, Cyane	95/32	64/12	5/2	$360,244	21
53. Al Nasr (Fr), 1978, Lyphard	43/15	22/3	2/2	$356,688	37
54. Transworld, 1974, Prince John	80/25	39/7	2/2	$345,461	41
55. Wavering Monarch, 1979, Majestic Light	66/22	43/10	5/4	$342,228	30
56. Valid Appeal, 1972, In Reality	118/32	70/6	5/2	$336,778	15
57. Pirateer, 1975, Roberto	54/4	26/2	1/1	$335,390	53
58. Golden Act, 1976, Gummo	86/31	49/13	2/0	$333,130	29
59. Sir Ivor Again, 1976, Sir Ivor	20/4	9/3	2/1	$329,154	50
60. Fabulous Dancer, 1976, Northern Dancer	10/7	5/2	1/1	$327,235	86
61. Secretariat, 1970-89, Bold Ruler	68/23	35/6	2/1	$323,617	27
62. Compliance, 1978, Northern Dancer	71/21	35/5	1/1	$323,359	36
63. Little Current, 1971, Sea-Bird	86/26	53/5	3/1	$321,165	30
64. Lydian (Fr), 1978, Lyphard	55/15	27/4	2/2	$309,713	47
65. Big Spruce, 1969, Herbager	77/28	41/4	2/1	$308,909	36
66. Great Above, 1972, Minnesota Mac	116/26	63/9	5/1	$305,975	22
67. Qui Native, 1974, Exclusive Native	27/8	20/2	2/1	$300,186	57
68. Hold Your Tricks, 1975, Hold Your Peace	35/10	22/3	2/1	$300,121	43
69. Encino, 1977, Nijinsky II	47/9	25/3	3/1	$300,059	40
70. Topsider, 1974, Northern Dancer	71/34	40/9	6/2	$299,449	16

Courtesy of *The Blood-Horse* Magazine

My favorite turf sires include His Majesty, Prince John, Stage Door Johnny, Lyphard, Nijinsky II, Hoist The Flag, Secretariat, Vaguely Noble, Roberto, Round Table, Majestic Light and Majesty's Prince. Some lesser known turf sires of merit include Sea-Bird, Diplomat Way, Speak John, Transworld, Sassafrass, Mr. Leader, Laomeholli and The Bart.

Is it reasonable to expect other bettors not to zero in on the same information? Many times, the answer is a resounding "yes."

Bolt From The Blue, a 4-year-old filly who began 1984 by winning the first division of the La Prevoyante Handicap at 1 1/2 miles on the turf, January 2, at Calder, came to Belmont Park the previous summer as a maiden, loser of her only three starts, each on dirt. She was entered by trainer Horatio Luro in a 1 3/8 mile maiden grass race, June 22, 1983, at Belmont.

This would be her first start on turf. Would she grass (do well on turf)?

Her sire, Blue Times, meant little to the average fan. Blue Times' bloodlines trace back to Princequillo, sire of Prince John, on his dam's side, but that information wasn't in the *Form*. What was readily available in the *Form* was Bolt From The Blue's immediate breeding. Her dam was Berkut, a daughter of Sea-Bird, a proven turf broodmare sire.

Bolt From The Blue was expected to grass, and she certainly did.

Her previous racing record suggested she would like the distance of her first turf race. Bolt From The Blue had raced once as a 2-year-old. In a four furlong maiden race at Timonium, she had finished ninth in a field of ten by twenty- five lengths at odds of 116 to 1. From that awful debut, however, Bolt From The Blue had done measurably better in her first two starts as a 3-year-old, each seven furlong maiden races on the main track at Hialeah: Bolt From The Blue closed seventeen and a half lengths to finish fourth by three-quarters of a length at 45 to 1, then closed four and a half lengths to finish fourth by two lengths at 5 to 1. Clearly, Bolt From The Blue had shown signs of life with added distance.

Despite being off two months, a negative factor we acknowledge and react to by reducing the amount of our wager, Bold From The Blue is an excellent overlay in her first turf start. The price at 10 to 1 was too high to resist.

Eleventh early in a field of fourteen, Bolt From The Blue won by a length, paying $22.80.

Even in her next start, a turf allowance race at Belmont Park, Bolt From The Blue was again allowed to go off as an overlay at 5 to 1. She returned $13.40 after winning by one and a half lengths. The comment after each victory in the *Form* was identical: "Going away."

Let's look at a $1^1/_{16}$ mile turf race at Saratoga, Aug. 5, 1983, an allowance for non-winners of two.

7 SARATOGA

INNER TURF COURSE — 1 1-16 MILES — SARATOGA — START — FINISH

1 1/16 MILES. (INNER-TURF). (1.41) ALLOWANCE. Purse $21,000. 3-year-olds an which have never won a race other than Maiden, Claiming or Starter. Weights: 3-y olds, 117 lbs.; older, 122 lbs.; non-winners of a race other than claiming at a mile or since July 15 allowed 3 lbs.; of such a race since July 1, 5 lbs.

Coupled—The Ghost and Imperial Realm.

Monkey Bread — B. c. 3, by Dewan—Baobab, by Pronto
Own.—Rosbash J — Br.—Cherry Valley Farm Inc-Marjory Corp (Ky) — Tr.—Hawkins Luke X — **112**
Lifetime 17 1 2 1 $14,885 — 1983 10 1 2 0 $11 — 1982 7 M 0 1 $3 — Turf 3 0 0 0 $1

15Jly83- 8Bel	hd	1⅜	[T]:11 .2:01 2:14	3↑Alw 21000	6 3 35½ 67½ 99¼ 98	Maple E	112	50.40	79-15	New Discovery 117hd Native Raid 112nk Tampa Town 113¾	Tire
1Jly83- 5Bel	hd	1 1/16	(T):45 1:09 1:40⅗	Clm 50000	10 5 712 611 613 59½	Smith A Jr	117	15.80	83-16	Native Raid 1133½ Speier's Luck 1132 Lutyens 1142¾	No excus
25May83- 1Bel	gd	1 1/16	[T]:49 1:14⅕ 1:47⅕	Clm 45000	3 6 53 2½ 41 42	Hernandez C	113	16.80	63-32	Chaudiere 117no Oliver List 1081½ Case Back 114½	Tire
13Apr83- 7Key	fst	7f	:22⅗ :45⅕ 1:24⅕	Alw 11000	6 12 106¾ 108¼ 74¾ 85¼	Ruane J	117	61.00	81-22	My Boy Neal 112½ Rapid Wing 120½ Norway 114nk	Outru
26Mar83- 1Aqu	fst	1⅛	:48⅕ 1:13⅖ 1:53⅕	Clm 45000	4 7 77¼ 89 812 712	Smith D L	115	30.20	57-19	Bishen 113nk Very Competable 1174 Medieval's Son 117¾	Outru
15Mar83- 3Key	fst	170	:47⅘ 1:14⅘ 1:46	Md Sp Wt	8 2 23 11 11 11¾	Smith D L	118	4.10	70-22	Monkey Bread 1181¾ Attilio 1186 Mr. Boojie 118½	Drivin
2Mar83- 1Key	my	1 1/16	:47⅖ 1:14⅕ 1:47⅖	Md Sp Wt	6 5 68½ 42½ 25 28	Rivera J	118	9.60	59-30	DreamOnAWing1138MonkeyBread118½MountinFreeze118¾	Rallie
18Feb83- 8Suf	my	6f	:24⅕ :50 1:18⅕	Md Sp Wt	7 5 712 611 68¾ 411	Smith D L	118	*1.50	39-57	Third And Inches 11810 Cyandi 118nk Milestone 1181	Outru
13Jan83- 4Aqu	fst	1⅛	[•]:48⅕ 1:15⅕ 1:55⅖	Md 45000	1 1 33 33 46½ 38½	Smith D L	118	4.40	60-26	[D]LordHtchet117hdOutnumbered1188½MonkyBrd1183¼	Weakene
13Jan83-Placed second through disqualification											
1Jan83- 6Aqu	fst	6f	[•]:23⅖ :47⅗ 1:14	Md 50000	13 2 63¼ 1010 89 88¾	Smith D L	122	28.60	65-25	HndsomeDncer111¾PersonlityCrisis122½SwetAffilition1222¾	Wid

LATEST WORKOUTS Aug 1 Bel tr.t 4f gd :49 h — Jly 26 Bel tr.t 3f fst :35⅗ b — Jly 9 Sar tr.t 5f fst 1:01⅖ h — ●Jun 24 Sar tr.t 5f fst 1:01⅖ b

Chica's Prince — Ch. c. 3, by Dactylographer—Chica Linda, by Grey Dawn II
Own.—Longford K Stable — Br.—Royal Palm Breeders (Fla) — Tr.—Cincotta Vincent J — **112**
Lifetime 15 2 1 2 $37,380 — 1983 13 2 1 1 $34 — 1982 2 M 0 1 $2 — Turf 6 1 1 0 $20

13Jly83- 8Bel	fm	1¼	[T]:47 1:35⅖ 2:00⅗	Lexington	9 5 510 811 915 914	Samyn J L	b 114	19.50	77-12	Kilauea 114hd Fortnightly 1263½ Top Competitor 114hd	Tired
3Jly83- 7Bel	fm	1 1/16	(T):46⅕ 1:10⅖ 1:42⅖	3↑Alw 21000	7 5 32 52¾ 21½ 2hd	Samyn J L	b 111	12.80	84-15	JeffersWest117hdChic'sPrinc111hdHyprt113nk	Came out, bumpe
19Jun83- 5Bel	fm	1	(T):46⅗ 1:11⅖ 1:38⅘	Clm 70000	8 9 610 57 43½ 12½	Samyn J L	b 113	21.80	71-25	Chic'sPrinc1132½Broodr'sTip114noQuickDip1071	Lckd rm st.,clea
11Jun83- 2Bel	fm	1¼	[T]:47⅘ 1:36⅕ 2:01	3↑Alw 21000	3 2 32 89 814 916	Migliore R	b 111	63.50	73-06	Charging Through 1142½ PacMania112hdLooseCannon111nk	Tired
26May83- 2Bel	gd	1½	(T):48⅗ 2:06⅘ 2:34	3↑Alw 21000	6 4 46 78 811 814	Migliore R	b 110	12.80	40-33	Soudan 1122½ Benefit Performer 1241¾ Green Pocket 1191½	Tired
19May83- 3Bel	fm	1	(T):46 1:11⅖ 1:38	3↑Alw 21000	6 9 95¾ 67 57½ 46¾	Migliore R	b 113	9.90	68-24	StoneyLonesome1112¾ColdRemark110hdToughMickey1084	Rallie
11May83- 6Aqu	fst	1⅛	:49⅘ 1:15⅕ 1:54⅕	Md Sp Wt	3 5 4¾ 2hd 2½ 1¾	Migliore R	b 122	12.10	64-30	Chica's Prince 122¾ Sweet Affiliation 1221¼ Terse 1222½	Driving
30Apr83- 4Aqu	fst	6f	:22⅘ :46⅖ 1:11⅗	Md Sp Wt	3 8 32 42½ 44½ 57½	Davis R G	b 122	9.10	75-22	Spring Fever 1221¾ Naskra's Gold 1223¾HailColumbus122hd	Tired
15Apr83- 6Aqu	fst	7f	:22⅘ :45⅘ 1:24⅕	Md Sp Wt	5 9 95¼ 99½ 814 812	Migliore R	122	23.20	68-29	Intention 1221½ Pac Mania 1222¼ Au Point 122½	Steadied
30Mar83- 6Aqu	fst	7f	:23 :46⅖ 1:25⅖	Md Sp Wt	3 12 69¼ 56½ 54½ 3nk	Migliore R	122	78.90	74-24	Chaudiere 117hd Scarlet Hobeau 122nkChica'sPrince122nk	Rallied

LATEST WORKOUTS Aug 3 Sar tr.t 5f fst 1:02⅖ b — Jly 28 Sar tr.t 5f fst 1:01⅖ b — Jly 11 Bel 4f fst :49⅕ b — Jun 30 Bel tr.t 5f fst 1:01⅗ h

Movable Feast

Own.—Verulam Farm

B. c. 3, by Banquet Table—Delimit, by Key to the Mint
Br.—Burch & Ewald (Ky)
Tr.—Burch William E

112

	Lifetime	1983	2	0	1	0	$5,820
	5 1 1 0	1982	3	1	0	0	$10,800
	$16,620	Turf	3	1	1	0	$15,420

24Jly83- 9Bel sly 7f	:23% :46% 1:24% 3 + Alw 20000	5 1 53½ 53½ 34½ 47	Sa. vn J L	111	2.40	71-22 Lutyens 111½ Special Notice 117⁵ Nivernay 111¹½	Wide 8
25Jun83- 9Bel fm 1 ①:45¾ 1:09¾ 1:34½ 3 + Alw 21000	12 8 64 56½ 46½ 24½	Samyr J L	109	20.30	89-12 Kilauea 109⁴¼ Movable Feast 109ⁿᵏSpecialNotice117⁴	Raced wide 12
12Nov82- 4Aqu fm 1½ ①:49% 1:14% 1:54¾	Alw 20000	8 711 75½ 65½ 52½	Samyn J L	119	7.50	68-27 AncientBarrister117ᵐᵈCgleSprings117ʰᵈNiverny122²	Lacked a bid 8
10Oct82- 6Bel fm 1½ ①:49 1:13½ 1:44%	Md Sp Wt	4 35½ 32½ 2½ 13½	Samy ₁ L	118	3.10	77-17 Movable Feast 118³½ Chaudiere 118² Moon Spirit118²	Ridden out 8
19Sep82- 6Bel fst ⁶f :22¾ :46% 1:12½	Md Sp Wt	3 10¹³ 108¼ 89 87½	McCarron G	118	28.20	73-20 Galaxy Guide 118² Balancing Act 1181½ Law Talk 1151½	No factor 11

LATEST WORKOUTS Aug 1 Sar 3f fst :35% h   Jly 21 Bel 5f fst 1:0'₄s h   Jly 11 Bel 4f fst ·50½ h   Jly 6 Bel 3f fst :36% h

Tanyosho

Own.—Al-Jo Stable

Dk. b. or br. c. 3, by The Minstrel—Fleet Treat, by Fleet Nasrullah
Br.—Hackman W M (Va)
Tr.—Campo John P

112

	Lifetime	1983	8	1	1	0	$41,₄⁶
	11 1 1 3	1982	3	M	0	3	$₃₀,₇₀₆
	$17,935						

7Jly83- 7Bel fm 1½ :23¾ :46½ 1:23¾ 3 + Alw 20000	3 10 109 10⁷½109¼109½	Samyn J L	b 111	20.30	76-19 Galaxy Guide 106ʰᵈ Waitlist 117¹¼ Believe The Queen111¾	Traded 8
30May83- 8Bel my 7f :22¼ :45% 1:23½ 3 + Alw 20000	2 8 913 89¼ 79½ 66¾	McCarron G	b 112	23.10	75-11 Cold Remark 108² Eskimo 112¹¾ Private Sun 114⁴	Broke slow 9
21May83- 6Bel gd 6f :22½ :45½ 1:09½ 3 + Alw 20000	2 6 711 67½ 58½ 57	McCarron G	b 112	6.50	89-07 Agile Shoebill 107⁴½ Private Sun 114¹ HeldBlameless113½	Outrun 7
28Mar83- 6Hia fst 1½ :47¾ 1:11¾ 1:49¾	Alw 10500	10 8 41½ 41½ 37	McCauley W H b 114	16.20	78-19 AwesomeCount114¹T.G.'sPrince114²WhoCouldForgt114½	Faltered 10
5Mar83- 8GP fst 1½ :48 1:12¾ 1:44½	Alw 16000	7 8 87½ 711 714 619	Bailey J D	117	4.40	59-19 I Really Will 117⁵ Runderbar 117² Oh My Windland 117½	Outrun 11
21Feb83- 7GP fst 1½ :48½ 1:13 1:45%	Alw 15000	2 8 83½ 53 56 43½	Bailey J D	117	3.40	68-24 High Honors 117¹ Wild Chorus 122½ Moon Spirit 119²	Mild bid 9
8Feb83- 4GP fst 7f :22½ :45% 1:24%	Md Sp Wt	9 2 43½ 42 13 17	Bailey J D	122	*.80	80-25 Tanyosho 122⁷ Press Agent 122¹½ Intrepid Wind 122³	Handil 9
19Jan83- 4GP fst 7f :22½ :45% 1:24½	Md Sp Wt	9 9 76½ 55 34½ 2ⁿᵏ	Bailey J D	122	*1.70	83-20 Jungle Minister 122ⁿᵏ Tanyosho 122⁴ Now's The Time 122¹	Wide 12
16Oct82- 2Aqu fst 1 :46¾ 1:11½ 1:37%	Md Sp Wt	3 3 31 45½ 47½ 35½	McCarron G	118	2.90	71-26 Pitchpipe 118⁷ Seligman 118³½ Tanyosho 118¹	Weake. 7
8Oct82- 4Bel fst 1 :47 1:13 1:39½	Md Sp Wt	5 8 66 62½ 32½ 32½	McCarron G	118	*2.80	63-25 Chumming118½MomentofJoy118²Tnyosho118¹	Lacked a response 11

LATEST WORKOUTS Aug 3 Sar tr.t 4f fst :50 b   Jly 21 Bel tr.t 4f fst :48½ h   Jly 14 Bel ① 5f fm 1:02 h (d)   ●Jly 1 Bel 7f fst 1:26¾ hg

Tampa Town

Own.—Pascuma W J

Ch. c. 3, by Nodouble—Sociable Angel, by Social Climber
Br.—Fuentes & Hayman Alice (Fla)
Tr.—Pascuma Warren J

112

	Lifetime	1983	8	1	2	1	$24,280
	12 1 5 1	1982	4	M	3	0	$11,440
	$35,720	Turf	2	0	1	0	$5,420

15Jly83- 8Bel hd 1¾ ①:11 2:01 2:14 3 + Alw 21000	3 4 49½ 23 21½ 3ⁿᵏ	MacBeth D	1i5	21.10	87-15 New Discovery 117ʰᵈ Native Raid 112ⁿᵏ TampaTown113¾	Rallied 9
3Jly83- 7Bel fm 1¾ ①:46½ 1:10¾ 1:42% 3 + Alw 21000	1 7 64¼ 73½ 97 75½	MacBeth D	116	12.30	78-25 JeffersWest117ʰᵈChic'sPrince111ʰᵈHyprt113ⁿᵏ	Lacked a response 9
26Jun83- 4Bel fst 1½ :47¾ 1:12 1:51¾ 3 + Md Sp.Wt	4 3 21½ 21 12½ 1⁵½	MacBeth D	114	*1.90	69-24 Tampa Town 114²½ HailColumbus114²Cyanesong114ⁿᵒ	Drew clear 7
13Jun83- 3Bel fst 6½f :22½ :45¾ 1:16¾ 3 + Md Sp.Wt	4 2 3ⁿᵏ 2ʰᵈ 2ʰᵈ 2ⁿᵏ	Maple E	114	*1.30	92-12 Halo's Comet 122ⁿᵏ Tampa Town 114⁴ Antigua 114½	Gamely 6
4May83- 2Aqu my 1 :45 1:09¾ 1:34%	Md Sp.Wt	4 5 53 25 2e 28	MacBeth D	122	2.00	86-18 Au Point 122⁸ Tampa Town 122⁵SwcetAffiliation122¹½	Drew clear 8
15Apr83- 6Aqu fst 7f :22½ :45% 1:24½	Md Sp Wt	8 6 74½ 53 55½ 55½	MacBeth D	122	6.70	55-29 Intention 122¹½ Pac Mania 122²¾ Au Point 122½	Steadied st. 10
30Mar83- 6Aqu fst 7f :23 :46¾ 1:25%	Md Sp Wt	4 5 35 25 11½ 4½	Maple E	122	*3.10	73-24 Chaudiere117ʰᵈScarletHobeau122⁶Chic'sPrince122ⁿᵏ	Weakened 13
14Mar83- 8Aqu gd 1½ ⑤:48 1:12¾ 1:44%	Md Sp Wt	2 3 42 2ʰᵈ 36 411	Smith A Jr	b 122	8.00	61-20 FstJohn122¹LordHtcht122⁵SwtAffiton122²²	Lacked a response 7
25Feb83- 6Aqu my 1 :46½ 1:11½ 1:37%	Md Sp Wt	7 4 43 42 32 2¹½	Fell J	b.118	3.20	81-24 Stoney Lonesome 118¹TampaTown118¹Chaudiere118ⁿᵏ	Gamely 9
11Nov82- 6Aqu fst 6f :22½ :45½ 1:11%	Md Sp Wt	11 2 41½ 31 32¹ 22½	Fell J	b 118	22.40	82-19 SplendidMoment118ⁿᵈ¹PacMania118¹½TampaTown118¹½	Even try 12

¹¹Nov82-Placed second through disqualification

LATEST WORKOUTS Jly 29 Sar 6f fst 1:15% h   Jly 22 Bel tr.t 4f my :49½ h (d)   Jly 10 Bel 5f fst 1:01¾ h   Jun 25 Bel tr.t 3f fst :35% h

The Ghost

Own.—Schwartz B K

Ro. c. 3, by Crow—Promised Woman, by Promised Land
Br.—Hedgewood Farm (Ky)
Tr.—Trovato Joseph A

112

	Lifetime	1983	5	1	0	1	$17,160
	5 1 0 1	1982	0	M	0	0	
	$17,160	Turf	3	1	0	0	$13,820

12Jly83- 6Bel fm 1½ ①:45% 1:09¾ 1:41% 3 + Alw 21000	3 1 11½ 1ʰᵈ 24 411	Cordero A Jr	113	*1.40	78-14 Unmistaken106³½ValLegendryWelth1115½	Swerved 8
3Jly83- 8Bel fm 1¾ ①:46½ 1:10¾ 1:42% 3 + Alw 21000	4 3 42 1ʰᵈ 41½ 4½	Murphy D J⁵	111	*1.30	63-15 Jeffers West 117ʰᵈ Chica's Prince 111ʰᵈHypertee113ⁿᵏ	Weakened 9
22Jun83- 6Bel fst 7f :22½ 1:09¾ 1:41 3 + Md Sp Wt	4 2 22½ 21 12 11½	Vasquez J	115	8.70	91-14 The Ghost 115¹½ Penzance 114ʰᵈ Rogues' Walk 122²½	Ridden out 12
3Jun83- 6Bel fst 7f :22¾ :45% 1:23% 3 + Md Sp Wt	4 1 2½ 21 34 43½	Vasquez J	115	2.40	76-19 Daring Groom 109⁵ Spring Commander122⁴TheGhost114½	Tired 7
25May83- 6Bel fst 6f :22½ :46 1:11½ 3 + Md Sp Wt	8 4 43 43½ 33 43½	Vasquez J	115	5.50	82-16 Cozzene 113⁵ Gallant Minded 113¹½BigMcCoy113ⁿᵏ	Lacked a rally 9

LATEST WORKOUTS ●Aug 1 Sar ① 7f fm 1:25½ h   Jly 27 Sar ① 5f fm 1:00¾ h   ●Jly 11 Aqu ① 6f fm 1:15 h   ●Jun 30 Aqu ① 5f gd 1:01¾ h (d)

Val De La Meuse

Own.—Mereworth Farm

B. c. 3, by Val De L'Orne—Hasty Flapper, by Hitting Away
Br.—Mereworth Farm (Ky)
Tr.—Nesky Kenneth A

112

	Lifetime	1983	5	1	1	1	$18,540
	8 1 1 3	1982	3	M	0	0	
	$18,540	Turf	1	0	1	0	$4,620

17Jly83- 6Bel fm 1½ ①:45% 1:09¾ 1:41¾ 3 + Alw 21000	2 7 65½ 66½ 34½ 23½	Samyn J L	b 111	33.80	85-14 Unmistaken106³½ValDeLaMeuse111²LegendryWelth1115½	Rallied 8
25Apr83- 5Aqu gd 1½ :47¾ 1:13 1:52	Alw 21000	3 5 59 35½ 33 38	Cordero A Jr	b 119	12.30	67-23 Bishen 112ⁿᵒ Wild Chorus 117½ValDeLaMeuse119³½	Weakened 7
25Mar83- 6Aqu fst 1½ :49 1:13¾ 1:56	Alw 21000	4 4 59½ 42 12 1⁷	Cordero A Jr	b 122	6.00	55-36 VlDeLMeus122⁷LordHtcht122⁵½ScrltHobu122²	Lugged in, drvng 6
24Feb83- 4Aqu fst 1½ ⑤:48½ 1:13¾ 1:54%	Md Sp Wt	8 3 32 32½ 33½ 56½	Cordero A Jr	b 122	7.20	66-24 Dirge 122⁷½ Fast John 122¹½ Lead The Way1122½	Tired 11
15Jan83- 8Aqu my 170 ⑤:49½ 1:15½ 1:46½	Md Sp Wt	9 9 76 78 510 511	Migliore R	118	40.80	60-22 Shamrocky 122⁵ Shock Wave 115½Tina'sDouble122²½	No threat 9
30Dec82- 6Aqu fst 7f ⑤:23½ :47½ 1:27%	Md Sp Wt	2 6 62½ 64½ 712 816	Cordero A Jr	118	16.40	65-24 Stshed118²½BelieveTheQueen118²DoubleExplosion118³½	No rally 14
22Dec82- 6Aqu fst 6f :23 :48½ 1:14½	Md Sp Wt	9 9 73½ 88½ 88½ 55½	Miranda J	118	16.60e	67-24 NoblePocket118⁵SpiffyAndCool118ⁿᵏNorthGlade118¹½	No excuse 10
8Dec82- 6Aqu fst 6f ⑤:23 :46½ 1:12%	Md Sp Wt	12 2 11¹⁴ 10¹⁴ 9¹⁴ 99½	Miranda J	118	34.60e	72-21 But Who Knows 118¹¹Unmistaken118¹½WhatMommy118¹½	Outrun 13

LATEST WORKOUTS Jly 27 Aqu ⑤ 6f fst 1:16¾ b   ●Jly 14 Aqu ⑤ 4f fst :48½ h   Jly 9 Aqu ⑤ 6f fst 1:15% h   Jly 3 Aqu ⑤ 6f fst 1:15¾ h

Outpost

Own.—Hirsch Mrs W J

Dk. b. or br. g. 4, by Distant Land—I Deceive, by Bagdad
Br.—Hirsch W M J (Ky)
Tr.—Hirsch William J Jr

117

	Lifetime	1983	3	0	0	0	$1,680
	11 1 4 0	1982	8	1	4	0	$26,440
	$28,120	Turf	8	1	4	0	$26,920

3Jly83- 7Bel fm 1½ ①:46½ 1:10¾ 1:42% 3 + Alw 21000	10 8 74½ 63½11¹²111¹¹	Maple E	117	5.40	73-15 Jeffers West 117ʰᵈ Chica's Prince 111ʰᵈ Hypertee 113ⁿᵏ	Outrun 9
25Jun83- 9Bel fm 1 ①:45¾ 1:09¾ 1:34½ 3 + Alw 21000	10 11 11¹¹ 98½ 511 58½	Maple E	117	*3.20	85-12 Kilauea 109⁴¼MovbleFest109ⁿᵏSpeciNotice117⁴	Squeezed back erly 12
13Jun83- 2Bel hd 1 ①:45¾ 1:08¾ 1:33%	Clm 20000	11 11 119 97½ 47½ 46½	Maple E	114	4.90	91-08 King's Glory 117⁵Deedee'sDeal116½FabulousFur113½	Bid evenly 11
31Oct82- 8Aqu yl 1½ ⑤:50½ 1:15½ 1:48% 3 + Alw 20000	6 6 52½ 41½ 42 2ⁿᵒ	Maple E	114	*2.30	63-29 Tufts 114ⁿᵒ Outpost 114½ Swallanga 117ⁿᵏ	Sharp 9
16Oct82- 5Aqu fst 1½ :48 1:12½ 1:37%	Alw 20000	6 6 52½ 41½ 42 2ⁿᵒ	Bailey J D	114	*2.30	73-26 NathanDetroit114½ReservationAgent114²BeauBidder114⁵	Evenly 9
30Aug82- 8Sar fm 1½ ①:48½ 1:12½ 1:43%	Alw 20000	2 4 42½ 2½ 1ʰᵈ 2¾	Maple E	117	*2.80	86-09 Sir Pele 122½ Outpost 117¹ Mr. Peruser 122⁴	Weakened 9
1Aug82- 9Sar fm 1½ ①:48 1:12 1:49½ 3 + Md Sp Wt	9 7 94½ 64½ 2¹ 2¹½	Maple E	117	4.40	81-11 Outpost117¹½LetterPerfect117ⁿᵒStarofHeven117ⁿᵒ	Blocked, clear 8
1Aug82- 7Sar fm 1¼ ⑤:23¾ :47½ 1:24% 3 + Md Sp Wt	8 5 99½ 46 22 21½	Maple E	114	18.80	81-20 My Right Hand 117¹OutpostStarofHeaven114½	2nd best 8
17Jly82- 6Mth fm 1¾ ①:48¼ 1:12¾ 1:43% 3 + Md Sp Wt	1 5 99¹ 46 22 2ⁿᵏ	Nemeti W	116	15.80	84-11 Pride Of Satan 115⁵¹ Outpost 115⁵ Gallant Minded 114½	Best of others 8
23Jly82- 6Bel fm 1½ ①:45¾ 1:10½ 1:41%	Md Sp Wt	3 3 34 38 614 815	Fell J	114	12.90	73-22 I'm So Merry 116³½ Spark Chief116³¹WordsByTheWise111½	Tired 11

LATEST WORKOUTS Aug 3 Sar 3f gd :36½ b   ●Jly 27 Sar 6f fst 1:12¾ h   Jly 21 Bel 6f fst 1:01¾ h   Jly 14 Bel 4f fst :47¾ h

***Special Notice** Ch. g. 4, by Sassafras—Collatteral, by Jim J
Own.—Luckman S M Br.—Firestone B R & Mrs (Ire) Tr.—Pagano George
117 Lifetime 24 2 2 3 $32,397 | 1983 16 2 2 2 $31,060 | 1982 6 M 0 1 $1,337 | Turf 12 1 0 2 $17,177

24Jly83-	9Bel	sly	7f	:23⅗	:46⅗	1:24⅘	3↑ Alw 20000	7	2	1½	1^{1}	1½	2¾	MacBeth D		117	6.40	77-22	Lutyens 111¾ Special Notice 117^{5} Nivernay 111^{1¼}	Gamely	8
9Jly83-	3Mth	fm	1$\frac{1}{16}$	Ⓣ:47⅗	1:11⅗	1:43⅖	3↑ Oceanport H	1	2	1^{hd}	1^{1}	10^{9¼}	11^{11}	Gomez E R		108	36.90	73-17	Fray Star 114^{1¼} Domynsky 112^{1½} And More 117^{1¼}	Stopped	12
25Jun83-	9Bel	fm	1	Ⓣ:45⅗	1:09⅖	1:34⅕	3↑ Alw 21000	4	3	3^{2}	3^{4½}	3^{5½}	3^{5}	Graell A		117	7.00	89-12	Kilauea 109^{4¾} Movable Feast 109^{nk} Special Notice 117¾	Evenly	12
16Jun83-	2Bel	fm	1$\frac{1}{16}$	Ⓣ:46	1:09⅖	1:41⅗	Clm 45000	3	1	1½	1½	1^{1}	1^{nk}	MacBeth D		113	14.00	88-14	Special Notice 113^{nk} Clarinet King 119^{1¼} Big Ding 110½	Driving	12
6Jun83-	2Bel	gd	1⅜	[T]:48⅖	1:39⅕	2:18	3↑ Hcp 16000s	9	3	3^{7½}	2^{2½}	3^{3}	4^{5¼}	Graell A		112	21.80	62-31	Campus Capers 122^{1} Could It Be 114^{1¼} ArdentBid120^{3}	Weakened	11
19May83-	6Bel	fm	1	Ⓣ:46⅖	1:11⅗	1:39	3↑ Alw 21000	6	9	9^{5¾}	9^{6¾}	5^{3½}	4^{3¼}	Graell A		119	96.00	67-24	Bundle of Kisses 119^{hd}FeloniousFellow114^{1½}Eskimo113^{1¾}	Rallied	11
7May83-	9Aqu	fst	7f	:22⅗	:45⅗	1:23⅕	Clm 22500	11	11	10^{6½}	8^{6½}	11^{11}	11^{12}	Hernandez C		117	47.50	73-19	Quick Rotation 117^{1} Mingo 110^{1} Hot Words 112no	Raced wide	12
27Apr83-	2Aqu	fst	6f	:22⅘	:46⅗	1:12⅖	Md 20000	10	4	3^{2}	2^{1}	2^{1}	1^{1}	Graell A		122	*2.50	79-17	SpecialNotice122^{1}SwiftAndProud122^{nk}[DH]DanceCritic113	Driving	12
13Apr83-	2Aqu	fst	6f	:23⅕	:46⅕	1:11⅘	Md 30000	8	3	4^{2½}	4^{7½}	3^{5}	3^{3}	Cordero A Jr		118	4.90	79-19	Hail the Hero 118^{1¾} ArcticBlast118^{1¼}SpecialNotice118^{3¾}	Mild bid	9
[illegible]	4Aqu	fst	7f	:22⅗	:45⅗	1:24⅗	Md Sp Wt	5	3	6^{9}	7^{9½}	7^{10}	6^{8¾}	Rogers A		122	20.50	69-25	WingedUnivrs117^{3¼}PrciousPrl122^{2}SpringCommndr122^{3}	No factor	10

LATEST WORKOUTS Jly 21 Bel [T] 4f yl :48⅕ h (d) Jly 6 Bel 4f fst :46⅗ h Jun 22 Bel 4f fst :46⅗ h

Into The Current Dk. b. or br. c. 3, by Little Current—Turbinia, by Hail To Reason
Own.—Darby Dan Farm Br.—Galbreath J W (Ky) Tr.—Ronindello Thomas L
112 Lifetime 8 1 1 1 $17,940 | 1983 8 1 1 1 $17,940 | 1982 0 M 0 0 | Turf 3 1 0 0 $11,400

15Jly83-	8Bel	hd	1⅜	[T]:11	2:01	2:14	3↑ Alw 21000	1	6	7^{14}	7^{8}	6^{7}	7^{5¾}	Velasquez J	b	112	4.40	81-15	New Discovery 117^{hd} Native Raid 112^{nk} TampaTown113^{3¾}	Outrun	9
3Jly83-	7Bel	fm	1$\frac{1}{16}$	Ⓣ:46⅕	1:10⅖	1:42⅖	3↑ Alw 21000	9	10	10^{6¾}	10^{4½}	8^{6½}	6^{4¾}	Velasquez J	b	113	7.60e	79-15	JeffersWest117^{hd}Chica'sPrince111^{hd}Hypertee113^{nk}	Mild response	12
15Jun83-	2Bel	fm	1$\frac{1}{16}$	Ⓣ:46⅘	1:10⅘	1:43⅖	3↑ Md Sp Wt	3	10	8^{6¾}	8^{5¾}	3^{3½}	1^{1¾}	Velasquez J	b	114	5.90	79-19	IntoTheCurrent114^{1¾}MassAppel122½Dr.DvidNthn114^{1¼}	Drew clear	12
23May83-	6Bel	my	1$\frac{1}{16}$	:46⅕	1:11⅖	1:44⅗	3↑ Md Sp Wt	5	6	8^{7½}	8^{5¼}	5^{4½}	2^{6}	Velasquez J	b	113	*3.00	73-16	Ennoble 113^{6} Into The Current 113^{hd}StraightTalk113^{nk}	Game try	9
9May83-	4Aqu	fst	1	:47⅗	1:12⅗	1:38⅕	3↑ Md Sp Wt	4	5	5^{2¼}	7^{5¾}	6^{11}	6^{10}	Hernandez C	b	113	4.00e	65-25	Scarlet Hobeau 115^{1¾} Crazy Moon113^{no}HailColumbus113^{7}	Outrun	7
30Apr83-	6Aqu	fst	6f	:22⅖	:45⅘	1:12⅗	Md Sp Wt	4	5	7^{6½}	6^{9}	7^{4¾}	4^{1}	Hernandez C	b	122	48.70	77-22	Entropy122^{no}RelStubborn122^{1}[D]ConchYToro122^{hd}	Wide,impeded	8
30Apr83-Placed third through disqualification																					
29Mar83-	6Hia	fst	6f	:22⅖	:46	1:10⅕	Md Sp Wt	7	8	8^{14}	8^{17}	8^{16}	8^{22}	Bailey J D		120	12.40	70-19	U. S. Flag 120^{11} Beseige 120^{1} Gamblers Image 120^{4}	Outrun	12
16Mar83-	6Hia	fst	6f	:22	:45⅖	1:11	Md Sp Wt	7	12	10^{13}	11^{20}	10^{13}	8^{12}	Hernandez C		120	13.10	76-19	Northern Best 120^{hd} Beseige 120^{2} Kings Row120^{2}	Squeezed start	12

LATEST WORKOUTS Aug 3 Sar 4f gd :50⅖ b Jly 28 Sar 5f fst 1:02 b Jly 22 Bel 4f sly :54 b Jly 10 Bel 4f fst :50⅘ b

The field:

Monkey Bread—Only one-for-seventeen lifetime, Monkey Bread had won his only race on the main track. His only three turf starts were his last three races. The first one wasn't bad, a fourth by two lengths after making up a bit of ground to temporarily grab second. The other two turf tries were poor, although we note he had a poor outside post position (10) in one, and was asked to go one and three-eighths miles, probably too long for him, in the other.

Chica's Prince—After breaking his maiden on the main track, Chica's Prince's next six starts were on grass with a win, a second by a head, a fourth and three dreadful lines including the last when he was overmatched in stakes company, finishing ninth by fourteen lengths in the 1¼ mile Lexington.

Movable Feast—Showed sharp improvement—and was bet as if it was expected—in his second lifetime start in 1982 when he won by three and a quarter lengths on grass after an eighth place finish on dirt. He had one more start as a 2-year-old, finishing fifth by two and a half lengths at one and an eighth miles on grass. In his first start in 1983, he drew the outside No. 12 post in a one mile grass allowance, raced wide, yet still got second, four and three-quarters lengths behind Kilauea, whom we note came back to win the Lexington beating

Chica's Prince by fourteen lengths. Movable Feast's last race was a fourth by seven lengths on a sloppy track at Belmont. We'll discard this mediocre performance because it was on dirt. Since that race, Movable Feast worked well at Saratoga, three furlongs in :35 2/5.

Tanyosho—One-of-eleven lifetime and has never been on turf. The son of Minstrel, a son of Northern Dancer, is bred for grass, but not on his dam side. Pass.

Tampa Town—One-of-ten lifetime on dirt before his last two races on grass, a seventh by five and a half lengths at one and one-sixteenth miles (Chica's Prince was second by a head in the same race) and an improved third by a neck in a longer turf race at one and three-eighths miles. He seems to want more distance.

The Ghost—Also showed sharp improvement when switched to grass for the third of his five lifetime races. He won his maiden on grass by one and a half lengths, then led and finished fourth by a half of a length, beaten by Chica's Prince, and tired badly in his last start, finishing fourth by eleven lengths with an excuse: the *Form*'s comment was "swerved."

Val De La Meuse—One-of-seven on dirt before his turf debut in his last race when he finished second by three and three-quarters lengths, beating The Ghost by seven and a quarter lengths. Val De La Meuse must be considered.

Outpost—He broke his maiden on the turf at Saratoga in 1982, but in three 1983 starts—each on turf—was fourth, fifth and eleventh, beaten soundly by Chica's Prince and Movable Feast in separate races.

Special Notice—One-of-twelve lifetime on turf and was third, beaten by a quarter of a length by Movable Feast three starts back, while giving him eight pounds. Today he gives him five.

Into The Current—He won his turf debut then was sixth and seventh in two grass allowance races, losing to Chica's Prince and Tampa Town in different races.

Conclusion? Four of the ten in here would seem to have little chance, leaving Monkey Bread, Movable Feast, Chica's Prince, The Ghost, Val De La Meuse and Special Notice.

Of the six, Movable Feast and Val De La Meuse have shown the best turf form. Both are 3-year-olds facing two 4-year-olds, but we don't handicap those horses, Outpost and Special Notice, as prime contenders; Outpost because of his three consecutive poor races and Special Notice because of his difficult post position, No. 9, on the inner turf course. Special Notice has shown speed on grass, but so has The Ghost.

The Ghost's narrow loss to Chica's Prince would tend to equate their abilities. The other contenders have more to offer.

Monkey Bread was beaten by seven and three-quarters lengths in his last race on the turf by Tampa Town, and must be eliminated. We had already discarded Tampa Town because he seems to need more distance.

We've now handicapped the race down to two horses, Movable Feast and Val De La Meuse. The latter has a worse post, but has a slightly better jockey in Jean-Luc Samyn. Jerry Bailey, capable but not as good as Samyn on the green, will ride Movable Feast. Val De La Meuse goes off the 5 to 2 favorite; Movable Feast as the 7 to 2 second choice. The better post, good work for the race, and a better price persuades us to bet Movable Feast. He wins by one and three-quarters lengths and pays $9.60. Monkey Bread runs second at 42 to 1 and teams with Movable Feast for an exacta worth $526.60. Into The Current finished third, three-quarters of a length behind Monkey Bread and a head in front of Val De La Meuse.

SEVENTH RACE
Saratoga
AUGUST 5, 1983

1 1/16 MILES. (INNER TURF) (1.41) ALLOWANCE. Purse $21,000. 3-year-olds and up which have never won a race other than Maiden, Claiming or Starter. Weights: 3-year-olds, 117 lbs.; older, 122 lbs.; non-winners of a race other than claiming at a mile or over since July 15 allowed 3 lbs.; of such a race since July 1, 5 lbs.

Value of race $21,000, value to winner $12,600, second $4,620, third $2,520, fourth $1,260. Mutuel pool $144,076, OTB pool $197,611. Track Exacta Pool $172,894. OTB Exacta Pool $281,082.

Last Raced	Horse	Eqt. A. Wt. PP St	1/4	1/2	3/4	Str	Fin	Jockey	r	Odds $1
24Jly83 9Bel 4	Movable Feast	3 112 3 2	5-1½	5-1	6-1	1 ½	1-1¾	Bailey J D		3.80
15Jly83 8Bel 9	Monkey Bread	3 112 1 1	7-1½	7-1½	7-2	6-1	2 ¾	Smith A Jr		42.60
15Jly83 8Bel 7	Into The Current	3 112 10 10	10	9-2	8 ½	5hd	3hd	Cruguet J		18.30
17Jly83 6Bel 2	Val De La Meuse	b 3 112 7 7	6-2	6-1	5-1½	4hd	4-1¾	Samyn J L		2.70
15Jly83 8Bel 3	Tampa Town	3 112 5 6	3hd	3hd	4-1	3-1½	5 ¾	MacBeth D		5.60
24Jly83 9Bel 2	Special Notice	4 117 9 3	1-1	1-1	1-1	2 ½	6hd	Vergara O		14.20
13Jly83 8Bel 9	Chica's Prince	b 3 112 2 8	8-1½	8hd	9-3	7-2	7-7	Fell J		7.30
3Jly83 7Bel11	Outpost	4 117 8 4	2-3	2-1	2 ½	8-1	8 ½	Cordero A Jr		6.80
17Jly83 6Bel 4	The Ghost	3 112 6 5	4-5	4-6	3hd	9-2½	9 ½	Velasquez J		5.20
7Jly83 7Bel10	Tanyosho	b 3 112 4 9	9hd	10	10	10	10	Lovato F Jr		25.20

OFF AT 4:39. Start good, Won driving. Time, :23 3/5, :47 3/5, 1:12 2/5, 1:37 2/5, 1:43 4/5 Course firm.

Veteran handicappers will tell you there is no substitute for watching the races live, getting to see the race as opposed to forming your opinions from only reading the *Form*. If your handicapping is on the mark in one race, as this was, you frequently may deduce other subsequent winners. In other words, one winner can lead to many winners. This race was one of them.

While Movable Feast was a convincing winner, it was worth noting the performances of two other horses in the race, each of whom came back to win a subsequent grass race at Saratoga at a lucrative mutuel.

One of the final horses discounted in our handicapping was Monkey Bread. Remember Monkey Bread's first race on turf? It wasn't bad at all, a fourth by two lengths. In his next two races, he had a poor post and then tried a longer distance. But in this race against Movable Feast, he raced extremely well, going from sixth by two and a half at the head of the stretch to finish second by one and three-quarters. He did this while racing wide, wide enough for the chart in the *Form* to comment "very wide." And he was 42 to 1 for Alfredo Smith, Jr., a competent jockey but certainly not in the upper echelon of the talent rich Saratoga riding colony.

After this improved turf performance, trainer Luke Hawkins entered him in an easier spot, a $60,000-$65,000 claiming race for 3-year-olds only, August 21, at Saratoga. The comment from his race against Movable Feast was "rallied" in the *Form*, but we know the move was more impressive since he rallied wide, a distinct disadvantage on a turf course, let alone the inner turf course he raced on.

Since that race, Monkey Bread worked twice at Belmont, a bullet six furlongs on a sloppy track in 1:14 3/5 and a breeze on a muddy track, three furlongs in :38 1/5. It's always a positive sign if a horse follows a good race with a good work. Monkey Bread did.

In this start at Saratoga, Monkey Bread would have several things going for him: 1) easier competition; 2) racing on the main turf course which would penalize him less if he rallied wide again, and 3) by far the most important, a jockey switch to Samyn.

There were other horses in the race who had credentials, including Chaudiere, who had beaten Monkey Bread by two lengths in the latter's turf debut at Belmont. But Monkey Bread seemed ready to put in a strong race, especially with the services of Samyn.

The price would be nowhere near 40 to 1, yet at 9 to 2 Monkey Bread had as much right to win this race as any of the other seven horses entered. Monkey Bread did win, paying $11.

Remember our evaluation of Tampa Town? He had two previous turf races before the one against Movable Feast, having finished a dull seventh at 1 1/16 miles then a much better third by a neck at 1 3/8 miles. Against Movable Feast at 1 1/16 miles, Tampa Town was third early, third by a length at the top of the stretch, and fifth by four and a quarter lengths at odds of 5 to 1. Our opinion of Tampa Town was he needed more distance on grass as shown by the discrepancy of performance at the two different distances. If that was true—and his okay if unspectacular effort against Movable Feast at a shorter distance won't dispute that—he would be more effective in a longer turf race.

Ten days later at Saratoga, Tampa Town was entered in a similar level allowance race at 1 1/2 miles on the inner turf course. At a greater distance, he seemed an overlay when let off at 4 to 1.

FIRST RACE		1 1/2 MILES. (INNER TURF) (2.28 2/5) ALLOWANCE. Purse $21,000. 3-year-olds and upward which have never

FIRST RACE
Saratoga
AUGUST 15, 1983

1 1/2 MILES. (INNER TURF) (2.28 2/5) ALLOWANCE. Purse $21,000. 3-year-olds and upward which have never won a race other than Maiden, Claiming or Starter. Weights, 3-year-olds, 117 lbs. Older, 122 lbs. Non-winners of a race other than claiming over a mile and a furlong since July 15 allowed 3 lbs. Of such a race since July 1, 5 lbs. (18th Day. WEATHER CLEAR. TEMPERATURE 76 DEGREES.)

Value of race $21,000, value to winner $12,600, second $4,620, third $2,520, fourth $1,260.   Mutuel pool $96,524, OTB pool $178,599

Last Raced	Horse	Eqt. A. Wt. PP	1/4	1/2	1	1 1/4	Str	Fin	Jockey	r	Odds $1
5Aug83 7Sar 5	Tampa Town	3 112 5	4-7	4-3	4-1	2-1	1hd	1-2½	MacBeth D		4.20
15July83 8Bel 6	Benefit Performer	4 112 3	7	6-1½	5-2	5 ½	3hd	2nk	Murphy D J-5		1.30
1Aug83 1Sar 4	Could It Be	4 119 2	1-5	1-5	1-2	1 ½	2-2½	3-1½	McCarron G		6.80
1Aug83 1Sar 3	Imperial Realm	b 3 114 4	6-1½	7	6 ½	6-1½	4hd	4-1½	Velasquez J		8.00
23July83 4Atl 5	Bannow Rambler	b 3 112 6	3-1½	2hd	2 ½	3-2	5-3	5-1½	Rogers K L		29.40
23July83 7Mol 8	Upper Court	3 112 7	5 ½	5hd	7	7	7	6no	Cordero A Jr		7.00
1Aug83 1Sar 2	Treacle Tom	3 112 1	2hd	3-4	3-2½	4 ½	6hd	7	Smith A Jr		3.90

OFF AT 1:30 Start good, Won driving. Time, :25 2/5, :49 3/5, 1:14 3/5, 1:39 4/5, 2:05 2/5, 2:32, Course firm.

$ 2 Mutuel Prices:	5-	TAMPA TOWN	10.40	4.40	3.20
	3-	BENEFIT PERFORMER		3.40	2.60
	2-	COULD IT BE			3.80

Ch. c, by Nodouble-Sociable Angel, by Social Climber. Trainer Pascuma Warren J. Bred by Fuentes & Hayman Alice (Fla).

TAMPA TOWN, reserved for a mile, made a run from the outside approaching the stretch and proved clearly best under brisk urging. BENEFIT PERFORMER rallied leaving the far turn and wore down COULD IT BE for the place without menacing the winner. COULD IT BE rated along on the lead while saving ground, remained prominent to midstretch and weakened. IMPERIAL REALM rallied approaching the final furlong but lacked a further response. BANNOW RAMBLER went after COULD IT BE nearing the final turn, remained a factor to the stretch and gave way. UPPER COURT was always outrun. TREACLE TOM rallied approaching the end of the backstretch the final time but was finished nearing the stretch.

As the chart shows, we were correct as Tampa Town won easily by two and a half lengths, returning $10.40.

Thus from correctly handicapping one race, we can identify other winners. These opportunities do repeat themselves. So when you're right in a race, take note of all the horses you were right about. It could lead to other winners.

If there is a single lesson to be remembered from this chapter, it is that the form of a horse on dirt and turf are many times separate. Sometimes, the two have so little in common it's almost as if you were handicapping two different horses.

A case in point: on May 7, 1983, a 6-year-old gelding named Campus Capers was entered in a one mile turf allowance at Belmont. He had been claimed two starts earlier, when he ran second by a nose, by the very capable trainer, Sue Sedlacek. In two starts for his new connections, Campus Capers ran nearly identical races, fifth place finishes by nine and a half and nine and three-quarters lengths. Those performances, however, were on the main track, as were the only lines Campus Capers showed in the *Form* that day. Campus Capers was, though, a proven winner on turf with a lifetime record of 8-3-1-3, seven of eight races in the money on grass. Campus Capers' two previous dull races meant nothing in the context of his ability to perform this day on grass. Sedlacek, one of the leading trainers at Aqueduct (she's the wife of Woody and the mother of Mike, both trainers), had to be figured to at least keep Campus Capers at his previous ability. More likely, she'd improve it. That ability was on grass. Campus Capers went off at a whopping overlay of 9 to 1 and won by a one and a half lengths. He was again an overlay when he made his next start in an allowance race on grass at Belmont, finishing second by a head at 6 to 1 against multi-stakes winner Open Call. Then, everybody remembered Campus Capers' ability on turf. He was third and first his next two starts on turf at odds of 8 to 5 and 6 to 5. Odds of 9 to 1 were a gift.

Our last turf sample came in the fifth race at Belmont Park, July 23, 1989. A field of ten went to post in the $1^{1}/_{4}$ mile allowance for non-winners of three races.

Fast 'N' Gold had one turf race, winning a $1^{1}/_{4}$ mile allowance at Belmont Park, June 11. That was in a race for New York-breds, and it was over a soft course. Handicappers can interpret that win two ways: 1) it was in a softer field over a soft course, therefore, it's not an indication Fast 'N' Gold can win again; or, 2) there's no reason he can't repeat because he won his lone try at the same distance at the same track. While we'll excuse a poor performance on a soft course, there's no reason to dismiss an impressive one, if that's the only PP on turf.

In his eight other PPs, Fast 'N' Gold didn't show a bad line, getting a check, by finishing in the top four, each time. Including the turf race, he was 2-3-1 in nine PPs, finishing fourth in the other three.

At 2 to 1 or 5 to 2, Fast 'N' Gold wouldn't be much of an overlay. At post time, however, he was 4 to 1. He romped by five and a quarter, paying $10.80 to win.

FIFTH RACE
Belmont
JULY 23, 1989

1¼ MILES.(InnerTurf). (1.58⅘) ALLOWANCE. Purse $31,000. 3-year-olds and upward which have never won two races other than Maiden, Claiming or Starter. Weights: 3-year-olds, 116 lbs.; older, 122 lbs. Non-winners of a race other than maiden or claiming over a mile since July 1 allowed 3 lbs.; of such a race since June 15, 5 lbs.

Value of race $31,000; value to winner $18,600; second $6,820; third $3,720; fourth $1,860. Mutuel pool $274,781. Exacta Pool $563,994.

Last Raced	Horse	Eqt.	A.Wt	PP	¼	½	¾	1	Str	Fin	Jockey	Odds $1
7Jly89 ⁵Bel²	Fast 'N' Gold		3 111	6	4^{3}	3^{1}	3^{2}	$1^{1\frac{1}{2}}$	1^{6}	$1^{5\frac{1}{4}}$	Samyn J L	4.40
28Jun89 ⁸Mth¹	Queen's Rook	b	4 119	1	7^{2}	7^{2}	7^{hd}	6^{1}	3^{3}	$2^{\frac{1}{2}}$	Santos J A	7.00
23Jun89 ⁸Bel²	Pacific Spy	b	5 117	5	9	$8^{\frac{1}{2}}$	8^{4}	4^{2}	$2^{\frac{1}{2}}$	$3^{5\frac{1}{2}}$	Cordero A Jr	3.10
30Jun89 ⁸Bel⁵	Elite Regent		4 117	2	10	10	9^{1}	$8^{1\frac{1}{2}}$	$6^{1\frac{1}{2}}$	4^{2}	Bailey J D	5.60
29Jun89 ⁴Bel¹	John's Concorde		4 117	3	3	4^{3}	$4^{\frac{1}{2}}$	$5^{\frac{1}{2}}$	4^{hd}	$5^{\frac{1}{2}}$	Maple E	14.90
14Jly89 ⁸Pha²	Northern Chateau		3 106	8	5^{1}	$6^{2\frac{1}{2}}$	$6^{\frac{1}{2}}$	$7^{\frac{1}{2}}$	8^{2}	6^{hd}	Carle J D⁵	20.90
4Jly89 ⁵Bel³	Soupcon		3 112	4	$8^{2\frac{1}{2}}$	9^{2}	10	9^{16}	7^{hd}	7^{3}	Romero R P	14.20
12Jun89 ⁴Bel²	Drums in the Night		4 117	7	1	$1^{1\frac{1}{2}}$	$1^{1\frac{1}{2}}$	2^{5}	$5^{\frac{1}{2}}$	8^{hd}	Migliore R	8.30
23Jun89 ⁸Bel¹¹	Tizo		4 117	10	6^{3}	$5^{1\frac{1}{2}}$	5^{2}	$3^{\frac{1}{2}}$	9	9	Perret C	14.60
30Jun89 ⁸Bel⁹	Brahma		5 117	9	2^{6}	2^{7}	2^{5}	10	—	—	Vasquez J	5.20

Brahma, Eased.

OFF AT 3:10. Start good, Won driving. Time, :23⅖, :47, 1:12⅕, 1:37⅗, 2:02⅘ Course firm.

$2 Mutuel Prices:				
	6-(F)-FAST 'N' GOLD	10.80	5.80	3.40
	1-(A)-QUEEN'S ROOK		7.00	5.00
	5-(E)-PACIFIC SPY			2.60

$2 EXACTA 6-1 PAID $67.80.

B. c, by Fast Gold—Maid for All, by One For All. Trainer Baillie Sally A. Bred by Baillie Sally A (NY).

FAST 'N' GOLD moved fast to catch DRUMS INTHE NIGHT approaching the stretch, drew off quickly while racing well out in the course and held sway under strong handling. QUEEN'S ROOK angled out leaving the far turn and continued on gamely to gain the place. PACIFIC SPY split horses while moving nearing the stretch but lacked kthe needed late response. ELITE REGENT passed tired horses. JOHN'S CONCORDE saved ground to no avail. DRUMS IN THE NIGHT was used up making the pace. TIZO rallied from between horses approaching the stretch but had nothing left. BRAHMA stopped suddenly after prompting the pace to the far turn and was eased late.

Inside with P.G. Johnson

CHAPTER 14 Trainer Phil G. Johnson has won more than $20 million in purses and has been the leading trainer at eight NYRA meets including Saratoga in 1983. He's twice ranked in the top twelve in the national trainer standings in the 1980s and is arguably New York's second finest trainer—after Mack Miller—in getting a horse to perform well on turf. P.G., as he's popularly known on the backstretch, is also a sweetheart of a human being, frequently helping Cerebral Palsy, Cystic Fibrosis and other charities.

His greatest training feat was winning twelve straight stakes races in which he entered a horse during a two-year period, 1978 to 1979.

A native of Chicago, Johnson, sixty-four, broke into racing by purchasing a horse named Song Master. "I got him for $75 at an auction in Chicago in 1942, and finally won a race with him at Hawthorne in the spring of 1944," Johnson said. The winning purse was $900.

Johnson trained at the Detroit Fair Grounds in the mid-1940s before returning to Chicago at Arlington Park in 1948. In 1962, he moved to New York where he's carved out an excellent career. Besides his own accomplishments, Johnson helped launch the career of another top trainer, Tom Skiffington, a former steeplechase jockey who led the nation in earnings three straight years. After working for trainer Frank Whiteley for one year, Skiffington started on his own in the winter of 1979. "I had one of Frank Whiteley's horses and one of my mother's," Skiffington said. "I was in P.G. Johnson's barn, and he was going to Florida for the winter. Every day, P.G. would bring me another horse and tell me what to do with it. I paid attention and won a lot of races that winter. I owe a lot to him, and I still go to him when I have a problem with a horse."

Johnson's list of stakes winners include Dismasted, Geraldine's Store, High Schemes, Match The Hatch, Ms. Eloise, Naskra, Naskra's Breeze, Nasty And Bold, Possible Mate, Told, and Tough Mickey. Much of Johnson's success has been on grass. His understanding of the nuances of turf racing is considerable.

"I like to run horses on turf," he said. "They last longer, and it's safer."

Miller, the only trainer to saddle three different grass champions, concurred: "I love turf racing. There is more traction. Horses have more confidence on the turf. Some horses are timid about sand in the face. It has a cutting effect or a stinging effect. They won't tolerate it."

Here, Johnson disagrees: "I don't subscribe to the theory that dirt hits them in the face, and that's why they don't like dirt. I don't think that's anywhere near the main reason. In super slow motion replays, if you watch, a horse extends on dirt so much that when his front foot hits the ground, the pastern flexes and the ankle drops and practically hits the ground. Then the feet will slide an inch or two forward before his next stride. Racing on dirt does two things: No. 1, it tends to make the horse use more energy to get the foot back in the air, so it tires him quicker or discourages him quicker, and, No. 2, if a horse has any ligament problem, the over-flexation of those joints could bring on the pain sooner that way. Now, when the horse gets on the turf, when his hoof hits, there's hardly any slide forward. Consequently, there's less flexation and less extension, so his foot gets back in action sooner. It helps the horse that loses his confidence from the first situation [No. 1]. It's like you running in the deep sand on the beach. It's a real strain. If you see a horse showing speed on the dirt and backing off for no reason, when that horse first makes his appearance on turf, I'd be very interested. He may improve a lot.

"On firm turf, horses hit the surface and they're immediately into the next stride. There's no slide. Turf is firmer and more natural for the horse to stride on, so consequently you don't have to have them wound up as tightly. The horse really doesn't have to be as fit. You might go an eighth of a mile further on the turf with a horse. Say his limitation is a mile on the dirt. He may need a race to get up to the mile. That same horse off a layoff, if he has established turf form, can probably go a mile and an eighth on firm turf without the need of a race, just off average training because turf races don't take so much out of him."

Johnson traditionally preps horses for their initial grass race with two sprints. "I like to sprint them," he said. "And I like to have them gallop out strongly after the sprint. Say my horse ran his last eighth in thirteen seconds. I'd like him to gallop out another quarter in twenty-eight seconds. I do that the second time he's in a sprint. Now the horse has had the equivalent of a mile work. When he goes on turf at a mile, a mile and a sixteenth or a mile and an eighth, he probably won't need a race at the distance to be ready. He just needs to handle the turf and be in a class he's competitive in."

Johnson thinks it's best to ignore a horse's first grass race if it was over a soft or yielding course: "I've seen some very good horses run horrible on the turf when it was soft and it was their first time on grass. They'll disappear on the turf, go back on dirt and continue their careers. Then, at some moment in time, either with that trainer or another trainer, they'll try turf when it's firm and turn out to be a very good turf horse. So I would throw out the first one on turf if it was soft and definitely stay with him."

On a sunny, unseasonably warm Saturday morning—Oct. 28, 1989—Johnson shared his handicapping opinions of a solid group of grass horses contesting a $50,000, $1^1/_{16}$ mile handicap at Aqueduct.

Scratches of Sea Symphony and Slew The Knight left a field of nine. The horses are discussed in post position order.

Johnson's thoughts:

Fourstardave—"He comes out of a Laurel sprint only beaten five lengths by a good English horse, Cricket Ball. He has enough speed to be close up. He was beaten one and a half lengths in his race against I Rejoice giving two pounds. Now he gets two. In New York-bred races, he's shown speed. He's an honest horse. He gets a piece of the purse all the time. Have to leave him in."

Soviet Lad—"I thought he was going to be real good here, but he's been disappointing. He was a speedy horse in France. He's coming out of the same race as Fourstardave. He's not generous. He's not consistent. That's a danger sign. How can he be second to Steinlen, only a half-length off him at the top of the stretch and then lose to weaker horses? I don't think he has a preference in tracks. I would take Fourstardave over this horse. His last two races, he's been in a position to win and hasn't gotten the job done. I don't like this horse."

7 **AQUEDUCT** TURF COURSE 1 1/16 MILES AQUEDUCT START FINISH

1 1/16 MILES. (Turf). (1.41) HANDICAP. Purse $50,000. 3-year-olds and upward. Weights Wednesday, October 25. Nominations close Wednesday, October 25, 1989. Declarations by 10:00 A.M. Thursday, October 26. Closed with 32 nominations.

Fourstardave — Ch. g. 4, by Compliance—Broadway Joan, by Bold Arian

Own.—Bomze R — Br.—Bomze Richard M (NY) — Tr.—O'Brien Leo — **120**

Lifetime 34 8 9 8 $828,310 — 1989 12 3 3 2 $234,425 — 1988 13 2 1 6 $377,139 — Turf 12 3 3 1 $249,436

22Oct89- 6Lrl sf 6f Ⓣ:23 :47⅗ 1:14 3↑Laurel Dash 12 1 97¾ 1014 118¾ 95 Cordero A Jr 122 7.90 67-28 Cricket Ball 120¾ Oraibi 1221 Point Of Light 120hd Outrun 14

7Oct89- 7Bel gd 1 Ⓣ:47 1:11⅗ 1:36⅖ 3↑Kelso H 8 6 63 63 62¾ 71½ Migliore R 116 5.10 81-18 I Rejoice 114hd Quick Call 113hd Wanderkin 118hd Lacked a rally 9

7Oct89-Grade III

27Sep89- 8Bel fst 7f :22⅕ :45⅕ 1:22⅖ 3↑Ⓢ Hudson H 3 6 76½ 75½ 99¼ 910½ Migliore R 124 3.60e 79-10 Scottish Monk 120no Banquo 110½ Crafty North 116no No excuse 11

23Aug89- 8Sar fm 1⅛ Ⓣ:47 1:10⅖ 1:46 3↑Ⓢ West Point H 2 1 11½ 11½ 14 11 Migliore R 121 2.10 97-15 Fourstardve1211Kte'sVlentine1091G'DyMte1151¾ Drifted out,drvg 9

13Aug89- 8Sar sf 1⅛ Ⓣ:50⅕ 1:14 1:51 3↑B Baruch H 4 2 21½ 21 31 47¾ Migliore R 117 10.90 64-28 Steinlen 1215 Soviet Lad 111¾ Brian's Time 1122 Gave way 8

13Aug89-Grade I

2Aug89- 7Sar fm 1 1/16 Ⓣ:48 1:11⅗ 1:41⅗ 3↑Daryls Joy 7 3 22½ 2hd 21 2½ Santos J A 122 *1.10 88-08 Highland Springs 122½ Fourstardave1221¼SovietLad115no Gamely 7

2Aug89-Grade III; Run in two divisions

4Jly89- 7Bel fm 1 Ⓣ:46⅕ 1:09⅗ 1:33⅕ 3↑Poker 1 2 11 1hd 13 12¼ Santos J A 117 3.30 99-13 Fourstardave 1172¼ Feeling Gallant 1171¾ Valid Fund117¾ Driving 9

4Jly89-Grade III

21Jun89- 8Bel gd 1 Ⓣ:45⅖ 1:10⅕ 1:35⅖ 3↑Handicap 2 4 34 2hd 12 12¾ Santos J A 115 4.60 88-18 Fourstardave 1152¾ Closing Bid 112½ War 1121½ Driving 10

7Jun89- 8Bel sf 7f Ⓣ:23⅘ :48 1:27 3↑Jaipur 8 1 41½ 32 22 21¾ Santos J A 119 3.20 67-31 Harp Islet 1171¾ Fourstardave 1192¼ Down Again 1143¼ Gamely 10

7Jun89-Grade III

17May89- 8Bel my 1 1/16 :45⅗ 1:10 1:41⅕ 3↑Handicap 3 2 2½ 2hd 31½ 38½ Antley C W 115 2.30 87-15 Lay Down 1145 Hill Slide 1133½ Fourstardave 1156½ Weakened 5

Speed Index: Last Race: -1.0 3-Race Avg.: +1.0 6-Race Avg.: +2.8 Overall Avg.: +0.1

LATEST WORKOUTS Sep 22 Bel 5f sly 1:01⅖ B ●Sep 14 Bel 6f fst 1:11 H ●Sep 7 Bel Ⓣ 6f fm 1:13⅖ H (d) Sep 2 Bel 4f fst :52 B

Soviet Lad — B. g. 4, by Nureyev—Green Valley II, by Val de Loir

Own.—La Presle Farm — Br.—Wertheimer J (Ky) — Tr.—Stephens Woodford C — **115**

Lifetime 15 3 3 3 $122,063 — 1989 7 1 1 2 $74,818 — 1988 6 1 1 1 $30,413 — Turf 14 3 3 3 $122,063

7Oct89- 7Bel gd 1 Ⓣ:47 1:11⅗ 1:36⅖ 3↑Kelso H 7 7 85 73¼ 41¾ 4nk Maple E 111 13.30 83-18 I Rejoice 114hd Quick Call 113hd Wanderkin 118hd Fin. well 9

7Oct89-Grade III

30Sep89- 9Med yl 1 1/16 Ⓣ:47 1:11⅕ 1:42⅕ 3↑Cliff Hng H 6 5 45 42 31½ 32 Maple E 112 5.10 89-14 Ten Keys 114¾ Wanderkin 1211¼ Soviet Lad 1125 Rallied 7

30Sep89-Grade III

18Sep89- 7Bel gd 1 1/16 :46 1:10⅘ 1:43 3↑Alw 50000 8 4 77 74½ 67¾ 710 Maple E 122 8.60 77-22 Gremm1133TheMdDoctor1151¼Bldski'sStr1152 Lacked a response 10

26Aug89- 7Sar fm 1 1/16 Ⓣ:45⅕ 1:09⅕ 1:39⅕ 3↑Bd Brd Cp H 6 3 33 42½ 63¾ 56½ Maple E 111 6.60 94-10 Highland Springs 117nk Maceo 1131¼ Slew City Slew 118hd Tired 6

26Aug89-Grade III

13Aug89- 8Sar sf 1⅛ Ⓣ:50⅕ 1:14 1:51 3↑B Baruch H 1 1 11½ 11 2½ 25 Maple E 111 11.30 67-28 Steinlen 1215 Soviet Lad 111¾ Brian's Time 1122 No match 8

13Aug89-Grade I

2Aug89- 7Sar fm 1 1/16 Ⓣ:48 1:11⅗ 1:41⅗ 3↑Daryls Joy 2 1 12½ 3nk 42½ 31¾ Maple E 115 1.80 87-08 HighlndSprings122½Fourstrdv1221¼SovitLd115no Tried to get out 7

2Aug89-Grade III; Run in two divisions

9Jly89- 7Bel fm 1 1/16 Ⓣ:47⅘ 1:11⅗ 1:41⅖ 3↑Alw 33000 4 1 11 11 13½ 13¼ Maple E 117 1.90 94-11 Soviet Lad 1173¼ Hodges Bay 117no DonMarioII1171¾ Ridden out 7

9Oct88♦5Longchamp(Fra) yl*1¼ 2:12⅗ Ⓣ Prix de Ranelagh 44 Guignard G 128 9.50 — — Nediym 119½ Robore 1191½ Fantastic Bird 1232 Prom, led 8

29Jly88♦5Evry(Fra) gd*1⅛ 1:51⅖ Ⓣ Prix Daphnis(Gr3) 52¾ Moore G W 126 4.00 — — Bricassar1201 Gerrnas120½ DrapeuTricolore120nk Set pace, wknd 7

23Jun88♦6Longchamp(Fra) gd*1 1:42 Ⓣ Prix de Pontarme 12 Moore G W 123 *1.30 — — Soviet Lad 1232 Academic 123¾ NiceAndLucky123no Led thruout 7

Speed Index: Last Race: +1.0 3-Race Avg.: +2.6 6-Race Avg.: +0.5 Overall Avg.: +0.2

LATEST WORKOUTS Oct 23 Bel 5f fst 1:02⅕ B Oct 15 Bel 4f fst :50 B ●Oct 6 Bel 3f fst :34⅘ H Sep 28 Bel 4f fst :48 H

I Rejoice—"He's an interesting horse. All he does is go out and battle every race. He got beat a nose by Wanderkin, who's a real nice horse, then beat him by a head. Now he's up to 122 pounds [from 114 in his last race]. I think it's a big jump. My conclusion is you definitely use him in exotics because he'll fight his way and get up."

Impersonator—"His wins aren't that exciting. He can be placed better. Last time, he raced against Easy Goer on dirt. He's not in this league here. I think he's overmatched."

I Rejoice *

B. g. 6, by Lord Gaylord—Imaglee, by Grey Dawn II
Br.—Isaacs Harry Z (Ky)
Own.—Brookfield Farms
Tr.—Kelly Edward I
122
Lifetime 30 12 6 4 $425,296 | 1989 4 3 1 0 $138,500 | 1988 8 2 1 2 $73,700 | Turf 15 9 2 1 $299,980

7Oct89- 7Bel gd 1 ⓣ:47 1:11⅗ 1:36⅖ 3↑Kelso H 3 4 3¹ 4¹ 2hd 1hd Bailey J D 114 4.10 83-18 I Rejoice 114hd Quick Call 113hd Wanderkin 118hd Driving 9
7Oct89-Grade III
28Aug89- 7Sar hd 1 3/16 ⓣ:49 1:13 1:54 3↑Handicap 3 1 2½ 1hd 11½ 12¼ Bailey J D 113 2.40 96-09 I Rejoice 1132¼ My Big Boy 1161½ Bally Blue 1124½ Driving 5
19Aug89- 5Sar fm 1 1/16 ⓣ:46⅘ 1:10⅖ 1:40⅖ 3↑Handicap 3 3 31½ 1hd 2hd 2no Samyn J L 113 *1.80 95-08 Wanderkin 122no IRejoice1132TurningForHome114nk Just missed 8
26Jly89- 8Bel fm 7f ⓣ:22⅘ :46 1:21⅖ 3↑Alw 41000 1 5 53¼ 3½ 1hd 1nk Samyn J L 115 *.50 97-13 I Rejoice 115nk Quick Call 11710 Marabeau Special 1093 Driving 6
8Nov88- 1Aqu fst 1 :45⅘ 1:10⅖ 1:36⅕ 3↑Alw 47000 5 3 3³ 5⁴ 57½ 510 Fox W I Jr 122 2.10 75-25 Scottish Monk 1152ForeverSilver113hdPurpleMountain1157 Tired 5
27Oct88- 8Aqu fm 1⅛ ⓣ:48⅖ 1:13⅕ 1:52 3↑Handicap 1 4 42¼ 41¾ 3nk 12¼ Fox W I Jr 112 6.00 75-29 IRejoice1122¼ArrivedOnTime1111CatchTheMoon110nk Drew clear 9
12Oct88- 8Bel gd 1 1/16 [T]:48⅘ 1:13 1:44⅖ 3↑Alw 47000 6 2 3¹ 31½ 5⁴ 64¾ Romero R P 115 *.80 74-25 OleAtocha112nkChristianHundred115½LordOfTheNight115nk Tired 7
18Sep88- 3Bel gd 1 1/16 [T]:49⅕ 1:13⅕ 1:43⅗ 3↑Handicap 3 2 1½ 1¹ 1hd 31½ Romero R P 113 *1.50 81-30 Wanderkin 1221¼ Yucca 114nk I Rejoice 1135 Weakened 8
9Sep88- 7Bel fm 7f ⓣ:23 :46 1:23 3↑Alw 41000 4 7 4⁴ 2½ 12½ 18¾ Romero R P 115 *.90 89-16 IRejoice1158¾DanceCrdFilled115nkExplosiveDncer115nk Drew off 12
23Jly88- 3Bel gd 7f :22⅘ :45⅗ 1:23 3↑Alw 41000 2 5 52¾ 4² 32½ 33¼ Venezia M 115 3.30 84-24 Uncle Ho 115hd Forest Fair 1153¼ I Rejoice 1151¾ Evenly 6
Speed Index: Last Race: +1.0 3-Race Avg.: +3.0 6-Race Avg.: +3.8 Overall Avg.: +4.6
LATEST WORKOUTS Oct 26 Bel [T] 4f gd :49 B (d) Oct 17 Bel [T] 3f fm :37 B Oct 6 Bel [T] 3f fm :37 B ●Sep 29 Bel 7f fst 1:25⅕ H

Impersonator

B. g. 4, by Sham—Totie Fields, by Ridan
Br.—Kellman Joseph (Ky)
Own.—Plaza Gold Stable
Tr.—Quick Patrick J
113
Lifetime 32 6 1 2 $138,247 | 1989 16 4 0 1 $95,340 | 1988 16 2 1 1 $42,907 | Turf 11 3 1 1 $75,037

7Oct89- 8Bel fst 1½ :48⅗ 2:05 2:29⅕ 3↑J C Gold Cp 2 1 1⁵ 728 — — Migliore R b 126 48.90 — — Easy Goer 1214 Cryptoclearance 12619½ Forever Silver126¾ Eased 7
7Oct89-Grade I
30Sep89- 6Bel gd 1¼ [T]:50⅘ 1:40⅕ 2:04⅘ 3↑Handicap 1 2 2¹ 1⁴ 1² 1nk Samyn J L b 112 5.10 70-27 Impersonator 112nk Crystal Moment 1142¾BallyBlue1112½ Driving 7
14Sep89- 8Bel sly 1⅜ :49⅕ 1:38⅖ 2:17⅕ 3↑Handicap 1 1 1² 1hd 12½ 1⁶ Krone J A b 109 5.50 94-16 Impersonator 1096 Bally Blue 11410 Waki River 1153 Driving 4
27Aug89- 9Sar hd 1⅜ [T]:48⅗ 1:38 2:15 3↑Clm 35000 1 2 2² 2½ 1½ 12¼ Migliore R b 117 3.80 93-10 Impersonator1172¼Dr.Evans117½OnBorrowedTime117¾ Drew clear 9
9Aug89- 2Sar fm 1⅝ ⓣ:50⅖ 1:41 2:42 3↑Clm 35000 8 4 2² 42½ 53½ 43¾ Migliore R b 117 12.90 71-10 Uncompromise 1172 High Policy1171¾SmartSaint117no Weakened 10
27Jly89- 4Bel fst 1 1/16 :47⅕ 1:12⅘ 1:45⅖ Clm c-25000 2 2 1hd 2½ 4⁶ 413¼ Migliore R b 117 4.30 62-27 Ells Blue Ribbon 1156 SlickJack1176½GoforCommadore119¾ Tired 6
22Jly89- 3Bel fst 7f :22⅗ :45⅗ 1:23 Clm 70000 6 8 89¼ 811 824 829¾ Rodriquez E M b 113 24.40 57-23 Gold Pack 113hdScavengerHunt1133DiamondAnchor113no Trailed 8
2Jun89- 5Bel fm 1¼ [T]:48⅕ 1:37⅕ 2:01⅖ 3↑Alw 33000 3 6 53½ 77¾ 710 711 Migliore R b 117 15.80 76-11 Safety Catch 117no Storada 1171¼ American Bred 117nk Outrun 7
19May89- 2Bel fst 1 :44⅖ 1:09⅕ 1:35 Clm 75000 1 9 811 84¾ 74½ 56¾ Migliore R 117 17.10 83-16 PledgeCrd114hdSummerTle1154½StrongPrformnc115no No threat 9
26Apr89- 8Aqu fm 1 1/16 ⓣ:48⅖ 1:12 1:43 3↑Alw 33000 8 6 6⁶ 5⁴ 511 59½ Migliore R 119 6.00 80-11 Closing Bid 1197½HodgesBay119nkFluorescentLou119hd No threat 8
Speed Index: Last Race: -3.0 3-Race Avg.: -6.3 5-Race Avg.: -8.2 Overall Avg.: -7.0
LATEST WORKOUTS ●Oct 25 Bel 5f fst 1:00⅗ H

River of Sin—"He's a tough, hard-hitting horse. His best race was against Yankee Affair. He's got speed. He's got serious speed. If he gets the lead, he'll have to work for it. He'll be used hard to maintain the lead around the turn. I think I Rejoice or Impersonator will press him."

Turning For Home—"Another one in that cavalry charge won by I Rejoice. It was a mess through the stretch, but if you saw the race, the horse that got in trouble was Wanderkin. I Rejoice beat Turning For Home by eight and a quarter the race before and by two, three races back. I don't honestly think he's good enough."

River of Sin

Dk. b. or br. g. 5, by Shenadoah R.ver—Satans Sin, by Ambernash
Br.—Gilmour Doug (Fla)
Own.—Meltzer Elaine
Tr.—Serpe Philip M
121
Lifetime 40 13 5 5 $256,394 | 1989 12 4 2 2 $114,919 | 1988 13 3 1 1 $52,020 | Turf 28 11 4 3 $239,859

13Oct89- 8Med fm 1 1/16 ⓣ:48 1:11⅖ 1:41⅕ 3↑John Henry 4 1 1⁴ 1⁴ 1⁶ 14½ Migliore R 119 3.60 91-10 River of Sin 1194½StrongRebound1151½Alwasmi112hd Going away 8
30Sep89- 9Med yl 1 1/16 [T]:47 1:11⅕ 1:42⅕ 3↑Cliff Hng H 7 1 1² 1½ 41¾ 5⁹ Ferrer J C 116 4.00 82-14 Ten Keys 114¾ Wanderkin 1211¼ Soviet Lad 1125 Tired 7
30Sep89-Grade III
4Sep89-10Med fm 1 1/16 ⓣ:46 1:10 1:40⅕ 3↑Manila 3 1 1² 11½ 11½ 11½ Wilson R 117 4.50 96-09 River of Sin 1171½ Good For Sky 115no Kings RiverII1153 Driving 6
18Aug89- 7Sar fm 1 1/16 ⓣ:46⅖ 1:10⅕ 1:40⅖ 3↑Alw 47000 9 1 1¹ 1½ 2½ 54¾ Cordero A Jr 122 15.40 90-13 Scottish Monk 1151 Maceo 115½ Sovereign Justice 1151½ Tired 10
4Aug89- 7Sar fm 1 1/16 ⓣ:47 1:11⅕ 1:43⅘ 3↑Alw 47000 8 2 2hd 2hd 31½ 75½ Perret C 115 15.80 72-18 TurningForHome1171¼SovereignJustice115nkRacingStr115¾ Tired 10
23Jly89- 7Bel fm 1 1/16 [T]:48⅖ 1:12 1:42⅘ 3↑Handicap 2 1 11½ 1¹ 1¹ 3⁴ Santos J A 115 *1.40 83-18 Hittias 1112 Eagle Watch 1122 River of Sin 1151½ Weakened 7
8Jly89-10Mth gd 1 1/16 ⓣ:49⅖ 1:12⅘ 1:43⅖ 3↑Oceanport H 3 1 11½ 1½ 1hd 2⁵ Wilson R 116 2.80 83-12 Yankee Affair 1215 River of Sin 1162½ Primino 110nk 2nd best 7
8Jly89-Grade III
27Jun89- 9Mth fm 1 1/16 ⓣ:47⅕ 1:10⅗ 1:41⅖ 3↑[R]Bet Twice 7 1 11½ 12½ 1⁵ 1⁵ Wilson R 115 3.70 98-08 River of Sin 1155CopperCup113½MasterSpeaker1133¼ Going away 7
19Jun89- 8Mth gd 1 [T]:48⅕ 1:13⅖ 1:39⅖ 3↑Alw 29000 1 1 1² 1³ 1³ 1³ Wilson R 115 *2.00 77-23 River of Sin 1153 Lyphard Line 115½ Master Speaker1175 Driving 8
29May89- 8GS sf 1 1/16 ⓣ:50⅕ 1:14⅘ 1:46⅕ 3↑[R]Chapel 3 1 1² 1¹ 12½ 2nk Wilson R 116 *1.40 77-29 Roundwood116nkRiverofSin1165CrystalMoment1162½ Just missed 7
Speed Index: Last Race: +1.0 3-Race Avg.: +0.6 10-Race Avg.: +0.3 Overall Avg.: +0.3
LATEST WORKOUTS ●Sep 24 Med 3f fst :36 B Aug 29 Mth ⓣ 4f fm :50 B (d)

Turning For Home B. g. 5, by Circle Home—Barbara's Reason, by Hail to Reason
Br.—ANW Enterprises Inc & Winick (Fla)
Own.—Cedar Valle Stable Tr.—Lenzini John J Jr
116 Lifetime 70 11 14 15 $295,931 | 1989 17 3 3 2 $116,560 | 1988 19 2 2 6 $80,580 | Turf 37 7 4 9 $213,580

7Oct89- 7Bel gd 1 Ⓣ:47 1:11⅗ 1:36⅖ 3↑Kelso H 6 8 74½ 84¾ 73¾ 61 McCauley W H b 113 29.20 82-18 I Rejoice 114hd Quick Call 113hd Wanderkin 118hd Fin. well 9
7Oct89-Grade III
28Aug89- 7Sar hd 1 3/16 Ⓣ:49 1:13 1:54 3↑Handicap 2 3 43½ 43 45 48¼ McCauley W H b 113 8.60 88-09 I Rejoice 1132¼ My Big Boy 1161½ Bally Blue 1124½ Gave way 5
19Aug89- 5Sar fm 1 1/16 Ⓣ:46⅘ 1:10⅖ 1:40⅖ 3↑Handicap 5 6 54 42½ 31½ 32 Cordero A Jr b 114 6.60 93-08 Wanderkin 122no I Rejoice1132TurningForHome114nk Evenly late 8
4Aug89- 7Sar fm 1 1/16 Ⓣ:47 1:11⅕ 1:43⅘ 3↑Alw 47000 9 9 812 68 53 11¼ Antley C W b 117 18.20 78-18 TurningForHome1171¼SovereignJustic115nkRcingStr115¾ Driving 10
24Jly89- 3Bel fm 1 1/16 Ⓣ:47⅗ 1:11⅖ 1:42⅕ Clm 100000 6 4 42½ 42½ 44 54¾ Samyn J L b 122 *2.00 80-19 Sovereign Justice 1221¾ MagnetCove118nkConquilot122nk Evenly 8
1Jly89- 5Bel fm 1 1/16 [T]:48⅖ 1:11⅘ 1:42⅕ 3↑Alw 47000 1 6 42½ 41¾ 41¾ 4½ Cordero A Jr b 117 6.50 89-15 Major Beard 115hd High Browser 105no Win 122½ Altered course 7
18Jun89- 6Bel fst 1 :45⅕ 1:09⅘ 1:35⅗ 3↑Alw 37000 5 4 44½ 44½ 56¼ 49 McCauley W H b 117 9.80 78-21 Fast Play 1094¼ Cefis 1171¾ Mister Modesty 1173 Evenly 6
10Jun89- 5Bel sf 1 1/16 Ⓣ:50⅗ 1:16⅕ 1:48⅕ 3↑Handicap 1 6 62¼ 62¾ 65 47¼ Cordero A Jr b 113 *1.20e 48-43 All Hands On Deck 1062¼Whodam1144½ForestFair116½ Poor start 6
29May89- 4Bel sf 1 1/16 [T]:50 1:13⅘ 1:44 3↑Alw 37000 6 5 52 31½ 1hd 2no McCauley W H b 119 2.80 81-21 Lord Bud119noTurningForHome1191¼StrongRebound119½ Gamely 7
19May89- 8Bel fst 1 :47 1:10 1:35 3↑Handicap 2 3 43½ 33½ 54 64 Samyn J L b 112 17.50 86-16 True and Blue 119¾ Forever Silver 1222 Its Acedemic 121hd Tired 6
Speed Index: Last Race: 0.0 3–Race Avg.: –0.6 8–Race Avg.: –1.2 Overall Avg.: –0.9
LATEST WORKOUTS Oct 22 Aqu 6f fst 1:14 H ●Sep 30 Aqu 6f fst 1:12⅖ H Sep 14 Aqu 5f fst 1:00⅘ H Sep 8 Aqu 5f fst 1:02 B

Turkey Point—"He's improving. He hasn't been tested yet. In his last race, he was driving to do what he did. Next year, he may be a nice turf horse. He's a late developer."

Lay Down—"They never put him back on the turf since his January 21 race at Gulfstream. I don't really understand why. That was a good effort. He's a longshot with a chance."

Turkey Point Ch. g. 4, by Dancing Count—Short Of Change, by Royal Orbit
Br.—Bowman Thomas (Md)
Own.—MacMillen W C Jr Tr.—Watters Sidney Jr
116 Lifetime 17 4 3 3 $91,720 | 1989 11 3 1 2 $58,100 | 1988 6 1 2 1 $33,620 | Turf 5 3 1 1 $56,180

13Oct89- 7Bel fm 1 Ⓣ:46⅕ 1:10⅕ 1:35⅕ 3↑Alw 32000 3 6 66½ 43 1hd 11¼ Castillo R E 117 *1.70 89-15 Turkey Point 1171¼ Sasquash 1146 Sunrise Willie 1161 Driving 8
6Oct89- 2Bel gd 1 Ⓣ:47⅕ 1:13⅗ 1:37⅗ 3↑Clm 35000 10 8 63¼ 41½ 2hd 11 Castillo R E 119 *1.70 77-24 Turkey Point 1191 Ashumet 1171 Fearless Leader 1176 Driving 10
14Sep89- 3Bel fm 1 1/16 Ⓣ:46⅗ 1:11⅕ 1:42⅘ 3↑Clm 35000 10 4 52¼ 1½ 13 11½ Castillo R E 117 3.50 82-18 Turkey Point 1171½VienneseCross1173½[D]IfYouPlease1174 Driving 11
1Sep89- 3Bel fm 1 1/16 [T]:47⅕ 1:11 1:41⅘ 3↑Clm 45000 6 7 812 74¾ 32 3nk Fox W I Jr 113 10.70 92-10 Avatar's Note 113no InAllRespects115nkTurkeyPoint1131½ Rallied 9
17Aug89- 7Sar fst 7f :22⅘ :45⅕ 1:23⅗ 3↑Alw 27000 4 7 97¾ 811 913 711¾ Antley C W 117 11.70 72-17 Twombly 1131 Paul's Way 107hd Craftmaster 117nk Outrun 9
6Aug89- 7Sar fst 6f :22 :44⅘ 1:10 3↑Alw 27000 1 8 88½ 713 79¼ 58 Antley C W 117 8.50e 82-19 Surgeon's Care 1132½ Twombly 1123¼ Sworn In 114½ Outrun 11
27Jly89- 9Bel fst 7f :23⅘ :47⅘ 1:25⅘ 3↑Alw 27000 4 6 51¾ 52¼ 64½ 77 Carle J D5 112 4.10 66-27 Reluctant Gambler 1171 Farewell Wave 1112 Libretto 117½ Tired 10
17Jly89- 7Bel fst 6f :22⅕ :45⅗ 1:11 3↑Alw 27000 4 6 79¾ 47 24 32 Carle J D5 112 6.40 82-24 Pitino Ball 1122 Silken Saber 112hd Turkey Point 1122¾ Wide 7
22Feb89- 8Aqu sly 6f [•]:22⅘ :46⅖ 1:11⅗ Alw 23000 7 3 54½ 52¾ 21 21½ Fox W I Jr 124 14.90 84-19 Buddah Luke1171½TurkeyPoint124noOccultism1171¼ Up for place 8
22Jan89- 6Aqu fst 6f [•]:22⅕ :45⅖ 1:11⅗ Alw 23000 3 6 79 67¼ 611 67 Santagata N 117 12.40 79-21 MajorMccallum117nkSpecilRuler117nkHoldtheSuce1173 No factor 8
Speed Index: Last Race: +4.0 3–Race Avg.: +1.6 4–Race Avg.: +1.7 Overall Avg.: –0.1
LATEST WORKOUTS Oct 25 Bel 4f fst :48⅘ H Oct 5 Bel 3f fst :37 B Sep 30 Bel 4f fst :49⅗ B Sep 25 Bel 4f fst :49 B

Lay Down * B. g. 5, by Spectacular Bid—Impish, by Majestic Prince
Br.—Phipps O M (Ky)
Own.—Phipps O M Tr.—McGaughey Claude III
115 Lifetime 19 8 0 1 $275,593 | 1989 9 2 0 1 $123,793 | 1988 6 4 0 0 $124,980 | Turf 3 0 0 1 $2,800

4Sep89- 8Pha fst 1⅛ :48⅕ 1:12⅕ 1:49⅖ 3↑Norristwn H 2 6 69¼ 67¼ 511 612 Molina V H 114 6.30 76-28 DrpeuTricolore1135½Homebuilder1161Xnomni1132¼ Showed little 6
4Sep89-Grade III
19Aug89- 9Tdn fst 1⅛ :45⅗ 1:09⅗ 1:49 3↑Bud Brd Cp H 6 5 513 411 34 42½ Lovato F Jr 118 3.90 89-11 Simply Majestic 122½ Stop the Stage 1141 Rosen Warrior 1121 8
22Jly89- 8Bel fst 1½ :50⅗ 2:04⅕ 2:28⅗ 3↑Brooklyn H 6 6 68½ 33 44 47¾ Cordero A Jr 113 4.80 69-23 ForeverSilver1164½DrapeauTricolore1121¼JckOfClubs1122 Rallied 6
22Jly89-Grade I
9Jun89- 8Bel sly 1⅛ :46⅗ 1:10⅕ 1:46⅘ 3↑Nassau Co H 3 3 32½ 32½ 410 515½ Santos J A 114 *1.50 77-23 Forever Silver 1144 Baltic Fox 1123 Brian's Time1176½ Weakened 7
9Jun89-Grade II
17May89- 8Bel my 1 1/16 :45⅗ 1:10 1:41⅕ 3↑Handicap 2 4 31 41½ 11½ 15 Santos J A 114 *1.70 96-15 Lay Down 1145 Hill Slide 1133½ Fourstardave 1156½ Driving 5
29Apr89- 8Aqu fst 1¼ :49⅕ 1:38⅕ 2:02⅗ 3↑Excelsior H 4 1 11 2hd 43 45½ Cordero A Jr 114 *.60 77-27 Forever Silver 1111¾ Its Acedemic 1131 Jack Of Clubs1132¾ Tired 5
29Apr89-Grade II
18Mar89- 8Aqu gd 1⅛ :48⅗ 1:12⅘ 1:50 3↑Grey Lag H 2 1 1½ 32 21 1¾ Santos J A 112 3.20 85-30 Lay Down 112¾ Its Acedemic 1164¼ Congeleur 1135 Going away 6
18Mar89-Grade III
5Feb89-10GP fst 1⅛ :47⅘ 1:11⅗ 1:50⅕ 3↑Donn H 2 3 44½ 54 1112 1115½ Samyn J L 111 18.20 65-25 Cryptoclearance1211½SlewCitySlew1183½Primal1174½ Fin. after 6f 12
5Feb89-Grade I
21Jan89- 9GP fm 1 1/16 Ⓣ:46⅘ 1:10⅖ 1:42 Alw 28000 8 3 35½ 53¼ 65¾ 31½ Samyn J L 119 8.40 88-09 Jimmy's Bronco 122¾ Kings River II 115¾LayDown119hd Checked 11
24Nov88- 8Aqu fst 1 3/16 :48⅘ 1:13⅖ 1:57⅕ 3↑Quens Cty H 4 2 21½ 2hd 13 1hd Samyn J L 109 14.90 76-26 Lay Down 109hdNostalgia'sStar1135PleasantVirginian113¾ Driving 6
24Nov88-Grade III
Speed Index: Last Race: –3.0 1–Race Avg.: –3.0 1–Race Avg.: –3.0 Overall Avg.: +1.5
LATEST WORKOUTS Oct 25 Bel 4f fst :48⅖ B Oct 19 Bel 4f sly :50⅖ B Oct 15 Bel 4f fst :51⅗ B Sep 3 Bel 3f fst :35⅕ H

Block Trader—"He seems a notch below these. He's had one start since April, and it wasn't a hard win. He's got the outside post, and I'd rather be on the outside at Belmont than Aqueduct at a mile and sixteenth on the turf. He's going to have to pick his way through horses. I'd put him as a closer."

lock Trader — **Ro. c. 4, by Wavering Monarch—Lady Taurian Peace, by Peace Corps**
Br.—Glencrest Farm & Moffitt B (Ky)
Own.—Dee-Ann Stabble — **Tr.—Tesher Howard M** — **109**

Lifetime							
15 3 3 1	1989	7	2	1	1	$44,550
$74,350	1988	7	1	2	0	$29,800
	Turf	8	3	1	1	$60,150

ct89-	5Bel	gd	1 1/16	Ⓣ:49	1:13 1/5	1:43 2/5	3↑Alw 34000	6	7	8^{9}	$6^{5\frac{3}{4}}$	$3^{3\frac{1}{2}}$	$1^{1\frac{1}{4}}$	Santos J A	117	4.40	84–18 Block Trader $117^{1\frac{1}{4}}$ Valid Fund $117^{1\frac{1}{4}}$ Royal Ninja 119^{nk}	Driving	8
pr89-	8Aqu	fm	1 1/16	Ⓣ:49 4/5	1:13 1/5	1:44 2/5	3↑Alw 31000	3	5	$6^{3\frac{1}{2}}$	$6^{5\frac{1}{2}}$	$4^{5\frac{1}{2}}$	$2^{2\frac{1}{4}}$	Antley C W	119	2.50	81–24 Ashumet $119^{2\frac{1}{4}}$ Block Trader 119^{nk} Finnegan'sPride114^{2}	Steadied	8
Apr89-	9Hia	fm	*1 1/16	Ⓣ		1:42 2/5	Alw 16000	3	8	9^{10}	9^{8}	$5^{6\frac{1}{2}}$	$3^{3\frac{3}{4}}$	Castaneda M	122	*2.80	82–17 Great Normand 116no Valid Fund $116^{3\frac{3}{4}}$ Block Trader122^{1}	Rallied	10
ar89-	9Hia	fm	*1 1/16	Ⓣ		1:43 1/5	Alw 19100	3	9	$10^{8\frac{1}{2}}$	$10^{9\frac{1}{2}}$	$8^{5\frac{3}{4}}$	$5^{3\frac{1}{2}}$	Perret C	122	6.10	78–17 ⒹAl Azim 116^{hd} Nisswa 119^{hd} Temperley 116^{nk}	Hung	10
24Mar89-Placed fourth through disqualification																			
eb89-	7GP	fm	*1 1/16	Ⓣ		1:45 1/5	Alw 24000	2	8	$9^{7\frac{1}{2}}$	8^{8}	$7^{2\frac{3}{4}}$	$1^{\frac{1}{2}}$	Santos J A	119	4.50	80–21 Block Trader $119^{\frac{1}{2}}$ Allsaw 117^{nk} Russian Affair 117^{hd}	Driving	10
eb89-	6GP	fm	*1 1/16	Ⓣ		1:45 1/5	Alw 19000	7	7	$8^{8\frac{1}{2}}$	$7^{6\frac{3}{4}}$	$7^{3\frac{3}{4}}$	$5^{2\frac{3}{4}}$	Romero R P	117	3.90	77–19 Lord Of Winloc117^{hd}NavelAcademy$117^{1\frac{3}{4}}$Stealroid117^{1}	Stride late	10
an89-	6GP	fm	1 1/16	Ⓣ:47 3/5	1:12 2/5	1:43 4/5	Alw 18000	4	3	4^{6}	$8^{8\frac{1}{2}}$	$8^{8\frac{1}{2}}$	8^{7}	Chavez J F	117	2.80	74–15 Biographer 117^{1} Finnegan's Pride 117^{2} Brave Bit $117^{1\frac{3}{4}}$	Tired	12
ov88-	7Aqu	sly	1 1/8	:48	1:12 4/5	1:53	3↑Alw 29000	7	5	$6^{3\frac{1}{2}}$	$5^{3\frac{3}{4}}$	5^{7}	$6^{6\frac{1}{4}}$	Santagata N	115	*1.40	64–29 Briskeen 117^{2} Benvolio 120^{1}RoadGameJohnny$110^{\frac{3}{4}}$	Wide 1st turn	7
ov88-	5Aqu	fst	1 1/8	:48 3/5	1:13 2/5	1:51 1/5	3↑Alw 29000	5	4	$4^{2\frac{1}{2}}$	$3^{2\frac{1}{2}}$	$2^{2\frac{1}{2}}$	$2^{2\frac{3}{4}}$	Antley C W	115	2.80	76–20 Binn's Fargo$115^{2\frac{3}{4}}$BlockTrader115^{3}SpectacularSon$117^{2\frac{1}{2}}$	2nd best	9
ov88-	5Aqu	my	1	:45 2/5	1:10 4/5	1:37 1/5	3↑Alw 29000	5	3	$2^{1\frac{1}{2}}$	$2^{3\frac{1}{2}}$	2^{5}	2^{4}	Antley C W	115	5.00	76–26 HsFrqntflyr112^{4}BlockTrdr$115^{\frac{3}{4}}$RodGmJohnny$107^{4\frac{1}{2}}$	Best of others	6

Speed Index: Last Race: +2.0 3–Race Avg.: +2.0 7–Race Avg.: –1.8 Overall Avg.: –2.2
LATEST WORKOUTS Oct 22 Bel tr.t 5f fst 1:01 H ●Sep 28 Bel 7f fst 1:23 4/5 H Sep 22 Bel tr.t 4f gd :49 B ●Sep 13 Bel 6f fst 1:11 1/5 H

Johnson identified three contenders: Fourstardave, I Rejoice and Slew The Knight, who was a late scratch. "I think Fourstardave will be an overlay because they'll all get on I Rejoice because he wins a lot."

The closing odds: Fourstardave 6 to 1; Soviet Lad 2 to 1; I Rejoice 7 to 2; Impersonator 14 to 1; River of Sin 9 to 1; Turning For Home 9 to 2; Turkey Point 16 to 1; Lay Down 14 to 1; Block Trader 10 to 1.

Fourstardave broke in front before River of Sin took the lead entering the clubhouse turn. Fourstardave settled in second, a length and a half back, with I Rejoice on his flank. Soviet Lad was a well placed fourth with Impersonator, taken off the pace by Jean-Luc Samyn, alongside in fifth.

Loose on the lead, River of Sin set slow fractions (:24 1/5, :48 1/5, 1:12 3/5) yet offered no resistance when the field bunched on the final turn. Fourstardave, I Rejoice and Impersonator took the outside route, two, three and four wide, while Eddie Maple shot Soviet Lad through the inside of River of Sin. At the top of the stretch the group of five stretched across the width of the course. River of Sin stopped badly and Fourstardave weakened to fourth. Impersonator outkicked I Rejoice by a length with Soviet Lad another one and a quarter lengths back in third.

While Johnson wasn't right about the winner (the author was wrong, too), he correctly labeled Soviet Lad as a beatable underlay at 2 to 1.

SEVENTH RACE
Aqueduct
OCTOBER 28, 1989

1 $\frac{1}{16}$ MILES.(Turf). (1.41) HANDICAP. Purse $50,000. 3–year–olds and upward. Weights, Wednesday, October 25. Nominations close Wednesday, October 25, 1989. Declarations by 10:00 A.M. Thursday, October 26. Closed with 32 nominations.

Value of race $50,000; value to winner $30,000; second $11,000; third $6,000; fourth $3,000. Mutuel pool $327,644. Exacta Pool $607,831.

Last Raced	Horse	Eqt.	A.	Wt	PP	St	¼	½	¾	Str	Fin	Jockey	Odds $1
7Oct89 ^{8}Bel	Impersonator	b	4	113	4	5	$4^{\frac{1}{2}}$	5^{2}	5^{2}	$4^{2\frac{1}{2}}$	1^{1}	Samyn J L	14.20
7Oct89 ^{7}Bel^{1}	I Rejoice		6	122	3	4	3^{2}	3^{1}	3^{1}	1^{hd}	$2^{1\frac{1}{4}}$	Bailey J D	3.80
7Oct89 ^{7}Bel^{4}	Soviet Lad	b	4	115	2	3	5^{1}	4^{1}	4^{hd}	$2^{\frac{1}{2}}$	$3^{4\frac{1}{2}}$	Maple E	2.10
22Oct89 ^{6}Lrl^{9}	Fourstardave		4	120	1	1	2^{hd}	2^{1}	2^{hd}	3^{hd}	4^{nk}	Cordero A Jr	6.70
4Sep89 ^{8}Pha^{6}	Lay Down		5	115	8	6	9	9	6^{hd}	5^{hd}	5^{nk}	Krone J A	14.30
13Oct89 ^{7}Bel^{1}	Turkey Point		4	116	7	7	7^{hd}	6^{hd}	$7^{2\frac{1}{2}}$	$6^{2\frac{1}{2}}$	$6^{1\frac{3}{4}}$	Castillo R E	16.50
7Oct89 ^{5}Bel^{1}	Block Trader		4	109	9	8	8^{2}	7^{1}	8^{3}	7^{1}	7^{1}	Rojas R I	10.10
7Oct89 ^{7}Bel^{6}	Turning For Home	b	5	116	6	9	$6^{\frac{1}{2}}$	$8^{1\frac{1}{2}}$	9	8^{1}	$8^{5\frac{1}{4}}$	McCauley W H	4.60
13Oct89 ^{8}Med^{1}	River of Sin		5	121	5	2	$1^{1\frac{1}{2}}$	1^{1}	$1^{1\frac{1}{2}}$	9	9	Migliore R	9.60

OFF AT 3:41 Start good, Won driving. Time, :24⅕, :48⅕, 1:12⅗, 1:38⅕, 1:44⅗ Course firm.

$2 Mutuel Prices:				
	5–(F)–IMPERSONATOR	30.40	10.20	5.40
	4–(E)–I REJOICE		5.20	3.20
	2–(C)–SOVIET LAD			2.80

$2 EXACTA 5–4 PAID $151.40.

B. g, by Sham—Totie Fields, by Ridan. Trainer Quick Patrick J. Bred by Kellman Joseph (Ky).

IMPERSONATOR, reserved early, lodged his bid outside horses on the far turn came five wide into the stretch, gained the lead outside horses in midstretch then drew clar of I REJOICE late. I REJOICE in good early position outside FOURSTARDAVE, came four wide into the stretch, gained a short lead nearing the furlong pole but could not keep pace with the winner. SOVIET LAD, never far back, slipped through along the inside entering the stretch bid for the lead inside horses nearing the furlong pole then was outfinished. FOURSTARDAVE, just off RIVER OF SIN while under snug restraint early came three wide into the stretch, then tired in the final furlong. TURNING FOR HOME was outrun. RIVER OF SIN took the early lead outside FOURSTARDAVE, showed the way to the stretch then gave way suddenly.

Trips

15 Trip handicapping is hardly a revelation to those handicappers familiar with harness racing. One of its basic tenets is evaluating trips, especially on half-mile tracks. Bettors note difficult trips, for example, a move while racing wide. The small circle mark in a past performance line in a harness racing program indicate the horse made its move parked out, racing two-wide. Two circles mean three-wide or four-wide.

Even the novice harness racing fans know a horse racing wide on one or two turns loses a lot of ground. Literally, the horse is racing a greater distance than a horse racing along the rail. Racing two-wide an entire mile on a half-mile harness track actually means racing one mile and sixty-two feet, according to the United States Trotting Association, the governing body of harness racing. In a game of photo finishes, inches can decide winning and losing.

What we're interested in, here, is how trips can be used in thoroughbred handicapping.

First, we must acknowledge the different aspects of harness and thoroughbred racing. In harness racing, races are almost always the same distance: one mile. Horses on a half-mile track go around turns four times in a one mile race. Horses in harness racing actually race physically closer to each other than their thoroughbred counterparts. Thus in harness racing, traffic problems are constantly created, usually for at least a couple of horses in each race. Thoroughbreds run into traffic problems as well, but in general, harness racing will produce one close mass of several horses bunching on the final turn with less room for horses to maneuver, especially on a half-mile track.

Evaluating trips in thoroughbred racing can be more difficult. There is no substitute for seeing the races, watching replays and taking in as much information as possible. Trying to handicap trips solely by reading PPs in the *Form* is limited to the *Form's* observations. Usually, yet certainly not 100 percent of the time, the *Form's* evaluation of what happened is accurate. Yet 100 percent of the time, that evaluation is limited by space requirements to one or two words for a comment in a horse's PPs.

Remember when we discussed the inherent disadvantages of outside post positions in a turf race? Those outside post positions many times result in difficult, if not impossible, trips.

Evaluating trips entails asking the question, Does everybody see the same race the same way? Hardly.

The 1984 Flamingo Stakes at Hialeah, March 3, was a spectacular race in which Time For A Change defeated Dr. Carter by a neck while previously unbeaten Devil's Bag limped home a well beaten fourth. That night, I ran into a friend who said, "Dr. Carter was much the best. He had the toughest trip."

Had he seen the same race? He based his opinion on the fact Dr. Carter's jockey, Jorge Velasquez, tried moving through on the inside of Time For A Change and Devil's Bag, who were head-to-head on the backstretch battling for the lead. Finding too little room inside them, Velasquez then eased Dr. Carter back, taking him three-wide into the turn around the frontrunners. In doing so, in my friend's opinion, Dr. Carter had the most difficult trip.

Not so. Replays showed Dr. Carter was only two to two and a half paths wide on the turn because Devil's Bag had already tired and jockey Jerry Bailey had moved Time For A Change in from the outside of Devil's Bag to the rail. With at least a sixteenth of a mile remaining in this important Kentucky Derby prep, Dr. Carter had dead aim on Time For A Change and couldn't get by him.

Time For A Change had run a brilliant race despite a much more difficult trip than Dr. Carter. Time For A Change had been rushed to the front around several horses on the first turn. He then engaged Devil's Bag head-to-head through a moderate first quarter in :23 2/5. But the two then sped to the three-quarters in 1:09 3/5, a torrid pace for a mile and an eighth race. Time For A Change literally ran Devil's Bag, regarded by some as unbeatable at the time, into the ground. As soon as he got done with Devil's Bag, Time For A Change had Dr. Carter at his throat. Thus, Time For A Change had survived a wicked front end duel—enough of one to exhaust Devil's Bag—and had enough courage to dig in and hold off Dr. Carter. Time For A Change's trip was one without an instant of rest, a remarkably difficult effort.

Giving Dr. Carter an excuse of a poor trip is an exaggeration of a poor ride and an injustice to understanding the difficulty of a trip laced with constant pressure every step of the way. Dr. Carter came back in the Florida Derby to run second to Woody Stephens' other 3-year-old star, Swale. Again, Dr. Carter had dead aim and again didn't get the job done, this time at odds of 3 to 5. This time, there were no excuses to be made. He hung.

Misreading trips, or giving them greater meaning than they deserve, is a dangerous booby trap. We must define and evaluate excuses.

Does the first-time starter who raced wide have an excuse? Yes, if he had a poor post position on the extreme outside. Does it mean he won't race wide again? No. The *Form* is filled with charts of horses who consistently race wide or get away from the gate slowly, chronic bad actors with chronic bad habits. Avoid them.

More valid excuses come when a horse is physically impeded, pinched or squeezed back, crowded on the turn or just plain blocked by a wall of horses in front of him. Such bad trips are usually noted by the comment in the *Form*.

It's not all that easy, however. We must determine if the bad trip or excuse significantly compromised the chances of a horse who was making a move when he encountered trouble. What difference does it make if a horse was steadied, checked or blocked if he wasn't gaining ground? Additionally, it's important to establish whether an excuse for a horse is an isolated case or an indication of a bad habit.

There are two classic examples to illustrate each concern.

In 1973, Secretariat became the first Triple Crown winner in twenty-five years. The following spring, no overwhelming favorite emerged. In fact, the crop of 3-year-olds was so evenly matched that twenty-three horses were entered in the Kentucky Derby (including eventual winner Cannonade).

There's no way twenty-three horse fields don't produce bad trips. The difficult questions were, who was affected the most, and who displayed a good effort despite it.

The answer became blatantly clear after the other two legs of the Triple Crown. Little Current closed a ton of ground but failed to light the board in the Derby. In the Preakness and Belmont Stakes, he posted impressive victories. He could have, and perhaps should have, won the Triple Crown. If only he had a better trip in the Derby.

Gate Dancer was a tremendously talented colt whom Jack Van Berg, one of the nation's best trainers, couldn't teach to run in a straight line. Gate Dancer won $2.5 million, compiling a career record of 7-8-7 in twenty-eight starts.

Van Berg tried everything to improve his colt's bad habits: blinkers, a white hood covering his ears, and several of the best jockeys anywhere including Eddie Delahoussaye, Angel Cordero, Jr., Laffit Pincay, Jr., and Chris McCarron. Gate Dancer treated them all the same, lugging in and leaning on horses continually. Of course, it cost Van Berg and owner Kenneth Opstein plenty.

In the 1984 Kentucky Derby, Gate Dancer broke terribly in another oversized field of twenty. He rallied to finish fourth by five and a half to Swale, but was disqualified for bearing in and placed fifth.

For the Preakness, Van Berg switched jockeys from Delahoussaye to Cordero. Gate Dancer again lugged in, but he did it clear of other horses, not only winning by a length and a half, but setting a stakes and track record.

In the inaugural $3 million Breeders' Cup Classic at Hollywood Park, Gate Dancer got even with Cordero for having the audacity of keeping him out of trouble in the Preakness.

Cordero was on the 3 to 5 favorite, Slew O' Gold. Gate Dancer was pounded down to 7 to 2 with Pincay aboard. Wild Again was a 31 to 1 longshot.

The three of them raced as a team the entire length of the stretch with Pat Day trying to keep Wild Again together on the inside. Slew O' Gold was in between horses. And the horse outside them was Gate Dancer, who seemed to have dead aim on both. But Gate Dancer once again began bearing in, squeezing Slew O' Gold into Wild Again. The three made contact repeatedly with Wild Again holding on by a desperate head, Gate Dancer second and Slew O' Gold just half a length back in third.

Gate Dancer was correctly disqualified for initiating the contact and placed third. The difference in the share of the purse was $351,000. After the race, Pincay said, "I thought I was going to win easy, then he started leaning on the horse inside me. I had the stick in my left hand, and I was showing it to him. But the way he holds his head so high, it's hard to get him straight."

A year later at Aqueduct in the same $3 million Breeder's Cup Classic, Gate Dancer, sent off at 3 to 1 with Chris McCarron riding, gained a clear lead in the field of eight before Proud Truth charged up from last place and ever so slowly nudged his way past to win by a head. In his account of the race for *The Blood-Horse*, Edward L. Bowen said, Gate Dancer "seemed to raise his head in the air briefly to notice some swirling sea gulls overhead, but ran straight and true and gamely."

Even so, Gate Dancer was an underlay simply because of his proclivity for causing problems. Recognize a bad actor, and remember our goal of finding value. It's hard enough being right about horses without factoring in whether or not he's going to get disqualified.

Problem horses come at all levels of racing. Let's consider the PPs of Self Pressured.

Self Pressured — Own.—Schwartz B K
Dk. b. or br. g. 6, by The Pruner—Self Made, by Gun Bow
$25,000 Br.—Peters L J (Fla)
Tr.—Trovato Joseph A
117 — Lifetime 73 6 12 10 $129,710
1983 13 0 2 1 $10,530
1982 13 0 2 3 $12,160
Turf 4 0 0 0 $1,020

27Jly83- 1Sar	fst	6f	:22⅖	:45⅗	1:10⅖	3↑ Clm 25000	9	9	11^{13}	10^{13}	$8^{8\frac{1}{2}}$	5^{3}	Cruguet J		117	11.90	85-13	Timeless Ride 117^{1} Fanny's Fox $117^{1\frac{1}{4}}$ Duck Call $117^{\frac{3}{4}}$	Wide Str 11
22Jly83- 9Bel	fst	6½f	:24	:47⅘	1:19⅗	Clm 20000	1	6	$3^{1\frac{1}{2}}$	$5^{1\frac{3}{4}}$	4^{3}	3½	Cordero A Jr		117	*2.60	78-26	Mingo 112no Come Up Pence 108½SelfPressured$117^{4\frac{3}{4}}$	Broke slow 7
13Jly83- 2Bel	fst	7f	:23⅕	:46⅗	1:24⅗	Clm 25000	10	12	12^{13}	$11^{9\frac{1}{4}}$	$10^{6\frac{1}{2}}$	$5^{3\frac{1}{4}}$	Smith A Jr	b	117	11.00	76-24	DlingDiplomt117^{nk}Fnny'sFox$112^{1\frac{1}{2}}$TimlssRd117^{nk}	Off slowly, wide 12
26Jun83- 2Bel	fst	6f	:23⅖	:46⅘	1:11⅗	Clm 25000	2	8	8^{8}	7^{7}	6^{6}	$4^{1\frac{3}{4}}$	Cordero A Jr	b	117	*2.20e	82-24	Bright Search 117^{1} Come Up Pence 108^{nk} Mingo 115½	Wide str. 9
29May83- 9Bel	fst	7f	:22⅘	:45⅗	1:22⅕	Clm 30000	5	7	9^{7}	8^{10}	8^{9}	$5^{8\frac{1}{4}}$	Cordero A Jr	b	113	11.10	83-11	Duck Call $106^{1\frac{1}{4}}$.Minced Words $108^{2\frac{1}{4}}$ ColdTrailin'$113^{1\frac{3}{4}}$	No factor 9
18May83- 3Bel	fst	6½f	:23	:46⅖	1:17	Clm 25000	8	14	$10^{5\frac{1}{4}}$	$10^{7\frac{1}{4}}$	$7^{6\frac{3}{4}}$	$5^{3\frac{1}{4}}$	Cordero A Jr		117	4.10	88-15	Cold Trailin' 117^{1} DealingDiplomat115^{nk}HerefordMan117½	Rallied 14
5May83- 9Aqu	fst	7f	:22⅕	:44⅘	1:22⅖	Clm 32500	4	10	10^{14}	6^{12}	$5^{5\frac{1}{2}}$	$4^{6\frac{3}{4}}$	Santiago A	b	115	6.30	82-21	Fanny's Fox 117^{5} Alec George 117½ RaiseABuck$106^{1\frac{1}{4}}$	No menace 10
14Apr83- 5Aqu	fst	7f	:23⅗	:46⅗	1:24	Clm 32500	2	8	8^{11}	$8^{9\frac{1}{2}}$	8^{6}	5^{2}	Santiago A		115	10.30	79-25	Rigid 117¾ Really Smart 117^{nk} Fanny's Fox 117^{1}	Wide Str. 8
16Mar83- 3Aqu	fst	1	:45⅕	1:11⅕	1:37⅗	Clm 35000	8	6	$2^{1\frac{1}{2}}$	3^{5}	10^{11}	10^{13}	McCarron G		117	11.60	65-27	Hugh Capet115¾Startop'sAce$112^{2\frac{1}{4}}$LetterFromLucy115^{no}	Faltered 14

His ability is reflected in his record of 6-12-10 in seventy-three lifetime starts. He also had two bad habits: getting off slowly and racing wide. Before the July 27 race, three of his ten PPs in the *Form* had the comment "Wide." Two recent lines had the comments "Broke slow" and "Off slowly, wide." Despite the poor starts, Self Pressured had finished a close fifth by three and a quarter lengths and third by half a length in his last two races before July 27. Did he have excuses for not doing better? Yes, but in this case the excuse is an entrenched habit, actually two habits, not conducive to maximizing performance. On July 27, at 11 to 1, he would break ninth in a field of eleven and rally to finish fifth by three lengths. The comment in the chart was "wide into the stretch, found best stride too late." It wasn't the first time it happened.

Remembering our contention younger horses may frequently display more consistent performances at the start of their careers, let's look at a couple of 2-year-olds who raced at Saratoga in 1983.

Bottle Top was entered in the Grade III, six furlong Schuylerville Stakes for 2-year-old fillies.

Bottle Top — B. f. 2, by Topsider—Rhubarb, by Barbizon — Lifetime 1983 3 1 1 1 $27,7[illegible]
Br.—Bwamazon Farm (Ky) — **114** — 3 1 1 1 $27,743
Own.—Bwamazon Farm — Tr.—Basile Anthony

6Jly83- 8Bel	fst	5½f	:22⅕	:45⅕	1:04⅘	Ⓕ Astoria	5	8	6^{5}	$7^{6\frac{1}{4}}$	$4^{5\frac{1}{2}}$	$3^{2\frac{3}{4}}$	Brumfield D	114	*2.20	89-10 Hot Milk 112^{nk} Terrible Terri T. $122^{\frac{1}{2}}$ Bottle Top $114^{1\frac{1}{2}}$	Checked
15Jun83- 8Bel	fst	5½f	:22⅗	:45⅗	1:05⅗	Ⓕ Fashion	9	8	$6^{2\frac{1}{2}}$	$5^{2\frac{3}{4}}$	$3^{3\frac{1}{2}}$	$2^{\frac{1}{2}}$	Brumfield D	115	14.50	86-20 Mink Hat $115^{\frac{1}{2}}$ Bottle Top 115^{2} Buzz My Bell $115^{\frac{1}{2}}$	Rallied
12Apr83- 3Kee	fst	4½f	:23⅗	:46⅘	:52⅘	Ⓕ Md Sp Wt	4	2		1^{2}	1^{5}	1^{9}	Brumfield D	118	*.40	91-09 Bottle Top 118^{9} Jay Parce 118^{4} Identity Crisis 118^{1}	Handily

LATEST WORKOUTS Jly 26 Sar 3f fst :38⅗ b ● Jly 18 Bel 5f fst :59⅘ hg Jly 13 Bel tr.t 4f fst :50⅘ b Jly 3 Bel 5f fst 1:00⅖ h

Copyright© by News America Publications Inc. Reprinted with permission of the copyright owner

Bottle Top's career consisted of three races. In her debut as a maiden at Keeneland, April 12, Bottle Top was bet down to 2 to 5 and won the four and a half furlong race by nine lengths. Her next start was June 15 at Belmont in the Fashion Stakes at five and a half furlongs. Sent off at 14 to 1, Bottle Top broke eighth, raced two and a half to three and a half lengths off the pace in the middle of a field of eleven, and rallied to finish second by half a length, closing three lengths in the stretch. Off that strong race, Bottle Top was sent off as the 2 to 1 favorite in the five and a half furlong Astoria Stakes at Belmont, July 6. Again breaking eighth in the field of nine, Bottle Top was five lengths off the lead when sixth after the first quarter, then seventh by six and a quarter lengths after the half. She moved up to fourth by five and a half at the top of the stretch and finished third by two and three-quarters lengths. The comment was "Checked." Is it a legitimate excuse? Sure. The correct assumption is to evaluate the race as an exception since Bottle Top hadn't encountered such traffic problems in her other two races. In the Schuylerville, Bottle Top won by four lengths as the 2 to 1 second choice, not an overlay.

Two days later at Saratoga, a 2-year-old colt named Gifted Bird appeared in a maiden race for 2-year-old New York-breds at six furlongs.

EIGHTH RACE
Saratoga
JULY 27, 1983

6 FURLONGS. (1.08) 66th Running THE SCHUYLERVILLE (Grade III). $50,000 added. Fillies. 2-year-olds. Weight 119 lbs. By subscription of $100 each which should accompany the nomination; $400 to pass entry box, with $50,000 added. The added money and all fees to be divided 60% to winner, 22% to second, 12% to third and 6% to fourth. Winners of two sweepstakes an additional 2 lbs.; non-winners of a sweepstakes allowed 3 lbs.; of a race other than maiden or claiming, 5 lbs.; maidens, 7 lbs. Starters to be named at the closing time of entries. A trophy will be presented to the winning owner. Closed Wednesday, July 13, 1983 with 31 nominations.

Value of race $56,700, value to winner $34,020, second $12,474, third $6,804, fourth $3,402. Mutuel pool $161,692, OTB pool $144,802.

Last Raced	Horse	Eqt.	A.	Wt.	PP	St	1/4	1/2	Str	Fin	Jockey	r	Odds $1
6Jly83 8Bel 3	Bottle Top	b	2	114	5	3	2-2½	2-5	1hd	1-4	Brumfield D		2.00
15Jly83 4Bel 1	Officer's Ball		2	114	1	6	1hd	1 ½	2-4	2nk	Cruguet J	a-	1.00
7Jly83 8CD 2	Ark		2	114	2	4	5hd	5-3	4-3	3no	MacBeth D		11.00
8Jly83 5Mth 1	Tony's Jig	b	2	116	3	2	6-3	4hd	3hd	4-8¾	Velasquez J		15.90
16Jly83 1Bel 1	Millionaire Jen	b	2	116	7	1	3-3	3hd	5-4	5no	Cordero A Jr		4.30
9Jly83 8Hol 4	Linda's Leader		2	114	4	7	7	7	7	6 ½	Guerra W A		17.80
6Jly83 4Bel 1	Amdala		2	114	6	5	4hd	6-1½	6 ½	7	Vasquez J	a-	1.00

a-Coupled: Officer's Ball and Amdala.
OFF AT 5:25. Start good for all but LINDA'S LEADER, Won driving. Time, :22, :45 2/5, 1:11 2/5 Track fast.

$ 2 Mutuel Prices:	6-	BOTTLE TOP	6.00	2.80	2.40
	1-	OFFICER'S BALL (a-entry)		2.60	2.20
	2-	ARK			2.60

B. f, by Topsider–Rhubarb, by Barbizon. Trainer Basile Anthony. Bred by Bwamazon Farm (Ky).

BOTTLE TOP showed good early foot while getting out slightly approaching the end of the backstretch, was strongly handled while bearing out around the turn, took over from OFFICER'S BALL with a furlong remaining and drew away. The latter rushed along early, made the pace into the stretch while saving ground and weakened under pressure. ARK finished evenly between horses. TONY'S JIG raced wide into the stretch but lacked the needed rally. MILLIONAIRE JEN tired badly. LINDA'S LEADER broke in the air. AMDALA failed to be a serious factor.

Owners– 1, Bwamazon Farm; 2, Brant P M; 3, Benckart D; 4, Campbell G; 5, Saj Stable; 6, Jones A U; 7, Cooke J K.
Trainers– 1, Basile Anthony; 2, Jolley Leroy; 3, McGaughey Claude III; 4, Allard Edward T; 5, Campo John P; 6, Barrera Lazaro S; 7, Jolley Leroy.
Scratched– Some For All(15Jly83 6Bel 1); Mrs. Flagler(16Jly83 1Bel 2).

Gifted Bird came to Saratoga off two interesting past performances at Suffolk Downs in Boston. In his debut, Gifted Bird was bet strongly at 5 to 2; broke last in a field of eight; ran third by five and a quarter lengths and was placed second because of a disqualification. The *Form's* comment: "Slow start, steadied." Having to steady, we must assume, was a direct result of the disqualified second horse's action. A slow start, however, is never a positive attribute in the debut of a 2-year-old.

In his second and only other start, Gifted Bird was placed in an open stakes race at Suffolk, the Mayflower, and went off at 6 to 1 with this important equipment change: blinkers added. With the change in equipment, Gifted Bird broke much better, fourth, got the lead by a length at the top of the stretch, and finished second by half a length, beating the third place finisher by seven and a half lengths in the field of ten.

The improved performance, in stakes company no less, forces us to assume the blinker change had corrected the problem of the slow start. We then evaluate his being steadied as a legitimate excuse. Again, neither problem reappeared in his next race. Off a stakes-placing, Gifted Bird figured much the best of a maiden race restricted to New York-breds. He was, winning easily and paying $5.80, again not much of an overlay. By the way, Gifted Bird won easily despite bearing out extremely wide in the stretch, the start of a new bad habit.

What of more experienced horses with bad habits? Deal with each one individually and take your own chances.

Hypertee appeared in an allowance race at 1³/₁₆ miles on the main turf course at Saratoga, July 31, 1983. The 3-year-old had eight previous starts and problems galore: 1) off slowly in his debut as a 2-year-old; 2) bore in and was disqualified from third to fourth in his next start as a 2-year-old; 3) in his turf debut as a 3-year-old, was jammed back early when sixth by nine and a half lengths; and 4) in his next try on turf, bumped when third by a neck. Trainer Angel Penna had tried adding blinkers, taking them off, adding them and taking them off again in an effort to improve Hypertee's manners. Here was a horse who was obviously a handful to ride.

Angel Cordero, Jr., apparently thought he could handle him when he took the mount in Hypertee's last race, a debut in stakes turf company in the 1¹/₄ mile Lexington Stakes at Belmont. Way back—as far as ninth by nineteen lengths—Hypertee rallied to finish fourth by three and a half lengths. For this easier allowance race at Saratoga, Hypertee again had the services of Cordero. Hypertee not only won this race, returning $7.40, but took another allowance race at Saratoga nineteen days later on the turf. The assumption: Hypertee had grown out of his early bad habits as a 2-year-old. Was he a good investment at 5 to 2 in his first win at Saratoga? No. Hypertee could have just as easily encountered or created problems again. It's always easy to look back after the fact. The fact we'll use is that Hypertee at 5 to 2 was not an overlay given his previous bad trips, some of them self-induced.

In his first victory at Saratoga, which was by a head, the chart said Hypertee was "strongly handled while lugging in." Maybe the habits were still there.

Our search for overlays leads us to horses whose odds are higher than they should be when bettors place too much emphasis on a bad race, which may have been caused by a bad trip.

If a closer has had a reasonably good performance on a speed-favoring track and then ships to a track with no bias, his chances will improve. If a speed horse was cooked in a three-way duel and now is in a race with little early speed, he has a better chance. If a horse was making a move and had to be stopped because of traffic problems, he's likely to improve in his next start.

Conversely, when a horse enjoys a good trip, let's say an uncontested wire-to-wire attempt on a speed-favoring track, and can't do the job, we'll place significance on that, too.

How about horses who aren't pushed in a moderate or poor finish? Many trainers use a race as a workout and don't ask much of their horses, especially if a high-priced stakes race looms immediately on the horizon. Also, jockeys on horses who are obviously not going to win—for example, a horse on the lead who is passed by three horses at the top of the stretch—may not persevere the final eighth or sixteenth of a mile, creating a worse PP. Finishing seventh by eight lengths or ninth by twelve doesn't automatically make a significant difference.

A final word about trips. In the 1982 Kentucky Derby, one horse had an incredibly difficult trip, racing maybe a sixteenth of a mile extra because he had started from an extremely disadvantageous outside post and raced wide on both turns. That horse, Gato del Sol, won anyway in a remarkable display, bad trip and all.

Inside with Richard Migliore

CHAPTER 16 Because he's been a regular in New York for a decade, Richard Migliore conjures an image of a seasoned old pro despite his boyish good looks. Only twenty-six, Migliore is nonetheless one of the nation's top jockeys.

Migliore's meteoric career began Sept. 29, 1980. A month later, he won his first race on Good Grip at The Meadowlands. Four months later, the sixteen-year-old began an assault on Steve Cauthen's record for earnings by an apprentice jockey in a single season. It took him only eight and a half months to break Cauthen's 1977 mark. He concluded 1981 as the leading rider in New York with 269 victories, and won the Eclipse Award as the nation's top apprentice.

Two years later, his career spiraled downward. Migliore lived through the glory of the apprentice system and the shocking agony which frequently accompanies the loss of the bug, the five to ten pound weight allowance granted apprentice riders.

An apprentice gets a weight allowance of ten pounds until he rides five winners; seven pounds until he wins thirty-five, and then five pounds for a calendar year from the date of his fifth winning race. The lure of having their horses carry less weight is a mighty incentive for trainers to try young, inexperienced riders.

"With my bug, I won $5 million in 1981," Migliore said. "The next season, as a journeyman, I won $2 million. It wasn't a bad year. The next year was bad all around."

In 1983, Migliore won sixty-seven races and $1.4 million. He estimated his average number of mounts per week dropped to ten to twelve. Two years earlier, it had been thirty-five to forty. "I knew it would be a tough period losing my bug," Migliore said. "But if I wasn't tough enough to make it through, I didn't deserve to make it."

Migliore was plenty tough enough. In 1985, he returned to the top, again leading the New York jockey colony with 257 victories.

He could have packed it in. At 5-feet-4 and 110 pounds, Migliore seems destined to battle weight for the duration of his career.

A frightening neck injury from a spill at Belmont, May 30, 1988, could have ended his career, but the Mig was back riding in six months.

He cultivated his solid 1989 season last fall by doing double duty: afternoons at Belmont/Aqueduct and evenings at The Meadowlands, where he won on eleven of thirty-one mounts in one streak.

On a rare day of rest, Tuesday, October 24, Migliore shared his thoughts about handicapping.

"I've always looked at the *Form*," he said. "I use it to refresh what I have already stored in my mind. I have a great memory for horses. I check, who has speed? Who closes? Who lugs in? Who lugs out? It's little things. They make a big difference. I look for clear cut speed or a clear closer.

"As a rider, you can overanalyze a race. Horses aren't machines. A lot of times you go to the paddock thinking you'll be laying fourth or fifth and the trainer says you should be on the lead. Or vice versa. The other night was a perfect example."

Migliore was named to ride Pete The Chief in the $50,000 1 1/16 mile Palisades Breeders' Cup Handicap at The Meadowlands, October 20. When the race was taken off the turf, three scratches reduced the field to five.

"I never rode the horse before," Migliore said. "He always showed early speed. I thought I'd be in front, but the trainer, Phil Serpe, said in the paddock, 'The one thing you have to do is keep this horse four or five lengths off the lead because he'll get rank.' So I didn't warm the horse up hard. I didn't want to get him excited."

Migliore saw the race unfold beautifully for his mount. "Everything went perfectly," he said. "I was behind three horses on the lead dueling."

There was only one other horse in the race, Silver Survivor, who was behind Pete The Chief. "I moved, got the lead, and Silver Survivor followed me," Migliore said. "He was going to beat us."

He did. But in the process, Silver Survivor bore sharply into Pete The Chief, forcing Migliore to take up his horse to avoid being knocked into the rail. Silver Survivor won easily by two and a half lengths, but was correctly disqualified to second behind Pete The Chief because of the blatant foul.

At home four nights later, Migliore shared his handicapping notes as he prepared for the $50,000, 1 1/8 mile handicap the following afternoon at Aqueduct. A field of six were entered. Weights had been assigned by the racing secretary four days earlier.

"It's a real good field," Migliore said. It was one he knew well. "Launching is the only one I've never ridden," Migliore said.

For this race, he'd ride Wind Chill, a 6-year-old gelding trained by Loretta Lusteg.

Migliore went over the field, horse by horse, and the notations he'd made on his copy of the *Form*.

In post position order:

8 AQUEDUCT — 1⅛ MILES AQUEDUCT — START FINISH

1 ⅛ MILES. (1.47) HANDICAP. Purse $50,000. 3–year–olds and upward. Weights Saturday, October 21. Declarations by 10:00 A.M. Monday, October 23. Closed Saturday, October 21 with nominations.

King's Swan X — **B. g. 9, by King's Bishop—Royal Cygnet, by Sea–Bird**
Br.—Kerr Mrs D K (Ky)
Own.—Akman A — **Tr.—Dutrow Richard E** — **117**

	Lifetime					
95 28 16 15	1989	10	1	3	1	$65,814
$1,746,270	1988	14	5	1	3	$539,681
	Turf	6	1	0	0	$9,630

4Oct89-	8Bel	fst	1 1/16	:48	1:13 3/5	1:44 4/5	3↑ Alw 50000	9	1	1hd	1hd	2 2 1/2	2 4 3/4	McCauley W H	119	17.50	73-36	Homebuilder 119 4 3/4 King's Swan 119 3/4 Gay Rights115 2 1/2	Held place	9
10Sep89-	8Pim	fst	6f	:22 3/5	:44 4/5	1:09 1/5	3↑ [R]Sprint H	4	11	11 13	11 16	10 18	10 13 3/4	Bracciale V Jr	116	10.00	86-09	Deputy Shaw 119 4 1/4 Turn to Dancin113nkBornToShop118 2	Outrun	11
5Aug89-	7Sar	fst	6f	:22	:44 4/5	1:08 4/5	3↑ A Phenomenon	2	2	3 1 1/2	4 6	6 9 1/2	6 13 1/4	Migliore R	117	13.80	83-12	Mr. Nickerson 112 3 1/2 Quick Call 115 2 1/2 MiamiSlick119 2	Tired badly	6
16Jun89-	8Bel	fst	1 1/16	:46 2/5	1:10 3/5	1:42	3↑ Alw 47000	5	1	1 1	1 1 1/2	1 1/2	1 1	Migliore R	117	4.80	92-19	King's Swan 117 1 Feeling Gallant 112 1 PassingShips117nk	Driving	7
1Jun89-	8Bel	fst	7f	:22 4/5	:45 3/5	1:22 2/5	3↑ Alw 41000	4	2	3 1	2 1 1/2	2 1/2	2 2	Santos J A	117	2.10	88-16	Crusader Sword 117 2 King's Swan117 1/2 PassingShips117no	Gamely	6
28Apr89-	1Aqu	fst	7f	:22 2/5	:45 1/5	1:22 4/5	Clm 100000	6	3	4 3 1/2	5 4	6 5 3/4	3 3 1/4	Antley C W	122	*.90e	84-24	SocillyInformed111 1 3/4 IrishChili114 1 1/2 King'sSwn122 2 1/4	Belated rally	6
17Apr89-	8Aqu	fst	6f	:21 4/5	:45 1/5	1:09 3/5	3↑ Alw 41000	4	5	4 5	4 2	4 2	2 2 3/4	Santos J A	121	2.70	89-15	Seattle Knight 121 2 3/4 King'sSwan121nkFourstardave121 2 1/2	Wide str	7
12Mar89-	8Aqu	fst	6f	[•]:22 3/5	:46 2/5	1:10 2/5	3↑ Toboggan H	7	1	5 6	5 3	7 4 1/2	6 4 1/2	Migliore R	114	12.20	87-29	LordOfTheNight114nkTeddyDron117hdVinnithVipr115 1 3/4	No factor	7
12Mar89-Grade III																				
25Feb89-	8Aqu	fst	6f	[•]:22 4/5	:46 2/5	1:11	3↑ Sprtng Plt H	2	5	7 3 3/4	6 5 3/4	5 5	4 6	Antley C W	116	7.10	83-21	ProudndVlid110 3/4 VinnietheViper115 2 3/4 TruendBlu113 2 1/2	No menace	7
7Jan89-	8Aqu	fst	1 1/16	[•]:46 4/5	1:11 1/5	1:42 4/5	3↑ Aqueduct H	6	2	4 4 1/2	5 9	6 9	6 15 1/4	Krone J A	118	*1.10	80-19	Lord Of The Night 114 1 ItsAcedemic110 4 3/4 TrueandBlue113 2 3/4	Wide	6
7Jan89-Grade III																				

Speed Index: Last Race: +9.0 3–Race Avg.: +6.3 3–Race Avg.: +6.3 Overall Avg.: +4.5
LATEST WORKOUTS Sep 3 Aqu 5f fst 1:02 1/5 B

King's Swan—SP (speed)—"He's at home at Aqueduct. It's the track he trains over. His last race was good. He'll probably show speed, be on the lead or close to it. Obviously, it looks like he's lost a step. It looks like his best races are at a mile and over. Tomorrow, you have to think the pace will be to his liking."

K. C.'s Best Turn — **Gr. h. 5, by Best Turn—Ky Cut Up, by Hatchet Man**
Br.—Lundy & Whiteley Jr (Ky)
Own.—Baker Farm — **Tr.—Bailie Sally A**

109 — Lifetime 31 4 5 5 $189,434

1989	10	1	1	3	**$59,220**
1988	9	0	0	2	**$11,880**
Turf	6	0	0	1	**$8,760**

4Oct89- 8Bel	fst	1 1/16	:48	1:13⅗	1:44⅘	3↑Alw 50000	6	9	99½	75¾	69½	612¾	Samyn J L	122	13.10	65-36 Homebuilder 1194¾ King's Swan 119¾ Gay Rights 1152½	Outrun	9
17Sep89-10FL	sly	1 1/16	:47	1:12	1:47	3↑Rochester Cp	4	6	611	713	613	415¼	Santagata N	116	4.30	66-25 Packett's Landing 1104½ Pauly Boy107nkLaunching10710½	Outrun	7
9Aug89- 7Sar	fst	1⅛	:46⅘	1:11⅕	1:50⅖	3↑Alw 47000	3	6	69½	66½	54	1½	Samyn J L	115	8.90	83-17 K.C.'sBestTurn115½GayRights1152½DrapeauTricolore122nk	Driving	6
20Jly89- 8Bel	gd	1 1/16	:46	1:10⅖	1:43⅕	3↑Alw 47000	1	4	42	31	22½	3½	Samyn J L	115	7.80	85-26 J. B. Tipton 115no Lord March115½K.C.'sBestTurn1155	Weakened	7
7Jly89- 8Bel	fst	1⅛	:45⅘	1:10⅕	1:48⅘	3↑Alw 33000	1	6	65½	56	25	27½	Samyn J L	117	3.00	75-23 DrpeuTricolore1197½K.C.'sBstTurn1174½Fstiv1171½	Best of others	6
24Jun89- 7Bel	sf	1⅜	Ⓣ:50⅘	1:42⅕	2:21⅕	3↑Alw 47000	5	2	31½	64¾	47½	412	Rogers K L	117	15.20	44-39 Three Engines 1171½ Waki River 1172½ Balsam 1178	Tired	7
14Jun89- 7Bel	fst	1⅛	:46⅕	1:09⅘	1:47⅗	3↑Alw 47000	5	4	43	41½	31	32¾	Samyn J L	117	4.40	86-17 SilverComet1171AdvncingEnsign1171¾K.C.'sBstTurn1174½	Evenly	6
31May89- 7Bel	fst	1 1/16	:46⅘	1:11⅗	1:43⅕	3↑Alw 33000	1	7	75¾	62¾	54½	34½	Samyn J L	119	8.60	81-21 Chinese Gold 1103¼ Garemma 1101¼K.C.'sBestTurn119½	Mild rally	7
22May89- 8Bel	fm	1¼	[T]:50	1:38⅖	2:02⅗	3↑Handicap	4	6	63½	68½	624	629¾	Antley C W	112	3.50e	51-21 Win 114hd Three Engines 112½ Rambo Dancer 1126	No factor	7
14May89- 7Bel	fst	1 1/16	:45⅗	1:09⅗	1:40⅖	3↑Alw 47000	6	8	75½	75½	610	714¾	Samyn J L	119	7.10e	85-13 Tour d'Or 1191¾ Silver Comet 1193 ScavengerHunt121¾	No factor	9

Speed Index: Last Race: +1.0 3–Race Avg.: –2.6 8–Race Avg.: +0.5 Overall Avg.: –4.1
LATEST WORKOUTS Oct 23 Bel 4f fst :49⅘ B Oct 17 Bel 5f fst 1:05⅖ B Oct 1 Bel 5f fst 1:02⅗ B Sep 25 Bel 4f fst :49⅖ H

K.C.'s Best Turn—CL (closes)—"His last race wasn't that good. It looks like he may have peaked at Saratoga. As a 3-year-old, he won the Colin in the summer. He seems to be better in the summer. He'll be running late."

Launching * — **Gr. c. 4, by Relaunch—Barona, by Cougar II**
Br.—Bradley Mary & Lavin (Ky)
Own.—I'll Wait Stable — **Tr.—Trovato Joseph A**

110 — Lifetime 43 5 5 9 $160,167

1989	8	2	1	1	**$62,420**
1988	28	2	4	7	**$82,747**
Turf	5	0	0	1	**$3,927**

5Oct89- 8Bel	fst	7f	:23	:46⅗	1:24⅗	3↑Alw 45000	2	2	11	3nk	615	624¼	Romero R P	b 115	8.40	55-26 Whiz Along 1173½ Pete The Chief1136¼SilentWoods1154	Checked	6
17Sep89-10FL	sly	1 1/16	:47	1:12	1:47	3↑Rochester Cp	7	2	21	21	24	34¾	Carr D	b 107	3.20	76-25 Packett'sLanding1104½PaulyBoy107nkLaunching10710½	Weakened	7
28Aug89- 8Mth	fst	6f	:21⅘	:44⅖	1:09⅕	3↑Alw 27000	4	2	32½	44½	46½	611½	Chavez J F	b 117	2.80	82-17 Castle Park 1193¼ Cutter Sam 1151 Sorry About That 1175¾	Tired	7
12Aug89- 7Sar	my	6½f	:22⅕	:45	1:16⅕	3↑Handicap	7	2	1hd	1hd	32	55	Santos J A	b 113	3.70	86-13 Quick Call 116nk Banker's Jet 1191¾CraftyNorth1132¾	Sp'd, wknd	7
6Apr89- 8Aqu	my	6f	:22⅕	:45	1:09	3↑Handicap	6	2	2½	21½	22½	23	Maple E	b 114	8.70	92-21 Dr. Carrington 1113 Launching 1144 Proud andValid1153	2nd best	6
20Feb89- 8Aqu	fst	1⅛	⊡:48⅗	1:13⅕	1:51⅕	3↑Stymie H	5	1	11½	3nk	612	724¼	Santagata N	b 112	9.80	62-27 Its Acedemic 1132¼ Congeleur1137LordOfTheNight1155	Gave way	7
20Feb89-Grade III																		
30Jan89- 8Aqu	my	1 1/16	⊡:47⅕	1:12⅖	1:45⅗	Handicap	2	1	15	14	13	11	Cordero A Jr	b 114	2.30	81-22 Launching 1141 Big Mukora 1103 Feeling Gallant 1224	Driving	6
13Jan89- 1Aqu	my	1 1/16	⊡:46⅖	1:11	1:41⅗	Alw 29000	2	1	12	14½	13	14	Cordero A Jr	b 117	2.70	101-14 Launching 1174 Ogle 1178¼ Crown the Leader117nk	Kept to drive	5
30Dec88- 7Aqu	fst	170	⊡:47⅖	1:11⅗	1:41⅖	3↑Alw 29000	5	1	15	12½	21	25	Cordero A Jr	b 115	4.20	88-16 Worryation1175Lunching1155CrowntheLeder117nk	Best of others	7
16Dec88- 7Aqu	fst	1 1/16	⊡:46⅗	1:11⅖	1:44⅕	3↑Alw 29000	4	1	12½	11	23½	33¾	Santos J A	b 117	2.60	84-22 Ucancountonme 1171¼ Landyap 1122½ Launching 117½	Gave way	7

Speed Index: Last Race: +1.0 3–Race Avg.: –2.3 6–Race Avg.: +3.0 Overall Avg.: +1.0
LATEST WORKOUTS ●Sep 9 Aqu 4f fst :47⅖ Hg

Launching—MSP (main speed)—"He's a fast horse, going short or going long. He'll be on the lead."

Congeleur — **B. g. 4, by L'Enjoleur—Double Dairya, by Tentam**
Br.—Ryehill Farm (Md)
Own.—Cap-Rus Stable — **Tr.—O'Connell Richard**

122 — Lifetime 39 9 8 7 $449,799

1989	14	4	3	2	**$212,241**
1988	24	5	5	5	**$237,558**
Turf	2	0	0	0	

12Oct89- 8Bel	fst	1	:46⅘	1:11⅗	1:37	3↑Handicap	4	4	32½	3nk	1½	1no	McCauley W H	b 122	10.80	80-24 Congeleur 122no Silver Comet 1151½ Activado 1162½	Driving	6
30Sep89-10Pim	fst	1 1/16	:47⅕	1:11⅕	1:41⅗	3↑Polynesian H	4	4	44½	44½	46½	512¼	Desormeaux KJ	b 114	3.00	84-16 LittleBoldJohn121¾MsterSpeker1173Bldski'sChoic1127	Weakened	6
16Sep89- 5Bel	my	1 1/16	:46⅖	1:11	1:43⅖	3↑Alw 50000	2	1	11½	11½	12	13	McCauley W H	b 115	3.70	85-17 Congeleur 1153 Drapeau Tricolore 1221¼ Gay Rights 1152	Driving	6
10Sep89- 7Bel	fst	7f	:23⅖	:46⅗	1:22⅕	3↑Alw 41000	6	1	21½	21½	31½	44	Migliore R	b 119	*2.10	87-14 Scottish Monk 122¾ Garemma 1181 Seattle Knight 1172¼	Tired	6
12Aug89- 7Sar	my	6½f	:22⅕	:45	1:16⅕	3↑Handicap	3	5	53½	43½	54	44¾	McCauley W H	b 115	7.20	86-13 Quick Call 116nk Banker's Jet 1191¾ CraftyNorth1132¾	Lkd a rally	7
29Jly89- 2Mth	fst	1	:47⅖	1:11⅗	1:36⅖	3↑Elkwood	4	5	52½	31	21½	23	Krone J A	b 117	*1.40	84-14 Timely Warning 1153 Congeleur 117no Loyal Pal 1195	Held place	8
15Jly89-10Det	fst	1⅛	:47⅗	1:12⅕	1:49⅕	3↑Mich Mile H	5	5	54½	41	45½	410¼	McCauley W H	b 113	9.10	81-21 Present Value 111¾ Proper Reality 1205 Mi Selecto1164½	Gamely.	9
15Jly89-Grade II																		
29Jun89- 8Bel	fst	7f	:23⅕	:46	1:22⅘	3↑Alw 41000	2	5	31½	1hd	14	13½	McCauley W H	b 117	3.90	88-16 Congeleur 1173½ Gay Rights 117½ Hittias 1176	Ridden out	5
21Jun89- 8Bel	gd	1	Ⓣ:45⅖	1:10⅕	1:35⅖	3↑Handicap	8	8	911	1016	917	925¼	McCauley W H	b 113	16.10	63-18 Fourstardave 1152¾ Closing Bid 112½ War 1121½	Outrun	10
1Apr89- 8Aqu	fst	1	:46⅕	1:10⅗	1:35⅗	3↑Westchstr H	6	5	53½	52	42	34¾	McCauley W H	b 112	4.10	83-20 Lord Of The Night 115hdDancingSpree1124¾Congeleur1121¾	Wide	8
1Apr89-Grade III																		

Speed Index: Last Race: +4.0 3–Race Avg.: +2.0 6–Race Avg.: +1.5 Overall Avg.: –0.6
LATEST WORKOUTS Sep 29 Bel 3f fst :37 B Sep 6 Bel 4f fst :49⅗ B Sep 1 Bel 4f fst :47⅗ H

Congeleur—LCL (lays close)—"He'll be stalking. I broke his maiden when he was a colt [he was subsequently gelded]."

Wind Chill — **Dk. b. or br. g. 6, by It's Freezing—Hour Serenade, by Bold Hour**
Own.—Topofthepines Farm — **Br.—Allor Fred M (Mich)** — **Tr.—Lusteg Loretta** — **113**
Lifetime 52 14 7 7 $428,422 — 1989 6 1 0 0 $24,780 — 1988 14 4 3 1 $169,889 — Turf 1 0 0 0

4Oct89- 8Bel	fst	1 1/16	:48	1:13⅗	1:44⅘	3↑Alw 50000	4	4	31½	31	45	48	Migliore R	115	7.80	70-36	Homebuilder 1194¾ King's Swan 119¾ Gay Rights 1152½	Tired	9
4Sep89- 5Bel	fst	1	:45⅕	1:09⅖	1:34⅖	3↑Clm 75000	1	7	74	42¼	1½	13¾	Migliore R	117	3.40	93-07	Wind Chill 1173¾ Heliport 113¾ Clos Nardon 113hd	Drew clear	8
9Aug89- 7Sar	fst	1⅛	:46⅘	1:11⅕	1:50⅖	3↑Alw 47000	5	5	54½	44	21½	43¼	Migliore R	115	22.80	80-17	K. C.'s BestTurn115½GayRights1152½DrapeauTricolore122nk	Hung	6
22Jly89- 3Bel	fst	7f	:22⅗	:45⅗	1:23	Clm 75000	2	5	42¾	53¼	44¼	43	Santos J A	117	7.90	84-23	GoldPack113hdScvengerHunt1133DimondAnchor113no	No excuse	8
4Jly89- 6Bel	fst	1 1/16	:46	1:10⅘	1:43⅕	3↑Alw 47000	5	2	2hd	2hd	57	511½	Migliore R	115	10.80	74-21	Tinchen's Prince 1151¼ J. B. Tipton 115nk RonStevens1158½	Tired	5
24Jun89- 4Bel	gd	7f	:22⅗	:45⅗	1:22⅘	Clm 90000	5	3	32	42	76¾	77	Migliore R	118	10.30	81-19	Conquilot 1222 Scottish Monk 120hdScavengerHunt1161	Stopped	8
8Oct88- 9Beu	fst	1 1/16	:46⅕	1:10⅘	1:42⅗	3↑Bud Brd Cp H	7	4	32	2½	23½	46½	Judice J C	115	9.90	87-14	Blue Buckaroo 1231½ Parochial 1183½ Clever Secret 1211½		9
5Sep88-11Det	fst	1⅛	:47⅖	1:12⅖	1:51⅗	3↑[S]Frontier H	8	6	54	51½	32	35	Judice J C	126	*1.50	74-29	MykkJoe1153PrivteExpress1162WindChill1262½	Lugged in stretch	10
4Jly88- 9Det	fst	1 1/16	:48⅕	1:13	1:45⅗	3↑[S]Brd Gov CpH	5	4	32½	22	22	23	Judice J C	126	*1.00	72-26	De Jeau 1253 Wind Chill 126nk Myakka Joe 1183		5
25Jun88- 9CD	fst	1⅛	:47⅕	1:11⅕	1:50⅗	3↑S Foster H	4	1	2½	1½	31	45¼	Judice J C	119	23.60	84-15	Honor Medal 123hd Outlaws Sham 1155 Momsfurrari 109hd		10

25Jun88-Grade III; $1,350 foal and stallion awards to Honor Medal and Outlaws Sham
Speed Index: Last Race: +6.0 — 3–Race Avg.: +1.0 — 8–Race Avg.: –0.1 — Overall Avg.: +0.6
LATEST WORKOUTS Oct 23 Bel 4f fst :48 H — Oct 13 Bel 4f fst :49 B — Sep 29 Bel 3f fst :36 H — Sep 24 Bel 4f fst :49 B

Wind Chill—Migliore's mount—"He used to be a speed horse. He seems better now running at a horse. The trainer and I have discussed the horse a lot.

"On June 24, he was close to the lead in fast fractions (:22 3/5, :45 3/5).

"On July 4, he got away from me. He was fighting me the whole way.

"July 22, I was out of town at Monmouth [Santos substituted].

"August 9, at a mile and an eighth, he put in a good run on the inside. I had no choice. He was on by far the worst part of the track.

"September 4 was by far his best race. When I set him down, he just exploded.

"October 4, it was just a funny race. There was a slow half [:48—the three-quarters was an equally slow 1:13 3/5]. It wasn't a fast enough pace for my horse."

Heritance — **Dk. b. or br. h. 5, by Silver Buck—Instant Hit, by Secretariat**
Own.—Garren M M — **Br.—Carrion Jaime S (Fla)** — **Tr.—Garren Murray M** — **107**
Lifetime 66 7 9 11 $227,900 — 1989 18 2 1 3 $45,580 — 1988 31 1 3 7 $94,820 — Turf 23 0 3 1 $33,320

12Oct89- 1Bel	fst	1⅛	:47⅘	1:12⅖	1:50	3↑Clm 35000	9	9	98¾	94¾	48½	310	Beitia A 05	b	114	6.50	67-24	Diamond Anchor 1171 Waterzip 1089 Heritance 114hd	Very wide	9
1Oct89- 5Bel	fst	1 1/16	:46⅖	1:11	1:43	3↑Clm 30000	6	4	65½	32	1hd	1½	Beitia A 05	b	108	4.20	87-18	Heritance 108½ Boutinierre 1083 Waterzip 1172¼	Driving	6
22Sep89- 1Bel	gd	7f	:22	:45⅕	1:24⅖	3↑Clm 30000	6	4	59	48	31½	12½	Beitia A 05	b	109	15.90	80-25	Heritance 1092½ Hot Amber 114no Mae Van 11319	Driving	6
7Sep89- 5Bel	fm	1¼	[T]:48	1:36⅗	2:01⅘	3↑Clm 35000	11	11	1123	1124	1122	1121	Belmonte J F	b	117	45.70	64-17	MkeSttement117nkMjesticRoberto110nkConteDMont1175	Trailed	11
27Aug89- 4Sar	hd	1⅜	[T]:48⅖	1:38⅘	2:14⅘	3↑Clm 35000	5	8	76	99	914	814	Santiago A	b	117	23.60	80-10	GallntHelio1193¾MkeSttement117¾Uncompromise1191½	No factor	10
17Aug89- 9Sar	fst	1 3/16	:47⅗	1:12⅕	1:58	3↑Clm 25000	6	9	911	810	48	46¾	Fox W I Jr	b	117	19.50	76-17	SummerTale1152½SlickJck1171½MkeSttement1192¾	Lkd late resp.	10
22Jun89- 6Bel	fm	1¼	[T]:48⅗	1:38⅗	2:03⅕	Clm 45000	7	12	1222	1227	1236	1251	Santos J A	b	113	16.70	27-24	Classic Move 117no Finnegan's Pride 113hd Man Ray1171½	Outrun	12
22May89- 8Bel	fm	1¼	[T]:50	1:38⅖	2:02⅗	3↑Handicap	6	7	716	725	732	731¾	Graell A	b	108	32.40	49-21	Win 114hd Three Engines 112½ Rambo Dancer 1126	Trailed	7
7May89- 8Aqu	sf	1 1/16	[T]:52⅖	1:18	1:50⅕	3↑Ft Marcy H	2	5	518	517	519	58¼	Graell A	b	107	6.90e	46-46	Arlene'sVlentine112¾Fourstrdve113¾SunshineForevr1263¾	Outrun	5
7May89-Grade III																				
23Apr89- 7Aqu	fm	1⅛	[T]:47⅖	1:12⅕	1:50⅕	Clm 75000	4	8	711	85¾	76¾	77½	Belmonte J F	b	112	32.10	76-14	Turning For Home 120hd FreeColony1221¾ClassicMove112¾	Tired	10

Speed Index: Last Race: –9.0 — 3–Race Avg.: –3.6 — 3–Race Avg.: –3.6 — Overall Avg.: –13.2
LATEST WORKOUTS Sep 18 Bel tr.t 3f fst :38 B — Sep 5 Bel tr.t 4f fst :49 B

Heritance—"He looks over his head."

Migliore's conclusions: "I expect my horse to race much better. Congeleur and King's Swan are the class of the field. My horse is getting nine pounds from Congeleur. I think nine pounds are significant at a mile and an eighth."

The odds the next day at Aqueduct: King's Swan, 2 to 1; K.C.'s Best Turn, 4 to 1; Launching, 8 to 1; Congeleur, 9 to 5; Wind Chill, 3 to 1; Heritance, 22 to 1.

Wind Chill was not an overlay at 3 to 1, especially since King's Swan had beaten him soundly, by three and a quarter lengths, in their last race while spotting him the same weight, four pounds, as today. Additionally, three starts back, Wind Chill was beaten three and a quarter lengths by K.C.'s Best Turn in a $1^1/_8$ mile allowance race at Saratoga at equal weights. Today, Wind Chill gave K.C.'s Best Turn four pounds.

Migliore's handicapping was excellent; his horse wasn't.

Launching quickly sprinted to a clear lead with King's Swan settled in second and a gap of two lengths to Wind Chill on the inside and Congeleur alongside. K.C.'s Best Turn and Heritance were fifth and sixth.

EIGHTH RACE
Aqueduct
OCTOBER 25, 1989

1 ⅛ MILES. (1.47) HANDICAP. Purse $50,000. 3-year-olds and upward. Weights Saturday, October 21. Declarations by 10:00 A.M. Monday, October 23. Closed Saturday, October 21 with 11 nominations.

Value of race $50,000; value to winner $30,000; second $11,000; third $6,000; fourth $3,000. Mutuel pool $179,478. Exacta Pool $290,660.

Last Raced	Horse	Eqt.	A.	Wt	PP	St	¼	½	¾	Str	Fin	Jockey	Odds $1
4Oct89 ^{8}Bel^{2}	King's Swan		9	117	1	2	$2^{1\frac{1}{2}}$	2^{2}	$1_{\frac{1}{2}}$	1^{1}	1^{3}	Santos J A	2.10
12Oct89 ^{8}Bel^{1}	Congeleur	b	4	122	4	3	$3^{1\frac{1}{2}}$	$3_{\frac{1}{2}}$	3^{hd}	2^{2}	2^{nk}	McCauley W H	1.90
4Oct89 ^{8}Bel^{6}	K. C.'s Best Turn		5	110	2	4	$5_{\frac{1}{2}}$	5^{hd}	$5_{\frac{1}{2}}$	4^{5}	$3^{4\frac{3}{4}}$	Samyn J L	4.00
4Oct89 ^{8}Bel^{4}	Wind Chill		6	113	5	6	$4^{3\frac{1}{2}}$	4^{4}	$4^{2\frac{1}{2}}$	$3^{1\frac{1}{2}}$	4^{4}	Migliore R	3.00
12Oct89 ^{1}Bel^{3}	Heritance	b	5	107	6	5	6	6	6	5	5	Graell A	22.30
5Oct89 ^{8}Bel^{6}	Launching	b	4	113	3	1	1^{2}	1^{2}	$2_{\frac{1}{2}}$	—	—	Cordero A Jr	8.40

Launching, Eased.

OFF AT 3:55. Start good, Won ridden out. Time, :23⅗, :47⅖, 1:12⅕, 1:37⅖, 1:50⅗ Track fast.

$2 Mutuel Prices:				
	1-(A)-KING'S SWAN	6.20	3.00	2.20
	4-(D)-CONGELEUR		3.00	2.20
	2-(B)-K. C.'S BEST TURN			2.20

$2 EXACTA 1–4 PAID $13.20.

B. g, by King's Bishop—Royal Cygnet, by Sea-Bird. Trainer Dutrow Richard E. Bred by Kerr Mrs D K (Ky).

KING'S SWAN stalked LAUNCHING to the far turn, gained the lead from the outside on the turn, drew clear, then widened his advantage over CONGELEUR in the final furlong to finish under a hand ride. CONGELEUR, unhurried early, lodged his bid after the winner three wide on the far turn, remained a strong factor in the upper stretch then falttened out. K. C.'S BEST TURN outrun early finished with a belated bid. WIND CHILL moved just inside CONGELEUR on the far turn, then tired in the drive. LAUNCHING set the pace to the far turn took up while dropping back on the turn, then was eased in the stretch. The stewards conducted an inquiry into the far turn but found no wrong doing.

Approaching the far turn, Jose Santos sent King's Swan after Launching as the field bunched. Congeleur and Wind Chill both moved to within two lengths of the leader, Congeleur on the outside and Wind Chill inside.

Launching offered little resistance and King's Swan quickly gained the lead. Congeleur moved toward him on the outside. Wind Chill, in a position to win along the rail, didn't sustain his momentum. As King's Swan increased his lead on Congeleur, Wind Chill tired and K.C.'s Best Turn rallied. With little difficulty, King's Swan won the twenty-ninth race of his carer by three lengths. Congeleur saved second by a neck in front of K.C.'s Best Turn, who finished four and three-quarters ahead of fourth place Wind Chill. Heritance was fifth another four lengths back, and Launching was eased.

Bits and Pieces

17

Weight

Does weight make a ton of difference? Of all the well-known factors of handicapping, weight more times than not carries the least significance, or is significant far fewer times than other considerations. Racing Secretary Hale says, "If a horse is right, a pound or two won't make a difference."

In general, weight has the least influence in sprints, which again, is just common sense. The farther a horse has to go carrying more weight, the more tired he becomes.

Weight becomes a serious consideration when horses carry different weight in a race. A 3-year-old may find difficulty carrying the 126 pounds of the Triple Crown races if he's never done it before, but all the 3-year-olds in the Triple Crown, (barring fillies who carry 121) carry that same impost. There is no advantage for any of the horses. However, we can handicap an advantage if we see a 3-year-old who has already carried that much weight and still raced well. His proven ability, contrasted with other horses who haven't carried as much weight successfully, can be an important handicapping factor.

Weight is important enough in the rules of racing to favor apprentice jockeys with a weight allowance of ten, then seven, then five pounds as they learn their craft.

Many times, we see the red-hot apprentice, riders such as Steve Cauthen, Richard Migliore and Declan Murphy, enjoy extreme success with the bug, the so-called asterisk (*) which denotes an apprentice jockey in the racing program. Is this success because their mounts are carrying less weight?

A simplistic answer is it certainly doesn't hurt. In reality, though, these apprentices bring in winners by the bundle because their success has a snowballing effect. Once they demonstrate they can handle a horse, the quality of their mounts naturally improves as more trainers seek their services. Within weeks, the young apprentice suddenly has an agent choosing two or three of the top mounts in many races when weeks before he couldn't get a single mount. When the apprentice weight allowance is waived—the allowance is five pounds for a calendar year from the date of an apprentice's fifth win— the effect can be devastating. It was bad enough that a high-quality rider such as Cauthen was saddled with a horrendous slump. Presumably, it was one of the reasons Cauthen abandoned the United States for Europe. Other riders such as Migliore, who broke Cauthen's apprentice earnings record for one year, stay and fight it out, determined to prove they can win though they've lost the weight allowance. The late Mike Venezia rode for years in New York, but never matched the eye catching success he enjoyed as an apprentice.

Another racing rule reflecting a consideration of weight is that older horses are asked to concede five pounds to 3-year-olds. Similarly, colts and geldings spot fillies and mares five pounds.

Weight becomes most important in handicap races when weight differences are used by a racing secretary to enhance the competitiveness of the race. With thoroughbreds, it's done by giving the top horse enough weight to slow him down in relation to the ability of the other horses in the race. The general rule used by racing secretaries in assigning weight is one pound equals one length in a distance race and two pounds equals one length in a sprint.

The better the horse in handicap racing, the more weight he carries. The ones who win anyway, a Kelso, a Forego and a John Henry, are usually geldings whose lack of stud potential allows them to continue racing. One of the great sins of thoroughbred racing is the across-the-board damage huge syndications have done by robbing thoroughbred racing of many of its greatest stars. Secretariat, the greatest horse of our time, never got the opportunity to race as a 4-year-old and prove if he could carry weight as well as Forego, whom you might not know finished fourth in Secretariat's Kentucky Derby victory in 1973.

Despite the initiation of the Breeders' Cup in 1984, which encourages owners to race their horses as 4-year-olds, syndications still steal thoroughbred stars. Risen Star, the son of Secretariat who won the 1988 Preakness and Belmont Stakes, is a telling example.

We'll use weight as a handicapping tool principally in distance races as a comparative measure.

Let's look at the 1983 running of the $150,000-added 1⅛ mile Whitney Handicap at Saratoga.

8 SARATOGA 1⅛ MILES SARATOGA Start & Finish

1 ⅛ MILES. (1.47) 56th Running THE WHITNEY (Grade I). Purse $150,000 added. 3-year-olds and upward. By subscription of $300 each, which should accompany the nomination; $1,200 to pass the entry box, with $150,000 added. The added money and all fees to be divided 60% to the winner, 22% to second, 12% to third and 6% to foruth. Weights Monday, July 25. Starters to be named at the closing time of entries. Trophies will be presented to the winning owner, trainer and jockey. Closed with 33 nominations Wednesday July 13, 1983.

Island Whirl B. h. 5, by Pago Pago—Alitwirl, by Your Alibhai
Own.—Elcee-H Stable Br.—Elcee-H Stable & Breeding Farm Inc (Fla) Tr.—Barrera Lazaro S
123 Lifetime 31 10 5 6 $984,310 | 1983 4 2 2 0 $325,900 | 1982 11 3 1 1 $269,730 | Turf 8 1 3 3 $44,660
26Jun83- 8Hol fst 1¼ :46⅕ 1:34⅘ 1:59⅖ 3+Gold Cup H 3 1 12½ 11½ 1½ 12 Delahoussaye E 120 3.00 94-09 Island Whirl 120² Poley 116² Prince Spellbound 120no Driving 6
12Jun83- 4Hol fst 6½f :22⅕ :44⅖ 1:14⅕ Alw 38000 2 3 1½ 13 15 18 Pincay L Jr 122 *.40 99-14 Island Whirl 122⁸ Laughing Boy115hdHaughtybutnice119nk Easily 6
15May83- 8Hol fst 1 :45⅗ 1:10 1:35⅘ 3+M Leroy H 5 2 2½ 1hd 1hd 21½ Lipham T 122 3.80 85-23 Fighting Fit 1151½ Island Whirl 122³ KangrooCourt116² Game try 7
30Apr83- 8Hol gd 7f :22⅕ :45⅗ 1:23⅖ 3+Triplebend H 3 3 2hd 1½ 12 2½ Lipham T 123 2.70 79-33 Regal Falcon117½IslandWhirl123¾KangrooCourt118⁴ Forced wide 5
14Nov82- 9Hol fst 6f :21⅗ :44⅕ 1:08⅗ 3+Nat Sprint C 8 2 53 41½ 43 63 Hawley S 124 4.20 91-12 Unpredictable 1201½ RememberJohn120½ChinookPass112hd Tired 8
14Nov82-Run in two division 8th & 9th races
3Nov82- 8Hol fst 1⅛ :46⅖ 1:10⅖ 1:41 3+Citation H 2 1 12 11 2hd 32½ Pincay L Jr 123 *2.30 87-18 Caterman 121½ Cajun Prince 118² Island Whirl 1234½ Weakened 5
9Oct82- 8Bel fst 1½ :47⅗ 2:04 2:31⅕ 3+J C Gold Cup 10 1 18 24 413 424 Pincay L Jr 126 5.30 40-25 Lemhi Gold 1264½ Silver Supreme 126² ChristmasPast118¹⁷ Tired 10
4Sep82- 8Bel fst 1⅛ :46⅖ 1:10 1:46⅘ 3+Woodward 6 1 12½ 13½ 17 15 Cordero A Jr 123 11.00 93-13 Island Whirl 123⁵ Silver Buck 126⁴ Silver Supreme 1262½ Driving 7
26Aug82- 8Dmr fm 1⅙ Ⓣ:49⅖ 1:13 1:43⅖ 3+Alw 30000 3 1 11 1½ 1hd 22 Pincay L Jr 119 *1.30 90-13 Regalberto 119² Island Whirl 119² Monarch 115½ Tired 6
7Aug82- 7Dmr fst 6f :22⅕ :44⅗ 1:08⅗ 3+Alw 24000 5 3 31 2hd 11½ 13½ Pincay L Jr 122 2.70 95-13 Island Whirl 1223½ Shady Fox 117² Amen Brother 116¾ Handily 8
LATEST WORKOUTS ●Jly 27 Sar 5f fst :58 h ●Jly 21 Bel tr.t 5f fst :59 h Jly 14 Bel 5f fst :59⅖ h

Muttering Ro. c. 4, by Drone—Malvine, by Gamin
Own.—Tartan Stable Br.—Tartan Farms (Fla) Tr.—Nerud Jan H
113 Lifetime 21 7 3 0 $490,208 | 1983 7 1 0 0 $31,359 | 1982 7 3 2 0 $350,420 | Turf 3 1 0 0 $31,359
17Jly83- 7Bel fm 1 Ⓣ:45 1:08⅖ 1:34 3+Handicap 7 2 47 716 515 412 Cordero A Jr 117 *.70e 83-14 Disco Count 1113¾ Ten Below 1135½ AskClarence109³ Forced out 8
3Jly83- 8Bel fm 1⅜ [T]:48⅗ 1:36⅘ 2:12⅘ 3+Tidal H 1 4 45 42 42¾ 44 Migliore R 119 3.70 89-15 Hush Dear 117hd John's Gold 1171½ Late Act 1112½ Weakened 8
11Jun83- 3Bel fm 6f Ⓣ:21⅘ :44⅗ 1:09⅕ 3+Alw 40000 11 8 68 65¾ 53½ 11 Migliore R 122 *1.70e 97-06 Muttering 122¹ Mayanesian 117no Ski Jump 114¾ Driving 11
26May83- 8Bel fst 7f :22⅗ :45⅕ 1:23 3+Alw 35000 5 5 54½ 66½ 612 615 Cordero A Jr 124 1.90e 72-21 Guyana 1191½ Winter's Tale 124½ Will Of Iron 1194½ Tired 6
15May83- 1Aqu fst 1 :46 1:09⅘ 1:35 3+Handicap 4 5 64½ 66½ 69 69¾ Fell J 118 5.30 81-18 West On Broad 1092½ Star Choice1151¾OtterSlide113nk No factor 6
15Apr83- 8Aqu fst 1 :46⅖ 1:10⅗ 1:37 3+Handicap 1 3 53¼ 56½ 58½ 58½ Cordero A Jr 122 *1.50 72-29 Parfaitement 1072½ Mouse Corps 1161½ Tumarshua 111² Tired 5
31Mar83- 8Aqu fst 6f :22⅖ :45⅗ 1:10 Alw 35000 7 6 612 713 711 711 Cordero A Jr 122 *.60e 80-21 Main Stem 112hd Maudlin 1123½ And More 117¾ Outrun 7
30Sep82- 6Med fst 1⅛ :47⅗ 1:11⅖ 1:49 Pegasus H 6 3 21 2hd 21½ 23¼ Cordero A Jr 120 2.00 85-15 Fast Gold 1103¼ Muttering 120² Exclusive One 116³ 2nd best 8
18Sep82- 8Bel fst 1¼ :47⅗ 1:36 2:01 3+Mrlbro Cup H 6 4 44 614 621 623 Shoemaker W 118 4.10 70-17 Lemhi Gold 1158¾ Silver Supreme 117¾ Pair of Deuces 116⁹ Tired 8
6Sep82- 8Dmr fst *1¼ :46⅗ 1:34⅘ 1:57 3+Dmr Inv H 1 2 21½ 21 1hd 12 Shoemaker W 117 3.20 92-17 Muttering 117² Regalberto 1194½ Exploded 121nk Drew clear 9
LATEST WORKOUTS Jly 27 Sar 4f fst :48 b Jly 11 Bel 4f fst :50⅕ b Jun 30 Bel [illegible] :47⅗ b Jun 25 Bel 5f fst :59⅖ h

Sunny's Halo * Ch. c. 3, by Halo—Mostly Sunny, by Sunny
Own.—Foster D Br.—Foster D J (Ont-C) Tr.—Cross David C Jr
116 Lifetime 16 8 2 $907,019 | 1983 5 3 0 0 $671,190 | 1982 11 5 2 1 $235,829
12Jun83- 8AP fst 1⅛ :46⅘ 1:10⅘ 1:49 Arl Classic 7 4 33 41¾ 42½ 47 Delahoussaye E 126 *.20 79-27 Play Fellow 123³ Bet Big 1143½ Passing Base 114½ Steadied str 9
12Jun83-Disqualified from purse money
21May83- 8Pim sly 1³⁄₁₆ :46⅘ 1:10⅗ 1:55⅖ Preakness 11 3 21½ 2½ 45 611 Delahoussaye E 126 *1.10 82-11 DeputedTstmony1262¾DsrtWin126⁴HighHonors1261¾ Speed, tired 12
7May83- 8CD fst 1¼ :47⅕ 1:36⅘ 2:02⅕ Ky Derby 10 2 21½ 1hd 1½ 12 Delahoussaye E 126 2.50 86-10 Sunny's Halo 126² Desert Wine 126nk Caveat 126¹ Steady urging 20
16Apr83- 9OP fst 1⅛ :46⅖ 1:11⅗ 1:49⅖ Ark Derby 13 1 15 15 14 14 Delahoussaye E 126 *2.90 96-19 Sunny's Halo 126⁴ Caveat 1201½ Exile King 1171½ Handy score 14
26Mar83- 9OP gd 170 :46⅖ 1:12⅕ 1:42⅕ Rebel H 2 3 41¾ 51½ 1hd 13 Snyder L 121 2.60 85-15 Sunny's Halo 121³SlighJet1171¾LeCouCou1151½ Boxed in str turn 11
4Nov82- 6Med fst 1⅙ :45⅘ 1:09⅗ 1:43⅖ Yng Amer'a 10 3 31 34½ 47½ 69 Penna D b 122 29.60 83-14 Slewpy 1193½ Bet Big 122¹ El Cubanaso 1192½ Tired 11
23Oct82- 8Lrl fst 1⅙ :46⅗ 1:12⅗ 1:45 Lrl Futurity 9 2 1hd 42 811 916 Bracciale V Jr b 122 *2.20 67-21 Cast Party 122¹ Pax In Bello 122¾ Primitive Pleasure 122⁵ Tired 11
11Oct82- 9WO sly 1⅛ :47⅖ 1:12⅖ 1:53⅗ [S]Coro'n Fut'y 3 1 14 16 16 17½ Penna D b 122 *.25 72-29 Snny'sHlo1227½RsngYongStr1224¾HlbrtonHsk122³ Drifted, easily 8
25Sep82- 9WO sly 1⅙ :47⅖ 1:12⅘ 1:45⅖ Grey 1 1 11½ 13 15 16½ Penna D 123 *.35 82-28 Sunny'sHalo1236½RisingYoungStr1179½HrdScrmbler115hd Handily 9
12Sep82- 9WO fst 7f :23⅘ :45⅘ 1:23⅘ Swynford 4 2 1½ 11½ 13½ 17½ Penna D b 122 *.90 90-20 Sunny's Halo1227½SecretWard117¹RisingYoungStar1153½ Handily 6

Deputy Minister — Dk. b. or br. c. 4, by Vice Regent—Mint Copy, by Bunty's Flight
Own.—Brennan R — Br.—Centurion Farms (Ont-C) — Tr.—Nobles Reynaldo H — 126
Lifetime 16 12 0 0 $568,135 — 1983 3 3 0 0 $150,900 — 1982 4 1 0 0 $10,621

17Jly83- 8Bel fst 7f :22⅘ :45⅗ 1:21⅕ 3↑Tom Fool 5 8 85½ 42½ 12½ 14¾ MacBeth D 126 3.40 91-13 Deputy Minister 1264¾ Fit to Fight119noMaudlin126hd Ridden out 9
12Feb83-10GP fst 1⅛ :47⅕ 1:11 1:48⅗ 3↑Donn H 7 7 66½ 31 1hd 11½ MacBeth D 122 *1.10 89-17 Deputy Minister 1221½ Key Count 1133½Rivalero1212½ Ridden out 16
29Jan83-10GP fst 7f :22 :44⅘ 1:22⅘ 3↑Sprnt Chmp H 4 9 1113107 5½ 1½ MacBeth D 122 5.50 90-20 Deputy Minister 122½ Wipe 'Em Out 1092½ CenterCut118½ Driving 12
21Nov82- 8Aqu fst 6f :22⅗ :45⅖ 1:09⅖ 3↑Sport Page H 3 9 94¾ 87½ 87½ 78½ MacBeth D 124 *1.60 86-24 Maudlin 1154 ⒹKing's Fashion117hdTopAvenger115nk No menace 11
28Oct82- 8WO fst 6f :22⅘ :45⅗ 1:09⅖ 3↑Alw 16000 6 1 1½ 12½ 16 16½ Platts R 115 *.30 96-19 Deputy Minister1156½ToutOuRien1231½ReddyRoadster1262 Easily 6
24Feb82- 9Hia fst 7f :23⅖ :46 1:22⅕ Alw 25000 8 2 31½ 21 44½ 99 MacBeth D 122 4.70 83-19 Distinctive Pro 1194½ D'Accord 1192½ Cecis Lil Bandit 115½ Tired 9
27Jan82- 9Hia fst 7f :22⅗ :45⅕ 1:22⅕ Bahamas 5 9 76 57 55½ 59¼ MacBeth D 122 *1.10 82-19 Alom'sRuler117hdDistinctivePro1174LetsDontFight1193 Steadied 9
5Nov81- 6Medfst 1⅟₁₆ :47⅕ 1:11⅗ 1:44⅗ Yng America 7 5 42 11 14 13 MacBeth D 122 *1.90 86-17 Deputy Minister 1223 Laser Light 1191 Real Twister 1192 Driving 14
24Oct81- 8Lrl gd 1⅟₁₆ :47 1:12⅘ 1:44⅗ Lrl Fut'y 3 4 42½ 1hd 11½ 1no MacBeth D 122 *1.60 85-18 Deputy Minister122noLaserLight1229ⒹCageyCougar122hd Driving 8
10Oct81- 7Bel fst 1 :46⅘ 1:11⅕ 1:36⅘ Champagne 11 6 52 41¾ 44 48 Cordero A Jr 122 3.50 78-14 TimelyWriter1224¾BeforeDawn1193NewDiscovery122nk Weakened 13
LATEST WORKOUTS Jly 25 Sar 7f fst 1:26⅕ b — Jly 16 Bel 3f fst :36⅗ b — ●Jly 11 Bel 7f fst 1:24⅘ hg — ●Jly 6 Bel 6f fst 1:11⅕ h

Bold Style — B. c. 4, by Bold Commander—Marianna Trench, by Pago Pago
Own.—Mayer L — Br.—Mayer L (Ky) — Tr.—McGaughey C R III — 114
Lifetime 24 7 3 4 $443,366 — 1983 9 3 1 1 $306,385 — 1982 8 3 0 1 $115,650 — Turf 6 3 0 0 $95,745

4Jly83- 8AP sf 1⅛ Ⓣ:49⅗ 1:15 1:48⅘ 3↑Strstripe H 6 1 1hd 2½ 53 67½ Patterson G 118 4.60 58-35 Rossi Gold 122½ Who's For Dinner 1103 Lucence 1151 Tired 7
19Jun83- 8Hol fm 1⅛ Ⓣ:47⅘ 1:11⅗ 1:41⅖ 3↑Inglewood H 8 1 1hd 2hd 1½ 12 Day P b 115 21.30 92-11 Bold Style 1152 Noalto 115½ Western 116no Drew clear 8
29May83- 8GG fm 7½f Ⓣ:23⅖ :46⅘ 1:29⅖ 3↑All Amercn H 11 6 2hd 2hd 44 65½ Judice J C b 119 3.30 87-16 Major Sport 115no Aristocratical 1141½ Take The Floor1151 Tired 11
7May83- 8Hol fm 1⅛ Ⓣ:46⅖ 1:10⅗ 1:47⅕ 3↑Century H 4 2 2½ 2hd 11½ 43 Day P b 115 14.20 91-11 The Wonder 1232½ Twin's Tornado 118no Lithan 115½ Weakened 9
15Apr83- 9OP fst 1⅛ :47⅕ 1:11⅗ 1:43 Oaklawn H 1 1 21 23 22 1½ Day P b 113 8.30e 93-16 Bold Style 113½ Eminency 1233½ Listcapade 1231½ Driving 8
2Apr83- 9OP fst 1⅛ :46⅗ 1:11⅗ 1:43⅗ Razorback H 3 4 42 53½ 33½ 32½ Lively J b 113 7.80e 87-21 Eminency 1202½ Cassaleria 115nk Bold Style 1135 Bumped start 10
20Mar83-10FG fst 1¼ :46⅗ 1:38⅗ 2:03⅕ N Orleans H 7 3 37 31 35½ 211 Moyers L b 113 6.20 82-19 Listcapade 12111 Bold Style 1131 Aspro 114¾ Bore out 9
27Feb83-10FG fm *1 Ⓣ 1:37⅗ Alw 12000 4 4 34 2½ 21½ 13 Moyers L b 113 *1.20e 91-11 Bold Style 1133 Up Limit 1212 Prince Freddie 1143 Driving 8
6Feb83- 8FG fst 6f :22⅖ :46⅗ 1:11 Alw 11500 1 2 31½ 52½ 54 43¾ Moyers L b 113 2.40 86-19 Another Bid 1162 Spoonful Of Honey 1131 Really Royal 111¾ 7
3Jly82- 9Aks fst 1⅛ :46⅖ 1:10⅗ 1:43⅕ Omaha Gld Cp 4 6 69 53½ 57 411 Hall D C b 123 3.90e 76-21 WveringMonrch1176½DropYourDrwrs1172EnrgticKing1172 Evenly 9
LATEST WORKOUTS Jly 27 Sar 5f fst 1:00 h — Jun 15 Hol Ⓣ 5f fm 1:03 h (d) — ●Jun 6 Hol 6f fst 1:12⅖ h

Star Choice — B. c. 4, by In Reality—Some Swinger, by Tirreno
Own.—Genter Frances A — Br.—Frances A Genter Stable (Fla) — Tr.—Veitch John M — 114
Lifetime 18 8 4 1 $273,081 — 1983 7 2 1 0 $181,636 — 1982 9 6 1 1 $88,115

23Jly83- 8Bel fst 1½ :48⅗ 2:04 2:31 3↑Brooklyn H 3 7 89½ 91210161119 Velasquez J b 114 9.00 46-30 Highland Blade 1171½ Sing Sing 118hd SilverSupreme1133 Outrun 13
23Jun83- 8Bel fst 1⅛ :47⅗ 1:11⅘ 1:43⅗ 3↑Alw 37000 6 3 32 32 32½ 53¼ Velasquez J b 119 *.50 81-22 Bounding Basque 1111¾ Nice Pirate 117¾ExclusiveOne117hd Tired 6
30May83- 8Bel my 1 :44⅗ 1:08⅕ 1:33⅗ 3↑Metroplt'n H 2 3 32½ 21½ 1hd 11¼ Velasquez J b 113 17.00 96-11 Star Choice 1131¼ Tough Critic 1103½ John's Gold 1112 Driving 13
15May83- 1Aqu fst 1 :46 1:09⅘ 1:35 3↑Handicap 5 3 32 2½ 22 22¼ Velasquez J b 115 *1.70 88-18 West On Broad 1092¼ StarChoice1151¾OtterSlide113nk Bid,evenly 6
15Apr83- 9OP fst 1⅛ :47⅕ 1:11⅗ 1:43 Oaklawn H 6 4 41½ 43 [illegible] [illegible] Velasquez J 116 4.90 87-16 Bold Style 113½ Eminency 1233½ Listcapade 1231½ Evenly 8
26Mar83- 8Aqu fst 1 :45⅗ 1:09⅗ 1:35⅘ 3↑Westchester 2 6 77½ 45 45 44 Brumfield D 116 2.50 86-19 Singh Tu 109½MasterDigby114¾FabulousFjnd1142¾ Lacked a rally 10
10Mar83- 9Hia fst 6f :22⅕ :45⅖ 1:10 Alw 14000 2 6 62¾ 53½ 31 1hd Brumfield D 119 *1.20 93-17 Star Choice 119hd Bill Wheeler 122½ Spirited Boy 122hd Driving 7
17Jly82- 6Atl fst 1⅛ :46 1:10 1:49⅗ Jersey Dby 2 4 39 36 31 2no Thomas D B 116 4.50 90-16 Aloma's Ruler 126no StarChoice1162SpanishDrums1264 Came out 8
10Jly82- 8Key fst 1⅟₁₆ :46⅗ 1:10⅘ 1:42⅘ Devon 1 9 99¾ 55 31½ 11½ Thomas D B 117 *1.70 90-19 Star Choice 1171½LordLister1172ThunderRunner1156½ Drew clear 10
26Jun82- 6Mth fst 1⅟₁₆ :47⅗ 1:11⅕ 1:42⅗ 3↑Alw 16000 3 5 35 41¾ 31 1hd Fann B 110 *.80 92-12 Star Choice 110hd CenturyBanker1192DynamicMove1152¾ Driving 6
LATEST WORKOUTS Jly 22 Bel 3f sly :37 b — Jly 18 Bel 1¼m fst 2:08⅗ b — Jly 15 Bel 6f fst 1:13⅖ h — Jly 10 Bel 5f fst 1:01 b

Kleiglight — B. c. 4, by Majestic Light—In Hot Pursuit, by Bold Ruler
Own.—Phipps O M — Br.—Phipps O M (Ky) — Tr.—Penna Angel — 107
Lifetime 3 2 1 0 $29,060 — 1983 3 2 1 0 $29,060 — 1982 0 M 0 0

20Jly83- 1Bel gd 1⅛ :48⅗ 1:12⅖ 1:50 3↑Alw 23000 5 2 2hd 2hd 2hd 2hd Cordero A Jr 122 *1.20 77-25 Galaxy Guide 106hd Kleiglight 1226½ Luv A Libra 1114¾ Brushed 5
1Jly83- 1Bel fst 1⅟₁₆ :47⅗ 1:12⅖ 1:43 3↑Alw 21000 2 4 43½ 3½ 1hd 1hd Cordero A Jr 122 *.40 87-16 Kleiglight 122hd Inner Circuit 1101½ Halo's Comet 1173½ Driving 6
16Jun83- 6Bel fst 1⅛ :45⅗ 1:09⅘ 1:49⅘ 3↑Md Sp Wt 1 5 31½ 2hd 13 16¾ Cordero A Jr 122 *1.20 78-22 Kleiglight 1226¾ Rue Lauriston1222¾BelmontBall114nk Ridden out 8
LATEST WORKOUTS Jly 19 Bel 4f sly :48⅗ b — Jly 13 Bel 4f fst :47⅘ b — Jun 30 Bel 4f fst :48⅗ b — Jun 14 Bel 4f fst :49⅗ b

Linkage — B. c. 4, by Hoist the Flag—Unity Hall, by Dyane
Own.—Christiana Stable — Br.—Lunger Jane DuPont (Ky) — Tr.—Clark Henry S — 116
Lifetime 16 11 3 0 $379,301 — 1983 3 3 0 0 $51,000 — 1982 11 6 3 0 $320,201

9Jly83- 1Bel fst 7f :23⅖ :46 1:22⅘ 3↑Alw 35000 1 4 1[illegible] 1hd 1hd 1no McCarron G 117 *.40 88-23 Linkage 117no Danebo 1171 Guyana 1173¾ Long,hard drive 5
18Jun83- 7Bel fst 6f :22⅖ :45⅘ 1:10⅖ 3↑Alw 35000 2 3 22 2½ 13 18 McCarron G 117 *.40 90-18 Linkage 1178 Prosper 117nk Mayanesian 119¾ Handily 8
23May83- 8Mth sly 6f :22⅘ :45⅗ 1:11 3↑Alw 15000 4 3 21 2hd 1½ 13½ McCarron G 115 *.70 85-21 Linkage1153½BoldAdonis1225JewelrySale115nk Loose band., clear 5
31Jly82- 8Mth fst 1⅛ :47⅘ 1:10⅗ 1:47⅘ Haskell H 5 2 41 41½ 48 514 Shoemaker W 122 *1.50 82-08 WveringMonrch117¾Alom'sRuler1269Lejoli1122 Drifted out, wide 7
5Jun82- 8Bel sly 1½ :47⅕ 2:03⅕ 2:28⅕ Belmont 7 5 34½ 24 311 422 Shoemaker W 126 *2.20 57-17 ConquistadorCielo12614GatoDelSol1264Illuminate1263¾ Gave way 11
15May82- 8Pim fst 1³⁄₁₆ :48 1:12 1:55⅖ Preakness 6 4 31½ 32 21½ 2½ Shoemaker W 126 *.50 92-16 Aloma's Ruler 126½ Linkage 1266¾ Cut Away 1262 Game effort 7
22Apr82- 7Kee fst 1⅛ :46⅗ 1:10 1:48 Blue Grass 5 2 1hd 11 12½ 15½ Shoemaker W 121 *.90 97-13 Linkage 1215½GatoDelSol121½WaveringMonarch1217½ Ridden out 9
15Apr82- 7Kee fst 7f :22⅗ :45⅕ 1:22⅘ Alw 30200 2 7 44½ 42½ 1½ 1½ Shoemaker W 123 *.40 92-18 Linkage 123½ Royal Roberto 1204 Center Cut 1231½ Driving 9
28Mar82-10FG fst 1⅛ :46⅘ 1:11⅖ 1:50⅗ La Derby 2 1 11 11½ 2hd 2½ Smith G P 120 *.90 90-21 El Baba 123½ Linkage 1204 Spoonful Of Honey 1133½ Gamely 8
13Mar82- 9FG fst 1⅟₁₆ :47⅗ 1:12 1:44⅖ Handicap 4 1 12½ 11½ 12½ 14 Smith G P 122 3.20e 90-18 Linkage 1224 El Baba 1252 Spoonful Of Honey 112½ Driving 8
LATEST WORKOUTS Jly 26 Sar 1 fst 1:39⅗ b — Jly 16 Pim 1 fst 1:41⅖ h — ●Jly 5 Pim 5f fst 1:00⅖ h — Jun 25 Pim 7f fst 1:25 h

Fit to Fight — B. c. 4, by Chieftain—Hasty Queen II, by One Count
Own.—Rokeby Stable — Br.—Congleton & Courtney (Ky) — Tr.—Miller Mack
114
Lifetime 14 7 1 3 $256,242 — 1983 5 1 1 2 $63,786 — 1982 6 4 0 1 $173,436

17Jly83- 8Bel	fst	7f	:22⅘	:45⅗	1:22⅕	3↑Tom Fool	2	6	74	64¼	54½	24¾	Maple E	119	6.50	86–13	Deputy Minister 1264¾ Fit to Fight 119no Maudlin 126hd	Rallied	9
26Jun83- 8Bel	fst	6f	:22⅖	:45⅕	1:10⅖	3↑True North H	5	8	66	56½	45	33½	Bailey J D	113	5.30	86–24	Gold Beauty 1212¼ Singh Tu 1111¼ Fit to Fight 1132	Wide str.	8
30May83- 8Bel	my	1	:44⅖	1:08⅕	1:33⅘	3↑Metropl't'n H	9	7	65	69	89¾	89½	Bailey J D	115	*1.50	86–11	StrChoic1131½ToughCritc1103¾John'sGold1112	Lacked a response	13
7May83- 8Aqu	fst	7f	:22⅖	:44⅗	1:22⅘	3↑Carter H	2	8	73¾	64½	71¾	33	McCarron G	116	*1.50	84–19	Vittorioso 113nk Sing Sing 1222¾ Fit to Fight 116¾	Blocked	9
22Apr83- 8Aqu	fst	6f	:22⅖	:45⅗	1:09⅖	3↑Alw 35000	4	9	43	42½	1hd	11½	Bailey J D	121	4.40	94–16	Fit to Fight 1211½ Star Gallant 1213¼ Sepulveda 119nk	Drew clear	11
30Oct82- 8Aqu	fst	1⅛	:47⅘	1:11⅗	1:49⅗	3↑Stuyvesant H	3	2	2½	21	33½	34	Bailey J D	118	2.40	83–16	Engine One 1232 Bar Dexter 1122 Fit to Fight 1182	Weakened	6
30Sep82- 6Med	fst	1⅛	:47⅗	1:11⅖	1:49	Pegasus H	1	2	31½	33	68½	48¼	Bailey J D	118	*1.30	80–15	Fast Gold 1103¼ Muttering 1202 Exclusive One 1163	Weakened	8
6Sep82- 8Bel	fst	1	:45⅘	1:10⅕	1:35⅖	Jerome H	1	2	1hd	1½	13½	16	Bailey J D	112	1.60	88–17	Fit to Fight 1126 John's Gold 1152¾ Lord Lister 1071	Ridden out	6
19Aug82- 7Sar	fst	6f	:22	:45	1:09⅖	3↑Alw 32000	1	4	45	32	21½	1¾	Fell J	117	*1.60	93–17	Fit to Fight 117¾ Hat Room 1151¼ Ring of Light 1191	Driving	6
7Aug82- 5Sar	fst	5½f	:22⅗	:45⅕	1:16⅖	3↑Alw 23000	3	10	75	43	1hd	1¾	Fell J	112	*.80	90–14	Fit to Fight 112¾ Jet Steam 112no GrandCourant117no	Ridden out	11

LATEST WORKOUTS Jly 27 Sar 5f fst 1:01 h — Jly 9 Bel 6f fst 1:14 b — ●Jun 20 Bel 6f gd 1:12⅘ h — Jun 13 Bel 5f fst 1:00⅘ b

The Whitney attracted an interesting, varied field. The starting high weight of 126 pounds was Deputy Minister, the 2-year-old champion of 1981 who was twelve for sixteen lifetime. He had come back from an assortment of injuries to win his first start in five months, the Tom Fool Handicap at Belmont, by four and three-quarters lengths, carrying the same impost. That was at seven furlongs.

Two of the horses he beat in the Tom Fool were entered in the Whitney: Fit To Fight, dropping 5 pounds to 114 after finishing second by four and three-quarters in the Tom Fool, and Danebo, who was scratched.

The second high weight was trainer Laz Barrera's Island Whirl, winner of the 1982 Woodward by five lengths while carrying 123 pounds, the same impost he had in the Whitney. While he was in benefit of three pounds from Deputy Minister, Island Whirl was picking up three pounds from his last start, a wire-to-wire, two length win in the $1^1/_4$ mile Hollywood Gold Cup.

Making the race most interesting was the presence of the 1983 Kentucky Derby winner, Sunny's Halo, and Linkage, the beaten favorite in the 1982 Preakness. Coming off two poor races following the Kentucky Derby, a sixth by eleven lengths in the Preakness and a fourth by seven in the Arlington Classic, Sunny's Halo was weighted at 116 for the Whitney, thus getting 10 pounds from Deputy Minister and 7 from Island Whirl.

In his ten PPs, Sunny's Halo had never carried less weight than 121.

Was it the reason he ran an impressive third in the Whitney? It didn't hurt, that's for sure. But Sunny's Halo was a horse of considerable ability as he showed in Kentucky and again in Louisiana when he romped to a ten length victory against Travers winner Play Fellow.

Island Whirl went wire-to-wire in the Whitney on Saratoga's

speed-favoring track, holding off 29 to 1 longshot Bold Style by a nose. Carrying 114 pounds, Bold Style got 9 from the winner. Would 10, 11 or 12 have been enough of a difference to reverse the nose margin? Most likely, yes.

Did 126 pounds slow down Deputy Minister as much as the speed-favoring surface worked against his late-run style? Probably not. It didn't help him, though, as he dead-heated for fourth with Fit To Fight, two and three-quarters lengths behind the winner.

Using weight exclusively would've tempted an overlay bettor to go to Sunny's Halo at 7 to 1 or perhaps Fit To Fight at 19 to 1. It would not have magically drawn us to Bold Style, who carried the same weight as Fit To Fight and had proven less in his career. Linkage, who ran a well-beaten sixth by four and a half lengths at 7 to 1, was also in light at 116 pounds. But if we had liked Bold Style for other handicapping factors, the 9 pound weight advantage against Island Whirl and 12 pound pull against Deputy Minister would've been decided pluses.

EIGHTH RACE
Saratoga
JULY 30, 1983

1 1/8 MILES. (1.47) 56th Running THE WHITNEY (Grade I). Purse $150,000 added. 3-year-olds and upward. By subscription of $300 each, which should accompany the nomination; $1,200 to pass the entry box, with $150,000 added. The added money and all fees to be divided 60% to the winner, 22% to second, 12% to third and 6% to fourth. Weights Monday, July 25. Starters to be named at the closing time of nominations Wednesday July 13, 1983. Trophies will be presented to the winning owner, trainer and jockey. Closed with 33 entries.

Value of race $173,100, value to winner $103,860, second $38,082, third $20,772, fourths $5,193 each. Mutuel pool $265,186 OTB pool $375,685.

Last Raced	Horse	Eqt. A. Wt. PP St	1/4	1/2	3/4	Str	Fin	Jockey	r	Odds $1
26Jun83 8Hol 1	Island Whirl	5 123 1 1	1-1½	1 †	1 †	1 †	1no	Delahoussaye E		1.30
4Jly83 8AP 6	Bold Style	b 4 114 8 6	5-1½	5-1	5hd	3hd	2 †	Day P		29.90
12Jun83 8AP	Sunny's Halo	b 3 116 3 3	3hd	4-2	4-1½	2-1½	3-2	Maple E		7.00
17Jly83 8Bel 1	dh-Deputy Minister	b 4 126 7 7	7-3	6hd	6 †	6-1½	4	MacBeth D		1.70
17Jly83 8Bel 2	dh-Fit to Fight	4 114 9 5	4-1½	3 †	3-1½	4hd	6-1½	Bailey J D		19.60
9Jly83 1Bel 1	Linkage	4 116 6 2	2hd	2 †	2hd	5-2	6-1½	McCarron G		7.80
23Jly83 8Bel 11	Star Choice	4 114 4 8	8-3	8-6	7-4	7-4	7-9	Velasquez J		41.40
17Jly83 7Bel 4	Muttering	4 113 2 4	6-1	7-1½	8 †	9	8hd	Migliore R		33.70
20Jly83 1Bel 2	Kleiglight	4 107 5 9	9	9	9	8-2	9	Samyn J L		18.00

dh-Dead heat.

OFF AT 5:25 Start good, Won driving. Time, :23 2/5, :46 4/5, 1:10 4/5, 1:35 3/5, 1:48 2/5 Track fast.

$ 2 Mutuel Prices:	1- ISLAND WHIRL	4.60	3.60	2.80
	2- BOLD STYLE		16.60	6.60
	3- SUNNY'S HALO			4.00

B. h, by Pago Pago-Alitwirl, by Your Alibhai. Trainer Barrera Lazaro S. Bred by Elcee-H Stable & Breeding Farm Inc (Fla).

ISLAND WHIRL came out while sprinting away to a clear lead racing into the first turn made the pace while remaining well out from the rail, responded gamely when challenged by SUNNY'S HALO with a furlong remaining and after turning back that rival, lasted over BOLD STYLE while drifting out under pressure. BOLD STYLE eased back around the first turn, came out between horse while moving leaving the far turn and finished strongly from the outside, just missing. SUNNY'S HALO eased back when ISLAND WHIRL came out racing into the first turn, was reserved behind the leaders while saving ground, was steadied along looking for room approaching the stretch, got through along the inside to loom boldly a furlong out but weakened slightly in deep stretch. DEPUTY MINISTER commenced to rally while racing well out in the track approaching the end of the backstretch, continued wide into the stretch and finished on even terms with FIT TO FIGHT while failing to seriously menace with a mild late response. FIT TO FIGHT, prominent from the outset, raced well out in the track while remaining a factor to midstretch and weakened. LINKAGE prompted the pace while racing between horses remained a factor until near the final furlong and gave way. STAR CHOICE moved menacingly around horses at the far turn but lacked a further response while continuing very wide. MUTTERING tired. KLEIGLIGHT was always outrun.

Owners- 1, Elcee-H Stable; 2, Mayer L; 3, Cross David C Jr; 4, Nobles Reynaldo H; 5, Miller Mack; 6, 8, Tartan Stable; 9, Phipps O M.

Trainers- 1, Barrera Lazaro S; 2, McGaughey C R III; 3, Cross David C Jr; 4, Nobles Reynaldo H; 5, Miller Mack; 6, Clark Henry S; 7, Veitch John M; 8, Nerud Jan H; 9, Penna Angel.

Scratched- Danebo(17Jly83 8Bel 4); Acaroid(2Jly83 8Atl 1).

The bottom line on weight: Use it as a positive factor in any race when it gives one horse a decided, comparative edge, or if it is a measure of proven ability in comparison to other horses. You can use weight as a legitimate question mark when a young horse is carrying more of it than he's ever won or raced with before.

Trainer Patterns

"The first thing I look for is trainers," jockey Angel Cordero, Jr., said as he discussed his priorities in choosing a mount. "They're just like jockeys and horses. There are trainers who like to win; horses that like to win. I like winning trainers. When they win, they get hot."

Trainers develop certain patterns, modes of behavior, which reflect the tenets they have come to believe to be the best way to train their horses. Some, such as Leroy Jolley, blaze them in the morning. Others, such as Charlie Whittingham and Mack Miller, give a horse all the patience in the world. Still others, such as Phil Johnson, are golden when they switch a horse to the turf. Others, such as Oscar Barrera, have poor results on the turf: in 1983, Oscar won twenty-one percent of his starts, but only three percent (one for twenty-nine) on turf. Understanding these patterns will be another valuable tool in our handicapping.

Let's examine patterns at Saratoga, the nation's premier race meet, in 1988 as well as the total 1988 and 1989 New York Racing Association final trainer standings and the 1989 national trainer standings.

John Angelo, author of *Saratoga Scorecard*, analyzed the performance of trainers at Saratoga in 1988. Several trainers have a second listing for 1987.

Trainer	Starts	Wins	Win %	In $ %	Avg. win	Jockey (# wins)
DiMauro, Stephen	31	7	22.5	35.4	$13.05	Cordero (2), Peck (2), Samyn (2), Maple
DeStasio, Richard	25	4	16.0	48.0	$9.45	Vasquez (2), Lovato, Day
Dutrow, Dick	34	2	5.8	47.0	$16.60	Bailey, McCarron
	73	10	13.6	45.2	$10.68	
Hertler, John	23	5	21.7	39.1	$9.48	Davis (2), Cordero, Velasquez, Cruguet

Trainer	Starts	Wins	Win %	In $ %	Avg. win	Jockey (# wins)
Jacobs, Eugene	11	3	27.2	45.4	$40.86	Cruguet (2), Velasquez
Jerkens, Allen	10	1	10.0	30.0	$12.40	Santos
	20	3	15.0	35.0	$7.52	
Johnson, P.G.	21	3	14.2	28.5	$11.46	Cordero (2), Samyn
	49	6	12.2	28.5	$15.56	
Jolley, Leroy	27	3	11.1	18.5	$9.33	Santos (2), Cordero
	53	6	11.3	26.4	$9.70	
Kelly, Pat	25	3	12.0	48.0	$12.40	Bailey, Romero, Davis
Klesaris, Bob	15	5	33.3	33.3	$11.44	Santos (3), Cordero (2)
Lake, Bob	22	5	22.7	40.9	$13.48	Davis (2), Santos, Romero, Bailey
Lenzini, John	30	2	6.6	30.0	$6.10	Peck, Velasquez
	53	4	7.5	30.1	$5.25	
Lukas, D. Wayne	65	16	24.6	67.7	$5.61	Santos (8), Cordero (4), Day (4)
	104	23	22.1	64.4	$5.26	
Lundy, Richard	23	4	17.3	47.8	$6.80	Bailey (4)
	40	8	20.0	47.5	$6.80	
Martin, Jose	11	3	27.2	45.4	$7.06	Cordero (2), Hernandez
	21	5	23.8	42.8	$7.40	
McGaughey, Shug	17	6	35.2	64.7	$7.03	Romero (3), Day (2), Cordero
	34	9	26.4	47.0	$6.60	
Miller, Mack	14	5	35.7	57.1	$8.40	Davis (3), Day (2)
	36	14	38.8	55.5	$8.44	
Moschera, Gasper	28	6	21.4	35.7	$10.93	Antley (3), Peck (2), Santos
	71	14	19.7	42.7	$8.31	

Trainer	Starts	Wins	Win %	In $ %	Avg. win	Jockey (# wins)
Mott, Bill	19	5	26.3	57.8	$14.08	Davis (2), Day (2), Antley
	38	9	23.6	63.1	$13.75	
Penna, Jr., Angel	9	4	44.4	55.5	$8.40	Hernandez (2), Santos, Cordero
	20	5	25.0	55.0	$8.12	
Schulhofer, Scotty	31	2	6.4	32.2	$7.80	Day, Santos

1989 FINAL
NATIONAL TRAINER STANDINGS

Trainer	Starts	1sts	2nds	3rds	Purses	Win %	In $ %
D. Wayne Lukas	1,398	305	231	162	$16,103,998	21.8	49.9
Charlie Whittingham	436	86	68	51	11,402,231	19.7	47.0
"Shug" McGaughey	178	55	30	30	8,306,888	30.9	64.6
Neil Drysdale	263	69	41	33	5,514,265	26.2	54.4
Ron McAnally	460	93	55	55	4,751,503	20.2	44.1
Roger Attfield	308	61	57	41	4,114,824	19.8	51.6
Scotty Schulhofer	410	59	64	49	3,560,624	14.4	42.0
William Mott	424	103	75	66	3,546,046	24.3	57.6
Robert Klesaris	729	187	108	92	2,748,667	25.7	53.1
Thomas Skiffington	429	82	55	48	2,748,636	19.1	43.1

NEW YORK RACING ASSOCIATION
1989 FINAL TRAINER STANDINGS

Trainer	Starts	1sts	Win Percentage
D. Wayne Lukas	410	101	24.6
Robert Klesaris	322	83	25.8
Gasper Moschera	391	65	16.1
Peter Ferriola	319	60	18.8
Robert Barbara	242	52	21.5
Richard Dutrow	401	50	12.5
John J. Lenzini	239	47	19.7

Trainer	Starts	1sts	Win Percentage
Steve DiMauro	337	43	12.8
Frank Martin	273	40	14.7
Robert Lake	312	39	12.5
"Shug" McGaughey	123	37	30.0
Bruce Levine	203	37	18.2
H. Allen Jerkens	290	35	12.0
Richard DeStasio	332	35	10.5
Phil Johnson	223	34	15.2
Mack Miller	140	34	24.3
William Mott	157	34	21.7

NEW YORK RACING ASSOCIATION
1988 FINAL TRAINER STANDINGS

Trainer	Starts	1sts	Win Percentage
D. Wayne Lukas	535	140	26.1
Peter Ferriola	533	135	25.3
Richard Dutrow	611	103	16.8
John J. Lenzini	384	76	19.7
Gasper Moschera	434	76	17.5
H. Allen Jerkens	289	59	20.4
Robert Klesaris	281	50	17.7
Frank Martin	388	47	12.1
Richard DeStasio	410	44	10.7
"Shug" McGaughey	160	43	26.8
Scotty Schulhofer	218	39	17.8
Robert Lake	273	39	14.2
Bruce Levine	278	39	14.0

Dosage

Since 1981, dosage has received considerable attention pertaining to the Kentucky Derby and Belmont Stakes. Dosage is a comprehensive evaluation of a horse's breeding through analysis of four generations of his pedigree. That analysis is called a dosage profile, which reveals both the quality of his pedigree and its focus ranging between two opposite poles, one representing speed and the other stamina.

There are subjective evaluations of breeding inherent in the dosage profile, yet it nonetheless provides an accurate assessment of a horse's breeding profile.

The pedigree is examined for the presence of proven dominant stallions, each termed a chef-de-race. There are five aptitude classes chefs-de-race can be placed in: speed, speed/middle distance, middle distance, middle distance/stamina and stamina. These classes are termed Brilliant, Intermediate, Classic, Professional and Solid.

Using a mathematical scale, points are awarded in a horse's pedigree for the presence of each chef-de-race in decreasing importance from the first to the last of the four generations based on the concept that the influence of a chef-de-race in one generation is twice that of a chef-de-race in a previous generation.

There are sixteen points maximum awarded for the number of chefs-de-race in each of the four generations. Thus a chef-de-race in the first generation is given sixteen points in whichever aptitude category he's designated. The presence of a chef-de-race in the second generation is worth eight points, in the third generation, four, and in the fourth, two each.

A dosage index is then determined by adding the points from Brilliant, Intermediate and half of Classic, and dividing that sum by the total of points from half the Classic, the Professional and the Solid. The resulting figure is the dosage index.

Developed by Dr. Steven Roman, Ph.D., as a variation of the dosage concept of Dr. Franco Varola, and popularized via Leon Rasmussen's breeding column in the *Form*, the Dosage Index (DI) has been a near-perfect guideline of whether 3-year-olds will be successful in their first attempt at going the distance of a mile and a quarter in the Kentucky Derby and a mile and a half in the Belmont Stakes. The ideal dosage is 1.0, reflecting a balanced pedigree with chefs-de-race on each of the two wings, speed and stamina. Since 1929, no winner of the Kentucky Derby has a DI higher than 4.0. Applied in the same manner to the Belmont Stakes, there have been just three exceptions: Damascus, Conquistador Cielo and Creme Fraiche. Interestingly, the latter two were on a sloppy track. Both were trained by Woody Stephens, another testament to Stephens' greatness. He conditioned two horses who weren't ideally bred to even make a mile and a quarter and got both of them to win at a mile and a half.

What's fundamentally important here is realizing that each year the DI was correct, it wasn't correct for simply one horse, the winner, but all the horses with DIs higher than 4.0 who were losers. If there were five horses, a conservative guess, with DIs higher than 4.0 each year, then there were 300 horses entered in the sixty runnings of the Derby. The DI guideline was correct for 300 of a possible 300. In the Belmont Stakes, where we'll tone down our estimate to two high DI horses each year to reflect the historically smaller fields the Belmont Stakes has than the Derby, the guideline was correct for 117 of 120.

How could DI not be beneficial in our handicapping?

Another worthwhile benefit of dosage is determining how many chefs-de-race are in a horse's four-generation pedigree. This isn't a kitchen. The more chefs, the better.

Dosage detractors disagree with the classification of certain chefs-de-race and/or dispute which sires are listed as chefs. Roman and "Bloodlines," written now by Dan Liebman after Rasmussen retired four years ago, have dealt with disagreements on the classification of chefs by sometimes placing one chef in two different aptitude classes and halving their numerical influence.

Critics also claim dosage is a self-fulfilling prophecy, with sires being labeled as chefs after their progeny perform well at a given distance, since dosage was introduced in 1981 and then researched back to 1929. If your knowledge of breeding is extensive enough to dispute the placement and/or inclusion of chefs, make your own adjustments and still use the framework of dosage to make your own DI calculation.

In recent years, the DI principle has been tied to the Experimental Highweight Handicap, where all top performers are evaluated on a mythical scale of weights in accordance to their performance in a single season. There is a recent claim that contenders for the Derby had to be pared to those horses with a proper DI *and* who were also weighted within ten pounds of the 3-year-old highweight in the Experimental Free Handicap. That's a connection we'll avoid because the Experimental Free Handicap can't help but be subjective and occasionally doesn't award the prestige earned by a lightly raced horse or one who blossomed late in the calendar year. Using dosage solely to eliminate non-qualifiers (DIs higher than 4.0), two losing favorites in the Derby, Snow Chief and Chief's Crown, were avoided. Additionally, dosage deemed 1985 winner Spend A Buck capable of making the Derby distance.

Jockeys

The best jockeys at major tracks have little separating their abilities. However, when there is a jockey switch either to a top jockey or from a top jockey, evaluate accordingly.

If a jockey is listed on two horses and chooses one, don't necessarily throw the other horse out. Jockeys and their agents don't always make the right choice between two mounts, and there may be other mitigating factors you have no chance of knowing regarding one jockey's relationship with the two trainers he's choosing between. A classic example from the Triple Crown races is Eddie Maple, trainer Woody Stephens' regular rider, who chose to ride Chumming instead of Caveat in 1983 and Devil's Bag rather than Swale in 1984. Caveat won the Belmont Stakes and Swale the Kentucky Derby and Belmont Stakes.

Here's how the top jockeys in America fared in 1989:

1989 FINAL NATIONAL JOCKEY STANDINGS

Jockey	Mounts	1sts	2nds	3rds	Purses	Win %	In $ %
Jose Santos	1,454	285	238	218	$13,838,389	19.6	51.0
Pat Day	1,349	383	255	198	13,313,946	28.4	62.0
Angel Cordero, Jr.	1,224	246	212	165	12,219,159	20.1	51.0
Chris McCarron	1,153	232	190	146	11,554,202	20.1	49.3
Eddie Delahoussaye	1,371	248	216	203	11,511,616	18.1	48.7
Laffit Pincay, Jr.	1,594	298	224	212	11,361,610	18.7	46.1
Gary Stevens	1,553	262	268	208	10,271,281	16.9	47.5
Kent Desormeaux	2,312	597	385	309	9,069,623	25.8	55.8
Pat Valenzuela	984	147	142	113	8,209,535	14.9	40.9
Julie Krone	1,673	368	287	235	8,031,445	22.0	53.2

Mudders

Here's a list of proven mud sires: Graustark, Key To The Mint, Czaravich, Nijinksy II, Grey Dawn II, Secretariat, Cormorant, Air Forbes Won, King's Bishop, Mr. Prospector, In Reality, Bold Forbes, Master Derby, Pleasant Colony and The Pruner.

In the *Form*, horses who have performed well on muddy tracks are indicated by one of three marks: * – fair; X – good; ⊗ – superior.

Keep in mind the difference between a sloppy and muddy track. Sloppy tracks can be wet-fast. Muddy tracks are drying out and tiring. Horses on the lead get an advantage on sloppy/muddy tracks of not having mud kicked in their faces, which can easily discourage horses, especially younger and/or inexperienced ones.

Blinker Change

Here are four examples of different results from blinker changes.

Stage View — Ch. f. 4, by Stage Door Key—Rose View, by Reviewer
Br.—Laurin Roger (NY)
Own.—Laurin R — Tr.—Destasio Richard A
115 — Lifetime 6 1 0 2 $23,640 — 1989 2 1 0 0 $17,4 — 1988 4 M 0 2 $6,2 — Turf 4 1 0 2 $23,6

3Jly89- 9Bel fm 1 1/16 [T]:46 1:10 1:41⅕ 3↑[F][S]Alw 29000 8 1 11½ 11½ 11 12 Carle J D5 b 112 12.70 90-11 Stage View 1122 Banded 1117 Quick Match 1114 Driving

12Jun89- 6Bel gd 1 1/16 [T]:46⅘ 1:12 1:44⅖ 3↑[F]Md Sp Wt 2 1 1hd 812 1119 1130¾ Castillo R E5 117 28.70 44-23 Tune Up 122¾ Secret Circle 109hd Mabuya 1223¾ Jostled turn

25Sep88- 9Bel fm 1 1/16 [T]:46⅕ 1:10⅘ 1:44⅕ 3↑[F][S]Md Sp Wt 11 2 1hd 1hd 21 34½ Castillo R E7 111 6.00 70-20 She'sHalfIced1183SpiritualWings1181½StageView111no Weakened

29Jly88- 4Bel gd 1 :45⅘ 1:11⅖ 1:36 3↑[F]Md Sp Wt 2 2 11 36½ 520 631¼ Peck B D5 111 8.00 54-17 For Kicks 11615 Natural Forest 1162½ Time forTommie1163 Tired

1Jly88- 6Bel fm 1 1/16 [T]:48 1:13⅕ 1:46 3↑[F]Md Sp Wt 3 1 11 11 1½ 32 Peck B D5 111 12.10 64-25 ComorinCape116nkArcticEvening1161¾StageView1112¼ Weakened

9Jun88- 9Bel fst 6f :23 :47 1:12⅖ 3↑[F][S]Md Sp Wt 2 3 21½ 43½ 815 924 Nuesch D 114 3.00 53-13 Cliffie 1142¼ Bold And Bossie 1141¼ Overrule 1171½ Tired

LATEST WORKOUTS Jly 11 Bel tr.t 4f fst :48⅕ H Jun 26 Bel tr.t 5f fst 1:01 H Jun 20 Bel tr.t 5f fst 1:01⅗ B Jun 2 Bel tr.t 4f fst :48⅗ H

Marine Band — B. f. 4, by Fifth Marine—Jazzerciser, by Tarleton Oak
Br.—Sussex Racing Group (NY)
Own.—Hundredhorn Stable — Tr.—Hushion Michael
115 — Lifetime 12 2 1 0 $42,100 — 1999 5 1 1 0 $26,08 — 1988 6 1 0 0 $14,40 — Turf 3 1 1 0 $26,08

1Jly89- 7Bel fm 1¼ [T] 46⅕ 1:37⅖ 2:03⅕ 3↑[F][S]Alw 31000 9 1 12 12 15 2½ Migliore R 117 4.10 77-15 Sa Marche 117½ MarineBand1173¾MaggieTonight1171½ Weakened 1

3Jun89- 7Bel fm 1 1/16 [T]:46⅗ 1:10⅘ 1:42 3↑[F][S]Alw 31000 10 2 21 21 1hd 45¾ Lovato F Jr 119 3.50 80-14 My Lady's Wim 1101¼ Warfie 113½ Pennways 1124 Weakened 1

29Apr89- 5Aqu fm 1 1/16 [T]:48 1:12⅖ 1:45⅘ 3↑[F]Alw 29000 9 1 2hd 2hd 1½ 11¼ Lovato F Jr 119 36.70 76-18 Marine Band 1191¼ Dayzac 1191 Windy Surf 1101¼ Driving 1

19Apr89- 7Aqu fst 6f :22⅗ :46⅘ 1:12⅗ 3↑[F][S]Alw 27000 3 2 52 42½ 107¾ 1112¼ Krone J A 119 17.30 65-28 Angela Serenity 1142¼ Wee Lass 119no Oh Betty 1123¾ Tired 1

16Jan89- 9Aqu gd 6f [•]:22⅗ :46⅖ 1:12 [F][S]Alw 23000 10 1 42½ 44 55 54¾ Migliore R 117 8.70 79-10 ChangeHands112nkEstatesJewel1174VideoCassette117½ Even trip 1

29Dec88- 8Aqu fst 6f [•]:22⅗ :46⅖ 1:12⅕ 3↑[F]Alw 23000 3 2 41½ 63¼ 66¾ 58 Migliore R 115 28.80 75-18 Aspen Alley 117nk Sunny Her 1173 Periapt 115nk No factor

19Dec88- 5Aqu fst 6f [•]:22⅗ :46⅖ 1:12⅘ 3↑[F]Alw 23000 5 8 75 79¾ 710 56½ Migliore R 115 15.30 74-23 Chilam Balam 117no Aspen Alley 1201ScaryLaugh115nk No factor

23Nov88- 7Aqu fst 6f :22⅕ :46 1:12⅕ 3↑[F][S]Alw 27000 7 2 1½ 23 36 77¼ Migliore R 120 *2.00 72-23 Lady Mulholland 117hd Video Cassette 1172¾ Cliffie 115½ Tired 1

6Nov88- 9Aqu fst 6f :22⅗ :46⅗ 1:12⅗ 3↑[F][S]Md Sp Wt 11 3 62¾ 42 1½ 12¼ Vega A 120 7.40 77-26 Marine Band 1202¼ Launchable 1201¼ Change Hands1204¼ Driving 1

23Oct88- 7Aqu fst 6f :22 :45⅘ 1:12 3↑[F]Md Sp Wt 1 3 1hd 54½ 918 814½ Vega A b 119 34.10 65-23 Solemn Vows 1194¾ MissyValentine119¾BrightMorning119¾ Tired 1

LATEST WORKOUTS May 27 Bel tr.t 5f fst 1:02 B

Golden Bubby — Ch. f. 3(May), by Dust Commander—Regal Line, by Viceregal
Br.—Belle A Enterprises (Fla)
Own.—Omni Belle Stable — Tr.—Martin Jose
121 — Lifetime 8 0 0 1 $4,140 — 1989 3 M 0 1 $3,1 — 1988 5 M 0 0 $1,0

19Jly89- 6Bel fst 7f :22⅘ :46⅗ 1:26 3↑[F]Md Sp Wt 4 2 65½ 68 513 416¾ Martinez JRJr5 b 111 27.40 55-25 I Like That 1169¾ Private Theatrics 1166Allego1221½ Raced green

26Jun89- 2Bel fst 6½f :22⅘ :47 1:19⅗ 3↑[F]Md 50000 9 3 33 54½ 64¼ 39¼ Martinez JRJr5 b 109 35.30 68-21 DancehallJne1146Mdeline'sGirl1073¼GoldenBubby1091¼ No threat

22May89- 3Bel fst 6f :22⅗ :46⅗ 1:13 3↑[F]Md 50000 1 2 66 76½ 66½ 79¼ Castillo R E5 b 110 6.90 65-24 Past Remembered 115no DameFortune1156GunnySac1151 Outrun

8Dec88- 2Aqu fst 6f [•]:22⅘ :46⅘ 1:12⅘ [F]Md 45000 8 7 66 411 512 513½ Cordero A Jr b 114 25.10 66-21 MissBettyBenson1152¾PrtyWidow1142UnitndConqur1176½ Outrun

26Nov88- 9Aqu fst 7f :22⅘ :46⅕ 1:26⅗ [F]Md 70000 8 5 65½ 79 917 911¾ Bailey J D b 113 24.30 56-22 Windy Surf 1142¼ Bounty Search 113no Key Flight 117nk Outrun

12Nov88- 4Aqu fst 7f :22⅗ :45⅘ 1:26⅘ [F]Md 70000 1 7 64½ 812 68½ 46¾ Centeno V R 113 45.10 60-24 East of Rome 1171¼ Pure Vanilla 1132¼WindySurf1143¼ No factor

24Oct88- 3Aqu fst 6f :22⅕ :46⅕ 1:13 [F]Md 70000 2 5 810 1119 914 96½ Imparato J 114 54.60 68-21 Racing Cosmic 117hd GreekPorche117nkTrueRoyalty113nk Outrun

8Oct88- 4Bel sly 6f :22⅗ :46⅕ 1:12 [F]Md Sp Wt 1 4 718 826 837 842½ Maple E 117 19.00 36-21 Surging 1175 Windy Surf 1171 Play Moon 1177½ Outrun

LATEST WORKOUTS Jly 9 Bel tr.t 4f fst :47⅗ H ●Jun 19 Bel tr.t 4f fst :47⅘ H ●Jun 10 Bel tr.t 4f my :48 H

op Letter B. g. 3(May), by Arts and Letters—New Orleans Gal, by Cannonade
Own.—Kingsford Stable **$45,000** Br.—Flynn & Questroyal Farm (NY) Tr.—Lake Robert P **113**

Lifetime	1989	19 1 0 1	$17,880	
25 1 0 2	1988	6 M 0 1	$2,880	
$20,760	Turf	2 0 0 0		

89- 2Bel	gd	7f	:22⅘	:46⅗	1:26⅖	Clm 15500	3	7	78¾	813	815	817½	Rogers K L		113	25.60	52-28	Speculatif 1171¾	McAva 117½	Overdrawn Account 1126¼	Outrun	8
89- 6Bel	gd	1 1/16 Ⓣ	:47⅖	1:12⅗	1:45⅗	3↑ [S]Alw 29000	9	12	1213	1017	714	712¾	Castillo R E		111	96.10	55-34	In the Groove111¾	DaringYouth1176	DanceAtSea1133	Lacked room	12
89- 2Bel	fst	7f	:24	:47⅘	1:25⅗	Clm 15500	3	4	42½	55¼	612	517¼	Rojas R I		113	29.70	57-29	Double Out 1197½	Jupiter Inlet 1172½	Myriad Right 1135	Outrun	6
89- 1Bel	fst	6f	:22⅖	:46⅖	1:13	Clm 15500	3	7	78½	611	612	613	Romero R P	b	113	17.90	61-21	Soccer Tour 117no	BelieveTheKing1133	McAva1121½	Broke slowly	7
89- 5Bel	fm	1 1/16 [T]	:48⅖	1:12⅗	1:44⅖	Clm 45000	5	8	86½	913	917	917½	Romero R P	b	113	30.10	61-16	Winloc'sBigLou113hd	RichN'Classy108nk	DistinctIntent1133	Outrun	10
89- 2Bel	my	7f	:23⅕	:46⅖	1:25⅘	Clm 15500	2	8	85½	611	66¾	58¼	Romero R P	b	113	16.00	65-17	Winloc'sBigLou117¾[DH]	BlvThKng113[DH]	MyrdRght1072½	No factor	9
89- 2Bel	fst	6f	:22	:45⅘	1:11⅘	Clm 15500	6	9	812	86½	95½	84¾	Nelson D		113	34.80	75-17	McAva 117nk	Cala Le Mani 108½	Full Beat 113hd	Outrun	9
89- 7Bel	fst	6f	:22⅕	:45⅗	1:10⅗	3↑ [S]Alw 27000	12	10	119	1111	129½	1215½	Laboccetta F Jr10		100	99.80	70-13	UncleHugo1141½[DH]	PrinceNapsalot110[DH]	LeadingAppel1101	Wide	12
89- 9Aqu	fst	1⅛	:48	1:12⅘	1:52⅕	3↑ [S]Alw 29000	7	7	79	710	817	1027½	Maple E		112	34.90	46-19	Flinty 1088	Joint Verdict 114no	Perpetual Optimist 114½	Outrun	10
89- 2Aqu	fst	7f	:22⅘	:45⅘	1:25	3↑ [S]Alw 27000	5	9	85	95¾	78¼	79¼	Castaneda M		115	40.80	67-24	Match the Mouse 1162¼	Marrone 1101¼	Crown Land 1152	Outrun	10

ATEST WORKOUTS Jun 11 Aqu 5f fst 1:02 H

Stage View won with blinkers on. Marine Band won with blinkers off. Golden Bubby failed to improve with blinkers added. Hoop Letter failed to improve with blinkers added and then removed. All four horses raced in late July 1989.

One key to remember is searching for recent workouts which may indicate the effect of the blinker change.

First-Time Starters

When there's no form to evaluate, handicappers are left to assess five factors in making decisions about 2-year-old—and occasionally 3-year-old—first-time starters.

1. Workouts—Firsters with excellent works in the *Form* will be obvious. Those with excellent works not included in the *Form* will usually show up on the tote board as the firster's odds diminish. We can look for two factors in workouts which will be helpful. Good or decent workouts at today's distance or farther tell you this isn't the first time this horse is being asked to run today's distance. Steady good works, say a couple at four furlongs in :47 and a five furlong work in 1:00, indicate consistency which can be equated into a good effort in his debut.

2. Post position—Outside posts in five and five and a half furlong races can be extremely difficult for first-time starters or more experienced horses because of the short run into the turn. If a first-time starter races wide in his debut yet still shows hints of ability, it may be profitable to bet this horse if he draws an inside or middle post in his next start. Also, the No. 1 post can be an obstacle for firsters because they're loaded into the gate first and many times have to wait two to

four minutes while the other starters are loaded. This prolonged wait for a horse making its debut can only make him more nervous and/or unruly when the gate finally opens.

3. Trainers—Many of the best trainers, including Shug McGaughey, Woody Stephens and D. Wayne Lukas are also the best with first-timers. Be wary when such a trainer doesn't use his regular jockey with a firster, especially if that jockey is on another horse in the race. Also be wary of firsters asked to go more than six furlongs in their debut.

4. Odds—Try to get a feel for what odds you'd expect from a top trainer off the workouts in the *Form*. If the horse is getting much more action than you'd figured on the tote board, be wary of betting against this horse. These hot first-timers are always underlays, but that doesn't decrease their chances. Think about reducing a wager against such horses or sitting the race out.

5. Breeding—The list of leading 2-year-old sires in the appendix is helpful.

If you're intimidated by too many firsters in a 2-year-old maiden race, you've got plenty of company. Look at this race from Belmont:

3 BELMONT

5½ FURLONGS. (1.03) MAIDEN SPECIAL WEIGHT. Purse $24,000. Fillies, 2-year-olds. Weigh5, 117 bls.

Cuillin
Ch. f. 2(Mar), by Topsider—Bluemonte, by Shirley Heights
Br.—Moseley Mrs J B (Ky)
Own.—Moseley Mrs J B — Tr.—Bush Thomas M — 117 — Lifetime 0 0 0 0 — 1989 0 M 0 0
LATEST WORKOUTS Jly 15 Bel 3f fst :36⅗ H — Jly 7 Bel 6f fst 1:17⅖ B — Jun 25 Bel 4f fst :49⅘ Bg — Jun 19 Bel 3f fst :36⅗ Hg

Hot n'Wild
Dk. b. or br. f. 2(Mar), by Wild Again—Hot Love, by What a Pleasure
Br.—Calumet Farm (Ky)
Own.—Calumet Farm — Tr.—Zito Nicholas P — 117 — Lifetime 0 0 0 0 — 1989 0 M 0 0
LATEST WORKOUTS Jly 12 Bel 4f fst :48⅗ H — ●Jly 8 Bel 4f fst :47⅕ H — Jly 3 Bel 5f fst 1:02 H — Jun 28 Bel 5f fst 1:01⅕ H

Smartly Styled
Ch. f. 2(May), by Cox's Ridge—Smart Heiress, by Vaguely Noble
Br.—Ryehill Farm (Md)
Own.—Ryehill Farm — Tr.—Stephens Woodford C — 117 — Lifetime 0 0 0 0 — 1989 0 M 0 0
LATEST WORKOUTS Jly 18 Bel 4f fst :51⅗ B — Jly 9 Bel 5f fst 1:03⅘ B — Jly 4 Bel 4f fst :49⅘ Bg — Jun 26 Bel 4f fst :50 B

Mt. Gibson Gold
Ch. f. 2(Mar), by Cox's Ridge—Tommy's Date, by Tom Rolfe
Br.—Cox Jr & Hermitage Farm Inc (Ky)
Own.—Reynolds D P — Tr.—Kelly Thomas J — 117 — Lifetime 0 0 0 0 — 1989 0 M 0 0
LATEST WORKOUTS Jly 16 Bel 5f fst 1:01⅖ H — Jly 9 Bel 4f fst :50⅖ B — Jun 30 Bel 5f fst 1:00⅖ H — Jun 14 Bel tr.t 4f gd :50 B

Miss Dolly D.
Dk. b. or br. f. 2(Feb), by Aloma's Ruler—Miss Marked, by Raise a Cup
Br.—Spiegel R (Ky)
Own.—Spiegel R — Tr.—Schaeffer Stephen — 117 — Lifetime 0 0 0 0 — 1989 0 M 0 0
LATEST WORKOUTS Jun 26 Bel tr.t 4f fst :49⅘ H — Jun 5 Bel tr.t 5f fst 1:02⅕ H — May 29 Bel 4f fst :49 Hg

Saratoga Style
B. f. 2(Apr), by Conquistador Cielo—Saratoga Fleet, by Sir Gaylord
Br.—Ryehill-Kirkham Partnership (Md)
Own.—Young W T — Tr.—Lukas D Wayne — 117 — Lifetime 0 0 0 0 — 1989 0 M 0 0
LATEST WORKOUTS Jly 12 Bel 5f fst 1:03⅖ B — Jly 2 Bel 4f fst :49⅕ B — Jun 11 Bel 4f fst :49 B — May 27 Bel 4f fst :50⅖ B

Sarolucy
B. f. 2(Jan), by Saros—Lucy, by El Virtuoso
Br.—Scheib E A (Cal)
Own.—Scheib E A — Tr.—Hirsch William J Jr — 117 — Lifetime 0 0 0 0 — 1989 0 M 0 0
LATEST WORKOUTS Jly 13 Bel 5f fst 1:02 H — ●Jly 6 Bel 4f sly :48⅕ Hg — Jun 29 Bel 4f fst :47⅘ Hg — Jun 23 Bel 4f fst :48 H

Leavealittleforme — B. f. 2(Feb), by Desert Wine—Miss Tres, by Secretariat
Own.—Link Helen P — Br.—Indian Creek & Louis Rowan (Ky) — Tr.—Connors Robert F
117 — Lifetime 1 0 0 0 $450 — 1989 1 M 0 0 $450
20Jun89- 1Mth fst 5f :22 :45⅘ :58⅘ ⒻMd Sp Wt 8 6 84¼ 43½ 57 59 Castaneda K 117 4.80 82-15 Big Pride 1174½ Socialite Belle 1172¼ Royal Peace 1171 Tired 8

Virgin Michael — Ch. f. 2(Mar), by Green Dancer—Virginiana, by Sir Ivor
Own.—Middletown Stable — Br.—Joseph & William Stavola Inc (NJ) — Tr.—Jerkens H Allen
107[10] — Lifetime 0 0 0 0 — 1989 0 M 0 0
LATEST WORKOUTS Jly 15 Bel 5f fst 1:01 H Jly 11 Bel 5f fst 1:03⅘ B Jly 1 Bel tr.t 4f fst :47⅖ H Jun 28 Bel tr.t 4f fst :51⅘ B

Here's how they finished:

THIRD RACE **Belmont** **JULY 20, 1989** — **5 ½ FURLONGS. (1.03) MAIDEN SPECIAL WEIGHT. Purse $24,000. Fillies, 2-year-olds. Weigh5, 117 bls.**

Value of race $24,000; value to winner $14,400; second $5,280; third $2,880; fourth $1,440. Mutuel pool $151,658. Exacta Pool $357,640

Last Raced	Horse	Eqt.A.Wt	PP	St	¼	⅜	Str	Fin	Jockey	Odds $1
	Sarolucy	2 117	7	7	3½	2 1½	1 2½	1 8	Perret C	6.30
	Hot n'Wild	2 117	2	1	1 1	1 1½	2 4	2 ¾	Romero R P	1.60
	Cuillin	2 117	1	2	4 hd	4 1	3 4	3 6¾	Cordero A Jr	15.50
	Smartly Styled	2 117	3	4	6 hd	6½	4 1½	4 3	Maple E	6.70
	Virgin Michael	2 107	8	8	8	8	7 2½	5 ¾	Singh D10	9.00
	Mt. Gibson Gold	2 117	4	3	5 6	5 5	6 1½	6 5	Bailey J D	9.70
	Miss Dolly D.	2 117	5	5	7 6	7 4	8	7 hd	Migliore R	13.30
	Saratoga Style	2 117	6	6	2 1½	3 2	5½	8	Santos J A	3.10

OFF AT 2:05 Start good, Won driving. Time, :22⅖, :46⅖, :59⅕, 1:05⅗ Track good.

$2 Mutuel Prices:

7-(G)-SAROLUCY	14.60	6.60	4.00
2-(B)-HOT N'WILD		3.40	2.80
1-(A)-CUILLIN			6.40

$2 EXACTA 7-2 PAID $51.60.

B. f, by Saros—Lucy, by El Virtuoso. Trainer Hirsch William J Jr. Bred by Scheib E A (Cal).

SAROLUCY quickly reached contention from the outside, caught HOT N' WILD entering the stretch and drew away under brisk urging. The latter raced well out from the rail while showing speed to the stretch but was no match for the winner. CUILLIN saved ground into the stretch and continued on with good energy. SMARTLY STYLED was always outrun. VIRGIN MICHAEL fell while acting up when being loaded into the gate, broke out of hand and was never close. MT. GIBSON GOLD was finished early. SARATOGA STYLE tired badly from her early efforts.

Physical Handicapping

Physical handicapping, judging a horse by its physical appearance, is difficult even for public handicappers. There are few experts. One is John Pricci, handicapper for *Newsday*.

In thoroughbred racing, horses casually saunter away after the post parade. Almost all gallop easily. Because thoroughbred tracks are routinely much larger in circumference than harness tracks, bettors only see thoroughbreds for a few seconds before they gallop away. Unlike harness horses, they don't make another appearance in front of the fans even if they're in a distance race which requires the starting gate being at or near the finish line. By the time thoroughbreds approach the gate, they've slowed to a walk.

But there are still several things you look for in watching a thoroughbred before his race. Mostly, you watch for negatives.

If you're at a track where you can watch horses get saddled in the paddock, look for a horse that is washed out or lathered around the neck, which means he's already broken a strong sweat. If he's also acting up, bucking up and down, that means he may already be expending too much energy even before the post parade. Common sense enters your consideration, too. If it's ninety degrees and humid, a lot of horses will be sweating before the race. You still want to avoid betting ones washing out profusely.

In the post parade, look for horses who are alert, ears cocked, showing signs of enthusiasm and perhaps nipping at the saddle pony, if there is one. These horses are ready to race. A bad sign is a horse throwing his head about wildly. Bandages are never a good sign but distinguish between routine run-down bandages (on a horse's back legs) and ones on his front legs.

Jargon

Dead on the Board—The horse is getting little action on the tote board, producing significantly higher odds than expected.

KOD—The kiss of death, usually applied by a friend or stranger standing next to you proclaiming during the race that the horse you bet is a winner, which instantaneously makes that horse stop dead as if he was harpooned in the heart.

Inquiry—The stewards are investigating the race just run for possible interference or other fouls which could result in a disqualification. The program number of the horse under suspicion flashes on the tote board indicating the result of the race is NOT official; hold your tickets.

Objection—A jockey has made a claim of foul against another jockey in the race; that horse's program number flashes on the tote board, too. The race isn't official; hold your tickets until it is.

If you missed the wedding, don't be there for the funeral—A horse you liked went off as an enormous overlay, raced great but didn't quite win, maybe because of a poor start or traffic problems; you've missed this golden opportunity and shouldn't bet him again solely to get even because said horse will bury you (and your wallet).

The Ultimate Overlay

CHAPTER 18 When we handicap a race and identify the two or three top contenders, then see that one of them is a gigantic longshot, what do we do? One school of thought about this situation says, "Back off," because the horse is "Dead on the Board." Such thinking has merit with first-time starters in a maiden race, especially one for 2-year-olds. As many as three-fourths of a field of 2-year-old maidens may be first-time starters. Other than workouts, trainer patterns, breeding and physical appearance, there is little else to handicap since the horse has never raced. When we see, for example, five first-time starters in a race and one of them being bet heavily, we can conclude this horse has done well in his preparation for his debut. Perhaps there are workouts not in the *Form* which have significance (the *Form* lists a horse's four most recent works). Dead on the Board, however, should never deter us from playing overlays. If we've handicapped a horse as a top contender in a race, we'll hope his odds go up as betting continues until post time. Remember, we're looking for a contender in a race whose odds are higher than we believe they should be in relation to his chance of winning. If the odds are 10 to 1, so be it. Ditto 15 to 1, 20 to 1 or even higher. If we're wrong in our evaluation of the horse, we lose. Our perspective about handicapping has losses built into its framework. We understand that playing overlays doesn't spew out winner after winner. We're looking for a few good horses with the mettle to be successful overlays. When we hit a good one, we'll be more than compensated for the ones we lose. It's always possible we'll be rewarded more than our wildest dreams.

The $500,000, 1 1/8 mile Florida Derby at Gulfstream Park attracted ten 3-year-olds in 1988. Here they are in post position order:

10 GULFSTREAM

1 ⅛ MILES. (1.46⅖) 37th Running THE FLORIDA DERBY (Grade I). Purse $500,000 guaranteed. 3-year-olds. By subscription of $1,000 each, which shall accompany the nominations, $4,000 to pass the entry box and $4,000 additional to start, with $500,000 guaranteed. All fees to be divided $300,000 to first; $95,000 to second, $50,000 to third, $30,000 to fourth; $15,000 to fifth and $10,000 to sixth. Weights, 122 lbs. Non-winners of a sweepstakes allowed 4 lbs. Horses finishing first, second or third in the Spectacular Bid Stakes, Hutcheson Stakes and/or Fountain of Youth Stakes, will automatically be nominated to the Florida Derby. Early bird nominations to Florida Derby series closed Saturday, October 10, 1987. Supplementary nominations may be made at time of entry. Thursday, March 3, on payment of $20,000 each. This event will not be divided. Starters to be named through the entry box by the usual time of closing. Florida Derby Trophy to winning owner. Nominations closed Saturday, January 23 with 138 nominations. (Preference to winners).

Twice Too Many — Dk. b. or br. c. 3, by Maudlin—Twicebefore, by Noholme II
Own.—Hilton T L — Br.—Ocala Stud Farms Inc (Fla) — Tr.—Mitchell Stephen — **118**
Lifetime 16 3 1 4 $56,651 — 1988 4 0 1 1 $9,880 — 1987 12 3 0 3 $46,771 — Turf 3 0 0 2 $11,386

24Feb88- 9GP	fm 1 1/16 Ⓣ	:46⅘ 1:11⅖ 1:42⅕	Gldn Grass	3	3	3¹½	4¹½	5³¾	3²½	Bain G W	115	32.40	86-13	Tanzanid 119¹¾ Cefis 113¾ Twice Too Many 115no	Shuffled bk.st.	10
6Feb88- 9Tam	gd 7f	:23 :46⅕ 1:24⅕	3↑ Gasparilla	8	6	5⁶½	5⁵	6⁴¾	2⁴½	Sanchez H A	110	8.70	94-13	Bold Midway113⁴½TwiceTooMany110hdPleasureCourt113¾	Rallied	10
24Jan88-10GP	fm 1 Ⓣ	:46⅕ 1:10⅕ 1:35⅗	Palm Beach	5	3	4³½	5⁶	9¹¹	11¹¹¼	Ward W A	115	20.30	81-11	Tanzanid 115½ Cefis 113nk Denomination 113¹½	Tired	12
2Jan88-10Hia	fst 1⅛	:46⅘ 1:11 1:49⅘	Flamingo	8	4	4²½	4²	6⁶½	7¹¹¾	Perret C	118	50.10	70-14	Cherokee Colony 118¹ Sorry About That 122hd Cefis 118²½	Tired	14
2Jan88-Grade I																
20Dec87- 9Hia	fst 1⅛	:46⅖ 1:10⅘ 1:50	Everglades	7	1	1hd	1¹	2½	3²½	Ward W A	112	20.20	-21	SorryAboutTht111½PositionLedr116²TwicTooMny112³	Weakened	8
20Dec87-Grade II																
6Dec87- 9Hia	fm 1 1/16 Ⓣ	1:43⅗	Citation	11	7	6²½	3²½	3¹½	3⁶	Duarte J C	114	24.30	74-25	Be A Natural 116⁵ Lover's Trust 120¹TwiceTooMany114¹½	Evenly	14
28Nov87-10Hia	fst 7f	:22⅖ :45⅕ 1:24	Bahamas	4	7	8⁷¾	6⁵½	4⁷	4²¾	Castillo H Jr	112	13.00	80-21	Position Leader118¹AboveNormal112nkMiamiSlick118¹½	Steadied	8
20Nov87- 8Hia	fst 7f	:23⅖ :46⅘ 1:24⅗	Alw 15200	3	4	3³	4¹½	1½	1¹	Castillo H Jr⁵	115	5.10	80-28	Twice Too Many 115¹ Evening Kris 114¾ Break Par 117²½	Driving	6
6Nov87- 9Crc	fst 6f	:22⅖ :46 1:11⅗	Alw 11500	2	5	4³	4⁴	4⁴	4⁵½	Castillo H Jr⁵	108	12.80	87-19	Tanzanid114¹¼AboveNorml116¹¼Cook'sBrownRice116³	No excuse	5
10Oct87- 9Crc	fst 7f	:22⅖ :46 1:26	Alw 12300	4	6	6⁸½	6⁵	3¹	1hd	Castillo H Jr⁵	108	19.40	86-19	TwiceTooMny108hdJudy'sotherbrothr116¹PurplPtuni112½	Driving	7

LATEST WORKOUTS Feb 17 Crc 1 fst 1:43 b ● Jan 18 Crc 7f fst 1:29⅕ b

Sorry About That — B. c. 3, by Guilty Conscience—Running Naked, by Bold L B
Own.—Hine Carolyn & Savin&Waltuch — Br.—Jones Brereton C (Ky) — Tr.—Hine Hubert — **122**
Lifetime 4 3 1 0 $136,400 — 1988 1 0 1 0 $50,000 — 1987 3 3 0 0 $86,400

2Jan88-10Hia	fst 1⅛	:46⅘ 1:11 1:49⅘	Flamingo	10	7	3¹½	3²	2½	2¹	Cruguet J	122	*3.20	81-14	Cherokee Colony 118¹ Sorry About That 122hd Cefis118²½	Rallied	14
2Jan88-Grade I																
20Dec87- 9Hia	fst 1⅛	:46⅖ 1:10⅘ 1:50	Everglades	6	5	5⁵	3¹½	1½	1½	Cruguet J	111	3.30	81-21	SorryAboutThat111½PositionLeder116²TwiceTooMny112³	Driving	8
20Dec87-Grade II																
8Nov87- 5Aqu	fst 7f	:22⅘ :46⅕ 1:24⅖	Alw 30000	4	7	4¹½	2¹½	1¹½	1⁵½	Santos J A	122	6.30	79-27	Sorry About That122⁵½Estes122³½O.K.NoProblem117¾	Drew clear	9
30Oct87- 7Med	fst 6f	:22 :45⅖ 1:11⅗	Md Sp Wt	8	7	6⁶½	5⁶½	3¹½	1½	Santos J A	118	10.60	84-16	SorryAboutThat118½BluredMemory118³TwoMnhttns118nk	Driving	10

LATEST WORKOUTS ● Mar 2 GP 4f fst :46⅗ h ● Feb 23 GP 6f fst 1:13 h Feb 16 GP 6f fst 1:15 b ● Feb 12 GP 5f fst 1:01⅖ h

Ruhlmann — Dk. b. or br. c. 3, by Mr Leader—Indian Maiden, by Chieftain
Own.—Moss J S — Br.—North Ridge Farm (Ky) — Tr.—Frankel Robert — **122**
Lifetime 7 2 2 1 $166,363 — 1988 1 1 0 0 $137,500 — 1987 6 1 2 1 $28,863 — Turf 3 0 1 0 $5,163

24Jan88- 8BM	fst 1 1/16	:45⅕ 1:09⅕ 1:39⅖	Cm Rl Dby	6	3	3⁴	3²	1³	1⁶	Day P	b 117	3.60	95-15	Ruhlmann 117⁶ Havanaffair 117²½ Chinese Gold 119⁶	Ridden out	9
24Jan88-Grade III																
3Dec87- 7Hol	fst 1 1/16	:46⅗ 1:11⅘ 1:44⅗	Alw 36000	1	1	2hd	1½	1²	3⁵½	Stevens G L	120	*.80	74-19	Propost 117¹ Lively One 120⁴½ Ruhlmann 120¹½	Weakened	7
2Dec87- 7Hol	fst 1	:45⅘ 1:11⅕ 1:37⅘	Alw 31000	5	4	3nk	2¹	2¹	2¹¾	Black C A	119	*.60	72-16	Cougarized 114¹¾ Ruhlmann 119³½ Pain 114¾	Bumped st.	9
0Nov87- 6Hol	fst 1	:45⅖ 1:10⅕ 1:35⅘	Md Sp Wt	7	2	2¹	1¹½	1⁴	1⁷	Black C A	117	3.20	84-13	Ruhlmann 117⁷ Spotted Raj 117⁴ Worryation 117¹½		12
5Aug87♦2Clairefont'e(Fra	yl*1	1:41⅗ Ⓣ	Prix de Neptune						7⁸½	Boeuf D	119	4.50	— —	Quaff 120²½ Face Nord 116¹½ Tourmalet 119¹½	No threat	9
8Jly87♦2MLaffitte(Fra)	gd*5½f	1:05⅕ Ⓣ	PrixRadisRose(Mdn)						7⁸¾	Black C	123	2.50	— —	KentuckySlew123¹½ BonVent123hd BlduSeigneur123¹½	No threat	8
9Jun87♦6Chantilly(Fra)	sf*6f	1:17⅖ Ⓣ	Prix de Vineuil(Mdn)						2²	Black C	119	4.00	— —	Grangil 123³ Ruhlmann 119½ Bulrush 123¹½	Finished well	7

LATEST WORKOUTS ● Mar 1 GP 5f fst :58 h ● Feb 24 GP 6f fst 1:12⅖ h ● Feb 17 Hol 7f fst 1:24⅗ h ● Feb 11 Hol 6f fst 1:11⅖ h

Brian's Time — B. c. 3, by Roberto—Kelly's Day, by Graustark
Own.—Phillips J — Br.—Phillips J (Ky) — Tr.—Veitch John M — **118**
Lifetime 5 2 1 0 $41,619 — 1988 2 1 0 0 $18,599 — 1987 3 1 1 0 $23,020

15Feb88-10GP	fst 1 1/16	:46⅗ 1:10⅘ 1:43⅕	Fountin Yth	1	7	8⁹½	8⁹¾	6⁷¾	4³	Bailey J D	112	15.80	82-21	Forty Niner 122no Notebook 122¹ Buoy 119²	Rallied	9
15Feb88-Grade II																
6Jan88- 7GP	fst 1 1/16	:49⅕ 1:13⅗ 1:45⅖	Alw 17000	2	5	5⁵½	4³¼	2hd	1⁴½	Bailey J D	119	*.80	74-20	Brian's Time 119⁴½ GrayGardner122²MasteryPlay117¹	Ridden out	12
9Dec87- 5Aqu	fst 1 1/16 ⊡	:48⅘ 1:13⅗ 1:45⅗	Alw 31000	5	6	5²¾	5²¼	3nk	2hd	Bailey J D	117	4.80	81-17	Chicot County 117hd Brian's Time 117³ Dynaformer 117no	Sharp	9
3Nov87- 6Aqu	fst 7f	:23⅗ :47⅖ 1:26	Md Sp Wt	6	6	5⁴½	4²½	1hd	1³½	Velasquez J	118	7.70	71-23	Brian's Time118³½John'sConcorde113¹½Buckbean118½	Drew clear	8
0Aug87- 2Sar	my 6f	:22⅕ :45⅘ 1:11⅕	Md Sp Wt	9	11	6⁸	5⁶½	5⁵	5⁷	Bailey J D	118	12.10	77-16	Appiello 118⁵ Lucy's Hill 118nk Grumpy Miller 118¹½	No factor	11

LATEST WORKOUTS Mar 4 Hia 3f fst :36⅗ b Feb 28 Hia 7f fst 1:28 b Feb 23 Hia 4f fst :49⅕ b Feb 14 Hia 3f fst :35⅗ b

Frosty The Snowman — B. c. 3, by His Majesty—Frosty Skater, by Diplomat Way
Own.—Appleton A I — Br.—Appleton Arthur I (Fla) — Tr.—Alter Happy — 118
Lifetime 4 3 0 0 $30,100 — 1988 2 1 0 0 $10,800 — 1987 2 2 0 0 $19,300

15Feb88-10GP fst 1 1/16 :46⅗ 1:10⅘ 1:43⅕ Fountin Yth 2 4 5² 6³¾ 7¹² 8¹²¼ Valiente D b 112 4.10 73-21 Forty Niner 122ⁿᵒ Notebook 122¹ Buoy 119² Bumped, bobbled 9
15Feb88-Grade II
16Jan88- 5GP fst 1 1/16 :48 1:13 1:44⅖ Alw 18000 2 1 1ʰᵈ 1¹½ 1³ 1³¼ Valiente D b 119 *.90 79-20 FrostyTheSnowman1193¼GayRights1195StoptheStge1192 Driving 8
27Sep87- 3Crc fst 1 :48⅗ 1:13⅖ 1:40 Alw 16900 1 1 1¹ 1³ 1⁶ 1⁹ Valiente D b 116 *.70 88-15 Frosty The Snowman 116⁹ Stralli 112¹ Solid Bryan 112⁷ Easily 7
13Sep87- 7Crc fst 7f :23 :46⅘ 1:25⅘ Md Sp Wt 11 1 1³ 1³ 1⁴ 1³ Valiente D b 117 6.20 87-17 FrostyThSnowmn1173Crdnl'sKy1178SnsblBrd117½ Greenly,driving 11
LATEST WORKOUTS ●Mar 2 GP 4f fst :46⅗ b Feb 25 GP 1 fst 1:41⅘ b ●Feb 12 GP 4f fst :48 b ●Feb 5 GP 1 fst 1:39⅕ h

Buoy — Gr. c. 3, by Blue Ensign—Mop Mop, by Royal Union
Own.—Bollero Lois — Br.—Bollero Lois (Fla) — Tr.—Bollero Joseph M — 122
Lifetime 8 4 2 2 $136,611 — 1988 2 0 0 2 $20,687 — 1987 6 4 2 0 $115,924

15Feb88-10GP fst 1 1/16 :46⅗ 1:10⅘ 1:43⅕ Fountin Yth 5 5 4¹½ 4²½ 3²½ 3¹ Allen K K 119 7.20 84-21 Forty Niner 122ⁿᵒ Notebook 122¹ Buoy 119² Rallied 9
15Feb88-Grade II
20Jan88- 9GP fst 7f :22 :45 1:23⅘ [S]Floridian H 6 6 6⁸ 6⁵ 3⁵½ 3² Allen K K 123 *.80 85-20 Above Normal 1132EveningKris115ʰᵈBuoy1232 Stmbld st-bore in 8
30Dec87- 9Hia fst 6f :22⅕ :45 1:10⅘ J O' Farrell 5 3 4¹½ 3³ 2½ 1ʰᵈ Allen K K 119 2.00 89-23 Buoy 119ʰᵈ Hooting Star 113²½ Distinctintentions 113ⁿᵏ Driving 9
28Nov87- 8CD sly 1 1/16 :48 1:14 1:47⅘ Ky Jock Clb 5 3 3¹½ 2ʰᵈ 1ʰᵈ 1ʰᵈ Allen K K 122 6.70[D] 71-33 [D]Buoy 122ʰᵈ Notebook 122⁵ Hey Pat 119⁹ Ducked In 6
28Nov87-Grade II; Disqualified and placed second
15Nov87- 8CD fst 1 :45⅖ 1:11⅕ 1:37⅘ Iroquois 1 4 4³½ 1ʰᵈ 1½ 1ⁿᵒ Allen K K 116 3.20 80-19 Buoy 116ⁿᵒ Key Voyage 118½ Delightful Doctor 116² 12
13Oct87- 5Kee fst 7f :22⅘ :45 1:23⅕ Alw 17300 5 7 2¹ 2¹½ 1½ 1⁴ Fires E 115 *1.40 90-13 Buoy 115⁴ Hayes' Hope 115ʰᵈ Persian Medic 115³ 11
2Sep87- 1AP fst 7f :23 :46⅘ 1:25⅘ Md Sp Wt 2 3 1¹ 1¹½ 1¹½ 1⁴½ Fires E 118 *.70 74-24 Buoy 118⁴½ Sparkling Prospect 118⁷ Haye's Hope 118ⁿᵏ 9
17Aug87- 1AP fst 6½f :23⅘ :46⅘ 1:19⅘ Md Sp Wt 4 5 2ʰᵈ 2½ 2² 2¹¾ Fires E 117 2.30 75-26 Angel Bid 117¹¾ Buoy 117⁴ Prayett 117²½ 11
LATEST WORKOUTS Mar 4 GP 3f fst :37⅖ b ●Feb 28 GP 6f fst 1:13⅘ h ●Feb 23 GP 3f fst :35⅕ bg Feb 11 GP 4f fst :48⅖ h

Evening Kris — Dk. b. or br. c. 3, by Kris S—Evening Y'all, by Double Hitch
Own.—Pace H — Br.—Little James H (Fla) — Tr.—Mayberry John P — 118
Lifetime 14 3 6 0 $67,115 — 1988 3 0 2 0 $23,806 — 1987 11 3 4 0 $43,309 — Turf 1 0 0 0

15Feb88-10GP fst 1 1/16 :46⅗ 1:10⅘ 1:43⅕ Fountin Yth 6 9 7⁹ 7⁷¾ 4⁵½ 5³ Gonzalez M A 118 35.80 82-21 Forty Niner 122ⁿᵒ Notebook 122¹ Buoy 119² In tight 9
15Feb88-Grade II
20Jan88- 9GP fst 7f :22 :45 1:23⅘ [S]Floridian H 1 8 7¹⁴ 7¹⁰ 4⁵½ 2² Gonzalez M A 115 2.50 85-20 Above Normal 113² Evening Kris 115ʰᵈ Buoy 123² Rallied 8
8Jan88- 9GP fst 6f :21⅘ :45 1:11 Specta'r Bid 6 7 8¹⁴ 7¹¹ 3⁴ 2ⁿᵒ Gonzalez M A 112 4.70 84-20 Cook's Brown Rice 114ⁿᵒ Evening Kris 112⁴ Riff 112³ Just failed 8
30Dec87- 9Hia fst 6f :22⅕ :45 1:10⅘ J O' Farrell 4 7 9⁹¾ 9¹⁰ 6⁵½ 4²½ Gonzalez M A 115 11.60 86-23 Buoy 119ʰᵈ Hooting Star 113²½ Distinctintentions 113ⁿᵏ Rallied 9
15Dec87- 9Hia fst 7f :22⅘ :44⅘ 1:23⅘ Alw 15700 7 7 6⁷ 4³½ 1¹ 1¹½ Gonzalez M A 115 7.90 86-25 EveningKris115¹½Distinctintentions118²SecretFlotill115¹ Driving 8
6Dec87- 9Hia fm 1 1/8 (T) 1:43⅘ Citation 10 5 5²½ 7⁶ 10¹³ 10¹³ Lee M A 112 35.70 67-25 Be A Natural 116⁵ Lover's Trust 120¹ Twice TooMany114¹½ Tired 14
20Nov87- 8Hia fst 7f :23⅗ :46⅘ 1:24⅘ Alw 15200 6 2 2¹½ 1½ 2½ 2¹ Lee M A 114 4.90 73-28 Twice Too Many 115¹EveningKris114¾BreakPar117²½ Outfinished 6
6Nov87- 9Crc fst 6f :22⅘ :46 1:11⅘ Alw 11500 4 2 5⁵ 5⁴½ 5⁷ 5⁹½ Lee M A 114 4.10 83-19 Tanzanid 114¹½ Above Normal116¹½Cook'sBrownRice116³ Outrun 5
15Aug87- 9Crc fst 6f :22 :45⅘ 1:12⅘ Criterium 1 7 7⁷½ 6⁵¾ 4⁷½ 4⁴¾ Lee M A 116 9.10 83-17 Lover'sTrust116²½PositionLeder118½HousAccount118¹½ Mild gain 10
6Aug87- 8Crc fst 6f :22⅘ :46⅘ 1:13⅘ Alw 16100 7 2 3¹½ 2¹½ 1½ 1¹ Lee M A 114 *1.20 83-17 EveningKris114¹Distinctintentions112²RhumbaKing112ⁿᵏ Driving 8
LATEST WORKOUTS Feb 27 Crc 1 fst 1:43 b Feb 9 Crc 1 sly 1:43⅘ b

Notebook — B. c. 3, by Well Decorated—Mobcap, by Tom Rolfe
Own.—Klein E V — Br.—Eaton & Thorne (NY) — Tr.—Lukas D Wayne — 122
Lifetime 7 4 1 1 $252,620 — 1988 2 0 1 1 $48,919 — 1987 5 4 0 0 $203,701

15Feb88-10GP fst 1 1/16 :46⅗ 1:10⅘ 1:43⅕ Fountin Yth 9 3 2ʰᵈ 2ʰᵈ 2ʰᵈ 2ⁿᵒ Romero R P b 122 3.90 85-21 Forty Niner 122ⁿᵒ Notebook 122¹ Buoy 119² Just missed 9
15Feb88-Grade II
3Feb88- 9GP fst 7f :21⅘ :44⅘ 1:23 Hutcheson 7 3 3½ 4¹½ 3²½ 3¹½ Santos J A b 122 2.30 87-24 Perfect Spy 114¹ Forty Niner 122½ Notebook 122⁴ Rallied 7
3Feb88-Grade III
26Dec87- 8Aqu fst 1 1/8 [-]:48⅕ 1:12⅘ 1:50⅘ [S]B F Bongard 5 1 1¹ 1² 1¹² 1¹⁸ Santos J A b 122 *.20 89-17 Notebook 122¹⁸ Nessuno 113½ Whodam 117¹½ Ridden out 6
28Nov87- 8CD sly 1 1/16 :48 1:14 1:47⅘ Ky Jock Clb 4 2 1ʰᵈ 1ʰᵈ 2ʰᵈ 2ʰᵈ Santos J A b 122 2.40 71-33 [D]Buoy 122ʰᵈ Notebook 122⁵ Hey Pat 119⁹ Bumped 6
28Nov87-Grade II; Placed first through disqualification
2Nov87- 8Aqu fst 7f :22⅘ :45⅘ 1:22⅘ [S]DmonRunyon 4 3 1¹ 1³ 1⁵ 1⁷½ Santos J A b 117 *.70 89-21 Notebook 117⁷½ Ballindaggin 122⁸ Whodam 117² Ridden out 8
22Oct87- 5Aqu fst 6f :22⅘ :46⅘ 1:10⅘ [S]Md Sp Wt 7 6 6²¾ 2½ 1¹½ 1⁹½ Santos J A b 118 *1.10 88-16 Notebook 118⁹½ Three Gifts 118¾ Con Carne 118⁷ Strong urging 14
21Sep87- 4Bel fst 6f :22⅘ :46⅖ 1:12 [S]Md Sp Wt 14 14 13¹⁴ 9¹¹ 9⁸½ 7³½ Santos J A 118 *2.00 76-15 Whodam 118¹½ Enjoy The Moment118ⁿᵒThreeGifts118ʰᵈ Bumped 14
LATEST WORKOUTS Mar 1 GP 4f fst :48⅖ b Feb 24 GP 5f fst 1:03⅘ b Feb 11 GP 4f fst :50⅘ b Jan 30 GP 4f fst :50⅗ b

Forty Niner — Ch. c. 3, by Mr Prospector—File, by Tom Rolfe
Own.—Claiborne Farm — Br.—Claiborne Farm (Ky) — Tr.—Stephens Woodford C — 122
Lifetime 8 6 1 0 $759,444 — 1988 2 1 1 0 $124,536 — 1987 6 5 0 0 $634,908

15Feb88-10GP fst 1 1/16 :46⅗ 1:10⅘ 1:43⅕ Fountin Yth 7 1 1ʰᵈ 1ʰᵈ 1ʰᵈ 1ⁿᵒ Maple E 122 *.80 85-21 Forty Niner 122ⁿᵒ Notebook 122¹ Buoy 119² Driving 9
15Feb88-Grade II
3Feb88- 9GP fst 7f :21⅘ :44⅘ 1:23 Hutcheson 5 2 2ʰᵈ 2½ 2¹½ 2¹ Maple E 122 *.70 88-24 Perfect Spy 114¹ Forty Niner 122½ Notebook 122⁴ Couldn't gain 7
3Feb88-Grade III
30Oct87- 8Kee fst 1 1/16 :46⅘ 1:11 1:43⅘ Brd Fut 2 1 2¹ 2ʰᵈ 2ʰᵈ 1ⁿᵒ Maple E 121 *.40 87-18 Forty Niner 121ⁿᵒ Hey Pat 121²½ Sea Trek 121³ Driving 7
30Oct87-Grade II
17Oct87- 8Bel fst 1 :46⅘ 1:10⅘ 1:36⅘ Champagne 7 2 3¹½ 2ʰᵈ 1¹½ 1⁴½ Maple E 122 3.30 81-20 Forty Niner 122⁴½ Parlay Me 122¹½ Tejano 122⁵½ Drew away 11
17Oct87-Grade I
20Sep87- 6Bel gd 7f :22⅕ :45⅗ 1:22⅘ Futurity 1 2 1¹½ 1¹½ 1³ 1³ Maple E 122 4.50 89-14 Forty Niner 122³ Tsarbaby 122²½ Crusader Sword122⁴ Ridden out 5
20Sep87-Grade I
19Aug87- 8Sar sly 6f :21⅘ :44⅘ 1:10 Sanford 3 3 2² 2¹½ 1ʰᵈ 1³½ Maple E 115 6.10 90-15 Forty Niner 115³½ Once Wild 115³ Velvet Fog 115⁵½ Driving 6
19Aug87-Grade II
7Aug87- 8Sar fst 6f :21⅘ :45 1:10⅘ Sar Special 2 4 1½ 2ʰᵈ 3¹ 6¹⁰ Maple E 117 3.40 79-17 Crusader Sword 117ⁿᵏ Tejano 117⁵½ Endurance 119⁴ Tired 8
7Aug87-Grade II
17Jly87- 5Bel fst 6f :22⅘ :46 1:11⅘ Md Sp Wt 8 4 1½ 1¹½ 1³ 1³½ Maple E 118 *1.40e 82-20 Forty Niner 118³½ Dyna Former 118²¾ Tsarbaby 118¹½ Ridden out 13
LATEST WORKOUTS Mar 4 Hia 3f fst :35⅘ b Feb 29 Hia 6f fst 1:14⅘ b Feb 25 Hia 1 fst 1:40⅕ h Feb 21 Hia 6f fst 1:16⅘ b

Cherokee Colony — B. c. 3, by Pleasant Colony—Cherokee Phoenix, by Nijinsky II
Own.—Buckland Farm — Br.—Evans T M (Va) — Tr.—Campo John P — 122

Lifetime					
6 2 3 0	1988	1	1	0	0	$150,000
$272,200	1987	5	1	3	0	$122,200

2Jan88-10Hia	fst	1⅛	:46⅘	1:11	1:49⅘	Flamingo	11	12	95¾	77	32	11	Velasquez J	118	3.70	82-14 Cherokee Colony 1181 Sorry About That 122hd Cebis1182½	Driving 14
2Jan88-Grade I																	
30Oct87- 8Med	fst	1 1/16	:46⅗	1:11⅕	1:45	Yng America	7	10	97¾	75	32	21½	Migliore R	119	9.30	77-23 Firery Ensign 1191½ Cherokee Colony 1191½ Kingpost119¾	Rallied 10
30Oct87-Grade I																	
16Oct87- 8Med	fst	1	:47⅕	1:13⅕	1:39⅗	Alw 16000	9	8	713	54½	31½	1hd	Migliore R	113	3.10	77-27 CherokeeColony113hdTroupeTrain1175LearnbyHeart1172½	Driving 9
30Sep87- 2Bel	gd	1	:46⅘	1:11⅖	1:37⅗	Md Sp Wt	9	13	127	86	24	2¾	Vasquez J	118	*1.30	76-16 GennesseFr118¾ChrokColony118½PlsingMmoris1183¾	Closed well 14
9Sep87- 6Bel	fst	7f	:22⅘	:46⅕	1:23⅖	Md Sp Wt	12	10	98	68	35	22½	Vasquez J	118	14.10	82-15 FrryEnsgn1182½ChrokColony1185FolshMcDff1183¾	Best of others 13
12Aug87- 3Sar	gd	7f	:22⅗	:46⅗	1:24⅗	Md Sp Wt	6	8	1110	1011	89¾	410½	Vasquez J	118	22.80	68-22 FortRiley1186½John'sConcord118nkForeverSilvr1183½	Raced wide 12

LATEST WORKOUTS Feb 27 Crc 6f fst 1:14⅘ b — Feb 20 Crc 7f fst 1:29⅕ b — ●Feb 2 Crc 6f fst 1:14⅖ b — ●Jan 27 Crc 5f fst 1:01⅗ b

Twice Too Many—Moderately successful in winter racing in Florida, Twice Too Many's three lifetime wins in sixteen starts were in a maiden race and two allowances (we deduce this by subtracting the two wins shown in his PPs from his career total of three). In November, he beat Evening Kris by one length in an allowance race. Moved up to stakes company, he had one second and three thirds. His best race was in the Grade II Everglades when he finished third by two and a half lengths behind Sorry About That. But in his next start, the Grade I Flamingo, Twice Too Many ran a distant seventh at 50 to 1. Cherokee Colony won the race by a length; Sorry About That was second. We pass.

Sorry About That—Lightly raced and working superbly, Sorry About That had displayed impressive ability. He won his debut in a maiden race at The Meadowlands, shipped to Aqueduct for a five and a half length easy score in a $30,000 allowance, then went to Florida to begin the long, arduous route to the Triple Crown races. Sorry About That showed he just might be good enough to be a factor in the Triple Crown. He jumped up from his allowance win to the 1 1/8 mile Grade II Everglades and won by half a length. He then finished second by a length to Cherokee Colony in the Flamingo. But that was January 2, two months before the Florida Derby. His workouts are extremely rapid, six furlongs in a bullet 1:13 then another bullet, four furlongs in :46 3/5. Since he didn't race on the lead in any of his four career starts, we interpret the sharp workouts to mean he's fit and ready. Yet a two month layoff preceding the toughest competition he's encountered weighs heavily.

Ruhlmann—Sorry About That wasn't the only Florida Derby starter with fast works. Ruhlmann showed four bullet works: six furlongs in 1:11 2/5 and seven furlongs in 1:24 3/5 at Hollywood Park (a fast track, yet many six and seven furlong races are run in slower times than Ruhlmann's works), and six furlongs in 1:12 2/5 followed by five furlongs in :58 at Gulfstream.

Ruhlmann had seven races, the first three on turf in France. Given three months to adjust to the U.S. by trainer Bobby Frankel, Ruhlmann began his career on dirt by taking a maiden race by seven lengths. Next were a tiring second and third in allowance company, each as the odds-on favorite. Frankel added blinkers, and Ruhlmann exploded to a six length win in the Grade III Camino Real Derby, January 24. He hadn't raced since. Because he had won his maiden after a three month layoff, many handicappers didn't feel his two-months of rest before the Florida Derby would affect his performance. Noted handicapper Andy Beyer called him a mortal lock.

Brian's Time—He made his debut on a muddy track at Saratoga as a 2-year-old, breaking eleventh and finishing fifth by seven. Trainer John Veitch gave Brian's Time three months off. Brian's Time responded by taking a maiden race by three and a half and then finishing second by a head, three lengths in front of subsequent stakes winner and similarly bred Dynaformer in an allowance race. His fourth start was a four and a half length allowance win. Veitch, whose list of outstanding horses includes Alydar, Proud Truth and Davona Dale, saw enough improvement to enter Brian's Time in the Grade II Fountain of Youth at one and a sixteenth miles. Dismissed at 15 to 1, Brian's Time rallied from eighth to finish fourth by three against Forty Niner, Notebook, and Buoy. Brian's Time's breeding, by Roberto out of Kelly's Day by Graustark, suggests that he would race better as the distance increased. His come-from-behind style supported that contention. He had closed six and three-quarters lengths against last season's 2-year-old champ, Forty Niner, in the Fountain of Youth.

Frosty The Snowman—That it took trainer Happy Alter so long to try this horse on grass amazed me. A son of His Majesty out of a mare by Diplomat Way, Frosty's breeding cried for turf. And eventually, his human connections put Frosty on turf, where he quickly blossomed into a stakes winner. But that happened later in his career and is still happening. At the time of the Florida Derby, Frosty had shown enough ability on dirt to keep him there. He won his first three starts, wire-to-wire in each one, then tried the Fountain of Youth. In a rough trip, labeled "Bumped, bobbled" in the *Form*, Frosty finished eighth by twelve and a quarter lengths behind five of the horses in this race: Forty Niner, Notebook, Buoy, Brian's Time and Evening Kris. An extra sixteenth of a mile wouldn't help his chances, though he showed sharpness in a bullet four furlong workout of :46 3/5 breezing.

Buoy—In the money all eight starts, Buoy came into the Florida Derby off a solid third, a length off Forty Niner, in the Fountain of Youth. Despite the strong effort, trainer Joe Bollero added blinkers. Buoy responded with a pair of bullet works, three furlongs in :35 1/5 and six furlongs in 1:13 3/5. Previously, Buoy raced close to the front in six races, on the lead once and, in the Floridian Stakes for Florida-breds two starts ago, well back in sixth. What would the addition of blinkers do? Hard to tell since Buoy had enough speed to stalk the pacesetters anyway. With an abundance of early speed in the race, we conclude Buoy's chances won't be improved if he shows more speed. If the blinkers were used to get him to relax and rate farther than normal behind the leader, it wasn't evident from his fast works.

Evening Kris—A strong closer, Evening Kris was hampered by traffic problems, noted by "In tight" in the *Form*, when he finished fifth by three against Forty Niner in the Fountain of Youth. Previously, Evening Kris was beaten by Twice Too Many in an allowance and by Buoy in a minor stakes at Hialeah.

Notebook—When D. Wayne Lukas debuted this New York-bred, he broke fourteenth, was bumped, and rallied to finish seventh by three and a quarter in a state-bred maiden race. Lukas added blinkers, and Notebook improved by leaps, winning his maiden and then a New York-bred stakes, the Damon Runyon, by nine and a quarter and by seven and a half respectively. Lukas tried Notebook in open company, the Grade II Kentucky Jockey Club Stakes, and he was second by a head, losing to Buoy, but Buoy was disqualified for ducking in and bumping Notebook. Notebook returned to New York for an eighteen length stakes romp against New York-breds, then was pointed south to take on the big boys. In the Grade III Hutcheson, marking the 3-year-old debut of Forty Niner, Notebook ran third, one and a half lengths behind upset winner Perfect Spy and just half a length behind Forty Niner. Notebook tested Forty Niner again in the

Fountain of Youth, and they dueled head-to-head for almost every yard in the $1^1/16$ mile stakes. Forty Niner won by a nose; Notebook was second.

For the Florida Derby, Lukas changed jockeys, replacing Randy Romero, one of New York's top riders, with Laffit Pincay, Jr., widely regarded as either the best or second best jockey in the country.

Forty Niner—There is no trainer better than Woody Stephens at pointing a horse to a specific big race. Stephens' goal with Forty Niner was the obvious one of the Kentucky Derby. After his first two starts in 1989 in the Hutcheson (second by a length) and the Fountain of Youth (first by a nose), Forty Niner was primed for a strong race which would be his next-to-last prep for the Kentucky Derby.

In a single word, Forty Niner was a champion. He had won six of his eight races and would win more later in his 3-year-old campaign. Forty Niner was a fighter, one who'd slug it out through the stretch with the best 3-year-olds in the country. Trainers can't teach courage to a horse. He either has it or doesn't. Forty Niner had tons.

Cherokee Colony—He is one of an extremely rare group of horses who win their maiden race in allowance company. The John Campo-trained Cherokee Colony, a son of 1981 Kentucky Derby and Preakness winner Pleasant Colony out of a Nijinsky II mare, missed in three maiden starts, but then won a $16,000 allowance by a head. Off that effort, Campo put Cherokee Colony in the Grade I Young America for 2-year-olds. Cherokee Colony was second by one and a quarter lengths.

Campo laid his horse off for two months, bringing him back to win the Flamingo by a length, January 2. He hadn't raced since. A couple of good six furlong works in 1:14 2/5 and 1:14 4/5 were inconclusive for a horse with obvious physical problems gleaned from his two layoffs after extremely good races.

So we have three horses off layoffs (Sorry About That, Ruhlmann and Cherokee Colony), two horses apparently not good enough (Twice Too Many and Frosty), and one with an equipment change we're not sure will be an advantage. Of those six, Ruhlmann seemed the best because of his six length stakes win, excellent works and a previous victory off a layoff suggesting he could perform well again. Cherokee Colony and Sorry About That were a length apart in the Flamingo and idle since.

There were three horses left. Forty Niner was the obvious class and Notebook was inches off him twice. What of Brian's Time? He was a closer who had demonstrated considerable improvement by gaining six and three-quarters lengths to finish fourth behind Forty Niner and Notebook. His breeding suggested he'd benefit from the added distance. Would he have a reasonable chance? Yes he would, assuming there was enough speed in front of him to keep a lively pace. Forty Niner, Notebook, and Frosty wanted to race on the lead. Ruhlmann, Sorry About That and Buoy usually raced near the lead and had shown speed in their workouts.

Forty Niner was justifiably made the favorite as expected. When the odds of Brian's Time opened in double digits and began climbing, we had an overlay. The higher the odds got, the bigger the overlay became.

This was an improving horse who closed well against two of the horses he had to beat, Forty Niner and Notebook. An extra sixteenth of a mile would allow him to close more. Did he have enough class to do it? It's a tough question that only the race would reveal. But he certainly figured as a logical contender. So what if he was 30 to 1?

Brian's Time gamely wore down stubborn Forty Niner in the final yards by a neck, paying $68 to win. The exacta paid more than $220.

Nearly 1,500 miles away, the same day and at almost the same time, Dynaformer was winning a $1^{1}/_{8}$ mile stakes, equaling Aqueduct's track record in the Lucky Draw Stakes. Dynaformer, also a son of Roberto, is from the same maternal family as Brian's Time.

It was a good day for Roberto's sons. And it was a good day for an enormous overlay.

Money Management

Betting on horses used to be a simpler proposition twenty to twenty-five years ago. There were fewer options.

You bet to win, place or show and took your chances. Today, the bettor must decide between straight bets, a.k.a. win, place or show, multiple bets (the Daily Double) and exotic bets including exactas and triples. Lately, extremely difficult wagers, such as the pick three all the way up to the pick six, have become popular.

Which should you bet? And how?

Wagering is an individual decision, one which has absolutely nothing to do with the ability to handicap.

Handicapping means picking winners. Successful wagering means conquering the devil of money management. Winning at the races or just breaking even and having an enjoyable time entail both handicapping and money management.

Money management is defined as not only choosing the right type of bet, but also the right amount to bet and the number of bets to make in any given trip to the track.

It's not easy. Anyone who says it is qualifies to be the same person who brags about winning all the time at the track. Nobody wins at the track all the time, and nobody has an easy time every race making money management decisions.

The vital initial step is to decide how much money you're willing and financially able to gamble. Whether you bet $2,000 a race or $2, your success will hinge on setting acceptable limits and sticking by them. In other words, Joe Fan will not—under any circumstances—lose more than $1,000 any trip to the track. Freddie Fan has lower limits, say $50, but lives by them in the same manner.

Anyone who doesn't have limits is inviting disaster. Set realistic limits you're comfortable with and then discipline yourself into living by them. It's the same discipline you'll need to skip certain races. If you lack discipline, you're drastically reducing your chances of emerging a winner.

GUIDELINE NO. 1—Keep a record. A wise person once said too much of anything is no good. Gambling on horses easily fits that description. While gambling on horse racing is more fun than casino or sports betting, it can be just as damaging if you don't have a handle on it. Keeping a record of your bets will ultimately do two important things: 1) keep you informed on a daily basis of your progress or lack of it, and 2) help you in your betting by pointing out where you've been successful and what means you used to create that success. It's easy to keep a record, takes only a couple minutes from your daily routine, and will always help you to be realistic in your wagering.

GUIDELINE NO. 2—Live by the limits you set. It's useless to say your limit for one year is $2,500 and wind up down $3,000 by the end of March. Working within your comfortable framework will keep you in control of your wagering rather than vice versa.

GUIDELINE NO. 3—Always bet enough to win on a horse so that if your exotic bets don't cash you don't feel like a moron afterwards. How many times have you bet a 5 to 1 shot or a 10 to 1 shot in exactas, or triples or daily doubles, watched that horse win, but failed to catch the exotic or the double? If you've bet none of your total investment to win, you're going to feel—deservedly—like the world's biggest dope. If you like a horse enough to key your exotic wagers on him, then put at least a percentage of your total investment on a win bet if the horse is a decent price. The purpose? It's hard enough being right about 8 to 1 shots, let alone being right and not cashing because you were greedy and went after the big exotic pot. Still go for the pot, just cover yourself so you don't tout your friends for ten minutes on a 6 to 1 shot who wins while you didn't bet a single dollar to win. When that does happen, odds are about even money you convinced one of your friends to bet on the winning horse. He's the one talking about a smart bet, while you're ripping up triple tickets and muttering.

GUIDELINE NO. 4—Discipline, discipline and more discipline. A successful bettor maximizes his good plays and minimizes the number of times he makes poor plays. Zeroing in on the one or two good plays of an afternoon of racing is a prerequisite to succeeding at your wagering.

Again, we revert to the idea of realism woven through this book. Don't expect to get four or five winners a day because it won't happen. Maybe once or twice a year, but that's the same amount of times you'll go 0-for-9.

Don't allow yourself to be arrogant, because time after time the track will roll over your body and bring you back to reality.

Here are the realities of handicapping. Year in and year out, John Piesen of the New York *Post*, Russ Harris of the *Daily News* and John Pricci of *Newsday* are three of the nation's top public handicappers. At their best, they pick thirty percent winners. Three for ten. A .300 hitter. Year after year, thirty percent is outstanding for a public thoroughbred handicapper.

Here's how the author fared as a public handicapper at Saratoga in 1989 compared to others: Harris, 36.5 percent winners; Dave Litfin, *Daily News*, 33.8; Pricci, 32.1; Bill Heller, *Schenectady Gazette*, 30.2; Paul Moran, *Newsday*, 30.2; F.I.G.S. *Form*, 28.8; Richard McCarthy, *Newsday*, 28.2; Piesen, 26.4.

In 1988 at Saratoga, Ernie Munick, an outstanding young handicapper who retired a year ago to continue his education, tabbed 34.3 percent. Bill Heller checked in at 27.8.

The realities of horse racing are well documented.

Think about it. Assuming a measure of combined intelligence generated by thousands and thousands of bettors in any single race, that wisdom cashes in one of three times with a horse deemed as the most logical winner: the favorite.

That's one for three: .333.

Now consider the fact we don't usually play favorites. The whole substance of this book is to explain the idea of catching overlays. If we cash one of three bets, we're doing as well as chalk players who, by definition, are getting a lower percentage return than we are since they're playing horses at lower odds.

Can we connect on one of three plays solely on overlays? Yes. It takes discipline to recognize legitimate overlays and/or a weak favorite, one we can shoot holes in by thorough handicapping. We won't be right nine races a day, nor will we expect to be. We'll look for positive situations with several handicapping factors working for us or against the other contenders we identify in the race.

Is the favorite coming off a lengthy layoff? Does he have a poor turf post and/or a rider who is more accomplished on dirt? Is the horse we have to beat a first-time starter from a trainer who likes to take his time with beginners?

How many arguments can we make in favor of the overlay we're contemplating making a wager on? Is it one item, or five of them? The more the better.

You can never spend too much time with the *Form* before the races. Experience will teach you when the morning line is reasonable and when it's out of line. Experience will teach you when a horse is likely to be overbet, creating overlays for other contenders. A switch to Cordero, especially when he's on a win streak, produces many underlays.

Will we ever use underlay horses in exacta or Daily Double bets? If we perceive the combination to have value—judging from the potential payoffs shown on the TV monitors—we'll bet accordingly. But the important item is to cash when you're correct and not waste the opportunity.

In New York, the first betting flash of off-track betting money sporadically produces underlays of ridiculous proportions, particularly at Saratoga. Tens of thousands of dollars may have been pumped into OTB shops around New York City and Long Island on a clear, sunny afternoon. At Saratoga, 175 miles away, a vicious storm may have changed the condition of the track or the track bias, or forced racing officials to make late switches of turf races to a sloppy, main track. These are excellent advantages for on-track bettors. In this game, take any advantage you can get.

If you're selective enough, disciplined enough and become

knowledgeable enough, you will survive at the track. If you break even, you're among a small percentage of people who bet horse racing. We want better. Focus on intelligent overlays. Cash even one of them a day and you'll make money. Cash two of them and you'll be set. Overlay, overlay.

Appendix

The following reference lists compiled and published in *The Blood-Horse* can help your handicapping. They certainly can't hurt.

LEADING ACTIVE SIRES—LIFETIME

For stallions currently standing in North America, represented by at least 100 named foals of racing age, the leaders are arranged by lifetime Average-Earnings Index. Cumulative statistics account for all progeny raced here and abroad, and yearlings sold in North America, England, Ireland, and France through Dec. 25, 1989.

Stallion (Foreign foaled) Year, Sire	Where stands	Crops No.	Avg. Size	Named Foals	Yearlings Sold	Average	TNA	Runners	Stakes Winners	Graded Stakes Winners	Champions	Avg-Erngs Index	*Comp. Index
1. Alydar, 1975, Raise a Native	Ky.	7	.52	.364	208	$476,329	12.8	254-70%	35-10%	.21- 6%	4	7.53	4.40
2. Danzig, 1977, Northern Dancer	Ky.	6	.46	.274	149	$458,110	12.0	198-72%	45-16%	.27-10%	2	6.78	4.01
3. Nureyev, 1977, Northern Dancer	Ky.	7	.32	.224	102	$474,651	12.9	188-84%	50-22%	.27-12%	8	6.18	4.83
4. Seattle Slew, 1974, Bold Reasoning	Ky.	8	.42	.332	132	$606,585	17.4	236-71%	41-12%	.27- 8%	4	6.03	5.08
5. Fappiano, 1977, Mr. Prospector	Ky.	5	.41	.206	119	$191,199	5.5	161-78%	26-13%	.11- 5%	1	5.79	2.94
6. Nijinsky II, 1967, Northern Dancer	Ky.	16	.41	.659	272	$499,404	15.3	500-76%	.122-19%	.82-12%	14	5.42	4.40
7. Mr. Prospector, 1970, Raise a Native	Ky.	12	.47	.566	205	$434,270	11.6	450-80%	94-17%	.48- 8%	11	5.20	3.11
8. Deputy Minister, 1979, Vice Regent.	Ky.	3	.36	.108	84	$77,223	2.5	72-67%	10- 9%	2- 2%	1	5.00	2.99
9. Private Account, 1976, Damascus	Ky.	6	.38	.228	138	$100,599	2.8	161-71%	23-10%	.15- 7%	1	4.63	2.81
10. Relaunch, 1976, In Reality	Ky.	6	.38	.230	126	$45,609	1.2	170-74%	31-13%	6- 3%	1	4.57	2.24
11. Blushing Groom (Fr) 1974, Red God	Ky.	9	.42	.382	199	$305,984	8.1	295-77%	60-16%	.37-10%	7	4.37	3.41
12. Halo, 1969, Hail to Reason.	Ky.	12	.35	.415	225	$98,378	2.8	336-81%	40-10%	.16- 4%	5	3.80	2.43
13. Storm Bird, 1978, Northern Dancer	Ky.	5	.39	.197	132	$223,175	6.6	140-71%	21-11%	.15- 8%	5	3.78	3.95
14. Lyphard, 1969, Northern Dancer	Ky.	14	.40	.554	240	$275,596	8.7	436-79%	77-14%	.45- 8%	10	3.74	3.80
15. Buckaroo, 1975, Buckpasser	Fla.	7	.26	.184	77	$17,552	0.4	153-83%	10- 5%	3- 2%	1	3.59	1.73
16. Pleasant Colony, 1978, His Majesty.	Ky.	5	.30	.149	45	$88,376	2.5	114-77%	18-12%	6- 4%	0	3.58	2.33
17. Sportin' Life, 1978, Nijinsky II.	Ky.	4	.30	.121	92	$34,544	1.1	91-75%	4- 3%	1- 1%	0	3.50	1.71
18. Cox's Ridge, 1974, Best Turn	Ky.	7	.44	.310	191	$134,232	3.8	222-72%	21- 7%	.10- 3%	2	3.39	2.48
19. Alleged, 1974, Hoist the Flag	Ky.	8	.52	.417	241	$230,695	6.6	274-66%	42-10%	.26- 6%	5	3.36	3.72
20. Vice Regent, 1967, Northern Dancer	Can.	15	.29	.439	262	$82,812	2.4	355-81%	67-15%	7- 2%	9	3.27	1.79
21. Kris S., 1977, Roberto	Fla.	5	.27	.133	11	$5,291	0.2	110-83%	13-10%	4- 3%	0	3.26	1.71
22. Topsider, 1974, Northern Dancer.	Ky.	7	.38	.265	149	$120,667	3.3	214-81%	29-11%	.13- 5%	2	3.19	2.83
23. Silver Hawk, 1979, Roberto	Ky.	4	.29	.117	39	$26,290	0.4	80-68%	10- 9%	4- 3%	0	3.18	1.60
24. Affirmed, 1975, Exclusive Native	Ky.	7	.37	.256	129	$145,452	4.4	189-74%	34-13%	.14- 5%	7	3.09	3.74
Diesis (GB), 1980, Sharpen Up	Ky.	3	.36	.109	78	$166,561	4.7	80-73%	8- 7%	4- 4%	1	3.09	2.21
26. Sovereign Dancer, 1975, Northern Dancer .	Ky.	7	.39	.271	132	$84,712	2.4	210-77%	20- 7%	8- 3%	0	3.06	1.88
27. Sir Ivor, 1965, Sir Gaylord	Ky.	18	.37	.661	336	$119,844	5.2	503-76%	80-12%	.41- 6%	7	3.01	3.41
28. Saros (GB), 1974, Sassafras	Calif.	7	.20	.138	10	$8,180	0.3	100-72%	4- 3%	3- 2%	0	2.98	0.75
29. His Majesty, 1968, Ribot.	Ky.	14	.27	.379	171	$47,294	1.6	296-78%	36- 9%	.17- 4%	2	2.97	2.39
30. Crafty Prospector, 1979, Mr. Prospector.	Fla.	3	.40	.121	47	$26,737	0.8	93-77%	5- 4%	0- 0%	0	2.93	1.54
31. Majestic Light, 1973, Majestic Prince	Ky.	9	.41	.369	175	$87,664	2.7	264-72%	37-10%	.22- 6%	1	2.92	3.62
32. Riverman, 1969, Never Bend.	Ky.	14	.43	.608	243	$187,936	5.6	481-79%	75-12%	.32- 5%	7	2.88	2.92
33. Conquistador Cielo, 1979, Mr. Prospector.	Ky.	4	.42	.166	96	$202,776	6.6	121-73%	12- 7%	4- 2%	0	2.86	3.94
34. Rich Cream, 1975, Creme dela Creme .	Ky.	6	.38	.229	138	$30,756	0.9	156-68%	6- 3%	3- 1%	0	2.83	1.74
35. Key to the Mint, 1969, Graustark .	Ky.	13	.31	.402	204	$92,994	3.2	302-75%	36- 9%	.12- 3%	3	2.76	3.02
Stop the Music, 1970, Hail to Reason .	Ky.	11	.30	.331	174	$76,739	2.4	268-81%	27- 8%	.14- 4%	2	2.76	2.57
37. Miswaki, 1978, Mr. Prospector.	Ky.	5	.49	.245	165	$81,426	2.4	185-76%	25-10%	.12- 5%	0	2.74	2.19
38. Ack Ack, 1966, Battle Joined	Ky.	15	.33	.494	218	$47,856	1.9	392-79%	49-10%	.19- 4%	1	2.73	2.68
The Minstrel, 1974, Northern Dancer.	Ky.	9	.39	.349	204	$308,030	8.7	275-79%	43-12%	.27- 8%	9	2.73	3.59
40. Flying Paster, 1976, Gummo .	Calif.	5	.36	.181	54	$26,067	0.7	134-74%	19-10%	5- 3%	0	2.71	2.10
41. Air Forbes Won, 1979, Bold Forbes.	Ky.	4	.38	.151	86	$19,310	0.6	109-72%	10- 7%	4- 3%	1	2.67	1.47
Stage Door Johnny, 1965, Prince John .	Ky.	18	.27	.477	201	$49,396	2.1	341-71%	47-10%	.27- 6%	2	2.67	3.82
43. Assert (Ire), 1979, Be My Guest .	Ky.	4	.38	.150	94	$82,337	2.5	95-63%	12- 8%	4- 3%	0	2.64	1.82
44. Grey Dawn, 1962, Herbager	Ky.	20	.32	.639	261	$52,920	2.0	556-87%	66-10%	.27- 4%	5	2.61	2.30
45. Northern Baby, 1976, Northern Dancer .	Ky.	6	.40	.239	145	$107,485	3.1	181-76%	14- 6%	8- 3%	2	2.53	2.86
46. Bold Ruckus, 1976, Boldnesian	Can.	6	.33	.197	109	$31,134	0.8	161-82%	19-10%	1- 1%	0	2.52	1.57
Silver Buck, 1978, Buckpasser.	Fla.	4	.38	.152	66	$23,303	0.7	114-75%	10- 7%	1- 1%	0	2.52	2.02
48. Al Nasr (Fr), 1978, Lyphard .	Ky.	4	.38	.150	104	$76,658	2.4	109-73%	10- 7%	5- 3%	1	2.51	2.07
Spectacular Bid, 1976, Bold Bidder .	Ky.	6	.46	.273	150	$205,687	6.4	193-71%	30-11%	9- 3%	0	2.51	3.86
Talc, 1972, Rock Talk	N.Y.	9	.24	.214	51	$12,029	0.3	178-83%	12- 6%	1- 1%	0	2.51	1.49
51. Cormorant, 1974, His Majesty .	N.Y.	9	.28	.256	106	$18,767	0.5	195-76%	16- 6%	3- 1%	0	2.49	1.57
52. Foolish Pleasure, 1972, What a Pleasure . .	Ky.	10	.32	.316	165	$86,029	2.8	242-77%	30- 9%	.10- 3%	2	2.47	2.85
Valid Appeal, 1972, In Reality	Fla.	10	.35	.347	98	$39,426	1.1	260-75%	35-10%	7- 2%	0	2.47	1.71
54. Vigors, 1973, Grey Dawn	Ky.	8	.36	.286	162	$35,997	1.0	232-81%	28-10%	6- 3%	1	2.45	2.13
55. John Alden, 1974, Speak John	Md.	7	.17	.121	25	$4,224	0.1	86-71%	7- 6%	1- 1%	0	2.44	0.95
56. Lord Gaylord, 1970, Sir Gaylord.	Md.	12	.21	.252	57	$46,461	1.3	204-81%	26-10%	5- 2%	1	2.43	1.76
57. Known Fact, 1977, In Reality	Ky.	5	.34	.169	67	$83,764	2.5	129-76%	12- 7%	1- 1%	1	2.41	2.61
58. Irish Tower, 1977, Irish Castle .	Ky.	5	.34	.169	108	$29,170	0.8	125-74%	12- 7%	3- 2%	0	2.39	1.92
59. Bates Motel, 1979, Sir Ivor .	Ky.	3	.39	.116	84	$35,401	1.3	84-72%	6- 5%	0- 0%	0	2.38	2.18
60. Believe It, 1975, In Reality	Ky.	8	.40	.319	166	$51,870	1.5	255-80%	16- 5%	.12- 4%	0	2.37	2.87
Clever Trick, 1976, Icecapade .	Ky.	6	.50	.300	211	$59,693	1.7	231-77%	25- 8%	9- 3%	0	2.37	1.94
Smarten, 1976, Cyane	Md.	7	.33	.234	117	$35,364	1.0	182-78%	21- 9%	6- 3%	1	2.37	2.60
63. Stalwart, 1979, Hoist the Flag	Ky.	5	.42	.209	130	$35,313	1.0	165-79%	20-10%	2- 1%	0	2.33	2.05
64. Green Dancer, 1972, Nijinsky II	Ky.	11	.47	.517	238	$120,003	3.7	427-83%	48- 9%	.18- 3%	1	2.32	2.99
Lord Avie, 1978, Lord Gaylord	Ky.	5	.36	.182	110	$20,872	0.6	124-68%	19-10%	3- 2%	0	2.32	2.14
Sunny's Halo, 1980, Halo.	Ky.	3	.38	.116	81	$29,329	1.0	84-74%	5- 4%	1- 1%	0	2.32	2.15

***COMPARABLE INDEX:** The lifetime Average-Earnings Index indicates how much purse money the progeny of one sire has earned, on the average, in relation to the average earnings of all runners in the same years; average earnings of all runners in any year is represented by an index of 1.00. The Comparable Index indicates the average earnings of progeny (in North America only) produced from mares bred to one sire, when these same mares were bred to other sires. Only 32 per cent of all sires have a lifetime Average-Earnings Index higher than their mares' Comparable Index.

Courtesy of *The Blood-Horse* Magazine

LEADING SIRES BY 1989 EARNINGS

For stallions which stand or (deceased) stood in North America and have runners in North America, the leaders are arranged by earnings through Dec. 31, 1989, including all monies earned in England and Ireland, plus earnings from stakes and 2-year-old races in France, Italy, Germany, Puerto Rico, and Mexico, converted to dollars at the rate of exchange agreed upon by international racing authorities.

Stallion (Foreign foaled), Year, Sire	Where Stands	Rnrs	Wnrs/Wins	Stakes Wnrs/Wins	(Chief Earner, Earnings)	1989 Earnings	Named Foals	Stakes Wnrs	A-E Index	*Comp. Index
1. Halo, 1969, Hail to Reason	Ky.	102	53/120	4/18	(Sunday Silence, $4,578,454)	$7,554,354	415	40	3.80	2.43
2. Alydar, 1975, Raise a Native	Ky.	102	50/90	5/16	(Easy Goer, $3,837,150)	$6,881,161	364	35	7.53	4.40
3. Blushing Groom (Fr), 1974, Red God	Ky.	75	35/77	11/23	(Nashwan-Eng., $1,420,150)	$4,757,826	382	60	4.37	3.41
4. Fappiano, 1977, Mr. Prospector	Ky.	100	53/99	13/20	(Cryptoclearance, $1,059,010)	$4,677,826	206	26	5.79	2.94
5. Danzig, 1977, Northern Dancer	Ky.	94	60/108	14/25	(Polish Precedent-Fr., $578,305)	$4,575,938	274	45	6.78	4.01
6. Caro (Ire), 1967-89, Fortino	—	77	48/108	10/21	(With Approval, $1,772,150)	$4,023,583	507	68	3.40	2.38
7. Mr. Prospector, 1970, Raise a Native	Ky.	99	53/103	15/20	(Rhythm, $612,920)	$3,955,071	566	94	5.20	3.11
8. Seattle Slew, 1974, Bold Reasoning	Ky.	86	47/88	13/20	(Slew City Slew, $642,216)	$3,581,538	332	41	6.03	5.08
9. Nijinsky II, 1967, Northern Dancer	Ky.	83	43/75	11/22	(Dancing Spree, $992,903)	$3,540,892	659	122	5.42	4.40
10. Nureyev, 1977, Northern Dancer	Ky.	74	39/62	12/20	(Zilzal-Eng., $734,838)	$3,510,534	224	50	6.18	4.83
11. Deputy Minister, 1979, Vice Regent	Ky.	65	44/100	9/18	(Open Mind, $1,120,308)	$3,273,465	108	10	5.00	2.99
12. Kris S., 1977, Roberto	Fla.	73	41/80	6/11	(Prized, $1,888,705)	$3,227,044	133	13	3.26	1.71
13. Relaunch, 1976, In Reality	Ky.	98	65/127	16/24	(Special Happening, $386,455)	$3,185,866	230	31	4.57	2.24
14. Pleasant Colony, 1978, His Majesty	Ky.	80	51/117	10/18	(Colonial Waters, $440,178)	$3,133,034	149	18	3.58	2.33
15. Naskra, 1967-89, Nasram	—	138	79/177	12/17	(Rose's Cantina, $447,532)	$3,090,141	515	54	2.49	2.16
16. Mr. Leader, 1966, Hail to Reason	Ky.	138	72/173	4/9	(Martial Law, $577,825)	$2,917,517	679	65	2.27	1.85
17. Slew o' Gold, 1980, Seattle Slew	Ky.	39	20/44	5/16	(Awe Inspiring, $978,052)	$2,856,050	89	5	6.39	5.02
18. Nodouble, 1965, Noholme II	—	107	63/121	8/14	(No Review, $382,875)	$2,734,996	615	83	2.52	1.94
19. Private Account, 1976, Damascus	Ky.	93	51/104	9/16	(Chimes of Freedom-Eng., Ire., $277,526)	$2,691,890	228	23	4.63	2.81
20. Topsider, 1974, Northern Dancer	Ky.	102	56/110	9/14	(Assatis-Eng., It., $454,704)	$2,689,555	265	29	3.19	2.83
21. Miswaki, 1978, Mr. Prospector	Ky.	116	71/154	11/14	(Black Tie Affair, $167,682)	$2,686,725	245	25	2.74	2.19
22. Silver Hawk, 1979, Roberto	Ky.	55	28/53	5/12	(Hawkster, $834,352)	$2,573,509	117	10	3.18	1.60
23. Valid Appeal, 1972, In Reality	Fla.	127	78/166	5/9	(Valid Vixen, $294,585)	$2,570,087	347	35	2.47	1.71
24. Flying Paster, 1976, Gummo	Calif.	89	51/97	9/12	(Endow, $360,709)	$2,549,453	181	19	2.71	2.10
25. Explodent, 1969, Nearctic	Ky.	106	59/130	8/16	(Mi Selecto, $722,287)	$2,544,967	480	37	2.28	1.75
26. Baldski, 1974, Nijinsky II	Fla.	147	86/184	3/7	(Baldski's Choice, $237,543)	$2,495,238	329	24	1.84	1.64
27. Roberto, 1969-88, Hail to Reason	—	82	42/65	9/9	(Sweet Roberta, $415,800)	$2,484,125	416	69	3.85	3.25
28. Vigors, 1973, Grey Dawn	Ky.	114	70/142	4/5	(Hodges Bay, $688,240)	$2,477,445	286	28	2.45	2.13
29. Vice Regent, 1967, Northern Dancer	Can.	82	49/96	6/8	(Regal Intention, $266,049)	$2,382,687	439	67	3.27	1.79
30. It's Freezing, 1972, T. V. Commercial	Ky.	137	86/188	1/4	(Big Chill, $214,250)	$2,365,939	284	23	2.24	1.68
31. Icecapade, 1969-88, Nearctic	—	123	67/129	7/9	(Rue de Palm, $289,000)	$2,295,265	498	59	2.38	1.91
32. Clever Trick, 1976, Icecapade	Ky.	122	77/155	6/9	(Tricky Creek, $392,568)	$2,289,997	300	25	2.37	1.94
33. Affirmed, 1975, Exclusive Native	Ky.	85	41/82	11/17	(Charlie Barley, $525,616)	$2,243,432	296	34	3.09	3.74
34. Alleged, 1974, Hoist the Flag	Ky.	96	54/88	10/12	(Legal Case-Eng., $510,885)	$2,231,416	417	42	3.36	3.72
35. Green Dancer, 1972, Nijinsky II	Ky.	126	55/93	6/7	(Fantastic Look, $186,150)	$2,165,206	517	48	2.32	2.99
36. Smarten, 1976, Cyane	Md.	98	69/145	6/10	(Dance Teacher, $306,821)	$2,110,820	234	21	2.37	2.60
37. Silver Buck, 1978, Buckpasser	Fla.	85	53/97	5/8	(Forever Silver, $866,054)	$2,106,997	152	10	2.52	2.02
38. Sunny's Halo, 1980, Halo	Ky.	75	35/79	3/6	(Dispersal, $908,450)	$2,092,816	114	5	2.32	2.15
39. Darby Creek Road, 1975-88, Roberto	—	105	52/92	6/9	(Drag Race, $317,438)	$2,086,308	273	23	1.99	1.60
40. Tri Jet, 1969, Jester	Fla.	145	92/151	5/6	(Triteamtri, $258,289)	$2,072,583	403	36	2.29	1.93
41. Temperence Hill, 1977, Stop the Music	Ky.	118	67/146	4/5	(Imbibe, $160,680)	$2,060,091	234	6	2.24	2.04
42. Crafty Prospector, 1979, Mr. Prospector	Fla.	86	62/149	2/5	(Robyn Dancer, $187,228)	$2,057,188	121	5	2.93	1.54
43. Northern Baby, 1976, Northern Dancer	Ky.	86	44/94	3/7	(Michelozzo-Eng., $351,330)	$2,035,254	239	14	2.53	2.86
44. Bates Motel, 1979, Sir Ivor	Ky.	73	44/102	5/11	(Packett's Landing, $442,892)	$2,028,307	116	6	2.38	2.18
45. Sauce Boat, 1975, Key to the Mint	Ky.	123	77/155	3/6	(Its Acedemic, $662,602)	$2,006,763	372	21	1.85	2.19
46. Majestic Light, 1973, Majestic Prince	Ky.	96	46/83	5/13	(Simply Majestic, $729,968)	$1,962,231	369	37	2.92	3.62
47. Distinctive Pro, 1979, Mr. Prospector	N.Y.	79	51/102	5/9	(Big Stanley, $325,338)	$1,907,527	117	6	2.26	1.51
48. Bold Forbes, 1973, Irish Castle	Ky.	110	62/136	2/2	(Bold Wench, $224,287)	$1,892,248	386	26	2.17	2.78
49. Stop the Music, 1970, Hail to Reason	Ky.	83	41/70	3/5	(Music Merci, $714,240)	$1,871,584	331	27	2.76	2.57
50. Conquistador Cielo, 1979, Mr. Prospector	Ky.	87	47/82	4/5	(Norquestor, $227,780)	$1,861,739	166	12	2.86	3.94
51. Well Decorated, 1978, Raja Baba	Ky.	103	56/103	5/8	(Notation, $249,778)	$1,851,850	200	11	2.11	2.64
52. Irish Tower, 1977, Irish Castle	Ky.	88	46/121	6/10	(Irish Jade, $138,526)	$1,851,125	169	12	2.39	1.92
53. Full Pocket, 1969-88, Olden Times	—	158	92/203	5/7	(Pok Ta Pok, $226,788)	$1,840,366	557	49	1.69	1.68
54. Grey Dawn (Fr), 1962, Herbager	Ky.	82	43/86	5/5	(Single Dawn, $236,480)	$1,837,608	639	66	2.61	2.30
55. Overskate, 1975, Nodouble	N.Y.	91	51/108	3/11	(Capades, $509,676)	$1,836,460	177	9	2.11	2.26
56. Bold Ruckus, 1976, Boldnesian	Can.	93	55/115	7/8	(Inverawe, $134,825)	$1,831,836	197	19	2.52	1.45
57. Damascus, 1964, Sword Dancer	—	94	51/83	7/9	(Highest Glory, $165,330)	$1,823,150	684	65	2.96	3.78
58. Star de Naskra, 1975, Naskra	Ky.	109	60/109	4/7	(Sewickley, $568,682)	$1,819,981	279	20	2.24	1.93
59. Spectacular Bid, 1976, Bold Bidder	Ky.	96	49/85	8/9	(Bite the Bullet, $138,681)	$1,806,341	273	30	2.51	3.86
60. Northern Jove, 1968, Northern Dancer	Ky.	115	64/126	4/9	(Equalize, $421,948)	$1,767,490	399	29	1.81	1.66
61. Exuberant, 1976, What a Pleasure	Fla.	115	68/153	4/6	(Shot Gun Scott, $469,640)	$1,759,165	289	18	1.63	1.50
62. Quadratic, 1975, Quadrangle	Va.	127	72/151	5/5	(Speedratic, $329,720)	$1,751,561	290	19	1.71	1.81
63. Cox's Ridge, 1974, Best Turn	Ky.	97	56/91	3/3	(De Roche, $183,214)	$1,729,512	310	21	3.39	2.48
64. Horatius, 1975, Proudest Roman	Md.	100	50/116	1/8	(Safely Kept, $696,270)	$1,720,198	227	4	1.46	1.18
65. Talc, 1972, Rock Talk	Ky.	103	67/144	2/3	(Zee Best, $143,443)	$1,709,660	214	12	2.51	1.49

FOOTNOTE: Chief earner for Halo, which led all sires in 1989 by progeny earnings, was champion 3-year-old colt Sunday Silence, a leading contender for Horse-of-the-Year honors.

*COMPARABLE INDEX: The lifetime Average-Earnings Index indicates how much purse money the progeny of one sire has earned, on the average, in relation to the average earnings of all runners in the same years; average earnings of all runners in any year is represented by an index of 1.00. The Comparable Index indicates the average earnings of progeny produced from mares bred to one sire, when these same mares were bred to other sires. Only 32 per cent of all sires have a lifetime Average-Earnings Index higher than their mares' Comparable Index.

LEADING FIRST-CROP SIRES OF 1989

For stallions which stand or (deceased) stood in North America, and have runners in North America, the leaders are arranged by earnings through Dec. 31, 1989, including monies earned in England, Ireland, France, Italy, Germany, Puerto Rico, and Mexico.

Stallion (Foreign foaled), Year, Sire	Where Stands	2yos/ Rnrs	Wnrs/Wins	Stakes Wnrs/Wins	(Chief Earner, Earnings)	1989 Earnings
1. Chief's Crown, 1982, Danzig	Ky.	33/20	10/24	4/9	(Be My Chief-Eng., $342,544)	$818,866
2. Moscow Ballet, 1982, Nijinsky II	Calif.	33/13	10/15	1/4	(Dominant Dancer, $412,470)	$541,810
3. Premiership, 1980, Exclusive Native	Fla.	51/34	20/30	5/5	(American Dreamer, $87,695)	$477,363
4. Mt. Livermore, 1981, Blushing Groom	Ky.	33/20	11/22	4/8	(Circus Media, $123,360)	$407,631
5. Track Barron, 1981, Buckfinder	Ky.	34/19	8/13	2/2	(Champagneforashley, $138,030)	$406,497
6. Spend a Buck, 1982, Buckaroo	Ky.	36/18	8/13	2/2	(Table Limit, $182,054)	$404,666
7. Dauphin Fabuleux, 1982, Le Fabuleux	Can.	26/11	4/8	2/2	(French King, $211,425)	$390,497
8. Wild Again, 1980, Icecapade	Ky.	54/27	12/16	2/2	(A Wild Ride, $78,854)	$386,156
9. Carr de Naskra, 1981, Star de Naskra	N.Y.	27/16	7/9	1/2	(Sir Richard Lewis, $253,416)	$359,436
10. Timeless Native, 1980, Timeless Moment	Ky.	40/25	15/23	2/2	(Dee's Heart, $72,702)	$341,793
11. Tsunami Slew, 1981, Seattle Slew	Ky.	36/18	5/9	1/2	(Slew of Pearls, $127,318)	$257,215
12. Judge Smells, 1983, In Reality	Ky.	24/11	10/17	1/2	(Smelly, $115,370)	$248,662
13. Top Avenger, 1978, Staunch Avenger	Texas	28/17	10/20	3/4	(Avenging Ace, $56,220)	$242,257
14. Morning Bob, 1981, Blushing Groom	Fla.	33/26	10/17	1/1	(Seaport Mac, $75,030)	$217,518
15. Country Pine, 1980, His Majesty	Fla.	28/21	10/16	2/2	(Country Isle, $29,270)	$203,604
16. Imp Society, 1981, Barrera	Ky.	35/18	9/13	1/1	(Society Doon, $34,160)	$177,897
17. Fighting Fit, 1979, Full Pocket	Ky.	46/18	4/7	1/1	(Fighting Fantasy, $112,541)	$176,449
18. Hooched, 1982, Danzig	Fla.	47/24	8/14	2/2	(Dandy Shine, $59,285)	$176,437
19. Dr. Carter, 1981, Caro	Ky.	33/14	5/7	0/0	(Dr. Bobby A., $92,968)	$167,612
20. Carnivalay, 1981, Northern Dancer	Md.	37/14	4/6	2/2	(Valay Maid, $54,000)	$167,565
21. Minstrel Glory, 1980, The Minstrel	N.Y.	10/3	2/3	1/1	(Lucy's Glory, $125,519)	$145,979
22. Cozzene, 1980, Caro	Ky.	36/15	6/8	0/0	(Fearless Revival-Eng., $41,836)	$142,290
Mark of Nobility, 1981, Roberto	Fla.	21/11	7/15	1/1	(Weepeat-PR, $54,440)	$142,290
24. Image of Greatness, 1982, Secretariat	Fla.	40/20	5/7	0/0	(Image On High, $51,450)	$142,014
25. Prosperous, 1979, Mr. Prospector	Fla.	23/14	6/7	1/2	(Prospective Dolly, $123,576)	$142,000
26. Time for a Change, 1981, Damascus	Ky.	33/14	6/7	1/1	(Aspirations, $35,120)	$140,210
27. Entropy, 1980, What a Pleasure	Fla.	32/19	7/11	0/0	(Gray Touch, $37,775)	$135,872
28. Bounding Basque, 1980, Grey Dawn	Ky.	23/12	7/9	1/1	(Paper Trail, $48,572)	$134,081
29. Megaturn, 1980, Best Turn	Ky.	32/20	8/11	1/1	(Mega Fortune, $42,649)	$114,248
30. Bet Big, 1980, Distinctive	Fla.	18/9	5/7	1/1	(Theoddsonchoice, $63,777)	$111,823
31. King Alphonse, 1980, Ship Leave	Can.	2/2	2/6	1/4	(Lollipop Lorie, $102,929)	$111,699
32. Dancing Crown, 1981, Nijinsky II	La.	16/11	7/10	1/1	(I Do I Do I Do, $47,319)	$111,385
33. On the Sauce, 1981, Sauce Boat	Can.	13/11	9/13	3/3	(Bye Bye Mexico, $46,624)	$104,481
34. Marine Brass, 1979, Fifth Marine	Md.	19/8	5/7	0/0	(Fighting Brass, $47,380)	$104,310
35. Clever Champ, 1982, Clever Trick	Md.	30/15	8/11	0/0	(Stickers n Scuffs, $18,932)	$103,668
36. Distant Ryder, 1981, Red Ryder	Texas	17/9	6/10	1/1	(Rocket Gibraltar, $40,000)	$95,698
37. Mighty Appealing, 1982, Valid Appeal	Fla.	15/7	4/7	1/1	(Wedding Band, $59,025)	$92,409
38. Lord At War (Arg), 1980, General	Ky.	18/8	5/6	0/0	(Sleepy Princess, $26,680)	$84,676
39. Prince Forli, 1980, Broadway Forli	Minn.	8/2	2/3	1/1	(Timeless Prince, $78,647)	$84,096
40. Pax Nobiscum, 1980, Hold Your Peace	Can.	9/4	2/3	0/0	(Income Pax, $47,201)	$83,791
41. Island Champ, 1980, Dancing Champ	Md.	8/1	1/2	1/1	(She's a Champ, $78,150)	$78,150
42. Bionic Light, 1982, Majestic Light	Okla.	53/24	8/9	1/1	(Light Autumn, $12,063)	$77,847
43. Bayou Hebert, 1981, Hoist the Flag	La.	17/11	6/11	1/1	(Genuine Meaning, $49,233)	$76,987
44. Gato Del Sol, 1979, Cougar	Ky.	26/10	2/3	0/0	(Red Tiger, $30,136)	$74,930
45. Expressman, 1980, Gaelic Dancer	Calif.	16/5	2/2	0/0	(Express It, $59,944)	$70,444
46. Mythical Ruler, 1978, Ruritania	Can.	25/10	5/5	0/0	(Mr. R. Ruler, $26,666)	$69,030
47. Victorious, 1980, Explodent	Ky.	23/11	4/7	0/0	(Johnny Ross, $33,540)	$68,467
48. Colonel Stevens, 1981, Lt. Stevens	Wash.	3/2	1/4	1/2	(Military Hawk, $66,425)	$67,150
49. Exclusive Bidder, 1980-87, Our Native	—.	16/9	2/4	1/2	(Windsong Maria, $56,854)	$63,914
50. Kleven, 1981, Alydar	Calif.	9/3	2/2	0/0	(Kleven Up, $43,950)	$62,945
51. Fight Over, 1981, Grey Dawn	Fla.	30/9	2/2	0/0	(Pampered Beauty, $24,600)	$62,090
52. Fatih, 1980, Icecapade	Calif.	32/17	4/8	0/0	(Green's Leader-Eng., $39,864)	$61,993
53. Tank's Prospect, 1982, Mr. Prospector	Ky.	42/14	4/5	0/0	(Real Cash, $21,800)	$58,061
54. Unreal Zeal, 1980, Mr. Prospector	Fla.	17/9	4/7	0/0	(Unreal Glitz, $21,210)	$57,805
55. Mugassas, 1981, Northern Dancer	Fla.	15/10	4/6	0/0	(Seasabb, $22,375)	$57,549
56. Special Kinda Guy, 1981, Blushing Groom	Venez.	14/8	4/9	1/2	(Kinda Lucky, $23,980)	$55,325
57. Slew's Royalty, 1980, Seattle Slew	Calif.	32/7	4/4	0/0	(Slewrena, $21,750)	$51,334
58. Shadeed, 1982, Nijinsky II	Ky.	37/14	4/5	0/0	(Megyaas-Eng., $10,821)	$51,185
59. Star Choice, 1979, In Reality	Ky.	29/8	3/4	0/0	(The Great Carl, $32,058)	$50,518
60. Star of the Road, 1980, Ramirez	Texas	2/2	1/5	0/0	(Captain Storm, $49,383)	$49,823
61. Ankara, 1980, Northern Dancer	Fla.	20/11	3/6	0/0	(Night in Ankara, $23,665)	$49,814
62. Eskimo, 1980, Northern Dancer	Fla.	4/3	2/2	0/0	(Coby Escapade, $31,092)	$49,228
63. Tridessus, 1981, Northern Dancer	Fla.	26/11	4/8	0/0	(Lady Try On, $25,458)	$46,907
64. Tonzarun, 1978, Arts and Letters	Calif.	23/7	5/8	0/0	(Ton One, $15,515)	$43,740
65. Iron, 1980, Mr. Prospector	Md.	29/12	6/9	0/0	(Richard's Lady J., $14,013)	$43,151

FOOTNOTE: Runners sired by 1989 first-crop sire Chief's Crown earned more money than any runners since 1985, when progeny of Fappiano earned $1,234,315 that year. Chief earner for Chief's Crown was Be My Chief, undefeated in six races, including the Racing Post Trophy (Eng-I). Chief's Crown also was represented by French group II winner Dr. Somerville and other stakes winners Crown Quest and Crowned.

Courtesy of *The Blood-Horse* Magazine

LEADING SIRES OF 2-YEAR-OLDS BY EARNINGS

For stallions which stand or (deceased) stood in North America, and have runners in North America, the leaders are arranged by earnings through Dec. 31, 1989, including all monies earned in England and Ireland, plus earnings from stakes and 2-year-old races in France, Italy, Germany, Puerto Rico, and Mexico, converted to dollars at the rate of exchange agreed upon by international racing authorities. ¶ indicates a sire represented by his first crop to race.

Stallion (Foreign foaled), Year, Sire	Where Stands	2yos/ Rnrs	Wnrs/Wins	Stakes Wnrs/Wins	(Chief Earner, Earnings)	1989 Earnings	CUMULATIVE through 1988 2yos	2yo Wnrs	Per Cent
1. Mr. Prospector, 1970, Raise a Native	Ky.	.56/22	.12/19	.5/8	(Rhythm, $612,920)	$1,560,083	510	131	.26
2. Fappiano, 1977, Mr. Prospector	Ky.	.46/24	.11/17	.3/5	(Grand Canyon, $1,019,540)	$1,436,422	159	.36	.23
3. Danzig, 1977, Northern Dancer	Ky.	.48/25	.19/31	.4/5	(Adjudicating, $506,232)	$1,332,782	228	.46	.20
4. ¶Chief's Crown, 1982, Danzig	Ky.	.33/20	.10/24	.4/9	(Be My Chief-Eng., $342,544)	$818,866	—	—	—
5. Private Account, 1976, Damascus	Ky.	.45/17	.6/12	.2/4	(Chimes of Freedom-Eng., Ire., $277,526)	$781,495	182	.30	.16
6. Kris S., 1977, Roberto	Fla.	.43/30	.18/26	.4/6	(Cheval Volant, $379,762)	$755,602	90	.22	.24
7. Darby Creek Road, 1975-88, Roberto	—	.38/24	.9/16	.3/5	(Drag Race, $317,438)	$734,081	235	.56	.24
8. Nijinsky II, 1967, Northern Dancer	Ky.	.53/23	.10/14	.4/6	(Sky Classic, $350,938)	$713,162	606	.115	.19
9. Alydar, 1975, Raise a Native	Ky.	.57/25	.10/13	.1/3	(Stella Madrid, $519,096)	$710,364	306	.45	.15
10. Deputy Minister, 1979, Vice Regent	Ky.	.34/16	.7/11	.1/1	(Go for Wand, $548,390)	$710,092	72	.9	.13
11. Seattle Slew, 1974, Bold Reasoning	Ky.	.43/23	.12/17	.3/5	(Yonder, $201,900)	$631,334	289	.42	.15
12. Relaunch, 1976, In Reality	Ky.	.44/12	.5/13	.4/7	(Special Happening, $386,455)	$627,363	186	.43	.23
13. Pleasant Colony, 1978, His Majesty	Ky.	.31/13	.6/14	.3/5	(Roanoke, $233,066)	$627,043	117	.18	.15
14. Icecapade, 1969-88, Nearctic	—	.34/16	.10/15	.3/3	(Rue de Palm, $289,000)	$625,881	464	.110	.24
15. Roberto, 1969-88, Hail to Reason	—	.44/21	.7/9	.1/1	(Sweet Roberta, $415,800)	$599,489	372	.98	.26
16. Baldski, 1974, Nijinsky II	Fla.	.49/37	.18/29	.1/2	(Stacie's Toy, $230,185)	$547,663	278	.87	.31
17. Exuberant, 1976, What a Pleasure	Fla.	.37/22	.7/12	.1/2	(Shot Gun Scott, $469,640)	$546,048	248	.58	.27
18. ¶Moscow Ballet, 1982, Nijinsky II	Calif.	.33/13	.10/15	.1/5	(Dominant Dancer, $412,470)	$541,810	—	—	—
19. Diamond Prospect, 1978, Mr. Prospector	France	.46/26	.17/26	.2/2	(Cullinan-Eng., Ire., $294,826)	$539,249	166	.41	.25
20. Runaway Groom, 1979, Blushing Groom	Fla.	.48/28	.15/21	.1/1	(Miss Running Vany, $314,900)	$528,268	65	.14	.22
21. Riverman, 1969, Never Bend	Ky.	.57/20	.11/15	.3/3	(Qirmazi-Fr., $141,406)	$509,720	550	.97	.18
22. ¶Premiership, 1980, Exclusive Native	Fla.	.51/34	.20/30	.5/5	(American Dreamer, $87,695)	$477,363	—	—	—
23. Storm Bird, 1978, Northern Dancer	Ky.	.42/13	.6/13	.1/4	(Summer Squall, $288,622)	$469,636	655	.35	.23
24. Highland Park, 1980, Raise a Native	Ky.	.42/25	.16/25	.3/7	(Bluegrass Native-Ger., $181,986)	$453,272	52	.8	.15
25. Stutz Blackhawk, 1977, Mr. Prospector	Fla.	.42/33	.14/27	.3/3	(On the Scent, $101,040)	$424,617	132	.34	.26
26. Conquistador Cielo, 1979, Mr. Prospector	Ky.	.46/24	.12/18	.1/1	(Alexandrina, $137,712)	$420,126	120	.29	.24
27. Foolish Pleasure, 1972, What a Pleasure	Ky.	.39/16	.4/6	.1/2	(Filago-Fr., $362,664)	$410,405	276	.43	.16
28. ¶Mt. Livermore, 1981, Blushing Groom	Ky.	.33/20	.11/22	.4/8	(Circus Media, $123,360)	$407,631	—	—	—
29. ¶Track Barron, 1981, Buckfinder	Ky.	.34/19	.9/14	.2/4	(Champagneforashley, $138,030)	$406,497	—	—	—
30. ¶Spend a Buck, 1982, Buckaroo	Ky.	.36/16	.8/13	.2/2	(Table Limit, $182,054)	$404,666	—	—	—
31. Breezing On, 1976-86, Stewward	—	.9/3	.3/10	.2/6	(Appealing Breeze, $291,581)	$396,757	48	.15	.31
32. ¶Dauphin Fabuleux, 1982, Le Fabuleux	Can.	.26/11	.4/8	.2/2	(French King, $211,425)	$390,497	—	—	—
33. Grey Dawn (Fr), 1962, Herbager	Ky.	.26/14	.6/9	.2/2	(Single Dawn, $236,480)	$388,710	612	.126	.21
34. Crafty Prospector, 1979, Mr. Prospector	Fla.	.42/23	.13/22	.1/3	(Robyn Dancer, $187,228)	$387,984	77	.16	.21
35. ¶Wild Again, 1980, Icecapade	Ky.	.52/27	.12/16	.2/2	(A Wild Ride, $78,854)	$386,156	—	—	—
36. Dr. Blum, 1977, Dr. Fager	N.Y.	.49/27	.12/25	.3/5	(Richard R., $177,505)	$359,561	124	.38	.31
37. ¶Carr de Naskra, 1981, Star de Naskra	N.Y.	.27/16	.7/9	.1/2	(Sir Richard Lewis, $253,416)	$359,436	—	—	—
38. Distinctive Pro, 1979, Mr. Prospector	N.Y.	.38/24	.13/17	.1/1	(Fuerza, $149,184)	$351,245	78	.26	.33
39. Monetary Gift, 1978, Gold and Myrrh	Mich.	.20/9	.7/10	.3/4	(Natalee's Birthday, $95,504)	$343,958	17	.9	.53
40. Green Dancer, 1972, Nijinsky II	Ky.	.58/27	.9/10	.1/1	(Senor Pete, $163,680)	$343,283	457	.75	.16
41. Topsider, 1974, Northern Dancer	Ky.	.39/16	.6/11	.2/3	(Moreofthebest, $138,028)	$341,962	225	.60	.27
42. Green Forest, 1979, Shecky Greene	Ky.	.45/13	.5/10	.2/3	(Somethingdifferent, Eng., N.A., Ger, $186,299)	$338,930	117	.10	.9
43. Bel Bolide, 1978, Bold Bidder	Calif.	.42/19	.8/12	.2/2	(Bel's Starlet, $132,365)	$338,393	30	.1	.3
44. Diesis (GB), 1980, Sharpen Up	Ky.	.40/21	.12/20	.1/1	(Rootentootenwooten, $165,284)	$337,125	68	.15	.22
45. Cormorant, 1974, His Majesty	N.Y.	.38/15	.8/11	.2/2	(Applebred, $124,950)	$332,533	217	.37	.17
46. ¶Timeless Native, 1980, Timeless Moment	Ky.	.40/25	.15/22	.2/2	(Dee's Heart, $72,702)	$329,393	—	—	—
47. Wavering Monarch, 1979, Majestic Light	Ky.	.37/23	.9/18	.1/3	(Wavering Girl, $226,038)	$324,352	76	.13	.17
48. Miswaki, 1978, Mr. Prospector	Ky.	.58/26	.13/21	.2/2	(Look n Good Darlin, $64,720)	$323,840	186	.43	.23
49. Raised Socially, 1977, Raise a Native	Ky.	.60/27	.10/16	.2/2	(La Dolce Vita, $71,400)	$308,602	139	.34	.24
50. Vice Regent, 1967, Northern Dancer	Can.	.36/14	.4/8	.1/1	(Trumpet's Blare, $191,818)	$306,371	403	.108	.27
51. Far Out East, 1977, Raja Baba	Ky.	.48/26	.10/19	.3/3	(East Royalty, $66,508)	$302,264	154	.35	.23
52. Fast Gold, 1979, Mr. Prospector	Ky.	.39/21	.10/21	.2/3	(Portentum, $100,200)	$298,051	16	.3	.19
53. Nureyev, 1977, Northern Dancer	Ky.	.37/20	.12/14	.2/2	(Silk Slippers-Eng., $129,555)	$292,799	187	.52	.28
54. Limbo Dancer, 1982-86, Northern Dancer	—	.31/15	.10/11	.1/1	(Floral Dancer, $190,758)	$287,848	25	.2	.8
55. Marfa, 1980, Foolish Pleasure	Ky.	.38/15	.6/6	.0/0	(Farma Way, $192,650)	$287,495	50	.8	.16
56. Steady Growth, 1976, Briartic	Can.	.9/6	.2/5	.1/3	(Ever Steady, $269,068)	$281,668	52	.11	.21
57. Naskra, 1967-89, Nasram	—	.44/23	.10/10	.1/1	(Talltalelady, $112,218)	$279,829	469	.82	.17
58. Cresta Rider, 1978, Northern Dancer	Chile	.29/14	.7/11	.2/2	(Annual Reunion, $130,000)	$278,197	97	.14	.14
59. Tri Jet, 1969, Jester	Fla.	.41/30	.14/21	.1/1	(Hi Jac Jet, $57,087)	$274,613	361	.126	.35
60. Sunny North, 1979, Northern Dancer	S. Af.	.30/21	.13/22	.3/3	(Fiery Best, $71,250)	$268,424	105	.33	.31
61. Briartic, 1968, Nearctic	Ky.	.38/18	.5/10	.1/2	(Briar Bush, $182,203)	$265,633	341	.112	.33
62. Pirate's Bounty, 1975, Hoist the Flag	Calif.	.53/24	.6/7	.2/2	(Effusive Bounty, $81,950)	$259,777	185	.23	.12
63. ¶Tsunami Slew, 1981, Seattle Slew	Ky.	.35/18	.5/9	.1/2	(Slew of Pearls, $127,318)	$257,215	—	—	—
64. Fit to Fight, 1979, Chieftain	Ky.	.44/25	.11/15	.0/0	(Lethal Factor, $47,120)	$255,674	51	.8	.16
65. Lypheor (GB), 1975-86, Lyphard	—	.33/20	.10/11	.1/1	(Contract Law-Eng., $89,382)	$251,728	263	.37	.14

FOOTNOTE: Go for Wand, champion 2-year-old filly for 1989, was the only juvenile stakes winner this year for her sire, 10th-ranked Deputy Minister, which also was represented by champion 3-year-old filly Open Mind.

Courtesy of *The Blood-Horse* Magazine

SIRES OF BROODMARES—1989 EARNINGS

For stallions whose daughters are represented by at least one runner in North America in 1989, regardless of the stallion's origin or the country in which he stands or stood. The leaders are arranged by 1989 earnings in North America, England, and Ireland through Dec. 31, 1989.

Broodmare Sire	Dams	Rnrs	Wnrs	Stks Wnrs	(Chief Earner, Earnings, Sire)	1989 Earnings	Foals	Stks Wnrs	Cumulative Avg-Erngs Index	*Comp Index
1. Buckpasser, 1963	101	171	94	16	(Easy Goer, $3,837,150, by Alydar)	$9,526,942	895	102	4.03	2.19
2. Northern Dancer, 1961	133	227	111	17	(Rhythm, $612,920, by Mr. Prospector)	$5,850,222	1,082	117	2.73	1.99
3. Understanding, 1963	16	23	12	2	(Sunday Silence, $4,578,454, by Halo)	$4,768,310	150	3	2.69	1.31
4. Grey Dawn (Fr), 1962	153	279	138	10	(El Senor, $662,497, by Valdez)	$4,427,087	900	61	2.09	1.80
5. Hoist the Flag, 1968	77	125	66	10	(Cryptoclearance, $1,059,010, by Fappiano)	$4,028,412	435	38	4.61	2.40
6. Sir Ivor, 1965	128	194	98	9	(Goodbye Halo, $486,000, by Halo)	$3,984,368	854	59	2.54	2.10
7. Cornish Prince, 1962	153	285	167	11	(Packett's Landing, $442,892, by Bates Motel)	$3,816,581	1,116	63	1.61	1.81
8. Nodouble, 1965	114	190	99	11	(Proper Reality, $950,830, by In Reality)	$3,729,011	514	34	2.27	1.80
9. Graustark, 1963	115	189	94	11	(Pay the Butler, $272,742, by Val de l'Orne)	$3,608,592	816	82	3.36	2.13
10. In Reality, 1964	117	206	129	12	(Orange Sunshine, $202,541, by Linkage)	$3,583,343	617	53	2.39	2.01
11. Mr. Prospector, 1970	88	145	84	10	(True and Blue, $285,005, by Hurry Up Blue)	$3,541,982	354	32	2.76	2.25
12. Prince John, 1953	116	203	116	3	(Blushing John, $1,232,030, by Blushing Groom)	$3,534,213	1,809	152	2.25	1.74
13. Exclusive Native, 1965	122	213	112	11	(Judy's Red Shoes, $386,719, by Hold Your Tricks)	$3,529,333	691	41	1.81	1.85
14. Chieftain, 1961	130	237	138	8	(Hawkster, $732,887, by Silver Hawk)	$3,445,748	945	65	1.72	1.77
15. Olden Times, 1958	165	298	153	8	(Patchy Groundfog, $270,600, by Instrument Landing)	$3,442,844	1,286	72	1.58	1.76
16. Dr. Fager, 1964	79	155	94	9	(Sewickley, $568,682, by Star de Naskra)	$3,387,151	606	70	2.79	2.18
17. Damascus, 1964	136	222	112	5	(Capades, $509,676, by Overskate)	$3,386,439	794	56	2.09	2.14
18. Nijinsky II, 1967	121	192	98	9	(Sadeem-Eng., $209,251, by Forli)	$3,280,529	632	64	2.92	2.28
19. Diplomat Way, 1964	141	249	137	10	(Frosty the Snowman, $242,750, by His Majesty)	$3,266,138	736	36	1.44	1.56
20. Raise a Native, 1961	171	268	150	7	(Sunshine Always, $171,318, by Arts and Letters)	$3,250,770	1,338	98	2.02	1.90
21. Secretariat, 1970	112	188	94	8	(Summer Squall, $288,622, by Storm Bird)	$3,193,250	487	40	3.09	2.46
22. Viceregal, 1966	54	105	59	5	(Present Value, $938,319, by Halo)	$3,191,726	463	33	2.34	1.82
23. Silent Screen, 1967	114	222	129	10	(Secret Hello, $271,620, by Private Account)	$3,125,830	623	36	1.68	1.71
24. Gallant Romeo, 1961	102	161	88	6	(Awe Inspiring, $978,052, by Slew o' Gold)	$3,096,882	675	37	1.52	1.68
25. Tentam, 1969	74	144	87	10	(Dance Teacher, $306,821, by Smarten)	$3,030,506	299	19	2.52	1.91
26. Stage Door Johnny, 1965	88	143	78	4	(Open Mind, $1,120,308, by Deputy Minister)	$2,961,092	571	39	2.41	2.02
27. Arts and Letters, 1966	88	165	98	5	(Its Acedemic, $662,602, by Sauce Boat)	$2,912,207	501	31	1.80	1.94
28. Hail to Reason, 1958	75	139	74	6	(Sabona, $604,300, by Exclusive Native)	$2,905,548	1,021	95	2.43	1.93
29. Vaguely Noble (GB), 1965	132	220	101	12	(Homebuilder, $269,691, by Mr. Prospector)	$2,905,527	884	77	2.74	2.10
30. The Axe II, 1958	109	201	115	5	(Lively One, $454,500, by Halo)	$2,830,935	930	68	1.63	1.72
31. Reviewer, 1966	52	101	55	8	(Adjudicating, $506,232, by Danzig)	$2,806,902	357	30	2.13	2.24
32. Drone, 1966	113	190	107	6	(Thirty Eight Go Go, $201,861, by Thirty Eight Paces)	$2,772,139	626	41	2.39	1.95
33. Vice Regent, 1967	84	133	87	6	(Mr. Hot Shot, $264,711, by Brave Shot)	$2,739,632	292	19	2.11	1.82
34. Riva Ridge, 1969	61	102	52	6	(Dancing Spree, $992,903, by Nijinsky II)	$2,722,966	286	14	2.35	2.22
35. Crimson Satan, 1959	121	228	120	6	(Lady Annabelle, $209,008, by Sir Ivor)	$2,710,327	958	64	1.52	1.76
36. T. V. Lark, 1957	96	165	94	8	(Pleasant Variety, $433,000, by Pleasant Colony)	$2,700,098	1,006	76	1.87	1.74
37. Key to the Mint, 1969	72	102	63	8	(Gorgeous, $600,245, by Slew o' Gold)	$2,617,523	317	31	3.22	2.43
38. Iron Ruler, 1965	119	231	132	5	(Ingot's Ruler, $173,455, by Diplomat Way)	$2,593,962	652	37	1.70	1.79
39. Round Table, 1954	85	139	81	8	(Martial Law, $577,825, by Mr. Leader)	$2,571,481	1,199	99	2.34	2.00
40. Tom Rolfe, 1962	111	192	99	5	(Jack of Clubs, $150,500, by Sir Ivor)	$2,555,671	803	53	2.69	1.94
41. Mr. Leader, 1966	117	220	108	7	(Danzig's Beauty, $154,200, by Danzig)	$2,554,190	592	28	1.48	1.58
42. Forli (Arg), 1963	113	172	86	7	(Olympic Prospect, $265,080, by Northern Jove)	$2,529,941	785	48	2.32	2.01
43. Al Hattab, 1966	102	208	114	5	(Black Tie Affair, $167,682, by Miswaki)	$2,465,585	521	26	1.48	1.81
44. Quadrangle, 1961	89	178	96	5	(Houston, $213,032, by Seattle Slew)	$2,462,741	656	51	1.92	1.77
45. L'Enjoleur, 1972	67	109	72	4	(Grand Canyon, $1,019,540, by Fappiano)	$2,441,124	244	15	1.99	1.81
46. His Majesty, 1968	90	166	88	5	(Tricky Creek, $392,568, by Clever Trick)	$2,428,990	393	20	2.13	1.88
47. Jacinto, 1962	103	177	93	4	(Music Merci, $714,240, by Stop the Music)	$2,409,109	740	35	1.47	1.80
48. Hawaii (SAf), 1964	110	191	106	4	(Shy Tom, $304,090, by Blushing Groom)	$2,396,526	581	32	1.79	1.86
49. Le Fabuleux (Fr), 1961	77	131	66	5	(Zilzal-Eng., $734,838, by Nureyev)	$2,348,824	807	60	2.66	2.03
50. Cyane, 1959	98	162	86	7	(Go for Wand, $548,390, by Deputy Minister)	$2,319,673	744	40	1.73	1.86
51. Ack Ack, 1966	91	170	88	8	(Stylish Star, $220,600, by Our Native)	$2,310,486	454	35	2.43	2.01
52. My Dad George, 1967	49	79	37	1	(Prized, $1,888,705, by Kris S.)	$2,299,527	290	10	1.40	1.45
53. Verbatim, 1965	99	153	86	3	(Raise a Stanza, $279,700, by Raise a Man)	$2,250,826	436	21	1.66	1.64
54. Lyphard, 1969	84	118	58	4	(Claire Marine, $801,565, by What a Guest)	$2,224,198	525	49	1.93	2.23
55. Raja Baba, 1968	109	184	97	7	(Texian, $143,189, by Majestic Light)	$2,176,397	507	21	1.42	1.97
56. Bustino, 1971	40	57	23	3	(Nashwan-Eng., $1,407,440, by Blushing Groom)	$2,164,234	169	8	3.23	2.08
57. Bold Bidder, 1962	125	204	106	7	(Closing Bid, $138,710, by Fio Rito)	$2,138,258	856	51	1.72	1.89
58. Never Bend, 1960	87	152	86	11	(Nikishka, $247,300, by Nijinsky II)	$2,137,675	882	88	2.42	2.03
59. Roberto, 1969	76	122	55	8	(Sapience-Eng., $262,867, by Niniski)	$2,124,209	284	21	2.26	2.31
60. Fleet Nasrullah, 1955	119	203	102	3	(Iron Courage, $301,768, by Caro)	$2,124,088	1,568	132	1.62	1.66
61. Distinctive, 1966	86	147	83	5	(Broke the Mold, $139,850, by Nodouble)	$2,083,083	464	21	1.55	1.71
62. One for All, 1966	85	146	78	5	(Hodges Bay, $688,240, by Vigors)	$2,079,690	421	18	1.65	1.73
63. Speak John, 1958	87	153	86	5	(On the Line, $529,880, by Mehmet)	$2,071,197	602	38	2.20	1.66
64. What a Pleasure, 1965	145	245	128	4	(Once Wild, $74,800, by Baldski)	$2,025,701	912	40	1.50	1.66
65. King Emperor, 1966	73	114	55	6	(Simply Majestic, $729,968, by Majestic Light)	$1,969,227	443	22	1.62	1.56

FOOTNOTE: Second-ranked Northern Dancer in 1989 was represented by 17 stakes winners as a broodmare sire, more than any other sire on the list. His chief earner was champion 2-year-old colt Rhythm.

*COMPARABLE INDEX: The cumulative broodmare-sire Average-Earnings Index indicates how much money the progeny out of each broodmare sire's daughters has earned, on the average, in relation to the average earnings of all runners in the same years; average earnings of all runners in any year is represented by an Index of 1.00. The Comparable Index is the combined Average-Earnings Index for all stallions bred to a broodmare sire's daughters, reflecting the general quality of these stallions, and indicating whether the produce of a broodmare sire's daughters does better or worse than that of all mares bred to the same stallions.

Courtesy of *The Blood-Horse* Magazine

List of Chef-De-Race Sires

BRILLIANT

Abernant
Apalachee
Black Toney*
Bold Ruler*
British Empire
Bull Dog
Cicero
Court Martial
Double Jay
Fair Trial
Fairway
Gallant Man*

Grey Dawn II*
Grey Sovereign
Habitat
Heliopolis
Hoist the Flag*
Hyperion*
In Reality*
Intentionally*
Mr. Prospector*
My Babu
Nasrullah

Nearco*
Never Bend*
Noholme II*
Northern Dancer*
Olympia
Orby
Panorama
Peter Pan
Phalaris
Pharis
Pompey

Raise a Native
Reviewer*
Roman*
Royal Charger
Sharpen Up*
Sir Cosmo
Spy Song
Tudor Minstrel
Turn-to*
Ultimus
What a Pleasure

INTERMEDIATE

Ack Ack*
Ben Brush
Big Game
Black Toney*
Bold Ruler*
Broomstick
Caro*
Colorado
Congreve
Damascus*
Djebel

Eight Thirty
Equipoise*
Full Sail
Gallant Man*
Grey Dawn II*
Havresac II
Hoist the Flag*
Intentionally*
Khaled
King Salmon

Mahmoud*
Nashua*
Native Dancer*
Never Bend*
Petition
Pharos
Polynesian
Princequillo*
Riverman*
Roman*

Sir Gaylord*
Sir Ivor*
Star Kingdom*
Star Shoot
Sweep
The Tetrarch
Tom Fool*
Traghetto
Turn-to*
T.V. Lark

CLASSIC

Ack Ack*	Gainsborough	Navarro	Sharpen Up*
Alibhai	Graustark*	Nearco*	Sicambre
Aureole	Gundomar	Never Say Die	Sideral
Bahram	Hail to Reason	Nijinsky II*	Sir Galahad III
Blandford	Herbager*	Noholme II*	Sir Gaylord*
Blenheim II*	High Top	Northern Dancer*	Sir Ivor*
Blue Larkspur	Hyperion*	Persian Gulf	Star Kingdom*
Brantome	In Reality*	Pilate	Swynford
Buckpasser	Luthier	Prince Bio	Ticino*
Bull Lea	Lyphard	Prince Chevalier	Tom Fool*
Caro*	Mahmoud*	Prince John	Tom Rolfe*
Clarissimus	Midstream	Prince Rose	Tourbillon*
Count Fleet	Mill Reef*	Reviewer*	Tracery
Damascus*	Mossborough	Ribot*	Vaguely Noble*
Equipoise*	Mr. Prospector*	Riverman*	Vieux Manoir
Exclusive Native	Nashua*	Roberto	War Admiral
Forli	Native Dancer*	Rock Sand*	

SOLID

Asterus	Fair Play*	Princequillo*	Sunstar
Bachelor's Double	Graustark*	Relko	Tantieme
Ballymoss	Herbager*	Right Royal	Teddy
Blenheim II*	Man o' War	Rock Sand*	Ticino*
Bois Roussel	Mill Reef*	Round Table	Vatout
Chaucer	Nijinsky II*	Sea-Bird	Worden
Discovery	Oleander	Stage Door Johnny*	

PROFESSIONAL

Admiral Drake	Donatello II	Precipitation	Stage Door Johnny*
Alcantara II	Fair Play*	Rabelais	Sunny Boy
Alizier	Foxbridge	Ribot*	Tom Rolfe*
Alycidon	Hurry On	Run the Gantlet	Tourbillon*
Bayardo	La Farina	Sardanapale	Vaguely Noble*
Bruleur	Le Fabuleux	Solario	Vandale
Chateau Bouscaut	Massine	Son-in-Law	Vatellor
Crepello	Mieuxce	Spearmint	Wild Risk
Dark Ronald	Ortello		

*Sire is listed in 2 classes

Sample Dosage: Brian's Time

```
                                                          Royal Charger
                                           Turn-to
                                                          Source Sucree
                         Hail to Reason
                                                          Blue Swords
                                           Nothirdchance
                                                          Galla Colors
           Roberto
                                                          Nasrullah
                                           Nashua
                                                          Segula
                         Bramalea
                                                          Bull Lea
                                           Rarelea
                                                          Bleebok
Brian's Time
                                                          Tenerani
                                           Ribot
                                                          Romanella
                         Graustark
                                                          Alibhai
                                           Flower Bowl
                                                          Flower Bed
           Kelly's Day
                                                          Roman
                                           Hasty Road
                                                          Traffic Court
                         Golden Trail
                                                          Eight Thirty
                                           Sunny Vale
                                                          Sun Mixa
```

(Chefs underlined)

Brian Time's Dosage Profile

Brilliant	Intermediate	Classic	Solid	Professional
2	2	16	4	2
2	2	8		
2	1	4		
1	2	2		
		2		
		2		
		2		

Breakdown of points by Chefs by Generation

1st Generation — Roberto 16 points in Classic

2nd Generation — Hail To Reason 8 points in Classic
Graustark 8 points split, 4 in Classic, 4 in Solid

3rd Generation — Turn-to 4 points split, 2 in Brilliant,
2 in Intermediate
Nashua 4 points split, 2 in Intermediate, 2 in Classic
Ribot 4 points split, 2 in Classic, 2 in Professional

4th Generation — Royal Charger 2 points in Brilliant
Nasrullah 2 points in Brilliant
Bull Lea 2 points in Classic
Alibhai 2 points in Classic
Roman 2 points split, 1 in Brilliant,
1 in Intermediate
Eight Thirty 2 points in Intermediate

Brian's Time's Dosage Profile by classes is 7-7-36-4-2 derived by adding
the points in each class.

Calculating Brian's Time's Dosage Index:

Brilliant + Intermediate + $1/2$ of Classic = 7 + 7 + 18 = 32

$1/2$ of Classic + Solid + Professional   = 18 + 4 + 2 = 24

32 divided by 24 = 1.33

Brian's Time's Dosage Index is 1.33
